Social groups and identities

INTERNATIONAL SERIES IN SOCIAL PSYCHOLOGY
Series Editor: Professor W. Peter Robinson, University of Bristol, UK

Adolescence: From Crisis to Coping (Gibson-Cline)
Assertion and its Social Context: (Wilson and Gallois)
Children's Social Competence in Context: The Contributions of Family, School and Culture (Schneider)
Emotion and Social Judgments (Forgas)
Game Theory and its Applications in the Social and Biological Sciences (Colman)
Genius and Eminence, 2nd edition (Albert)
Making Sense of Television: The Psychology of Audience Interpretation (Livingstone)
The Psychology of Gambling (Walker)
Social Dilemmas: Theoretical Issues and Research Findings (Liebrand)
The Theory of Reasoned Action: Its Application to AIDS Preventative Behavior (Terry, Gallois and McCamish)

To obtain copies of any of the above books approach your bookseller or, in case of difficulty, contact the Sales Department, Butterworth-Heinemann, Linacre House, Jordan Hill, Oxford OX2 8DP, UK. If you wish to contribute to the series please send a synopsis to Matthew Deans, Commissioning Editor, at the same address, or to Professor Peter Robinson, University of Bristol, Department of Psychology, 8 Woodlands Road, Bristol BS8 1TN.

For order or further details you may also contact Butterworth-Heinemann on e-mail: matthew.deans@bhein.rel.co.uk.

Social Groups and Identities

Developing the Legacy of Henri Tajfel

Edited by
W. PETER ROBINSON

Department of Psychology, University of Bristol, UK

International Series in Social Psychology

To the Memory of Henri Tajfel

Butterworth-Heinemann
Linacre House, Jordan Hill, Oxford OX2 8DP
A division of Reed Educational and Professional Publishing Ltd

A member of the Reed Elsevier plc group

OXFORD BOSTON JOHANNESBURG
MELBOURNE NEW DELHI SINGAPORE

First published 1996

British Library Cataloguing in Publication Data
Social groups and identities: developing the legacy of
Henri Tajfel
1 Tajfel, Henri – Criticism and interpretation
2 Group identity 3 Social interaction 4 Intergroup
relations 5 Social psychology
I Robinson, W. P. (William Peter)
302

ISBN 0 7506 3083 3

Library of Congress Cataloguing in Publication Data
Social groups and identities: developing the legacy of Henri Tajfel/
edited by W. Peter Robinson.
p. c.m. – (International series in social psychology)
Includes bibliographical references and indexes.
ISBN 0 7506 3083 3
1 Tajfel, Henri. 2 Social groups. 3 Group identity.
4 Social psychology. I Robinson, W. P. (William Peter)
II Tajfel, Henri. III Series.
HM131.S5835
305–dc20 96–7631
CIP

Printed and bound in Great Britain by
Hartnolls Limited, Bodmin, Cornwall

Contents

Contributors

DOMINIC ABRAMS gained his undergraduate degree at the University of Manchester (1979), an MSc in social psychology at the London School of Economics and Political Science (1980), and a PhD in social psychology at the University of Kent (1984). He has held lectureships at the Universities of Bristol, Dundee and Kent, where he is Professor of Social Psychology and was until recently, Head of Department. He is now Director of the Centre for the Study of Group Processes there.

MICHAEL BILLIG is Professor of Social Sciences at Loughborough University. He was both an undergraduate and postgraduate at Bristol University. His recent books include *Arguing and thinking*, *Talking of the Royal Family* and *Banal nationalism*.

RICHARD BOURHIS was educated in the French and English school system in Montreal. He obtained a BSc in psychology at McGill University in 1971. He pursued his graduate studies in social psychology at the University of Bristol where he obtained a PhD in 1977. As Associate Professor, Bourhis taught social psychology at McMaster University in Ontario and then moved to the Université de Québec at Montreal where he is now a full professor. Recently (1994), Richard Bourhis and Jacques-Philippe Leyens published a volume entitled: *Stereotypes, discrimination et relations intergroups*.

RUPERT BROWN is Professor of Social Psychology. After completing his PhD with Henri Tajfel at Bristol he moved to Sussex and subsequently to Kent where he helped to establish the Department of Psychology there. His research interests are in the area of group processes generally, and specifically in intergroup relations. He has held numerous grants from the ESRC and other funding agencies, the most recent being "Cognitive Processes Underlying Prejudiced and Non-Prejudiced Beliefs". He is the author of *Group processes* (Blackwell, 1988) and *Prejudice* (Blackwell, 1995).

SUSAN CONDOR completed her PhD with Henri Tajfel and Howard Giles. After leaving Bristol, she worked at the Universities at Kent and Loughborough. She is now Lecturer in Psychology and in Culture and Communication at Lancaster University.

RICHARD EISER obtained his BA from Oxford in 1966 and his PhD from the London School of Economics and Political Science in 1969. He was a lecturer in psychology at the University of Bristol from 1968 to 1975, and has been Professor of Psychology at the University of Exeter since 1979.

SUSAN FOX is Assistant Professor in Communication at Western Michigan University, Kalamazoo. She has published research from a social identity perspective in areas of intergenerational and interability communication.

HOWARD GILES obtained his PhD in social psychology at the University of Bristol in 1971. Since then, and amongst other projects, he has been pursuing social identity ideas into intercultural and intergenerational areas. He is currently Professor and Chair of Communication at the University of California, Santa Barbara.

MICHAEL A. HOGG obtained his BSc in 1977 from the University of Birmingham, and his PhD in 1983 from the University of Bristol. After lecturing for three years at Bristol University he moved to Australia in 1985 to take up a postdoctoral fellowship at Macquarie University, Sydney. In 1986 he moved to a lectureship at the University of Melbourne, and in 1991 to the University of Queensland, Brisbane, where he is now Reader in Social Psychology, and Director of the Centre for the Study of Group Processes. He has been centrally involved in the development of social identity theory and self-categorization theory, and has published widely on these topics and group processes generally.

DAVID MILNER was awarded his first degree at the University of Wales (Cardiff) moving to Bristol in 1967 and becoming Henri Tajfel's first postgraduate student there. While not actually a member of the Bristol School, he admits that some of his best friends were, and that his own work was compatible with that perspective. This has centred on racism in general and developmental aspects in particular, with a strong emphasis on application and policy in multiracial education. He has lectured and broadcast widely in this country and in the USA and is currently Professor of Social Psychology at the University of Westminster.

SIK HUNG NG was awarded a PhD supervised by Henri Tajfel and went from Bristol to New Zealand in 1976 to take up a lectureship at Otago University. He received the 1986 Hunter Award of distinction in research, and was later elected Fellow of both the New Zealand and British Psychological Societies. Since 1992 he has been Professor of Psychology at Victoria University of Wellington. His publications include *The social psychology of power*, *Nurses and their work* and *Power in language*.

Penny Oakes was an undergraduate, research assistant and postgraduate at Bristol University from 1975 until 1983, and is now Senior Lecturer in Social Psychology at the Australian National University in Canberra. She has published extensively on stereotyping and group membership and is author (with Alex Haslam and John Turner) of *Stereotyping and social reality*, and editor (with Russell Spears, Naomi Ellemers and Alex Haslam) of *The social psychology of stereotyping and group life*.

Stephen Reicher was an undergraduate and postgraduate with Henri Tajfel at Bristol University where he did his thesis on crowd behaviour. He has since developed this interest and is currently researching into the construction of social categories. Stephen has been a senior lecturer in psychology at Exeter University and is now Reader at the University of St Andrews.

W. Peter Robinson is currently Professor of Social Psychology at the University of Bristol, having previously been Professor of Education there. Current research interests include truthfulness of authorities and citizens in the public domain, and self-perception and self-evaluation of low achieving adolescents. He is editor of the *International Series in Social Psychology*, in which this volume is included.

John C. Turner is Professor of Psychology at the Australian National University. He obtained his BA at the University of Sussex and PhD at the University of Bristol with Henri Tajfel and has held academic appointments at the University of Bristol and Macquarie University in Sydney. His research interests are in intergroup relations, group processes and social cognition.

Margaret Wetherell is senior lecturer in the social sciences at the Open University, having been supervised for a PhD by Henri Tajfel and John Turner. Her main research interests lie in the development of discourse analysis as a theoretical and methodological approach within social psychology. She is the author (with Jonathan Potter) of *Discourse and social psychology* and *Mapping the language of racism*, and (with Nigel Edley) of *Men in perspective*.

Preface

The idea of a Festschrift for Henri Tajfel was first mooted around the time of his retirement from Bristol. What was envisaged as a happy celebration in which Henri would have duly revelled became untimely in the wake of his premature death. To be issuing an appreciation so many years later hints of unnecessary delay, but it is a testimony to the power of his work that social identity theory and its associated ideas continues to be one of the dominant themes in social psychology in Europe.

It is appropriate that the volume should emanate from the university and city which served as the base for Henri's most productive years. Social psychology seems to have had peculiar birth pangs in Britain, and with very few but notable exceptions, it is thanks to the émigrés of Henri's generation that the field gained a foothold in the academic world. In spite of its current popularity among the student body, social psychology in Britain has clearly been squeezed, and not surprisingly so in an era in which the leader of the repeatedly elected government pronounced that there was no such thing as society, only individuals. Simultaneously and sadly, in the world at large this is also an age marked by ferocious intergroup conflicts involving mass slaughtering of peoples, apparently on the basis of their social identity. That has been happening periodically on a majority of the world's continents throughout the century. Perhaps before too long, and as its knowledge and power base grows, social psychology will begin to inform political-decision making and influence the course of history. If it does, then the work of Henri Tajfel will be seen as one of the foundations from which intergroup conflict came to be better understood, reduced and prevented.

The worst part of taking the editorial initiative with this volume has been the selection of authors. It is a mark of Henri's charisma that a three volume work would have been feasible. I can only apologize to those associates of Henri who were not invited to contribute. The first filter used was to think of those who followed doctoral studies with Henri as supervisor and are still actively pursuing research related to social identity theory, but records had been lost and not all were known to me until too late. And then there were also vigorous academics supervised by supervisees. Further, there were academic colleagues in the Bristol department who have maintained research influenced by Henri. In the end, a Bristol PhD and continuing work in the field of social identity were the two main criteria—and being on the departmental files. I am now aware that there are distinguished colleagues in continental Europe who meet those criteria. There are also distinguished colleagues who were inspired to become social psychologists as a result of Henri's lectures to undergraduates. Yet others worked with Henri, but have shifted fields. I can only express my regrets that ignorance and the pragmatics of publishing took precedence over criteria of academic appropriateness and personal preference.

I do not consider it necessary to write those ingenuous integrative paragraphs that point out the commonalities and contrasts which bind the chapters together. There are omissions from the original editorial plan; the absence of a chapter focusing on the process of comparison is one such gap. On balance it seemed better to let authors select their own titles and trust that the quality thus generated would be preferable to a more comprehensive coverage. The advantages of this decision are apparent in the originality of the essays.

The general structure of the chapters is similar. Authors set Henri Tajfel's contribution to their particular concern in its historical context and then show how that contribution has fared since its initial publication, often as a direct result of the author's personal research. The theme is therefore one of progress. How have his ideas, insights and interpretations been superseded, modified, expanded, subordinated, challenged or developed? The limitations of his frame of reference are also discussed, especially in the later chapters. The concerns are not to show in how many respects Henri Tajfel was correct in his analyses, but to demonstrate how his activities have served as a significant source of inspiration for others. The common attitude is not one of reverence, but of gratitude for intellectual stimulation that encouraged the pursuit of research within, without and beyond his own work. What is the current state of the art and the prognosis for the future study of the issues he considered? The last fifteen years have witnessed a dramatic growth in the number of people working in the area, and it is to be hoped that they will benefit particularly from reading his collection.

Peter Robinson
Bristol, UK

Henri Tajfel: An Introduction

JOHN C. TURNER

Division of Psychology, The Australian National University

Contents

> It is difficult to do justice to the calibre of someone like Henri Tajfel the man and social scientist. He will occupy a very important place in the history of psychology in the 20th century when this comes to be written and he occupies it now in the minds and hearts of the many who have worked with him and are numbered among his friends
>
> Hilde Himmelweit, 1982

It is indeed difficult to do justice to Henri Tajfel, as the late Hilde Himmelweit wrote in her obituary. He died in 1982, over thirteen years ago, and yet his influence on social psychology remains as strong as ever. The years since his death have revealed the magnitude of his contribution. They have also shown the continuing relevance of his particular vision of social psychology. He has proved quite irreplaceable in his intellectual and personal role in the science. Social psychology needs the ideas of Tajfel as much today as it did in the 1970s and 1980s. It has understood and absorbed some, absorbed but not understood others, and neglected much that was most important and difficult. I think that Himmelweit was right in her judgement of his intellectual stature. He will prove to be one of the most important and seminal figures in social psychology for several reasons, not least the fact that he has already changed the international character of the discipline. But his future reputation will rest fundamentally on his intellectual contribution. This

Festschrift cannot and does not intend to substitute for Tajfel's own writings. However, in celebrating and remembering Henri, it is important that it encourage today's researchers and students, those who knew him and those who did not, to pick up his books and articles, again or for the first time, to study his rich and powerful point of view.

In this brief introduction I shall provide a capsule sketch of his career and point to some of his major contributions to social psychology. I knew Henri (and in this context it is unnatural for me to refer to him unrelentingly in the impersonal style of "Tajfel") as his PhD student, collaborator, colleague and friend from 1971 until his death. Although we were close, I am not an expert on his early or personal life. My knowledge of him comes primarily from a working relationship that lasted a decade in a life of nearly 63 years. This is not therefore an attempt at biography, personal or intellectual, and nor am I trying to provide a comprehensive summary of his work. What follows is a short sketch of his life and work intended to serve no more than an introductory purpose. Henri has provided his own introduction to his work, and some comments on its relationship to his life, in his 1981 book *Human groups and social categories*, in which he collected his most significant papers. That introduction and the book are both strongly recommended.

Life: Jewish, Polish, French, British and "European"

Henri Tajfel was born on the 22nd June 1919 in Wloclawek, Poland; his family were Jewish and his father a businessman. He left Poland when he was eighteen, after attending secondary school in Wloclawek, because it was almost impossible for Jews to receive a university education in Poland at that time. He went to France where, after obtaining his baccalaureate in Paris, he studied chemistry for two years (1937–1939) at the Universities of Toulouse and Paris (Sorbonne).

According to Himmelweit (1982) he found chemistry boring and neglected his university studies in favour of "becoming bilingual, and savouring French culture and Parisian life" (p. 288). This would not have surprised those who knew him later. Henri never ceased to savour French culture and life. He remained closely attached to Paris all his life and loved to share his familiarity with that city with his colleagues and students.

In 1939 came the Second World War. His brief career in chemistry ended. Henri was called up to serve in the French army in November 1939 and a year later was taken prisoner by the German army. He spent from 1940 to 1945 in various German prisoner-of-war camps in Germany and Austria, being released only with the end of the war. All through this period he lived under the false identity of being French: had it been discovered by the German authorities that he was a Polish rather than a French Jew he would have been killed.

He sometimes referred to this experience of living under a false identity, on guard against an ever-present danger of discovery, in his later academic life. He used it to illustrate his distinction between interpersonal and intergroup behaviour and what he meant by an "interpersonal–intergroup continuum" (Tajfel, 1974, 1978). The point he made was that no matter what his personal characteristics were or the quality of his personal relationships with the German guards, once his true identity had been discovered, it was that social category membership (of being Polish) which would have determined the reaction of the guards and his ultimate fate. His personal attributes and identity as a unique individual would have proved unimportant and irrelevant to their response.

His more formal idea of an interpersonal–intergroup continuum, developed in the early 1970s as part of the evolution of social identity theory (Tajfel, 1974; Tajfel and Turner, 1979), refers to the assumption that social interaction between people varies along a continuum defined at one extreme by purely interpersonal behaviour and at the other by purely intergroup behaviour. Purely interpersonal behaviour is conceptualized as being based solely on the individual characteristics and personal relationships of the interactors (such as their personalities and interpersonal attitudes), whereas purely intergroup behaviour is seen as solely determined by their respective social category memberships (such as being Polish or French). Henri first conceptualized the distinction between interpersonal and intergroup behaviour in terms of "acting in terms of self" versus "acting in terms of [one's] group" (1974, pp. 87–89). Subsequently, the distinction has become associated with a closely related one between personal and social identity in self-categorization theory, in which both poles are seen as forms of acting in terms of self (Turner, 1982).

In May 1945 he was "disgorged with hundreds of others from a special train arriving at the Gare d' Orsay in Paris with its crammed load of prisoners-of-war returning from camps in Germany . . . [he] soon discovered that hardly anyone I knew in 1939—including my family—was left alive" (Tajfel, 1981a, p. 1). His social and cultural background had been wiped out, literally. The vibrant pre-war community of Polish Jews had largely ceased to exist, along with millions of other Jews. His parents, brother and other members of his family were killed.

He then spent six years in the immediate post-war period working for organizations which tried "with insufficient means to stem the flood of misery" (1981a, p. 1). From 1945 until 1949 he was education officer, then later director (successively in Lyons, Paris and Brussels) of various rehabilitation centres for children and adolescents, who were victims of the war, mostly orphans and survivors of concentration camps. Under the auspices of an international relief agency (Oeuvre de Secours aux Enfants), he worked to supervise their studies and restore their confidence and capacity to face the future. From 1949 to 1951 he then worked as a rehabilitation officer for disabled refugees in the British Zone of West Germany, under the International Refugee Organization of the United Nations. He was responsible for the administration of arrangements for the vocational training and rehabilitation of refugees from several countries.

It was during this period of his life that he developed his interest in social psychology. He resumed his university studies part-time in Paris (1946–7) and Brussels (1947–9), but now in psychology, not chemistry. He obtained a "Certificat de Psychologie Générale" from the University of Paris in 1947 and a "Candidature [Diploma] des Sciences de l'Education" from the University of Brussels in 1949.

It was also during this period that his new family life began. In 1948 he married Anne Tajfel (née Anna Eber in Hamburg) and after his time in West Germany he moved, in 1951, to Britain where Anne's family now lived. His two sons, Michael and Paul, were born in 1949 and 1955. From 1951 to 1954 he pursued part- and full-time studies and research in psychology at Birkbeck College, University of London. He worked part-time to begin with, but eventually won one of the Ministry of Education's very rare state scholarships for mature students for 1953–4. He won the scholarship with an essay on "Prejudice". He states in *Human groups and social categories* (1981a) that he suspects that the interviewers who awarded him the scholarship gave it to him because they thought that he must know what he was talking about. This early essay, in reflecting his life, was a harbinger of scientific interests that never left him. "Prejudice" remained a central theme of his whole research career.

He emerged from Birkbeck with a first class honours degree in psychology in 1954. He then went to work as a research assistant for two years at the University of Durham and in 1956 he moved to the University of Oxford. He stayed at Oxford for eleven years as university lecturer in social psychology in the Department of Social and Administrative Studies and as Fellow of Linacre College. He obtained his PhD from the University of London on the topic, "The role of value in the formation of a scale of judgements". From the mid-1950s his life finally began to take on a more conventional academic form:

> The ivory towers, more solid then than they are now, had a way of smothering one with their benevolent warmth and comfort. Very soon . . . I was talking a new language, I learned a new jargon and discovered "problems" which I never knew existed. The "academic" psychology took full hold of me.
>
> (1981a, p. 2)

However, for those who knew Henri, it was always clear that, much more than for most, his social psychology, the problems he studied, the theories he proposed and the approaches he saw as necessary and significant, remained closely bound up with the tragedies and experiences of his earlier life. This is much more than a matter of the unifying theme of his research, variously defined as "group prejudice" (Bruner, 1981, p. xii), or the "pervasiveness of, and the mechanisms whereby, social values distort judgement and behaviour" (Himmelweit, 1982, p. 288), or the "more general question of the sensitivity of people to the social climate of group differentials as they exist in the broader social setting" (Bruner, 1981, p. xii), or "the relationship between human psychological functioning and the large-scale social processes and events which shape this functioning and are shaped by it" (Tajfel, 1981a, p. 7). It refers as well to his commitment to a

"European" social psychology, his beliefs about what was theoretically important and what was trivial and his metatheoretical vision and definition of social psychology:

> He wrote, "We all have a kind of intellectual history; I know that mine has been deeply enmeshed with the traumatic events of long ago", events which he suggests gave focus to his work and also led him to wage a passionate war against the neglect by orthodox social psychology of the social dimension and against its failure to capitalize on the richness and diversity of European culture.
>
> (Himmelweit, 1982, p. 289).

In 1957 he acquired British citizenship, his third nationality, having been born a Pole and become a French citizen soon after the war. In that year too he published his first papers: "Hobbes and Hull—metaphysicians of behaviour" (Peters and Tajfel, 1957), and "Value and the perceptual judgement of magnitude" (Tajfel, 1957). The joint paper with Richard Peters, one of his Birkbeck teachers, was a critique of reductionist, mechanistic accounts of behaviour. The other was a major statement of theory in *Psychological Review*, dealing with the problem of perceptual overestimation. Both were indicative of what was to come. The Peters and Tajfel paper was about metatheory and expressed an abiding distaste for the simple-minded "psychologizing" of human social behaviour:

> The article attempted to present a case against certain forms of reductionism in psychology. I now know what outraged me about Hull was his bland indifference to all that one knew about human society while he was weaving his web of "hypothetico-deductive" over-simplifications, claiming at the same time that they provided the basis for insights about the complexities of human social behaviour.
>
> (Tajfel, 1981a, p. 2)

The other was a first step in a long journey that led him from a "New Look" problem to do with the perception of physical magnitudes to a categorization analysis of stereotyping and cognitive aspects of prejudice and then finally to a rejection of *purely* cognitive analysis in favour of a full-blown social psychology of stereotyping (Tajfel, 1981a, pp. 57–161; see Oakes, Haslam and Turner, 1994). Tajfel was not the first to grasp the significance of categorization for social psychology (he was much influenced by G. W. Allport, Bruner and Sherif), but he has certainly provided the clearest and most influential analysis of its relationship to perceptual accentuation phenomena, and more than anyone else is responsible for the increase in its explanatory significance in contemporary social psychology. Current work on stereotyping, impression formation, attitude judgement, group formation and polarization, social influence and intergroup relations, which employs the categorization process as a central theoretical tool, can almost without exception be traced back to Tajfel's theorizing and direct research inspiration.

During his appointment at Oxford he spent a year working with Jerome Bruner at the Center for Cognitive Studies at Harvard (1958–1959) and a year as Fellow of the Center for Advanced Study in the Behavioral Sciences at Stanford (1966–1967). In 1967, a year in which he had a severe heart attack, he moved from Oxford to the Department of Psychology at the University of Bristol on his appointment to the first Chair of Social Psychology at that university. Henri remained at Bristol as Professor of Social Psychology for virtually the remainder of his life. He retired from Bristol in 1982 to resettle in Oxford just a few weeks before his death on May 3rd 1982 at the age of 62.

From 1967 until 1982 Henri led the social psychology group at Bristol, creating a major centre of social psychology where highly influential work was done. During the 1960s his research had become more overtly social psychological. It shifted from perceptual issues to focus on problems of stereotyping, prejudice, ethnocentrism and group identity, although it still made free use of ideas derived from the perceptual work. It was also in the early 1960s that he began his labours to create a "European" social psychology, playing a leading role in the very first efforts to bring European scholars together. From the late 1960s through the 1970s he developed his work on social categorization and social identity, and created at Bristol what in retrospect was the most exciting place for research on intergroup relations in the world. Also through the 1970s he clarified and elaborated his metatheory of social psychology (in Tajfel 1972a, 1979, 1981b and other articles).

The emergence of Bristol as a centre of social psychology was bound up with Henri's active leadership in two key spheres: the development of European social psychology (the formation and growth of the European Association of Experimental Social Psychology, the EAESP, being one expression of this process) and experimental research on intergroup behaviour (which produced *inter alia* the "minimal group paradigm" and "social identity theory"). His efforts to build a European community of social psychologists began before he went to Bristol, but his time there saw the work come to fruition and the process of development become irreversible.

Whereas the European venture was strongly linked to Henri's own dynamism and the Bristol scene was shaped by that link and strengthened by it, the intergroup research was much more a product of Henri's presence at Bristol and his interactions with the research group and ambience he created there. He always acknowledged the contributions of others to the intergroup work, but there was never any doubt that he led it and that his contributions were fundamental. By the time of his death Henri "had become the most dynamic, productive and influential social psychologist not only in this country but in Europe" (Himmelweit, 1982, p. 289).

Tajfel's Role in the Development of European Social Psychology

From the early 1960s right through to his death, Tajfel played a leading role in the development of European social psychology. This took several forms: administrative, intellectual and personal.

In 1962 two Americans, John Lanzetta, who was spending two years in London, and John Thibaut, who was in Paris for a year, and three Europeans, Mauk Mulder from Utrecht, Robert Pagès from the Sorbonne and Henri Tajfel from Oxford, formed a small committee to work to identify and contact European social psychologists, a task that seemed strange only ten years later, as Henri wrote in his 1972 presidential report to the EAESP (Tajfel, 1972b). After working for over a year, their efforts led to the first-ever conference of European social psychologists in 1963 in Sorrento.

The Sorrento meeting attracted about forty participants, including several Americans, and was a great success. It had been encouraged and supported by the Committee on Transnational Social Psychology of the American Social Science Research Council. Soon afterwards the SSRC committee co-opted three Europeans (Koekebakker, Moscovici and Rommetweit) to help it continue its European activities. This enlarged SSRC committee and the original committee initiated by Lanzetta worked together to organize a second European meeting towards the end of 1964 at Frascati near Rome. This was the meeting at which the decision was taken to create the EAESP and at which its first planning committee was elected, of which Tajfel was a member. The Transnational Committee of the SSRC under the leadership of Leon Festinger and then Morton Deutsch continued its support for the development of social psychology in Europe for many years and Tajfel was co-opted as a member in 1966 and remained a member until 1974.

In 1965 the first joint conference of social psychologists from Europe, the United States and the socialist countries of Eastern Europe was held in Vienna, again with the active help of the SSRC committee. Henri was a member of the organizing committee of this first "East–West" meeting and subsequently chaired the committees which organized further East–West meetings in Prague in 1968 and Budapest in 1974. Around this time many discussions were taking place about the form the EAESP should take. The aim was clear:

> to encourage and instigate communication in Europe, to create a *milieu* of social psychologists which would become a breeding ground for more research, more training and more inventiveness in what was being done. The social, political and cultural diversity of Europe was seen as an advantage rather than a hindrance in the fostering of a second, independently creative, intellectual centre of social psychology.
>
> (Tajfel, 1972b, p. 309)

In the summer of 1965 the first European summer school in social psychology was held in The Hague and less than a year later in the spring of 1966 the first "official" plenary meeting of the EAESP was held in Royaumont. The first executive committee of the EAESP was elected and Serge Moscovici became first president. Tajfel was a member of the executive committee right through to 1972 and was re-elected in 1975 for a further period. He became second president of the EAESP at the next plenary meeting in 1969 and was president from 1969 to 1972. Appropriately, Leon Festinger, chairman of the SSRC committee, attended the 1966 meeting and John Lanzetta was guest of honour at the 1969 Louvain meeting, the second official EAESP plenary meeting and the first organized from the EAESP's own funds.

After 1966 European activities in the form of summer schools, East–West meetings, plenary meetings, small working group meetings and exchange visits continued unabated. Tajfel played a central role in the many activities of those years. Significant milestones were the founding of the *European Journal of Social Psychology* in 1971 during his term as president (he later became a member of the editorial board for a time) and the founding of the *European Monographs in Social Psychology* under his editorship, with the first volume by Carswell and Rommetweit published in 1971. By the time of his death he had produced as editor a total of 28 books in the European Monographs series, a series which quickly became the premier showcase for European work.

As well as being co-organizer of the first European conference, the first East–West meetings, co-founder of the EAESP, member of its executive committee for many years and second president, co-founder of the European Journal and founding editor of the European Monographs series, he engaged in many other roles and activities, formal and informal, too numerous to list, which contributed to the emergence and evolution of European social psychology. He was also, for example, a member of the executive committee of the European Laboratory of Social Psychology of la Maison des Sciences de l'Homme in Paris and of the editorial board of the related series of volumes, *European Studies in Social Psychology*.

The EAESP has now become a large and mature organization. It is difficult to think of anyone who played a more significant, sustained role in its creation than Henri Tajfel. As Himmelweit comments:

> There were a number of founders of the European Association for [*sic*] Experimental Social Psychology but without doubt he was its mainspring.
>
> (1982, p. 289)

Bruner echoes the same thought more broadly in his foreword to Tajfel's 1981 book:

> it is inconceivable how anybody could have done more to promote the cause [of "European" social psychology] . . . Tajfel sensed something deeper about the European scene, a point of view waiting to be expressed. And he more than any other helped to bring it into being.
>
> (Bruner, 1981, p. xiii)

Apart from Tajfel's unstinting administrative activity, there were also his intellectual and personal contributions. Along with others he provided the intellectual justification for distinctively European work. He produced a rationale for an alternative, different kind of social psychology from the North American mainstream. His vision was pluralistic, taking for granted the proposition that social science was not and could not be value-free. Social science is influenced by society's values and ideologies, by the social and cultural background of its practitioners. Researchers hold the views they do, not just as a function of an asocial, neutral appraisal of facts and evidence, but because of who and where they are, their ideology and social location. Things cannot be otherwise and hence social psychology must be pluralistic and varied to reflect and allow for the variety of human cultures and perspectives. A social psychology of one country must be intellectually limited:

> There cannot be, and should not be, any kind of a unified European, or any other social psychology. The acquisition of a new identity . . . must be understood instead in terms of two related developments. One of them was the progressive creation of actively interacting community of people . . . The channels of communication, so easily available to our American colleagues, had to be either created or unblocked in Europe. The second development consisted of the creation of a *diversity* of communicating viewpoints, trends of interest and research initiatives . . .
>
> . . . Why a *European* Association and a series of *European* Monographs in Social Psychology? These titles are not meant to reflect some new versions of a "wider" or "continental" nationalism—academic, intellectual or any other. The future of social psychology as a discipline and as a contribution to knowledge and society is no more "European", "American" or "African" than it is Basque, Welsh, Flemish, German or French . . . In the long run . . . an exclusive focus from, and on, one cultural context cannot escape being damaging to the healthy development of a discipline which is in the last analysis one of the social sciences. There was a time, not so long ago, when most of us were quite happy to accept the proposition that the social and human sciences can be "value free" and independent of their cultural and social framework. It is undoubtedly true that, whatever the case may be, this has become today a highly controversial issue, and not only for social psychology. Even the outwardly neutral description . . . of social psychology as the "scientific study of social behaviour" has not managed to remain *au-dessus de la mêlée* . . . For all these reasons, and many others, we must create a social psychology which grows simultaneously in many places . . . [We] do not set out to be "European" in explicit opposition, competition, or contradistinction to anything else . . . But a discipline concerned with the analysis and understanding of human social life must, in order to acquire its full significance, be tested and measured against the intellectual and social requirements of many cultures.
>
> (Tajfel, 1981a, pp. 5–6)

The last sentence in this quotation is important. In today's intellectual climate it is easy to misunderstand Tajfel's argument as a rejection of scientific truth in favour of some insipid relativism. His point is otherwise; that to reach scientific maturity the discipline needs to develop on the basis of and be consistent with the interacting insights, ideas and perspectives that derive from the whole human social experience. He also made clear that this was not a simple-minded call for a "cross-cultural" social psychology:

> The point is that *all* experiments are "cultural" and whether the "cross" adds to their value or not depends entirely upon the theoretical background from which they start. To go around looking for fortuitous similarities and differences may broaden the mind of the researcher as travel is presumed to do, but it will not add much to our fund of relevant knowledge.
>
> (Tajfel, 1981a, p. 22)

In his own work he provided European social psychology with an example of an alternative style and content, more compatible with the philosophical and ideological convictions of Europeans. Social identity theory was developed more or less self-consciously by Tajfel as an embodiment of his view of social psychology, a view which emphasized cumulative theory-driven research and a rejection of piecemeal empiricism. It was a cognitive perspective, rather than biological or behaviourist, which assumed that it was in people's active efforts to understand, to find meaning in, their situation that the explanation of their behaviour would be found. He rejected reductionism and individualism in the explanation of social conduct and argued that social psychology was discontinuous with general (individual) psychology in both phenomena and required theory. Social psychology proper, he believed, should focus on the socially shared aspects of human behaviour, the collective regularities, not the individual exception. It required explanatory concepts which had a social as well as psychological origin.

In method Tajfel rejected both the armchair philosophizing which never produced empirical results of some Europeans and the atheoretical empiricism characteristic of much experimental research on both sides of the Atlantic. He believed in close links between theory and experiment and argued that the value of experiments depended on the quality of the ideas they tested. Experiments were not good or bad in themselves; they produced trivial findings when they were guided by trivial ideas. Artificial experiments guided by powerful ideas could and did produce valuable theoretical insights. He never saw experimental data as having inductive or simple descriptive validity (Tajfel, 1972a), despite how his own research was sometimes interpreted by others.

He tried in social identity theory to create an intergroup theory that gave proper due to the social dimensions of social conflict, which inserted intergroup relations and group memberships into its macro-social context, but which nevertheless showed how the emergent psychological aspects of group relations and self-definition could have relatively autonomous and at times decisive consequences. He came to see the essence of a European perspective as being this focus on the social dimension of social psychology, a preoccupation with psychological functioning in its social context. Society, social structure, was the natural environment of human behaviour and social psychology's task was to relate psychological processes to that context. He elaborates this theme in all of his major books, in his volumes on social identity theory (Tajfel, 1978, 1982), in *Human groups and social categories* (Tajfel, 1981a) and in his pioneering "handbook" or compendium of European research activity, *The social dimension: European developments in social psychology* (Tajfel, 1984, published posthumously with the help of Colin Fraser and the late Jos Jaspars).

His important personal contribution was more diffuse, easier to take for granted at the time and perhaps easier to forget with the passing years, but it should not be ignored. Bruner (1981) captures well the points here. First, Henri was himself the canonical European social psychologist. As Jew, Polish, French and British, he was an internationalist, committed to the political and social unity of Europe, with ideals of co-operative, cultural pluralism, and just as at home on the continent as in the UK. He was cosmopolitan, humanistic and multilingual, a citizen *par excellence* of the new Europe, with friends and colleagues spread across the continent and around the world. For Tajfel Europe was not a divisive or chauvinistic concept. It was unifying and inclusive, a form of internationalism in science, culture and politics.

Second, there was his forceful, energetic, warm, hospitable and expansive personality, simultaneously cultured, sociable, charming and intellectually aggressive. He was a committed person, uncomfortable with faint-hearted loyalties. His personality created an immediate and strong impression. He visited and travelled seemingly continuously, inviting colleagues to Bristol and to his home, taking a personal interest in every contact or group that promised to aid the development of social psychology in Europe. He was at the centre of a large and complex web of personal contacts and interactions that put the flesh and muscle on the intellectual bone of a European community. It is hard to believe that any other person could have done the job and played the role that he did. Socializing and talking at Henri's house in the company of an endless variety of visitors from Europe, America, Canada, Australia and New Zealand was for his graduate students and colleagues a normal part of the Bristol scene.

Intellectual Contributions: From Perceptual Overestimation to the Social Context of Social Psychology

It is useful to think of Tajfel's academic research as falling into three periods. The division is crude because there was much overlap, continuity and parallel development. In the first period in the 1950s and early 1960s, his research revolved around issues of perceptual overestimation and judgmental accentuation. In the second period in the 1960s his work became more recognizably "Tajfellian". His explanation of perceptual accentuation was now developed into an analysis of stereotyping, a topic directly related to prejudice, group membership and intergroup relations. The culmination of this line of research was his classic paper "Cognitive aspects of prejudice", published in 1969, which heralded and paved the way for the "cognitive revolution" in the analysis of stereotyping.

Other projects in the 1960s were similarly dominated by the problems of prejudice, ethnocentrism and group identity. Tajfel and Dawson (1965) looked at the experience of coloured students from the British Commonwealth who arrived in Britain in the early sixties. This was before the time of the rapid growth of immigration and of the corresponding growing awareness of issues of "race relations" in the UK. Most of the students came not knowing what to expect, or expecting something rather different from what they found. They often came seeing themselves as "British" or part of the British family of nations and found themselves instead treated as outsiders. One result was a growing awareness of their minority group membership together with the development of new attitudes towards themselves and the host country.

Further studies (e.g. Tajfel *et al.*, 1970, 1972) examined the development of children's preferences for their own country, finding evidence of "ingroup devaluation" in groups defined as minorities socially rather than numerically in comparison with higher status groups in their societies. These studies showed the high sensitivity of children to the social climate of intergroup attitudes in society. The data confirmed the researchers' suspicion that the ethnocentrism of young children, as expressed in their preferences for their own nationals over foreigners, crystallized early in life, long before the concept of "nation" has been grasped even in a most rudimentary form. Other studies pursued the underlying general issue of the development of national attitudes in children, showing how children assimilated evaluative beliefs about groups as easily as factual beliefs (see Tajfel, 1981a). At the end of the 1960s he was writing about the formation of national attitudes and aspects of ethnic loyalty, social categorization and the cognitive aetiology of prejudice. Issues to do with the formation of group identity in the context of intergroup relations and social conflict had come to the fore.

Viewed with hindsight, there seems an inexorable movement to research which looked at the nexus between social categorization, ethnocentrism and intergroup relations, the focus which dominated the next period, beginning at the end of the 1960s and continuing through to his death. In 1970 and 1971 he published his seminal experimental studies of the effects of social categorization on intergroup discrimination (Tajfel, 1970; Tajfel *et al.*, 1971). Through the 1970s he developed his work on social categorization, social identity and intergroup relations (Tajfel, 1974, 1978, 1982). He also clarified and elaborated his metatheory of social psychology (e.g. Tajfel 1972a, 1979, 1981b).

It is worth outlining the most important of these contributions in a little more detail.

Perceptual accentuation, categorization and stereotyping

As noted above, Tajfel's first major paper (1957) dealt with the problem of perceptual overestimation. A succession of papers (Tajfel and Cawasjee, 1959; Tajfel, 1959, Tajfel and Wilkes, 1963, 1964; Tajfel *et al.*, 1964; Tajfel, 1969, 1981b) developed this line of work to provide a cognitive and then a social psychological analysis of stereotyping.

A major finding of the "New Look" research on perception was that estimates of the physical magnitudes of stimuli were affected by their value and emotional significance to the perceiver. Coins, for example, were perceived as larger than neutral disks of the same objective magnitude. Although the effect of values seemed definite there were some inconsistent results. Tajfel (1957) brought order into the findings, by arguing that so-called perceptual overestimation was in fact an expression of a perceptual exaggeration of the perceived differences between an ordered series of stimuli, where this series was systematically correlated with a relevant value dimension. Thus he hypothesized that where stimulus coins differed continuously in size in such a way that larger coins tended to have more value than smaller coins, subjects tended to exaggerate the differences between individual coins so that the size of larger coins was increased and the size of smaller coins decreased. The exaggeration of differences on one (focal) dimension as a function of its correlation with a superimposed (peripheral) value dimension had functional value for the perceiver in ensuring that differences were perceived more strongly when they contained more diagnostic information (i.e. the more the differences mattered). This exaggeration of correlated differences represented a systematic bias which, paradoxically, had functional value.

In Tajfel (1959), the same principles were transposed from judged differences between *individual* stimuli in a series endowed with value differentials to *groups* of stimuli. The subjective classification of stimuli into different classes, where there is a predictable relationship between their class membership and their positions on the correlated dimension, will lead to the accentuation of the judged differences between the different classes on that dimension. When the distinctions between the classes are also related to subjective differences in value, the judgmental accentuation of perceived interclass differences will be enhanced.

The next steps (Tajfel, 1981a, pp. 90–126; see Tajfel and Wilkes, 1963 in particular) were to argue that the subjective classification of stimuli led to enhancement of relevant intraclass similarities as well as interclass differences on the correlated dimension and that these effects apply equally well to the perception of people, where social group memberships could function as the basis of subjective classification.

These ideas and related research formed the basis of Tajfel's cognitive theory of stereotyping (Tajfel, 1969), the kernel of which is:

> personal traits or characteristics can be empirically treated as dimensions much in the same way as height and weight would be if we could conceive them only in comparative terms of "more" or "less", "shorter" and "longer", "heavier" and "lighter". This is the kind of statement that I make if I say that someone is "intelligent" or "honest" or "lazy" . . .
>
> . . . through personal and cultural experience, dimensions such as "intelligent", "lazy" or "honest" are subjectively associated with classifications of people into groups. As long as we have little specific knowledge about an individual, we shall tend to ascribe to him the characteristics which we derive from our knowledge of his class membership, be it a class of trade unionists, undergraduates, animal lovers, or Patagonians . . .
>
> The third statement refers to two consequences of the tendency to simplify in order to cope. They are but two aspects of the same phenomenon and can be described as follows: when a classification is correlated with a continuous dimension, there will be a tendency to exaggerate the differences on *that* dimension between items which fall into distinct classes, and to minimize these differences within each of the classes.
>
> (Tajfel, 1969, pp. 82–83).

Thus the perception of people in terms of their social group memberships leads to a tendency to exaggerate the perceived similarities within groups and the perceived differences between groups. This corresponds exactly to our understanding of the cognitive aspects of stereotyping.

He went on in "Cognitive aspects of prejudice" not only to elaborate this analysis, but also to discuss other normal cognitive processes involved in the generation of social prejudice, which he summarized by the concepts of "assimilation" (the processes by which the culturally generated norms, values and content of stereotypes are transmitted to individual members of society) and "the search for coherence" (the making of constant causal attributions about the processes responsible for social change within and between groups).

His general and highly influential point was to emphasize the importance of the adaptive cognitive functioning of humankind in the causation of prejudice, as opposed to accounts based on the evolutionary past or unconscious motivation. He developed powerfully the rationale for a cognitive social psychological perspective on intergroup relations: to predict intergroup relations, we should not assume that "social man . . . has lost his reason" (1969, p. 80), but find out "how he understands the intergroup situation" (p. 81).

As well as pioneering the cognitive approach to prejudice which became so dominant in North American work in the 1980s, he was also one of the first to reject the excesses of purely cognitive theory (Tajfel, 1981b). For Tajfel, unlike for many others, a cognitive perspective was a way of being *social* psychological. He never subscribed to the view that general (i.e. individual) cognitive mechanisms, understood as being basic and unmodified by the social world, could provide an adequate account of social psychological phenomena (see Tajfel, 1972a). In his 1981b chapter "Social stereotypes and social groups", he argued that individual cognitive and motivational processes such as categorization and the need for the preservation of individual values were a necessary part of the analysis of stereotyping, but not sufficient. Stereotypes were held and shared by people as members of social groups and reflected the nature of intergroup relations. They had social as well as individual functions; in particular they provided group members with positively valued intergroup differences which enhanced their social identity, and explained and justified intergroup relations. They served collective aspects of psychology, ideologizing and giving social meaning and value to collective action. We needed to understand how they evolved socially and became shared images and how their collective character shaped and interacted with their individual functions. Instead of proceeding from the individual to the social, which produced reductionist explanations, we needed to start from an analysis of social functions to reach the individual ones:

> We shall never be able to formulate adequate guidelines for research on collective social behaviour if we do not go beyond constructing sets of independent variables seen as functioning in a social environment which is assumed to be psychologically unstructured in its homogeneous and all-embracing "inter-individuality".
>
> (Tajfel, 1979, p. 189)

In the 1980s the sovereignty of social cognition was proclaimed with respect to stereotyping, but during the 1990s, as he presaged, it has become much harder to find true believers in the purely cognitive perspective (see Oakes *et al*., 1994).

Social identity and intergroup relations

> In our judgements of other people, in forming stereotypes, in learning a second language, in our work relations, in our concern with justice, we do not act as isolated individuals but as social beings who derive an important part of our identity from the human groups and social categories we belong to; and we act in accordance with this awareness.
>
> (Tajfel *et al*., 1984, p. 5)

Only a handful of experimental studies on intergroup behaviour (as opposed to stereotyping or prejudice) were conducted during most of the 1960s. After the pioneering work of the Sherifs and their colleagues in the 1940s and 1950s, there were a few follow-up studies and one or two other relevant lines of work, but nothing like the interest that one might have expected. Just as experimental intergroup research seemed almost to have disappeared, it was resurrected at the end of the 1960s by the activities of a number of scholars: Jaap Rabbie at Utrecht, Willem Doise in Paris and Henri Tajfel in Bristol. A tradition of interest in intergroup relations continued in the USA (e.g. LeVine and Campbell, 1972) and some useful studies were done, but there is no doubt that it was in Europe that the renaissance took place. It was Tajfel's work that had the biggest impact and that has continued to dominate the field subsequently. After twenty-five years his influence has become more diffuse as the circles have widened, but there is little doubt that it is there.

A number of studies had suggested that competitive biases emerged more easily in the relations between groups than they should have if Sherif's (e.g. 1967) conflict of interest theory was correct. Tajfel and his colleagues decided to see just how little it took to create discrimination between groups (Tajfel, 1970; Tajfel *et al.*, 1971). They created a stripped-down intergroup situation in which all the variables normally thought to determine group cohesiveness and intergroup attitudes had been eliminated. The situation was "intergroup" only because subjects had been classified into two distinct groups and therefore were able to perceive themselves as members of one group and not members of the other. This "social categorization" variable was considered a necessary part of any intergroup relationship. In what became known as the "minimal group paradigm", there was no interaction or contact between group members, no group goals linked to group action or personal self-interest, no history of hostility between the groups and who, other than self, was in which group was unknown to subjects. There was only the perception of ingroup–outgroup membership (where assignment to groups was on the basis of a trivial *ad hoc* criterion).

Subjects had to make decisions about allocating small monetary sums to anonymous other members of their own and the other group (in various combinations), with no guidance as to what the basis of their decisions should be. Tajfel did not expect intergroup behaviour to occur in this highly controlled situation. His idea was to establish a baseline of no intergroup behaviour and then to add variables cumulatively to see at what point intergroup discrimination occurred. He assumed subjects would be fair or award as much money as possible to everyone. In fact, subjects consistently discriminated in their choices, awarding more money to ingroup members than outgroup members, both in absolute and relative terms.

This and related findings inspired great interest, disbelief and controversy. Both the experimental paradigm and the findings have inspired a mass of later research (see Turner, 1981, 1983; Turner *et al.*, 1987). Whilst the controversy as to theoretical significance still continues (see Turner and Bourhis' chapter in this book), subsequent research has established that there is little doubt about the *fact* that under certain conditions social categorization alone—the mere perception of belonging to one group in contrast to another—can be sufficient for intergroup discrimination in which members favour their own group over the other.

In thinking about the social categorization data, Henri had what he described to me in my first PhD meeting with him in 1971 as his second great idea. I remember being slightly taken aback but also excited by his self-confidence as he told me that most social psychologists were lucky if they had one great idea, but that he had just had his second! It was the idea that social comparisons between groups were focused on the establishment of positive ingroup distinctiveness, unlike intragroup comparisons which, according to Festinger (1954), led to intragroup homogeneity. I wish I had asked him what had been his first great idea (something to do with his work on perceptual accentuation, certainly, but the whole body of related ideas, the first step or a later development?).

His "idea" was published in 1972(c) in a chapter reviewing social categorization processes. He suggested that there was a psychological requirement that groups provide their members with a positive social identity and that the positive aspects of social identity were inherently comparative in nature, deriving from evaluative comparisons between social groups. It followed that to provide positive social identity, groups needed to distinguish themselves positively from other groups and that intergroup comparisons were focused on the maintenance and establishment of positively valued distinctiveness for one's ingroup. A person's social identity comprised those social categories which defined his or her place in society and which had been internalized to define the self, together with their emotional and value significance. Apart from providing a succinct account of psychological pressures for ethnocentric biases in intergroup relations, his idea was a major revision of Festinger's (1954) social comparison theory. Festinger had ruled out comparisons *between* groups (they were by definition different and non-comparable) and supposed that social reality testing through social comparison only took place where physical testing was unavailable.

Tajfel had used the term social identity before and had also spoken of the role of the self-concept in shaping the search for meaning in intergroup relations, but there is no doubt that what is now known as social identity theory began with his 1972(c) chapter (appropriately enough published in French). He used the minimal group data as an empirical illustration of the search for positive distinctiveness. My own contribution began at this stage, developing the idea of "social competition" in contrast to Sherif's realistic competition as the process underlying minimal intergroup discrimination and related phenomena of ingroup bias (Turner, 1975). Tajfel quickly took things further (1974, 1978). The core psychological proposition of a causal sequence, from social categorization to social identity, to social comparison, to positive distinctiveness, was used to erect a theoretical framework for understanding intergroup relations and social change in society at large.

Social identity theory (Tajfel, 1974, 1978; Tajfel and Turner, 1979) is not easy to summarize in a few paragraphs. The ideas changed over time in some degree, they are complex and various and have many implications, and the theory was a developing one. Henri himself (Tajfel, 1979) described it as a conceptual tripod with three legs. One leg was the psychological sequence noted above. The basic psychological dynamic was that people with unsatisfactory social identity would seek to change that state of affairs by restoring positive distinctiveness to their relevant group memberships. Another leg was the complex set of social and psychological processes that shifted behaviour from an interpersonal to an intergroup level and the psychological consequences of such a shift. Thus social conflict, social stratification, impassable social barriers between groups, beliefs systems which defined social movement as a matter of large-scale collective action rather than individual mobility, etc. all made it more likely that people with unsatisfactory social identity would tend to act and seek solutions at the intergroup level (i.e. they would act collectively as group members rather than as individuals pursuing personal self-interest). In intergroup behaviour people act in terms of shared social category memberships, behaving similarly and treating outgroup members similarly and perceiving outgroup members as stereotypically homogeneous. It is the collective level of action and perception. The psychological dynamic of seeking positive social identity only came into play to the degree that social interaction moved to the intergroup level.

The third crucial leg of the tripod was the social contextualization of the psychological dynamic. As Deutsch and Krauss (1965) stated in a passage quoted approvingly by Tajfel (1981a, p. 19):

> . . . human relationships always occur in an organized social environment—in a family, in a group, in a community, in a nation—that has developed techniques, categories, rules and values that are relevant to human interaction. Hence the understanding of the psychological events that occur in human interactions *requires comprehension of the interplay of these events with the social context in which they occur* . . . the social psychologist must be able to characterize the relevant features of the social environment in order to understand or predict human interaction'.
>
> (Deutsch and Krauss, 1965, pp. 2–3; Tajfel's italics)

Tajfel did not see the psychological dynamic of social identity as an alternative explanation to conflicting group interests or the effects of the macro-social structure. It was a complementary process, an interacting part of the complex web of causation that determined intergroup relations. Intergroup relations exist in an objective social structure. People are defined in society as members of social groups and these social categorizations refer not only to objective groupings but are socially and historically evolved. People internalize these social categorizations to define themselves subjectively. Thus these social groupings and the political, sociological and economic relationships between them have psychological aspects and consequences. Social psychology makes a "modest" contribution to explaining intergroup behaviour by pointing to processes associated with these psychological aspects, of which the social identity dynamic is one.

To predict outcomes from this dynamic, it must be understood as being situated concretely in a specific societal context which provides the relevant social categories and their meanings, contents and values and the character of political, economic, etc. relations between them, and constrains the possible ways in which the dynamic can be worked out. Much of the complexity and richness of social identity theory comes from Tajfel's attempts to integrate the psychological core with the macro-social realities of group life in societies stratified by power, wealth and status. Two important notions here were his distinction between secure and insecure intergroup comparisons and his taxonomy of strategies by which subordinate and dominant groups could react to identity problems in a social hierarchy (later systematized in Tajfel and Turner, 1979).

"Secure" groups were those of different status which nevertheless saw no "cognitive alternatives" to the status quo; their relationship was in a quiescent state, with minimal active comparison between them. "Insecure" groups actively compared themselves to each other even where they were of different status; their relationship was perceived as unstable and illegitimate, from differing perspectives, and their social identities were in a state of active mutual threat. As a function of whether they were secure or insecure, of high or low social status, groups would have a range of specifiable problems to deal with in terms of the implications of their situation for the positive social identity of their members.

These problems again could be solved by a range of psychological and behavioural options constrained by the essential psychological structure of the identity dynamic and by the objective macro-social and ideological realities. An insecure subordinate group, for example, with unsatisfactory social identity, could engage in strategies of "individual mobility", "social creativity" or "social competition" (Tajfel and Turner, 1979). These notions were elaborated and tested in laboratory studies and in more descriptive studies of particular real-life intergroup relationships (Tajfel, 1978, 1982).

This is not the place to review subsequent research on social identity theory. Suffice to say that much has addressed its psychological core in isolation from Tajfel's metatheory. This has led to a misunderstanding of certain key ideas and even to suggestions that the theory is individualistic, reducing intergroup conflict to psychological causes. Tajfel (1979) answered this charge. It is not intended to be a macro-social theory. It is not intended to be an individual–psychological theory. It is *social* psychological, outlining concepts and processes which lend themselves to the job of integrating the psychological aspects of intergroup relations with the macro-social structure which provides their context and with which they interact. In terms of any real-life intergroup relationship, the theory provides a framework, a set of theoretical tools, for concrete analysis, not a set of ready-made empirical generalizations.

Social psychology and the social context

> Social psychology *can* and *must* include in its theoretical and research preoccupations, a direct concern with the relationship between human psychological functioning and the large-scale social processes and events which shape this functioning and are shaped by it.
>
> (Tajfel, 1981a, p. 7)

Tajfel wrote important papers about the nature of social psychology (1972a, 1979, 1981b) and made relevant points throughout his work. He criticized what he saw as a continuing tendency for social psychological theory to be reductionist and individualistic, as opposed to properly *social* psychological. He pointed out that our models seem to assume that we are describing and explaining the behaviour of randomly interacting individual persons, operating in an unstructured, homogeneous social medium:

> a clear distinction must be made between theories which are'individualistic' and one which is concerned with socially-shared patterns of individual behaviour. An'individualistic' theory contains the (most often) unstated assumption that individuals live and behave in a homogeneous social medium. This medium consists of a collection of undifferentiated individual particles which are assumed to relate to each other inter-individually following the laws of basic psychological processes. There is no room in this vision of randomly floating particles for the cognitive and socially-shared *organization* of the system within which the particles float.
>
> (1981a, p. 49)

The reality is of course quite otherwise. People live and act in a socially structured system and this social system has major psychological consequences. Social structure, society, provides the normal and ever-present environment of social behaviour. The interaction between society and the individual is expressed in socially-shared psychological regularities which are irreducible to biological, sociological or general–psychological mechanisms. They are expressed, for example, in our experimental data which are neither genotypic nor phenotypic, neither "general" nor "individual", but both socially systematic and variable:

> the general case is an impossible myth as long as human beings behave as they do because of the social expectations with which they enter an experiment—or any other social situation. If these expectations are shared—as they always are by definition to some degree in any social context—I shall obtain data from my experiment which are neither "general" nor "individual". The observed regularities of behaviour will result from the interaction between general processes and the social context in which they operate . . .
>
> . . . If . . . the background social context of the experiment and the social task that the experiment itself presents to the subjects provide enough common meaning to determine the observed regularities, then we must provide a kind of interpretation of the data that is specific to many problems in the social sciences . . . the observed regularities . . . fall somewhere in between the general case and the unknowable, individual case. Their range of application is determined by the nature of human social behaviour in which lawful but diverse modifications of pattern occur as a function of interactions between human groups and their social environment.
>
> (Tajfel, 1981a, p. 21)

These socially shared patterns of perception and conduct, the collective similarities and differences between human beings, are a result of interactions between the socially shared and derived properties of individuals and psychological processes functioning in specific social contexts. Thus social psychology is not about biology, sociology or general psychology. It is not simply the use of general psychology but incorporating people as social stimuli, or social factors as independent variables. We need theories which recognize the discontinuities between the psychological mechanisms involved in social and non-social behaviour and that qualitatively different kinds of theories are necessary to capture the interplay between psychology and the shared social properties of humans.

The proper and defining task of social psychology is to study the interplay between psychological functioning and social structure and propose theories consistent with and explanatory of such an interplay.

Social identity provides one illustration of a properly social psychological concept (see Oakes and Turner, 1986; Turner and Oakes, 1986). Social categories are socially evolved representations of social structure, that define an individual in terms of a common social location and are shared with others in that location. They can be internalized to change the psychology and conduct of the individual, producing a qualitative shift to a collective psychology:

> Any society which contains power, status, prestige and social groups differentials (and they all do), places each of us in a number of *social* categories which become an important part of our *self*-definition. In situations which relate to those aspects of our self-definition that we think we share with others, we shall behave very much as they do . . . They acted together, but it was not because of any *individual* facts of their personal psychology.
>
> (Tajfel, 1977, p. 66)

Similarly, intergroup relations, as the very opposite of individual behaviour, is a quintessential problem of social psychology. It is fine for social psychologists to be interested in explaining idiosyncratic, exceptional behaviour, but much more important in terms of their special task is for them to find out "why so many people behave in unison—which they often do" (Tajfel, 1977, p. 66). Social psychology is not about individual differences, but the socially shared. The focus must be on the collective aspects of conduct, the socially shared, derived and systematic, on how social forces shape the many, not the individual exception.

To address the collective aspects of psychology, our theories need to employ concepts that are as much socially derived and meaningful as psychological and the explanatory process should work from the social to the psychological, not try to build up the social from the individual–psychological. In this sense, all social psychology is "cultural", not meaning that it should simply study cross-cultural differences, but that it should employ concepts and theories which allow for the integration of cultural products and patterns with psychological explanation.

Tajfel's discussions of social identity theory, intergroup relations and the social functions of stereotypes show how he tried to put these ideas into practice. He also discussed the social normative character of social conduct, its relationship to socially created rules, norms and values, as a fundamental argument against reduction to biological or asocial/presocial psychological theory. He suggested that cognitive dissonance theory, for example, could be regarded as social psychological and not merely individual–cognitive because concepts of "commitment" and "justification" are inherent in it. These concepts "are capable of being analysed in terms of their social derivation and they have their own derivations in the sharing, diffusing and communicating of conflicting modes of social conduct" (Tajfel, 1981a, p. 39).

His general point is that human social conduct is fundamentally rule-governed. People seek to act appropriately (and evaluate themselves positively) in terms of the social norms and values of their social groups and the wider society. Such norms and values derive from social systems and ideologies. Thus social conduct is not based on a "hedonistic algebra of self-interest . . . based on a few universal human drives" (1981a, p. 36), as so many so-called social psychological theories seem to suppose:

> In the field of social conduct, rules can be described as notions about appropriateness. This means quite simply that social conduct is to a very large extent determined by what an individual deems to be appropriate to the social situation in which he finds himself. His conceptions of what is appropriate are in turn determined by the prevailing system of norms and values which must be analysed in the light of the properties of the social system in which he lives . . .
>
> . . . Values are the implicit and explicit ideologies of a society—political, social, moral or religious—and of the subgroups within it . . .
>
> . . . It is because of the socially derived, shared, accepted and conflicting notions of appropriateness of conduct, because of the social definition of the situations to which they apply, and of the social origin of their manner of changing and of relating to one another, that individual or inter-individual psychology cannot be usefully considered as providing the bricks from which an adequate social psychology can be built. The derivations need to be in the opposite direction.
>
> (Tajfel, 1981a, pp. 36–39)

Tajfel's conviction was that social psychology needed to reject individualism and reductionism not as a matter of idle philosophy but of good science. Unless we sought to explain human social behaviour in terms of the "cognitive and socially shared organization of the [social] system" within which people define themselves and interact (1981a, p. 49), our theories would not only remain misleading, they would also be irrelevant and weak.

Henri Tajfel's argument for a genuinely *social* psychology was not a call to study sociology or purely social processes, nor did it have anything to do with the notion that we should be studying social groups or institutions or culture in contrast to individuals, and least of all was it an argument against fully psychological analysis. It was a demand for a particular kind of psychological theory, one that was founded on, explanatory of and capable of integration with the socially-shared regularities of social conduct, deriving from the interaction between individuals and their societal form of organization.

Acknowledgements

I wish to thank Rachael Eggins, Rupert Brown and Peter Robinson for their help in preparing this chapter.

References

Bruner, J. S. (1981). Foreword to H. Tajfel's *Human groups and social categories*. Cambridge, UK: Cambridge University Press.

Deutsch, M., and Krauss, R. M. (1965). *Theories in social psychology.* New York: Basic Books.

Festinger, L. (1954). A theory of social comparison processes. *Human Relations*, **7**, 117–140.

Himmelweit, H. T. (1982). Obituary: Henri Tajfel, FBPsS. *Bulletin of the British Psychological Society*, **35**, 288–289.

LeVine, R. A., and Campbell, D. T. (1972). *Ethnocentrism: Theories of conflict, ethnic attitudes and group behaviour.* New York: Wiley.

Oakes, P. J., Haslam, S. A., and Turner, J. C. (1994). *Stereotyping and social reality.* Oxford, UK and Cambridge, MA: Blackwell.

Oakes, P. J., and Turner, J. C. (1986). Authors' rejoinder to Jahoda and Tetlock (the problem is not the level but the kind of analysis). *British Journal of Social Psychology*, **25**, 257–258.

Peters, R. S., and Tajfel, H. (1957). Hobbes and Hull—metaphysicians of behaviour. *British Journal for the Philosophy of Science*, **8**, 30–44.

Sherif, M. (1967). *Group conflict and co-operation: Their social psychology.* London: Routledge and Kegan Paul.

Tajfel, H. (1957). Value and the perceptual judgement of magnitude. *Psychological Review*, **64**, 192–204.

Tajfel, H. (1959). Quantitative judgement in social perception. *British Journal of Psychology*, **50**, 16–29.

Tajfel, H. (1969). Cognitive aspects of prejudice. *Journal of Social Issues*, **25**, 79–97.

Tajfel, H. (1970). Experiments in intergroup discrimination. *Scientific American*, **233**, 96–102.

Tajfel, H. (1972a). Experiments in a vacuum. In J. Israel and H. Tajfel (Eds), *The context of social psychology.* London: Academic Press.

Tajfel, H. (1972b). Some developments in European social psychology. *European Journal of Social Psychology*, **2**, 307–321.

Tajfel, H. (1972c). La catégorisation sociale. In S. Moscovici (Ed.), *Introduction à la psychologie sociale*. Paris: Larousse.

Tajfel, H. (1974). Social identity and intergroup behaviour. *Social Science Information*, **13**, 65–93.

Tajfel, H. (1977). Social psychology and social reality. *New Society*, **39**, 65–66.

Tajfel, H. (1978). (Ed.), *Differentiation between social groups: Studies in the social psychology of intergroup relations*. London: Academic Press.

Tajfel, H. (1979). Individuals and groups in social psychology. *British Journal of Social and Clinical Psychology*, **18**, 183–190.

Tajfel, H. (1981a). *Human groups and social categories*. Cambridge: Cambridge University Press.

Tajfel, H. (1981b). Social stereotypes and social groups. In J. C. Turner and H. Giles (Eds), *Intergroup behaviour.* Oxford: Blackwell, and Chicago: University of Chicago Press.

Tajfel, H. (1982). (Ed.) *Social identity and intergroup relations*. Cambridge: Cambridge University Press, and Paris: Editions de la Maison des Sciences de l'Homme.

Tajfel, H. (1984). (Ed.) *The social dimension: European developments in social psychology.* Cambridge: Cambridge University Press, and Paris: Editions de la Maison des Sciences de l'Homme.

Tajfel, H., and Cawasjee, S. D. (1959). Value and the accentuation of judged differences. *Journal of Abnormal and Social Psychology*, **59**, 436–439.

Tajfel, H., and Dawson, J. K. (Eds) (1965). *Disappointed guests*. Oxford: Oxford University Press.

Tajfel, H., Flament, C., Billig, M. G., and Bundy, R. F. (1971). Social categorization and intergroup behaviour. *European Journal of Social Psychology*, **1**, 149–177.

Tajfel, H., Jahoda, G., Nemeth, C., Rime, Y., and Johnson, N. B. (1972). Devaluation by children of their own national or ethnic group: Two case studies. *British Journal of Social and Clinical Psychology*, **11**, 235–243.

Tajfel, H., Jaspars, J. M. F., and Fraser, C. (1984). The social dimension in European social psychology. In H. Tajfel (Ed.), *The social dimension: European developments in social psychology.* Cambridge: Cambridge University Press, and Paris: Editions de la Maison des Sciences de l'Homme.

Tajfel, H., Nemeth, C., Jahoda, G., Campbell, J. D., and Johnson, N. B. (1970). The development of children's preferences for their own country: A cross-national study. *International Journal of Psychology*, **5**, 245–253.

Tajfel, H., Sheikh, A. A., and Gardner, R. C. (1964). Content of stereotypes and the inference of similarity between members of stereotyped groups. *Acta Psychologica*, **22**, 191–201.

Tajfel, H., and Turner, J. C. (1979). An integrative theory of intergroup conflict. In W. G. Austin and S. Worchel (Eds), *The social psychology of intergroup relations.* Monterey, CA: Brooks/Cole.

Tajfel, H., and Wilkes, A. L. (1963). Classification and quantitative judgement. *British Journal of Psychology*, **54**, 101–114.

Tajfel, H., and Wilkes, A. L. (1964). Salience of attributes and commitment to extreme judgements in the perception of people. *British Journal of Social and Clinical Psychology*, **2**, 40–49.

Turner, J. C. (1975). Social comparison and social identity: Some prospects for intergroup behaviour. *European Journal of Social Psychology*, **5**, 149–178.

Turner, J. C. (1981). The experimental social psychology of intergroup behaviour. In J. C. Turner and H. Giles (Eds), *Intergroup behaviour.* Oxford: Blackwell, and Chicago: University of Chicago Press.

Turner, J. C. (1982). Towards a cognitive redefinition of the social group. In H. Tajfel (Ed.), *Social identity and intergroup relations.* Cambridge: Cambridge University Press, and Paris: Editions de la Maison des Sciences de l'Homme.

Turner, J. C. (1983). Some comments on . . ."the measurement of social orientations in the minimal group paradigm". *European Journal of Social Psychology*, **13**, 351–367.

Turner, J. C., Hogg, M. A., Oakes, P. J., Reicher, S. D., and Wetherell, M. S. (1987). *Rediscovering the social group: A self-categorization theory.* Oxford and New York: Blackwell.

Turner, J. C., and Oakes, P. J. (1986). The significance of the social identity concept for social psychology with reference to individualism, interactionism, and social influence. *British Journal of Social Psychology*, **25**, 237–252.

1

Social Identity, Interdependence and the Social Group: A Reply to Rabbie *et al.*

JOHN C. TURNER

Division of Psychology, The Australian National University
and

RICHARD Y. BOURHIS

Département de Psychologie, Université du Québec à Montréal

Contents

> Only because individuals are capable of realizing the possibilities of joint action do these possibilities become real; on this basis arise actions having a mutual reference. To say this is fundamentally different from asserting that group facts are subjective constructions in the minds of individuals. They achieve objective expression because we are capable subjectively of

> grasping them . . . we must grasp the unusual process that gives rise to groups at the human level . . . It is the only part–whole relation that depends on the recapitulation of the structure of the whole in the part.
>
> (Asch, 1952, pp. 252–257)

> The processes of social categorization, social identity and social comparison, as used in the theory, cannot be conceived to originate outside of their social contexts.
>
> (Tajfel, 1979, p. 185)

> Social groups are not "things"; they are processes . . . the psychological existence of a group for its members is a complex sequence of appearances and disappearances, of looming large and vanishing into thin air . . . In the static conception, the groups are seen as "being there" side by side, almost like herrings packed in a box, coming to life to "perceive" each other whenever prodded into doing so by the researchers. In the dynamic conception, groups (and intergroup relations) come to life when their *potential* designations as such have acquired a psychological and behavioural reality.
>
> (Tajfel, 1982, p. 485)

Introduction: Social Identity versus Interdependence

In a series of papers (Horwitz and Rabbie, 1989; Rabbie, 1991; Rabbie and Horwitz, 1988; Rabbie *et al.*, 1989), Rabbie and his colleagues have argued against the analysis of the social group and intergroup relations provided by social identity and self-categorization theories (Tajfel and Turner, 1979; Turner *et al.* 1987). Their two most important assertions are (1) that Tajfel and Turner have failed to make a fundamental distinction between social categories of similar individuals and social groups as dynamic wholes or behaving social systems and (2) that social identity research over the last twenty-five years has been based on a major misinterpretation of the results of the minimal group paradigm (MGP). They argue, and claim to provide data to demonstrate, that ingroup favouritism in the minimal group paradigm is not a function of social categorization or social identification but is purely rational, instrumental, utilitarian and (economically) self-interested.

The significance of their claims, if proved valid, is beyond doubt. Social identity ideas have made a large and growing contribution to social psychology in the last twenty-five years, especially in Europe but also in North America, Australia and elsewhere, in research on group processes, social influence, intergroup relations and social cognition. Much current research is based on social identity theory's interpretation of intergroup behaviour and self-categorization theory's reconceptualization of the psychological group. The critique of the interdependence model of group processes explicit in these theories is widely accepted. Rabbie *et al.*'s papers represent the first systematic attempt by interdependence theorists to respond to the ideas and data of social identity and self-categorization theories. It is important to assess the success and usefulness or otherwise of the theory (the behavioural interaction, or group interdependence, model, BIM) they propose.

In addition, many researchers—whether or not working from a social identity perspective—have been influenced by the standard interpretation of the minimal group paradigm, accepting that social categorization can alone, under certain conditions, lead to intergroup discrimination. The paradigm has been widely used as a methodological tool, in the belief that minimal groups do capture key psychological aspects of group formation under controlled conditions. It is also true that many researchers have been influenced by the metatheory of the social identity perspective, its rejection of reductionism and individualism and its demand for genuinely social psychological explanations (see Tajfel, 1979, 1981; Turner and Oakes, 1986).

According to Rabbie *et al.*, all this is based on error. The minimal group paradigm, they state, is so confounded as to show nothing more than simple instrumental self-interest at work, albeit in a form which mirrors ordinary group formation. The confusion of groups with categories of similar individuals means that social identity ideas are *de facto* reductionist and individualistic, unable to cope with group-level phenomena and providing "intrapsychic", "cognitive" explanations of intergroup relations. A genuine social psychology, it seems, requires a return to interdependence theory. Turner's (1985) argument that interdependence theory has become an individual-level perspective is apparently flawed.

Are Rabbie *et al.* correct? A clear answer is required if group research is to progress. The analysis of the social group is central to social psychology, and the conflict of views between Rabbie *et al.* and social identity theorists revolves around major theoretical issues in the field. Empirical dispute between different theories is healthy and to be welcomed, but conceptual and semantic confusion and the prevalence of flawed interpretations of significant data can only sabotage the scientific effort. Fortunately, a definite answer is possible. We shall show that Rabbie *et al.* are victims of a "semantic confusion" (Tajfel, 1982), that their arguments are inconsistent and self-contradictory, that their own studies show that MGP responses cannot be explained in terms of instrumental self-interest, and that Rabbie *et al.* are forced to adopt *post hoc* key social identity and self-categorization ideas to explain their data. The suggestion that social identity ideas are intrapsychic and reductionist is mere sloganizing based on a refusal to confront the published literature. Throughout their critique Rabbie *et al.* deal with awkward facts and ideas simply by ignoring them.

Rabbie *et al.* make their points frankly but without personal animus. This reply is made in exactly the same spirit. We shall explain why we reject their critique, however, it should not be inferred that we do not esteem our colleagues and their many contributions to social psychology.

Social Categories versus Social Groups?

Rabbie *et al.* pose the difference between social identity and interdependence theories in terms of a contrast between social categories and social groups (we shall often use social identity theory as a generic term to include self-categorization theory). Rabbie and Horwitz (1988, p. 117) state that a "social group can be considered as a "dynamic whole" or social system, characterized by the perceived interdependence among its members, whereas a social category can be defined as a collection of individuals who share at least one attribute in common". A category becomes a group, they say, when people act "as a locomoting entity" (p. 119). They suggest that social identity theory blurs the distinction between categories and groups and supposes that groups can be equated with social categories.

In fact, it is difficult to think of anyone in social psychology who has ever believed that a social group is only a category, that there is no difference between a sociological category (or membership group) and a psychological (or reference) group characterized by organized social activity. From Le Bon and McDougall onwards, social psychologists have made a basic distinction between a group defined by outsiders which has no psychological implications for its members and one which has a psychological and social reality for them (Turner, 1991; Turner *et al.*, 1987). Tajfel and Turner are not an exception. The distinction is explicit in Tajfel's discussions (e.g. 1978) and is the *whole subject* of self-categorization theory. The aim of the latter is to understand the social psychological processes whereby individuals are able to form a behaving social group. Moreover, the theory explicitly assumes a metatheory of "interactionism" in which the social reality of groups is taken for granted as interacting with psychological processes (Turner and Oakes, 1986, 1989).

Rabbie *et al.* first mooted the idea that social identity theory reduced groups to categories in Tajfel's 1982 book (see Horwitz and Rabbie, 1982). Tajfel spent part of his concluding chapter pointing out that this was a "semantic confusion" (1982, p. 500). He pleaded that discussion of substantive issues not be side-tracked by such an obvious misconception. The semantic confusion was to fail to discriminate two different theoretical usages of the term "category". On the one hand, social categories can refer to objective collections of similar individuals as defined by outside observers, i.e. objectively defined groupings which may not be subjectively significant for their members (e.g. some sociological category such as single income families in rural areas). On the other hand, social categories are also shared *cognitive representations*, *psychological concepts* which can play a part in the analysis of the group as a *social psychological process*. Turner's usage in his 1982 chapter in the book, Tajfel pointed out, was plainly not the former one, but a dynamic, psychological one, in which *the capacity of people to represent themselves cognitively as members of social categories* is part of the process whereby sociological categories become genuinely psychological groups (cf. the quotation from Asch above).

The very premise of Turner's chapter, apparently not understood by Rabbie *et al.*, was that *externally defined, objective categories were not psychological groups* and that there was a need to develop a theory of the psychological processes which made the transition from category to group possible:

> We are concerned here with group membership as a psychological and not a formal–institutional state, with the subjective sense of togetherness, we-ness, or belongingness which indicates the formation of a psychological group. What are the necessary and sufficient conditions for some aggregate of individuals to feel themselves to be a group and act accordingly?
>
> (Turner, 1982, p. 16)

Tajfel referred Horwitz and Rabbie to his own discussions of the problem of defining a group, in which he stressed that psychological group formation had to be defined from the subjective perspective of the participants, in terms of the *internal psychological criteria* of group membership (Tajfel, 1978, 1981). Tajfel was fond of the definition of a group as a collection of people who feel that they are a group (cf. McDougall, 1921). This definition stresses the psychological and subjective aspects of group belongingness, defining a social group from the perspective of its participants, not from that of some outside sociological observer. It is the opposite of the idea of the group as a category in the crucial respect which Rabbie *et al.* gloss over: *it is the members who are using the category to define themselves* and hence are able to bring into being an emergent collective life. Rabbie *et al.* leave out the essence of social identity and self-categorization theories in their critique, namely the psychological role of social categories *in defining and transforming the individual self* into one based on collective, shared social identity. Rabbie *et al.* fail to understand the role of *self-categories* in the *psychological processes* by which members form an emergent social entity and confuse self-categories with sociological categories.

Tajfel also reminded them of the research conducted within the MGP in which the hypothesis that group membership can be equated with similarity between individual persons had already been tested and rejected (Billig and Tajfel, 1973). That is, contrary to the view attributed to them by Rabbie *et al.*, social identity researchers long ago rejected the idea that group formation could be understood as interpersonal similarity (Turner, 1975, 1982; Turner *et al.*, 1983).

The distinction between categories and groups is also apparent in the first discussions by Tajfel *et al.* (1971) and Turner (1975) of the minimal group findings. They always supposed that the explanation of minimal intergroup discrimination could not be simply attributed to experimenter-imposed social categorization. This merely redescribes the independent variable. The theoretical issue was the nature of the social psychological processes operating in the subjects which explained how and why they accepted the social division imposed by the experimenter as a relevant basis for their behaviour. That is, what processes intervened between social categorization and the actions of the subjects as a "behaving social system"? Tajfel *et al.* (1971) talked of the "subject effect". Turner (1975) stated:

> Whilst it is true empirically that *under certain conditions* categorization *per se* is sufficient for intergroup discrimination, the proposition may be theoretically misleading to the extent that it suggests that "acceptance" by subjects of a categorization is automatic and its use inevitable rather than indicating that "acceptance" itself is to be explained in terms of how the category is used.
>
> (p. 17)

The explanation of minimal intergroup discrimination is to be found in the psychological processes underlying acceptance of the social categorization by the subjects as self-defining and the attendant psychological consequences, not in the simple imposition of a social classification, as if psychological groups were nothing but externally designated categories (Turner and Oakes, 1989). This is a confusion in the minds of Rabbie *et al.* that was never in the minds of Tajfel and Turner. The intellectual proof is that self-categorization theory was developed to make sense of the former processes (see the Preface in Turner *et al.*, 1987) and social identity theory originated to deal with the "attendant psychological consequences".

Group Definitions and the Metatheory of Social Identity

It is noticeable that Rabbie *et al.* are nowhere able to cite Tajfel and Turner to the effect that a social group is only a category. Tajfel (1982) specifically denied such a view. Tajfel and Turner (1986) define a group as follows: "a collection of individuals who perceive themselves to be members of the same social category, share some emotional involvement in this common definition of themselves, and achieve some degree of social consensus about the evaluation of their group and of their membership in it" (p. 15). Another definition (Turner, 1978, 1982, p. 15) is that a psychological group is a collection of people "who share a common identification of themselves or . . . perceive themselves to be members of the same social category" (see Turner and Oakes, 1989). To read these definitions as blurring the distinction between group and category is superficial and unjustified. They must be read in the context of the metatheory of social identity.

Rabbie *et al.* routinely imply that social identity theory is reductionist and asocial because it is psychological (whilst getting the substance of the psychology wrong). They ignore statements that social identity and self-categorization theories are concerned not with the complete scientific explanation of the human group but with its psychological aspects. The theories are deliberately selective, limited, and specialized in being social psychological. They do not deny the role of social processes because they focus on psychological ones, but assume their role as part of their "interactionist" metatheory (Oakes and Turner, 1986; Tajfel, 1979, 1981; Turner and Oakes, 1986). This perspective proposes a dynamic interaction between the psychological and social reality of groups. A social psychological theory is neither sociological nor an eclectic combination of sociological and individual–psychological elements, but one that addresses the functional interaction between psychological and social processes. It must show how the psychological processes invoked cannot be conceived to operate outside the contexts of social reality. This is not the same as a theory which simply incorporates social factors as independent variables affecting individual–psychological processes or conceives of such processes as operating outside a socially structured organization of life (Tajfel, 1979, 1981). Tajfel made these points over and over again.

Thus Tajfel and Turner's definitions do not indicate a reductionist view that groups are to be explained in terms of individual psychology. They are to be understood as focusing on the psychological aspects of society in a way that takes for granted the role of social reality and seeks to formulate psychological theories consistent with such a "taking-for-granted" and explanatory of it. For example, Turner and Giles (1981) argued that there was a continual causal interplay between social identity as a cognitive representation and as a social product:

> The group is both a psychological process and a social product . . . the psychological hypothesis is that group behaviour and relationships are mediated by a cognitive redefinition of the self in terms of shared social category memberships and associated stereotypes.
>
> On the other hand, however, the group is a social reality. It refers to real interrelated people engaged in concrete social activities as a function of their social relationships and goals . . . The cognitive processes instigate collective interaction and thus the emergence of social processes. The latter produce social structures, roles, norms, values, purposes, etc. which in turn become determinants of individual psychological functioning. The same also applies to the development of social identity itself . . . This is apparent in that the theory takes for granted that real intergroup relations presuppose *shared* social categorizations and stereotypes, with a specific *sociocultural* content, related to members' *collective purposes* and the explanation, justification and evaluation of *concrete political and historical contexts* . . . the group is a product of social influences as well as cognitive and motivational processes.
>
> (Turner and Giles, 1981, p. 27)

Similarly, in response to a continuing tendency to vulgarize social identity theory as if it were a psychologizing and reductionist theory, Tajfel (1979) made a specific point of explaining why social identity theory could not be reduced to an "intrapersonal" need for self-esteem or cognitive simplicity or solely to the psychological sequence of "social categorization–social identity–social comparison" (p. 184).

This latter sequence is merely one leg of the theory's "conceptual tripod". For the theory to contribute to explaining "certain selected uniformities of social behaviour . . . we must know (i) something about the ways "groups" are constructed in a particular social system, (ii) what are the psychological effects of these constructions; and (iii) how the constructions and their effects depend upon, and relate to, forms of social reality" (1979, p. 185). The psychological sequence leading to the search for positive ingroup distinctiveness and positive social identity is part of the answer to (ii); self-categorization theory and other explanations of variation along the interpersonal–intergroup continuum of social behaviour are relevant to (i); and the "relationships between . . . social intergroup constructions and their effects . . . and . . . various forms of social reality" (p. 186) are relevant to (iii). In relation to (iii), Tajfel stated: "'Social reality' can be described or analysed in terms of socio-economic, historical or political structures. Such descriptions or analyses are not within the competence of the social psychologist", but he or she *can* ascertain the "shared interpretations of social reality" held by group members, and such shared perceptions of intergroup relations as being secure or insecure, legitimate or illegitimate, and so on, in combination with the perceived location of groups within the particular system, can be used to formulate testable hypotheses.

In line with this same metatheory, self-categorization theory relates the cognitive activity of self-categorizing to changes in the social relationships between self and others in varying social contexts. The theory shows how self-categories are social contextual definitions of the individual (Turner *et al.*, 1994). It supposes that the self-process works to socialize cognitive functioning and individual behaviour and ensure that cognitive activity is tied closely to the current realities of the individual's social environment. In its application to stereotyping, for example, it takes for granted the reality of the social group and collective relationships (Oakes *et al.*, 1991, 1994).

When we focus on social identification to explain group behaviour, it is a focus on certain selected psychological processes which exist as part of a complex interplay between the realities of social life and the properties of social individuals, living not in a social vacuum or a homogeneous medium of interindividuality, but in a definite social and historical time and place, in a society which is socially structured and specific. This is why social psychology cannot explain everything about how a group forms. What it can do is to show the processes which translate social and historical realities into individual perceptions and behaviour. The theory is not therefore reductionist or purely "cognitive", but explains exactly how the psychological processes of individuals can give rise in concrete social contexts to the emergent social and psychological reality of groups.

From this perspective, the group definitions of Tajfel and Turner cited above indicate that social identity is *social consensual* (i.e. shared, related to processes of social influence), *social comparative* (related to perceived social relationships), *self-evaluative* (affective, related to social values and motivation and self-defining) and that it has a specific *social content* (i.e. it is defined by particular dimensions of comparison), related to the realities of the society in which people actually live. The purposive, goal-oriented aspects of self-categorization are also explicit in Bruner's notion of a "perceptual readiness" to categorize taken over in the explanation of group formation by self-categorization theory (Oakes, 1987).

The other major point completely ignored by Rabbie *et al.* is that self-categorization theory shows how the transition from personal to social identity gives rise to the emergent, higher-order properties of group life. The group forms a psychological system which transforms qualitatively interpersonal into intra- and intergroup behaviour. For example, the theory explains group norms as a dynamic and emergent property of the group as a whole (just as Kurt Lewin would have understood). It is a "field" theory not only in seeing the psychological and social as functioning within a unified field but also in being more consistent with Lewin's own *Gestalt* idea of interdependence than BIM. The key point in its psychological analysis is not the simple fact that people represent social groups in terms of categories but the *qualitative transformation of the self and social behaviour* produced by the self-categorization. A group is not a category, but a group may emerge from social and psychological processes which lead a collection of people to invent, create and use a social category as a shared definition of themselves in such a way as to transform "qualititatively" their social relationships.

Perceived Interdependence and Group Formation

Another basic theoretical issue which Rabbie *et al.* confuse is the relationship between interdependence and group formation. On the one hand, they tell us that BIM is a "group-interdependence theory" (Horwitz and Rabbie, 1989, p. 107), that a "dynamic whole" is a group where the members are interdependent with respect to outcomes and that people seek positive outcomes from their group membership. On the other hand, they imply that social identity theory is preoccupied with similarity and ignores, neglects or denies the role of interdependence. They try to draw a stark contrast between BIM as a theory which acknowledges the importance of objective and perceived interdependence (in terms of goals, outcomes, needs, the reward structure of the situation), and social identity theory as one which ignores all forms of interdependence. The truth is quite otherwise.

Thus Turner (1981, p. 100) stated:

> There is no doubt at all that people's objective interests (economic, political, etc.) play a major role in social conflict . . . There is also no doubt that that individuals' goals or purposes do contribute to group formation;

and Tajfel (1982), in replying in part to Horwitz and Rabbie (1982), reminded them that:

> Intergroup comparisons reflect a pattern in which both instrumentality and social identity must be taken into account. As we once wrote (Tajfel and Turner, 1979), the perspective stressing the functioning of social categorization, social identity and social comparison in intergroup relations must be conceived as *complementary* to the views emphasizing the importance in these relations of the "objective" conflict of interests, rather than as aiming to be a substitute for these views.
>
> (p. 499)

Far from ignoring interdependence, its relationship to group formation has been spelled out in some detail by self-categorization theory. This relationship is one of the cornerstones of the theory. Firstly, it is important to note (Turner *et al.*, 1987) that the meaning of interdependence is both varied and has changed significantly over the years. Originally it had a field–theoretical or *Gestalt* quality and indicated the idea of groups as dynamic social systems with emergent whole-properties. Members who were interdependent parts of such systems were qualitatively changed by their membership in the whole. From this perspective, self-categorization theory is an interdependence theory (see Preface, Turner *et al.*, 1987), since it holds that groups are organized wholes which are more than the sum of their parts and that members are changed psychologically by their interrelationships. Another more general meaning shared by the theory is the idea of psychological interdependence as the reciprocal psychological influence of one member on another (see McDougall, 1921).

If we turn specifically to goal interdependence, we find that self-categorization theory always explicitly proposed that the perceived interdependence of people could function as both a cause and an effect of psychological group formation (Turner, 1981, 1982, 1985). It was hypothesized that any variable such as common fate, shared threat, proximity, similarity, shared interests, co-operative interaction or positive interdependence which could function *cognitively as a criterion of social categorization to produce an awareness of shared social identity* could lead to group formation. We can define ourselves as a distinct we-group on the basis of our shared interests in contrast to others. Similarity of fate, shared goals, etc. can directly create a group through social identification prior to any experience of positive outcomes mediated by group membership. It is also made clear in our contemporary work that a psychological readiness to categorize oneself socially is related to the motives, values, expectations and goals served by the social categorization (Oakes *et al.*, 1994; Turner *et al.*, 1994).

Similarly, it was hypothesized long ago that group formation could produce perceived interdependence:

> The social group can be an independent variable in the perception of co-operative and competitive interdependence . . . we can derive from the social identity principle the hypothesis that . . . social categorization *per se* should cause individuals to perceive their interests as co-operatively linked within groups and competitively linked between groups . . . the formation of a common or superordinate group tends to induce and stabilize co-operative behaviour in the same way that an ingroup–outgroup division elicits competitive tendencies: not merely through the need for positive distinctiveness, but more basically, because social categorization directly influences individuals' perceptions of their goals.
>
> (Turner, 1981, pp. 97–98).

This explanation of social co-operation was elaborated further as self-categorization theory developed. It is assumed that a salient social identity *depersonalizes* the self and so transforms differing personal self-interests into a collective we-group interest (Turner, 1985; Turner *et al.*, 1987). These ideas have been applied and tested in research on social co-operation and conflict–resolution and contact (e.g. Brewer and Schneider, 1990; Caporael *et al.*, 1989; Gaertner *et al.*, 1989, 1990).

The disagreement between self-categorization theory and BIM is *not* about the empirical importance of interdependence *but its theoretical role. Is perceived interdependence the necessary and sufficient causal basis for psychological group formation?* Does group belongingness represent the development of mutual co-operation and social cohesion between persons based on the mutual satisfaction of their individual needs? Self-categorization theory holds that interdependence, like many other variables, *can* lead to group formation, but only where it leads to mutual social identification. It proposes that the underlying psychological process is the emergence of shared social identity, not the development of reward-based cohesiveness.

This is not playing with words. If interdependence only leads to group formation where it is associated with the development of a shared social identification, then it is not necessary and neither, under certain conditions, will it be sufficient. Such a view produces distinctive empirical predictions. For example, can people who mediate costs for each other form a psychological group? Self-categorization theory supposes that shared negative outcomes can sometimes produce a group (Turner *et al.*, 1983, 1984). What if identity is only based on being in a common situation rather than positive or negative outcomes? Self-categorization theory supposes that this kind of similarity can lead to group belongingness, as in the MGP. What if positive interdependence and co-operative interaction fail to eliminate important cognitive boundaries between the groups; does this reduce intergroup conflict? There is evidence (see Worchel, 1979) that superordinate goals and co-operation do not always reduce intergroup competition. Does group cohesiveness always increase with mutual need satisfaction? It would be hard to follow Lewin's (1948) analysis of the formation of the Jewish group identity as a result of oppression and deprivation by the majority group if this were always so. How can one create social co-operation? Does group formation produce social co-operation or is it merely a consequence of co-operation (reflecting objective interdependence)? Self-categorization theory argues that there is no one-to-one correspondence between objective interests and social relationships. Before a group will co-operate in its own interests, it must define itself as a group (Turner *et al.*, 1987, pp. 31–35, 65–66).

Self-categorization theory, therefore, holds that goal interdependence is neither necessary nor sufficient for co-operation and group formation, but that *once a group is formed* (and one *empirical* factor could be the awareness of interdependent goals or of a common fate), it will directly affect how people perceive their interests and in particular will lead to the development of collective, shared interests. BIM argues in contrast that outcome interdependence is the fundamental underlying process in group formation. Or does it? What is striking in the papers of Rabbie *et al.* is how far they have come to accept the social identity view despite their clamour about group interdependence. They apparently no longer believe that interdependence is necessary for group formation—"cognitive boundaries" they now agree are sufficient—and they completely agree that social categorization *per se* directly modifies perceived interdependence amongst group members through a "groupness norm".

Thus Rabbie *et al.* (1989) state:

> Explicit social categorization is only one of the many factors which may contribute to the perception of a bounded social group or system which is characterized by perceived interdependence among its members. Other unit forming factors include common fate and perceived interdependence, proximity, a shared territory, similar preferences and shared labels,

> shared threat . . . the greater the salience, importance and number of these *unit forming factors* within the group, the greater the ingroup–outgroup differentiation or ingroup–outgroup favouritism.
>
> (p. 179)

This unit formation hypothesis is simply the social categorization hypothesis by another name. Implicitly or explicitly, a factor which leads to the perception of a bounded, distinct social unit is a cognitive criterion of social categorization. To group people perceptually as social units is to categorize them. The list of determinants of social categorization is almost identical to that provided in social identity writings ten years earlier. So now BIM seems to have abandoned its key idea that interdependence for positive outcomes is necessary for group formation and agrees that cognitive boundaries are sufficient. It also (finally) seems to agree that perceived interdependence can be an effect of cognitive unit formation, just as in self-categorization theory. This is absolutely clear and explicit in Rabbie *et al.*'s analysis of their empirical research (to which we turn in the following sections), where various *ad hoc* notions are introduced to redescribe the social identity prediction that social categorization *per se* leads to an assumed identity of interests within the ingroup.

BIM, Self-Categorization and Common Fate

At this point the question is raised: What exactly is BIM? The answer is difficult because, as argued above, the theory is inconsistent and self-contradictory. On the one hand it argues that perceived interdependence is fundamental to group formation and that group behaviour is purely instrumental, rational and self-interested. On the other hand, it advances ideas consistent with self-categorization theory that cognitive unit-forming factors (such as similarity of fate) may produce a group and that groupness affects perceived self-interest and interdependence by generating differential expected ingroup–outgroup consequences and a norm of ingroup bias (i.e. perceived interdependence is not necessary for but an effect of group formation).

In yet a third form of BIM, it is argued that common fate (i.e. *similarity* of fate, and presumably other unit-forming factors) directly *gives rise* to perceived interdependence, the latter being the crucial process in group formation. Note how Rabbie *et al.* are trying to have their cake and eat it too. They argue, on the one hand, that perceived interdependence is necessary for group formation and that self-categorization theory is wrong and, on the other, that perceived interdependence is crucial and always present in groups because they agree with self-categorization theory that similarity and group formation produce perceived interdependence.

The same inconsistency is apparent in their treatment of common fate, a central concept in their analysis. The best thing to do seems to be to point out the inconsistencies and try to indicate what BIM needs to be arguing if it wants to be considered a genuinely distinctive analysis from self-categorization theory as opposed to merely a terminological reworking of social identity ideas.

Rabbie *et al.* begin strongly by arguing that it is the experience of a common fate which transforms a sociological category into a psychological group (Rabbie and Horwitz, 1988, p. 119). They cite Lewin to the effect that common fate, and not similarity, is basic to group belongingness:

> "Similarity between persons merely permits their classification, their subsumption under the same abstract concept, whereas belonging to the same social group means concrete, dynamic interrelations between persons" (Lewin, 1948, p. 184) . . . the fact that it is classified by the majority as a distinct group is what counts . . . the main criterion of belongingness is *interdependence of fate* . . . the experience of a common (or an interdependence of) fate
>
> (Rabbie *et al.*, 1989, p. 172)

The problems here are immediately apparent. Lewin equates "common fate" with "interdependence of fate" (1948, pp. 165–166), but his concept of common fate is also linked closely to the idea of social categorization by a majority:

> It is easy enough to see that the common fate of all Jews makes them a group in reality (p. 166) . . . the fact that it is classified by the majority as a distinct group is what counts.
>
> (p. 184)

It is clear from reading the discussions from which these extracts are taken that Lewin's point was not to make an argument about social categorization versus common fate. His point was that group membership does not depend upon *interpersonal* similarities and attraction (just as Tajfel and Turner have consistently argued), but that the similarity of fate, of problems, dangers and challenges which faced all Jews, which required them to develop shared, collective goals and a collective response, is a similarity of fate *based on* their social categorization by others as Jews. Their interdependence arises from an externally imposed group-level similarity, not personal similarities of individual character and temperament.

Thus what Lewin is saying is that the social categorization of people as "Jews" by society (reflecting historical, political, cultural, religious and other processes) creates for them a common, shared fate in reality, which leads them to become a psychological group characterized by various forms of interdependence. Jews are interdependent in their fate as a group in the sense that their individual characteristics are irrelevant: they are to be treated alike solely as a function of their classification as Jews:

> If it has ever been a question whether the Jewish problem is an individual or social one, a clear-cut answer was provided by the SA men in the streets of Vienna who beat with steel rods any Jew irrespective of his past conduct or status.
>
> (Lewin, 1948, p.161)

Lewin's concept of common fate therefore cannot be equated with some form of perceived interpersonal interdependence, which exists prior to social categorization. Dorwin Cartwright (a leading student of Lewin's) quite appropriately, therefore, makes a distinction between common fate and interdependence. According to Rabbie *et al.* (1989, pp. 173–175):

> Cartwright (1968, pp. 56–57) has suggested that the "external designation" of members into a "socially defined category" imposes a "common fate" upon them in the sense that opportunities are given or denied to them "simply because of their membership in the category". He argued that "interdependence among members develops because society gives them a 'common fate' " ... We have proposed that perceived interdependence, for example as a consequence of experiencing a "common fate" ... or a "common predicament" (Sherif, 1966), is a crucial precondition for the formation of social groups ... Turner ... disagrees with this position.

This quotation is highly revealing. Note here that whereas Rabbie *et al.* began by equating common fate with perceived interdependence (supposedly following Lewin), they now distinguish it as a *consequence* of common fate! It is *not* common fate after all which creates a psychological group, but a consequence which is crucial (i.e. perceived interdependence, which as a consequence can plainly no longer be the same thing). They do not explain what common fate is if it is not perceived interdependence. The answer of course is obvious: it is a social category-based *similarity* of fate (the same similarity which they have already dismissed on the basis of a misunderstanding of Lewin). Previously, they implied that common fate and perceived interdependence were the same thing. Now they say one leads to the other. They agree with Turner (1982) that common fate is empirically sufficient for group formation, but want to claim that perceived interdependence is the hypothetical *intervening* process to maintain their interdependence theory.

What must be pointed out is that:

(1) Common fate is not the outcome of interdependence. They mean two different things. Common fate is shared fate, "being in the same boat", "sinking or swimming together", *sharing* the *same* positive or negative outcomes (what matters is that the outcomes are *shared*, *similar*, not that they are positive or negative). Interdependence of outcomes is a functional relationship in which one's own outcomes depend instrumentally on the actions of the other and the other's outcomes depend on one's own behaviour. It is not the case that Brand X toothpaste users who find that their toothpaste is toxic (an example of common fate provided by Rabbie and Horwitz, 1988, p. 119) are instrumentally responsible for each other's outcomes. What happens to one does not depend on the actions or outcomes of another simply because they all use the same toothpaste. Rabbie *et al.* have overlooked the simple point that their much-touted common fate is in fact precisely a *similarity* variable—it is similarity of fate, outcomes or situations that they are in fact conceding is a first crucial step in group formation.

If Rabbie *et al.* agree that common fate produces group formation directly, then they agree after all that similarity between people, even a similarity associated with negative outcomes in the case of the minority group examples cited by Lewin (see Turner *et al.*, 1983), can create a psychological group. Similarity, of course, is a key feature of categorization, both as cause and effect.

(2) For both Lewin and Cartwright, common fate is a group-based similarity; it is closely linked to social categorization. The imposed common fate depends upon a prior social categorization. If perceived interdependence develops from shared fate, the critical issue is: Is this development mediated by social identification? Self-categorization theory readily accepts that people forming a collective identity on the basis of shared fate would, as a consequence and at the same time, begin to develop shared goals and interests reflecting their collective self-definition. Hence perceived interdependence would also develop.

But if BIM wishes to remain a distinctive theory, it must argue that common fate directly leads to perceived interdependence prior to and independent of group formation and that group formation reflects perceived interdependence. It cannot argue, as Rabbie *et al.* seem to have realized belatedly, that common fate is the same as interdependence. This is patently untrue (common goals, for example, are not necessarily superordinate goals, as Sherif, 1967, pointed out). Therefore BIM needs to argue and show (a) how common fate leads to perceived interdependence independent of intervening group formation and (b) that group formation always *follows* perceived interdependence. If it does not make these points, it is merely a confused restatement of the social identity analysis. If it does, it will, we argue, move away from the spirit of Lewin's analysis, and more to the point, in the following section, Rabbie *et al.*'s own data will prove it wrong.

(3) Despite the references to Lewin, his analysis of group formation and belongingness is close in spirit to the theory of self-categorization. Lewin's (1948) discussion of the Jewish group emphasizes the varying salience of different group memberships in different situations, the idea of the group as a process rather than as a reified "thing", the role of social, physical and cognitive boundaries and group symbols, of intragroup similarities and intergroup differences, of external categorization, and the idea of intense group affiliations associated with negative outcomes. He does state that the satisfaction of individual needs by a group is a major factor in attraction to a group (and who would argue?), but he also recognizes that there are constraining forces which induce group membership independent of personal need satisfaction (p. 191).

Our view is that self-categorization theory provides a more detailed and systematic perspective for understanding how the processes described by Lewin actually operate: how a shared group-level fate in reality, not personal similarities, can produce subjective group belongingness and lead to the development of collective goals and intragroup interdependence. The price of a more systematic understanding of Lewin's insights and hypotheses is that one must jettison the particular theory developed through the 1950s and 1960s which posits initial outcome interdependence between individuals as the crucial antecedent process in group formation.

So where are we theoretically? First, the idea that self-categorization theory rejects the importance of common fate and interdependence is wrong in point of fact and theory. It provides an analysis of how they may be both causes and effects of group formation. Second, for BIM to be a different theory rather than merely a confused rehash of social identity ideas, it must argue and show that perceived interdependence exists prior to and determines psychological group formation and that group formation always reflects perceived interdependence. It cannot simply argue that common fate produces a group from a sociological category. It must demonstrate that there is an intervening process of perceiving interdependence prior to group formation. Self-categorization theory explained over fifteen years ago how common fate could produce a mutual social identification between people which would lead to perceived co-operative interdependence by means of a collective redefinition of self and self-interest. Third, for this reason, it is Rabbie *et al.* (1989) who seem to be in some danger of agreeing with Turner (1981, 1982), who argued that common fate, as a cognitive basis of shared self-categorization, is sufficient for group formation and the production of co-operative intragroup interdependence.

Finally, the suggestion that Tajfel (1982) dissociated himself from Turner's position that "the formation of social identity is a pre-condition for the formation of groups", instead endorsing the idea that interdependence of fate is "needed . . . for the development of social identity" (Rabbie and Horwitz, 1988, p. 120), seriously misrepresents what Tajfel actually said. In was in this chapter that Tajfel criticized Horwitz and Rabbie (1982) for their semantic confusion between static, sociological and dynamic, psychological conceptions of group membership. He then argued for a complementary, sequential view of instrumentality and identity in group formation and explained how notions of common fate and interdependence could be integrated theoretically into Turner's formulation (consistent with the discussion above). Tajfel commented on what was needed as a *precondition for social identity* (a comment completely in line with Turner, 1982); Rabbie *et al.* suggest he disagreed about *the role of social identity in group formation.* In fact, his integration was to point out to Horwitz and Rabbie that common fate, similarity, interdependence, proximity, etc. had a role in the formation of identity, as part of the "pre-history" (p. 502) of group formation, and that social identity was crucial to group formation proper. He therefore embraced Turner's position, but not the straw man version depicted by Rabbie *et al.* Nowhere in this chapter did Tajfel agree with Rabbie *et al.* that perceived interdependence could lead to group formation without the formation of a shared social identity.

Social identity theory acknowledges the importance of goal interdependence in group processes but describes its role in a more complex and unified manner than traditional theory. It can explain how interdependence and a whole range of other factors can produce group formation and how the latter can produce shared and superordinate goals. The problem for BIM is that there are data which demonstrate unequivocally that social categorization independent of the perceived reward structure can lead to psychological group formation. The next section pursues this issue in relation to Rabbie *et al.*'s own research.

The Minimal Group Paradigm

A very large part of Rabbie *et al.*'s critique is given over to their reinterpretation of the results of the minimal group paradigm; (see Turner's introductory chapter in this book for a brief description of the paradigm). The standard interpretation of these results is that they show that social categorization *per se* is sufficient for ingroup favouritism (FAV) uncontaminated by any rational link between subjects' personal self-interest and a strategy of FAV (Bourhis *et al.*, 1994; Tajfel, 1972; Turner, 1975). In line with BIM, Rabbie *et al.* state that the main aim of their 1989 paper is to show that there is such a link:

> The main aim of this paper is to show that in the standard MGP, there *is* a rational link between economic self-interests and the two major allocation strategies which are often found in MGP experiments: the strategy of ingroup favouritism and the "influential strategy of fairness" (Tajfel and Turner, 1979, p. 39): to give the ingroup about as much as the outgroup.
>
> (1989, pp. 175–176)

They claim that their reinterpretation and the data they present demonstrate that MGP responses are "perfectly rational, instrumental and utilitarian" (p. 197) and that subjects' behaviour in the paradigm is overwhelmingly determined by the perceived reward structure in the MGP, a structure of positive interdependence with the ingroup (dictating intragroup co-operation) and negative interdependence with the outgroup (producing intergroup competition).

This is a strong claim, but they fail to review the mass of evidence on which their monetary self-interest interpretation was discounted by earlier reviewers. For example, it is well known that FAV in the MGP is made up of both MIP (maximizing absolute ingroup profit) and MD (maximizing the difference between ingroup and outgroup in favour of the ingroup, a purely *relative* bias strategy). It has been demonstrated routinely that subjects pursue MD even at the cost of absolute monetary gain for the ingroup (Bourhis *et al.*, 1994; Turner, 1983). That is, subjects sacrifice (ingroup) economic self-interest to pursue a gratuitously competitive "winning" strategy. In an early study, Turner (1978) showed that FAV persisted even when subjects distributed points with no monetary value. Ingroup bias has been shown on many measures which do not involve monetary rewards or economic outcomes, e.g. on evaluative and attitudinal dimensions, or in memory for positive and negative traits. Some studies have pitted social categorization against perceived interdependence (like the study in Rabbie *et al.*, 1989) and found FAV in conflict with economic self-interest (as they do). Turner (1978), for example, found that, under conditions of salient ingroup membership, subjects favoured ingroup over outgroup others even where they could award money directly to themselves personally and when personal self-interest required no differential treatment of ingroup and outgroup others (see also Brewer and Silver, 1978; Turner *et al.*, 1979).

Rabbie *et al.* imply quite falsely that Tajfel *et al.* (1971) overlooked the possible role of economic self-interest in the MGP, the possible influence of the fact that subjects would receive what others awarded them. In fact Tajfel and

Turner and others were fully aware that, since subjects would receive what others awarded them (*all* others not merely ingroup members), the economically rational strategy was for subjects to act in terms of their real-life group membership as experimental subjects and give away as much of the experimenter's money as possible to others. This is the MJP strategy (maximizing the joint, or combined total, profit of the recipients). For subjects to maximize personal self-interest, the obvious thing to do was for them to give as much money away as possible to others (i.e. pursue MJP) in the hope that others would do likewise.

However subjects did not (significantly) use the MJP strategy (Turner, 1983). The finding of FAV (MIP+MD) in terms of the ingroup–outgroup categories was of theoretical interest and important because it sacrifices MJP and economic self-interest to favour the ingroup. If subjects had followed MJP or even fairness (parity of outcomes for the recipients of each choice) or just responded randomly, no one would have been interested in the data. Given that MJP is collectively and individually rational, why do subjects not follow it? This is the question that Rabbie *et al.* must answer. They seek to suggest that Tajfel *et al.* created a perceived interdependence structure in the MGP which required FAV. How?

Firstly, Rabbie and Horwitz (1988) suggest that social categorization directly creates expectations of differential consequences for ingroup and outgroup members:

> The experimenter's interest in dividing them [the subjects] into two groups could have suggested that differential consequences might befall each group as a whole . . . Neither Tajfel's nor our minimal conditions provide evidence that ingroup favouritism is produced by classifying people into categories that have no perceived consequences for themselves or other individuals (or for their own or other groups).
>
> (p. 118)

The latter statement uses a straw man to hide the adoption of social identity ideas. Tajfel did not suggest that social categorization had no perceived consequences. As discussed above, self-categorization theory predicts that group formation is likely to affect the perception of self-interest and to link it with the collective interests of the group. People in the same group are likely to adopt and expect a positive and co-operative orientation from others. This follows from social identity ideas. It is difficult to see how it follows from BIM, whose main argument is that expected differential outcomes are prior to and causal of group formation.

The original social identity interpretation of MGP responses was that, *as a consequence* of defining oneself in terms of the social categorization, self-evaluative intergroup comparisons were stimulated, leading to the development of social competition (Turner, 1975). Again, social categorization was the basis of the perceived consequences.

The only evidence Rabbie *et al.* cite for their suggestion is consistent with social identity theory. Initially they refer to the Rabbie and Horwitz (1969) study. Their interpretation of this study has now changed markedly since 1969. In 1969 the study manipulated group classification without common fate (the control condition) and several experimental common fate conditions in which minimal groups shared positive or negative outcomes.

The result was that one experimental condition (one in which group members shared a common fate of winning or losing a prize by chance) showed significant ingroup bias. The control condition did not. Rabbie and Horwitz (1969) concluded that social categorization *per se* was not sufficient for FAV and that common fate (i.e. perceived interdependence of fate in their terms) was necessary. There was no suggestion that social categorization directly created expectations of differential consequences. Rabbie and Horwitz in 1969 were content with the finding that social categorization without common fate had no effect on ingroup bias.

However, as everyone now knows, Rabbie and Horwitz had got it wrong. Tajfel *et al.* and other researchers not only found something different, but pointed to various methodological weaknesses in the 1969 study. Rabbie and Horwitz (1988) now inform us (citing Horwitz and Rabbie, 1982) that they decided to run some more subjects and that as a consequence they found a different result from the one they published. They did after all find that group classification *per se* produced significant ingroup bias in subjects' ratings. [In Horwitz and Rabbie (1982), the new finding is attributed to Rabbie (1972), who ran sixteen extra subjects in the control condition in response to the criticisms noted above.]

They now claim that in some sense they did show that social categorization *per se* (the control manipulation) was sufficient for FAV. Such a claim (and let us welcome it even if it is belated) is nonetheless incompatible with their original theoretical conceptualization of the control condition (no common fate) and implies that social categorization without perceived interdependence is sufficient for bias. The solution adopted by Rabbie and Horwitz is apparently to revise their original view; now they say that the control condition, which they themselves designed to manipulate *mere* categorization, was an interdependence condition after all. They berate Tajfel *et al.* for not seeing what they themselves did not see until, *post hoc*, it became necessary.

Apparently, their control condition leads to expected differential consequences because one is dependent on the evaluations of others. The dependent variable in Rabbie and Horwitz (1969) is social evaluation rather than monetary allocation. They suggest that because subjects evaluate each other, just as in the MGP they award money to each other, they are dependent on each other for positive outcomes (in this case positive ratings). They imply that this fact of being dependent on others for a positive evaluation creates a perceived differential dependence on ingroup and outgroup, a positive interdependence within the ingroup, leading to instrumental intragroup co-operation, and a negative interdependence between the groups, leading to instrumental intergroup competition. One co-operates with the ingroup or competes with the outgroup for a positive self-evaluation, just as one co-operates or competes for monetary rewards.

The major flaw in this argument is so blatant that we ought to note it in passing even though we shall return to it presently. Since subjects are actually dependent on both ingroup and outgroup members for a positive evaluation (they are rated by both), the structure of mutual dependence in the situation provides no basis for a differential treatment of ingroup and outgroup members.

Let us also note that what Rabbie *et al.* are actually saying in their reinterpretation of the 1969 control condition is that, as a result of social categorization, people seek competitively to evaluate the ingroup more positively than the outgroup, reflecting a need for positive self-evaluation induced by the situation. Just as in the MGP one supposedly competes for monetary rewards, so in a setting of mutual evaluation, one's group competes for a positive evaluation. This, of course, is pretty much the social identity theory/social competition explanation of ingroup bias (Tajfel, 1972; Turner, 1975).

Rabbie *et al.* seek to assimilate social competition to a goal interdependence model, as if evaluative and instrumental competition were identical, but, as was pointed out by Turner (1975), there is a major conceptual difference between "social" or "relational" competition and "instrumental" competition based on negative goal interdependence (conflict of group interests). The critical point is that social competition is not competition for a goal or outcome which exists in principle outside and prior to the intergroup situation. The "goal" of "being better", "superior", "winning" or "positively distinctive", etc. is inherently comparative and relational. There is no goal which is an absolute end in itself, motivating the intergroup relationship from outside. It is *produced by and inherent in* the intergroup situation. It follows from social categorization and does not exist prior to it!

The distinction between instrumental and social competition is one that Rabbie *et al.* themselves accept later in the 1989 paper. Once again, we have to point out that they cannot have it both ways. If they accept the distinction, any social competition induced in Rabbie and Horwitz's (1969) control condition cannot be properly described as *instrumental and based on outcome interdependence*. This is competition for positive social identity which is comparative and relational and arises directly from a prior social categorization into groups—it cannot therefore be used to explain away the effects of social categorization. If the 1969 control condition produced social competition, as they now seem to be arguing, this is not evidence for an interdependence interpretation, but the very opposite. Group classification produces a competitive bias which derives not from prior outcome interdependence but from the psychological consequences of being categorized into groups.

The idea that the "perceived differential consequences" of social categorization introduce a reward structure into the MGP does not, therefore, serve the purpose they intend. The consequences appear to be the relational form of intergroup competition for positive social identity that is the core of the social identity interpretation and/or the intragroup co-operative and intergroup competitive orientations which self-categorization theory derives from social categorization. In neither case is there a confounded instrumental reward structure which provides an alternative explanation of the social categorization effect.

Rabbie *et al.*'s second suggestion is that dependence on others for rewards in the MGP induces an expectation of within-group reciprocity which produces a form of implicit intragroup co-operation. People assume rationally that by giving more to ingroup members than to outgroup members they will maximize their personal gain:

> Although subjects in the standard MGP cannot directly allocate money to themselves, they can do it indirectly, on their reasonable assumption that the other ingroup members will do the same to them. By giving more to their ingroup members than to the outgroup members—in the expectation that the other ingroup member will reciprocate this implicit co-operative interaction—they will increase their chances of maximizing their own outcomes. This notion is analogous to the concept of "reciprocal altruism" . . .
>
> . . . They "tacitly" seem to co-ordinate their responses with each other (Schelling, 1963) in trying to maximize their own individual self-interests and probably the interests of their group as a whole.
>
> (Rabbie *et al.*, 1989, p. 176)

There is a major logical flaw at the heart of this suggestion which Rabbie *et al.* never resolve, but sink deeper into. Mutual dependence in the MGP is not defined in terms of the ingroup–outgroup categories, but in terms of the experimental subjects as a whole. As Rabbie *et al.* agree, in the standard MGP people are equally dependent on ingroup and outgroup members for the receipt of rewards. Since mutual dependence is in terms of the superordinate subject group and since there is no differential dependence on ingroup than outgroup members, perceived interdependence predicts MJP and group formation at the level of the superordinate group, not FAV at the level of the imposed minimal categories.

The whole problem is to explain FAV instead of MJP. Perceived interdependence predicts MJP. Rabbie *et al.* simply assert that people perceive dependence on the basis of the social categorization rather than reality, but why should they? Why don't people assume reciprocity and tacitly co-operate in terms of the real-life grouping of all subjects in the experiment (or experimental session)? Rabbie *et al.*'s assertion is not an explanation but a redescription of what has to be explained. It is also an assertion inconsistent with the objective reward structure of the situation. It may well be that people do define themselves as interdependent within the ingroup, but this is consistent with the social identity argument that psychological group membership influences perceived interdependence and that social categorization is sufficient for group formation. It is Rabbie *et al.* who want to argue that perceived interdependence determines group formation. They must explain, therefore, why perceived interdependence appears to follow social categorization, rather than group formation follow objective interdependence.

Rabbie *et al.* want to say that the effect of social categorization is an artifact, a product of a confounding between social categorization and perceived interdependence. What looks like the effect of social categorization is really the effect of a different, correlated variable. Thus they must show that perceived interdependence produces social categorization effects. They *cannot argue* that the perceived interdependence structure is dependent on social categorization. If it is social categorization that alters subjects' perceptions of interdependence from the objective structure to a differential intergroup one, then this is evidence for the determining role of social categorization and confirms the analysis provided by self-categorization theory. It is inconsistent with BIM. In fact, as we shall see, Rabbie *et al.* have no explanation for why equal dependence on ingroup and outgroup members should produce FAV, other than a belated, *post hoc* acceptance of the causal role of social categorization.

That this is so is confirmed by the major study reported in Rabbie *et al.* (1989). In this study Rabbie *et al.* hypothesize explicitly both that dependence on others produces favouritism towards those others and that in the standard MGP there is an equal dependence of subjects on ingroup and outgroup members. It follows logically for the relevant predictions that dependence on the ingroup should lead to FAV, dependence on the outgroup should lead to outgroup favouritism (–FAV) and that equal dependence on the ingroup and outgroup should lead to no favouritism towards either group (zero FAV or fairness). Unfortunately, of course there is FAV in the standard MGP, a setting of equal dependence. Rabbie *et al.* respond by fudging their predictions and evading the logic of their own analysis. They predict a moderate degree of ingroup bias (FAV) in the (control) condition of their study which is defined as one of equal dependence on ingroup and outgroup and identical to the standard MGP. Even with this major fudging they are still forced to introduce other *ad hoc* notions unrelated to their theory to explain their data, notions which are just the social categorization hypothesis by another name.

The Experiments

Experiment 1

Rabbie *et al.* report three studies as directly relevant to their critique (Horwitz and Rabbie, 1989). Only experiment 1 is described in any detail (Rabbie *et al.*, 1989). Subjects in each session are divided into a "preference" (PREF) ingroup and outgroup. There are three dependence conditions (ID, OD, IOD). They are told that they are dependent on the PREF ingroup (ID—"the subjects were instructed that they would receive, at the end of the experiment, the amount of money the ingroup members had awarded them"; p. 182), the PREF outgroup (OD—"they would receive the money the outgroup members had awarded them", p. 182) or on both ingroup and outgroup members (IOD—"they would receive the amount of money the others had awarded them. In this control condition, the subjects received the same instructions as in the Tajfel *et al.* (1971) "experiment"; p. 182).

They are also divided within each PREF category into two spatial (SPAT) triads, all assigned to different rooms, so that each subject is a member of a SPAT ingroup triad and a SPAT outgroup triad within their PREF ingroup and is also aware of two SPAT outgroup triads within their PREF outgroup. Subjects all make three types of choice: BOTH, between the PREF and SPAT ingroup triad and a PREF and SPAT outgroup triad; SPAT, between a SPAT ingroup triad and SPAT outgroup triad within the same PREF ingroup; and PREF, between a PREF ingroup but SPAT outgroup triad and a PREF and SPAT outgroup triad.

The researchers' basic predictions were that subjects would show ingroup FAV in ID, outgroup FAV in OD and an intermediate level of FAV in IOD (presumably on PREF and BOTH choices). The third prediction, as we have pointed out, is flawed and inconsistent: they should predict no FAV in IOD since subjects are equally dependent on both ingroup and outgroup. To make such a prediction in the IOD control condition, however, which they equate with the standard MGP, would reveal that they have no explanation for the standard finding. Nevertheless, as the paper progresses, it becomes harder and harder for them to deny the obvious. Ultimately at the end of the paper (and in Horwitz and Rabbie, 1989) they cannot but point to the evidence of FAV in IOD as a bias which cannot be explained by dependence—a stance which completely undermines their original prediction and reveals the emptiness of their explanation of the standard MGP finding.

According to BIM there should also, obviously, be no bias in the SPAT choices within the same PREF ingroup, since the dependence structure is linked to the PREF categorization. There is no reason to differentiate between ingroup and outgroup spatial triads in the PREF ingroup, since one is either dependent on them both (ID and IOD) or dependent on neither (OD). This prediction follows straightforwardly from BIM, but is never made clearly. It is submerged in a discussion of the role of group boundaries and cognitive unit-forming factors, which are beside the point if BIM is supposed to be making the distinctive hypothesis that interdependence is primary (cognitive unit-forming factors are more consistent with self-categorization theory). There is also a group polarization phase to the study which can be ignored for the moment.

What were the main results? Firstly, manipulation checks reveal that subjects perceive the manipulated interdependence structure exactly as intended. They do not perceive themselves as more dependent on the ingroup than the outgroup in IOD but equally dependent. Nevertheless, contrary to the reciprocity argument, subjects expected to gain more from ingroup than outgroup members in the IOD condition. Also, subjects expected to gain more from the ingroup in the OD condition than from the outgroup in the ID condition, again suggesting a tendency to expect more from ingroup than outgroup members irrespective of the dependence structure. Rabbie *et al.* (p. 186) state:

> These findings may reflect the operation of a normative orientation to expect more of one's own group than from an outgroup, e.g. according to the generic "groupness" norm of Tajfel *et al.* (1971), or the moral notion that more weight should be given to the desires of the ingroup and its members than to the outgroup and its members . . .

It could also be of course that, independent of the explicit dependence structure, social categorization *per se* is sufficient to produce an expectation of mutual co-operation between ingroup members, just as self-categorization theory would predict. After all, in a "we-group", others' interests become our own interests (Turner, 1981, 1982, 1985). Puzzlingly, Rabbie *et al.* do not seem to understand that both of the explanations they proffer assume that psychological group formation has taken place in line with social categorization but independent of the objective reward structure.

Secondly, on BOTH choices, there is strong FAV in ID, strong outgroup FAV in OD and a moderate level of FAV in IOD. The same seems to be largely true in PREF choices, although there are some differences suggesting that the SPAT division into triads had some effect on top of the PREF categorization. Interestingly, there is significant MD in the IOD condition in both PREF and BOTH choices—a finding which is inexplicable in terms of any notion of economic self-interest. There is also significant FAV in SPAT choices in ID and IOD conditions (only fairness is significant in OD SPAT choices).

The findings of FAV and MD in the IOD condition in any choices and of FAV in the ID condition in SPAT choices are completely inconsistent with BIM. These data provide evidence for social categorization effects independent of the manipulated reward structure. The data (including the ID and OD findings) are consistent with social identity and self-categorization theories for all the reasons given previously. Self-categorization theory accepts that an explicit co-operative dependence on others can function as a cognitive basis for social identification. If co-operative dependence is correlated with a minimal group membership, then the minimal categorization ceases to be minimal and is likely to become a more salient and powerful basis for self-definition (see the concept of "fit" in self-categorization theory: Oakes, 1987; Oakes *et al.*, 1994). This is the ID condition. If a real and strong co-operative dependence is opposed to a *minimal* group membership, then the prior social categorization should become less salient and subjects may identify instead with the group they depend on. This is the OD condition. Where social categorization is neither explicitly based upon nor opposed by dependence on others, then psychological group formation *per se*, based solely upon self-categorization, can shape allocation behaviour as an outlet for either social or instrumental competition, depending on how the dimension of intergroup comparison is defined and linked to collective self-interest. This is the IOD and standard MGP condition.

Another explanation of the data is provided by the "power differential" studies of Sachdev and Bourhis (1985, 1991). Sachdev and Bourhis conceptualize the issue of dependence on ingroup or outgroup from a power perspective using social identity theory as their theoretical framework. In their 1985 power differential study they created *ad hoc* minimal groups whose degree of control over the allocation of course credits to group members varied systematically from 0% power to 100%. Three types of intergroup power differential were created: (1) a situation in which both the ingroup and outgroup had 50% power, as in the usual MGP; (2) a situation in which one group had 70% control over the distribution of resources while its outgroup had only 30% control; (3) an extreme power differential situation in which one group had total 100% control while its outgroup had 0% or no control. Subjects in each group were asked to distribute resources to ingroup and outgroup others using the MGP matrices. These behavioural measures were supplemented with perceptual items which included subjects' degree and quality of ingroup identification, intergroup perceptions and self-reports of matrix-strategies.

It is clear that Rabbie *et al.*'s (1989) ID condition corresponds closely to the Sachdev and Bourhis (1985) 100% power condition, since relevant subjects in both studies are in complete control of their own group fate within the experiment and need not depend at all on the outgroup for the final allocation of resources. Similarly, subjects in the OD condition are in the same boat as the 0% group members in Sachdev and Bourhis' study, since both groups are at the total mercy of the dominant outgroup for the final allocation of resources in the experiment. As in the standard MGP studies, the IOD condition corresponds to the 50% power condition since subjects in both depend equally on ingroup and outgroup decisions.

Sachdev and Bourhis (1985) argued that intergroup power enables group members to actualize and achieve a positive social identity by successfully establishing favourable intergroup comparisons with outgroups through discriminatory behaviour. Increasing group power should lead to concomitant increases in discrimination such that dominant group members (100%, 70% groups) should discriminate more against outgroups than subordinate group members (0%, 30%). This is basically what they found: more power led to more discrimination, with 50% groups also showing FAV as in IOD and the standard MGP. Interestingly, however, 70% groups were most discriminatory, followed by the 100% power groups. Also, in addition to using FAV, all group members who discriminated in the study also employed MD, favouring the ingroup even at the cost of absolute ingroup profit. The data are similar but not identical to those obtained by Rabbie *et al.* (1989)—the 0% power groups, for example, did not favour the outgroup as in the OD condition but were almost completely fair, failing to discriminate at all—but they provide some corroboration for the later pattern of results. The key point is the very different explanation provided by Sachdev and Bourhis, which sees the power differences in FAV as consistent with social identity theory (the experimental design and hypotheses were derived from a social identity framework). It is worth noting too that the detailed perceptual data they gathered imply strongly that power or "dependence" variations almost certainly affect subjective ingroup identification, just as we have argued above. It is most unlikely that Rabbie *et al.*'s study varied the interdependence structure between groups whilst "holding category differentiation constant" as they claim. Rabbie *et al.*'s failure to include detailed post-experimental measures of identification and group formation in their study weakens any conclusions they can draw about the implications of their data for social identity ideas.

Despite their data and these points, Rabbie *et al.* try to have it both ways. They conclude as follows:

> In their early work Tajfel *et al.* (1971, p. 174) emphasized the "'non-rational', 'non-instrumental' and 'non-utilitarian' character" of the allocation behaviour in their experiments. In contrast with this view we have shown that the allocation behaviour in the MGP is *perfectly* [emphasis added] rational, instrumental and utilitarian at least when monetary outcomes are involved.
>
> (1989, p. 197)

Then *on the very same page* they make it clear that biases remain which are not perfectly instrumental:

> Subjects expected more of ingroup members than outgroup members, even in conditions in which these expectations were not instrumental in maximizing their financial outcomes . . .
>
> . . . even in subgroups within the same preference group some ingroup favouritism was observed, although this strategy did not have any utilitarian value to the subjects in maximizing their outcomes, but can probably be best understood as a consequences [*sic*] of the normative orientation to give greater weight to the desires of ingroup than outgroup members . . .
>
> (p. 197)

In this paper, they are still trying to claim that FAV in IOD is consistent with BIM. Indeed they even suggest that BIM is more parsimonious than social identity theory, because it can explain the greater fairness in IOD than ID or OD as well as the more moderate level of FAV. It predicts greater fairness, of course, for the same reason that it should not be predicting FAV at all, which is that there is no differential dependence on I over O in that condition (and as the manipulation check confirmed). Horwitz and Rabbie (1989), however, finally abandon this absurdity and at the same time grasp again at the straw of the generic "groupness" norm to rescue their position from demonstrable falsification. After summarizing the results of Experiment 1 they state:

> The results should not be taken to mean that subjects in the minimal intergroup situation act only to maximize their individual gains and are indifferent to the outcomes of others in their groups. *Biases in favour of ingroup members remain evident in these data* [emphasis added]. In the condition in which subjects were dependent on both the ingroup and outgroup, they allocated as usual more money to ingroup than outgroup members. In the conditions in which subjects were solely dependent on either the ingroup or outgroup, they allocated significantly more money to ingroup than outgroup members. Their behaviour could reflect the fact that they expected ingroup members to be more likely than outgroup members to co-operate with themselves (Hornstein, 1982). It could also reflect the other side of this "generic" norm, namely that as group members they ought to give more consideration to the interests of the ingroup and its members than to the interests of the outgroup and its members
>
> (p. 111)

Rabbie *et al.* focus on the ID and OD data to claim that their predictions are confirmed and that MGP responses are perfectly rational (even though these are not distinctive predictions), while aware that bias in the IOD condition, in ID SPAT choices and the stronger bias in ID than OD are all findings inconsistent with the interdependence structure! They appear not to know what the word "perfectly" means, but they do appreciate its polemical value.

Faced with these effects of social categorization they revise BIM to incorporate these findings through an addition both *post hoc* and *ad hoc*, the supposed generic "groupness" norm of Tajfel *et al.* (1971). Their version of the norm (different from Tajfel's), which has no obvious organic relationship to BIM, is that people give more weight to the desires of ingroup members than outgroup members. This norm simply acknowledges what is already obvious, that it is the social categorization of subjects into ingroup and outgroup, as well as the manipulated reward structure, which determines how they define their interests and with whom they expect to co-operate or compete. The "norm" is merely a restatement of the psychological effect of social categorization and redescribes a causal process consistent with social identity insights but completely at odds with the logic of BIM.

When Rabbie *et al.* state that Tajfel was premature in abandoning the groupness norm, they are only admitting that they were premature in rejecting the social categorization hypothesis. If there were no social categorization effect, if responses were purely instrumental, rational, and so on, what need of a groupness norm to explain them? Tajfel's initial notion of a groupness norm was a first attempt at explaining the effect, not discarding it. The norm is overt recognition that social categorization plays an autonomous role in ingroup bias (the norm is an unsatisfactory *explanation* of the effect exactly because it is largely a redescription—see Tajfel, 1978; Turner, 1975, 1980).

At this point BIM gives up any pretence of offering any new insights into the MGP. It is merely a rhetorical preference for describing the findings and hypotheses generated by social identity research in the language of interdependence. Unfortunately it is a rhetorical preference that is conceptually confused and generates no new or heuristic understandings of its own. This preference for redescribing what social identity theorists have already said in different terminology is taken even further in Rabbie and Horwitz's later contributions to the controversy (Horwitz and Rabbie, 1989; Rabbie, 1991), in areas to be mentioned briefly below.

The group polarization aspect of the study can be dealt with briefly. After making individual choices, subjects discussed their PREF choices to consensus in their triads. As expected, there was some evidence of polarization, that is, groups moved in the direction to which they were already tending as individuals (see Turner, 1991, for a review of this area of research). Rabbie *et al.* argue that polarization indicates a shift to becoming more rational (basing themselves on one particular theory of polarization and ignoring the criticisms made of it). On this basis they try to argue, for example, that when people in ID polarize to more FAV, this indicates that the original FAV response was rational. It is an unconvincing argument given the problems with the theory of polarization they espouse, but one need only note that, by the same logic, MJP is rational in IOD, since subjects polarize to MJP in that condition. If MJP is rational in IOD, then why do subjects show FAV at the individual level? Plainly, from their perspective, FAV in IOD cannot be strictly rational and so their interpretation of the key condition falls to the ground.

The theoretical discussion of group polarization is highly confused. They contrast the group polarization hypothesis (that groups tend to become more extreme than their average member but in the same direction) with the supposed view of Tajfel and Turner that groups are always inherently more competitive than individuals. This is an odd argument even conceding its usual straw man quality, since Turner has developed an explanation of group polarization in terms of self-categorization theory. What Turner actually said in the passage cited by Rabbie *et al.* was *not* that groups were inherently more competitive than individuals, but that there was evidence that groups tended to be more competitive than individuals *under the same functional conditions*, where the conditions in question were mixed-motive and liable to induce competition at both the individual and group level. There was no suggestion that co-operative individuals could not polarize to even greater co-operation as a group.

Experiments 2 and 3

Experiments 2 and 3 are described extremely briefly (Horwitz and Rabbie, 1989), much too briefly to be sure of what is going on, but Horwitz and Rabbie (1989) nevertheless cite them as support for their position. It is therefore worth spending a few words to demonstrate the ambiguity of their data.

Experiment 2 apparently shows that subjects given instructions to pursue self-interest respond similarly to subjects in the standard MGP. Horwitz and Rabbie conclude that the data demonstrate by inference that standard MGP responses are self-interested. The alternative conclusion is that since standard MGP responses are not primarily self-interested, as we have shown, and since subjects given self-interest instructions respond similarly, this may imply that social categorization is sufficiently powerful to override these instructions (see Turner *et al.*, 1979) or that, as intended, there is no simple way to express self-interest in this paradigm.

Experiment 3 shows that people sacrifice personal self-interest for the sake of group interest and that this may be stronger where the ingroup–outgroup boundary is more salient. The fact that people sacrifice personal self-interest in the standard MGP presumably implies that personal self-interest is not the driving force behind intergroup behaviour in the MGP. These data confirm the results of Turner *et al.* (1979).

The Gagnon and Bourhis study

Recently, Gagnon and Bourhis (1992) conducted a laboratory study specifically to test the validity of Rabbie *et al.*'s interdependence interpretation of the MGP, in competition with the social identity account. Using the MGP, they categorized Quebec francophone undergraduates as members of *ad hoc* groups (Group K, Group W) using the toss of a coin. The study was presented as a decision-making task in which subjects made decisions on how to distribute an extra five course credits for taking part in the study. The course credit distributions were made using the MGP matrices and a 100–point zero-sum distribution. The first condition embodies the usual minimal group procedure in which subjects' final point awards depended on the combined allocation decisions of anonymous ingroup and outgroup others. For the specific purposes of this study, this was labelled the "interdependent" condition. The second condition was exactly the same as the first except for one important difference. Prior to their decision task, individual subjects were secretly told that in their personal case the experimenter had already decided to give them the total possible five credit points for taking part in the study. Thus subjects in this "autonomous" condition had their personal interests settled before decision-making, since they were awarded the five points regardless of the allocation decisions made by ingroup or outgroup others.

According to Rabbie *et al.*, subjects in the autonomous condition have no reason to discriminate in favour of the ingroup, since their personal self-interest is not involved in their decisions and they have nothing to gain from any tacit intragroup co-operation or from any other form of intergroup behaviour. However, according to social identity theory, "autonomous" subjects should still compete socially by discriminating in favour of their own group relative to the outgroup. Even with instrumental self-interest maximally satisfied, social identity needs created by the situation will still lead categorized subjects to show FAV as a way of positively differentiating own group from the other group.

The results were completely clear-cut. Interdependent and autonomous subjects identified equally strongly with their respective ingroup categories. Both showed significant ingroup favouritism on the standard MGP measures (FAV, MD) and on the 100–point zero-sum allocation. There was no difference between the conditions in the strength of intergroup discrimination. Gagnon and Bourhis also used a post-session item on degree of ingroup identification to assign subjects to high or low social identification conditions, creating a 2 × 2 factorial design with four conditions: interdependent/high identification; interdependent/low identification; autonomous/high; and autonomous/low. The additional result to emerge, fully supporting social identity theory, was that high identifiers were significantly more discriminatory and less fair than low identifiers. Thus identification with the minimal ingroup category, but not personal self-interest, predicted FAV.

Remaining Issues

Rabbie *et al.* raise an almost endless series of issues in their relentless rejection of social identity ideas. They fall into two groups. Some raise matters of genuine interest which deserve to be discussed in their own right at some point but which are not strictly relevant to the central themes of their critique. Some are relevant to themes already discussed but revolve around arguments supposedly supportive of BIM but in fact virtually indistinguishable from social identity ideas. Both sets of issues are liable to add confusion to the social identity versus interdependence controversy and need addressing. To discuss them fully, however, would try the patience of even the most tolerant reader. We shall comment on them as briefly as we possibly can, grouping them together where possible, summarized as series of points.

The self-concept issue

> . . . the first crucial assumption in the chain or [*sic*] arguments [in the social identity account of FAV], namely that subjects' categorization into, say a blue or a green group is internalized by them to define their selves has not been adequately tested to our knowledge. Abrams and Hogg (1988) have seriously questioned the validity of Turner's assumption and the studies which have been quoted in support of his proposal . . . They have also pointed out that it is unclear whether self-esteem is to be considered primarily as a cause or an effect of discrimination.
>
> (Rabbie *et al.*, 1989, p. 175)

> On that interpretation [the use of minimal categories to define the self], the subjects' self-concepts would have to be extraordinarily malleable. One would have to suppose in the treatment in which subjects evidenced outgroup favouritism, their self-concepts were as easily dissolved and replaced as they were initially formed.
>
> (Horwitz and Rabbie, 1989, p. 111)

Self-categorization theory does suppose that the self-concept is highly malleable. The self, like group formation itself, is understood as a fluid and flexible process. This point is central to recent work (Oakes *et al.*, 1994; Turner *et al.*, 1994). There is evidence for changes in self-definition in studies which have showed changes in self-esteem (e.g. Lemyre and Smith, 1985; Oakes and Turner, 1980; Turner *et al.*, 1984) and that self-categorization affects the perception of similarities and differences between self and others (Haslam and Turner, 1992, 1995; Oakes *et al.*, 1994). Other studies have measured identification directly in minimal group studies in tests of social identity theory (Bourhis, 1994; Ellemers, 1991; Gagnon and Bourhis, 1992; Sachdev and Bourhis, 1985, 1987, 1991).

As for the "self-esteem hypothesis", we must dissent from the view that social identity theory ever supposed that intergroup behaviour was motivated by a need for individual self-esteem, as if the latter were some kind of fixed or global personality structure and as if there were no difference between personal and social identity. The need for positive social identity arises from an interaction between social categorical self-definition, shared social values and intergroup comparison. The self-esteem hypothesis as commonly interpreted is based on a basic misunderstanding of the theory. As for causal direction, it was always perfectly clear that unsatisfactory social identity (in interaction with other conditions) could motivate intergroup discrimination and that the latter could make social identity more positive.

The categorization versus attribution issue

In their enthusiasm for demonstrating that category differentiation plays no role in intergroup conflict (note the confusion between category differentiation and social identity theory), Rabbie *et al.* argue that group-level attribution processes in conflicting intergroup relations are crucial to the development of intergroup hostility and that social categorization processes involve only the generalization of already formed traits from individual to individual, supposedly as in stereotyping, and do not explain the formation of negative beliefs about groups as a whole.

The former point is unexceptionable and would certainly not have been disputed by Tajfel, who played a major role in advancing our understanding of intergroup attribution and showing the links between group-level attributions, stereotypes and the formation of shared social beliefs and myths (1969, 1981, 1984). The suggestion that Tajfel denied the role of group-level attributions in intergroup hostility is based on a failure to understand his point in a particular argument in a particular context (his response to the chapter by Horwitz and Rabbie in his 1982 book).

The second point is quite wrong and theoretically absurd. Stereotyping is about the perception of people as group members, not just person-to-person generalization. Without categorization and stereotyping, there would be no perceived group-level entities to which attributions could be made. Stereotyping in any case is closely related to attribution, as is categorization. Oakes *et al.* (1991), for example, in elaborating self-categorization theory, have argued that social categorizations become salient to explain people's collective actions and beliefs, when they demonstrate systematic *social* similarities and differences from others. Oakes *et al.* (1994), in their recent analysis of stereotyping, have proposed that it is a flexible and fluid process of categorical judgement, in which the collective realities of group behaviour are represented and explained in terms of perceivers' background theories and knowledge. In this analysis it is meaningless and foolish to draw sharp lines between attribution, categorization and stereotyping (see too Hewstone and Jaspars, 1982; Hewstone *et al.*, 1982).

Tajfel's misunderstood point in 1982 (and here we must perforce speculate) was the idea that categorization of others as beyond the pale of "self", "us", "human", carried with it a ready-made explanation of the worthlessness of others, leading to indifference at best and a readiness to justify inhuman cruelty at worst. Tajfel's argument was that the group-level attributions about Jews made by Nazis were implicit in and made possible by the fundamental prior categorization of Jews as beyond the pale of "us". Once this fundamental rejection and derogation had taken place, the finding of "reasons" for hostility followed logically and easily. To suppose that the provided "reasons" were causal and primary is to accept the propaganda that "justified" the slaughter to others. After all it is not true that the negative attributions made about Jews as a whole by the Nazis reflected an objective conflict of interests between Jewish and non-Jewish Germans. The negative beliefs that justified cruelty and murder did not derive from rational explanations of the groups' conflicting behaviours. They were made possible by and inherent in the prior categorization of the Jews as "them", "different", less than human. We think that Tajfel's point should be read as similar to Oakes' (1987) later argument that social categorizations *are* explanations.

The fixing of a rigid distinction between categorization and stereotyping on the one hand and group-level beliefs and attributions reflecting intergroup relations on the other is untenable and runs counter to much contemporary research.

Identification with the group versus identification with group interests

In their 1988 paper Rabbie and Horwitz distinguish between social identity and group identification:

> One difficulty in using social identity as a "simple and sovereign principle" . . . is the fact that persons can positively identify with one group or negatively identify with another without belonging to either of them . . . She obviously shares no social identity with either group, but she identifies positively with the outcomes of one and negatively with the outcomes of the other.
>
> Heider (1958) treats one's positive or negative identification with another party as a form of interdependence whereby one is satisfied or dissatisfied by the other party's good or bad outcomes, holding constant whatever outcomes may accrue to oneself . . .
>
> (1988, p. 120)

They argue that social identity is not the same as identifying with a group and that the latter is a matter of identifying with group interests. This is an odd point. There is no difficulty for self-categorization theory in the example they provide. Reference groups need not be membership groups and social identity is addressed to psychological or reference group membership. To identify with the outcomes of another is to identify with the other and one can do this in terms of higher-order social categories, such as humanity, which imply many lower-level differences. There is no difficulty in knowing that one is different from others at one level whilst identifying with them and their outcomes at a higher level. The Heider hypothesis suggests a close connection between identification and identifying with others' outcomes just as in self-categorization theory. The difference is that self-categorization theory has an explanation of this connection, whereas simply to define identification as a form of interdependence is pointless. It stretches the interdependence perspective to the point where it explains everything by definition. Self-categorization theory explains that to identify with others is not to hold "self" and "own outcomes" constant but to re-categorize self, and it is this re-categorization of others as self that is the basis of altruistic co-operation and empathy (see Gaertner *et al.*, 1989).

The same purely terminological victories are multiplied in a later paper. Horwitz and Rabbie (1989) suggest that social identity theory does not distinguish between individual and group-level interaction, between attitudes and reactions to individuals and to groups as whole entities. This is supposedly because Tajfel and Turner think that groups are only categories of similar individuals. In fact this distinction is fundamental to social identity ideas. It was Tajfel who originated the concept of the interpersonal–intergroup continuum and argued endlessly, following Sherif, that one could not extrapolate from theories of interpersonal behaviour to intergroup relations. Self-categorization theory elaborated this distinction. It explained the emergent properties of group-level behaviour in terms of the psychological consequences of moving from defining self and acting in terms of personal identity to defining self and acting in terms of social identity. Extraordinarily, however, Horwitz and Rabbie lay claim to this basic distinction as a derivation from BIM.

They explain that the concept of the interpersonal–intergroup continuum needs to be redefined. Instead of Tajfel's definition (see Tajfel, 1978, p. 41), we are given:

> If "group identification" is treated as "identifying with group interests", interindividual and intergroup behaviour can be ordered along a continuum. An interaction is wholly interindividual where one attributes the causes of others' actions to their individual interests rather than to their identifying with group interests. The interaction is wholly intergroup, where one attributes the causes of others' actions to their identifying with group interests rather than to their individual interests.
>
> (p. 120)

This "conceptual" improvement is nowhere justified in any empirically testable terms (and indeed ignores the evidence that attribution of people's behaviour is influenced by the level at which they are categorized). It simply borrows Tajfel's basic idea that people can vary in the extent to which they act at an individual or group level and asserts that these levels are bound up with attributions to individual or group "interests".

Similarly, they inform us that the concept of "depersonalization", central to social identity ideas and understood as the perception of self and others in terms of the shared characteristics of a social category membership, needs to be understood as "the degree that the others are perceived to act as agents or pawns of their group's interests" (p. 119), as if the perception of others as group members rather than individuals were not relevant to such an inference.

They even inform us that a major problem with the contact hypothesis is that researchers have not taken into account the interpersonal–intergroup distinction and have assumed that attitudes to individuals *qua* individuals will generalize to attitudes to people as group members; apparently because researchers have thought that groups were only categories of individuals. They go on to advocate three principles based on their distinction between individual and group behaviour that "may be used to facilitate cordial interpersonal interaction across antagonistic group lines": (1) reducing the salience of intergroup conflicts; (2) use of overlapping group memberships; and (3) increasing the salience of superordinate structures (i.e. common group identifications).

All these contributions of BIM rest on little more than the assertion that intergroup behaviour is not a matter of identifying with the group but of identifying with group interests. The problem is that none of them is new in essence. They are all to be found in theory and research in the social identity tradition. The distinction between individual and group-level behaviour, the interpersonal–intergroup continuum, the critique of the contact hypothesis in these terms, the concept of depersonalization, the role of salient group boundaries in shaping interaction, etc. have all been prominent and elaborated in social identity research, taking over as it did (with acknowledgement) the contributions of Sherif in this regard. All BIM does is take an idea already proposed and replace "identification with the group" with "identification with group interests".

Do Rabbie and Horwitz believe that people identify with group outcomes but not with groups? If people identify with groups, i.e. define themselves in terms of a group membership, is this not social identity? Self-categorization theory argues that the process of identification with group goals is two-way, from group to goals and from goals to group. All we get from BIM is the supposed precedence of interests over social identity, with the *ad hoc* resort to Heider and unit-forming factors whenever the data show otherwise.

The tendency to adopt the substance of the social identity perspective whilst flailing it in public is particularly clear in a more recent article by Rabbie (1991) on the causes of intragroup co-operation. Here is a slightly fuller version of what Turner said in 1981 under the heading "An alternative perspective: group-formation as a determinant of social co-operation":

> . . . we can derive from the social identity principle the hypothesis that, under conditions where objective functional relations are ambiguous, indirect or mixed co-operative and competitive . . ., social categorization *per se* should cause individuals to perceive their interests as co-operatively linked within groups and competitively linked between groups. The implication is that the formation of a common or superordinate group tends to induce and stabilize co-operative behaviour in the same way that an ingroup–outgroup division elicits competitive tendencies: not merely through the need for positive distinctiveness, but more basically, because social categorization directly influences individuals' perceptions of their goals.
>
> . . . The fundamental point is that the processes implicated in group-formation *per se* may also tend to dictate the co-operative and competitive orientations characteristic respectively of intragroup and intergroup relations.
>
> (1981, pp. 98–99)

In 1987, after reviewing evidence from research on experimental games, he stated:

> What seems to matter for co-operation, the decisive condition, is the intervention of social psychological variables that produce a mutually co-operative relationship. If one looks carefully at the relevant variables—a shared self-definition as partners, being oriented to the common interest, shared goals and experiences, similarity, reduced social distance and increased social contact, empathy and trust, mutual attraction, the salience of shared norms and values, acting in "public" (a shared social field) as opposed to as an isolated private individual, etc.—there is a strong implication that the general process underlying mutually co-operative intentions and expectations is the extent to which players come to see themselves as a collective or joint unit, to feel a sense of "we-ness" . . . the fundamental process is one of becoming a psychological group.
>
> . . . Instead of social co-operation producing the group, it may well be that, psychologically, the group is the basis of co-operation.
>
> (Turner *et al.*, 1987, p. 34)

Here is what Rabbie says in 1991 reviewing the same literature on experimental games and in the immediate context of *contrasting* his position with social identity ideas:

> A group becomes a compact "we-group" or "social group" to the extent that individuals are subjected to the experience of a common fate, perceive themselves to be interdependent with

> respect to their common goals and means to attain those goals, view themselves (and are also considered by others) as a distinctive social unit, can directly communicate with one another and engage in co-operative face-to-face interactions in an effort to achieve a group product or common outcomes . . .
>
> Our central hypothesis is that the more a collection of people begins to share the features of a compact social group, as we have defined it, the more mutual intragroup co-operation will occur . . .
>
> The opportunity to communicate, the information that others have co-operated in the past, the trust in other group members, shared social values and responsibility for the group's welfare and obviously [*sic*] the awareness of a common group identity encourage the arousal of co-operative orientations and consequent behaviour.
>
> (1991, pp. 238–240 and 253)

The similarity behind the terminological veneer is striking. The central hypothesis reverses the direction of causality from co-operation to the group that is the essence of reward structure theories like BIM (e.g. see Deutsch, 1949; Sherif, 1967) and basically adopts Turner's earlier position (viz., "the more a collection of people resembles a compact social group, the more intragroup co-operation will occur", Rabbie, 1991, p. 260). Yet later in the paper Rabbie goes on once more to argue that co-operation in social dilemma tasks is perfectly rational and instrumental and determined by interpersonal interdependence, just as he goes on once more to differentiate BIM from social identity theory, castigating the latter for defining groups as categories and misunderstanding the MGP. Whilst claiming that interdependence is primary and rejecting social identity ideas on this basis, he nevertheless adopts an hypothesis from self-categorization theory, whilst ignoring its origins in the opposed perspective.

Does Rabbie now accept that group formation *produces* co-operation (when we had all thought that his re-interpretation of the MGP was to assert the opposite)? If so, he must explain how it does so and how group formation takes place prior to rational co-operation on the basis of personal self-interest. Self-categorization theory has already answered these questions. Rabbie *et al.* seem to have little to offer when they confront these questions, but the very fact that they are arriving at them is a tribute to the influence of social identity ideas.

Conclusion

Rabbie *et al.* argue that social identity theory blurs the distinction between social categories and groups and that intergroup discrimination in the MGP reflects perceived interdependence rather than social categorization *per se.* We have shown that their argument in both respects is fallacious. They have failed to understand the theory of the group provided by social identity ideas and have directed their critique at a straw man, seeing no difference between the psychological role of self-categories in the emergence of groups as behaving social systems and the definition of a group as an objective sociological category. Their explanation of MGP responses in terms of perceived interdependence is logically inconsistent and does not work. Their own data (and other more recent data) demonstrate that social categorization *per se* under certain conditions can produce ingroup bias irreducible to personal self-interest.

Rabbie *et al.* seem gradually to become aware of the weakness of their position. Whereas they begin by bravely telling us that MGP responses are completely rational, self-interested and instrumental, by the end of their 1989 paper BIM has become a supposedly integrative theory that includes not only goal interdependence but the cognitive role of common fate, the salience of social categorizations and other cognitive boundaries, a generic groupness norm and identification with group interests, i.e. all the concepts that it supposedly rejected in social identity theory.

Despite this plethora of *ad hoc* additions there seem to be no new distinctive predictions generated by the theory. The only really distinctive idea is the classic one that they seem to want to obscure, that goal interdependence is the basis of cohesiveness and group formation. Despite their theoretical rhetoric, they come to distinguish goal interdependence from common fate (it is a "consequence"), common fate they accept as a cognitive criterion of group formation and the latter (through the groupness norm) they agree creates perceived interdependence. In other words, they agree that group formation can precede and produce perceived interdependence. The only evidence they once had that social categorization unconfounded by interdependence did not lead to discrimination (the control condition of Rabbie and Horwitz, 1969), they have now themselves abandoned. Their strong claim that social categorization without perceived consequences *never* leads to discrimination is hollow, since they have redefined "perceived consequences" to be consistent with a social identity rather than an interdependence perspective.

In rejecting Rabbie *et al.*'s claims, we are neither devaluing nor rejecting the contribution to social psychology of the classic Gestalt/interdependence perspective and the research which has flowed from it, including the important work of Rabbie, Horwitz and colleagues. Social identity and self-categorization theories are, in fact, a return to the classic interdependence idea of the group as an evolving social and psychological system, characterized by whole-properties, that transforms the behaviour of its members, a system in which the psychological is genuinely social–psychological because it is conceived as taking place within a social field that modifies the psychological processes of individuals (e.g. Asch, 1952; Sherif, 1936). The emphasis on self-categorization does not imply that a group is purely psychological or cognitive. The aim in recent work is to show how self-categories are intrinsically social comparative and social contextual, reflexively representing the individual in terms of his or her social contextual properties, not reified intrapsychic structures activated by but pre-existing such contexts (Turner *et al.*, 1994). A social psychological analysis of self-categorization is a necessary part of the story whereby individual becomes group behaviour and individual psychology becomes social psychology.

References

Asch, S. E. (1952). *Social psychology.* Englewood Cliffs, NJ: Prentice-Hall.

Billig M. G., and Tajfel, H. (1973). Social categorization and similarity in intergroup behaviour. *European Journal of Social Psychology,* **3**, 27–52.

Bourhis, R. Y. (1994). Power, gender and intergroup discrimination: Some minimal group experiments. In M. Zanna and J. Olson (Eds), *The psychology of prejudice: The Ontario symposium,* Vol. 7. Hillsdale, NJ: Lawrence Erlbaum, pp. 171–208.

Bourhis, R. Y., Gagnon, A., and Moise, L. (1994). Discrimination et les relations intergroupes. In R. Y. Bourhis and J. P. Leyens (Eds), *Stéréotypes, discrimination et les relations intergroupes.* Liège, Belgium: Mardaga, pp. 161–200.

Bourhis, R. Y., Sachdev, I., and Gagnon, A. (1994). Intergroup research with the Tajfel matrices: Methodological notes. In M. Zanna and J. Olson (Eds), *The psychology of prejudice: The Ontario symposium,* Vol. 7. Hillsdale, NJ: Lawrence Erlbaum, pp. 209–232.

Brewer, M. B., and Schneider, S. K. (1990). Social identity and social dilemmas: A double-edged sword. In D. Abrams and M. A. Hogg (Eds), *Social identity theory: Constructive and critical advances.* London: Harvester-Wheatsheaf.

Brewer, M. B., and Silver, M. (1978). Ingroup bias as a function of task characteristics. *European Journal of Social Psychology,* **8**, 393–400.

Caporael, L. R., Dawes, R. M., Orbell, J. M., and van de Kragt, A. J. C. (1989). Selfishness examined: Co-operation in the absence of egoistic incentives. *Behavioral and Brain Sciences,* **12**, 683–699.

Deutsch, M. (1949). A theory of co-operation and competition. *Human Relations,* **2**, 129–152.

Ellemers, N. (1991). Identity management strategies. Unpublished PhD thesis, Rijksuniversiteit Groningen, The Netherlands.

Gaertner, S. L., Mann, J., Dovidio, J., Murrell, A., and Pomare, M. (1990). How does co-operation reduce intergroup bias? *Journal of Personality and Social Psychology,* **59**, 692–704.

Gaertner, S. L., Mann, J., Murrell, A., and Dovidio, J. (1989). Reducing intergroup bias: The benefits of recategorization. *Journal of Personality and Social Psychology,* **57**, 239–249.

Gagnon A., and Bourhis, R. Y. (1992). Discrimination in the minimal group paradigm: Social identity or self-interest? Paper presented to the 53rd Annual Conference of the Canadian Psychological Association, Quebec City, Canada.

Haslam, S. A., and Turner, J. C. (1992). Context-dependent variation in social stereotyping 2: The relationship between frame of reference, self-categorization and accentuation. *European Journal of Social Psychology,* **22**, 251–277.

Haslam, S. A., and Turner, J. C. (1995). Context-dependent variation in social stereotyping 3: Extremism as a self-categorical basis for polarized judgement. *European Journal of Social Psychology,* **25**, 341–371.

Hewstone, M., and Jaspars, J. (1982). Intergroup relations and attribution processes. In H. Tajfel (Ed.), *Social identity and intergroup relations.* Cambridge: Cambridge University Press.

Hewstone, M., Jaspars, J., and Lalljee, M. (1982). Social representations, social attribution and social identity: The intergroup images of "public" and "comprehensive" schoolboys. *European Journal of Social Psychology,* **12**, 241–269.

Horwitz, M., and Rabbie, J. M. (1982). Individuality and membership in the intergroup system. In H. Tajfel (Ed.), *Social identity and intergroup relations.* Cambridge: Cambridge University Press.

Horwitz, M., and Rabbie, J. M. (1989). Stereotypes of groups, group members, and individuals in categories: A differential analysis. In D. Bar-Tal, C. F. Grauman, A. W. Kruglanski, and W. Stroebe (Eds), *Stereotyping and prejudice: Changing conceptions.* New York: Springer Verlag.

Lemyre, L., and Smith, P. M. (1985). Intergroup discrimination and self-esteem in the minimal group paradigm. *Journal of Personality and Social Psychology,* **49**, 660–670.

Lewin, K. (1948). *Resolving social conflicts.* New York: Harper and Brothers.

McDougall, W. (1921). *The group mind.* Cambridge: Cambridge University Press.

Oakes, P. J. (1987). The salience of social categories. In J. C. Turner, M. A. Hogg, P. J. Oakes, S. D. Reicher, and M. S. Wetherell. *Rediscovering the social group.* Oxford: Blackwell.

Oakes, P. J., Haslam, S. A., and Turner, J. C. (1994). *Stereotyping and social reality.* Oxford, UK, and Cambridge, MA: Blackwell.

Oakes, P. J., and Turner, J. C. (1980). Social categorization and intergroup behaviour: Does minimal intergroup behaviour make social identity more positive? *European Journal of Social Psychology*, **10**, 295–301.

Oakes, P. J., and Turner, J. C. (1986). Authors' rejoinder to Jahoda and Tetlock. *British Journal of Social Psychology*, **25**, 257–258.

Oakes, P. J., Turner, J. C., and Haslam, S. A. (1991). Perceiving people as group members: The role of fit in the salience of social categorizations. *British Journal of Social Psychology*, **30**, 125–144.

Rabbie, J. M. (1972). Experimental studies of intergroup relations. Paper presented to EAESP Conference on the Experimental Study of Intergroup Relations, University of Bristol, UK.

Rabbie, J. M. (1991). Determinants of instrumental intra-group co-operation. In R. A. Hinde and J. Groebel (Eds), *Co-operation and prosocial behaviour.* Cambridge: Cambridge University Press.

Rabbie, J. M., and Horwitz, M. (1969). The arousal of ingroup–outgroup bias by a chance win or loss. *Journal of Personality and Social Psychology*, **13**, 269–277.

Rabbie, J. M., and Horwitz, M. (1988). Categories versus groups as explanatory concepts in intergroup relations. *European Journal of Social Psychology*, **18**, 117–123.

Rabbie, J. M., Schot, J. C., and Visser, L. (1989). Social identity theory: A conceptual and empirical critique from the perspective of a behavioural interaction model. *European Journal of Social Psychology*, **19**, 171–202.

Sachdev, I., and Bourhis, R. Y. (1985). Social categorization and power differentials in group relations. *European Journal of Social Psychology*, **15**, 415–434.

Sachdev, I., and Bourhis, R. Y. (1987). Status differentials and intergroup behaviour. *European Journal of Social Psychology*, **17**, 277–293.

Sachdev, I., and Bourhis, R. Y. (1991). Power and status differentials in minority and majority group relations. *European Journal of Social Psychology*, **21**, 1–24.

Sherif, M. (1936). *The psychology of social norms.* New York: Harper.

Sherif, M. (1967). *Group conflict and co-operation: Their social psychology.* London: Routledge and Kegan Paul.

Tajfel, H. (1969). Cognitive aspects of prejudice. *Journal of Social Issues*, **25**, 79–97.

Tajfel, H. (1972). Social catègorization. In S. Moscovici (Ed.), *Introduction à la psychologie sociale*, Vol. 1. Paris: Larouse.

Tajfel, H. (Ed.) (1978). *Differentiation between social groups: Studies in the social psychology of intergroup relations.* London: Academic Press.

Tajfel, H. (1979). Individuals and groups in social psychology. *British Journal of Social and Clinical Psychology*, **18**, 183–190.

Tajfel, H. (1981). *Human groups and social categories.* Cambridge: Cambridge University Press.

Tajfel, H. (1982). Instrumentality, identity and social comparisons. In H. Tajfel (Ed.), *Social identity and intergroup relations.* Cambridge: Cambridge University Press.

Tajfel, H. (1984). Intergroup relations, social myths and social justice in intergroup relations. In H. Tajfel (Ed.), *The social dimension: European developments in social psychology*, Vol. 2. Cambridge: Cambridge University Press.

Tajfel, H., Flament, C., Billig, M. G., and Bundy, R. F. (1971). Social categorization and intergroup behaviour. *European Journal of Social Psychology*, **1**, 149–177.

Tajfel, H., and Turner, J. C. (1979). An integrative theory of intergroup conflict. In W. G. Austin and S. Worchel (Eds), *The social psychology of intergroup relations.* Monterey, CA: Brooks/Cole.

Tajfel, H., and Turner, J. C. (1986). The social identity theory of intergroup behaviour. S. Worchel and W. G. Austin (Eds), *Psychology of intergroup relations*, 2nd edn. Chicago: Nelson-Hall.

Turner, J. C. (1975). Social comparison and social identity: Some prospects for intergroup behaviour. *European Journal of Social Psychology*, **5**, 149–178.

Turner, J. C. (1978). Social categorization and social discrimination in the minimal group paradigm. In H. Tajfel (Ed.), *Differentiation between social groups: Studies in the social psychology of intergroup relations.* London: Academic Press.

Turner, J. C. (1980). Fairness or discrimination in intergroup behaviour? A reply to Branthwaite, Doyle and Lightbown. *European Journal of Social Psychology*, **10**, 131–147.

Turner, J. C. (1981). The experimental social psychology of intergroup behaviour. In J. C. Turner and H. Giles (Eds.), *Intergroup behaviour.* Oxford: Blackwell, and Chicago: University of Chicago Press.

Turner, J. C. (1982). Towards a cognitive redefinition of the social group. In H. Tajfel (Ed.), *Social identity and intergroup relations*. Cambridge: Cambridge University Press.

Turner, J. C. (1983). Some comments on . . . "the measurement of social orientations in the minimal group paradigm". *European Journal of Social Psychology*, **13**, 351–367.

Turner, J. C. (1985). Social categorization and the self-concept: A social cognitive theory of group behaviour. In E. J. Lawler (Ed.) *Advances in group processes*, Vol. 2. Greenwich, CT: JAI Press.

Turner, J. C. (1991). *Social influence*. Buckingham, UK: Open University Press and Pacific Grove, CA: Brooks/Cole.

Turner, J. C., Brown, R. J., and Tajfel, H. (1979). Social comparison and group interest in ingroup favouritism. *European Journal of Social Psychology*, **9**, 187–204.

Turner, J. C., and Giles, H. (1981). Introduction: The social psychology of intergroup behaviour. In J. C. Turner and H. Giles (Eds.), *Intergroup behaviour*. Oxford: Blackwell, and Chicago: University of Chicago Press.

Turner, J. C., Hogg, M. A., Oakes, P. J., Reicher, S. D., and Wetherell, M. S. (1987). *Rediscovering the social group: A self-categorization theory*. Oxford and New York: Blackwell.

Turner, J. C., Hogg, M. A., Turner, P. J., and Smith, P. M. (1984). Failure and defeat as determinants of group cohesiveness. *British Journal of Social Psychology*, **23**, 97–111.

Turner, J. C., and Oakes, P. J. (1986). The significance of the social identity concept for social psychology with reference to individualism, interactionism, and social influence. *British Journal of Social Psychology*, **25**, 237–252.

Turner, J. C., and Oakes, P. J. (1989). Self-categorization theory and social influence. In P. B. Paulus (Ed.) *The psychology of group influence*. Hillsdale, NJ.: Erlbaum.

Turner, J. C., Oakes, P. J., Haslam, S. A., and McGarty, C. A. (1994). Self and collective: Cognition and social context. *Personality and Social Psychology Bulletin*, **20**, 454–463.

Turner, J. C., Sachdev, I., and Hogg, M. A. (1983). Social categorization, interpersonal attraction and group formation. *British Journal of Social Psychology*, **22**, 227–239.

Worchel, S. (1979) Co-operation and the reduction of intergroup conflict: Some determining factors. In W. G. Austin and S. Worchel (Eds), *The social psychology of intergroup relations*. Monterey, CA: Brooks/Cole.

2

Intragroup Processes, Group Structure and Social Identity

MICHAEL A. HOGG

Department of Psychology, The University of Queensland

Contents

Henri Tajfel has touched the lives, both professionally and personally, of all of us who have contributed to this book. In the autumn of 1981 I took up my first lecturing appointment—it was at Bristol University where I had been a postgraduate since 1978. I was required primarily to replace Henri Tajfel who was on leave, and my main responsibility was to teach his advanced social psychology course to final year students. I still clearly recall making the sad announcement in this class, Henri's class, that social psychology had lost one of its greatest scholars and one of its most effective champions.

Henri Tajfel has left his mark on social psychology in at least three important, and interrelated, ways: (1) the establishment of a functional infrastructure for social psychology in Europe (Doise, 1982; Jaspars, 1980, 1986; Tajfel, 1972); (2) the development of a characteristically European perspective on social psychology (e.g. Tajfel, 1984)—one which, for example, distinctively frames European social psychology textbooks (e.g. Hewstone *et al.*, 1988; Hogg and

Vaughan, 1995; Tajfel and Fraser, 1978); and (3) the development of social identity theory as a non-reductionist analysis of intergroup behaviour.

In this chapter I focus on social identity theory, with the aim of showing how it has grown into a significant international perspective on group-mediated social psychological phenomena. My main emphasis is on understanding processes that occur within groups, and on how groups may be internally structured and differentiated. In doing this I have intentionally focused upon my own research over the past fifteen years or so, and have highlighted current ongoing research in which I am involved. I consider this work to be strongly and continuingly influenced by Henri Tajfel's insights.

The chapter has ten sections. The first three overview my interpretation of social identity theory and self-categorization theory, and describe how, taken as an integrated whole, they increasingly function as a general perspective on group-mediated social psychological phenomena. The fourth section focuses on the study of processes and structures within groups, and the remainder of the chapter deals with specific areas of research. In the fifth section I briefly overview work on group cohesiveness and social attraction, which feeds into a discussion of psychological group formation, identity salience, and identity motivation in the section which follows. The seventh section covers, in more detail, the issue of intragroup differentiation, and in the eighth section I discuss some recent work on leadership as a differentiated role within a salient group. The penultimate section explores work, again recent, into how groups influence the attitudes of their members and how groups influence attitude–behaviour relations. The chapter finishes with some brief concluding comments in the final section.

Social identity theory

Social identity theory has its origins in early work in Britain by Henri Tajfel on social factors in perception (e.g. Tajfel, 1959, 1969a), and on cognitive and social belief aspects of racism, prejudice and discrimination (e.g. Tajfel, 1963, 1969b, 1970), but was fully formulated and developed in collaboration with John Turner and others in the mid to late 1970s at Bristol University (e.g. Tajfel, 1974, 1978, 1982; Tajfel and Turner, 1979; Turner, 1982). Although from the outset it was primarily a theory of intergroup relations between large scale social categories (e.g. races, nations, ethnic groups, socio-economic classes), it can be more broadly considered as a social psychological theory of the social group (e.g. Hogg and Abrams, 1988; Tajfel, 1978, 1982; Tajfel and Turner, 1979; Turner, 1982; Turner and Giles, 1981).

The core idea is that a self-inclusive social category (e.g. nationality, political affiliation, sports team) provides a category-congruent self-definition that constitutes an element of the self-concept. People have a repertoire of such discrete category memberships that vary in relative overall importance in the self-concept. The category is represented in the individual member's mind as a social identity that both describes and prescribes one's attributes as a group member. When a specific social identity is the salient basis for self-regulation, self-perception and conduct become ingroup stereotypical and normative, perceptions of relevant outgroup members become outgroup stereotypical, and intergroup behaviour acquires, to varying degrees depending on the history of relations between the groups, competitive and discriminatory properties. Social identities are not only descriptive and prescriptive, but also evaluative. They furnish a relatively consensual evaluation of a social category, and thus its members, relative to other relevant social categories. Because social identities have important self-evaluative consequences, groups and their members are motivated to adopt strategies for achieving or maintaining intergroup comparisons that favour the ingroup, and thus the self.

To account for social identity phenomena, social identity theory invokes the operation of two underlying processes. (1) *Categorization*, which clarifies intergroup boundaries by producing group stereotypical and normative perceptions and actions, and assigns people, including self, to the contextually relevant category. Categorization is a basic cognitive process which operates on social and non-social stimuli alike, to highlight and bring into focus those aspects of experience that are subjectively meaningful in a particular context. (2) *Self-enhancement*, which guides the social categorization process such that ingroup norms and stereotypes are largely ingroup favouring. It is assumed that people have a very basic need to see themselves in a relatively positive light in relation to relevant others (i.e. have an evaluatively positive self-concept), and that in group contexts self-enhancement can be achieved through evaluatively positive social identity in relation to relevant outgroups (but see Grieve and Hogg, submitted; Hogg and Abrams, 1993; Mullin and Hogg, submitted).

An important feature of social identity theory is that in order to explain the behaviour of group members, it formally articulates (cf. Doise, 1986; Lorenzi-Cioldi and Doise, 1990) categorization and self-enhancement processes with *subjective belief structures*. The latter refer to people's beliefs about the nature of relations between their own group and relevant outgroups. These beliefs (which are not necessarily accurate reflections of reality) concern the stability and legitimacy of intergroup status relations, and the possibility of social mobility or social change. They influence the specific behaviours that group members adopt in the pursuit of self-enhancement through evaluatively positive social identity.

Although social identity researchers often consider the theory to be a general framework for the analysis of the social group, much of the research has actually emphasized intergroup behaviour rather than what goes on among individuals within a group—witness the pervasive presence of the word 'intergroup' in articles and books adopting a social identity perspective (e.g. Hogg and Abrams, 1988; Tajfel, 1978, 1982; Tajfel and Turner, 1979; Turner and Giles, 1981). Research has tended to dwell on crowd behaviour (e.g. Reicher, 1987), stereotyping (e.g. Oakes *et al.*, 1994; Tajfel, 1981), the way in which subjective belief structures influence intergroup behaviour (e.g. Brown, 1978; Sachdev and

Bourhis, 1991; Taylor and McKirnan, 1984; van Knippenberg and Ellemers, 1993), the role of ethnolinguistic vitality perceptions in interethnic relations and language behaviour (e.g. Giles and Johnson, 1987; Sachdev and Bourhis, 1993), and so forth. Even the minimal group studies, which are often invoked as critical evidence for social identity, are studies of intergroup behaviour between social categories (e.g. Diehl, 1990; Tajfel *et al.*, 1971).

Nevertheless, the social identity concept can be used very effectively as a general perspective on group-mediated social psychological phenomena (e.g. Hogg, 1996; Hogg and Abrams, 1988; Hogg *et al.*, 1995b; Hogg and Vaughan, 1995). This has, perhaps paradoxically at first sight, been facilitated enormously by the development of self-categorization theory.

Self-Categorization Theory

Self-categorization theory (Turner, 1985; Turner *et al.*, 1987) is an important theoretical development of social identity theory. It elaborates in detail the social–cognitive basis of group membership. Because it focuses upon the individual cognitive process of categorization, because it talks mainly about categories rather than groups, and because much of its research base is non-interactive individuals, there has been a general tendency for people to treat self-categorization theory simply as part of social cognition. In one sense, of course, it is. However, there is an important difference in metatheoretical emphasis: traditional social cognition tends to focus on the unidirectional effect of cognitive processes and structures on information processing about people (cf. Fiske, 1993; Fiske and Taylor, 1991), while self-categorization theory, as a social–cognitive theory, also emphasizes emergent cognitive and behavioural outcomes of human interaction (cf. Levine *et al.*, 1993; Sherif, 1936).

Self-categorization theory represents a shift in emphasis from intergroup relations, social change, and so forth, to intragroup processes (e.g. conformity, cohesiveness), and the social–cognitive basis of group membership and group phenomena. As such, it is quite distinct from social identity theory. However, it is closely related in many other respects—both theories come from the same stable and are part of the same broader theoretical and metatheoretical enterprise (cf. Hogg and Abrams, 1988; Hogg and McGarty, 1990).

Self-categorization theory elaborates the operation of the categorization process as the cognitive basis of group behaviour. Categorization accentuates both similarities among stimuli (physical, social, or aspects of the self) belonging to the same category and differences among stimuli belonging to different categories on dimensions believed to be correlated with the categorization. This process clarifies intergroup discontinuities, and ultimately serves the function of rendering experience of the world subjectively meaningful, and identifies those aspects relevant to action in a particular context.

When people categorize themselves and others in terms of ingroup–outgroup (defining one's social identity) there is, therefore, an accentuation of the perceived group prototypicality, stereotypicality or normativeness of people. The individual is perceptually and behaviourally depersonalized in terms of the relevant ingroup prototype. It is this process of depersonalization of self which underlies group phenomena such as social stereotyping, group cohesion and ethnocentrism, co-operation and altruism, collective behaviour, and shared norms and mutual influence process. Nothing negative is implied by the term "depersonalization". It contains none of the implications of "dehumanization" or "deindividuation", but simply refers to a contextual *change* in the level of identity, not to a loss of identity.

For self-categorization theory, people cognitively represent social groups in terms of prototypes. A prototype is a subjective representation of the defining attributes (beliefs, attitudes, behaviours, etc.) of a social category, which is actively constructed and is context dependent. Because common group members generally find themselves relatively similarly placed within the same social field, their prototypes will usually be very similar—i.e. shared. Prototypes are ordinarily unlikely to be checklists of attributes (though they can of course be elicited in this form by probing); rather, they are fuzzy-sets which capture the context-dependent features of group membership often in the form of exemplary members (actual group members who best embody the group) or ideal types (an abstraction of group features). People are able to assess the prototypicality of real group members, including self—that is, the extent to which a member is perceived to be close or similar to the group prototype.

The social self-concept is context dependent insofar as specific social self-categorizations are brought into play (i.e. become the basis of perception and conduct) by the social field. The cognitive system, in seeking to maximize meaning in a specific context, engages whatever categorization best accounts for the similarities and differences among stimuli. This categorization seeks a balance between minimization of perceived *intra*category differences and maximization of perceived *inter*category differences, with respect to relevant prototypes, within the social frame of reference. Once formed on the basis of perceived similarities and differences among stimuli, categories are consequently used as a basis for the perceptual accentuation of these similarities and differences, thereby maximizing separateness and clarity. The subjective salience of social categories is not only governed by the mechanics of stimulus–category fit, but also by the motivated availability of social categories. By this I mean that people actively engage in more or less competitive (and more or less successful) re-negotiation of the frame of reference in order to achieve a self-categorization that is relatively more favourable for conceptualization of self in that context.

Self-categorization research has been most evident in perhaps three areas: (1) social influence, including the study of conformity and group polarization (e.g. Abrams and Hogg, 1990; Turner, 1991; Turner and Oakes, 1989); (2) social perception, including the study of stereotyping, relative homogeneity effects and illusory correlation (e.g. Haslam *et al.*, in press; Oakes *et al.*, 1994); and (3) group solidarity and cohesiveness (e.g. Hogg, 1992, 1993).

A Social Identity Approach to Social Psychology

Tajfel's influence is strong and evident in both social identity theory and self-categorization theory. Indeed, there are distinct benefits from treating these two theories as complementary aspects, albeit with differences in conceptual emphasis, of one and the same broader social identity analysis of group-mediated behaviour (see Hogg, 1992, 1995; Hogg and Abrams, 1988; Hogg *et al.*, 1995b). This raises the possibility of social identity becoming a mid-range or even higher order theory that is applicable not only to the traditional areas of stereotyping, prejudice, intergroup relations and conformity, but also to the study of, for instance, small group processes, intragroup structure and attitude change.

To some extent this has already happened. The concepts of a wider social identity perspective are used in undergraduate texts to explain a range of phenomena (e.g. Hogg and Vaughan, 1995); they crop up in organizational psychology (e.g. Ashforth and Mael, 1989), and sociology (e.g. Hogg *et al.*, 1995b); and they have been influential to varying degrees in a range of contemporary social psychological theories—examples include Brewer's (e.g. 1991, 1993) optimal distinctiveness theory, Crocker's (e.g. Crocker *et al.*, 1993) model of collective self-esteem, and Moreland and Levine's (e.g. Moreland *et al.*, 1993) model of group socialization. In fact, in a recent analysis of publication trends over 20 years (since 1974) for group research in the three main American social psychology journals, Moreland *et al.* (1994) found evidence for a vigorous revival during the 1990s—a revival that was significantly influenced by social identity research.

For the remainder of this chapter, however, I focus only on how this broader social identity perspective may help to understand processes and structures within groups (e.g. small group processes, cohesiveness and social attraction, group formation, group motivation, social differentiation, roles, leadership, norms, group-mediated attitude change, group-mediated attitude–behaviour relations).

Processes and Structures Within Groups

The metatheoretical orientation and the explanatory concepts of a social identity perspective do away with distinctions between large scale social categories and small interactive groups, and so allow transcendance of the historical separation in social psychology between the study of social categories (e.g. prejudice, discrimination, identity, conflict) and the study of small groups (e.g. decision making, roles, cohesiveness). However, most social identity research more directly addresses social categories and traditional topics such as stereotyping (e.g. Oakes *et al.*, 1994) than small group processes and less traditional topics such as leadership.

The social identity analysis of small group processes, which is only in its infancy (e.g. Hogg's 1992, analysis of intragroup attraction phenomena, and

Moreland *et al.*'s 1993, analysis of group socialization), is likely to confront a number of issues (Hogg, 1996). On the one hand, application of the theory to small groups is straightforward. People in small groups categorize themselves as members of that group, construct a contextually appropriate ingroup prototype from salient ingroup–outgroup comparative information, perceive themselves and others in terms of this prototype, and conform, attitudinally, behaviourally and emotionally, to the prescriptions of the prototype. However, there are specific features of small groups that may raise problems. For instance, in small groups interpersonal relations among all members are not only possible but relatively more salient, and so interpersonal and group processes may interact in ways not yet explored by social identity theory.

The extension of social identity concepts to intragroup, especially small group, phenomena, may also confront another set of issues. Social identity theory tends to focus on intergroup differentiation and intragroup homogenization, and has not fully explored intragroup differentiation. Yet, research on relative homogeneity effects shows that ingroups are usually perceived to be relatively more differentiated than outgroups (Simon, 1993; Simon and Brown, 1987), and research on small groups has emphasized the structural differentiation of groups into roles (e.g. leadership)—in fact many definitions of the social group include group structure as a crucial feature that distinguishes a group from an aggregate (e.g. McDavid and Harari, 1968; Sherif and Sherif, 1956).

Social identity concepts may be able to explain intragroup differentiation in terms of social identity processes, via the notion of relative prototypicality. This may circumvent having to invoke notions of subgrouping, or of personal identity or individual differentiation from the group. However, this has not yet been fully explored (Hogg, 1996; Hogg *et al.*, 1995b).

In suggesting that social identity theory can explicate intragroup phenomena, small group processes, and intragroup differentiation, it needs to be kept clearly in mind that any such analyses will still have the following essential properties: (1) a group is a collection of people who categorized themselves in terms of the same social categorization; (2) interpersonal processes are conceptually separate from group processes; (3) the intergroup social comparative context is an integral feature of the analysis; and (4) a complete explanation requires articulation of cognitive and social processes.

Cohesiveness and Social Attraction

In contrast to traditional explanations of large scale group phenomena which focus, for example, on personality dynamics (e.g. Adorno *et al.*, 1950; Dollard *et al.*, 1939) or goal relations (e.g. Deutsch, 1949, 1973; Sherif, 1967; Sherif and Sherif, 1969), small group research has historically placed an emphasis on interpersonal attraction as an important dimension of group membership and solidarity. Since Festinger *et al.*'s (1950) elaboration of the psychological construct of cohesiveness to explain adherence to group norms, attraction has assumed a central explanatory role in many treatments of small group dynamics (e.g. Lott and Lott, 1965). Critics have felt, however, that although small groups may be characterized by interpersonal attraction and friendship, something is being missed if *group* cohesiveness is no more than aggregated *interpersonal* attraction (e.g. Evans and Jarvis, 1980; Hogg, 1987, 1992; Mudrack, 1989; Turner, 1984).

This problem can be resolved by adopting a conceptual separation of interpersonal attraction from group-mediated attraction, and then analysing group-mediated attraction as one of a range of effects of self-categorization and social identification (Hogg, 1983, 1987, 1992, 1993). The former, *personal attraction*, is true interpersonal attraction grounded in specific interpersonal relationships and idiosyncratic preferences. The latter, *social attraction*, is group membership based regard, including attraction, which is grounded in depersonalized prototype-based perception of self and others—positive regard for ingroup members and negative regard for outgroup members. Social attraction can be generated by the self-categorization process in a number of co-occurring ways (see Hogg, 1992, 1993, for full details):

(1) Since ingroup prototypes are perceived to be more favourable than outgroup prototypes (cf. ethnocentrism—Sumner, 1906), depersonalization renders ingroupers more likeable than outgroupers—more ingroup prototypical ingroupers and less outgroup prototypical outgroupers are liked more.

(2) Self-categorization is associated with heightened concern for intergroup distinctiveness (cf. Hogg and Abrams, 1993)—more ingroup prototypical ingroupers and more outgroup prototypical outgroupers are liked more.

(3) Self-categorization accentuates perceived prototypical (not interpersonal) similarity between self and fellow ingroupers and difference between self and outgroupers—intragroup attraction is accentuated and intergroup attraction reduced (e.g. Hogg *et al.*, 1995a).

(4) Self-categorization depersonalizes self-perception in terms of the evaluatively positive ingroup prototype. This enhances self-liking which is generalized to fellow ingroup members as a function of their perceived prototypical similarity to self (cf. LeVine and Campbell, 1972).

(5) Self-categorization brings into play relevant social belief structures (cf. Hogg and Hains, 1996). These prescribe strategic behaviours that may, in some intergroup contexts, include overt expression of ingroup solidarity which might enhance ingroup liking, perhaps through mutual reciprocation of expressed positive regard—people tend to like those who express liking for them (e.g. Lott and Lott, 1965).

This analysis of group-mediated attraction accomplishes a number of things. It separates the attraction dimension of group solidarity from interpersonal attraction, such that group-mediated attraction is independent of both group size and interindividual interaction. Solidarity/cohesiveness is recognized to involve interindividual feelings, but it is not purely a matter of such feelings, and it is not an aggregate of interindividual processes. By linking social attraction to prototypicality, it recognizes group structure—at the most basic level it recognizes that within groups there may be more and less popular group members—less prototypical members may have lower status, and may become effectively marginalized and possibly rejected from the group (cf. the black sheep effect—Marques and Paez, 1994).

Direct support for the social attraction hypothesis comes from a programme of research which has mainly addressed the focal prediction that in salient groups, ingroup liking is depersonalized in terms of the ingroup prototype, and is independent from interpersonal attraction (see reviews in Hogg, 1992, 1993, 1996). Taken together, these studies (Hogg *et al.*, 1993; Hogg and Hardie, 1991, 1992, in press) reveal that in salient groups people like one another on the basis of how ingroup prototypical they are perceived to be rather than how interpersonally similar they are, and that this effect is stronger for people who identify more strongly with the group. Intergroup relations do not impact on these intragroup attraction dynamics directly, but through the mediation of social identification (Hogg and Hains, 1996). There is also some evidence that if perceived similarity is one process that underlies group-mediated attraction, then in salient groups it is specific prototypical, not general interpersonal, similarity that is responsible (Hogg *et al.*, 1995a).

Group Formation and Identity Salience

One consequence of social identity research into cohesiveness is that attraction is no longer a likely contender for the process of psychological group formation—interpersonal attraction has been shown to be neither sufficient or necessary for group formation (see empirical overviews by Hogg, 1987 and Turner, 1984, of early research), and social attraction is clearly a consequence of group formation. Self-categorization is a better contender. However, the question remains as to what are the conditions under which people categorize themselves and thus psychologically become group members. Social identity theory has approached this question in a variety of ways.

Some early explanations of the minimal group effect suggested that people might identify with groups in order to impose structure on intrinsically uncertain circumstances (e.g. Tajfel and Billig, 1974). Very soon, however, evaluatively positive social identity became the main motivation behind social identification, and it in turn was explicated in terms of the operation of an individual motive to maintain or enhance self-esteem (e.g. Tajfel and Turner, 1979; Turner, 1982)—described as the self-esteem hypothesis by Abrams and Hogg (1988). It was this formulation that inspired most social identity research that dealt with intergroup relations, intergroup conflict, ethnolinguistic identity, and so forth (e.g. Giles and Johnson, 1987; Hogg and Abrams, 1988; Tajfel, 1982; Taylor and McKirnan, 1984; Turner and Giles, 1981). Although unquestionably useful at the macrosocial level, it has proven difficult to establish exactly how self-esteem is related to social identification or self-categorization at a more fundamental social–cognitive level (Abrams and Hogg, 1988; Hogg and Abrams, 1990, 1993).

Self-categorization theory (Turner, 1985; Turner, *et al.*, 1987) has changed the emphasis from self-esteem to categorization, from motivation to process, and from group formation to salience. In a given social comparative context the human cognitive apparatus brings to bear an array of cognitively accessible social categorizations to try to make sense of interindividual similarities and differences—the categorization that accounts for the most variance (best "fits" the data) becomes the salient basis for self-categorization (e.g. Oakes, 1987; Oakes *et al.*, 1994).

This perspective has tended to focus on how immediate situational factors render pre-existent contextually relevant social self-categorizations salient (e.g. bring into play an existing identification as, say, a University lecturer giving a class). The emphasis has been on the contextual responsiveness of self-categorizations. Taken too far, this perspective runs the risk of grounding itself on the shifting sands of social constructivism. The group-mediated self-concept becomes too closely tied to immediate situational factors and thus becomes fragmentary and kaleidoscopic—an ever changing reflection of infinitely unique situations. Given that no two people are going to interpret the same situation identically, self-conceptions within the group also become synchronically fragmented, which of course precludes the possibility of shared self-categorization and renders self-categorization theory no longer a theory of the group.

This danger may be avoided by being careful to distinguish between salience and group formation. People form relatively enduring group memberships/identities (e.g. British, male, lecturer) which prescribe situationally appropriate behaviours. Such identities are constructed and cognitively represented in memory in the form of self-inclusive group prototypes that are more or less cognitively accessible. Social comparative contexts make salient such identities and provide them with more or less finely grained nuances of situational/contextual appropriateness.

For self-categorization theory there is no explicit motivational analysis to account for salience and group formation. Rather, it is implicit that salience is partially governed by maximization of situational meaningfulness/minimization of situational variance. It can, however, be proposed that the individual motivation underlying both group formation and salience is subjective uncertainty reduction (cf. Turner, 1985, 1991).

Drawing on social comparison theory (Festinger, 1954; Suls and Wills, 1991) and early writings on social influence by Moscovici (1976), as well as social identity theory and self-categorization theory, Hogg and colleagues (Grieve and Hogg, submitted; Hogg and Abrams, 1993; Mullin and Hogg, submitted) argue that people need to be certain that their perceptions, attitudes and behaviours in subjectively important domains are "correct" so that they may ascribe meaning to their world and interact appropriately with their environment. People seek subjective certainty—to believe they are correct. Correctness cannot be "objective", but rather is a product of social agreement with others who are perceived as similar to self in the particular context. Thus, subjective uncertainty about subjectively important matters motivates uncertainty reduction, which can be resolved in different ways including self-categorization. Self-categorization reduces uncertainty because it changes perceptions, beliefs, attitudes, and behaviours in line with a self-inclusive prototype. It replaces relative diversity and disagreement among people, and thus subjective uncertainty, with relative homogeneity and agreement among ingroup members, and thus subjective certainty. As the ingroup prototype changes (as a function of situational or historical changes in social context) uncertainty may arise once again—to be resolved perhaps by self-categorization in terms of the changed prototype.

Uncertainty reduction has implications for self-esteem and for one's feelings about other people. People feel good when they are certain about their attitudes, beliefs, perceptions and behaviour in subjectively important domains, and uncomfortable when they are uncertain. Thus, certainties, and those responsible for the consensus upon which certainty rests (i.e. ingroup members including self), are imbued with a positive valence (cf. Hogg, 1992, 1993). In this way uncertainty reduction through self-categorization can account for self-esteem, social attraction, positive social identity and ethnocentrism. Furthermore, strong group identification should better satisfy the motive than weak identification, and should, accordingly, accentuate group behaviours.

Grieve and Hogg (submitted) conducted a preliminary test of this idea in the very specific context of the minimal group paradigm. We argued that social categorization *per se* does *not* produce intergroup discrimination, but rather that social categorization under subjective uncertainty, as opposed to subjective certainty, produces identification which in turn produces discrimination. Discrimination is not an inevitable consequence of social categorization. In a 2 $\times$ 2 minimal group study, subjects were explicitly randomly categorized into X and Y group, or were not categorized. This was done under normal minimal group conditions, which we felt embodied relatively high subjective uncertainty, or under conditions where subjects had been given a number of practice trials on the matrices (low uncertainty). On a composite measure of ingroup bias (representing use of favouritism strategies on the minimal group matrices) we found significant discrimination only among those subjects who were categorized under uncertainty ($F(1144) = 4.55$, $p<.05$)—see Figure 2.1. These subjects also showed significant reduction in uncertainty (uncategorized subjects did not), and significantly higher self-esteem (as measured by a single item focusing on transitory and specific self-esteem) than subjects who were categorized under low uncertainty. There was also some indication that these subjects identified more strongly with their group, as measured by a five-item identification scale.

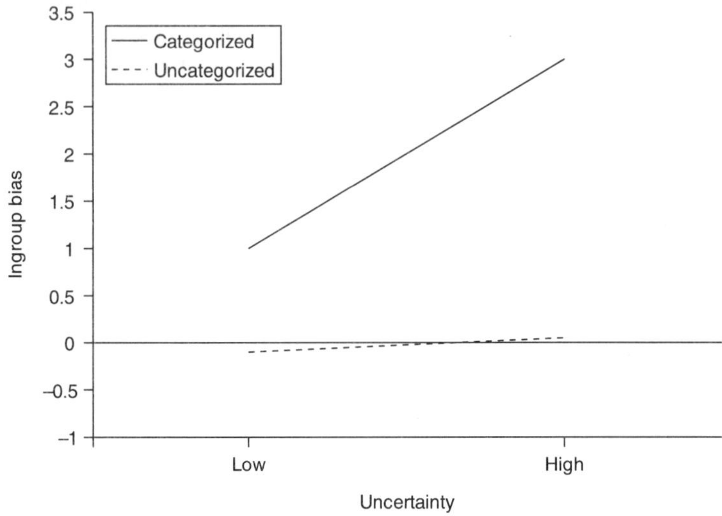

FIG 2.1 Ingroup bias as a function of categorization and subjective uncertainty. Ingroup bias is a composite scale with a range from –12 to +12. (Data from Grieve and Hogg, submitted.)

Differentiation Within Groups

The principle of metacontrast (e.g. Hogg *et al*., 1990; cf. Tajfel's, 1959, accentuation effect) identifies an important feature of social identity dynamics— there is greater perceived difference between than within salient groups. Indeed, social identity theory has mainly been concerned with intergroup differentiation. Self-categorization theory has also mainly focused on intergroup differentiation. Few groups, however, are homogeneous. Most are differentiated into roles, and most group members can readily recognize the way in which their group is structured. Some aspects of group structure are actually due to cross-cutting categorization (e.g. in my department there are social psychologists, clinical psychologists, cognitive psychologists, and so forth). Other aspects are due to nested subgroups (in my department we have various subcommittees), while yet other aspects are due to behavioural roles (e.g. leader, social event organizer, comedian, grumbler).

Intragroup structure and differentiation has been a traditional focus of small groups research (Levine and Moreland, 1990, 1994; Moreland and Levine, 1982, Moreland *et al*., 1993) and of sociological approaches to roles, for example identity theory (e.g. Burke, 1980; McCall and Simmons, 1978; Stryker, 1968: cf. Hogg *et al*., 1995b). Intergroup research, including social identity and self-categorization theory, have paid it scant attention. Self-categorization theory seems to imply that intergroup and intragroup differentiation are inversely related—greater differentiation between groups is associated with less differentiation within the ingroup and greater ingroup identification. Ingroup differentiation is associated with low identification and thus, ultimately, not with groups at all.

This idea has been explored more fully by Brewer in her optimal distinctiveness theory (Brewer, 1991, 1993; Brewer and Weber, 1994). Brewer suggests that human beings are driven by conflicting motives for inclusion/sameness (satisfied by group membership) and for distinctiveness/uniqueness (satisfied by individuality). People try to strike a balance between these two motives by striving to achieve optimal distinctiveness. Brewer's research has tended to focus on group size—small groups oversatisfy the need for distinctiveness and so people strive for greater inclusiveness, while large groups oversatisfy the need for inclusiveness and so people strive for distinctiveness. In small groups, then, people should identify strongly and there should be little evidence of intragroup differentiation. It is less clear what happens in large groups—one reading of optimal distinctiveness theory is that identification will weaken and the group will fragment into individuals; another reading is that identification will weaken and optimally distinctive subgroups will form. In either case, intragroup differentiation associated with reduced identification will arise—but in the former it is differentiation into discrete individuals (an interpersonal process), and in the latter into subgroups (a group process).

Identification and intragroup differentiation may not, however, be inevitably antagonistic. Armies or churches, for example, are large groups which are highly differentiated (at both the inter- and intragroup level) but exact high levels of identification. Indeed, in a study, conducted during the 1993 Australian federal election, of how influenced by political media campaigns self, political ingroup and political outgroup members were perceived to be, Duck *et al.* (1995a) found that subjects who identified more strongly with their political ingroup tended not only to accentuate perceived ingroup–outgroup differences (on the dimension of perceived influence by the campaign), but also to accentuate the perceived difference between self and other ingroup members (cf. Duck *et al.*, 1995b). Figure 2.2 shows selected means for high and low political identifiers' perceptions of how influenced by media campaigns self, political ingroup members, and political outgroup members were.

One way to explain how a positive relationship between identification (inclusion) and intragroup differentiation can occur comes directly from the notion of prototypicality described by self-categorization theory (Hogg, 1996; cf. Codol, 1975, 1984). In groups people strive to conform to their representation of the group norm (i.e. the subjective prototype). Thus, if there is virtual consensus on the prototype, self-categorization will produce homogeneity of attitudes, opinions and behaviours. If there is a diversity of representations of the prototype, then self-categorization will produce heterogeneous behaviour as individuals conform to their own subjective and different prototypes. Consensual prototypes are likely to arise under conditions in which all group members are

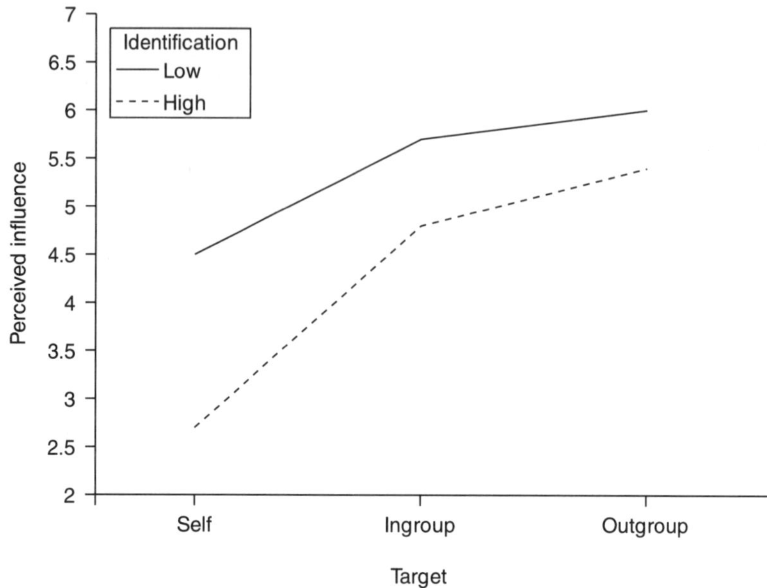

FIG 2.2 Perceived influence of political advertising on self and political ingroup and outgroup members as a function of own political ingroup indentification. Scale range for perceived influence is 1 to 9. (Data from Duck *et al.*, 1995a.)

exposed to the identical social comparative context—i.e. they have identical information from which to construct the prototype. These are the sorts of conditions that might prevail in, for example, highly orthodox, rigid, ideologically controlled groups (e.g. religions, cults, military groups, adolescent gangs, totalitarian regimes), active sociopolitical minorities (e.g. environmental groups, ethnic minorities), *ad hoc* groups used in laboratory research into group processes, and, all things being equal, smaller groups where all members can communicate with one another. Non-consensual prototypes are likely to arise under conditions in which group members are exposed to different social comparative contexts—i.e. they have different information from which to construct the prototype. These are the sorts of conditions that might prevail in, for example, groups which contain factions (e.g. a social movement that is undergoing ideological change), democratic, *laissez-faire* societies or organizations, and, all things being equal, larger groups where all members cannot communicate with one another.

The process of social differentiation within groups described here is not produced by interpersonal processes, but by characteristics of intergroup relations and the immediate or larger scale social comparative context that influences the degree of intragroup consensuality of the subjective prototype. People differentiate because they are conforming to different representations of the group. From the perspective of self-categorization theory this is a relatively new idea which remains to be explored (cf. Hogg, 1995; also see Duck *et al.*, submitted).

A second way in which intragroup differentiation may arise rests on the social attraction hypothesis described earlier (e.g. Hogg, 1992, 1993). When group membership is a salient basis for self-perception, less prototypical members will be liked less than more prototypical members. In this way, self-categorization produces intragroup evaluative and affective structuring. In smaller groups where prototypes may be more consensual, this structuring itself may be more consensual—some people may become socially unpopular or consensually disliked in group terms. This process may go so far as effectively to exclude the most unpopular members from membership at all. They become "black sheep" who are ostracized and rejected (c.f. Marques, 1990; Marques and Paez, 1994; Marques and Yzerbyt, 1988; Marques *et al.*, 1988).

A third way owes more, perhaps, to social identity theory than to self-categorization theory or optimal distinctiveness theory. People in groups, irrespective of group size, identify more or less strongly as a complex function of uncertainty reduction and positive distinctiveness considerations, with sociostructural factors residing in the nature of intergroup relations determining the extent and nature of intragroup differentiation into subgroups and roles. Important groups with which you identify strongly may or may not be best served by functional, role or subgroup differentiation.

Finally, intragroup differentiation is not only in degree (e.g. degree of liking, favourability of attitude, extent of prototypicality), but also very much in content (i.e. roles, with important evaluative connotations, that prescribe different types of behaviour as group members). In their diachronic model of group socialization in small groups, Moreland and Levine (e.g. Levine and Moreland, 1994; Moreland and Levine, 1982, 1984, 1989) identify a number of generic roles (i.e. prospective member, new member, full member, marginal member, ex-member) that people can occupy at different stages of their passage through the group. At any given time, then, the group is differentiated into different roles, and members' commitment to the group is reflected in role-consistent behaviour. Recently, Moreland *et al.* (1993) have identified ways in which their notion of commitment may be approached from a self-categorization perspective. Specifically, they suggest that the group's commitment to members may depend on the perceived prototypicality of members, and members' commitment to the group on their perceived self-prototypicality. The sort of behaviour that commitment produces depends on how group membership is defined from the perspective of the member, and this in turn is influenced by the member's role in the group. In terms of the earlier discussion of prototypical consensuality, social comparative information influences the subjective, or self-relevant prototype of group membership, and self-categorization produces prototype-consistent behaviour.

Leadership

One of the most obvious ways in which groups are internally structured is into leaders and followers. Leadership has been an important focus of small group research (e.g. Bass, 1981, 1990; House and Baetz, 1990), as well as wider social science perspectives (e.g. Graumann and Moscovici, 1986; Hunt *et al.*, 1988; cf. Levine and Moreland, 1990), but has simply not been systematically addressed by social identity theory. The history of leadership research in social psychology has largely been a struggle between personality and situational perspectives, culminating in Fiedler's (1965, 1971) interactionist perspective. In recent years there has been very little attention paid to leadership in mainstream social psychology, with perhaps one notable exception—leader categorization theory (Lord, 1977, 1985; Lord and Alliger, 1985; Lord *et al.*, 1984; Nye and Forsyth, 1991; Palich and Hom, 1992; Phillips and Lord, 1981). Leader categorization theory states that people have preconceptions about situationally appropriate leadership behaviours. These preconceptions are cognitive schemas (stereotypes or prototypes) which operate in the same way as do other schemas (cf. Fiske and Taylor, 1991)—when someone is categorized as a leader in a particular situation the situationally appropriate leadership schema comes into play to generate further assumptions about the person's behaviour. Good leaders are people who have the attributes of a leader that are stereotypical for a particular type of group context. This analysis treats leadership as a product of individual information processing, and largely not as a structural property of groups nor as an intrinsic or emergent property of psychological group membership (see Hains *et al.*, submitted).

The group-mediated nature of leadership may be better understood in terms of a broadly self-categorization analysis (Hains *et al.*, submitted; Hogg, 1992, 1996)—Figure 2.3 portrays some of the potential main features of this model. Leaders are individuals who have disproportionate influence, often through possession of consensual prestige and/or the exercise of power, over the attitudes, behaviours and destiny of group members. The group leader would thus be expected to be the individual who occupies the contextually most prototypical group position—as this is the position that embodies the behaviours to which most group members conform. If the comparative context remains relatively stable, so does the prototype and thus the same person remains in the leadership (most influential) position. Thus far this is a relatively passive process, and the "leader" does not lead in an active sense but merely embodies the aspirations, attitudes and behaviours of the group.

Leadership is, however, more than merely being prototypical—it also involves the active exercise of individual power. People occupying prototypical positions may acquire such power to influence in at least two ways: (1) They are socially attractive (cf. Hogg, 1992, 1993) and thus, because they are liked, people in the group are more likely to comply with their suggestions, requests and orders. (2) They are perceived to have charismatic/leadership personalities, due to the

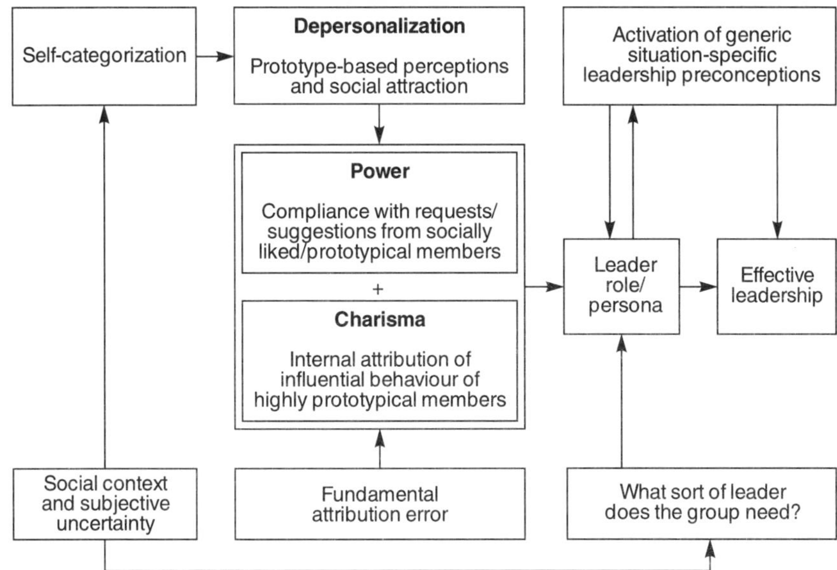

Fig 2.3 A Self-categorization model of leadership.

operation of attribution processes that cause members to attribute the leader's apparent influence to the person rather than the prototypicality of the position they occupy (cf. the fundamental attribution error—Ross, 1977). Indeed, since prototypical members are quite probably figural against the background of less prototypical members, the fundamental attribution effect may be especially strong (cf. Taylor and Fiske, 1978).

The longer a specific individual remains in a leadership position the more that person will be socially "liked", the more consensual will social attraction be, and the more entrenched will the fundamental attribution effect be. Having acquired power in these ways, the person occupying the prototypical position will be able to adopt the more active aspects of being a leader, including the power to maintain his/her leadership position by influencing the social comparative context and thus his/her prototypicality. In addition, groups with consensual prototypes are more likely to have entrenched leaders due to the consensuality of perceptions of and feelings for the leader by the group. In groups with less consensual prototypes, there will be greater dissensus of perceptions of and feelings for the leader and thus the leader may have less power and may occupy a less stable position. Preconceptions about leadership (cf. leadership categorization theory) will no doubt have a role to play—once someone has been categorized as a leader on the basis of the processes just described, situation-specific leadership schemas may generate additional assumptions about that person's personality and behaviour.

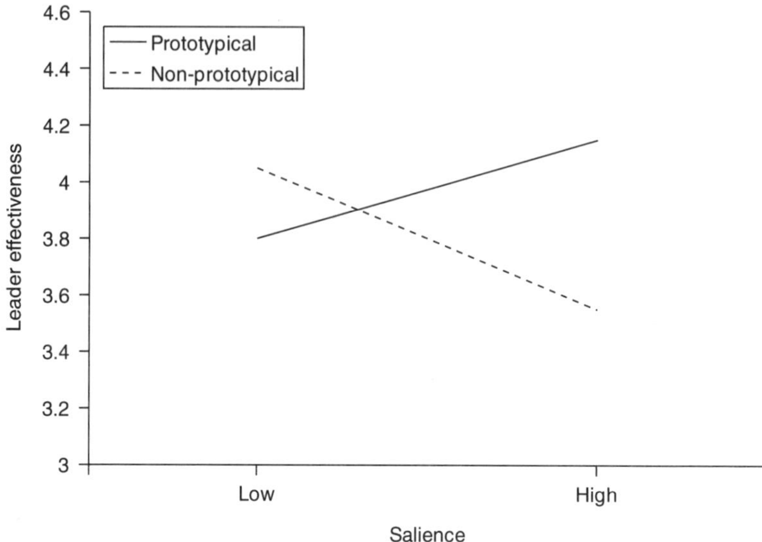

FIG 2.4 Leader effectiveness as a function of salience and group prototypicality. Leader effectiveness is a weighed average of ten nine-point items. (Data from Hains *et al.*, submitted.)

We have recently conducted a study of these ideas—specifically the idea that, in salient groups, group prototypicality plays a significant role, possibly more significant than leader stereotypicality, in determining leadership (Hains *et al.*, submitted). The three independent variables of group salience, group prototypicality and leader stereotypicality were orthogonally manipulated in a $2 \times 2 \times 2$ design. Under conditions of high or low group salience, subjects anticipated joining a discussion group formed on the basis of attitudinal congruence regarding attitudes towards "increased police powers". Subjects were given information about the randomly appointed group leader that described him/her as being group prototypical or non-prototypical (group prototypicality) in terms of the attitudinal dimension, and as having a behavioural style (on the basis of a pretest) that was stereotypical or non-stereotypical of a leader (leader stereotypicality). Group identification and perceived leader effectiveness were each measured by at least ten items which comprised reliable scales. As we predicted, group prototypicality was a significant basis for perceived leadership among subjects who identified with the group, but not for those who did not. Figure 2.4 shows the interactive effect for salience and group prototypicality on the composite index of perceived leader effectiveness ($F(1176) = 18.63$, $p<.001$)—only the low salience prototypical and non-prototypical means did not differ significantly by Newman Keuls. Also as predicted, there was a tendency for leader stereotypicality to assume less importance in perceived leadership among high than low salience subjects. Figure 2.5 shows the interactive effect of

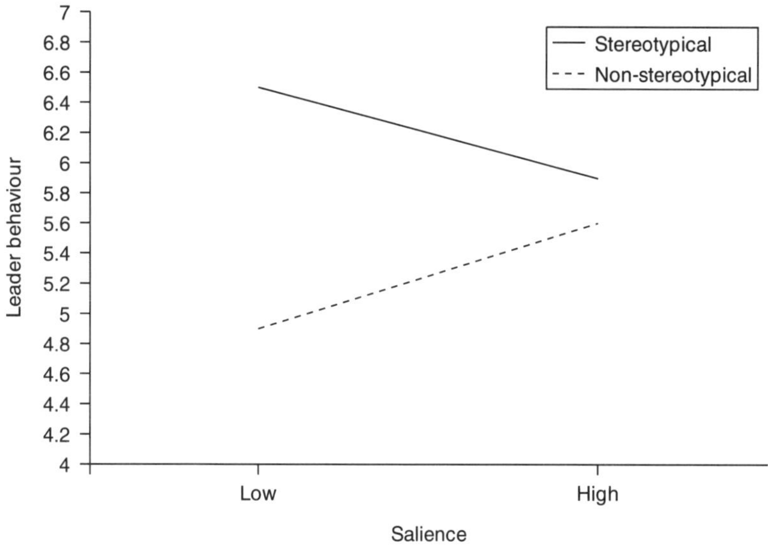

FIG 2.5 Leader behaviour as a function of salience and leader stereotypicality. Scale range for leader behaviour is 1 to 9. (Data from Hains *et al.*, submitted.)

salience and leader stereotypicality on a measure of leader behaviour ($F(1176) = 7.65$, $p<.01$)—only the high salience stereotypical and non-stereotypical means did not differ significantly by Newman Keuls.

Attitudinal Effects of Social Influence Within Groups

In dealing with social influence, social identity and self-categorization theory have generally taken a conformity perspective which focuses on overt behaviour or expressed attitudes (e.g. Abrams and Hogg, 1990; Hogg and Turner, 1987; Turner, 1991; Turner and Oakes, 1989). From this perspective, however, the actual mechanism of social influence/conformity in salient groups is one that produces true internalized cognitive change (prototype-based depersonalization) rather than mere surface behavioural compliance. As such, group influence affects attitudes as internalized cognitive structures.

In an ongoing programme of research, Terry and Hogg and their associates have explicitly treated self-categorization induced social influence as an attitude phenomenon, and have found that this focus may help better understand important issues in the study of attitude–behaviour relations (Terry and Hogg, 1996, submitted; White *et al.*, 1994) and attitude change (Masel *et al.*, submitted). In the light of evidence for generally poor attitude–behaviour relations (see Eagly and Chaiken, 1993), two major contemporary theories of attitude–behaviour relations, the theory of reasoned action (Fishbein and Ajzen,

1975) and the theory of planned behaviour (Ajzen and Madden, 1986), have introduced social norms as a predictor (in addition to attitudes) of behaviour. Empirical research has, however, largely failed to find evidence for significant normative influence on attitude–behaviour relations (Ajzen, 1991; Farley, Lehmann, and Ryan, 1981).

Terry and Hogg (1996) suggest that this may be because norms and attitudes are treated as quite different sorts of things—essentially independent constructs. Attitudes are viewed as being "in here" (internalized, private, cognitive constructs), while norms are largely viewed as being "out there" (public, external pressures, representing other people's expectations of self). This distinction maps remarkably well onto the general distinction made in the social influence literature between informational and normative social influence (e.g. Deutsch and Gerard, 1955; Kelley, 1952). Informational influence is driven by a need to be objectively correct—thus effective informational influence affects/changes attitudes, while normative influence is driven by a need for social acceptance and approval—thus effective normative influence affects overt behaviour, not covert attitudes. From an attitude–behaviour perspective, then, attitudes are influenced/changed via informational influence, while behaviour is influenced by normative influence (i.e. norms). The conceptual separation of attitudes from norms, taken together with the conceptual separation of informational and normative social influence, makes it very difficult to conceptualize how attitudes relate to norms and behaviour.

Social identity theory may provide a way around this problem: (1) by treating norms as a property of attitudes and behaviours, rather than as a separate construct—attitudes and behaviours become normative (or become norms) when they prescribe/describe the properties of a social group; and (2) by treating group mediated social influence as a single process which affects both attitudes and behaviours, provided that the attitudes and behaviours are normative. It can thus be predicted that the attitude–behaviour relationship will become stronger under conditions where people self-categorize in terms of a salient group membership which is defined in terms of normative behaviours and/or attitudes that prescribe behaviours. Thus, the norms of a behaviourally-relevant reference group will independently predict behaviour, but only for people who identify strongly with the reference group. Norms are tied to specific groups and they influence behaviour if the group is a contextually salient basis for self-categorization and the norm/group is behaviourally-relevant.

This general idea has now attracted some support from a series of studies (Terry and Hogg, 1996, submitted; White *et al.*, 1994). For example, Terry and Hogg (1996) conducted two longitudinal questionnaire studies with university students—one examining the relationships among attitudes, perceived group norms, and intentions and behaviours relating to regular exercise, and the other examining the relationship among the same variables in relation to sun-protective behaviour. In both cases, behavioural intentions (i.e. to take regular exercise or to adopt sun-protective behaviours) were stronger for subjects whose attitudes

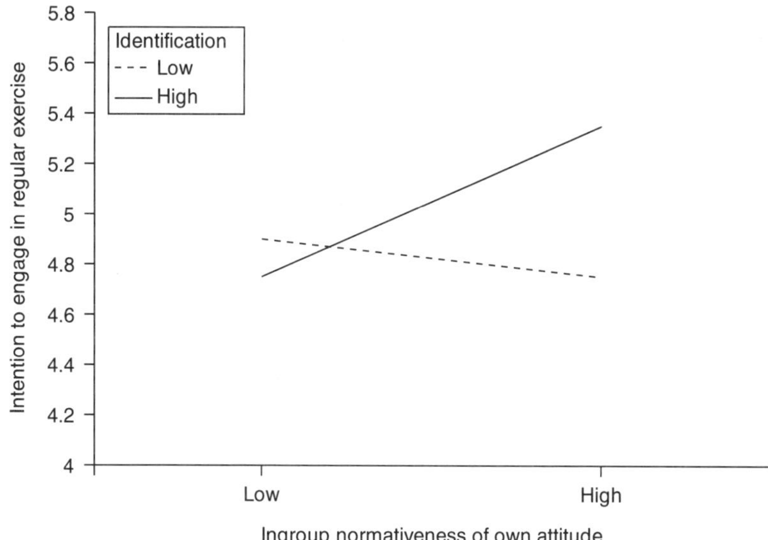

FIG 2.6 Intention to engage in regular excercise as a function of identification and ingroup normativeness of own attitude. Scale range for intention to engage in regular excercise is 1 to 7. (Data from Terry and Hogg, 1996, study 1.)

towards exercise or sun-protection were normative (i.e. were the group norm) for an ingroup (peers and friends at university) with which subjects identified strongly. Figure 2.6 shows the interactive effect of identification and attitudinal normativeness on intention to engage in regular exercise behaviour (i.e. study 1)—using an hierarchical regression procedure in which the identification by norm interaction term was entered after the relevant main effect terms (identification, attitude, and group norm), the interaction term accounted for a significant increment in variance in behavioural intention ($r^2_{change} = .03$, $F(3126) = 3.79$, $p<.05$). This result was replicated in Terry and Hogg's (1996) second study, and has gained further support from the most recent study in our research programme (Terry and Hogg, submitted).

Attitude change through persuasion can also be understood from an attitude perspective on self-categorization induced social influence. A recent perspective on persuasive communication is Petty and Cacioppo's (1984, 1986; Petty *et al.*, 1981) elaboration likelihood model (ELM). According to this model, attitude change can occur via one of two cognitive processing routes: (1) peripheral route processing–attitude change occurs as a consequence of surface consideration of simple contextual cues; (2) central route processing–attitude change occurs as a consequence of detailed and deep consideration of the persuasive arguments themselves (the better the argument, the greater the likelihood of attitude change). The degree of central route processing that occurs is affected by people's motivation and ability to engage in central route processing. Attitudes formed via central route processing tend to be more persistent over time, show greater attitude–behaviour consistency, and are more resistant to counter-persuasion. For the ELM, group membership is a contextual cue and thus affects attitude change via the peripheral route (cf. Pallak, 1983). Only a handful of studies have tested this idea (Mackie *et al.*, 1990, 1992). They confirm that ingroup messages are more persuasive than outgroup messages, but are less clear about cognitive processing route—ingroup messages appear to be processed both peripherally and centrally.

From a social identity perspective ingroups persuade via self-categorization which produces contextually enduring internalized attitude change in line with the ingroup prototype. As long as self-categorization occurs, attitude change will occur irrespective of whether one processes the persuasive information carefully (central route) or whether one simply responds to contextual cues (peripheral route). There is, however, the possibility that processing route does have a role to play in self-categorization mediated attitude change in response to a persuasive communication. Masel *et al.* (submitted) have suggested that there may be an ingroup–outgroup asymmetry in message processing. Both ingroup and outgroup messages can be processed peripherally—people automatically accept "on trust" an ingroup message (attitude change occurs), and reject out-of-hand an outgroup message. However, people prefer to process ingroup messages centrally because such messages have important self-definitional implications—people like to think carefully about information that defines who they are. The prediction that flows from this is that where group membership is salient, ingroup messages that are centrally processed will be significantly more persuasive (in terms of attitude change) than outgroup messages or peripherally processed ingroup messages.

Masel *et al.* (submitted) tested this idea in a 2 × 2 × 2 factorial experiment on attitudes towards a vegetarian diet. Under high or low social identity salience, student subjects were exposed to a relatively high quality pro-vegetarian message from their ingroup (city campus of the university) or from an outgroup (rural campus of the university), and were given ample or insufficient time to process the message fully (i.e. central versus peripheral route processing). We found that subjects exposed to an ingroup message were most persuaded when they could process a salient ingroup message under low time pressure (see Figure 2.7): this was as predicted and was associated with elevated ingroup identification and with central route processing. However, contrary to prediction, subjects exposed to an ingroup message were also strongly persuaded when they had to process a non-salient ingroup message under high time pressure. Identification and processing route data (these subjects identified strongly and tended to process the message peripherally) suggest an explanation which is consistent with our general analysis—under high time pressure these subjects used available information, in this case latent ingroup cues, to help make a rapid attitudinal decision (i.e. via a peripheral processing route), which in turn was associated with heightened

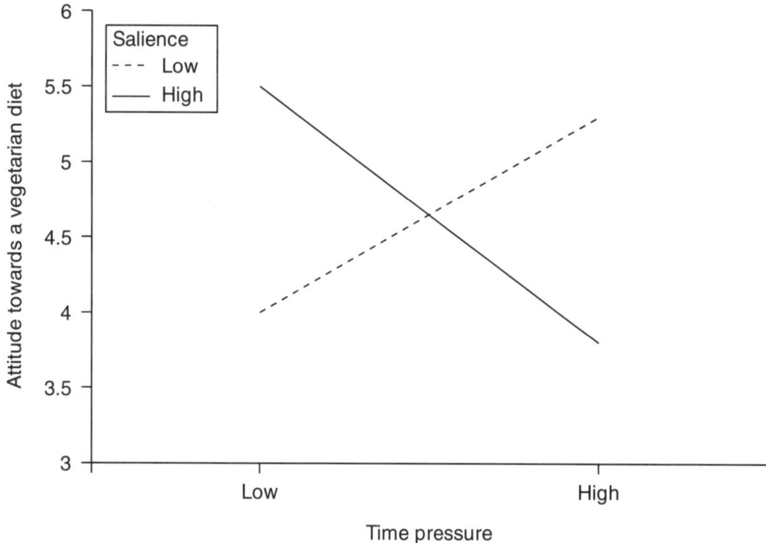

FIG 2.7 Ingroup subjects' attitude towards a vegetarian diet as a function of identity salience and time pressure. Scale range for attitude towards a vegetarian diet is 1 to 9. (Data from Masel *et al.*, submitted.)

ingroup identification. This is only a preliminary study, but it does suggest an interesting interplay of processing route and self-categorization in group-mediated persuasion.

Conclusions and Prospects

Social identity theory and self-categorization theory can, with care, and despite important differences in emphasis, quite comfortably be integrated under the umbrella of a general social identity perspective on group-mediated phenomena in social psychology. Such an integration produces a theoretical framework which has the potential to become a broad-ranging perspective on group-mediated phenomena. In this chapter I have focused mainly on processes and structures within groups to illustrate how a social identity perspective may be able to help us address phenomena which in many cases have not been the main focus of social identity research. Some of these phenomena (e.g. small interactive groups, intragroup social differentiation, roles, leadership, cognitive processing of persuasive ingroup messages) may pose new theoretical challenges. In many respects these are fresh new future directions for social identity research, which still clearly owe their origins to the metatheoretical convictions and early theoretical insights of Henri Tajfel.

Acknowledgements

I wish to acknowledge the Australian Research Council for their grant support of my research programme since 1987, and I would like to thank Julie Duck, Sarah Hains and Deborah Terry for their comments on sections of this chapter.

References

Abrams, D., and Hogg, M. A. (1988). Comments on the motivational status of self-esteem in social identity and intergroup discrimination. *European Journal of Social Psychology*, **18**, 317–334.

Abrams, D., and Hogg, M. A. (1990). Social identification, self-categorization, and social influence. *European Review of Social Psychology*, **1**, 195–228.

Adorno, T. W., Frenkel-Brunswik, E., Levinson, D. J., and Sanford, R. M. (1950). *The authoritarian personality*. New York: Harper.

Ajzen, I. (1991). The theory of planned behaviour. *Organizational Behavior and Human Decision Processes*, **50**, 179–211.

Ajzen, I., and Madden. T. J. (1986). Predictions of goal-directed behavior: Attitudes, intentions, and perceived behavioral control. *Journal of Experimental Social Psychology*, **22**, 453–474.

Ashforth, B. E., and Mael, F. (1989). Social identity theory and the organization. *Academy of Management Review*, **14**, 20–39.

Bass, B. M. (1981). *Stogdill's handbook of leadership*. New York: Free Press.

Bass, B. M. (1990). *Bass and Stogdill's handbook of leadership: Theory, research and managerial applications* New York: Free Press.

Brewer, M. B. (1991). The social self: On being the same and different at the same time. *Personality and Social Psychology Bulletin*, **17**, 475–482.

Brewer, M. B. (1993). The role of distinctiveness in social identity and group behaviour. In M. A. Hogg and D. Abrams (Eds), *Group motivation: Social psychological perspectives*. London: Harvester Wheatsheaf, pp. 1–16.

Brewer, M. B., and Weber, J. G. (1994). Self-evaluation effects of interpersonal versus intergroup social comparison. *Journal of Personality and Social Psychology*, **66**, 268–275.

Brown, R. J. (1978). Divided we fall: An analysis of relations between sections of a factory workforce. In H. Tajfel (Ed.), *Differentiation between social groups*. London: Academic Press, pp. 395–429.

Burke, P. J. (1980). The self: Measurement requirements from an interactionist perspective. *Social Psychology Quarterly*, **43**, 18–29.

Codol, J.-P. (1975). On the so-called "superior conformity of the self" behaviour. *European Journal of Social Psychology*, **5**, 457–501.

Codol, J.-P. (1984). Social differentiation and non-differentiation. In H. Tajfel (Ed.), *The social dimension: European developments in social psychology*, Vol. 1. Cambridge: Cambridge University Press, pp. 314–337.

Crocker, J., Blaine, B., and Luhtanen, R. (1993). Prejudice, intergroup behaviour and self-esteem: Enhancement and protection motives. In M. A. Hogg and D. Abrams (Eds), *Group motivation: Social psychological perspectives*. London: Harvester Wheatsheaf, pp. 52–67.

Deutsch, M. (1949). A theory of co-operation and competition. *Human Relations*, **2**, 129–152.

Deutsch, M. (1973). *The resolution of conflict*. New Haven, CT: Yale University Press.

Deutsch, M., and Gerard, H. B. (1955). A study of normative and informational influences upon individual judgement. *Journal of Abnormal and Social Psychology*, **51**, 629–636.

Diehl, M. (1990). The minimal group paradigm: Theoretical explanations and empirical findings. *European Review of Social Psychology*, **1**, 263–292.

Doise, W. (1982). Report on the European Association of Experimental Social Psychology. *European Journal of Social Psychology*, **12**, 105–111.

Doise, W. (1986). *Levels of explanation in social psychology*. Cambridge: Cambridge University Press.

Dollard, J., Doob, L. W., Miller, N. E., Mowrer, O. H., and Sears, R. R. (1939). *Frustration and aggression*. New Haven, CT: Yale University Press.

Duck, J. M., Hogg, M. A., and Terry, D. J. (1995a). Me, us and them: Political identification and the third-person effect in the 1993 Australian federal election. *European Journal of Social Psychology*, **25**, 195–215.

Duck, J. M., Hogg, M. A., and Terry, D. J. (submitted). Social comparison, social identity and group distinctiveness. Manuscript submitted for publication, University of Queensland.

Duck, J. M., Terry, D. J., and Hogg, M. A. (1995a). The perceived influence of AIDS advertising: Third-person effects in the context of positive media content. *Basic and Applied Social Psychology*, **17**, 305–325.

Eagly, A. H., and Chaiken, S. (1993). *The psychology of attitudes*. Fort Worth, TX: Harcourt, Brace, Jovanovich.

Evans, N. J., and Jarvis, P.A. (1980). Group cohesion: A review and re-evaluation. *Small Group Behavior*, **11**, 359–370.

Farley, J. U., Lehmann, D. R., and Ryan, M. J. (1981). Generalizing from "imperfect" replication. *Journal of Business*, **54**, 597–610.

Festinger, L. (1954). A theory of social comparison processes. *Human Relations*, **7**, 117–140.

Festinger, L., Schachter, S., and Back, K. (1950). *Social pressures in informal groups*. New York: Harper and Row.

Fiedler, F. E. (1965). A contingency model of leadership effectiveness. *Advances in Experimental Social Psychology*, **1**, 149–190.

Fiedler, F. E. (1971). *Leadership*. Morristown, NJ: General Learning Press.

Fishbein, M., and Ajzen, I. (1975). *Belief, attitude, intention, behaviour: An introduction to theory and research*. Reading, MA: Addison-Wesley.

Fiske, S. T. (1993). Social cognition and social perception. *Annual Review of Psychology*, **44**, 155–194.

Fiske, S. T., and Taylor, S. E. (1991). *Social cognition*, 2nd edn. New York: McGraw-Hill.

Giles, H., and Johnson, P. (1987). Ethnolinguistic identity theory: A social psychological approach to language maintenance. *International Journal of the Sociology of Language*, **68**, 256–269.

Graumann, C.F., and Moscovici, S. (Eds) (1986). *Changing conceptions of leadership*. New York: Springer-Verlag.

Grieve, P., and Hogg, M. A. (submitted). Subjective uncertainty and intergroup discrimination in the minimal group situation. Manuscript submitted for publication, Griffith University and University of Queensland.

Hains, S. C., Hogg, M. A., and Duck, J. M. (submitted). Self-categorization and perceived leadership: Effects of group prototypicality and leader stereotypes. Manuscript submitted for publication, University of Queensland.

Haslam, S. A., Oakes, P. J., Turner, J. C., and McGarty, C. (in press). Social identity, self-categorization and the perceived homogeneity of ingroups and outgroups: The interaction between social motivation and cognition. In R. M. Sorrentino and E. T. Higgins (Eds), *Handbook of motivation and cognition*, Vol. 3. New York: Guilford.

Hewstone, M., Stroebe, W., Codol, J.-P, and Stephenson, G. M. (Eds) (1988). *Introduction to social psychology*. Oxford: Blackwell.

Hogg, M. A. (1983). Investigations into the social psychology of group formation: A cognitive perspective. Unpublished doctoral dissertation, University of Bristol.

Hogg, M. A. (1987). Social identity and group cohesiveness. In J. C. Turner, M. A. Hogg, P. J. Oakes, S. D. Reicher, and M. S. Wetherell (Eds), *Rediscovering the social group: A self-categorization theory*. Oxford and New York: Blackwell, pp. 89–116.

Hogg, M. A. (1992). *The social psychology of group cohesiveness: From attraction to social identity*. London: Harvester Wheatsheaf, and New York: New York University Press.

Hogg, M. A. (1993). Group cohesiveness: A critical review and some new directions. *European Review of Social Psychology*, **4**, 85–111.

Hogg, M. A. (1996). Social identity, self-categorization, and the small group. In J. Davis and E. H. Witte (Eds), *Understanding group behavior*, Vol. 2: *Small group processes and interpersonal relations*. Hillsdale, NJ: Erlbaum.

Hogg, M. A., and Abrams, D. (1988). *Social identifications: A social psychology of intergroup relations and group processes*. London and New York: Routledge.

Hogg, M. A., and Abrams, D. (1990). Social motivation, self-esteem and social identity. In D. Abrams and M. A. Hogg (Eds), *Social identity theory: Constructive and critical advances*. London: Harvester Wheatsheaf, pp. 28–47.

Hogg, M. A., and Abrams, D. (1993). Towards a single-process uncertainty-reduction model of social motivation in groups. In M. A. Hogg and D. Abrams (Eds), *Group motivation: Social psychological perspectives*. London: Harvester Wheatsheaf pp. 173–190.

Hogg, M. A., Cooper-Shaw, L., and Holzworth, D. W. (1993). Studies of group prototypicality and depersonalized attraction in small interactive groups. *Personality and Social Psychology Bulletin*, **17**, 175–180.

Hogg, M. A., and Hains, S. C. (1996). Intergroup relations and group solidarity: Effects of group identification and social beliefs on depersonalized attraction. *Journal of Personality and Social Psychology*, **70**.

Hogg, M. A., and Hardie, E. A. (1991). Social attraction, personal attraction, and self-categorization: A field study. *Personality and Social Psychology Bulletin*, **17**, 175–180.

Hogg, M. A., and Hardie, E. A. (1992). Prototypicality, conformity and depersonalized attraction: A self-categorization analysis of group cohesiveness. *British Journal of Social Psychology*, **31**, 41–56.

Hogg, M. A., and Hardie, E. A. (in press). Self-prototypicality, group identification, and depersonalization attraction: A polarization study. In K. Leung, Y. Kashima, V. Kim and S. Yamaguichi (Eds), *Progress in Asian psychology*, Vol. 1. Singapore: Wiley.

Hogg, M. A., Hardie, E. A., and Reynolds, K. J. (1995a). Prototypical similarity, self-categorization, and depersonalized attraction: A perspective on group cohesiveness. *European Journal of Social Psychology*, **25**, 159–177.

Hogg, M. A., and McGarty, C. (1990). Self-categorization and social identity. In D. Abrams and M. A. Hogg (Eds), *Social identity theory: Constructive and critical advances*. London: Harvester Wheatsheaf, and New York: Springer-Verlag, pp. 10–27.

Hogg, M. A., Terry, D. J., and White, K. M. (1995b). A tale of two theories: A critical comparison of identity theory with social identity theory. *Social Psychology Quarterly*, **58**, 255–269.

Hogg, M. A., and Turner, J. C. (1987). Social identity and conformity: A theory of referent informational influence. In W. Doise and S. Moscovici (Eds), *Current issues in European social psychology*, Vol. 2. Cambridge: Cambridge University Press, pp. 139–182.

Hogg, M. A., Turner, J. C., and Davidson, B. (1990). Polarized norms and social frames of reference: A test of the self-categorization theory of group polarization. *Basic and Applied Social Psychology*, **11**, 77–100.

Hogg, M. A., and Vaughan, G. M. (1995). *Social psychology: An introduction*. London: Prentice-Hall/ Harvester Wheatsheaf.

House, R. J., and Baetz, M. L. (1990). Leadership: Some empirical generalizations and new research directions. In L. L. Cummings and B. M. Staw (Eds), *Leadership, participation, and group behavior*. Greenwich, CT: JAI Press, pp. 1–84.

Hunt, J. G., Baliga, B. R., Dachler, H. P., and Schriesheim, C.A. (Eds) (1988). *Emerging leadership vistas*. Lexington, DC: Heath.

Jaspars, J. M. F. (1980). The coming of age of social psychology in Europe. *European Journal of Social Psychology*, **10**, 421–429.

Jaspars, J. M. F. (1986). Forum and focus: A personal view of European social psychology. *European Journal of Social Psychology*, **16**, 3–15.

Kelley, H. H. (1952). Two functions of reference groups. In G. E. Swanson, T. M. Newcomb, and E. L. Hartley (Eds), *Readings in social psychology*, 2nd edn. New York: Holt, Rinehart and Winston, pp. 410–414.

Levine, J. M., and Moreland, R. L. (1990). Progress in small group research. *Annual Review of Psychology*, **41**, 585–634.

Levine, J. M., and Moreland, R. L. (1994). Group socialization: Theory and research. *European Review of Social Psychology*, **5**, 305–336.

LeVine, R. A., and Campbell, D. T. (1972). *Ethnocentrism: Theories of conflict, ethnic attitudes and group behavior*. New York: Wiley.

Levine, J. M., Resnick, L. B., and Higgins, E. T. (1993). Social foundations of cognition. *Annual Review of Psychology*, **44**, 585–612.

Lord, R. G. (1977). Functional leadership behavior: Measurement and relations to social power and leadership perceptions. *Administrative Science Quarterly*, **22**, 114–133.

Lord, R. G. (1985). An information processing approach to social perception, leadership and behavioral measurement in organizations. *Research in Organizational Behavior*, **7**, 87–128.

Lord, R. G., and Alliger, G. M. (1985). A comparison of four information processing models of leadership and social perceptions. *Human Relations*, **38**, 47–65.

Lord, R. G., Foti, R. J., and DeVader, C. L. (1984). A test of leadership categorization theory: Internal structure, information processing, and leadership perceptions. *Organizational Behavior and Human Performance*, **34**, 343–378.

Lorenzi-Cioldi, F., and Doise, W. (1990). Levels of analysis and social identity. In D. Abrams and M. A. Hogg (Eds.), *Social identity theory: Constructive and critical advances*. London, Harvester Wheatsheaf, and New York: Springer-Verlag, pp. 71–88.

Lott, A. J., and Lott, B. E. (1965). Group cohesiveness as interpersonal attraction. *Psychological Bulletin*, **64**, 259–309.

Mackie, D. M., Gastardo-Conaco, M. C., and Skelly, J. J. (1992). Knowledge of the advocated position and the processing of in-group and out-group persuasive messages. *Journal of Personality and Social Psychology*, **62**, 145–151.

Mackie, D. M., Worth, L. T., and Ascunsion, A. G. (1990). Processing of persuasive in-group messages. *Journal of Personality and Social Psychology*, **58**, 812–822.

Marques, J. M. (1990). The black-sheep effect: Out-group homogeneity in social comparison settings. In D. Abrams and M. A. Hogg (Eds), *Social identity theory: Constructive and critical advances*. London: Harvester Wheatsheaf, and New York: Springer-Verlag, pp. 131–151.

Marques, J. M., and Paez, D. (1994). The "black sheep effect": Social categorization, rejection of ingroup deviates and perception of group variability. *European Review of Social Psychology*, **5**, 37–68.

Marques, J. M., and Yzerbyt, V. Y. (1988). The black sheep effect: Judgmental extremity towards ingroup members in inter- and intra-group situations. *European Journal of Social Psychology*, **18**, 287–292.

Marques, J. M., Yzerbyt, V. Y., and Leyens, J.-P. (1988). The black sheep effect: Extremity of judgements towards in-group members as a function of group identification. *European Journal of Social Psychology*, **18**, 1–16.

Masel, C. N., Hogg, M. A., and Terry, D. J. (submitted). Group membership salience and dietary attitudes: A self-categorization analysis of attitude change through persuasion. Manuscript submitted for publication: University of Queensland.

McCall, G., and Simmons, R. (1978). *Identities and interactions*, revised edn. New York: Free Press.

McDavid, J., and Harari, H. (1968). *Social psychology: Individuals, groups, societies*. New York: Harper and Row.

Moreland, R. L., Hogg, M. A., and Hains, S. C. (1994). Back to the future: Social psychological research on groups. *Journal of Experimental Social Psychology*, **30**, 527–555.

Moreland, R. L., and Levine, J. M. (1982). Socialization in small groups: Temporal changes in individual–group relations. *Advances in Experimental Social Psychology*, **15**, 137–192.

Moreland, R. L., and Levine, J. M. (1984). Role transitions in small groups. In V. Allen and E. van de Vliert (Eds), *Role transitions: Explorations and explanations*. New York: Plenum, pp. 181–195.

Moreland, R. L., and Levine, J. M. (1989). Newcomers and oldtimers in small groups. In P. B. Paulus (Ed.), *Psychology of group influence*, 2nd edn. Hillsdale, NJ: Erlbaum, pp. 143–186.

Moreland, R. L., Levine, J. M., and Cini, M. (1993). In M. A. Hogg and D. Abrams (Eds), *Group motivation: Social psychological perspectives*. London, Harvester Wheatsheaf, pp. 105–129.

Moscovici, S. (1976). *Social influence and social change*. London: Academic Press.

Mudrack, P. E. (1989). Defining group cohesiveness: A legacy of confusion. *Small Group Behavior*, **20**, 37–49.

Mullin, B. A., and Hogg, M. A. (submitted). Dimensions of subjective uncertainty in social identification and minimal intergroup discrimination. Manuscript submitted for publication: University of Queensland.

Nye, J. L., and Forsyth, D. R. (1991). The effects of prototype-based biases on leadership appraisals: A test of leadership categorization theory. *Small Group Research*, **22**, 360–379.

Oakes, P. J. (1987). The salience of social categories. In J. C. Turner, M. A. Hogg, P. J. Oakes, S. D. Reicher, and M. S. Wetherell (Eds), *Rediscovering the social group: A self-categorization theory*. Oxford and New York: Blackwell, pp. 117–141.

Oakes, P. J., Haslam, S. A., and Turner, J. C. (1994). *Stereotyping and social reality*. Oxford: Blackwell.

Palich, L. E., and Hom, P. W. (1992). The impact of leader power and behavior on leadership perceptions: A lisrel test of an expanded categorization theory of leadership model. *Group and Organization Management*, **17**, 279–296.

Pallak, S. R. (1983). Salience of a communicator's physical attractiveness and persuasion: A heuristic versus systematic processing interpretation. *Social Cognition*, **2**, 158–170.

Petty, R. E., and Cacioppo, J. T. (1984). The effects of involvement on responses to argument quantity and quality: Central and peripheral routes to persuasion. *Journal of Personality and Social Psychology*, **46**, 69–81.

Petty, R. E., and Cacioppo, J. T. (1986). The elaboration likelihood model of persuasion. *Advances in Experimental Social Psychology*, **19**, 123–205.

Petty, R. E., Ostrom, T. M., and Brock, T. C. (1981). Historical foundations of the cognitive response approach to attitudes and persuasion. In R. E. Petty, T. M. Ostrom, and T. C. Brock (Eds), *Cognitive responses in persuasion*. Hillsdale, NJ: Erlbaum, pp. 5–29.

Phillips, J. S., and Lord, R. G. (1981). Causal attributions and perceptions of leadership. *Organizational Behavior and Human Performance*, **28**, 143–163.

Reicher, S. D. (1987). Crowd behaviour as social action. In J. C. Turner, M. A. Hogg, P. J. Oakes, S. D. Reicher, and M. S. Wetherell (Eds), *Rediscovering the social group: A self-categorization theory*. Oxford and New York: Blackwell, pp. 171–202.

Ross, L. (1977). The intuitive psychologist and his shortcomings. *Advances in Experimental Social Psychology*, **10**, 174–220.

Sachdev, I., and Bourhis, R. Y. (1991). Power and status differentials in minority and majority group relations. *European Journal of Social Psychology*, **21**, 1–24.

Sachdev, I., and Bourhis, R. Y. (1993). Ethnolinguistic vitality: Some motivational and cognitive considerations. In M. A. Hogg and D. Abrams (Eds), *Group motivation: Social psychological perspectives*. London: Harvester Wheatsheaf, pp. 33–51.

Sherif, M. (1936). *The psychology of social norms*. New York: Harper and Bros.

Sherif, M. (1967). *Group conflict and co-operation*. London: Routledge and Kegan Paul.

Sherif, M., and Sherif, C. W. (1956). *An outline of social psychology*. New York: Harper and Row.

Sherif, M., and Sherif, C. W. (1969). *Social psychology*. New York: Harper and Row.

Simon, B. (1993). On the asymmetry in the cognitive construal of ingroup and outgroup: A model of egocentric social categorization. *European Journal of Social Psychology*, **23**, 131–147.

Simon, B., and Brown, R. J. (1987). Perceived intragroup homogeneity in minority–majority contexts. *Journal of Personality and Social Psychology*, **53**, 703–711.

Stryker, S. (1968). Identity salience and role performance: The importance of symbolic interaction theory for family research. *Journal of Marriage and the Family*, **30**, 558–564.

Suls, J., and Wills, T. A. (Eds) (1991). *Social comparison: Contemporary theory and research*. Hillsdale, NJ: Erlbaum.

Sumner, W. G. (1906). *Folkways*. Boston, MA: Ginn.

Tajfel, H. (1959). Quantitative judgment in social perception. *British Journal of Psychology*, **50**, 16–29.

Tajfel, H. (1963). Stereotypes. *Race*, **5**, 3–14.

Tajfel, H. (1969a). Social and cultural factors in perception. In G. Lindzey and E. Aronson (Eds), *Handbook of social psychology*, Vol. 3. Reading, MA: Addison-Wesley, pp. 315–394.

Tajfel, H. (1969b). Cognitive aspects of prejudice. *Journal of Social Issues*, **25**, 79–97.

Tajfel, H. (1970). Experiments in intergroup discrimination. *Scientific American*, **223**, 96–102.

Tajfel, H. (1972). Some developments in European social psychology. *European Journal of Social Psychology*, **2**, 307–322.

Tajfel, H. (1974). Intergroup behaviour, social comparison and social change. Unpublished Katz-Newcomb lectures, University of Michigan at Ann Arbor.

Tajfel, H. (Ed.) (1978). *Differentiation between social groups*. London: Academic Press.

Tajfel, H. (1981). Social stereotypes and social groups. In J. C. Turner and H. Giles (Eds), *Intergroup behaviour*. Oxford: Blackwell, pp. 144–167.

Tajfel, H. (Ed.) (1982). *Social identity and intergroup relations*. Cambridge: Cambridge University Press.

Tajfel, H. (Ed.) (1984). *The social dimension: European developments in social psychology*. Cambridge: Cambridge University Press.

Tajfel, H., and Billig, M. (1974). Familiarity and categorisation in intergroup behaviour. *Journal of Experimental Social Psychology*, **10**, 159–170.

Tajfel, H., Billig, M., Bundy, R. P., and Flament, C. (1971). Social categorization and intergroup behaviour. *European Journal of Social Psychology*, **1**, 149–177.

Tajfel, H., and Fraser, C. (Eds) (1978). *Introducing social psychology*. Harmondsworth: Penguin.

Tajfel, H., and Turner, J. C. (1979). An integrative theory of intergroup conflict. In W. G. Austin and S. Worchel (Eds), *The social psychology of intergroup relations*. Monterey, CA: Brooks-Cole, pp. 33–47.

Taylor, D. M., and McKirnan, D. J. (1984). A five-stage model of intergroup relations. *British Journal of Social Psychology*, **23**, 291–300.

Taylor, S. E., and Fiske, S. T. (1978). Salience, attention, and attribution: Top of the head phenomena. *Advances in Experimental Social Psychology*, **11**, 249–288.

Terry, D. J., and Hogg, M. A. (submitted). Attitude—behaviour relations: The role of ingroup norms and mode of behavioural decision-making. Manuscript submitted for publication: University of Queensland.

Terry, D. J., and Hogg, M. A. (1996). Group norms and the attitude–behavior relationship: A role for group identification. *Personality and Social Psychology Bulletin*, **22**.

Turner, J. C. (1982). Towards a cognitive redefinition of the social group. In H. Tajfel (Ed.), *Social identity and intergroup relations*. Cambridge: Cambridge University Press, pp. 15–40.

Turner, J. C. (1984). Social identification and psychological group formation. In H. Tajfel (Ed.), *The social dimension: European developments in social psychology*, Vol. 2. Cambridge: Cambridge University Press, pp. 518–538.

Turner, J. C. (1985). Social categorization and the self-concept: A social cognitive theory of group behaviour. In E. J. Lawler (Ed.), *Advances in group processes: Theory and research*, Vol. 2. Greenwich, CT: JAI Press, pp. 77–122.

Turner, J. C. (1991). *Social influence*. Milton Keynes: Open University Press.

Turner, J. C., and Giles, H. (Eds) (1981). *Intergroup behaviour*. Oxford: Blackwell.

Turner, J. C., Hogg, M. A., Oakes, P. J., Reicher, S. D., and Wetherell, M. S. (1987). *Rediscovering the social group: A self-categorization theory*. Oxford and New York: Blackwell.

Turner, J. C., and Oakes, P. J. (1989). Self-categorization theory and social influence. In P. B. Paulus (Ed.), *The psychology of group influence*, 2nd edn. Hillsdale, NJ: Erlbaum, pp. 233–275.

van Knippenberg, A., and Ellemers, N. (1993). Strategies in intergroup relations. In M. A. Hogg and D. Abrams (Eds.), *Group motivation: Social psychological perspectives*. London, Harvester Wheatsheaf, pp. 17–32.

White, K., Terry, D. J., and Hogg, M. A. (1994). Safer sex behaviour: The role of attitudes, norms and control factors. *Journal of Applied Social Psychology*, **24**, 2164–2192.

3

The Categorization Process: Cognition and the Group in the Social Psychology of Stereotyping

PENELOPE OAKES

Division of Psychology, The Australian National University

Contents

Social psychologists have been trying to explain stereotyping for more than sixty years, but it is just about consensually acknowledged that the "modern era" of stereotyping research began in 1969, with the publication of Henri Tajfel's article "Cognitive aspects of prejudice". This paper revolutionized the field. Its major contribution was the systematic discussion of the way in which the very basic, functional process of *categorization* underpinned social stereotyping.

The subsequent literature devoted to the development of a categorization analysis of stereotyping is immense (for reviews see Hamilton and Sherman, 1994; Oakes *et al.*, 1994). We can look back over more than a quarter of a century's work and find that the categorization process has maintained a pivotal position in the social–psychological explanation of stereotyping. It is also apparent, however, that our understanding of that process and of its precise role in social stereotyping has developed and changed. Indeed, there is currently quite marked disagreement in the stereotyping literature over the nature and function of the categorization process in social perception (Oakes and Turner, 1990; Oakes *et al.*, 1994).

Many stereotyping researchers see categorization as, primarily, a tool for the *simplification* of perception (Tajfel, 1969; Taylor, 1981a). It is an information-reduction mechanism, designed to help the perceiver cope with limited information processing capacity. In simplifying social reality, categorization introduces distortions. In particular, it leads to an overgeneralization and exaggeration of individuals' true characteristics. This is seen as regrettable, but nonetheless inevitable given the demands of cognitive economy. For example, in their continuum model Fiske and Neuberg (1990) suggest that categorization and stereotyping are particularly likely when the perceiver is unable to invest the attention required for an accurate appraisal of others' attributes.

At the same time, categorization has also been identified as a key process in self-definition, and as the mechanism through which the self and the group come together (Tajfel, 1972, 1978; Tajfel and Turner, 1986; Turner, 1985). As developed in self-categorization theory (Turner, 1985), this idea has led to the argument that it is variation in the level of inclusiveness of the self-categorization process that both makes possible and reflects real and important qualitative differences between group and individual contexts (Tajfel, 1978). In other words, categorization enables the *veridical* selective representation of a complex and varying social reality, one comprising people who can be both individuals and group members.

The aim in this chapter is to uncover the roots of both of these views of the categorization process in Tajfel's own work, and then to trace their subsequent development in the work of others. We shall see that the idea of categorization as simplification has dominated the stereotyping literature, while the link between categorization and the self has transformed the social psychology of the group. It is when we bring these two traditions together, when we try to develop a categorization analysis of stereotyping which encompasses *the reality of group life*, that the tension between these differing views of categorization becomes apparent. I shall suggest that the way in which we resolve this tension has widespread implications for the social psychology of stereotyping.

Categorization as Cognitive Simplification

> Stereotypes arise from a process of categorization. They introduce simplicity and order where there is complexity and nearly random variation. They can help us to cope only if fuzzy differences between groups are transmuted into clear ones, or new differences created where none exist. . . . in each relevant situation we shall achieve as much stereotyped simplification as we can without doing unnecessary violence to the facts.
>
> (Tajfel, 1969, p. 82)

Tajfel was not the first to link stereotyping with categorization, and its apparent ability to simplify perception. In particular, Walter Lippmann (1922) had emphasized the simplification function of stereotypes, and Gordon Allport

(1954) had recognized that categorization was implicated in stereotyping and prejudice (see Oakes *et al.*, 1994 for further discussion). What was unique about Tajfel's contribution was that he turned to the explanation of stereotyping from a background of research on judgement processes, which had included the investigation of categorization effects (e.g. Tajfel, 1957, 1959, Tajfel and Wilkes, 1963; see Tajfel, 1981b). Thus he brought to the social psychology of stereotyping a more precise understanding of the perceptual and cognitive functioning of categorization and, importantly, clear empirical evidence that it could "be responsible . . . for biases in judgements of individuals belonging to various human groups" (1969, p. 85).

The seminal study, now a classic in the area, was carried out by Tajfel and Wilkes (1963). Three groups of subjects were presented with a series of eight lines differing from each other in length by a constant ratio. In one "classified" condition the four shorter lines were labelled "A" and the four longer "B" while in an "unclassified" condition no labels were presented and in a "random" condition there was no predictable relationship between the length of line and the label attached to it. It was found that when reporting the length of lines, subjects in the classified group, and these subjects alone, accentuated the difference between the two classes of lines by exaggerating the difference between the shortest of the longer four and the longest of the shorter four. In fact, subjects judged this difference to be over two times larger than it actually was. There was also some evidence to suggest that subjects in the classified condition minimized the differences between lines within each of the two classes.

The following principle emerged from this study:

> When a classification is correlated with a continuous dimension, there will be a tendency to exaggerate the differences on *that* dimension between items which fall into distinct classes, and to minimize these differences within each of the classes.
>
> (Tajfel, 1969, p. 83)

Tajfel saw this as a distortion of perception: stimuli were being perceived as more similar and different than they *really* were, than they would appear to be if the perceiver made more effort, or took "a closer look" (see Tajfel, 1972).

The next step was to demonstrate how these *accentuation effects* of the categorization process might account for some of the features of social stereotypes. If, for example, having white or black skin was thought to be correlated with certain personal characteristics (e.g. laziness, intelligence), then in terms of those characteristics members of one racial category would be seen as both *very similar to each other* and *very different from members of the other category*—blacks are all lazy, we whites are industrious; blacks are all stupid, we whites are intelligent, and so forth. Early research had demonstrated that perceivers, especially prejudiced perceivers, sometimes had considerable difficulty distinguishing between members of an outgroup (Malpass and Kravitz, 1969; Secord, 1959; Secord *et al.*, 1956). The latter paper also found a significant exaggeration of the *difference* between blacks and whites in skin colour and other physiognomic characteristics associated with race amongst prejudiced subjects (see also Pettigrew *et al.*, 1958; Seeleman, 1940). Much of the appeal of Tajfel's categorization analysis stemmed from the fact that the accentuation effects he identified provided such a simple and elegant explanation of these perceptual distortions: the accentuation of similarity within and difference between categories occurred as an automatic product of the categorization process itself. Not surprisingly, there have been many attempts to verify the effects' existence, and to demonstrate their relevance to the explanation of stereotyping (for reviews see Deschamps, 1984; Doise, 1978; Eiser and Stroebe, 1972; McGarty and Penny, 1988; Oakes *et al.*, 1994; Wilder, 1986).

Tajfel had suggested that stereotypes arose from categorization, and that we categorize because we have to "simplify in order to cope". This idea found a very receptive audience in the social psychology of the late 1970s, a social psychology which was becoming more explicitly concerned with the analysis of cognition, and particularly with the idea of the *limited capacity* of the information processing system (see Fiske and Taylor, 1991). Within this context, processes which allowed us to "simplify" perception were clearly of particular interest, and "a categorization approach to stereotyping" (Taylor, 1981a; see also Hamilton, 1979; Taylor *et al.*, 1978) developed rapidly, building on Tajfel's discussion of both the perceptual accentuation effects of categorization, and the ingroup bias that had been observed following "mere categorization" in the minimal group paradigm (Tajfel *et al.*, 1971). Other information processing "biases", thought to affect the encoding, interpretation and retrieval of information in ways that initiated and perpetuated social stereotyping, were soon identified (see Hamilton and Sherman, 1994; Oakes *et al.*, 1994, Chapter 3, for reviews).

Throughout this work ran the critically important idea that social perceivers categorized, despite all the attendant biases, errors and distortions of reality, *because* it enabled them to "simplify in order to cope" (e.g. see Hamilton, 1979, p. 80). Indeed, the need to reduce social reality to cognitively manageable proportions became such a central notion in the late 1970s and through the 1980s that, in an influential review of developments in social cognition, Taylor (1981b) dubbed this the age of the *cognitive miser*, conveying the idea that dealing with capacity limitations was seen as the driving force in human information processing. It certainly came to be seen as critical in the explanation of social stereotyping. The idea that we categorize, and hence stereotype "as a means of reducing the amount of information we must contend with" (Hamilton and Trolier, 1986, p. 128) is a mainstay of currently influential models of person perception, models which account for stereotyping within a general analysis of impression formation (Brewer, 1988; Fiske and Neuberg, 1990). For example, Fiske and Neuberg comment:

> We have neither the cognitive capacity nor the time to deal with all the interpersonal information we have available to us. . . . Given our limited cognitive resources, it is both simpler (requires less effort) and more efficient (requires less time) for a perceiver to use stereotyped information to make inferences about individuals belonging to a group than it is to analyse each person on an individual basis.
>
> (1990, p. 14)

Clearly, these models have embraced Tajfel's notion of stereotyping as an outcome of a social categorization process designed to *simplify* social perception, and they have elaborated and moved beyond it. Importantly, as models of impression formation, they draw out some implications of this view of social categorization and stereotyping for person perception in general. In particular, the critical association of categorization with simplification (i.e. with an at least incomplete and frequently distorted representation of social reality) has led to a sharp distinction being drawn between interpersonal perception and stereotyping, in terms of the *cognitive processes* thought to be involved in the two forms of person perception. Both models argue fairly explicitly that whilst stereotyping involves categorization, interpersonal perception does not.

Fiske and Neuberg (1990) distinguish between top-down, category-based impressions and data-driven, attribute-oriented impressions, placing them at opposite ends of their continuum of impression formation. The latter involve "an attribute-by-attribute consideration of isolated pieces of information" (Fiske *et al.*, 1987, p. 401), with no attempt to establish relationships between these pieces of information, that is no attempt to categorize. The final impression formed is then "relatively uncontaminated by category-based generalizations" (Fiske and Neuberg, 1990, p. 8); it is "more accurate but less efficient" (op. cit., p. 62) than stereotyping. Brewer's model contrasts top-down, category-based processing with bottom-up, person-based processing in which "specific behaviours are first encoded at a relatively concrete level" (1988, p. 24). Again, category-based processing is "efficient and functional" (1988, p. 29), but at the price of the richness and complexity which attention to specific behaviours and individuals would have revealed. In these models, then, interpersonal perception represents an accurate, almost unmediated appreciation of people's "true" characteristics, perhaps akin to the uncategorized "standard" condition in the Tajfel and Wilkes (1963) study. In contrast with this, stereotyping represents the unfortunate but inevitable distortion which simplification of this complex reality must entail.

Given the centrality of the limited capacity idea to this account of stereotyping, it is not surprising that an early tendency to treat the cognitive economy function of social categorization as self-evident (see Fiske and Neuberg, 1990, p. 14) has been replaced by attempts at direct empirical demonstration. Several recent papers report tests of the hypothesized relationship between available "cognitive resources" and the likelihood of stereotyping (e.g. see Gilbert and Hixon, 1991; Macrae *et al.*, 1993; Neuberg and Fiske, 1987; Pendry and Macrae, 1994; Ruscher *et al.*, 1991; Stangor and Duan, 1991). I cannot review this work in detail here, but would simply note that while some commentators conclude that we now have "solid evidence that stereotypes indeed function to preserve cognitive resources" (Hamilton and Sherman, 1994), others argue that the reported findings are neither robust nor unambiguously attributable to variation in "processing capacity". They may be accounted for by task-related and other contextual factors which co-vary with "capacity" manipulations and are known to affect the categorization process (Haslam, *et al.*, 1995a; Reynolds and Oakes, 1995; Spears and Haslam, in press).

In summary, the limited capacity/cognitive economy account of stereotyping portrays social categorization as unfortunate but unavoidable. It suggests that, if not for limited capacity, we could greatly increase the richness, validity and *accuracy* of social perception by always treating each person as a unique individual with a unique configuration of attributes—indeed, we could treat social reality as if it were made up of "freely-floating individual particles" (Tajfel, 1979, p. 188). However, we do have limited capacity, and as a consequence we have social categorization and stereotyping.

Categorization as Meaning and Identity

At the same time as this cognitive simplification approach to stereotyping was being developed, Tajfel was applying his interest in the categorization process to a different, though closely related, research problem—intergroup behaviour. Throughout the 1970s he had been mounting an offensive against individualistic perspectives on the group in social psychology. As part of this argument, he opposed the reduction of intergroup to interpersonal behaviour, suggesting instead that we must appreciate the qualitative difference between the two (see 1978, Chapter 2; 1979).

To emphasize this point, he suggested that interpersonal and intergroup behaviour might represent the extremes of a bipolar continuum upon which all instances of social behaviour could be placed. At the "intergroup" extreme all of the behaviour of two or more individuals towards each other would be determined by their membership of different social groups or categories (i.e. by group affiliations and loyalties to the exclusion of individual characteristics and interpersonal relationships). The "interpersonal" extreme referred to any social encounter in which all the interaction that took place was determined by the personal relationships between the individuals and their individual characteristics (i.e. idiosyncratic personal qualities were the overriding causal influences). More formally, the two extremes were distinguished in terms of the presence or absence of social categorizations and the degree of uniformity or variability in intra- and intergroup behaviour.

In essence, the continuum described the distinction between an intergroup social reality and an interpersonal social reality. The validity and usefulness of this distinction has been upheld in much subsequent research. For example, recent reformulations of the contact hypothesis of prejudice reduction recognize that to interact with an individual *as an individual* or *as a group member* are not the same thing, and do not have the same outcomes (Brown and Turner, 1981; Hewstone and Brown, 1986). The continuum represented a persuasive argument against individualism in theories of group behaviour, against the treatment of social reality as comprised of "freely-floating individual particles"—Tajfel's argument was that we have to take into account "the cognitive and socially-shared *organization* of the system within which the particles float" (1979, p. 187; cf. Asch, 1952; Sherif, 1967; see Turner and Oakes, 1986).

Tajfel's continuum was basically descriptive in character, and later work attempted to develop a causal analysis of variation between the interpersonal and the intergroup. This work has involved consideration of the part categorization processes play in the definition of the self, of *identity.* In *Differentiation between social groups*, Tajfel argued that categorization provides a system of orientation for *self-reference*, creating and defining the individual's place in society. Individuals' "self-definition in a social context" (1978, p. 61), the meaning and significance of their actions and attitudes in that context, depend upon social categorization. Where the relevant categorization divides individuals into social groups, identity and action within that context will take on the distinct character of intergroup relations, with profound effects on the nature of social interaction.

This proposed link between the self and social categorization was formalized in the concept of *social identity* (e.g. see Tajfel 1978, p. 63), and became an important foundation of social identity theory, Tajfel and Turner's (1986) more general theory of intergroup relations. However, the detailed exposition of just how categorization processes might affect self-definition, and in turn regulate the form of social interaction, has been the subject of *self-categorization theory,* initially developed by John Turner in the early 1980s (Turner, 1982, 1984, 1985; Turner *et al.*, 1987; Turner and Oakes, 1989; for a more recent account see Turner *et al.*, 1994). The theory begins with the assumption that self-conception reflects self-categorization, the cognitive grouping of the self as identical to some class of stimuli in contrast to some other class of stimuli. As is the case with all systems of natural categories (Rosch, 1978), self-categorizations can exist at different *levels of abstraction* related by *class inclusion.* That is, a given self-category (e.g. "scientist") is seen as more abstract than another (e.g. "biologist") to the extent that it can contain the other, but the other cannot contain it: all biologists are scientists, but not all scientists are biologists.

Going beyond the parameters of Tajfel's original interpersonal–intergroup continuum, self-categories both more and less abstract than personal and social identity are envisaged, but for purposes of theoretical exposition three levels of abstraction of self-categories are distinguished: the interpersonal (subordinate level of abstraction, personal identity, self as an individual person); intergroup (intermediate level of abstraction, social identity, self as a group member); and interspecies (superordinate level of abstraction, self as a human being). These are defined not by specific attributes but by the level at which people are being compared and categorized. For instance, "altruism" could function as a cue to an individual identity, to a particular social category, or to being human, depending on the context.

The theory regards categorization as a dynamic, context-dependent process, determined by *comparative relations within a given context.* Thus, to predict categorization, the entire range of stimuli under consideration, rather than

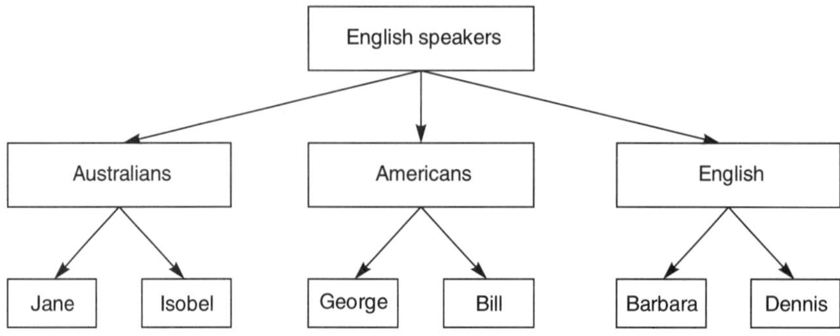

FIG 3.1 A hierarchy of English speakers.

isolated stimulus characteristics, must be taken into account. This point is formalized in the principle of *meta-contrast*, which is so called because it involves a contrast between contrasts, a judgement of difference between differences. The meta-contrast principle predicts that a given set of items is more likely to be categorized as a single entity *to the degree that differences within that set of items are less than the differences between that set and others within the comparative context* (cf. Campbell, 1958; Rosch, 1978; Tajfel, 1969; Tversky, 1977). This principle encapsulates but subtly transforms the classic idea that categories form on the basis of intraclass similarities and interclass differences. By proposing that categories form so as to ensure that the differences between them are larger than the differences within them, meta-contrast contextualizes categorization, tying it to an on-the-spot judgement of *relative differences*.

For example, consider the system of categories in Figure 3.1. Meta-contrast predicts that we would categorize and perceive an individual as "Australian" to the extent that, in the current comparative context, the differences between individual Australians (Isobel, Jane, etc.) are *less than* the differences between Australians and Americans. Alternatively, the salient category might be "English-speaking" in a context where the difference between various English-speaking groups (such as Americans and Australians) is *less than* the difference between English and non-English speakers.

Note, however that the meta-contrast principle provides only a partial account of categorization. It describes the *comparative relations* between stimuli which lead them to be represented by a category, but it is also important to take into account the *social meaning* of differences between people in terms of the normative and behavioural content of their actions, and the relative accessibility of particular categorizations (Oakes, 1987; Oakes *et al.*, 1991). In general terms, the theory explains the salience of any given category as a function of an interaction between its relative accessibility (the "readiness" of a perceiver to use a particular categorization) and the "fit" between the category and reality. Meta-contrast is the theory's principle of "comparative fit" (the match between category and the comparative properties of stimuli), but "normative fit" (the match between category and the content properties of stimuli) is also always inseparably at work (for relevant evidence see Blanz, 1995; Haslam *et al.*, 1995b; Oakes, 1994; Oakes *et al.*, 1991; van Knippenberg *et al.*, 1994).

This emphasis on categorization as highly variable and context-dependent produces a concomitant emphasis on the context-dependence of perceived similarity and difference, the major *outcome* of categorization. People who are categorized and perceived as different in one context (e.g. "biologists" and "physicists" within a science faculty) can be recategorized and perceived as similar in another context (e.g. as "scientists" rather than "social scientists" within a University) *without any actual change in their own positions*. This is the essence of categorization: it is a cognitive grouping process that transforms differences into similarities, and vice versa. We need some psychologically neutral term such as perhaps *distances* to indicate the nature of precognized stimulus relations. There are distances between people, but are they similarities or differences? Are physicists and biologists similar or different? Arising from the comparisons specified in the meta-contrast principle, categorization subjectively transforms "distances" into similarities and differences, and from perceived similarities and differences flow, amongst other things, perceptions of attraction and dislike, agreement and disagreement, co-operation and conflict.

In this way, our social orientation towards others varies with the functioning of the categorization process. Categorization depends on comparison, and as such is affected by the range of stimuli available in the context (see Haslam *et al.*, 1995b; Haslam and Turner, 1992). Importantly, *stereotyping* is simply the outcome of a salient categorization at the ingroup–outgroup level. It is distinguished from interpersonal perception only in terms of the level of abstraction at which the categorization process is operating—both stereotyping and individuation involve categorization (c.f. Fiske and Neuberg, 1990; see above). Indeed, the different levels of identity discussed in self-categorization theory are seen as closely related through the categorization process, and highly dependent upon each other. For example, social identity can be said to depend on individual differences, as the latter play an essential role in determining the meta-contrasts from which social categorizations arise. Perhaps more controversially, self-categorization theory also suggests that personal identity depends on social identity. Stimuli must share identity at some level in order to be compared, the nature of the shared identity defining the dimensions on which difference becomes apparent and relevant (see Medin *et al.*, 1993). In this way, individual self-categorizations are based on and constrained by intragroup comparisons. The way in which Isobel and Jane (from the example above) perceive themselves as individuals will be affected by the nature of the intragroup comparison providing the context for the interindividual distinctions: are they differentiating within the category Australian, or perhaps as women, or as physicists, and so on (Reynolds, 1995; see below)?

At the same time as emphasizing their interdependence in this way, self-categorization theory posits a conflicting, competitive relationship between different levels of categorization as representations of the same stimulus situation. Following the meta-contrast principle, *social* categorization of the self and others becomes more likely as intergroup differences increase and intragroup, interpersonal differences decrease. On the other hand, categorization at the *personal*, individual level becomes more likely as intergroup differences decrease and intragroup differences increase. Further, the accentuation *effects* of categorization work to enhance perceived differences between and similarities within categories associated with the salient level (e.g. the difference between Australians and Americans might be accentuated). At the same time they reduce perceived similarities and differences which are the basis of categorization at another level (e.g. differences between individual Australians may be minimized). There tends, therefore, to be an inverse relationship between self-perception as a unique individual and as an ingroup category—the more Isobel perceives herself as similar to other Australians, the less she will be aware of her personal, idiosyncratic differences from them (and vice versa; cf. Doise, 1988; Duck *et al.*, 1995; Simon, in press; see Turner, 1988).

This idea of social and personal levels of self-categorization as in some sense in conflict, mutually antagonistic in their effects, brings us back to Tajfel's interpersonal–intergroup continuum, but in a more complex form. In its account of the psychological basis of group behaviour, self-categorization theory maintains the idea of such a continuum, hypothesizing that shift along it is a matter of the varying outcome of a continual conflict between personal and social identity as they vary in relative salience. Shifts towards social identity produce the *depersonalization* of self-perception and behaviour as a direct consequence of the accentuation effects of self-categorization at the ingroup–outgroup level. The outcome is *self-stereotyping*, perception of increased identity between the self and ingroup members and increased difference from outgroup members (on relevant dimensions). Most importantly, self-categorization theory proposes that it is this process of depersonalization that makes group behaviour possible and produces its emergent, irreducible properties.

Thus, for some purposes self-categorization theory does retain Tajfel's contrast between social and personal identity. At the same time, however, one of the essential points of its analysis of the categorization process is that *the appropriate level of categorization varies with the context*, in a way that cannot be captured by a simple personal/social comparison. The idea of a given level is useful to indicate a theoretical extreme, and to emphasize the qualitative distinctions between interpersonal and group behaviour, but in reality there is a perceptual continuum that never fully embodies any one level but arises from a dynamic, fluid process through which tensions between different levels of abstraction are resolved. Human beings are both individual persons and social groups, but the extent to which they are one or the other varies. We see them as both, but represented in a single unique configuration at any given instant.

In sum, self-categorization theory explains stereotyping as one outcome of a dynamic and variable categorization process, a process designed to give perceivers access to the context-dependent meaning of stimuli—meaning which is only given through appreciation of the way in which individual stimuli *relate to each other* in the present context. The theory sees all impression formation as arising from this same categorization process, operating at varying levels of inclusiveness. Following the principles of comparative (meta-contrast) and normative fit (in interaction with relative accessibility), when the perceived relations between people are appropriately represented in terms of interindividual similarities and differences, categorization and impression formation will tend to occur at the interpersonal level; when the perceived pattern of similarities and differences fits categorization at an ingroup–outgroup level, stereotyping is more likely, and so on. Importantly, I might also note here that, in common with social identity theory, self-categorization theory takes for granted the social and psychological reality of groups (see Oakes *et al.*, 1994, Chapter 4). Its initial aim as a theory was to explain the psychological emergence of the *group-level properties of social behaviour.* It is these group-level properties—the reality at the intergroup end of Tajfel's continuum—that stereotypes describe.

Issues in the Categorization Approach to Stereotyping

Thus far, I have outlined two quite distinct views of the functioning of the categorization process in social perception. At the most general level, we can say that one view emphasizes simplification and the consequent distortion of social perception, while the other sees categorization as enabling veridical impression formation which takes into account people's context-specific, relational characteristics.

Initially at least, these views developed in somewhat distinct areas of social psychology—as we have seen, the emphasis on the simplification function seemed particularly useful as an explanation of stereotyping, whereas the relevance of categorization for identity, particularly group identification, was elaborated in the intergroup literature. However, given that stereotyping *is* the perception of people as group members, it was inevitable that these literatures would come into close contact with each other. More specifically, in the course of developing the self-categorization analysis of stereotyping very briefly outlined in the preceding section (Oakes *et al.*, 1994) we became aware of some incompatibilities between the two views of categorization, and of the distinctive implications of the categorization-as-identity emphasis for the social psychology of stereotyping (see also Spears *et al.*, in press). Here, we simply try to convey the flavour of this analysis by focusing on two related questions which we see as particularly important in the current literature: How does categorization achieve perceptual selectivity?—is it necessarily through information reduction? What is the relationship between stereotyping and individuation?—is the former necessarily a simplified distortion of the latter?

Categorization and perceptual selectivity

The issue here is precisely *how* categorization effects perceptual selectivity. That it does so is not in question. We have long understood that perception is a selective process, in the sense that we do not passively record every detail of the world presented to our senses, but rather construct a *meaningful* representation which necessarily encodes some stimulus features but not others. What is the role of categorization in this perceptual selectivity? From the cognitive miser perspective, categorization effects selectivity through *information reduction.* In the case of social categorization and stereotyping, the complexity of individual differences and interpersonal relationships is reduced to the more manageable but inevitably somewhat distorted proportions of category memberships (see Brewer, 1988, p. 28–29; Fiske and Neuberg, 1990, p. 14). However, we have argued (see Oakes *et al.*, 1994, Chapter 5; Oakes and Turner, 1990) that there is an alternative way of thinking about the link between categorization and the introduction of "simplicity and order where there is complexity and nearly random variation" (Tajfel, 1969, p. 82).

We have drawn heavily on Jerome Bruner's (1957) discussion of categorization and perceptual selectivity. He argued that there is never perception without categorization: "all perception is necessarily the end product of a categorization process" (1957, p. 124; see also McCauley, 1987; cf. Neisser, 1987). The major reason for this is that it is the placing of percepts in general classes, of which the defining properties are already known, which gives "stimuli" identity. Raw, uncategorized stimulus information may be abundant in quantity but it is entirely lacking in human relevance, in meaning. Far from reducing or impoverishing perceptual experience, categorization enriches and expands it, allows the perceiver to, in Bruner's famous phrase, "go beyond" (1957, p. 129) mere sensory stimulation to the identity of objects and events with "*more elaborated*, connotative meaning" (1957, p. 148, emphasis added). Similarly, in his comments on the "goals and purposes of social categorization", Medin (1988) expresses some scepticism about the idea that categorization works to cope with information overload. He feels that "categorization, including social categorization, is primarily to cope with the problem of too little rather than too much information" (1988, p. 122). He emphasizes the vital ability of categorization to generate expectations about a stimulus, and notes the importance of paying due regard to context in this process, noting that the same category can have different implications in different contexts (see Haslam *et al.*, 1992).

Thus Bruner and others argue that the principal purpose of categorization is to turn "stimuli" into objects and events with human relevance and elaborated meaning. If our experience of the world is so dependent upon categorization, understanding the origins and nature of our category systems obviously becomes a priority—why do we categorize in certain ways rather than others? This issue has received considerable attention in cognitive psychology in recent years (e.g. Medin *et al.*, 1993; Murphy and Medin, 1985; the chapters edited by Neisser,

1987), with researchers emphasizing both "ecological" and "intellectual" factors in the definition of what makes a category a category, what holds it together (Medin and Wattenmaker, 1987 refer to this as "category cohesiveness"), and thus why we categorize the world in the way we do.

The ecological arguments can be traced to what Neisser (1987, p. vii) refers to as the "Roschian revolution" in our understanding of categorization processes. Rosch (1978) suggested that the category systems we employ are not arbitrary, purely subjective constructions. Rather, they represent real and relevant invariances in the material world, "natural discontinuities". The commonly used example is the category "bird" which reflects, among other things, the fact that wings and feathers really do co-occur far more frequently than do wings and fur. Neisser develops a similar argument in his own approach to categorization, where he discusses the importance of "the ecological distribution and characteristics of the to-be-categorized domain itself" (1987, p. 3) as a vital determinant of the category systems we develop and use. Indeed, Bruner also touches on this idea when he notes that perceivers develop "a system of categories-in-relationship that fit the nature of the world in which [they] must live" (1957, p. 127), and it is more generally implicated in his concept of "fit" between stimulus input and category specifications as one determinant of category activation. "Fit" clearly implies that there is actual invariance in stimulus input which cognitive categories represent and make meaningful and, as outlined above, our own adaptation of Bruner's fit hypothesis occurred within the explicit context of arguments supporting the psychological reality and distinctiveness of group identification and behaviour. In summary, several writers argue that categorization does not impose purely subjective structure on "nearly random variation", but rather selectively draws our attention to aspects of real, material structure. Reality, with its natural "joints", is the source of conceptual order (see McCauley, 1987, for a review).

On the other hand, the "intellectual" argument is that abstract, idealized "theories" about the world and the way it works mediate between reality and the categories used to represent it. These ideas become critically important when one considers the inadequacy of similarity-based models of category cohesiveness (Medin and Wattenmaker, 1987; see also Medin, 1989; Medin *et al*., 1993; Murphy and Medin, 1985). To use Murphy and Medin's example (1985, p. 292), consider the relationship between a plum and a lawnmower. Clearly these are "similar" on a number of dimensions (both weigh less than 1000 kg, both cannot hear, both have a smell, both can be dropped, . . .) but these "similarities" do not define any meaningful categorical identity shared by a plum and a lawnmower. What is lacking here is a way of defining *relevant attributes*, on the basis of which a meaningful categorization decision can be made. How do we decide that some similarities between objects are decisive for a given categorization decision, whereas others are irrelevant? Medin and Wattenmaker argue that it is consistency with people's "background theories or naive knowledge of the world" that determines what qualifies as a good category and what does not (and see Turner *et al.*, 1994), and they discuss some fascinating empirical illustrations of the influence of background theories in the categorization process (see Oakes *et al.*, 1994, Chapter 5). For example, in one study subjects' task was to identify the features used to sort a set of children's drawings into two categories. Some were given the background information that mentally healthy versus disturbed children had provided the two sets of drawings, while others were told they came from farm versus city children, still others that the artists were creative and non-creative children, and so on.

These "background theories" substantially affected subjects' derivation of categorization rules. For instance, subjects given the farm/city theory might note the use of animal parts in some of the children's drawings, and develop an abstract rule along the lines of "each drawing reflects some aspect of farm life"—no subject given an alternative theory would mention animal parts at all. Furthermore, the *same* features could be interpreted quite differently across conditions in order to validate different categorization rules. For example, homogeneously smiling faces in one set of drawings was interpreted as evidence that they were the work of mentally healthy (versus disturbed) children in one condition, but supported their attribution to non-creative (versus creative) children in another. The same "attribute" meant something quite different across the two theoretical contexts.

This research allows us to understand the role of categorization in perceptual selectivity in a new way. Medin and Wattenmaker conclude that, when we categorize, it is not a matter of selective attention to a fixed set of attributes, such that some become more salient than others, some are perceived whereas others are "lost". They suggest that a given stimulus array can "'support" a limitless set of properties" (1987, p. 49), that the very existence and identity of "attributes" is context-specific, and emerges from the *interaction between the stimulus and the theoretical perspective of the perceiver*, i.e. categorization. Categorization does not delete or reduce "information"—it actually creates and defines it.

In summary, there is contemporary and influential work within the psychological literature which portrays the selectivity of categorical perception in ways quite other than information reduction. Taking this work together with self-categorization theory, we have argued that "there is . . . no important sense in which categorization functions as an information-reduction mechanism" (Oakes *et al.*, 1994, pp. 113–114). We agree with Neisser that "selection is a positive process, not a negative one" (1976, p. 80), and suggest that categorization effects selectivity through the perceiver engaging with and elaborating reality as construed *at one particular level of abstraction*. In principle, no one level is more or less informative than another. Indeed, we would argue that, through the interactive influence of fit and relative accessibility (see Blanz, 1995) categorization (at whatever level) selectively makes salient a representation of the stimulus context which is, from the perceiver's perspective, the *most informative* representation possible.

Categorization and individuation

In the discussion of categorization-as-simplification, it became clear that recent theoretical accounts of stereotyping which draw on this principle make a sharp and explicit contrast between stereotyping on the one hand—category-based, simplified, efficient but inaccurate—and individuated impression formation on the other—piecemeal analysis of real, objective attributes, no categorization, attention demanding but rich and accurate. The argument is that in perceiving individual differences we see the "real" person, but that we often have to forgo this "luxury" (see Pendry and Macrae, 1994, p. 304) because of time and capacity limitations. The general idea that, relative to individuated impressions, stereotypes represent simplified distortion, has widespread appeal. Again, however, we feel that the categorization-as-identity perspective has profound implications for this view. This section focuses on three relevant issues: the reality and distinctiveness of group contexts, the involvement of categorization in interpersonal impression formation, and the nature of categorical accentuation effects.

First, and as we have seen, the categorization-as-identity perspective argues for the reality and distinctiveness of group behaviour and identity (Oakes *et al.*, 1994, Chapter 4; Turner and Oakes, 1986). I have noted Tajfel's insistence on the *irreduceability* of group phenomena to the individual, to interpersonal processes. This means that there are group-level instances of behaviour, and group-level characteristics of persons, to which perception must give us direct access if it is to be veridical. The general point here was perhaps most graphically stated by Solomon Asch:

> Group-properties are the forms that interrelated activities of individuals take, not simply the actions of separate individuals. A flying wedge of policemen has a quality of power or threat that is a direct consequence of its organization. A picket line in front of a plant has a quality of unity that is a product of its organization. In each of these instances the group property cannot be rediscovered in the individuals taken singly.
>
> (1952, p. 225)

Note that Asch locates these distinctive group properties in the "*interrelated* activities of individuals", in other words it is the contextual relations between people which must be apprehended in order to access these group properties. We have argued that, through meta-contrast, it is precisely these context-specific relationships which categorization represents.

Interestingly, some work testing the categorization-as-simplification approach to stereotyping has recently come into direct contact with the distinction between group and individual contexts. From their continuum-model analysis of the conditions encouraging stereotyping or individuation, Neuberg and Fiske (1987) have argued that *interdependence* (i.e. outcome dependency) between individuals encourages individuation because it "increases perceiver's attention to attribute information with the goal of increasing accuracy" (p. 440). They suggest that perceivers are particularly concerned to form accurate impressions of others on whom their outcomes depend, because they need to be able to predict and perhaps control their behaviour. To this end, they avoid categorization, and invest attentional capacity in the task of discovering the other's true attributes. Both positive and negative interdependence, i.e. both co-operative and competitive relationships with a target, are expected to have this individuating effect, because both should instigate the accuracy-oriented attention to individual attributes.

However, we have known for a long time that inter*group* negative interdependence (i.e. intergroup competition) tends to produce highly stereotypical rather than individuated impressions of opponents (e.g. Sherif, 1967). This apparent inconsistency with predictions from the continuum model has been confronted by Ruscher *et al.* (1991), who attempt to accommodate the differential effects of intergroup and interpersonal competition on the impression formation process within the categorization-as-simplification approach.

Their first experiment reproduced the intergroup–interpersonal difference, showing that interpersonal competitors tended to individuate their opponents to a greater degree than did intergroup competitors. Following the continuum model emphasis on the relationship between attention and stereotyping/individuation (i.e. more attention, more individuation), Ruscher *et al.*'s interpretation of their finding was that, "individuation of opponents during intergroup encounters is hampered because perceivers use their attentional resources to individuate team-mates" (p. 601). Their second study tested this interpretation, predicting that individuating processes (indicated by attention to and dispositional inferences about stereotype-inconsistent attributes, and more variability in impressions formed) would be used more in forming impressions of team-mates than opponents.

This prediction was confirmed—analysis of the number of seconds subjects spent considering information about team-mates and opponents revealed that indeed more attention was paid to stereotype-inconsistent (i.e. individuating) than consistent information about team-mates. However, it also revealed that more attention was paid to stereotype-consistent than inconsistent information about opponents, and overall there was no difference in the amount of attention paid to team-mates and opponents. In other words, there was evidence suggesting relatively individuated impressions of team-mates and relatively stereotypical impressions of opponents, but this could not be attributed to the hypothesized enhanced attention to team-mates. A similar pattern of findings had been reported by Ruscher and Fiske in 1990. Ruscher *et al.* interpret their findings thus:

> Situational constraints (created by being in an experiment or otherwise) may require some attention to attribute information. . . . given one has to attend to something beyond the category, but also given a lack of major motivation to be accurate, a perceiver may simply focus on category-consistent attributes to reconfirm the category. . . . intergroup competitors were unwilling to expend the major effort to incorporate inconsistent information into their impressions of opponents. However, they complied with the experimenter's requirement to form impressions of their opponents by simply reconfirming their expectancies . . . through increased attention to expectancy-consistent information'.
>
> (1991, p. 603)

But why is attention to consistent information simply compliance with experimenter demands, whereas attention to inconsistent information represents effort towards accuracy? Both types of information were presented as descriptive of the targets by the experimenter. Also, there is actually no evidence at all that individuation required a "major effort" relative to stereotyping—the apparently individuated impressions of team-mates and apparently stereotypical impressions of opponents required, by the evidence of Ruscher *et al.*'s reading time measures, exactly the same amount of attention.

Alternatively, we could offer a self-categorization interpretation of Ruscher *et al.*'s findings, one which takes into account the *real, qualitative difference* between impression formation in interpersonal as compared to intergroup contexts. We would argue that judgements of team-mates represented interpersonal differentiations within an ingroup, and therefore focused on characteristics which could differentiate between group members—inconsistent information—and were relatively variable. On the other hand, judgements of opponents were made on an ingroup–outgroup basis, and focused on characteristics which differentiated between the ingroup and the outgroup—consistent attributes—and were less variable.

Kate Reynolds and I have recently carried out a series of studies testing this re-interpretation and exploring some of its implications (Oakes and Reynolds, 1995; Reynolds, 1995; Reynolds and Oakes, 1995). For example, one study manipulated interdependence versus no interdependence (as a manipulation of high versus low attentional investment, following Ruscher *et al.*), together with the interpersonal versus intergroup context in which subjects considered a description of one constant target, characterized by stereotype-consistent, inconsistent and neutral attributes. We predicted no effect of interdependence on stereotyping (given the way it was manipulated in line with previous work in this area), but rather a main effect for comparative context, indicating relative individuation in the interpersonal conditions, and stereotyping in the intergroup conditions. This prediction was strongly confirmed, and we have consistently found that the tendency to stereotype or individuate a target (both ingroup and outgroup members) varies reliably with comparative context (in interaction with normative fit; see also Blanz, 1995; Hogg and Turner, 1987; Oakes *et al.*, 1991). Under these conditions (i.e. where group contexts and interpersonal contexts are contrasted), we have found that the type of capacity or attention-related variables often manipulated in this area (e.g. interdependence, accuracy goals) have no effect on the level of stereotyping or individuation.

In summary, the contrast between group and individual contexts, and the recognition that group behaviour stems from the "real" person (their social identity) just as much as does idiosyncratic behaviour (personal identity) is one of the critical legacies of Tajfels' work. It means that to perceive people as group members (to stereotype) is not, by definition, to distort their "true" individuality. In some contexts (specified within self-categorization theory) it is entirely appropriate to perceive individuals in terms of group relationships rather than personality. Both our own recent work, and some of that reported by Ruscher and colleagues, supports the sensitivity of the impression formation process to the individual–group distinction.

Second, the idea that stereotyping involves categorization whereas individuation does not is critical to the understanding of stereotyping as *relatively* distorted. Again, I have outlined our argument that all impression formation involves categorization, that categorization varies with context, and therefore that the validity of *all* impression formation is relative to context. Importantly, this implies that individuated impressions (i.e. of another's personality) have no more stable, context-independent validity or usefulness, no more claim upon "reality" than do stereotypical impressions—or, rather, both have an equal claim. It is not the case that when we individuate a target we are dealing with real, absolute attributes without interference from cognitive inference (e.g. see Fiske and Neuberg, 1990, p. 8), whereas when we categorize we are imposing cognitively represented, abstract information upon reality*. I outlined above our view of categorization as active engagement involving an "interaction of intelligent systems with aspects of their perceptual world" (Medin and Wattenmaker, 1987, p. 50), and we see this process as equally at work in individuated impression formation.

This issue was also addressed in one of the experiments carried out with Kate Reynolds (see Reynolds, 1995). Subjects were female science students. They formed impressions of a single, constant target, identified as a female science student and characterized by female/arts-stereotypical (creative, tolerant), science/male-stereotypical (systematic, logical) and neutral attributes. Impressions were formed under conditions where the subject's identity as either a science student or a woman had been made salient, and where either an interpersonal (the context was restricted to the ingroup) or intragroup (the context involved direct comparison with either arts students or men) relationship between subject and target was emphasized.

As predicted (and consistent with Reynolds' earlier findings, described above), impressions of the target tended to be individuated in interpersonal conditions, stereotypical in intragroup conditions. Of particular interest, though, was the effect of the salient superordinate identity (science/female) on the nature of self–target differentiation. One dependent measure required subjects to represent both their own position and that of the target on a number of dimensions. Overall, self–other differentiation tended to be more marked in the interpersonal conditions and, most importantly, *the dimensions on which it occurred varied with the categorical frame of reference*. Specifically, where the science category provided the frame of reference, so that subject and target compared as fellow

*Part of the confusion here stems from very different conceptualizations of what categorization is. As we have seen, self-categorization theory (SCT) is very specific about the categorization process it envisages, in terms of both its determinants and its effects. However, models such as Fiske and Neuberg's are less detailed in this regard, and where categorization is described it is clearly quite different from the comparative, context-dependent process described in SCT. For example, Fiske *et al.* (1987, p. 401) refer to categorization as the invocation of a schema stored in memory. This suggests a rigidity and lack of context-sensitivity which SCT rejects, and which clearly relates to some other divergences of perspective in this area. However, the issue of categorization as process versus categories as structure is beyond the scope of this chapter (see McGarty, 1990).

science students, most interpersonal differentiation occurred on arts dimensions, i.e. subjects defined the distinctiveness between their personal self and that of the target in terms of their relative creativity and tolerance, rather than in terms of how relatively systematic or logical they were. On the other hand, when the context was defined in terms of being female, so that subject and target compared as women, most differentiation occurred on male dimensions, i.e. subjects emphasized their relative distinctiveness on systematic and logical, but not on creative and tolerant.

Recall that the actual attribute information provided about the target was constant across all conditions. In other words, given the same "objective" individual information, the attributes used to characterize the self and the target as distinct, "unique" individuals varied with the social–comparative context within which interpersonal differentiation was occurring, i.e. with the salience of their superordinate identities as either science students or women. This suggests that the nature of individual impressions is as category-based (involving the selective *accentuation* of self–other differences at the interpersonal level; see below) and relative to context as is stereotyping (Haslam *et al.*, 1992), and therefore that one type of impression is not, *by definition*, more subject to distortion than the other.

The findings of this study are also relevant to the third and final issue I wish to raise here—accentuation, one of the fundamentals of the categorization process. Surely categorization does not simply give us access to the reality of group-level phenomena. It unavoidably *distorts* our perception of reality by accentuating perceived similarity within and difference between categories (e.g. see Krueger and Rothbart, 1990, p. 651; Stephan, 1985, p. 611). This idea has been central to the classic condemnation of stereotypes as overgeneralizations, and might appear, at the very least, problematic for any attempt to advocate the ubiquity and veridicality of category-based representations.

The self-categorization analysis (e.g. see Haslam and Turner, 1992; Oakes *et al.*, 1994, Chapter 6; Turner and Oakes, 1989, p. 269) has in fact turned our understanding of accentuation effects on its head, and argued that an *absence* of what we have come to know as "accentuation" would indicate distortion, would reflect perception which was insufficiently sensitive to context. At the heart of this argument is a point already emphasized—that, through categorization, *all perception is relative to context*. If this is the case, how can we establish a "standard" in comparison to which other impressions are "distorted" or "accentuated"? Returning to the study by Reynolds just described, which is the accurate standard—differentiation between subject and target in terms of logicality or tolerance? In comparison to which image of the target would we define the enhanced similarity reported under intragroup conditions as "accentuation", and therefore distorted? In fact, we would argue that perception in all conditions of this study varied with context in a veridical manner. Theoretically, we could just as well define subjects' awareness of interindividual differences in the interpersonal conditions as an accentuated distortion of the "real" similarities perceived in the intragroup conditions. The fact that stereotyping and individuation have not been construed in this way simply indicates that researchers have, without explicit justification, defined interpersonal differences as the objectively accurate "standard".

We would argue that it is inappropriate to refer to the judgement effects of ingroup–outgroup categorization as "accentuation", because this suggests that to be non-accentuated (that is, accurate), impression formation should always proceed as if it were operating in an interpersonal context, with reference to individual differences. However, once we accept the real distinctiveness of group-level behaviour, we can see that it would make no sense to see people as individuals when they were behaving as group members, or as group members when they were behaving idiosyncratically. At the same time, we would emphasize that this re-analysis of accentuation is not restricted to conditions where group influences do in fact transform the character of individual "stimuli", such as where conformity processes produce relatively homogeneous behaviour within groups (Turner, 1991). This is, of course, part of a clear dynamic within which stereotyping processes operate (see Vinacke, 1956), but even where the stimulus is incapable of effecting change itself (as in most studies of social judgement), veridical perception will still involve accentuation (at some level of categorization), because accentuation simply reflects cognizance of the *relational* properties of stimuli within the current context.

Consider, for example, the results of the Tajfel and Wilkes' (1963) experiment outlined at the beginning of this chapter, where subjects apparently distorted reality by, amongst other things, representing the difference between the longest of the four short lines and the shortest of the four long lines as 1.9 cm when the "actual" difference was 0.9 cm. It can be argued, however, that 0.9 cm is a judgement of distance made in isolation, using a classification device—a ruler—designed and consensually employed to make judgements at that singular, isolated level of abstraction. This judgement is not, under all conditions, more valid, accurate or useful than judgements which reflect the category memberships of those lines. The "accentuated" judgements reflect the fact that there were *important and meaningful* differences between the two categories of lines (A and B), a significant higher-level structural property of the stimulus situation that *cannot be conveyed* by use of a ruler.

I can, perhaps, clarify this argument that accentuation is simply the necessary contextualization of perception by referring to a short verbal exchange that took place during the trial of the Black South African leader Steve Biko in 1976, sixteen months before his death in police detention.

> *Judge Boshoff* But now why do you refer to you people as blacks? Why not brown people? I mean you people are more brown than black.
>
> *Biko* In the same way as I think white people are more pink and yellow and pale than white.
>
> *Judge Boshoff* Quite . . . but now why do you not use the word brown then?

> *Biko* No, I think really, historically, we have been defined as black people, and when we reject the term non-white and take upon ourselves the right to call ourselves what we think we are, we have got available in front of us a whole number of alternatives . . . and we choose this one precisely because we feel it is most accommodating.
>
> (Biko, 1988, p. 121)

This extract provides a vivid example of the role of social context in determining accentuation. The judge's argument arises from a particular ideological position and reflects a conceptualization of the nature of social reality that is remote from the reality of intergroup relations and everyday life. In rejecting the judge's position, Biko argued that the accentuated representation of his own group as "black" (chosen from a range of alternatives and standing in opposition to the ruling "whites"), was the most valid, meaningful and appropriate representation, *even though* in an individualistic, decontextualized sense it might appear wrong.

Conclusions

Categorization involves the treatment of a number of individual items as in some way equivalent, interchangeable. When we do this with individual people (including ourselves) are we oversimplifying and distorting social reality, or are we reflecting and making possible the group-related aspects of that reality?

In this chapter I have very briefly outlined our argument that the conceptualization of categorization as information loss leads to an analysis of stereotyping which is inconsistent with the realities of group life. I have outlined an alternative view of the categorization process which we believe to be more fruitful for the explanation of stereotyping as impression formation in group contexts. Of course, there are other important issues raised by this analysis not discussed here. For example, what of the ethnocentrism, even hatred, represented in some intergroup stereotypes? Surely this betokens some element of motivated distortion in the stereotyper's view of reality? If not, are we left with social and political relativism? We have discussed these issues elsewhere (see Oakes *et al.*, 1994, Chapter 8; Oakes and Reynolds, in press), in the context of assessing the social validity of stereotypes. Our main concern here has been their psychological validity, the nature of the cognitive process universally accepted as the root psychological cause of social stereotyping (e.g. see Hamilton and Trolier, 1986, p. 134).

In his last published comments on stereotyping, Tajfel (1981a) made it quite clear that cognition was only a part of the stereotyping story. In identifying five functions of stereotypes, two individual-level and three group-level, he emphasized the need to link rather than set up false barriers between the group and the individual functions. Moreover, he suggested that attempts to make such links should "start with the group functions and then relate the individual functions to them" (p. 163). In other words, for Tajfel the group, and the "cultural traditions, group interests, social upheavals and social differentiations" (p. 163) that go with it, was the *primary* causal factor in stereotyping, and other factors had to be understood in light of the fact that stereotypes reflect and make possible *group life*. The aim here has been to outline a view of the categorization process compatible with, and capable of realizing, Tajfel's vision.

Acknowledgements

Preparation of this chapter was supported by a research grant from the Australian Research Council to P. J. Oakes, J. C. Turner and S. A. Haslam. I am grateful to Kate Reynolds for comments on an earlier draft.

References

Allport, G. W. (1954). *The nature of prejudice*. Cambridge, MA: Addison Wesley.

Asch, S. E. (1952). *Social psychology.* New York: Prentice-Hall.

Biko, B. S. (1988). *I write what I like*. London: Penguin (first published in 1978).

Blanz, M. (1995). When persons are perceived as group members: Experiments on the salience of social categories. Paper presented at the Third Muenster Workshop on the Social Identity Approach, Muenster/Rothenberge, March 22–24.

Brewer, M. B. (1988). A dual process model of impression formation. In T. K. Srull and R. S. Wyer (Eds), *Advances in social cognition*, Vol. 1. Hillsdale, NJ: Erlbaum, pp. 1–36.

Brown, R. J., and Turner, J. C. (1981). Interpersonal and intergroup behaviour. In J. C. Turner and H. Giles (Eds), *Intergroup behaviour.* Oxford: Blackwell, and Chicago: University of Chicago Press.

Bruner, J. S. (1957). On perceptual readiness. *Psychological Review*, **64**, 123–152.

Campbell, D. T. (1958). Common fate, similarity, and other indices of the status of aggregates of persons as social entities. *Behavioural Science*, **3**, 14–25.

Deschamps, J-C. (1984). The social psychology of intergroup relations and categorical differentiation. In H. Tajfel (Ed.), *The social dimension*, Vol. 2. Cambridge: Cambridge University Press, and Paris: Editions de la Maison des Sciences de l'Homme.

Doise, W. (1978). *Individuals and groups: Explanations in social psychology.* Cambridge: Cambridge University Press.

Doise, W. (1988). Individual and social identities in intergroup relations. *European Journal of Social Psychology*, **18**, 99–111.

Duck, J. M., Hogg, M. A., and Terry, D. J. (1995). Me, us and them: Political identification and the third-person effect in the 1993 Australian Federal Election. *European Journal of Social Psychology*, **25**, 195–215.

Eiser, J. R., and Stroebe, W. (1972). *Categorization and social judgement*. European Monographs in Social Psychology, No. 3; London: Academic Press.

Fiske, S. T., and Neuberg, S. L. (1990). A continuum of impression formation, from category-based to individuating processes: Influences of information and motivation on attention and interpretation. In M. P. Zanna (Ed.), *Advances in experimental social psychology*, Vol. 23. New York: Random House, pp. 1–73.

Fiske, S. T., Neuberg, S. L., Beattie, A. E., and Milberg, S. J. (1987). Category-based and attribute-based reactions to others: Some informational conditions of stereotyping and individuating processes. *Journal of Experimental Social Psychology*, **23**, 399–427.

Fiske, S. T., and Taylor, S. E. (1991). *Social cognition*. NY: McGraw-Hill Inc.

Gilbert, D. T., and Hixon, J. G. (1991). The trouble of thinking: Activation and application of stereotypic beliefs. *Journal of Personality and Social Psychology*, **60**, 509–517.

Hamilton, D. L. (1979). A cognitive–attributional analysis of stereotyping. In L. Berkowitz (Ed.), *Advances in experimental social psychology*, Vol. 12. New York: Academic Press.

Hamilton, D. L., and Sherman, J. W. (1994). Stereotypes. In R. S. Wyer, Jr. and T. K. Srull (Eds) *Handbook of social cognition*, 2nd edn. Hillsdale, NJ: Erlbaum.

Hamilton, D. L., and Trolier, T. K. (1986). Stereotypes and stereotyping: An overview of the cognitive approach. In J. F. Dovidio and S. L. Gaertner (Eds), *Prejudice, discrimination, and racism*. New York and Orlando, FL: Academic Press, pp. 127–163.

Haslam, S. A., Oakes, P. J., Rainbird, K. J., and Spears, R. (1995a). What is "cognitive load" and how does it affect stereotyping? Unpublished manuscript, The Australian National University.

Haslam, S. A., Oakes, P. J., Turner, J. C., and McGarty, C. (1995b). Social categorization and group homogeneity: Changes in the perceived applicability of stereotype content as a function of comparative context and trait favourableness. *British Journal of Social Psychology*, **34**, 139–160.

Haslam, S. A., and Turner, J. C. (1992). Context-dependent variation in social stereotyping 2: The relationship between frame of reference, self-categorization and accentuation. *European Journal of Social Psychology*, **22**, 251–278.

Haslam, S. A., Turner, J. C., Oakes, P. J., McGarty, C., and Hayes, B. K. (1992). Context-dependent variation in social stereotyping 1: The effects of intergroup relations as mediated by social change and frame of reference. *European Journal of Social Psychology*, **22**, 3–20.

Hewstone, M., and Brown, R. J. (Eds) (1986). *Contact and conflict in intergroup encounters*. Oxford: Basil Blackwell.

Hogg, M. A., and Turner, J. C. (1987). Intergroup behaviour, self-stereotyping and the salience of social categories. *British Journal of Social Psychology*, **26**, 325–340.

Krueger, J., and Rothbart, M. (1990). Contrast and accentuation effects in category learning. *Journal of Personality and Social Psychology*, **59**, 651–663.

Lippmann, W. (1922). *Public opinion*. New York: Harcourt Brace.

Macrae, N., Hewstone, M., and Griffiths, R. J. (1993). Processing load and memory for stereotype-based information. *European Journal of Social Psychology*, **23**, 77–87.

Malpass, R., and Kravitz, L. (1969). Recognition for faces of own and other race. *Journal of Personality and Social Psychology*, **13**, 330–334.

McCauley, R. N. (1987). The role of theories in a theory of concepts. In U. Neisser (Ed.), *Concepts and conceptual development: Ecological and intellectual factors in categorization*. Cambridge: Cambridge University Press.

McGarty, C. (1990). Categorization and the social psychology of judgement. Unpublished PhD thesis, Macquarie University.

McGarty, C., and Penny, R. E. C. (1988). Categorization, accentuation and social judgement. *British Journal of Social Psychology*, **27**, 147–157.

Medin, D. L. (1988). Social categorization: structure, processes and purposes. In T. K. Srull and R. S. Wyer (Eds), *Advances in social cognition*, Vol. 1. Hillsdale, NJ: Erlbaum, pp. 119–126.

Medin, D. L. (1989). Concepts and conceptual structure. *American Psychologist*, **44**, 1469–1481.

Medin, D. L., Goldstone, R. L., and Gentner, D. (1993). Respects for similarity. *Psychological Review*, **100**, 254–278

Medin, D. L., and Wattenmaker, W. D. (1987). Category cohesiveness, theories, and cognitive archaeology. In U. Neisser (Ed.), *Concepts and conceptual development: Ecological and intellectual factors in categorization*. Cambridge: Cambridge University Press.

Murphy, G. L., and Medin, D. L. (1985). The role of theories in conceptual coherence. *Psychological Review*, **92**, 289–316.

Neisser, U. (1976). *Cognition and reality*. San Francisco: W. H. Freeman.

Neisser, U. (ed.) (1987). *Concepts and conceptual development: Ecological and intellectual factors in categorization*. Cambridge: Cambridge University Press.

Neuberg, S. L., and Fiske, S. T. (1987). Motivational influences on impression formation: Outcome dependency, accuracy-driven attention, and individuating processes. *Journal of Personality and Social Psychology*, **53**, 431–444.

Oakes, P. J. (1994). A response to Biernat and Vescio. The effect of fit versus novelty on the salience of social categories. *Journal of Experimental Social Psychology*, **30**, 390–395

Oakes, P. J. (1987). The salience of social categories. In J. C. Turner, M. A. Hogg, P. J. Oakes, S. D. Reicher, and M. S. Wetherell (Eds), *Rediscovering the social group*. Oxford: Blackwell.

Oakes, P. J., Haslam, S. A., and Turner, J. C. (1994). *Stereotyping and social reality*. Oxford, UK: Blackwell.

Oakes, P. J., and Reynolds, K. J. (1995). Resources, reality, and the relationship between stereotyping and individuation. Paper presented at the Third Muenster Workshop on the Social Identity Approach, Muenster/Rothenberge, March 22–24.

Oakes, P. J., and Reynolds, K. J. (in press). Asking the accuracy question: Is measurement the answer? In R. Spears, P. J. Oakes, N. Ellemers, and S. A. Haslam (Eds), *The social psychology of stereotyping and group life*. Oxford, UK: Blackwell

Oakes, P. J., and Turner, J. C. (1990). Is limited information processing capacity the cause of social stereotyping? In W. Stroebe and M. Hewstone (Eds), *European review of social psychology*, Vol. 1. Chichester, UK: Wiley.

Oakes, P. J., Turner, J. C., and Haslam, S. A. (1991). Perceiving people as group members: The role of fit in the salience of social categorizations. *British Journal of Social Psychology*, **30**, 125–144.

Pendry, L. F., and Macrae, N. (1994). Stereotypes and mental life: The case of the motivated but thwarted tactician. *Journal of Experimental Social Psychology*, **30**, 303–325.

Pettigrew, T. F., Allport, G. W., and Barnett, E. O. (1958). Binocular resolution and perception of race in South Africa. *British Journal of Psychology*, **49**, 265–278.

Reynolds, K. J. (1995). Beyond the information given: Capacity, context, and the categorization process in impression formation. Unpublished PhD thesis, The Australian National University.

Reynolds, K. J., and Oakes, P. J. (1995). When do we stereotype or individuate others? An examination of context and attentional resources. Paper presented at the annual conference of the Society of Australasian Social Psychologists, Hobart, Tasmania.

Rosch, E. (1978). Principles of categorization. In E. Rosch and B. B. Lloyd (Eds), *Cognition and categorization*. Hillsdale, NJ: Erlbaum.

Ruscher, J. B., and Fiske, S. T. (1990). Interpersonal competition can cause individuating processes. *Journal of Personality and Social Psychology*, **58**, 832–843.

Ruscher, J. B., Fiske, S. T., Miki, H., and Van Mannen, S. (1991). Individuating processes in competition: Interpersonal versus intergroup. *Personality and Social Psychology Bulletin*, **17**, 595–605.

Secord, P. F. (1959). Stereotyping and favourableness in the perception of Negro faces. *Journal of Abnormal and Social Psychology*, **59**, 309–314.

Secord, P. F., Bevan, W., and Katz, B. (1956). The Negro stereotype and perceptual accentuation. *Journal of Abnormal and Social Psychology*, **53**, 78–83.

Seeleman, V. (1940). The influence of attitude upon the remembering of pictorial material. *Archives of Psychology*, **258**.

Sherif, M. (1967). *Group conflict and co-operation: Their social psychology*. London: Routledge and Kegan Paul.

Simon, B. (in press). Self in society: Ten theses on the individual self and the collective self. In R. Spears, P. Oakes, N. Ellemers, and S. Haslam (Eds), *The social psychology of stereotyping and group life*. Oxford, UK: Blackwell.

Spears, R., and Haslam, S. A. (in press). Why do we stereotype? The ups and downs of cognitive load. In R. Spears, P. Oakes, N. Ellemers and S. Haslam (Eds), *The social psychology of stereotyping and group life*. Oxford, UK: Blackwell.

Spears, R., Oakes, P. J., Ellemers, N., and Haslam, S. A. (in press). *The social psychology of stereotyping and group life*. Oxford, UK: Blackwell.

Stangor, C., and Duan, C. (1991). Effects of multiple task demands upon memory for information about social groups. *Journal of Experimental Social Psychology*, **27**, 357–378.

Stephan, W. G. (1985). Intergroup relations. In G. Lindzey and E. Aronson (Eds.), *Handbook of social psychology*, Vol. 2. New York: Random House.

Tajfel, H. (1957). Value and the perceptual judgement of magnitude. *Psychological Review*, **64**, 192–204.

Tajfel, H. (1959). Quantitative judgement in social perception. *British Journal of Psychology*, **50**, 16–29.

Tajfel, H. (1969). Cognitive aspects of prejudice. *Journal of Social Issues*, **25**, 79–97.

Tajfel, H. (1972). Social categorization. In S. Moscovici (Ed.), *Introduction a la psychologie sociale*, Vol. 1. Paris: Larouse.

Tajfel, H. (Ed.) (1978). *Differentiation between social groups: Studies in the social psychology of intergroup relations*. London: Academic Press.

Tajfel, H. (1979). Individuals and groups in social psychology. *British Journal of Social and Clinical Psychology*, **18**, 183–190.

Tajfel, H. (1981a). Social stereotypes and social groups. In J. C. Turner and H. Giles (Eds), *Intergroup behaviour*. Oxford: Blackwell; Chicago: University of Chicago Press, pp. 144–167.

Tajfel, H. (1981b). *Human groups and social categories*. Cambridge: Cambridge University Press.

Tajfel, H., Flament, C., Billig, M. G., and Bundy, R. F. (1971). Social categorization and intergroup behaviour. *European Journal of Social Psychology*, **1**, 149–177.

Tajfel, H., and Turner, J. C. (1986). The social identity theory of intergroup behaviour. In S. Worchel and W. G. Austin (Eds), *Psychology of intergroup relations*, 2nd edn. Chicago: Nelson-Hall.

Tajfel, H., and Wilkes, A. L. (1963). Classification and quantitative judgement. *British Journal of Psychology*, **54**, 101–114.

Taylor, S. E. (1981a). A categorization approach to stereotyping. In D. L. Hamilton (Ed.), *Cognitive processes in stereotyping and intergroup behaviour.* Hillsdale, NJ: Erlbaum, pp. 88–114.

Taylor, S. E. (1981b). The interface of cognitive and social psychology. In J. Harvey (Ed.) *Cognition, social behaviour and the environment.* Hillsdale, NJ: Erlbaum, pp. 189–211.

Taylor, S. E., Fiske, S. T., Etcoff, N. L., and Ruderman, A. J. (1978). Categorical and contextual bases of person memory and stereotyping. *Journal of Personality and Social Psychology*, **36**, 778–793.

Turner, J. C. (1982). Towards a cognitive redefinition of the social group. In H. Tajfel (Ed.), *Social identity and intergroup relations* Cambridge. Cambridge University Press.

Turner, J. C. (1984). Social identification and psychological group formation. In H. Tajfel (Ed.), *The social dimension: European developments in social psychology.* Cambridge: Cambridge University Press.

Turner, J. C. (1985). Social categorization and the self-concept: A social cognitive theory of group behaviour. In E. J. Lawler (Ed.), *Advances in group processes*,. Vol. 2. Greenwich, CT: JAI Press.

Turner, J. C. (1988). Comments on Doise's individual and social identities in intergroup relations. *European Journal of Social Psychology*, **18**, 113–116.

Turner, J. C. (1991). *Social influence*. Milton Keynes: Open University Press.

Turner, J. C., Hogg, M. A., Oakes, P. J., Reicher, S. D., and Wetherell, M. S. (1987). *Rediscovering the social group: A self-categorization theory.* Oxford: Blackwell.

Turner, J. C., and Oakes, P. J. (1986). The significance of the social identity concept for social psychology with reference to individualism, interactionism, and social influence. *British Journal of Social Psychology*, **25**, 237–252.

Turner, J. C., and Oakes, P. J. (1989). Self-categorization theory and social influence. In P. B. Paulus (Ed.), *The psychology of group influence*. Hillsdale, NJ: Erlbaum.

Turner, J. C., Oakes, P. J., Haslam, S. A., and McGarty, C. (1994). Self and collective: Cognition and social context. *Personality and Social Psychology Bulletin*, **20**, 454–463.

Tversky, A. (1977). Features of similarity. *Psychological Review*, **84**, 327–352.

van Knippenberg, A., van Twuyver, M., and Pepels, J. (1994). Factors affecting social categorization processes in memory. *British Journal of Social Psychology*, **33**, 419–431

Vinacke, W. E. (1956). Explorations in the dynamic process of stereotyping. *Journal of Social Psychology*, **43**, 105–132.

Wilder, D. A. (1986). Social categorization: Implications for creation and reduction of intergroup bias. In L. Berkowitz (Ed.) *Advances in experimental social psychology*, Vol. 19. New York: Academic Press.

4

Accentuation Revisited

J. RICHARD EISER

Department of Psychology, University of Exeter

Contents

It must have been some time around 1970. At any rate, it was before there was much talk about social identity theory. Whatever the date exactly, it was one of many evenings spent in Henri Tajfel's sitting room in Bristol, warmed by the after-glow of a good red wine. There were a number of us there, including I think some other contributors to this volume, following a colloquium by a visiting speaker. Henri, as was his wont, was in animated debate with the visitor when he suddenly checked himself and said, "You know, it's a lucky man who has one really good idea in his life—and I've just had another one." The rest, as the cliché goes, is history, and I'm afraid my memory of the remainder of the evening is rather hazy. However, I certainly remember his *first* "really good idea", for it was what had inspired me to take up social psychological research some years before. It is with this first source of inspiration that this chapter is concerned.

Picture another scene—a lecture room in Oxford in the mid-sixties, designed for examinations rather than teaching, an old blackboard on a wooden easel, poor acoustics, uncomfortable or absent seating, dark oak and the smell of floor wax. A few curious undergraduates, temporary fugitives from talk of herring gulls, rats' bolli and visual illusions, had gathered to hear a series of lectures on the social psychology of prejudice from someone with a funny name. Could it be, hope against hope, that psychology had something to say about real issues? We were not disappointed. Not only were we persuaded that psychology must study people in their social context, we were also shown, crucially, how an understanding of basic psychological processes, of cognition, perception and motivation, could contribute to an explanation of the society and the horrors of social conflict in particular—of war and the constant threat of war, of racial prejudice, of the holocaust. Society is a human construction and its construction reflects how human beings *think*. The most significant aspect of human thought, we were told, is the need to simplify, *to categorize*, and to base decisions on accentuated differences between categories.

This chapter will be organized into the following sections. First, I shall give a summary of Tajfel's account of categorization processes and the principle of accentuation. Then I shall briefly describe some of my own work developing this principle within the context of attitudes and social judgement. I shall then compare the accentuation tradition with treatments of the concept of categorization by other researchers. This will lead on to a reappraisal of the accentuation principle in terms of more recent developments in cognitive theory. I shall then conclude by hinting at ways in which a newer and more general conception of cognition can be at least as socially relevant as approaches more familiar to social psychologists over recent years.

Value as a Cue

Tajfel's experimental research on categorization started from an attempt to explain earlier findings suggesting that visual stimuli of emotional or monetary value were overestimated in size compared with control stimuli of the same physical dimensions but no evaluative significance (e.g. Bruner and Goodman, 1947). As is often the case in the field of social judgement, a rather narrow empirical question provided the focus for a testing of more general theoretical assumptions. For Bruner and Goodman and researchers that followed soon after, the effects they described were taken as evidence of values and motives *biasing* a more "basic" psychological process—that of perception. In a masterly critique of these studies, Tajfel (1957) disputed this account, arguing instead that subjects were using the value of stimuli such as coins as a cue to their size. The main piece of evidence was that valued stimuli were not all overestimated to the same extent. The most important limiting condition was that the value of the stimuli should co-vary predictably with their size (e.g. bigger coins should be worth more). Where there was no correlation between size and value, no overestimation occurred. Where there was such a correlation, it was the more valued (and larger) stimuli that were overestimated more. In short, the actual effect in need of explanation was not just a general overestimation of the size of emotionally significant stimuli, but an *accentuation of the differences* in size between more and less valued stimuli.

This was very much an information-processing account, although this label was not in currency at the time. Perceivers are assumed to combine different items of information together to form a concept of an object and choose an appropriate judgemental response. Value influences judgements of size if and only if value provides *information* about size. Relying on additional items of information, therefore, makes the task of judgement easier (although Tajfel was not too precise about whether this was because it improved discriminability or confidence in a discriminative response). Because what is crucial is information and how we use it, this principle can be applied far more widely than just to judgements of size and value. In fact, it can be applied to any situation where knowledge of one attribute of a stimulus can influence the judgement of that stimulus along another dimension. To keep things clear, let us use the term "focal" for the attribute being judged, such as size, and "peripheral" for the extra, unjudged attribute, such as value (see Eiser and Stroebe, 1972). All that is then required is that the focal and peripheral attributes are correlated. Significantly, neither need vary continuously. The peripheral cue can take the form of a discontinuous classification—such as membership of opposed groups. Superimposed classifications are merely a special case of superimposed cues. Nonetheless, partly for simplicity, and partly because he already had thoughts of social groups in mind, Tajfel tended to talk more of superimposed *classifications* than of continuous cues. This was despite the fact that the early empirical question concerning overestimation effects was concerned with the influence of the continuous cue of value. This emphasis had a profound influence on how his principle was later applied to categorization of social groups. With respect to judgements of physical stimuli, Tajfel (1959, p. 20) expresses the principle as follows:

> When a classification in terms of an attribute other than the physical dimension which is being judged is superimposed on a series of stimuli in such a way that one part of the physical series tends to fall consistently into one class, and the other into the other class, judgements of the physical magnitude of the stimuli falling into the distinct classes will show a shift in the direction determined by the class membership of the stimuli, when compared with judgements of a series identical with respect to this physical dimension, on which such a classification is not superimposed.

This "shift in the direction determined by the class membership of the stimuli" was predicted to consist of two complementary effects. The first is an *accentuation of interclass differences*, in other words a tendency to judge members of different classes as more distant from each other than in a control condition where no information about class membership is provided. The second effect predicted is a *reduction of intraclass differences*, in other words a tendency to judge stimuli as more similar to other members of the same class. These predictions were tested by Tajfel and Wilkes (1963), who had subjects estimate the lengths of eight lines, projected singly onto a screen. In the experimental condition, the four shortest lines were accompanied by a large A, and the four longest by a large B (or vice versa). The superimposed classification of the lines into As and Bs led to the two classes being judged as further apart that in the control condition. In particular, the estimated interval between the stimuli at the class boundary (i.e. between stimuli 4 and 5) was exaggerated. Thus the prediction of an accentuation of interclass differences was supported. Estimated intraclass differences were somewhat reduced in the experimental condition, but this second effect was non-significant.

It is important to remember that interclass and intraclass effects are logically as well as empirically distinct. Members of the same class could be seen as more similar ("assimilated") to each other without the different classes being judged as further apart. Conversely, two classes could be seen as more separated from each other without a reduction of the variance or heterogeneity within each class (unless a restricted number of categories on the response scale leads to an artefactual bunching of responses in the extreme categories). Nonetheless, *both* kinds of judgemental effects were seen as related to aspects of prejudice and stereotyping. Accentuation of interclass differences is the supposed basis for seeing other groups as exaggeratedly different from one's own, and the reduction of intraclass differences supposedly underlies the failure to differentiate members of the same group (and particularly the outgroup) from one another. A recurrent question in Tajfel's subsequent work, and much other research reviewed in this volume, was whether this essentially cognitive principle provided a sufficient or necessary condition for manifestations of intergroup discrimination and negative stereotyping. For purposes of this chapter, I am content to leave most of this debate to others. My own aim will be to re-examine the accentuation principle in terms of what was originally assumed, and what is now perhaps better understood, about the underlying cognitive processes.

Unfortunately, Tajfel's own assumptions about the cognitive processes were not altogether precisely stated, although we can make some reasonable inferences by comparing his approach with the dominant traditions in judgement research at that time. What makes his work stand out was that he was concerned with the judgement of *multi-attribute* objects, whereas most previous work was concerned with judgements of stimuli varying only along a single dimension. The goal of classical psychophysics was to describe lawful relationships between the magnitudes of stimuli on some physical dimension (e.g. weight) and their "psychological magnitudes" or associated sensations (e.g. perceived heaviness). Problems arise because such sensations are typically *inferred from* judgemental responses, and such responses may be affected by many biases or contextual factors other than the sensations themselves (Eiser, 1990). In particular, shifts in the judgement of stimuli can be observed in ways that suggest that subjects are merely re-anchoring their response categories (e.g. changing their minds about what weights to call "heavy") rather than "experiencing" the stimuli any differently. So, if we think of judgement as involving stimuli that vary (a) in their physical magnitude or intensity, (b) in the intensity of the sensations they produce, and (c) in how these sensations are described, where are we to locate the effects of superimposed cues and classifications?

This is a surprisingly difficult question to answer, if posed in this way. On the one hand, it seems clear enough that Tajfel was looking for more than mere semantic effects. In the broader context, he was deeply concerned with how different groups thought about and "saw" each other. In the narrower context, his experiments started from a focus on size *estimation*, and not just with the use of (more obviously) arbitrary response scales. The suggestion that accentuation effects might be dismissed as a kind of response "artefact" would have enraged him. Yet if accentuation is part of how stimuli are represented and not simply how they are rated, we need to be more specific about the kind of representation that is involved. Tajfel seemed to accept, as we did at the time (Eiser and Stroebe, 1972), the basic distinction between "focal" and "peripheral" stimulus dimensions. Judgement, in other words, reflects the representation of the stimulus *in terms of the focal dimension*. Peripheral attributes affect judgement by affecting this "focal" representation, in particular by increasing ease and certainty of discrimination:

> The class identification of a stimulus provides a *supplementary source of information* about the relationship of its magnitude to the magnitude of the other stimuli, whether identified as belonging to the same class or a different class.
>
> (Tajfel and Wilkes, 1963, p. 103)

An alternative point of view could be that stimuli are typically represented and judged *as* multi-attribute objects, so that the distinction between focal and peripheral dimensions is not absolute, but a reflection of the relative strength of their connections with the vector of response alternatives. It is also worth injecting into the discussion at an early stage a warning against depending too heavily on concepts drawn from research on perception and psychophysical judgement. These were especially important areas of "basic" psychological research when Tajfel was first formulating his theory, but they are far from being the only areas in which accentuation processes might be implicated. There is recent evidence, for instance, from Krueger and Clement (1994) that the accentuation principle may apply to certain kinds of memories; they had subjects try to recall high and low daily temperatures for different dates throughout the year. Differences between recalled temperatures on successive dates were accentuated if the dates were from different months but underestimated if both dates were from the same month.

Accentuation of Attitudinal Judgements

My own research into accentuation processes also started with a relatively narrow empirical problem. As part of standard methods of attitude scale construction devised by Thurstone (1928), measures are required of the extent to which different statements express favourable or unfavourable points of view on a given issue. These measures are called the "scale values" of the statements or items, and are derived from asking samples of independent "judges" to rate the items on a scale from, say "extremely unfavourable towards X" to "extremely favourable towards X". Note that this procedure does *not* require judges to say if they personally agree or disagree with the statements, but merely to say what kind of opinion it is which each statement *expresses*. For instance, rating a statement as "extremely unfavourable" should mean only that you think that *whoever made such a statement* would be extremely opposed to the issue or object in question. Such a rating should *not* be taken to mean that one personally disagreed or agreed with the statement. Indeed, Thurstone proposed that such ratings should be unaffected by judges' own attitudes on the issue.

This proposal was subsequently challenged, notably by Hovland and Sherif (1952), who used a previously devised attitude scale measuring "attitude toward the social position of the Negro", and showed that the scale values derived from ratings given by black and pro-black white student judges were radically discrepant from those given by anti-black or "average" whites. In particular, judges whose own attitudes were at the favourable extreme rated many more statements (including many receiving moderate ratings from the other judges) as expressing extremely anti-black opinions. There is some indication that a few of the more favourable statements showed a shift in the opposite direction being rated as even more favourable by the pro-black groups. On the basis of these data, Sherif and Hovland (1961) proposed their "assimilation–contrast" model, which predicts that judges with extreme and strongly held opinions should "assimilate" (rate as closer to their own position) statements that fall within the range of positions they would accept, and should "contrast" (rate as closer to the opposite extreme of the scale) statements that fell outside this "latitude of acceptance". This leads to a prediction of a relatively simple relationship between the extremity of judges' own positions and the extremity of their ratings of the opinions expressed by the statements. Compared with more moderate judges, both extremely pro and extremely anti judges shou!d rate more statements as close to the extremes of the scale—i.e. they should give more *polarized* ratings. This is because extremely pro judges should assimilate favourable items and contrast unfavourable ones, whereas extremely anti judges should contrast favourable items and assimilate unfavourable ones.

I was struck by two inadequacies in Sherif and Hovland's account. The first was an empirical one. In studies of ratings of attitudes towards black people, the predictions of the assimilation–contrast model work well enough when considering the ratings given by pro-blacks, but not at all for those given by anti-blacks. In fact, the latter group tend to give *less* polarized ratings than "moderate" judges (Selltiz *et al.*, 1965). The second problem was that Sherif and Hovland interpreted their findings in terms of an "anchoring" principle—i.e. a process of comparison of stimuli with an anchor or standard (in this case, the judge's own position). It did not seem to me that the derivation of this principle was entirely consistent with previous psychophysical data.

Tackling the second problem first, I proposed (Eiser, 1971) that differences in polarization of attitude judgement were a reflection of a subjective categorization process—in simpler terms, an accentuation of judged differences (in favourability) between statements that were personally acceptable and unacceptable to the judge. In other words, my interpretation was that judges would treat their own agreement and disagreement with the statements presented to them as a peripheral cue or classification *superimposed* on the focal dimension of favourability. As a first step in testing this interpretation, I showed that an experimentally superimposed classification (the supposed attribution of the statements to one of two newspapers) could produce an accentuation of interclass differences in a manner analogous to the Tajfel and Wilkes (1963) findings. So, the argument went, if judges will accentuate the differences between two classes of items defined in terms of an experimentally superimposed cue, they might also accentuate the differences between statements they agree with personally and those with which they disagree. This should lead to judges with more extreme opinions giving more polarized ratings, as Sherif and Hovland (1961) had predicted.

This, however, did not solve the empirical problem that, in previous research, such polarization effects had been found only for judges with attitudes at *one* extreme—those with pro-black attitudes on the issue of attitudes towards black people. In fact, I found a similar asymmetry in my own (1971) study. The issue was that of the non-medical use of drugs, and judges had to rate the items in terms of a scale labelled "extremely permissive" to "extremely restrictive". More polarized ratings were given by those with the most "permissive", or pro-drug, attitudes. There was no evidence that those with the most anti-drug opinions also showed more polarization than more neutral judges. This suggested that polarization of judgement was not related simply to extremity of attitude, but rather to attitude favourability *on the particular response scales used.* So was there something wrong with the accentuation principle, or did another factor have to be included to take account of the differences between those with pro and anti attitudes? I pursued the latter possibility, arguing that the response scales used both in my own study, and in previous ones, may have carried implicit *value connotations* which were consistent with the views of pro judges but inconsistent with the views of anti judges. In simpler terms, if words like "favourable" or "permissive" were implicitly more positive than "unfavourable" or "restrictive", pro judges would be able to attach a "good" label to statements with which they agreed and a "bad" label to statements with which they disagreed. Anti judges, on the other hand, would be required to attach a "bad" label to the anti statements with which they agreed and a "good" label to the statements with which they disagreed. An example of this would be someone who held racist views but denied that his or her opinions implied any personal antipathy towards black people.

This led on to a revised or expanded principle of accentuation of attitudinal judgement. Accentuation effects depend on the evaluative consistency between the judges' acceptance–rejection of the statements and the connotations of the terms used to label the extremes of the response scale. Judges will accentuate the judged differences between statements with which they agree and statements with which they disagree if their "own end" of the scale is the one defined by the more positive label, but will not do so if the labels imply a negative evaluation of their own position and of statements which they accept. Polarization of judgement, in other words, should depend on an interaction between two factors: judges' own attitudes and the way the response scale is labelled. Since the second of these factors had not been manipulated in previous experiements, this interaction had not been recognized.

Manipulating Response Language Connotations

A series of experiments was then conducted in which judges were presented with attitude statements to be judged in terms of *more than one* response scale. Typically, half the response scales (referred to as P+ scales) were ones designed so that the pro extreme was marked by an evaluatively positive label and the anti extreme by an evaluatively negative label, whereas the other half (A+ scales) were ones where the pro extreme was marked by a negative label and the anti extreme by a positive label. For instance, in the study by Eiser and Mower White (1974), the issue was that of adolescents' attitudes towards adult authority and teenage judges were asked to describe the kind of person who had made each of a series of ten statements, in terms of ten different scales. P+ scales were those that implied more positive evaluations of pro-authority viewpoints, for example "impatient–patient" and "disobedient–obedient". A+ scales implied approval of more anti-authority viewpoints, for example "adventurous–unadventurous" and "imaginative–unimaginative". The clear finding was that pro judges showed more polarized ratings than anti judges on P+ scales, whereas this difference was reversed on A+ scales. What this means essentially is that pro-authority judges would rate pro-authority items as very "patient", etc. but only moderately "unimaginative", whereas anti judges would rate anti statements as only moderately "impatient" but very "imaginative". Conversely, pro judges would be less inclined to rate anti statements as very "imaginative" whereas anti judges would be less inclined to rate pro statements as very "patient". These effects, however, did not produce any widespread tendency for judges to reverse the directions of the scales, i.e. pro judges tended to concede that their side was relatively less "imaginative", whereas antis conceded that their side was the less "patient".

This interaction between judges' own attitudes and the connotations of the response scale is a robust effect and has replicated with various procedural modifications and on different issues, including drug-use (Eiser and van der Pligt, 1982) and reactions of members of the general public to interpretations of the nuclear accident at Chernobyl (Eiser *et al.*, 1989). Such findings seem to reflect a more general tendency for individuals to use evaluatively-laden language rhetorically so as to commend their own opinions and discount those of their opponents (Eiser and van der Pligt, 1979). Such forms of language use can even have self-persuasive effects. In other words, individuals induced to apply evaluative-laden terms to an issue may change their attitudes so as to be more consistent with the language they have used (Eiser and Pancer, 1979; Eiser and Ross, 1977; van Schie *et al.*, 1994).

Explaining such interaction effects, however, is less straightforward than predicting them. Clearly, judges' ratings are some kind of combined effect of the descriptive differences between the items (e.g. which items are more pro-authority) and judges' own evaluations (e.g. which items deserve a "good" or "bad" label). But where does this leave the notion of accentuation of differences between subjective categories? One could say simply that polarization reflects the congruity of the response language with judges' attitudes, but an attempt could still be made to interpret such effects in terms of the influence of peripheral cues:

> This hypothesis may be related to the principle of accentuation of differences if one regards both the judge's own levels of agreement with the statements and the value connotations of the scale terms as peripheral cues superimposed on the focal dimension of favorability toward the issue. Since both of these cues are evaluative, one might expect their combined effect to be roughly additive. Polarization should then be directly related to the *net* difference in evaluation between the favorable and unfavorable extremes of the scale, which should be maximal for a judge whose own position was close to the more positive labeled extreme and minimal for a judge whose own position was close to the opposite extreme.
>
> (Eiser and Mower White, 1974, p. 351)

Something strange is happening, however, to the focal–peripheral distinction. The connotations of the scale terms are a feature of the response dimension, not a feature of the stimuli being judged. Thus they cannot be said to provide a "supplementary source of information" (to use Tajfel and Wilkes', 1963, phrase) about the relative degrees of favourability of the different statements. Another way of putting this would be that they are not obviously part of the representation of the statements themselves. It is much more as though different forms of response language are regarded as more *appropriate* for expressing the distinctions seen as important by the judges.

Subsequent findings further encourage this line of thought. Eiser and Mower White (1975), using the same ten statements about adult authority as in their 1974 study, introduced an additional manipulation. In one condition, the five pro statements were presented as having been made by girls, and the five anti statements by boys ("direct" condition). In a second ("reverse") condition, this association was the other way around. There was also a control condition in which neither boys' nor girls' names were attached to the statements (as in Eiser and Mower White, 1974). The gender of the supposed source of the statements thus constituted an experimentally superimposed classification. The response scales, as before, included both those with P+ and those with A+ value connotations. However, half the scales within each category were chosen, on the basis of piloting, to be "marked" for gender, such that the more pro-authority term was also seen as more applicable to girls (e.g. polite, timid) and the anti-authority term more applicable to boys (e.g. rude, bold). "Unmarked" scales were seen as carrying no such gender implications (e.g. creative–uncreative;

unhelpful–helpful). Applying the accentuation principle, one would expect more polarized ratings in the "direct" and "reverse" conditions that in the control condition, but the novel prediction was that this would depend on the congruity between the superimposed classification and the (gender) connotations of the response scale. This was confirmed. Compared with controls, judges in the "direct" condition showed accentuation on both "marked" and "unmarked" scales. Those in the "reverse" condition also accentuated on the "unmarked" scales but (crucially) *not* on the "marked" scales, where the terms would be incongruent with the sources of the statements. Crudely, this would mean that judges were reluctant to describe a boy who had supposedly made a pro-authority statement as "timid" because boys are (reputedly) less timid than girls. Eiser and van der Pligt (1982) also related polarization of judgement to whether scale terms were seen as appropriate to item distributions covering different ranges of positions between the pro and anti extremes.

From a different starting point, Romer (1983) re-examined the failure of previous studies (e.g. on attitudes towards black people) to find polarization or assimilation–contrast effects for judges with unfavourable attitudes. Whatever the possible role of value connotations in these studies, Romer argues that many judges behaved as though a rating of "favourable" meant "I agree" rather than "I think whoever said this had a favourable attitude". The interesting point here is not just that such an artefact may have been present, but that it depends on an implicit closeness of meaning between "favourable" and "acceptable". In other words, judges may have used the favourable–unfavourable scale to express their acceptance–rejection of the statements *directly.* On such an interpretation, it would not be that judges used the "peripheral" cue of acceptability to classify the items into distinct classes *and then* accentuated this "focal" distinctiveness in their favourability ratings. Rather, it is as though this "peripheral" classification became the "focal" dimension for some of the judges.

Intraclass Comparisons

Throughout the early days of research on accentuation processes, and indeed on social identity theory, the emphasis was on discrimination *between* groups and classes. Even so, the prediction of a reduction of intraclass differences, despite receiving mediocre empirical support, remained very much part of Tajfel's thinking. This was doubtless because of the intuition that prejudice and the perception of group homogeneity were closely connected. However, from a more narrowly cognitive perspective, it is unclear why this prediction should necessarily follow from the idea that people may use class membership as "a supplementary source of information" about relative stimulus magnitudes. Class membership may tell one something about the relative position of a stimulus compared with stimuli of *another* class, for example: "this line is an A, so it should be shorter than the Bs". However, it tells one nothing directly about the relative position of any stimulus to other stimuli of the *same* class, since, within any single class, there is, by definition, a zero correlation between the peripheral and focal attributes. Set against Tajfel's assumption that shared class membership should make stimuli be seen as more similar to each other, there is an equally plausible view that class membership tells one nothing about the relative positions of stimuli belonging to the same class, and should therefore be ignored when intraclass comparisons are made.

There is, however, a third possibility. This is that, when considering the positions of stimuli relative to other members of the same class, people invoke standards or norms appropriate to that class. In other words, knowing the class membership of an object tells one something about the range within which that object is likely to fall. For instance being told that an animal is a mouse rather than an elephant would certainly lead us to predict (if we were so asked) that it will be smaller than an elephant (an interclass comparison). We could also safely assume that it would be more similar in size to other mice than to elephants. But matters would not stop there. If we had to describe mice and elephants on a scale from "extremely small" to "extremely large" we could well describe a particular mouse as "extremely large" even though it was tiny in comparison to any elephant we would describe as "extremely small". The reason is obvious. What is "large" *for a mouse* is nowhere near as big as what is "small" *for an elephant.* In other words, as soon as we move from absolute estimates to the use of descriptive rating scales, we anchor these scales according to our expectations which take account of the class membership of the objects being judged. Obvious though this may be, this is not something easily incorporated into accentuation theory, which deals with relative judgements on scales defined in common for all stimuli regardless of class membership.

Other theorists have developed this idea more formally. Possibly the most ambitious statement is that of Kahneman and Miller (1986), whose "norm theory" specifies a number of psychological effects dependent on the perceived relationship of an object to "local norms" appropriate to objects of the same class. Essentially, these "norms" may be regarded as expectations, acquired through interactions with objects of a given class, concerning configurations and variations of stimulus attributes. The novel twist to Kahneman and Miller's approach, however, is their claim that these norms or expectations are recruited "after the fact" rather than being "precomputed". The picture suggested is that perceivers do *not* approach their environment with a pre-defined array of categories or identities into which they proceed to pigeon-hole individual objects. Rather, it is the experience of the objects themselves that evokes memories of similar objects, as well as leading, under some circumstances, to imaginary constructions of "counterfactual alternatives". The "normality" or (un)surprisingness of an object thus depends, supposedly, on the kinds of thoughts it activates *after* it is presented. This allows for far greater flexibity in subjective comparison processes, since it does not demand that we specify in advance what the dimensions of comparison should be. Clearly, all such comparisons depend on acquired expectancies, but the effect of such expectancies on judgemental and other reactions tends to be implicit unless they are directly violated. A mouse of about two inches in length (plus tail) is, I suppose, fairly normal as far as mouse sizes go, but normal in size or not, you would be startled enough if you now looked down and saw one at your feet!

Not all of what Kahenman and Miller (1986) propose relates directly to intraclass comparisons, but the main implication is clear. Judgements rarely involve just one kind of comparison or pre-established frame of reference. The interpretation of any piece of information depends on its context, but this context is itself a function of thoughts and memories that are called to mind or activated on presentation of the information. With respect to the question of which thoughts are activated, a great deal can depend, within any psychological research, on the specific way in which questions are directed by the researcher to the respondent. Providing information about the class membership of stimuli may thus not only prompt subjects to attend to differences between classes, but may also establish separate frames of reference for comparisons of stimuli with others in the same class.

One possibility this suggests is that, under some circumstances, processes of intraclass comparison can counteract simple interclass accentuation effects. Suppose we have two classes of stimuli varying in size which border onto each other, with class A containing the smaller stimuli and class B the larger ones. The accentuation principle clearly predicts that the difference between the A and B stimuli should be accentuated, so that the largest As are judged smaller and the smallest Bs longer (as in Tajfel and Wilkes, 1963). However, this process might be offset by a tendency to judge the largest As as even larger (because they are especially big *for As*) and the smallest Bs as even smaller, for similar reasons. This should result in the two classes being seen as closer together at the borderline, i.e. *interclass assimilation*.

Research by Manis *et al.* (1986) provides evidence of this latter effect. They presented student subjects with responses to diagnostic tests supposedly completed by patients at either of two hospitals. These responses (e.g. definitions of target words) had been prescaled to be indicative of greater or lesser degrees of psychopathology. In the crucial condition, the more disturbed responses were attributed to patients from one hospital, and the less disturbed ones to patients from the other hospital. Subjects then had to make paired comparison judgements between items ("test responses") which were similar and moderate in terms of implied pathology and had to say which of the two patients in each pair was the most disturbed. Critically, each pair contained one example of a relatively disturbed patient from the more "normal" hospital and a relatively "normal" patient from the hospital with more disturbed patients. Within this condition, there was a (weak) tendency for interclass assimilation—i.e. the midscale or borderline patients from the "normal" hospital tended to be judged as more disturbed than those from the other hospital.

A follow-up study by Manis *et al.* (1988) using the same stimulus materials, manipulated the extremity of difference between the two classes (i.e. hospitals).

If interclass assimilation is a result of contrast effects which distance borderline stimuli from the "local norms" of their own hospital, this should be stronger if these "local norms" (learned through presenting individual items before the paired comparison task) are more extremely distinct from each other. Under these conditions, the borderline stimuli should be "outliers" from their own class. Manis *et al.* (1988) observed interclass assimilation of borderline stimuli in a condition where the initial separation of the classes was extreme, but interclass accentuation (as in Tajfel and Wilkes, 1963) when the separation was moderate.

This apparently neat solution is complicated, however, by some of our own findings. Eiser *et al.* (1991), using the same items, found evidence of interclass assimilation but this was unrelated to the extremity of the ("induction") items presented prior to the paired comparison task. Moreover, the interpretation of this effect as reflecting intraclass contrast from "local norms" is undermined by the fact that interclass assimilation was found not only for the midscale items at the borderline, but also for the more discriminable "induction" items (Manis *et al.* had not tested for such an effect). The reasons for this are not altogether clear, but our tentative conclusion was that information about class membership may lead to interclass assimilation rather than accentuation in situations where subjects are relatively unsure about their discriminations and the stimulus information requires complex processing.

Category Identification and Representation

So much, then, for research conducted more or less directly within the framework of accentuation theory. On the whole, the predictions about interclass accentuation have been confirmed, particularly when account is taken of the nature of the response dimension, although there are exceptions. There are also ambiguities with respect to the question of comparison of individual stimuli with members of their own class. Curiously, though, this whole field has remained somewhat separate from research into categorization conducted within the predominantly American social cognition tradition. There is no special cultural significance to this, beyond the tendency for researchers from a similar background tending to be more likely to read and cite each others' work. The difference in emphasis is more mundane, although it has some implications for the applied problems considered.

The Tajfel tradition, broadly, is concerned with *classifications that are superimposed*, and with the effect of information about category membership on the discrimination of individual stimuli, objects or people. In other words, the classifications are given by the experimenter, and the research question is one of how subjects use this information. By contrast, much social cognition research has been concerned with how category membership is *inferred* from information about stimulus attributes, in other words, how individual stimuli are sorted into categories. The question addressed is (not exclusively, but predominantly) that of how individuals identify the category or class to which a given object or person belongs. The approach taken links in closely with work on perceptual object identification and with the use of linguistic categories, which may often be assumed to be organized into hierarchical structures. Both traditions converge on the question of how information about the class membership of an object is linked to information about its other attributes, or, to put it differently, what form of cognitive representation underlies the recognition and use of categories.

Approaches to this question have changed considerably over the years. The "taxonomic" approach regarded categorization as a form of logical problem solving, that is, of working out the "if–then" rules which determined category membership. Bruner *et al.* (1956) treated categorization as a form of concept attainment, based on a "process of finding predictive defining attributes that distinguish exemplars from nonexemplars of the class one seeks to discriminate" (p. 22). It is worth noting that, for Bruner *et al.*, categorization did not involve a *failure* to discriminate at an intraclass level, but rather a direction of attention away from *discriminable* intraclass distinctions towards more salient or significant information:

> To categorize is to render *discriminably different* things equivalent, to group the objects and events and people around us into classes, and to respond to them in terms of their class membership rather than their uniqueness.
>
> (Bruner *et a!.*, 1956, p. 1; emphasis added)

The notion of "defining attributes" was considered rather formally. For instance, attainment of a concept such as "three circles" would involve number and shape as defining attributes, but treat the attribute of colour as irrelevant. That is, although three red circles would be discriminable from three green circles, both patterns would be exemplars of the same concept or category and so would be *treated* as equivalent. However, when considering categorization of complex stimuli outside the laboratory, the "correct" rule-based "defining attributes" may not be the "criterial attributes" which people actually use, and which "affect the probability" (p. 31) of a particular category identification. Category learning is thus viewed as coming to recognize the attributes which in fact define a category, and to treat them as criterial.

> The distinction between defining attributes and criterial attributes . . . permits us to think of categorizing as a process of achievement: discovering the defining attributes of the environment so that they may serve with their proper values as the criteria for making judgments about identity.
>
> (Bruner *et al.*, 1956, p. 30)

This same distinction implies a differentiation between individuals' subjective representation of a category and the objective content or definition of the category itself. This differentiation, however, becomes less easy to sustain when the definition of a category becomes more a matter of social consensus and category boundaries become "fuzzy" or probabilistic. Furthermore, by considering categories in a more probabilistic way, one can ask whether particular objects are "better" (i.e. more easily identifiable) exemplars of a category than others.

This became the hallmark of the dominant tradition of categorization research in the 1970s—the view that category representations rested on notions of *prototypes* or "best examples" (e.g. Rosch and Lloyd, 1978). The precise nature of such representations was still a matter of debate, but there was a continued reliance on a modified form of rule-based reasoning involving general relationships between categories and attributes (e.g. "birds have wings") while allowing for exceptions (e.g. "except for kiwis"). Acknowledgement of the probabilistic nature of categories also led to a shift of emphasis from syllogistic or deductive reasoning to inductive information processing (Holland *et al.*, 1986).

Much of this work seemed to take its direction from an interest in semantics and how people learn the meaning of linguistic concepts. From the 1980s onwards, however, the interest shifted towards thinking of category representations as structures stored in memory and subsequently retrieved for purposes such as discrimination, pattern recognition and behavioural decision making. At the core of this new trend is the idea that memory depends on learned *associations* organized into a network where different thoughts or pieces of information can activate others. But associations between what? Probably the most influential approach so far has been the so-called *exemplar model* of (social) categorization. In simple terms, this states that people form associations between a category label and individual exemplars of that category. As a consequence, presentation of a category label should activate memories of specific exemplars of that category and vice versa. Also, thoughts of one exemplar should activate thoughts of other exemplars. Prototypicality can be neatly defined in terms of the strengths of these associations. The most prototypical exemplar is the one with the strongest associations to both the category label and most other exemplars of the same category. This does not demand that a prototypical exemplar is the most distinguishable from exemplars of other categories, although this assumption can be built into particular formulations (Smith and Zárate, 1992).

A more radical view is that people do not necessarily store information about exemplars *as such* (except perhaps for a limited number that are frequently encountered), but form associations between category labels and large numbers of stimulus attributes which are processed in parallel. This "parallel distributed processing" view of cognition is the foundation of contemporary *connectionist* or "neural network" research in cognitive science (Eiser, 1994). One of the main differences between this and some earlier associationist approaches is the idea that the "units" or "nodes" between which associations are formed within the network do not by themselves necessarily stand for any meaningful or symbolic concept. Different "meanings" are represented by different *patterns* of activation across the network, and any single unit or node may contribute to many different patterns. Knowledge is represented by the matrix of connection weights linking the separate units in the network to each other. These weights determine the response of the system to a given input and are modified through experience and feedback. Connectionism relies very largely on computer simulation in order to test theoretical principles. However, it must be stressed that there is no need to "pre-program" a definition of the categories to be learned or identified. The kinds of programs exploited by neural networks are general-purpose ones which allow the system to "learn" or derive its own solutions to discrimination or recognition problems. This constitutes a fundamental difference from earlier approaches where the meaning of a category depended on if–then rules and defining attributes.

Attempts are being made to reconcile the connectionist and exemplar-based approaches (Nosofsky *et al.*, 1992), since the learning algorithms used in connectionist modelling can be applied or adapted to the learning of exemplar associations and even prototype identification as a special case. The advantages of doing so are not altogether established, however. While "purer" connectionist approaches have the merits of greater generality and parsimony on their side, advocates of (more "localist") exemplar-based models argue that they can account better for data from specific tasks, including systematic errors people make with particular kinds of category discriminations (Kruschke, 1993). Both these approaches, however, differ markedly from earlier theories in terms of how categories are assumed to be represented and stored in memory. Within any parallel distributed system, these representations consist simply of network of learned associations between (separate or aggregated) stimulus features, contextual cues and response or output alternatives. They do *not* consist of formal definitions of the categories, since such definitions fulfil no extra informative role.

Must the Content of Categories be Pre-defined?

Connectionist research suggests that it is possible to simulate category learning, pattern recognition and discrimination without pre-programming the system with a formal definition of the categories to be learned. This raises a broader issue. If we go back to substantive research on accentuation and social categorization, how important is it to assume that people actually represent the *content* of categories to themselves? Do we need to carry around with us "in our heads" a repertoire or encyclopaedia of pre-existing definitions of alternative categories or identities into which we can fit the objects, events and people we encounter, as well as ourselves? Clearly we have repertoires of alternative *responses* to objects and events, either acquired from everyday experience or provided by researchers in experiments or surveys. These responses can include ordinary language descriptions and evaluations, as well as different points or categories on rating scales. A connectionist interpretation is that all these responses depend on learned (direct and indirect) associations with features of the object being judged and the context in which it is presented. These learned associations constitute the *knowledge* we use to make inferences to and from category membership, and so may be taken to reflect our *representation* of the categories in question. But "representation" is a dangerous word. Used loosely, it can suggest the existence of some mental "picture" of what is represented, leaving open the danger of infinite regress if we then ask how this "picture" is itself "represented" in order to be understood.

A close analogy can be drawn with visual pattern recognition. Indeed, as Lingle *et al.* (1984, p. 104) put it:

> In a sense, the process of assigning an entity to its appropriate category is one of pattern recognition, in which a set or pattern of attributes is identified as suggesting membership in a particular category.

Yet we no longer need to depend on theories which seek to explain pattern recognition in terms of matching perceived objects with pre-existing mental images or "templates". Such a view leads us to the implausible position that we should have a separate template for every pattern that we recognize. Prototype theories and, to some extent, exemplar models raise similar worries. When I recognize an object outside my window as a tree, am I comparing it with some image of a prototypical tree (a Platonic ideal perhaps)? Are memories of every other exemplar of the category "tree" I have ever come across activated as I identify what I now see? I don't think so. Or more cautiously, if this is what is happening, it doesn't seem to penetrate to my conscious thought. These are big issues, which could take me far beyond the scope of this chapter. For present purposes, I am simply warning against the tendency to assume that mental representations of information are any kind of recognizable "picture" of the objects or categories so represented. If we did have such recognizable "pictures", we would have to account for *how* they were recognizable, and the whole cycle would have to start again.

These questions nonetheless lie at the core of the theoretical and practical goals of Tajfel's own research and that inspired by his ideas. Discussing the relevance of mental representations for social cognition, Holyoak and Gordon (1984, p. 46) wrote:

> Progress in identifying representational formats may well have important implications for social–psychological models. Nonetheless, in many cases it seems that social psychologists can afford to treat the issues regarding format distinctions with a degree of benign neglect. Many of the central theoretical problems in social cognition hinge more on the content of social cognition than on its representational format.

To this I would counter, firstly, that there has been considerable progress in this direction over the last decade and it does have important implications for such models. Secondly, the predominance of content issues is far from universal in social psychology or even in work within the accentuation and social identity traditions. Indeed, it is not difficult to discern, even I expect within this volume, contrasting emphases either on the content or the form of representation of social (or socially valued) categories.

Tajfel himself was relatively *un*concerned with the content of social categories. This is suggested by his choice of rather sparse stimulus materials and experimental paradigms from size estimation studies through to minimal groups.

It is declared more explicitly in his manipulations of class membership—lines labelled A or B, school students divided supposedly on the basis of visual number estimation or artistic preference, even university students grouped according to their degree course subject. These bases for group classification were all (to use a favourite Tajfelian epithet) *trivial*. Yet what was sometimes missed in the ensuing debate about "experiments in a vacuum" and ecological validity of laboratory research is that this "triviality" was deliberate. More than this, it is essential to the theoretical and political significance of Tajfel's work.

To appreciate why this is so, let us remind ourselves of the question he never forgot—why conflict occurs and can lead to the atrocities of war and genocide. Let us allow this question to nag away at the back of our mind while we contrast Tajfel's "triviality" with more content-rich approaches. The work on "social representations" (e.g. Farr, 1984) provides an example of the latter kind. Of course there is a place for social research that documents beliefs that are widely held and shared within specific cultural communities, and of course it is worthwhile considering how such beliefs may reflect broader sociopolitical and historical processes. However, the intrinsic interest of such material does not lessen the obligation on theorists to offer a coherent account of how such "social representations" are accessed, experienced and *used* by individual people at the level of personal decision-making and social interaction. Without such an account, merely documenting the occurrence of specific social representations (or stereotypes) within a society or milieu is the social psychological equivalent of train-spotting. Whereas some researchers in the social representation tradition do respond to the challenge of specifying relevant psychological processes, others have been frustratingly silent on this issue.

It is, of course, possible to offer a theory of process while incorporating attention to the content of actual category representations. Turner's (e.g. 1982) self-categorization theory is a prime example. Granted the composition of this volume, any comments I can offer on his work are likely to be oversimplified, redundant, or both. Nonetheless, for me, Turner's original notion of self-categorization seems to imply that the content of specific category systems is extremely important. Through asking what it "means" to be a member of a given social group or category, people are assumed to arrive at a "cognitive definition" of the group, which carries with it many implications for social influence, for acceptance or rejection of potential group members, and for their own social identity. The flexibility of Turner's approach depended on the availability of alternative identities or bases for categorizing the self and others. It is the *content* of these alternative identities that prescribes different forms of positive and negative discriminatory behaviour. Recently, however, Turner has greatly modified his position and now strongly emphasizes the importance of ongoing cognitive processes rather than antecedent self-definitions.

> The concept of self as a separate mental structure does not seem necessary . . . Rather than a distinction between the activated self and the stored, inactive self, it is possible to think of *the self as the product of the cognitive system at work, as a functional property of the cognitive*

> *system as a whole* . . . We can suppose that we deploy cognitive resources flexibly to categorize self as and when appropriate . . . Therefore the notion of self-concepts as stored, invariant structures and the associated model of category use as a process of *activating an already existing representation* (or some subset of such representations) are both being rejected.
>
> (Turner *et al.*, 1994, p. 459; emphasis in original)

Categorization and Conflict

What does this knowledge tell us about why the holocaust occurred? No doubt something could be learned by searching the archives for research documenting contemporary social representations of "the Jew", or illuminating what it meant to categorize oneself as "German". Faced with such a question, any clues are welcome. But for Tajfel, this was not the place to concentrate one's efforts. To be a Jew in 1930s Germany and central Europe was to be somewhat different from non-Jewish citizens. But it was not *that* different—not different *enough* to account for what so few believed could happen. Set against the atrocities of the Nazi period, the Jew–Gentile distinction was *absolutely trivial*. Tajfel's simple but stunning insight was that even the most trivial of category distinctions can be the cue for the most extreme forms of discrimination. To draw this out even more pointedly for subsequent research, although stereotypes and forms of social identification can reflect categorization processes, intergroup conflict and discrimination cannot be attributed exclusively or mainly to the content of *pre-existing* stereotypes or the "meaning" of *pre-existing* social identities.

This is not a comfortable conclusion either to work or live with. It illustrates both the power and limitations of a purely psychological account of intergroup relations. If, as he proposed and the idea is still sustainable, there are fundamental psychological principles that underly phenomena as diverse as genocide and overestimation of the size of coins, we may be left with an account of all conflict and discrimination in general, but no one specific conflict in particular. If *any* category distinction can be a cue to conflict, we are faced with the happier, but just as difficult, question of why conflict is not universal (or universally severe). This is not simply a question for psychology, although it is a question psychology cannot ignore.

So Tajfel's account rested on assumptions about the process of categorization, rather than the content of categories. While the accentuation principle has stood the test of time pretty well, many of the implicit background assumptions (which are not his alone) need re-examination. Tajfel did not attribute discrimination to the content of pre-existing stereotypes, but he did regard stereotyping as the result of an accentuation of pre-existing group differences. Groups and categories were part of the informational *input* with which individuals had to deal, since category distinctions were superimposed through experimental manipulation. This does not actually constitute a test of the central idea that we *represent* our world categorically, since the category cues were given to start with. The question actually addressed is the narrower one of what *judgements* we make, once we are provided with such cues. Then there is the idea that relying on such cues leads to greater cognitive simplicity and economy of effort. This was always rather loosely argued (and I was as loose as the rest). What processes, exactly, are "simplified"? Are we talking about simplified representations, or merely simplified judgements? We have good evidence for the latter. It is unclear exactly what would count as evidence for the former.

I myself have come round to the view that accentuation and categorization are primarily characteristics of judgement, that is, of the *output* of our cognitive system. I would like to be able to claim that I realized this many years ago, when I first showed that accentuation effects depended on connotations of the response scale. However, to the extent that I recognized this as a question at all, I probably would have gone along with the traditional view that categories are part of the structure of the reality to which we are exposed, with processes such as accentuation serving only to exaggerate the categories that are somehow already "there".

I have since come to believe that this traditional view is thoroughly misdirected. Categories, as such, are not generally part of the "input" to social cognitive processes. They do not exist "out there" in any simple sense. This is not to say that there is not considerable covariation and redundancy within our stimulus environment. On the contrary, such covariation is essential for any mental life at all. Nor is it at all to deny that there are discontinuities. What I am saying is that categories as *meaningful concepts* are not to be defined in terms of antecedent rules, or even presorted catalogues of exemplars, but are expressions of cognitive operations performed on the input of our experience. This is very much in accordance with what Turner *et al.* (1994) argue with respect to the self-concept. What this leads on to, though, is a need for social psychological theory to be even more explicit about the kind of operations and cognitive system assumed to be involved. I personally have great hopes for connectionist approaches in cognitive science and for their potential applicability to social psychology (Eiser, 1994). These approaches can account for the judgemental phenomena discussed in this chapter while relating them to a more general context.

Henri Tajfel's life and work meant many things to a great many people. A very small part of what it meant to me was that it made sense to ask basic questions about how we think and use information about our social world. Daring to tackle such questions head-on is as vital now for social psychology as it ever was. The study of basic cognitive processes is very much our business as social psychologists, since social psychological processes are "basic" too. We need to be able to say that our questions are *psychological* ones, but, as *social* psychologists, we can go one step further. With Henri's intellectual legacy to guide us, we can affirm that our questions are ones that matter and that the answers (if we find them) really can offer insights into what is best and worst in the human condition.

References

Bruner, J. S., and Goodman, C. C. (1947). Value and need as organizing factors in perception. *Journal of Abnormal and Social Psychology*, **42**, 33–44.

Bruner, J. S., Goodnow, J. J., and Austin, G. A. (1956). *A study of thinking*. New York: Wiley.

Eiser, J. R. (1971). Enhancement of contrast in the absolute judgment of attitude statements. *Journal of Personality and Social Psychology*, **17**, 1–10.

Eiser, J. R. (1990). *Social judgment*. Buckingham: Open University Press.

Eiser, J. R. (1994). *Attitudes, chaos and the connectionist mind*. Oxford: Blackwell.

Eiser, J. R., Martijn, C., and van Schie, E. (1991). Categorization and interclass assimilation in social judgement. *European Journal of Social Psychology*, **21**, 493–505.

Eiser, J. R., and Mower White, C. J. (1974). Evaluative consistency and social judgment. *Journal of Personality and Social Psychology*, **30**, 349–359.

Eiser, J. R., and Mower White, C. J. (1975). Categorization and congruity in attitudinal judgment. *Journal of Personality and Social Psychology*, **31**, 769–775.

Eiser, J. R., and Pancer, S. M. (1979). Attitudinal effects of the use of evaluatively biased language. *European Journal of Social Psychology*, **9**, 39–47.

Eiser, J. R., and Ross, M. (1977). Partisan language, immediacy, and attitude change. *European Journal of Social Psychology*, **7**, 477–489.

Eiser, J. R., Spears, R., and Webley, P. (1989). Nuclear attitudes before and after Chernobyl: Change and judgment. *Journal of Applied Social Psychology*, **19**, 689–700.

Eiser, J. R., and Stroebe, W. (1972). *Categorization and social judgement*. London: Academic Press.

Eiser, J. R., and van der Pligt, J. (1979). Beliefs and values in the nuclear debate. *Journal of Applied Social Psychology*, **9**, 524–536.

Eiser, J. R., and van der Pligt, J. (1982). Accentuation and perspective in attitudinal judgment. *Journal of Personality and Social Psychology*, **42**, 224–238.

Farr, R. M. (Ed.) (1984). *Social representations*. Cambridge: Cambridge University Press.

Holland, J. H., Holyoak, K. J., Nisbett, R. E., and Thagard, P. R. (1986). *Induction: Processes of inference, learning and discovery*. Cambridge, MA: MIT Press.

Holyoak, K. J., and Gordon, P. C. (1984). Information processing and social cognition. In R. S. Wyer Jr., and T. K. Srull (Eds) *Handbook of social cognition*, Vol. 1. Hillsdale, NJ: Erlbaum. pp. 39–70.

Hovland, C. I., and Sherif, M. (1952). Judgmental phenomena and scales of attitude measurement: Item displacement in Thurstone scales. *Journal of Abnormal and Social Psychology*, **47**, 822–832.

Kahneman, D., and Miller, D. T. (1986). Norm theory: Comparing reality to its alternatives. *Psychological Review*, **93**, 136–153.

Krueger, J., and Clement, R. W. (1994). Memory-based judgments about multiple categories: A revision and extension of Tajfel's accentuation theory. *Journal of Personality and Social Psychology*, **67**, 33–47.

Kruschke, J. K. (1993). Human category learning: Implications for backpropagation models. *Connection Science*, **5**, 3–36.

Lingle, J. H., Altom, M. W., and Medin, D. L. (1984). Of cabbages and kings: Assessing the extendability of natural object concept models to social things. In R. S. Wyer, Jr., and T. K. Srull (Eds), *Handbook of social cognition*, Vol. 1. Hillsdale, NJ: Erlbaum, pp. 71–117.

Manis, M., Nelson, T. E., and Shedler, J. (1988). Stereotypes and social judgment: Extremity, assimilation and contrast. *Journal of Personality and Social Psychology*, **55**, 28–36.

Manis, M., Paskewitz, J., and Cotler, S. (1986). Stereotypes and social judgment. *Journal of Personality and Social Psychology*, **50**, 461–473.

Nosofsky, R. M., Kruschke, J. K., and McKinley, S. C. (1992). Combining exemplar-based category representations and connectionist learning rules. *Journal of Experimental Psychology. Learning, Memory and Cognition*, **18**, 211–233.

Romer, D. (1983). Effects of own attitude on polarization of judgment. *Journal of Personality and Social Psychology*, **44**, 273–284.

Rosch, E., and Lloyd, B. (Eds) (1978). *Cognition and categorization*. Hillsdale, NJ: Erlbaum.

Selltiz, C., Edrich, H., and Cook, S. W. (1965). Ratings of favorableness about a social group as an indication of attitude toward the group. *Journal of Personality and Social Psychology*, **2**. 408–415.

Sherif, M., and Hovland, C. I. (1961). *Social judgment. Assimilation and contrast effects in communication and attitude change*. New Haven, CT: Yale University Press.

Smith, E. R., and Zárate, M. A. (1992). Exemplar-based model of social judgment. *Psychological Review*, **99**, 3–21.

Tajfel, H. (1957). Value and the perceptual judgment of magnitude. *Psychological Review*, **64**, 192–204.

Tajfel, H. (1959). Quantitative judgement in social perception. *British Journal of Psychology*, **50**. 16–29.

Tajfel, H., and Wilkes, A. L. (1963). Classification and quantitative judgement. *British Journal of Psychology*, **54**, 101–114.

Thurstone, L. L. (1928). Attitudes can be measured. *American Journal of Sociology*, **33**, 529–554.

Turner, J. C. (1982). Towards a cognitive redefinition of the social group. In H. Tajfel (Ed.) *Social identity and intergroup relations*. Cambridge: Cambridge University Press, pp. 15–40.

Turner, J. C., Oakes, P. J., Haslam, S. A., and McGarty, C. (1994). Self and collective: Cognition and social context. *Personality and Social Psychology Bulletin*, **20**, 454–463.

van Schie, E. C. M., Martijn, C., and van der Pligt, J. (1994). Evaluative language, cognitive effort and attitude change. *European Journal of Social Psychology*, **24**, 707–712.

5

Social Identity, Self as Structure and Self as Process

DOMINIC ABRAMS

Department of Psychology, University of Kent

Contents

Social identity theory has contributed enormously to our understanding of intergroup relations and group processes. However, cast as it is within the framework of a conflict structuralist model of society (Hogg and Abrams, 1988), it leaves us with a rather heavily deterministic view of the impact of groups and categories on individuals. The later development of self-categorization theory (Turner *et al.*, 1987) moved the focus towards cognitive processes and developed the emphasis on categorization and contrast. There remain some difficult problems for both theories, such as the motivational components of group processes (cf. Hogg and Abrams, 1993). However, the issue addressed in this chapter is how best to conceptualize the relationship between social groups and self.

Given the context of this book it is unnecessary to redescribe the details of either social identity theory or self-categorization theory, but it is worth rehearsing some of the assumptions. Social identity theory (Tajfel and Turner, 1979) assumes that social categorization establishes a framework for engaging in social comparison, that identity becomes bound up in the category shared by oneself, and that individuals seek positive distinctiveness for that category in order to maintain or enhance self-esteem. Thus, the value attached to identity is established through relativistic judgements and depends on the features of the comparison category.

Social identity theory has helped us to understand how people come to act *as* group and category members, in the name of their group (Hogg and Abrams, 1988). However, it has left unresolved some tricky problems. First and foremost was determining which of the many available categorizations would become a basis for identity. Tajfel may not have considered this to be a key question because he was concerned with groups that self-evidently provided a rich and meaningful basis for identity: cultural, ethnic, religious, and other large scale social cleavages.* Tajfel's aim and contention was that social psychology had to provide a supra-individual level of analysis in order to account for the prejudice and discrimination it sought to explain. He wished to discredit explanations based on individual differences, individual drive and energy processes (such as frustration), and even structural conflicts of interests. Instead, social categorization, stereotyping, and identification were seen by Tajfel as providing an engine for collective attitudes and behaviour.

Self-categorization theory has addressed the problem of which group memberships will become ascribed to self, and also the impact of these self-categorizations on conformity, polarization, attitudes and stereotypes (e.g. Abrams and Hogg, 1990b; Oakes *et al.*, 1994; Turner, 1992; Turner *et al.*, 1987). Given the reification of self in the twentieth century (Baumeister, 1987) it comes as no surprise that much theorizing in social psychology treats the self as a well-defined entity which establishes stability and continuity to behaviour. This contrasts with the social identity approach, which holds that transitions occur between personal and social identifications, and with the self-categorization approach, which holds that changes in the comparative context result in changes in self-conception. Social identity theory and self-categorization theory have both neglected the question of *how* people retain psychological continuity when making transitions from behaving as a member of group X to behaving as a member of group Y, or indeed how and whether groups X and Y are psychologically integrated as potential components of the self. Some overarching motivational processes have been put forward as possible candidates. Social identity theory's original emphasis on self-esteem appears to have been moderated or abandoned in the light of conceptual and methodological obstacles (Abrams, 1992; Abrams and Hogg, 1988; Hogg and Abrams, 1990), and the relationship between strength of identification and intergroup discrimination has

* Although Tajfel did not analyse gender, this has also been addressed by other social identity researchers (Abrams, 1989; Brown and Williams, 1984; Condor, 1986; Skevington and Baker, 1989; Williams, 1984)

also been found to vary (Mullen *et al.*, 1992). More general motivations such as for the achievement of good psychological structure (Abrams and Hogg, 1988) or uncertainty reduction (Hogg and Abrams, 1993; McGarty, *et al.*, 1993) are currently being canvassed. Regardless of which motivational concept is appropriate, the issue may reflect the theoretical desire to provide an overarching theme or integrity to identity.

Structure versus Process Models of Self

It is possible to characterize theory as emphasizing two different questions about the self. Some theorists are concerned primarily with the structural properties of the self, whereas others are concerned with the processes involved in self-conception. Clearly, not all theories are restrictive in their scope, but it is my intention to highlight some different assumptions of the structure and process views.

A number of researchers have examined the enduring structures of the self. For example, Markus (1977) illustrated that some aspects of self are represented schematically. There is debate over the way information about the self is represented and retrieved (Srull and Wyer, 1993). One view is that we make trait inferences about ourselves using autobiographical behavioural exemplars (e.g. Keenan, 1993). That is, our ability to make summary descriptions of ourselves depends on the number of instances of relevant behaviours we can retrieve from memory. There is reasonable support for exemplar models in accounting for group categorization judgements (Judd and Park, 1988; Smith and Zárate, 1990), trait inferences about others (Kahneman and Miller, 1986), and stereotyping (Rothbart and John, 1985). Associative network models seem to be useful in accounts of impression formation (Hamilton, 1989) and the cognitive structure of social stereotypes (Andersen and Klatzky, 1987). However, in relation to self-judgements, the exemplar view has been rejected as being unwieldy and as involving an infinite regress to ever more restrictive categorizations (Bellezza, 1984, 1993). The more favoured view seems to be that trait judgements of self arise through some combination of behavioural exemplars and abstracted trait summaries. This latter approach can either rely on depth of processing (the dual exemplar/summary view espoused by Kihlstrom and Cantor, 1984) or quantity of information (the mixed model view espoused by Klein and Loftus, 1993) to account for transitions from exemplar to trait representation.

Klein and Loftus conducted a series of studies suggesting that, for judgements of self, trait representation can be functionally independent of autobiographical behavioural exemplars. They suggest that experimental judgemental tasks involving others are usually relatively devoid of context and involve retrieval of material very shortly after learning. In contrast, when people make self-judgements they typically have extensive information, acquired across contexts, and involving long retention intervals. All of these factors facilitate abstraction to summary traits. The various models do seem to converge in supporting the idea of self as a relatively stable, enduring, and quite abstractly represented structure. However, the dissociation of summary or abstract representations of self from behavioural exemplars has interesting implications for structural and process models of self, a point returned to later in this chapter.

Various motivational hypotheses have been advanced on the assumption that different components of the self-structure combine to embody differing goals. Different theorists emphasize different levels of specificity and temporal implications for the goals people set for themselves. For example, Higgins (1987) explores discrepancies between different "self-guides", Markus and Nurius (1986) outline the impact of people's conceptions of their "possible selves", and Cantor (1990) focuses on how individuals set different life tasks for themselves (see Knowles and Sibicky, 1990 for an overview of different perspectives on the self). Markus and Kitayama (1991) have highlighted cross-cultural differences in the content of self-definition. In the USA the self is conceptualized as an independent entity whereas in Japan it is more likely to be conceptualized as interdependent with other people. According to Markus and Kitayama this difference results in self-esteem being gained and sustained differently in the two cultures.

Buss (1980), Scheier and Carver (e.g. 1981), and Fenigstein *et al.* (1975) have all adopted a distinction between the private and public self, while Crocker and Luhtanen (1990) focus specifically on a generalized collective self (*cf* Greenwald and Pratkanis, 1984). Breckler and Greenwald (1986) describe the public, private, and collective selves as emerging in a developmental sequence and as setting different ego tasks. In common with many other theorists (e.g. Cheek and Briggs, 1992), Breckler and Greenwald equate the public self with interpersonally orientated issues, the private self with "internal standards", and the collective self with cognitions about group memberships. It is not always argued explicitly that these "motivational facets" of self are structurally independent, but this is an operating assumption shared by many researchers in areas ranging from self-presentation and self-awareness, to cross cultural differences (Triandis, 1989).

Collective versus private selves

An explicitly structural model is adopted by Trafimow *et al.* (1991) who argue that cognitions about the self are divided into two distinct components or "baskets". Private self-cognitions are thought to be organized around a general private self-concept and collective self-cognitions around a general collective self-concept. The collective self contains affiliations, group memberships and connections to collectives of all types. The private self contains knowledge of one's own attitudes, traits, feelings and behaviour.

Trafimow *et al.* (1991) conducted two experiments to demonstrate the structural discontinuity between the two self-concepts. Both experiments involved North American and Chinese students at the University of Illinois. In these experiments subjects were exposed to a prime and after a short delay were asked to complete a "Twenty statements test" (Kuhn and McPartland, 1954) in which they had to write down twenty self-descriptions beginning "I am . . .". In the first experiment the prime for private self asked subjects to think about. "What makes you different from your family and friends? What do you expect yourself to do?". A prime for collective self asked them to think of: "What have you in common with your family and friends? What do they expect you to do?". Responses were classified as reflecting idiocentric (traits, etc.) or social (common fate categories) self-descriptions.

It was proposed that, if the two types of self are represented in separate baskets, the two primes would result in selective accessing of the relevant, more than the irrelevant self. Further, it was argued that "the probability of someone retrieving a particular type of self-cognition, given that a similar type was previously retrieved, should be greater than if a different type of self-cognition had been previously retrieved" (Trafimow *et al.*, 1991, p. 650).

The results of the first experiment revealed that the overall number of social self-descriptions was very low. Compared with non-Chinese participants and subjects in the private prime condition, Chinese subjects (from a collectivist culture) and subjects in the collective prime condition, respectively, mentioned a higher proportion of social self-descriptions. More importantly for the "two baskets" hypothesis, analysis of conditional probabilities revealed that social self-descriptions tended to follow other social self-descriptions (rather than individual self-descriptions) at a higher than chance rate.

In the second experiment, the prime was more indirect. Subjects read a story about a warrior who appointed a general, either to increase his personal glory and power (private prime), or for the glory of his family (collective prime). The results were consistent with the first experiment. Trafimow *et al.* concluded that if a person happens to be thinking about a collective self-image (either spontaneously or as a result of a prime), other collective self-images also become more accessible than if they happen to have been thinking about a private self-image. In sum, Trafimow *et al.* adopt a basic structural model of self.

Hierarchical process model

Social identity theory and self-categorization theory both describe personal and social identifications as being *functionally* antagonistic. Early writings on social identity (e.g. Turner and Giles, 1981; Hogg and Abrams, 1988) described social and personal identity broadly as consisting of category memberships and traits, respectively. However, more recently (e.g. Abrams and Hogg, 1990a), particularly with the development of self-categorization theory (Turner *et al.*, 1987), this view has been modified and developed; personal and social identities are representations of self at different levels of abstraction relative to both one another and the social frame of reference.

Theoretically, only one self-image can be salient at any particular time. There is no requirement to specify the content of personal and social identifications, and indeed it is impossible to do so without knowledge of the subjective context (e.g. contrasting categories). It is, however, possible to specify the conditions under which different self-images will be made salient, and the kinds of information that might determine the central or criterial attributes of different category memberships. In fact, one of the theoretical advantages of the social identity approach is that apparent inconsistencies in individuals' behaviour can be interpreted as reflecting activation of different self-images framed by different social comparisons (Turner *et al.*, 1994).

The social identity approach thus assumes that the self is *potentially* multi-levelled and multi-faceted, but that at any particular moment, the self is a (highly flexible) specific product of a process of comparison (cf. Markus and Nurius, 1986; Fiske and Von Hendy, 1992). It follows that stability of self-conception can emerge from the frequency and richness of particular social comparisons which will affect the relative accessibility of different self-categorizations.

Despite superficial similarities between the social/personal identity distinction and Trafimow *et al.*'s (1991) distinction between private and collective selves, there are some important differences. The Trafimow *et al.* model claims that category labels (in the collective self basket) are more closely associated with one another than with the attributes which describe the categories (which cohere in the private self basket). In other words, the strongest associative connections are horizontal, between self-categorizations.

In contrast, following self-categorization theory, collective selves (social identifications) should not specifically imply one another. Instead, it can be argued, images of collective self should include the attributes associated with the particular categorization which is activated (Abrams, 1993). Thus, if self as "female" is salient, the collective (stereotypical) attributes of females should be more likely to be ascribed to the self. These attributes will appear as traits, behaviours, attitudes, etc. As coded within the Trafimow *et al.* approach, these attributes would, in fact, be indistinguishable from the content of the private self. In other words, the largest number of associative linkages will be vertical, between categorizations and category features (cf. Rosch, 1978). The social identity approach, therefore, posits a process generating varying content arrayed in a hierarchical way, and can be described as a hierarchical process model of self.

Hierarchical structure model

Deaux (1992) suggests an alternative to these two approaches and highlights problems with the assumptions within social identity/self-categorization theory of functional antagonism between personal and social identity. Deaux (1992) and Breakwell (e.g. 1986) have argued that self-images involving both social *and* personal features can be meaningful or salient in a social situation, and that many self-images cannot sensibly be described at a single level of abstraction. According to this view, the self has considerable stability and can usefully be described as a psychological structure. Deaux emphasizes the value of a more sociological perspective (e.g. Stryker, 1987) which suggests that each individual interprets his or her own identities and roles in a unique manner. Thus, for example, being a psychologist can mean different things to different psychologists. In particular, Deaux extends Rosenberg's (1988) hierarchical classification approach, suggesting that self-classifications (be they roles or social categories) correspond to social identity, while self-descriptions in terms of traits correspond to personal features of identity. The traits and categories are each structured hierarchically and traits and categories are linked, but the particular structure is different for each individual. Deaux claims that this analysis is useful when trying to predict attitudes and behaviour since it accepts that meanings of identity can change although the category label may remain constant. Moreover, the chronic accessibility of particular self-images (cf. Higgins and King, 1981) will reflect their vertical position in the hierarchy.

Deaux *et al.* (1995) set out to examine the parameters of social identity among students. Using various sorting procedures they found that there were five types of social identity: personal relationships, vocations/avocations, political affiliations, ethnic/religious groups and stigmatized groups. These differed along various dimensions, providing support for Deaux *et al.*'s view that "all social identities are not the same", and that interchangeability of identities may depend on their proximity in terms of defining dimensions. Deaux *et al* characterize social identity theory as conceiving of all social identifications as "collective and relational". However, their evidence suggested that few social identities were relational and only ethnic, religious, some stigmatized and some political identities were seen as collective. Occupational identities, in contrast, were perceived to be more individualistic.

Mutable Self-Categories: Extending the Self-Stereotyping Hypothesis

It is possible to accommodate the structural accounts of self by characterizing temporal and individual differences in self-conception as arising from variations in the particular social comparisons and particular social frames of reference. If people spend much of their time in stable social environments it is unsurprising that there is a structural stability to their self-conceptions. However, this does not rule out variation in meaning and importance of categories and attributes. For example, the self-categorization "parent" can be subjectively defined equally as a social category or group membership (e.g. at a parent–teachers Association meeting) or as a uniquely individuating aspect of self (e.g. recalling the moment the child was born). Moreover, in many apparently "interpersonal" situations we make reference to a higher level of abstraction of self to provide the context for our behaviour. Pursuing the present example, imagine the parent is faced with a decision as to what his or her child should be bought for Christmas. Personal finances may play a role in the decision, but the question of what kind of present to buy (toys versus flowers) is framed by the social category memberships parent and child. Further, the type of toy and the amount spent are also heavily influenced by normative expectations concerning the responsibilities and interests of the two categories. The fact that most other children are receiving *Power Rangers* exerts strong normative pressure on both parent and child. The parent may even justify not buying Power Ranger toys using subcategorizations ("you don't want to be like those kids. . .", and implicitly, "I don't want to be like those parents"). The point here is that whether a self-categorization is personal or social is determined not by a formal definition of the abstractness of the category, but by the subjective interpretation of its relevant social frame of reference. It follows that the level and content of self-categorizations are not determined by the category assigned to self but by the comparison categories in the particular context. There is evidence that this is true of ingroup and outgroup perceptions (Abrams and Hogg, 1987; Haslam and Turner, 1992; Haslam *et al.*, 1992; Oakes *et al.*, 1994).

A critical difference between structure and process models concerns the presumed stability in the relationship between different components of the self. For example, in the Trafimow model a self-conception is defined a priori as collective, private or public on the basis of its content. Thus college membership is always collective; being an intelligent person is always private. In contrast, a self-categorization approach allows for flexibility in the definition of whether a characteristic is private or collective.

The distinction between categories and attributes may itself be highly mutable (Abrams, 1993). First, a category at one level of abstraction can easily be seen to constitute an attribute in relation to a higher level of abstraction (Bellezza, 1993). Second, if the structure of attributes and categories is itself a product of context, it is not always easy to define a priori which features are categorical and which are attributes. For example, among academic scholars some may have a higher IQ than others; they share a category membership, "scholar", of which intelligence is one attribute. On the other hand, a set of people who categorize themselves as intelligent have formed an organization known as MENSA, and scholarliness may be one of their attributes, as illustrated in Figure 5.1.

If this analogy can be accepted as representative of category–attribute distinctions in general, it follows that collective and private self-conceptions do not have a structure which is definable by content alone. For example, one may be a member of a bridge club who happens to study psychology, or a psychologist who happens to play at a bridge club. Similarly, whether one self-categorizes, for example, as a member of Greenpeace, or England (or neither) for the purposes at hand will determine whether either one's objections to pollution or one's nationality are parts of the collective or private self. As a tourist one may be an English environmentalist who likes walking in mountains; at a global environment conference one might be representative of Greenpeace from England who is particularly concerned with ocean pollutants; at a general social

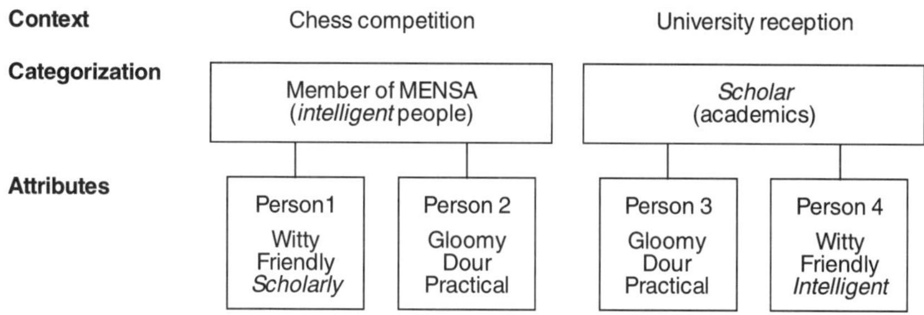

FIG 5.1 Categories and features can be interchangeable.

science conference abroad one could be a psychologist from England concerned with the psychological aspects of environmental issues, and so on.

A first step towards supporting this hierarchical process formulation is to demonstrate the existence of the inductive relationship posited between abstract (category) memberships and exemplars, features or attributes of the categories. Recall that structural models of self assume that summaries or abstractions about the self always result from behavioural exemplars but that, once developed, the abstractions can become functionally independent (e.g. Klein and Loftus, 1993; Trafimow *et al.*, 1991). Such functional independence could also arise, however, if the relationship between abstractions and exemplars was indeterminate, depending more on induction than deduction. This would be entirely consistent with the process described by self-categorization theory as self-stereotyping.

Evidence for self-stereotyping

Categorizations of others imply different attributes and invite different evaluations depending on the relation between that category and one's own (e.g. Abrams and Hogg; 1987, Hogg and Turner, 1985; Oakes *et al.*, 1994). The evidence is consistent with the view that the *self* is implicated in such judgements. However, it remains possible that contrasts between different pairs of categories make different sets of features salient without having any implications for self-conception. The more important evidence, therefore, is whether category salience makes people's self-images more aligned with the ingroup prototype; whether self-stereotyping actually takes place.

Abrams *et al.* (1990) found that when gender was made salient by the mere presence of outgroup members, females endorsed more traditional (stereotypically feminine) values. Abrams *et al.* (1985) found that female school pupils with larger numbers of male siblings (theoretically making their own gender more salient) opted for more traditional school subjects. Hogg and Turner (1987) manipulated gender salience in the context of a discussion group. When differences of opinion corresponded to gender differences, subjects endorsed self-descriptive (semantic differential) items that were more own-gender stereotypic. Other explorations of gender/sexuality-related self-stereotyping have yielded mixed results (Hardie and McMurray, 1992; Lorenzi-Cioldi, 1991; Simon *et al.*, 1991), providing little clear evidence that self-stereotyping arises in free self-descriptions in the absence of explicit categorizations.

Simon and Hamilton (1994) examined the impact of relative group size and group status on self-stereotyping. In one experiment subjects viewed some pictures, were asked to define themselves as either introvert or extrovert, and were then told that their artistic preferences were held by either a majority or minority of other people, and that artistic preferences were correlated with being either an introvert or an extrovert. Subjects then rated themselves on six rating scales tapping the introversion–extroversion dimension, rated their similarity to other ingroup members on those dimensions, and then similarity among ingroup and among outgroup members. As predicted, minority group members self-stereotyped more than majority members, but did not differ in the extent to which they saw themselves as belonging to a psychological group. In the second experiment, subjects were additionally told that their preferred painter was either distinguished or not (high versus low status). Self-stereotyping was increased for high relative to low status minority (but not majority) ingroup. Self-stereotyping appeared to be correlated with self-categorization (measured as self-reported psychological groupness) but it was not possible to decide which variable mediated the other.

While Simon and Hamilton's results at first seem impressive there is a drawback in their method. Specifically, because they required subjects to categorize themselves explicitly as introverted or extroverted, it is possible that the self-stereotyping reflected varying degrees of activation of a pre-existing self-schema. That is, people who were schematically "introverted" judged themselves and others more in terms of introversion as that schema was made more salient. Therefore, it is difficult to be sure whether the experiments demonstrated the application of a stereotype to self, or simply the increased accessibility of pre-existing self-knowledge. Moreover, while the experiments demonstrated variation in the intensity of self-stereotyping, together with some motivated biases, they did not demonstrate that it was possible to induce self-stereotyping in an experimenter-determined direction.

In sum, there is reasonably good indirect evidence consistent with self-stereotyping. Some of the available data concern contextual influences on judgements of ingroups and outgroups where the judgements of outgroups alter according to the relevant ingroup, and vice versa (Abrams and Hogg, 1987; Haslam and Turner, 1992; Haslam *et al.*, 1992). Other evidence reveals that factors affecting the salience of pre-existing category memberships do affect the amount of self-ascribed category-consistent features. However, there is a dearth of evidence supporting the possibility of qualitative changes in self-perception and not much evidence against the argument that the self is a reference point with relatively stable content and evaluation.

Collective and Private Selves Revisited

A self-categorization explanation for Trafimow *et al.*'s (1991) findings could be that in the collective prime condition, the clustering of self-descriptions in terms of social category memberships reflects the use of a frame of reference at a higher level of abstraction (e.g. American, or possibly human) than the self-descriptive categories listed by subjects (e.g. son, student). This is particularly likely given that the collective prime asked subjects to think about the attributes they had in common with their family. Judgement of similarity inevitably involves contrast with some alternative (Turner *et al*, 1987). Family members are more likely to share distinctive category memberships (e.g. ethnicity, religion, area of residence) than traits. The self-descriptions generated therefore contained as *attributes* the social categories which are made accessible. In contrast, when subjects were asked to think about ways they differed from their family they generated individuating attributes. The data, therefore, can be interpreted as showing that the same category (family) can be used to generate different features depending on the level of abstraction at which subjects consider it. In other words, subjects categorized themselves at different levels of abstraction in the two conditions.* This interpretation assumes that the primary linkages in the self-system are vertical (from category to attribute) rather than horizontal (from attribute to attribute, or category to category).

If this idea is correct, it should be possible to use a similar procedure to affect stereotype *specific* content in self-descriptions (Abrams, 1993). In some experiments conducted in the USA and England (Abrams *et al.*, in preparation), we obtained convergent evidence for this self-stereotyping interpretation. In a preliminary empirical test of our interpretation of the Trafimow *et al.* (1991) results, we (Abrams *et al.*, 1992) added a further condition to their design. Subjects either thought about animals (a control prime), ways they differed from their family (private self-prime from the Trafimow study) or about ways their family differed from other families. We hypothesized that this third prime would bring to mind category memberships because of a process of social differentiation rather than a focus on similarities. Moreover, we believed that this explicitly contrastive collective prime would result in subjects sampling a larger number of social categories than the standard collective prime. Finally, in line with our vertical linkage model and in contrast with the structural two-baskets model, we hypothesized that social self-descriptions should be more strongly associated with "private" self-descriptions than with each other.

* It is possible to offer some alternative interpretations of the Trafimow *et al.* data. First, the results may reflect some kind of incidental schematic thinking which bears no relation to the self-concept. Second, individuals may be able to think about society in different ways (e.g. in terms of groups and roles versus individuals and behaviours), and the fact that they write down several social category memberships in succession may reflect a processing choice rather than a cognitive structure.

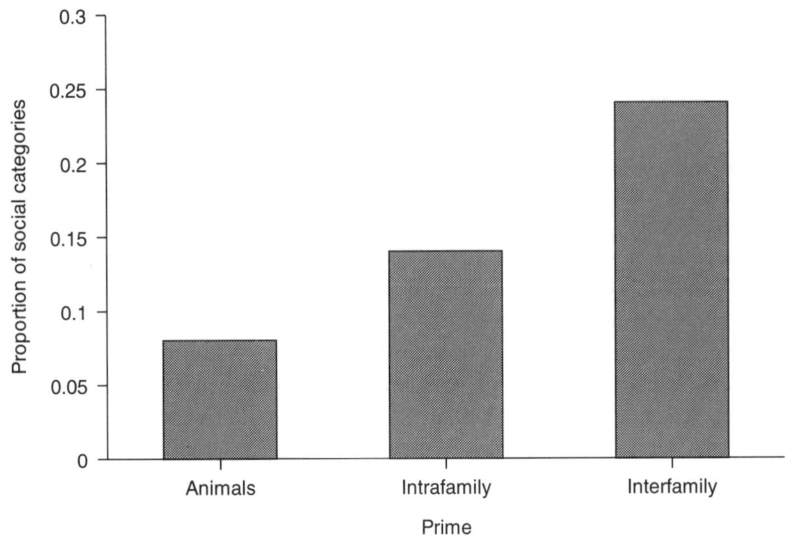

FIG 5.2 Social and personal self-descriptions. Data collected at the University of Illinois, 1992, with Bill Waterman and Wing Tung Au.

The results depicted in Figure 5.2, above, revealed that making the intercategory comparisons between own and other families more explicit did, as predicted, increase the use of "collective" self-descriptions. In addition, conditional probability analyses confirmed our prediction of vertical rather than horizontal linkages.

In a further study (Abrams *et al.*, in preparation) we explored this vertical-linkage idea more directly. We reasoned that priming particular categorizations should result in increased association between self and category-relevant attributes relative to category irrelevant attributes, i.e. we considered that self-stereotyping should be evident. Subjects considered either what they had in common with their family (Trafimow collective prime) or a target-specific collective prime, "think about the difference between the British and Italians". Unlike the previous studies we did not require subjects to write twenty statements, but simply as many as they could up to a limit of twenty. We predicted that this specific collective prime would result in more social self-descriptions but, more importantly, that these would be specifically relevant to the differences between the British and Italians. In order to determine this, we asked subjects to go back over their self-descriptions and indicate any that were stereotypically British.

The results supported our vertical linkage hypothesis in several respects. First the collective prime resulted in more private and social self-descriptions,

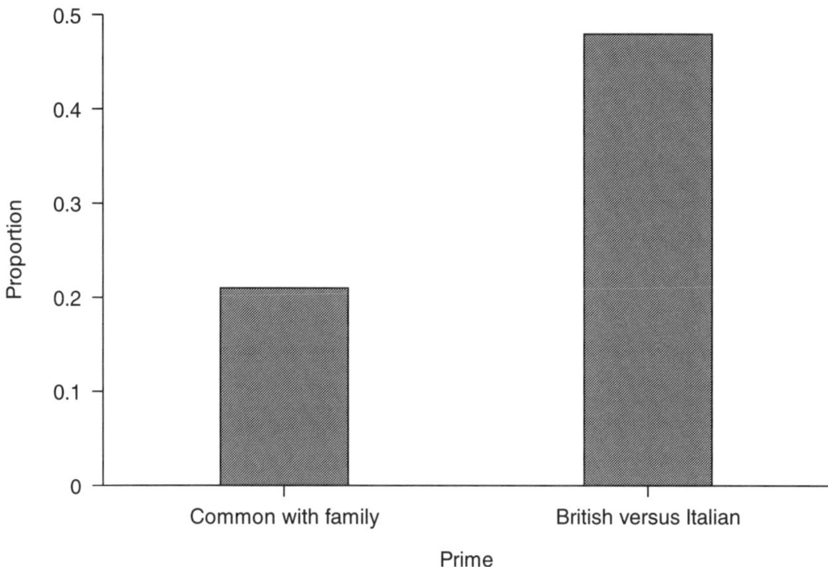

Fig 5.3 Proportion of stereotypically British self-ascribed traits. Data collected at the University of Kent, 1993, with Claire Mallett.

suggesting that the concrete categorization made it easier for subjects to retrieve attributes. Second, the specific collective prime did result in a higher proportion of British–Italian relevant self-descriptions and, crucially, these were at the level of traits rather than categories, as can be seen in Figure 5.3. Thus, the prime resulted in self-stereotyping as British relative to the standard collective prime. Third, as in the previous study, social self-descriptions were associated more strongly with "private" self-descriptions than with one another. When the results from our studies are laid over those of Trafimow *et al.* (see Figure 5.4) it appears that we have two very similar sets of data from two experiments conducted in different countries. Both Trafimow *et al.* and we find that I–I (trait followed by trait) pairings are more likely than I–S (trait followed by category) pairings. However, whereas Trafimow *et al.* find S–S to be more likely than S–I, we find the reverse. Since our first experiment was conducted at the same university and using the same subject population as Trafimow *et al.*, we are unsure as to the reasons for the differences. However, our data are consistent with the vertical structure we posited, and also with findings by Reid and Deaux (submitted).

These results seem to provide support for the view that the self is mutable and flexible. We are currently engaging in further research to see whether priming categories at different levels of abstraction results in different self-descriptions in terms of subcategories or traits.

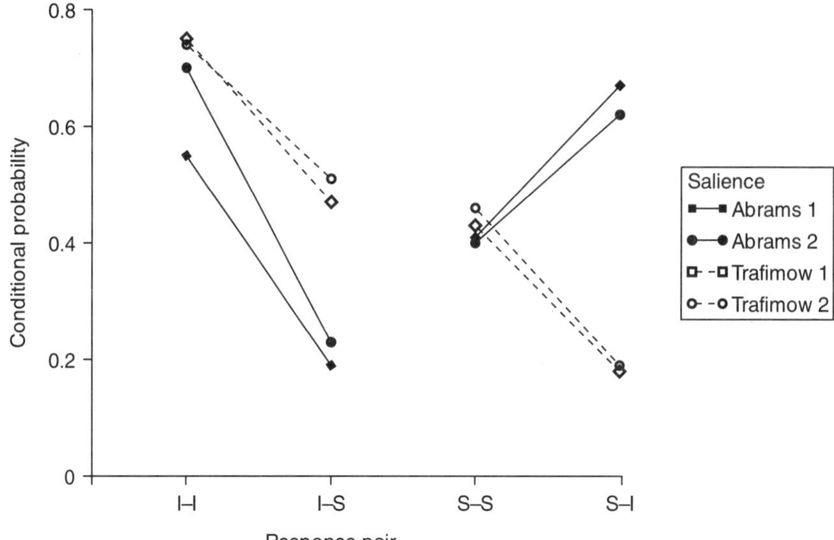

FIG 5.4 Conditional probability analysis of social and idiocentric self-descriptions: Comparisons of Abrams *et al.* (in preparation) and Trafimow *et al.* (1991) data. I, idiocentric self-description; S, social self-description. Data included only if Ss produce more than 2S. Abrams, $n = 41$; Trafimow *et al.*, $n = 37$.

Self-Process and Self-Regulation

We conclude from these studies that the self is indeed affected by the categorizations people use within particular contexts, and that the content of self is somewhat flexible in response to changes in categorizations. This conclusion is consistent with a "process" model of self. However, it would be rash to abandon structure models altogether. Thousands of studies of personality attest to the fact that there is continuity and stability in self-descriptions, and that these relate in predictable ways to behaviour. Moreover, there is a body of literature illustrating that people behave strategically (e.g. Batson, 1994), that people have generalized evaluations of themselves (Rosenberg, 1988) as well as more specific self-evaluations (e.g. Crocker *et al.*, 1994), and that there is some tendency to balance deficits and credits across different content areas of the self-system (Tesser and Cornell, 1991). Therefore, it seems useful to build some bridges between self-categorization theory and other approaches to individual psychological functioning.

One possibility is that the categorization processes determining the salience of self-images function at one level and the decision-making, attention-full processes involved in novel behaviour, planning, and consideration of outcome alternatives, operate at another. A salient categorization may imply a self-stereotype, but as one friend once remarked, "just because I'm American, doesn't mean I have to eat hamburgers!". The crux of the problem is that, while in principle the self can be defined in many different ways, it is in practice harder to offload the baggage of everyday life; roles, obligations, rituals, routines and material needs all have their own trajectories and momentum (Abrams, 1990; 1992). We are aware of these even when (perhaps especially when) they are at odds with one another or with our ideal self-images (Higgins, 1987).

To varying degrees it may be possible for people to select whether and when to adopt or reject the norms of a self-category. This entails considering alternative norms, and alternative categories (Markus and Nurius, 1986; Vorauer and Ross, 1993), a possibility which is not encompassed in self-categorization theory, because it conceives of the self as being a product of social categorizations, not as acting upon them.

Social self-regulation

Recently I outlined a social self-regulation model which attempts to embody the content-driving categorization process and the integrative meaning-providing selection process (Abrams, 1992, 1994). Originally intended to integrate self-attention theory with social identity theory (Abrams, 1990), the model more broadly sets some parameters around the possible linkages between self-categorization and behaviour. A distinction is made between salience of a self-image and attention devoted to regulating behaviour. A salient self-image provides a framework and the content for judgement and action. The self-image may be contextually determined and/or may comprise memories, experiences or stereotypes which have been accessed previously. Behavioural choices are then made with reference to a broader subjective context of endpoints, goals or motives (Fiske and Neuberg, 1990). Attention is generally required to respond in a way that satisfies these goals in relation to the normative implications of self-categorization. Theoretically, salience is determined in the manner specified by self-categorization theory and attention serves to regulate behaviour in the manner specified by self-attention theory (e.g. Carver, 1979).

The basic proposition is that salient categorization provides a self-definition, the implications of which can then be considered in the light of other self-relevant information. Unlike perceptions and judgements, behaviour is irreversible; it is necessarily woven into a temporally extended scenario or context. For this reason the behavioural implications of a self-image often need to be assessed in relation to broader concerns. It is proposed that this is a relatively conscious, attention-full process. Specifically, a superordinate "supervisory attention-full system" (Shallice, 1988) is responsible for this somewhat complex interpretive process and sets behavioural targets. The system mediates between higher level objectives such as ideological, strategic, moral concerns, and the immediate implications of salient self-images. As a result, the behaviours are directed and systematic but may not always correspond directly to stereotypical norms.

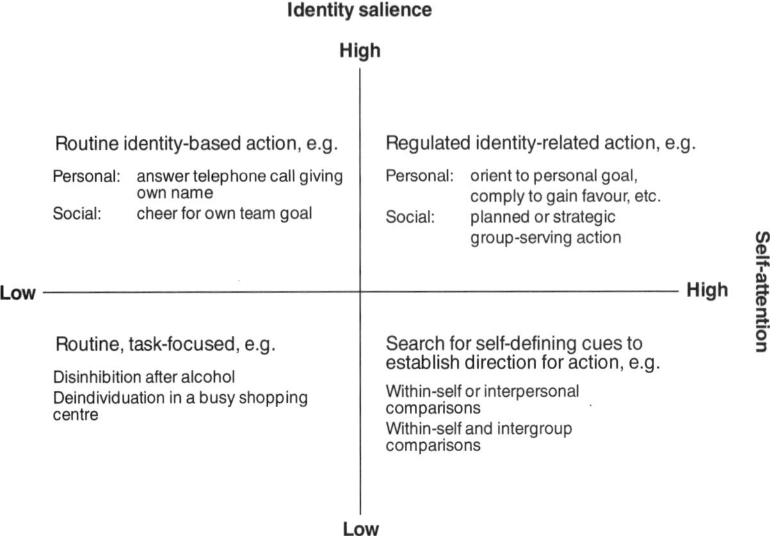

FIG 5.5 Social self-regulation.

The model, depicted in Figure 5.5, can be characterized as being composed of two continua: identity salience (low to high) and self-attention (low to high). For descriptive purposes it is useful to distinguish between different levels of self-categorization when discussing identity salience. Thus, within each quadrant one can describe (at least) the likely outcome for social and personal identifications.

When no self-image is salient and self-attention is low, behaviour is likely to be disinhibited, deindividuated and most likely routinized or task-focused. This kind of situation is represented by the deindividuation theory account of group behaviour (Diener, 1980; Reicher, 1984). If self-attention is increased it is likely to be because the person is searching for self-defining cues, perhaps to self-categorize and/or to locate an appropriate behavioural goal. For example, on arrival at an overseas airport passengers might start looking for signs that classify arriving passengers to determine which passport control exit they should use.

When personal features of identity are salient, behaviour will be routinely self-relevant, such as answering the telephone with one's name. Self-attention is increased when a non-routine or planned response is required in a situation, perhaps when considering what to wear at a dinner party, or trying to argue one's case at a meeting, contemplate one's feelings about something, or describe symptoms to a doctor. Some theories of conformity assume that behavioural compliance within groups results from self-regulation of behaviour in terms of personal self-presentational goals. These include a desire to be liked by other ingroup members (see Carver and Humphries, 1981; Froming and Carver, 1981; Prentice-Dunn and Rogers, 1989).

When social identifications are salient there may be occasions when ingroup norms are so clear and well-learned that people respond in a habitual or routine manner. For example, when watching a sports match, supporters of the home team all tend to cheer at the same time when that team scores a goal. This is likely to be unreflective and regulated only at a very low level. This situation corresponds closely to Turner *et al.*'s (1987) conception of depersonalization. In much of the social identity literature, social categorizations are depicted as having this relatively direct effect on behaviour.

Finally, there are occasions when social identity is salient but behavioural standards are ambiguous, problematic, non-achievable, or conflict with alternative demands. Under these circumstances, and when other factors induce it, self-attention will increase in order to regulate action. The supervisory system is particularly likely to be required when novel intergroup situations arise, or when behaviour has wider implications. Three instances where regulation is required are those involving intergroup turn-taking, historical conflict, and novel relations. For example, negotiators for management and unions have to moderate their actions in the context of a series of meetings, so each must plan ahead to deal with both their group's interests and the negotiating style of their counterpart (Stephenson, 1981; Kramer *et al.*, 1993). Even in the case of historical intergroup conflicts and aggression (e.g. civil wars in Yugoslavia) combatants need to decide about when and how to aggress. It is not possible to be aggressive continuously, so the person must orientate towards a plan of action that meets both normative and pragmatic requirements (including self-image preservation, survival, etc.). Finally, when people find themselves thrust into a new category with novel behavioural choices (e.g. in a minimal group situation), conscious effort is required to work out the implications of those choices for self.

There are several sources of evidence for the distinction between levels of attentional regulation in the context of a salient social identity. First, as evidence of the effects of salience without attention, it does appear that there are some automatic ingroup biases in many situations (Perdue *et al.*, 1990; Turner, 1991), and that increasing salience of social identity increases intergroup differentiation (Reicher, 1984; Spears *et al.*, 1990). However, it is likely that relatively little intergroup behaviour is unconscious or automatic (cf. Bargh, 1992; Jacoby, 1991). Providing evidence of the role of high salience with attention, Kakimoto (1994) found that in minimal group situations, perceptual differentiation between ingroup and outgroup categories is relatively unconscious, but behavioural responses such as reward allocations are under relatively conscious control (Kakimoto and Abrams, 1994). When social identity is salient, experimentally manipulated levels of self-attention affect the extremity and consistency of group-serving behaviour (Abrams, 1985; Hong and Harrod, 1988). There is also evidence that individuals adopt different standards or goals in expressing ingroup membership (Chin and McClintock, 1993; Mummendey and Schreiber, 1983; Mummenday *et al.*, 1992; Platow *et al.*, 1990). Furthermore, it appears that when individuals holding different standards in intergroup contexts are made more self-attentive they adhere to those standards more closely (Abrams, 1985, 1990; Abrams and Brown, 1989, 1992; Fenigstein and Abrams, 1993; Kernis *et al.*, 1988). Consistent with the idea of a "mutable self", and with the view that private psychological processes can nonetheless involve collective aspects of self, many of these studies indicated that attention to standards represented by the supposedly "private" self was responsible for these effects.

The advantage of adopting a self-attention X identity salience formulation is that it retains the psychological basis for collective behaviour (self-categorization and social identification), while also allowing for a degree of individual agency and psychological continuity across time and situations. The model encompasses the non-reductionist ambition of allowing the uniformity and co-ordination of collective action, whilst also allowing individuality and diversity in the particular enactment and manifestation of identity.

Expanding the conception of identity

Reid and Deaux (submitted) propose that individuals experience social identity as enduring relatively concrete, what can be termed "role-based", self-images restricted to a limited set of cognitive structures. The evidence for this seems strong, and appears to be at odds with self-categorization theory's emphasis on social identity, as what can be termed abstracted "conceptual" self-images. Role-based self-images appear to be well developed (e.g. one's occupation), have strong normative elements (e.g. one's status *vis à vis* occupants of other roles) and involve personal interpretations of value, meaning, performance styles and rituals (e.g. one's ways of enacting the roles). They are likely to involve specific relationships with occupants of other roles. Conceptual self-images are self-categorizations as a member of a particular social category in relation to a particular other category and/or task. They are likely to be specific, transient, mutable, even hypothetical. They involve relationships with others defined primarily in conceptual terms.

Reid and Deaux (submitted) concur with the view that social and personal features of identity are vertically connected, and also agree with some of the criticisms of the two-basket theory. However, they regard their evidence as being consistent with the existence of a stable and evolving self-structure and not with a mutable self. In their "integration model", Reid and Deaux retain the idea of a fixed relationship between categories and attributes. It may well be that most of the time this does provide a good description of most people's identity. However, it remains a structure model, and thus may be somewhat defeated by within-individual variations in behaviour as well as by variations in mass behaviour. These may well be better dealt with using a self-categorization and social identity perspective.

Role-based self-images may be on the threshold between social and personal identity. If this is so, they may be particularly vulnerable to contextual shifts which affect the relative importance of normative versus personal standards and goals. For example, at a wedding reception a male guest might be called upon to act as husband, cousin, brother, uncle, son, friend, best man, etc. in relation to particular other guests. In order to accomplish this it seems likely that his role-based self-images would have to be especially well represented in memory and contain both abstracted trait information (e.g. whether he has a good relationship with the other person) and behavioural exemplars (e.g. particular activities they have shared). Equally, as best man, he must follow the precisely prescribed rituals associated with the role. If Deaux *et al.* (1995) are correct in their depiction of social identity, much day to day self-regulation is likely to involve co-ordinating behaviourally among our role-based self-images. The role-based images sustain routinized behavioural objectives (e.g. a parent remembers to collect his or her child from school at the same time each day) and provide a longer term reference context for conceptual self-images.

Conceptual self-images are likely to arise in the course of role-related events. For example, at the wedding reception a discussion about an international soccer tournament may activate a self-categorization in terms of nationality with an associated norm to support ingroup competitors. If the discussants turn out to be from different countries (e.g. England and Scotland) they may engage in mutually derisive banter about their opposing teams. This illustration implies that conceptual selves might flicker in and out of consciousness as external cues make them more or less meaningful. Another situation which may give rise to a rapid succession of self-conceptualizations might be that of watching the television news, which frequently sets out stories in terms of different groups (victim/helper, criminal/police, left-wing/right-wing). Even the weather forecast involves transitory comparisons between different parts of a country.

An important point to be made about conceptual selves is that although they may be fleeting and trivial, they are also capable of becoming enduring and central to action. Lifton (1994) makes a similar point in discussing the protean self. In circumstances such as war, self-categorizations provide a basis for social order by specifying the normative framework or standards for behaviour. The fact that we are capable of conceptualizing ourselves so flexibly means that we can act as representatives of social categories and groups in ways that seem completely contradictory with our other roles and memberships. When inequalities are characterized in terms of social categories, the category memberships can become an overriding context for behaviour (Tajfel, 1981). For example, despite the many overlapping features and considerable intermarriage of Hutus and Tutsis, membership of one category is a sufficient basis to warrant murdering or being murdered by the other, as illustrated by the following excerpts.

> In pre-colonial times the Tutsi and the Hutu lived in relative peace, although the Tutsi were an elite and the Hutu a peasant class. The Germans took advantage of this relationship by appointing Tutsi as their representatives in Rwanda-Urundi. . .The Belgians introduced a system of identity cards showing a person's ethnic group, a system which continues to this day
>
> (Martin Bright, The Guardian, May 10th 1994)

> The cards are the only definitive proof of ethnic origin; though the archetypal Tutsi is taller and slimmer than his Hutu neighbour and has higher cheekbones and a bonier nose, years of intermarriage have blurred the distinction. The cards are a brutal form of passport: they gain the bearer access either to the next checkpoint or into a nearby ditch full of corpses
>
> (Mark Huband, The Observer, May 22nd 1994).

When people discover that they share a common disadvantage they have a basis for mobilizing to change their collective situation (Klandermans, 1989), and there is clear evidence that involvement reflects the strength with which people identify with a common social category (Abrams, 1990, 1992; Kelly, 1994). Protest can even arise when deprivation is experienced on behalf of others (Tougas and Veilleux, 1990). Moreover, there are many instances where people are willing to sacrifice personal gains for collective aims (e.g. Abrams and Emler, 1992; Crosby *et al.*, 1993). Yet, after the football match, the riot, or the battle, people do resume role-based activities; they focus on enduring tasks, goals and responsibilities. Tajfel made us aware of the pervasiveness and power of intergroup relations in human social life, and of the importance of understanding the social psychological mediation of those relations. Although he made the important distinction between personal and social identity, he did not fully explore how the two might be connected.

Psychological transitions between role-based and conceptual selves probably require considerable conscious effort and control. Given the pervasiveness of the self as an organizer and motivator for behaviour, this chapter has proposed that the self is best thought of in terms of processes rather than specific content, and that a superordinate regulatory process integrates across identifications. A fruitful avenue for future research will be the factors that sustain the normative power of conceptual self-images through time and across roles.

References

Abrams, D. (1985). Focus of attention in minimal intergroup discrimination. *British Journal of Social Psychology*, **24**, 65–74.

Abrams, D. (1989). Differential association: Social developments in gender and social identity in adolescence. In S. Skevington and D. Baker (Eds), *The social identity of women*. London: Sage

Abrams, D. (1990). How do group members regulate their behaviour? An integration of social identity and self-awareness theories. In D. Abrams and M. A. Hogg (Eds), *Social identity theory: Constructive and critical advances*. London and New York: Harvester Wheatsheaf and Springer Verlag, pp. 89–112.

Abrams, D. (1992). Processes of social identification. In G. Breakwell (Ed), *Social psychology of identity and the self-concept*. San Diego: Academic Press, pp. 57–99.

Abrams, D. (1993). From social identity to action. "British Invited Speaker" presentation, British Psychological Society, Social Psychology Section conference, Oxford, September.

Abrams, D. (1994). Social self-regulation. *Personality and Social Psychology Bulletin*, **20**, 273–483.

Abrams, D., Au, W., Waterman, W., Garst, J., and Mallett, C. (in preparation). The two baskets and one process views of self: three experiments on self-stereotyping (University of Kent).

Abrams, D., and Brown, R. J. (1989). Self-consciousness and social identity: Self-regulation as a group member. *Social Psychology Quarterly*, **52**, 311–318.

Abrams, D., and Emler, N. P. (1992). Self-denial as a paradox of political and regional identity: Findings from a study of 16- and 18-year olds. *European Journal of Social Psychology*, **22**, 279–295.

Abrams, D., and Hogg, M. A. (1987). Language attitudes, frames of reference and social identity: A Scottish dimension. *Journal of Language and Social Psychology*, **6**, 201–213.

Abrams, D., and Hogg, M. A. (1988). Comments on the motivational status of self-esteem in social identity and intergroup discrimination. *European Journal of Social Psychology*, **18**, 317–334.

Abrams, D., and Hogg, M. A. (1990a). An introduction to the social identity approach. In D. Abrams and M. A. Hogg (Eds), (1990). *Social identity theory: Constructive and critical advances*. London and New York: Harvester Wheatsheaf and Springer Verlag, pp. 1–9.

Abrams, D. and Hogg, M. A. (1990b). Social identification, self-categorization, and social influence. In W. Stroebe and M. Hewstone (Eds), *European Review of social psychology*, Vol. 1. Chichester, UK: John Wiley and Sons, pp. 195–228.

Abrams, D., Sparkes, K., and Hogg, M. A. (1985). Gender salience and social identity: the impact of sex of siblings on educational and occupational aspirations. *British Journal of Educational Psychology*, **55**, 224–232.

Abrams, D., Thomas, J., and Hogg, M. A. (1990). Numerical distinctiveness, social identity and gender salience. *British Journal of Social Psychology*, **29**, 87–92.

Abrams, D, Waterman, W., and Au, W. T. (1992). Testing a self-categorization explanation of the two-basket theory of self. (Unpublished manuscript, University of Illinois).

Andersen, S. M., and Klatzky, R. L. (1987). Traits and social stereotypes: Levels of categorization in person perception. *Journal of Personality and Social Psychology*, **53**, 235–246.

Bargh, J. A. (1992). The ecology of automaticity: Toward establishing the conditions needed to produce automatic processing effects. *American Journal of Psychology*, **105**, 181–199.

Batson, C. D. (1994). Why act for the public good? Four answers. *Personality and Social Psychology Bulletin*, **20**, 603–610.

Baumeister, R. F. (1987). How the self became a problem. A psychological review of historical research. *Journal of Personality and Social Psychology*, **52**, 163–176.

Bellezza, F. S. (1984). The self as a mnemonic device: The role of internal cues. *Journal of Personality and Social Psychology*, **47**, 506–516.

Bellezza, F. S. (1993). Does "perplexing" describe the self-reference effect? Yes! In T. K. Srull and R. S. Wyer Jr. (Eds), *The mental representation of trait and autobiographical knowledge about the self: Advances in social cognition*. Vol. V. Hillsdale, N. J.: Lawrence Erlbaum Associates, pp. 51–60.

Breakwell, G. (1986). *Coping with threatened identities*. London: Methuen.

Breckler, S., and Greenwald, A. (1986). Motivational facets of the self. In R. Sorrentino and T. Higgins (Eds), *Handbook of motivation and cognition*. New York: Guildford Press, pp. 145–164.

Brown, R. J., and Williams, J. A. (1984). Group identification: The same thing to all people? *Human Relations*, **37**, 547–564.

Buss, A. H. (1980). *Self-consciousness and social anxiety*. Glencoe: Free Press.

Cantor, N. (1990). From thought to behavior: "Having" and "doing" in the study of personality and cognition. *American Psychologist*, **45**, 735–750.

Carver, C. S. (1979). A cybernetic model of self-attention processes. *Journal of Personality and Social Psychology*, **37**, 1251–1281.

Carver, C. S., and Humphries, C. (1981). Havana daydreaming: A study of self-consciousness and the negative reference group among Cuban Americans. *Journal of Personality and Social Psychology*, **40**, 545–552.

Cheek, J. M., and Briggs, S. R. (1982). Self-consciousness and aspects of identity. *Journal of Research in Personality*, **16**, 401–408.

Chin, M. G., and McClintock, C. G. (1993). The effects of intergroup discrimination and social values on level of self-esteem in the minimal group paradigm. *European Journal of Social Psychology*, **23**, 63–76.

Condor S. G. (1986). Sex role beliefs and "traditional" women: Feminist and intergroup perspectives. In S. Wilkinson (Ed), *Feminist social psychology*. Milton Keynes: Open University Press.

Crocker, J.,and Luhtanen, R. (1990). Collective self-esteem and ingroup bias. *Journal of Personality and Social Psychology*, **58**, 60–67.

Crocker, J, Luhtanen, R., Blaine, B., and Broadnax, S. (1994). Collective self-esteem and psychological well-being among white, black, and Asian college students. *Personality and Social Psychology Bulletin*, **20**, 503–512.

Crosby, F., Cordova, D., and Jaskar, K. (1993). On the failure to see oneself as disadvantaged: cognitive and emotional components. In M. A. Hogg and D. Abrams (Eds), *Group motivation: Social psychological perspectives*. London: Harvester Wheatsheaf.

Deaux, K. (1992). Personalizing identity and socializing self. In G. Breakwell (Ed)., *Social psychology of identity and the self-concept*. San Diego: Academic Press, pp. 9–34.

Deaux, K., Reid, A., Mizrahi, K., and Ethier, K. A. (1995). Parameters of social identity. *Journal of Personality and Social Psychology*, **68**, 280–291.

Diener, E. (1980). Deindividuation: The absence of self-awareness and self-regulation in group members. In P. B. Paulus (Ed), *Psychology of group influence*. Hillsdale, NJ: Erlbaum.

Fenigstein, A., and Abrams, D. (1993). Self-attention and the egocentric assumption of shared perspectives. *Journal of Experimental Social Psychology*, **29**, 287–303.

Fenigstein, A., Scheier, M. F., and Buss, A. H. (1975). Public and private self-consciousness: Assessment and theory. *Journal of Consulting and Clinical Psychology*, **43**, 522–527.

Fiske, S. T., and Neuberg, S. L. (1990). A continuum of impression formation, from category-based to individuating processes: Influences of information and motivation on attention and interpretation. In M. P. Zanna (Ed), *Advances in experimental social psychology*, Vol. 23. New York: Academic Press, pp. 1–74.

Fiske, S. T., and Von Hendy, H. M. (1992). Personality feedback and situational norms can control stereotyping processes. *Journal of Personality and Social Psychology*, **62**, 577–596.

Froming, W. J., and Carver, C. S. (1981). Divergent influences of private and public self-consciousness in a compliance paradigm. *Journal of Research in Personality*, **15**, 159–171.

Greenwald, A. G., and Pratkanis, A. R. (1984). "The self". In R. S. Wyer and T. K. Srull (Eds), *Handbook of social cognition*, Vol. 3. Hillsdale, NJ: Erlbaum, pp. 129–178.

Hamilton, D. L. (1989). Understanding impression formation: What has memory research contributed? In P. R. Solomon, G. R. Goethals, C. M. Kelley and B. R. Stephans (Eds), *Memory: Interdisciplinary approaches*. New York: Springer-Verlag, pp. 221–242.

Hardie, E. A., and McMurray, N. E. (1992). Self-stereotyping, sex role ideology, and menstrual attitudes: a social identity approach. *Sex Roles*, **27**, 17–37.

Haslam, S. A., and Turner, J. C. (1992). Context-dependent variation in social stereotyping 2: The relationship between frame of reference, self-categorization and accentuation. *European Journal of Social Psychology*, **22,** 251–278.

Haslam, S. A., Turner, J. C., Oakes, P. J., McGarty, C., and Hayes, B. K. (1992). Context-dependent variation in social stereotyping 1: The effects of intergroup relations as mediated by social change and frame of reference. *European Journal of Social Psychology*, **22**, 3–20.

Higgins, E. T. (1987). Self-discrepancy: A theory relating self and affect. *Psychological Review*, **94**, 319–340.

Higgins, E. T., and King G. A. (1981). Accessibility of social constructs: Information processing consequences of individual and contextual variability. In N. Cantor and J. F. Kihlstrom (Eds), *Personality, cognition, and social interaction*. Hillsdale, NJ: Erlbaum,. pp. 69–122.

Hogg, M. A., and Abrams, D. (1988). *Social identifications: A social psychology of intergroup relations and group processes*. London: Routledge.

Hogg, M. A. and Abrams, D. (1990). Social motivation, self-esteem and social identity. In D. Abrams and M. A. Hogg (Eds), *Social identity theory: Constructive and critical advances*. London and New York: Harvester Wheatsheaf and Springer Verlag.

Hogg, M. A. and Abrams, D. (1993). Towards a single-process uncertainty-reduction model of social motivation in groups. In M. A. Hogg and D. Abrams (Eds), *Group motivation: Social psychological perspectives*. London: Harvester Wheatsheaf.

Hogg, M. A. and Turner, J. C. (1985). Interpersonal attraction, social identification and psychological group formation. *European Journal of Social Psychology*, **15**, 51–66.

Hogg, M. A., and Turner, J. C. (1987). Intergroup behaviour, self-stereotyping and the salience of social categories. *British Journal of Social Psychology*, **26**, 325–340.

Hong, O. P., and Harrod, W. J. (1988). The role of reasons in the ingroup bias phenomenon. *European Journal of Social Psychology*, **18**, 537–545.

Jacoby, L. L. (1991). A process dissociation framework: Separating automatic from intentional uses of memory. *Journal of Memory and Language*, **30**, 513–541.

Judd, C. M., and Park, B. (1988). Outgroup homogeneity: Judgements of variability at the individual and group levels. *Journal of Personality and Social Psychology*, **54**, 778–788.

Kahneman, D., and Miller, D. T. (1986). Norm theory: Comparing reality to its alternatives. *Psychological Review*, **93**, 136–153.

Kakimoto, T. (1994). *Social categorization, distraction, and intergroup discrimination*. Unpublished doctoral dissertation, University of Kent at Canterbury, UK.

Kakimoto, T., and Abrams, D. (1994). Measurement of the processes in intergroup discrimination. Paper presented at the 23rd International Congress of Applied Psychology.

Keenan, J. M. (1993). An exemplar model can explain Klein and Loftus's results. In T. K. Srull and R. S. Wyer Jr. (Eds), *The mental representation of trait and autobiographical knowledge about the self: Advances in social cognition*,. Vol. V. Hillsdale, NJ: Lawrence Erlbaum Associates, pp. 69–78.

Kelly, C. (1994). Group identification, intergroup perceptions and collective action. In W. Stroebe and M. Hewstone (Eds), *European review of social psychology*, Vol. 4. London: John Wiley and Sons, pp. 59–83.

Kernis, M. H., Grannemann, B. D., Richie, T., and Hart, J. (1988). The role of contextual factors in the relationship between physical activity and self-awareness. *British Journal of Social Psychology*, **27**, 265–274.

Kihlstrom, J. F., and Cantor, N. (1984). Mental representation of the self. In L. Berkowitz (Ed). *Advances in experimental social psychology*, Vol. 17., New York: Academic Press, pp. 145–177.

Klandermans, B. (1989). Grievance interpretation and success expectations: the social construction of protest. *Social Behaviour*, **4**, 113–125.

Klein, S. B., and Loftus, J. (1993). The mental representation of trait and autobiographical knowledge about the self. In T. K. Srull and R. S. Wyer Jr. (Eds), *The mental representation of trait and autobiographical knowledge about the self: Advances in social cognition*, Vol. V. Hillsdale, NJ: Lawrence Erlbaum Associates, pp. 1–50.

Knowles, E. S., and Sibicky, M. E. (1990). Continuity and diversity in the stream of selves: Metaphorical resolutions of William James's one-in-many-selves paradox. *Personality and Social Psychology Bulletin*, **16**, 676–687.

Kramer, R. M., Pommerencke, P., and Newton, E. (1993). The social context of negotiation: Effects of social identity and interpersonal accountability on negotiator decision making. *Journal of Conflict Resolution*, **37**, 633–654.

Kuhn, M. H., and McPartland, T. S. (1954). An empirical investigation of self-attitudes. *American Sociological Review*, **19**, 68–76.

Lifton, R. J. (1994). The protean self. Paper presented at the Social Science Research Council workshop on Conflict, Culture and Identity, University of Stanford, November.

Lorenzi-Cioldi, F. (1991). Self-stereotyping and self-enhancement in gender groups. *European Journal of Social Psychology*, **21**, 403–417.

Markus, H., (1977). Self-schemata and processing information about the self. *Journal of Personality and Social Psychology*, **35**, 63–78.

Markus, H. and Kitayama, S. (1991). Culture and the self: Implications for cognition, emotion, and motivation. *Psychological Bulletin*, **98**, 224–253.

Markus, H., and Nurius, P. (1986). Possible selves. *American Psychologist*, **41**, 954–969.

McGarty, C., Turner, J. C., Oakes, P. J., and Haslam, S. A. (1993). The creation of uncertainty in the influence process: The roles of stimulus information and disagreement with similar others. *European Journal of Social Psychology*, **23**, 17–38.

Mullen, B., Brown, R. J., and Smith, C. (1992). Ingroup bias as a function of salience, relevance and status: An integration. *European Journal of Social Psychology*, **22**, 103–122.

Mummendey, A., and Schreiber, H. J. (1983). Better or just different? Positive social identity by discrimination against or differentiation from outgroups. *European Journal of Social Psychology*, **13**, 389–397.

Mummendey, A., Simon, B., Dietze, C., Grunert, M., Haeger, G., Kessler, S., Lettgen, S., and Schaferhoff, S. (1992). Categorization is not enough: Intergroup discrimination in negative outcome allocation. *Journal of Experimental Social Psychology*, **28**, 125–144.

Neuberg, S. L., and Fiske, S. T. (1987). Motivational influences on impression formation: Outcome dependency, accuracy-driven attention and individuating processes. *Journal of Personality and Social Psychology*, **53**, 431–444.

Oakes, P. J., Haslam, S. A., and Turner, J. C. (1994). *Stereotyping and social reality*. Oxford: Blackwell.

Perdue, C. W., Dovidio, J. F., Gurtman, M. B., and Tyler, R. B. (1990). "Us" and "them": Social categorization and the process of intergroup bias. *Journal of Personality and Social Psychology*, **59**, 475–486.

Platow, M. J, McClintock, C. G., and Liebrand, W. B. G. (1990). Predicting intergroup fairness and ingroup bias in the minimal group paradigm. *European Journal of Social Psychology*, **20**, 221–239.

Prentice-Dunn, S., and Rogers, R. W. (1989). Deindividuation and the self-regulation of behaviour. In P. B. Paulus (Ed), *Psychology of group influence*, 2nd ed. Hillsdale, NJ: Erlbaum.

Reicher, S. D. (1984). Social influence in the crowd: Attitudinal and behavioural effects of deindividuation in conditions of high and low group salience. *British Journal of Social Psychology*, **23**, 341–350.

Reid, A., and Deaux, K. (submitted). The relationship between social and personal identities: segregation or integration? City University of New York.

Rosch, E. E. (1978). Principles of categorization. In E. E. Rosch and B. B. Lloyd (Eds), *Cognition and categorization*. Hillsdale, NJ: Erlbaum.

Rosenberg, S. (1988). Self and others: Studies in social personality and autobiography. In L. Berkowitz (Ed). *Advances in experimental social psychology*, Vol. 21. New York: Academic Press, pp. 57–95.

Rothbart, M., and John, O. P. (1985). Social categorization and behavioral episodes: A cognitive analysis of the effects of intergroup contact. *Journal of Social Issues*, **41**, 81–104.

Scheier, M. F., and Carver, C. S. (1981). Private and public aspects of self. In L. Wheeler (Ed)., *Review of personality and social psychology*, Vol. 2. London: Sage.

Shallice, T. (1988). From neuropsychology to mental structure. Cambridge: Cambridge University Press.

Simon, B., Glassner-Bayerl, B., and Statenwerth, I (1991). Stereotyping and self-stereotyping in a natural intergroup context: The case of heterosexual and homosexual men. *Social Psychology Quarterly*, **54**, 252–266.

Simon, B., and Hamilton, D. L. (1994). Self-stereotyping and social context: the effects of relative in-group size and in-group status. *Journal of Personality and Social Psychology*, **66**, 699–711.

Skevington, S., and Baker, D. (Eds), (1989). *The social identity of women*. London: Sage.

Smith, E. R. and Zárate, M.A. (1990). Exemplar and prototype use in social categorization. *Social Cognition*, **8**, 243–262.

Spears, R., Lea, M., and Lee, S. (1990). Deindividuation and group polarization in computer-mediated communication. *British Journal of Social Psychology*, **29**, 121–134.

Srull, T. K. and Wyer, R. S. Jr. (Eds), (1993). *The mental representation of trait and autobiographical knowledge about the self: Advances in social cognition*, Vol. V. Hillsdale, NJ: Lawrence Erlbaum Associates.

Stephenson, G. M. (1981). Intergroup bargaining and negotiation. In J. C. Turner and H. Giles (Eds), *Intergroup behaviour*. Oxford: Blackwell.

Stryker, S. (1987). Identity theory: Developments and extensions. In K. Yardley and T. Honess (Eds), *Self and identity: Psychosocial perspectives*. New York: Wiley, pp. 83–103.

Tajfel, H. (1981). *Human groups and social categories*. Cambridge: Cambridge University Press.

Tajfel, H., and Turner, J. C. (1979). An integrative theory of intergroup conflict. In W. G. Austin and S. Worchel (Eds), *The social psychology of intergroup relations*. Monterey, California: Brooks-Cole.

Tesser, A., and Cornell, D. P. (1991). On the confluence of self processes. *Journal of Experimental Social Psychology*, **27**, 501–526.

Tougas, F. and Veilleux, F. (1990). The response of men to affirmative action strategies for women: The study of a predictive model. *Canadian Journal of Behavioral Science*, **22**, 424–432.

Trafimow, D., Triandis, H. C., and Goto, S. G. (1991). Some tests of the distinction between the private self and the collective self. *Journal of Personality and Social Psychology*, **60**, 649–655.

Triandis, H. C. (1989). The self and social behaviour in differing cultural contexts. *Psychological Review*, **96**, 506–520.

Turner, J. C. (1991). *Social influence*. Milton Keynes: Open University Press.

Turner, J. C., and Giles, H. (Eds), (1981). *Intergroup behaviour*. Oxford: Blackwell.

Turner, J. C., Hogg, M. A., Oakes, P. J., Reicher, S. D., and Wetherell, M. (1987). *Rediscovering the social group: A self-categorization theory*. Oxford and New York: Blackwell.

Turner, J. C., Oakes, P. J., Haslam, S. A., and McGarty, C. (1994). Self and collective: Cognition and social context. *Personality and Social Psychology Bulletin*, **20**, 454–463.

Vorauer, J. D. and Ross, M. (1993). Exploring the nature and implications of functional independence: Do mental representations of the self become independent of their bases? In T. K. Srull and R. S. Wyer Jr. (Eds), *The mental representation of trait and autobiographical knowledge about the self: Advances in social cognition*, Vol. V. Hillsdale, NJ: Lawrence Erlbaum Associates,. pp. 157–170

Williams, J. A. (1984). Gender and intergroup behaviour: Towards an integration. *British Journal of Social Psychology*, **23**, 311–316.

6

Tajfel's Contribution to the Reduction of Intergroup Conflict

RUPERT BROWN

Centre for the Study of Group Processes, Department of Psychology, University of Kent

Contents

In 1966 Henri Tajfel published an article entitled "Cooperation between human groups" (Tajfel, 1966). In his long and prolific output it was a rare excursion into print analysing the factors which promote more positive intergroup relationships. The bulk of his work, particularly that which is most frequently cited today, was concerned with the origins of intergroup discrimination and prejudice, and only indirectly with the reduction of bias and co-operation. Nevertheless, despite this personal neglect, his ideas have had important implications for conflict reduction and in this chapter I shall try to show how.

Besides its rarity value in Tajfel's bibliography, that article is interesting in other respects. It is published in, of all places, a journal entitled *The Eugenics Review*! Whatever possessed him to write for such an outlet we shall probably never know, but the article itself does contain some intriguing hints of questions that would preoccupy social psychologists in the years to follow. In discussing the conditions which might facilitate co-operation, Tajfel placed some emphasis on finding ways to transform the outgroup psychologically so that it could be categorized as having something in common with the ingroup. Hostility towards an outgroup was, he believed, closely related to perceiving it as dissimilar from the ingroup. But then, and in apparent contradiction, he concluded his article with a plea for allowing groups to maintain their differences from one another. As I shall show, these issues of categorization and similarity have been at the forefront of research which has been addressing intergroup co-operation in recent years. My review begins with the ways categorization processes have been exploited with the aim of reducing ingroup bias. These include the effects of crossed categorization, recategorization, and decategorization. I then examine the concept of similarity. Similarity has been the focus of attention both as a criterion for and a competitor to categorization as the basis of prejudice. It has also been of interest at an intergroup level where rival hypotheses as to its effects on attitudes towards the outgroup have been extensively tested. In the final section I review recent theoretical and empirical developments on the contact hypothesis. Here, too, a central question turns out to be the practical benefit (or otherwise) of maintaining the salience of social categories.

Categorization and the Reduction of Ingroup Bias

One of Tajfel's most important legacies to social psychology was the identification and clarification of the categorization process. Although he was by no means the first social psychologist to recognize the importance of categorization—for example, Allport (1954), Bruner (1957) and Campbell (1956) all preceded him—his theoretical and empirical work proved to be highly influential, especially Tajfel (1959) and Tajfel and Wilkes (1963). As is well known, the two major principles to emerge from this research were those of accentuation and assimilation: people tend to exaggerate the differences between categories and simultaneously minimize the differences within categories.

These principles were useful in explaining various phenomena, not just the obvious ones in the field of social judgement but also many manifestations of ingroup bias, stereotyping, and intergroup discrimination (Doise, 1976; Tajfel, 1969). Indeed, so fundamental has categorization come to be viewed for these latter phenomena that at least one commentator has noted that it has led social psychologists to conclude (mistakenly in his view) that prejudice is inevitable (Billig, 1985).

In fact, there are good reasons for supposing that the very consequences of categorization that can so easily lead to prejudice can also be exploited for the purposes of prejudice reduction. Furthermore, it may be possible to contrive social situations in which categories are psychologically less in evidence, which can then result in some short-term benefits in the diminution of ingroup favouring biases. These various possibilities can be summarized under three main headings: crossed categorizations, recategorization, and decategorization.

Crossed categorizations

In most social situations there is more than one possible dimension of categorization available for use. The people present may be classified by ethnicity, gender, class, age and any number of other appropriate criteria. Very often these dimensions cut across one another so that, to the observer, any given person may share category membership in one respect but be excluded in another. They may also, of course, be excluded on both or all criteria. The potential of this crossed categorization scenario for the reduction of intergroup differentiation was first properly formalized in social psychological terms by Doise (1976). Drawing on ethnographic research which had noted a correlation between societies with cross-cutting kinship and tribal systems and a relative absence of internal conflict (e.g. Gluckman, 1956; LeVine and Campbell, 1972), Doise realized that a contributory explanation for this lay in the cognitive processes of accentuation and assimilation. Doise reasoned that where two (or more) category systems are orthogonal then the accentuation and assimilation associated with one should effectively cancel out the same processes associated with the other. The result should be lessened, or perhaps even completely abolished, bias in terms of each of the original categorizations.

There is a good deal of evidence which supports this hypothesis. In one study, Deschamps and Doise (1978) asked some teenage girls to rate "young people" and "adults", and "males" and "females" on a number of stereotype traits. Half rated these as dichotomous pairs; this was the simple categorization condition. The remainder rated the categories in conjunction: "young females", "male adults", etc.; this was the crossed categorization condition. In the latter, the perceived differences between both the age and the gender categories were consistently smaller than in the simple case. In a second study young girls and boys worked on a number of games. In the simple condition they were seated around a rectangular table such that the boys occupied two sides, the girls the other two sides. In the crossed condition, before starting the games the boys on one side of the table and the girls on the adjacent side were given red pens, and the other boys and girls given blue pens, the experimenter casually remarking that now "we have a group of blues and a group of reds". The children's estimations of each other's performance were radically altered by this intervention. In the simple condition both boys and girls believed that their own gender had performed better than the other; in the crossed case, however, this gender bias completely disappeared. In fact, even those of the opposite gender *and* in the other colour group were rated as favourably as those in the same category on both criteria.

These experiments stimulated a number of others. Brown and Turner (1979) pointed out that the two categories employed in Deschamps and Doise's studies might not have been of equal significance. Using two artificial categories we found evidence of the maintenance of some bias in the partially overlapping case (i.e. when one membership is shared but not the other). More importantly, in the completely non-overlapping case (i.e. sharing neither category) the bias was magnified. It is fair to say that the former result has not generally been replicated whilst the latter has. Perhaps the most definitive set of laboratory studies has been done by Vanbeselaere (1991). Using two equally important categorizations he confirmed Deschamps and Doise's (1978) original findings that bias against those who share at least one category membership is virtually eliminated. However, in accord with Brown and Turner (1979), against those who share neither category the bias seems to increase (see also Diehl, 1990).

These laboratory findings are interesting because of their potential significance for policies aimed at reducing prejudice. They suggest that if we can arrange social situations so that at least two (and perhaps even more) categorical dimensions cut across one another then, in principle, the likelihood of persistent prejudice between groups along any one of those dimensions should be reduced. Unfortunately, in the world outside the laboratory such a neat panacea for prejudice is not always so effective.

In a study in Hong Kong, for instance, Brewer *et al.* (1987) asked some Cantonese boys and girls to express their liking for each of eight hypothetical peers. These "stimulus" children were either male or female and were from one of four different ethnic groups: Cantonese (like themselves), Shanghai, American, and Indian. The children's responses showed two things very clearly. First, they preferred those of their own gender. This was the strongest single effect in the data. They also showed a clear preference for the two Chinese groups over the other two, but this preference was slightly stronger when evaluating same gender targets than opposite gender targets. Brewer *et al.* interpreted their findings as showing that for these children gender assumed greater importance than ethnicity and that, unlike in Deschamps and Doise's (1978) laboratory experiment, the addition of the second (ethnic) dimension was not enough to eliminate that potent gender bias.

This tendency for one categorical dimension to dominate in real-life contexts was confirmed in a study conducted amongst Bangladeshi Muslims and Hindus (Hewstone *et al.*, 1993). Here the cross-cutting categories were religion (Muslim versus Hindu), nationality (Bangladeshi versus Indian) and, in a second study, language use (Bengali versus other languages). In the Brewer *et al.* (1987) study gender had dominated; here it was religion. If people were seen as sharing the same religion they were always evaluated positively. If not, the ratings dropped sharply, no matter if they were of similar nationality or spoke the same language. A similar predominance of religious categories was observed by Hagendoorn and Henke (1991) in their study of religious and caste/class attitudes in Northern India. Upper class/caste Muslims and Hindus tended to derogate those from a different religion, especially if they came from a lower status group. However, the lower status groups (of both religions) were much less affected by either religion or status and, indeed, seemed to show something more nearly resembling the original crossed-categorization effect observed in the laboratory.

As one final illustration let me report the results of a recent survey of university academics in a Canadian university (Joly *et al.*, 1993). In the survey instrument we included a hypothetical scenario in which six candidates (described in brief curriculum vitae) were applying for a research assistantship. The curriculum vitae had been carefully prepared: four equally good ones differing only in gender and language preference, and two obviously inferior ones, both from men, one Anglophone, one Francophone. Our respondents, who also included both male and female Anglophones and Francophones, were asked to indicate their recommendation for a payment rate for these six candidates. Not surprisingly, the two weaker candidates were generally allocated lower salaries. However, amongst the "good" candidates there was some evidence of bias against Francophones even, it has to be said, from the Francophones themselves! Once again, then, the presence of two cross-cutting categories did little to diminish the historically rooted perception of Francophones as a lower status group.

These field studies serve as important reminders that which category dimension will assume pre-eminence in any situation is very dependent on particular local circumstances. In Northern Ireland, the Lebanon, and the Indian subcontinent, religion is often crucial. Elsewhere, however, religion can pale into insignificance against other more powerful social divisions. The fact that Iranians and Iraqis share the same (Muslim) religion did not prevent them killing each other in large numbers in their war during the 1980s. In this case the national conflicts of military and territorial interests overrode any psychological affiliations deriving from their shared religious category membership. Thus the complexities of intergroup situations in the real world, particularly where the groups are of different size or status and where they may be co-operatively or competitively interdependent, should lead us to be cautious about the efficacy of crossed categorization arrangements by themselves for reducing prejudice.

Recategorization

There is a second avenue by which categorization processes can assist in the reduction of bias. This is to find ways to redefine the conflictual situation so that those who are currently perceived as members of the outgroup can be subsumed into a new and larger category and thereby be seen as ingroup members (Turner, 1981). In this way, the very cognitive processes which contribute to the creation and maintenance of the existing intergroup differentiation are harnessed for its reduction. This is, of course, a classic propagandist technique used by ruling governments the world over when attempting to deflect demands for ethnic or regional autonomy. A common tactic is to make appeals to "nationhood" or "national unity", often reinforced with spectres of threats from external agencies.

There is some limited amount of research evidence which supports the recategorization hypothesis. An early field study by Minard (1952) provided the first clues. He noted how black and white miners in West Virginia, USA showed little ethnic animosity underground where their common category membership as coal miners was salient. Only when they returned to their communities did the old prejudices manifest themselves. Laboratory work subsequently confirmed the same idea. Worchel *et al.* (1978) found that co-operating *ad hoc* groups who wore similar clothing showed greater intergroup attraction than groups whose clothing was different and hence contributed to the maintenance of the group divisions.

A more systematic programme of work along the same lines has been mounted by Gaertner and his colleagues (e.g. Gaertner *et al.*, 1993). They have investigated the effects of manipulating social situations so that they are perceived as consisting of a single superordinate group, two groups, or merely as a collection of separate individuals. The experiment by Gaertner *et al.* (1989) provides a good example of how this was achieved. Using artificial group labels (different colour tags), six subjects were initially assigned to one of two groups and had to work together in those groups. The two groups were then brought together to work on a further task and the nature of this encounter was systematically varied. In the "two groups" condition the members of the group sat opposite each other at a table, keeping their original group labels, and interacted mainly amongst each other with a view to winning a prize for the best single solution to the task. In contrast, in the "one group" condition the members of the two groups sat in alternate places around the table, devised a new group label for the larger entity formed by the joining of the groups, and worked with each other to win a prize for the best *joint* group solution to the task. And in the "individual" condition each person sat at a separate table, was asked to think up an idiosyncratic name, and worked towards the best individual solution.

These manipulations had a marked effect on the way subjects categorized each other and, as expected, these altered perceptions were also associated with differences in ingroup bias, least being observed in the "one group" case, most in the "two groups" condition. These findings were corroborated in a field study conducted in a multi-ethnic American high school. Here they found that students' positive attitudes towards other groups were positively correlated with responses to items stressing a superordinate identity (e.g. "despite the different groups at school, there is frequently the sense that we are all just one group"), but negatively related to items emphasizing the existence of different groups. (Gaertner *et al.*, in press).

Although these findings are promising for conflict reduction purposes, once again we should be cautious in believing that they offer an easy panacea. One difficulty is to be able to achieve some generalization of the attitude change from the immediate intergroup context to outgroup members who have not yet been encountered. In a partial replication of Gaertner *et al.*'s (1989) study we confirmed that, indeed, favourable attitudes towards outgroup members in the experimental situation were correlated (positively) with a perception of those present as belonging to a single group. However, attitudes towards other members of the outgroup not yet met was more reliably associated with a "two groups" construal of the situation (Vivian *et al.*, in press). I shall return to the possible reasons for this apparently paradoxical result and to the whole question of generalization in a later section.

Decategorization

A third strategy suggested by the original findings on social categorization is the exact obverse of those I have discussed so far. Both the crossed and recategorization approaches rely for their success on the continued operation of the accentuation and assimilation processes. The decategorization approach, in contrast, seeks to reduce the emphasis on categorical judgement with the ultimate aim of dissolving the "problematic" category boundaries altogether (Brewer and Miller, 1984). In this way, it is hoped, the interactions will take place on an interpersonal level and the participants should be more likely to attend to idiosyncratic information about each individual and be correspondingly *less* attentive to group based—i.e. stereotypic—information. Repeated interpersonal contact of this kind is thought to result in the disconfirmation of pre-existing (negative) stereotypes of the outgroup which ultimately is

> . . . more likely to generalize to new situations because extended and frequent utilization of alternative informational features in interactions undermines the availability and usefulness of category identity as a basis for future interactions with the same or different individuals. Thus permanent changes occur in both the cognitive and motivational aspects of social interaction with outgroup members'.
>
> (Brewer and Miller, 1984, pp. 288–289)

In support of this model Brewer and Miller have carried out a number of studies using a similar paradigm (Bettencourt *et al.*, 1992; Miller *et al.*, 1985). Typically, two artificial categories are created (e.g. "overestimators" and "underestimators"). Then members of these two categories are brought together into co-operative work groups so that both overestimators and underestimators are represented in each group. The subjects are given different instructional sets for the group tasks: some are encouraged to focus on each other to find out what the "fellow team members must really be like" (Bettencourt *et al.*, 1992, pp. 305–306); others are told to concentrate particularly on the task at hand. In this way it is hoped to "personalize" or "depersonalize" the contact situation respectively. After the task the subjects allocate rewards to the members of their team and also to members of another team unknown to them, portrayed on a short video clip. The key dependent measure in these experiments is the degree of bias in these allocations between over- and underestimators, both for the known team members and the "strangers" shown on video. A consistent finding has been that those undertaking the task with the "personalization" instructions show less bias than those who are concentrating much more on the task.

It is clear that this approach has much to recommend it, at least in terms of short term interventions. It is also supported by distinguished theoretical and empirical precedent, most notably in the work of Cook (1962, 1978). However, as with the recategorization idea, a remaining problem concerns generalization. As Cook put it:

> Attitude change will result from co-operative (. . . . . .) contact only when such contact is accompanied by a supplementary influence that promotes the process of generalization from favourable contact with individuals to positive attitudes toward the group from which the individual comes.
>
> (Cook, 1978, p. 103).

In the third section I will examine just what that "supplementary influence" is most likely to be.

Similarity and Intergroup Attraction

If there is one "law" of social relations which is almost universally accepted in social psychology it is that similarity leads to attraction. Variously derived from principles of social comparison (Festinger, 1954), balance (Newcomb, 1961), or reinforcement (Byrne, 1971), the basic similarity–attraction hypothesis has received ample support in the field of interpersonal relationships (e.g. Byrne, 1971; Duck, 1977). However, Tajfel was never one to acquiesce unthinkingly to conventional wisdom. In some of his minimal group experiments he was concerned to rebut at least one of the corollaries of that seemingly self-evident idea (Billig and Tajfel, 1973). Subsequently, in social identity theory (Tajfel, 1978; Tajfel and Turner, 1986), which will surely be one of his most enduring contributions, he hinted at some further qualifications to it.

Categorization versus belief dissimilarity as a basis for prejudice

The most notable extrapolation of the similarity–attraction hypothesis to the field of intergroup relations was that proposed by Rokeach (1960). Following Festinger (1954), Rokeach believed that similarity of opinions leads to mutual attraction because of the validation that such agreement provides. On the other hand, disagreement leads to dislike because of the threat to our belief system that is posed by that discord. Rokeach went on to propose that various group prejudices have less to do with people's memberships of those groups and their associated intergroup relations, but are principally the result of "belief incongruence", a perception that the people concerned hold belief systems incompatible with our own:

> Belief is more important than ethnic or racial membership as a determinant of social discrimination.
>
> (Rokeach, 1960, p. 135).

To test this idea Rokeach *et al.* (1960) devised an experimental paradigm in which group membership and belief congruence are independently varied. Thus, subjects typically have to express their liking for various people who are alleged to belong to either the same or different group from themselves and who are also seen to hold similar or different beliefs. In a number of studies using this basic technique the belief factor usually emerges as a more powerful determinant of attitude than the categorical variable. Thus, white subjects will often say that they prefer a black person with similar beliefs to a white person with dissimilar beliefs (e.g. Byrne and Wong, 1962; Hendrick *et al.*, 1971; Rokeach and Mezei, 1966; Rokeach *et al.*, 1960). The exceptions to this conclusion appear to be for rather stronger measures of attraction (e.g. desire to have a close friendship) where several studies have found that the category difference assumes greater importance than belief dissimilarity (Insko *et al.*, 1983; Stein *et al.*, 1965; Triandis and Davis, 1965).

Despite the empirical support for Rokeach's theory, there are several grounds for doubting whether it offers an adequate account of prejudice, at least in the strong form in which he originally formulated it. To begin with, we should note that the theory involves some sleight of hand in explaining the occurrence of any kind of intergroup prejudice. If it is the case, as Rokeach argued, that we dislike people because we perceive them to hold different beliefs from us why should we assume that members of outgroups hold those different beliefs? Surely, if social categories are unimportant, then our liking for a person should be on a case-by-case basis, decided by that person's similarity to us. There should be no a priori reason why a whole group of people should share the same beliefs. And yet, prejudice *is* manifestly patterned along categorical lines, as Tajfel (1969) argued so convincingly. Thus, for Rokeach's theory to hold water we need to add the extra and *category-based* assumption that members of another group are likely to believe in different things from us. In fact, there is some evidence that this is exactly what people do perceive, but, note, such a perception is first predicated on the psychological reality of the ingroup–outgroup category difference (Allen and Wilder, 1979; Wilder, 1984a).

A second difficulty with Rokeach's theory is that it is limited by an important qualification. From the beginning he wished to exempt from the belief congruence explanation those situations in which the prejudice has become institutionalized by law or social custom, or where there exists significant social support for its expression. There, he conceded, people's respective group memberships would override belief congruence as the basis for prejudice (Rokeach, 1960, p. 164). Thus, for many of the most widespread and virulent manifestations of prejudice—against blacks in many parts of Britain and the USA, between different religions in Ireland, India and the Lebanon, and so on—it seems that Rokeach's theory is simply inapplicable.

A third criticism of the belief–congruence approach hinges on the typical experimental methodology used to substantiate it. I have presented this critique in more detail elsewhere (Brown, 1988; Brown and Turner, 1981). The central point is that the race-belief paradigm (as it has come to be known) does not usually present a properly intergroup situation to the experimental participants. Typically, subjects are confronted with a series of individuals (real or hypothetical) who just happen to endorse this or that set of beliefs and who, almost incidentally, share a category membership (or not) with the subject. In such circumstances, I have argued, it is little wonder that one of the major determinants of *interpersonal* attraction (i.e. attitudinal or belief similarity) comes to the fore as the principal causal factor. On the other hand, where the group-like nature of the situation is given equal weight to considerations of interpersonal similarity, the evidence for Rokeach's theory is much less strong.

The most direct evidence of this comes from an experiment by Billig and Tajfel (1973) which employed variants of the minimal group paradigm, (Tajfel *et al.*, 1971). Their objective was to examine the effects on intergroup discrimination of different methods of group formation. In one condition the subjects were informed only that some recipients were more similar to them than others because they had preferred the same kind of painting in the pretest. There was no mention made of groups. This, therefore, constituted a "pure" similarity condition. In a second condition, by contrast, there was no mention of any similarity; subjects were simply told that they had been assigned to two groups by the toss of a coin. This was a "pure" categorization condition. In a third variant the first and second conditions were combined so that similarity of picture preferences formed the basis for categorization. Finally, in a control condition there was neither similarity nor categorization. The first two conditions are the critical ones. If Rokeach is correct one would expect discrimination in the first and not the second. If, however, categorization does have an independent influence then one would expect more discrimination in the second than the first. The results clearly supported the latter interpretation. In the two conditions where a categorization was present, ingroup favouritism in the reward allocations was visible. The main effect of the similarity variable, although statistically significant, was much weaker than the categorization effect.

Other experiments using the minimal group paradigm have also generated findings which are difficult to reconcile with belief–congruence theory. Allen and Wilder (1975) independently varied the similarity of the ingroup and outgroup to the subject, apparently on the basis of artistic and political beliefs. Varying the perceived similarity of the outgroup had no effect on level of intergroup discrimination; subjects were as strongly biased against a "dissimilar" outgroup as they were against a "similar" outgroup. More problematic still were the findings from two experiments reported by Diehl (1988). In the first, Diehl varied the similarity between the individual subject and *one member* of each of the ingroup and outgroup. In this interpersonal situation there was some limited support for Rokeach's position, since those who were similar were liked, regardless of group membership. Nevertheless, on the measure of discrimination (allocation of monetary rewards) the similarity of the outgroup had little effect on the amount of bias displayed. Then, in the second experiment, Diehl varied the extent of perceived similarity between *the groups as a whole*, thus reducing the interpersonal nature of the situation. In these conditions similarity had exactly the opposite effect to that predicted by Rokeach: there was more discrimination against the "similar" outgroup than against the "dissimilar" outgroup.

It seems clear, therefore, that the original form of Rokeach's (1960) hypothesis is not tenable as an explanation for prejudice. In situations in which group memberships are psychologically salient, the idea that dissimilarity of beliefs is a more potent force than categorical differences simply cannot be sustained. Nevertheless, there is a weaker version of Rokeach's theory which may be more consistent with the evidence. In this form, some division into ingroup and outgroup is taken as read and what is then at issue is the effect of different degrees of intergroup similarity. Do people typically display less prejudice against outgroups which are seen as endorsing similar attitudes to those which prevail in the ingroup than against outgroups which seem to believe in quite different things? It is to that question that I now turn.

Effects of intergroup similarity

At the heart of social identity theory is the notion of positive distinctiveness (Tajfel, 1978; Tajfel and Turner, 1986). The theory proposes that it is psychologically important for group members to be able to view the ingroup as different from and better than other groups on some relevant dimensions. This immediately suggests a hypothesis concerning similarity. To the extent that outgroups are perceived to be similar—either in prevailing attitudes or in status, the same argument applies to both—then there should be motivational pressures towards increased differentiation from them and, perhaps, greater dislike for them (Brown, 1984b; Turner, 1978). Such a hypothesis obviously runs directly counter to the familiar similarity–attraction proposition with which I began this section.

My own interest in the similarity issue began with a field study of workers in an aircraft factory (Brown, 1978). In that research I observed substantial evidence of intergroup rivalry and lack of intergroup co-operation amongst three groups of shop stewards. This ingroup favouritism was all the more remarkable because the groups were similar on a number of dimensions: they belonged to the same trade unions (which cut across the three departmental boundaries—see section on crossed categorizations above), they were all committed union activists endorsing similar political ideologies, they all earned very similar wages, and they had the same employer. At about the same time, experimental evidence was emerging which also suggested that similarity might have repulsive, rather than attractive, effects on intergroup attitudes, although in these first studies it also interacted with the perceived stability of the intergroup system (Mummendey and Schreiber, 1984; Turner, 1978).

We followed these studies with a series of others on the effects of intergroup similarity (Brown, 1984b; Brown and Abrams, 1986). In these we led school children to believe that they were undertaking a task with members of another school. Depending on condition, members of that school were portrayed as being similar to them in status because they seemed to perform about as well as them academically, or were better or worse than them. In addition, the prevailing attitudes towards different academic subjects in the two schools were depicted as being either similar or different. Both variables had effects on the children's intergroup attitudes. The outgroup thought to hold similar attitudes was generally liked better than the outgroup that was believed to be different (Brown, 1984a; Brown and Abrams, 1986. See also Grant (1993) for identical results in a different context). A second finding was that when the children believed they were about to co-operate with the other school, their levels of ingroup bias against the similar status group were lower than the average of their biases against the higher and lower status group (Brown, 1984a). Both of these findings rather contradicted the social identity theory prediction that similarity would provoke a greater search for positive distinctiveness. However, a third finding was more in line with that hypothesis. This was that where the outgroup was very similar indeed to the ingroup because it had similar attitudes *and* was similar in status, then the amount of bias increased (Brown and Abrams, 1986). It was as if a certain threshold of similarity had been crossed beyond which the ingroup felt threatened by the psychological proximity of the outgroup (see also Diehl, 1988; Roccas and Schwartz, 1993).

Using a rather different paradigm we have found some comparable effects of role similarity (Brown and Wade, 1987; Deschamps and Brown, 1983). In these experiments, we arranged for groups to work together for real rewards under conditions in which the groups' contributions were distinctive and recognizable or similar and blurred. In general, we found more liking for the outgroup in the former than in the latter conditions. However, there is some recent evidence which suggests that these positive effects of role dissimilarity may be restricted to intergroup co-operative encounters; when the interaction is more personalized, the beneficial effects of such clear-cut divisions of role may be diminished (Marcus-Newhall *et al.*, 1993).

On the whole, then, the laboratory evidence suggests that similarity (whether of status or attitudes) seems to promote attraction between groups. A similar conclusion emerges from field studies of ethnic relations. For example, Brewer and Campbell (1976) found that ethnic groups in East Africa that were independently judged to be similar to one another tended to express friendlier attitudes towards one another than culturally more disparate groups. Similarly, Berry *et al.* (1977), in a large survey of Canadian interethnic attitudes, found a moderately strong positive correlation between respondents' evaluations of nine ethnic groups and their perceived similarity to themselves. Finally, Struch and Schwartz (1989) found that religious groups in Israel which were seen to have similar values to the respondents' own groups were viewed with less hostility than those seen as dissimilar.

On balance, therefore, there is support for a weaker and modified version of Rokeach's (1960) belief congruence theory. It is not the case, as he originally believed, that people's perception of interpersonal belief similarity can so easily override differences in category membership and reduce prejudice (see above). However, it may well be that outgroups which are seen as somewhat similar to the ingroup are treated more favourably than those which are perceived to be quite different. This runs rather counter to the idea derived from social identity theory that intergroup similarity will be regarded as threatening and hence be reacted to aversively. There *are* circumstances in which this seems to happen—when groups have arrived at some extreme of similarity and find themselves literally too close for comfort. But, at the more common intermediate levels of similarity, groups seem to appreciate being able to have at least something in common.

A recent idea of Brewer's (1991) may help us to understand why this might be. Brewer suggests that individuals seek a compromise between needs for uniqueness and countervailing desires for assimilation. The former motive, she argues, can best be met in small groups which are highly distinctive from others in society; the latter implies the categorization of self as similar to a reasonably large number of others for reasons of affiliation and self validation. The result is a choice of ingroups which provides the best trade-off between these two motives, what she calls the point of "optimal distinctiveness". It may be that this same compromise applies at the group level also. Perhaps people, as *group members*, want to be able to see that their group has sufficient in common with other groups to avoid feeling completely deviant and stigmatized but, at the same time, need to regard it as distinctive enough to retain its particular identity. This would suggest that prejudice will be least likely to be directed towards outgroups of intermediate similarity to the ingroup, groups that are neither so different as to have no points of contact with us nor so similar as to threaten our identity. Interestingly enough, such a hypothesis is exactly opposite to a prediction which can be derived from another quite different model, frustration–aggression theory (Dollard *et al.*, 1939). By a careful analysis of the concept of "displacement" in that theory, Brewer and Campbell (1976) derived an *inverted* U-shape curve for the hypothesized relationship between intergroup similarity and aggression towards the outgroup: highly similar or dissimilar outgroups should be preferred to those of moderate similarity. Doubtless, future research will reveal which of these contrary predictions best corresponds to reality.

Intergroup Contact and Attitude Change

A chapter on the reduction of intergroup conflict would not be complete without some discussion of that most well-known panacea of all: the contact hypothesis. First properly formalized by Allport (1954), whose intergroup relations prize Tajfel was later to win (Tajfel, 1969), its central premise is that the best way to reduce tension and hostility between groups is to bring them into contact with each other under appropriate conditions. The four most important of these are as follows: there should be social and institutional support for the contact; the contact should be of sufficient frequency, duration and closeness to permit the development of meaningful relationships; it should take place between equal status participants; and it should involve some co-operation over jointly desired goals (Allport, 1954; Cook, 1962; Pettigrew, 1971).

The contact hypothesis has generated an enormous literature in the forty years since it was first formulated. That literature has been sufficiently comprehensively reviewed elsewhere not to need its recapitulation here (Amir, 1976; Cook, 1978; Hewstone and Brown, 1986). However, as anticipated earlier, one outstanding problem in that literature concerns the generalization of attitude and stereotype change from the specific contact situation to other situations and to other members of the outgroup one has not already encountered.

In response to this problem, refinements to the contact hypothesis have been put forward in recent years. Two of these—Gaertner *et al* (1993) and Brewer and Miller (1984)—have already been considered (see above). In effect, both of them propose the dissolution of existing group boundaries. Although each has a sound rationale for this, one problem that it creates for both of them is that the process of generalization is made more difficult. Suppose I interact with an outgroup person under either decategorized or recategorized conditions. To the extent that these conditions have been successful in preventing me from perceiving that person as a member of an outgroup (or, indeed, any group at all), then any change in attitudes I experience towards that person cannot easily be extrapolated to other members of his or her group whom I have not yet met. Thus, my more general intergroup attitudes may remain intact, unaffected by the contact situation. It was this consideration which led Hewstone and I to propose a rather different model of intergroup contact (Hewstone and Brown, 1986; Vivian *et al.*, in press). We suggest that rather than attempting to eliminate the existing ingroup–outgroup division there may be some virtue in keeping it at least minimally salient whilst simultaneously optimizing the various Allport (1954) conditions for successful contact. In this way the contact will take place at an intergroup rather than an interpersonal level, between people acting as group representatives rather than unaffiliated individuals (Brown and Turner, 1981). If this can be successfully arranged then any positive change engendered during contact is likely to transfer readily to other members of the outgroup because one's contact partners are seen as somehow typical of that group (see Rothbart and John, 1985 for a similar argument).

In some ways this seems a somewhat paradoxical strategy. In order to reduce prejudice towards an outgroup we are suggesting that maintaining the psychological salience of the intergroup distinction can be advantageous. Nevertheless, various lines of evidence are beginning to converge to this conclusion. Wilder (1984b) varied how typical a member of a rival college was seen to be during a co-operative encounter. In addition, this outgroup member behaved pleasantly or unpleasantly. Only the pleasant encounter with a "typical" outgrouper produced significant improvements in the evaluation of the outgroup as a whole. Unpleasant encounters or encounters with an atypical person produced little change in attitude. Using the outgroup category, "former mental patient", DesForges *et al.* (1991) compared the efficacy of different kinds of co-operative learning situations. Although they did not vary the typicality of the confederate who was alleged to have had a history of mental illness, in all conditions she was portrayed as a typical former mental patient and this category remained salient during the experiment. As expected, co-operative encounters with this person produced more attitude change towards mental patients as a whole than the minimal contact control conditions. Studies of stereotype change also indicate that disconfirming information needs to be associated with people who are otherwise typical members of the category concerned if they are not to be subtyped and treated as exceptions, leaving the general category stereotype unchanged (Johnston and Hewstone, 1992; Weber and Crocker, 1983).

In an attempt to test our model directly we have carried out studies in which we could examine the effects of making group membership more or less salient (Vivian *et al.*, 1994). One was an experiment involving a co-operative encounter with someone of a different nationality. Our British subjects arrived at the laboratory and were required to work with a German confederate for a substantial joint reward (if successful). This confederate was depicted as someone who possessed some characteristics which were either stereotypical for how British people viewed Germans or rather atypical. In addition, we provided some bogus information about how homogeneous German people were on various attitudinal and personality characteristics. Depending on experimental condition, they were seen as homogeneous or heterogeneous. Our reasoning was that the situation would be seen in the most "intergroup" terms when typicality was combined with homogeneity, and that there the link between the target person and the group as a whole would be strongest. Conversely, if they met an atypical member of a heterogeneous group the encounter would be more "interpersonal" and the chances of generalization correspondingly lower. Our primary interest was in our subjects' subsequent perceptions of German people as a whole. These we divided into four groups of traits: positive and negative, and stereotypical or not of Germany (as determined by pre-testing). We found little change on the negative indices, but on the positive measures there was a more favourable perception after interaction with a "typical" rather than an "atypical" partner, and on one of these measures this was particularly pronounced in the "homogeneous" conditions.

In the Netherlands, using a different method of invoking category salience and a different intergroup context (Dutch–Turkish), Van Oudenhoven *et al.* (in press) have observed similar results. The ethnicity of Turkish confederate was either kept quite implicit by the experimenter never making reference to it (low salience), or was drawn to people's attention only at the end of the interaction (moderate salience), or was emphasized throughout (high salience). After two hours of working co-operatively with this confederate, the Dutch subjects evaluated both him and Turks in general. The individual confederate ratings did not vary across conditions but the general attitudes towards Turks were reliably more favourable in the two conditions where his ethnicity had been made salient than in the low salience condition.

We followed up these experiments with a survey conducted in six different European countries (Vivian *et al.*, 1994). One of the sections of the survey questionnaire asked respondents to think of a person from another country with whom they had had some contact. There then followed a series of questions exploring the nature of this contact—how frequent was it, was it competitive or co-operative, how typical of the country did they regard the person, and how salient was nationality in their conversations with this person? The final and crucial question asked how much they would like to live in the country concerned. We took this to be our index of a favourable and generalized intergroup attitude. Consistent with the traditional contact hypothesis, more frequent contact of a co-operative nature was positively correlated with positive attitudes. However, this was especially true if the contact person was seen as typical of the country (again we selected Germany so as to be consistent with the laboratory study) *and* if their respective nationalities featured regularly in their interactions (i.e. were salient). As we had predicted, therefore, positive attitudes towards the outgroup as a whole were associated with favourable *intergroup* contact with someone from that outgroup.

Although the Hewstone and Brown model seems to offer a promising way of tackling the generalization problem, it is an approach fraught with difficulties. One of these follows directly from the very same argument which provided the rationale for the model in the first place. If intergroup (as opposed to interpersonal) contact permits greater generalization of the attitudes promoted by the encounter then, in principle, both positive *and* negative attitudes can be generalized. Indeed, if the co-operative interaction goes wrong, perhaps in failing to achieve the common goal or because it turns competitive, then structuring the interaction at the intergroup level could well make matters worse. Not only might one's fellow interactant(s) be derogated but there is a risk of reinforcing negative stereotypes of the outgroup precisely because those people are seen as typical of it. This danger is heightened by a second problem. This is that intergroup encounters may be more anxiety-provoking than interpersonal ones and too much anxiety is usually not conducive to harmonious social relations (Stephan and Stephan, 1985; Wilder and Shapiro, 1989). Studying Muslim–Hindu contact in Bangladesh, Islam and Hewstone (1993) found that features indicative of intergroup relationships tended to be correlated with increased anxiety which, in turn, was correlated with less favourable attitudes towards the outgroups.

If this finding is replicated with other populations then it might suggest that the decategorization or recategorization models discussed earlier provide less hazardous strategies for prejudice reduction, especially since there is some evidence that decategorization is still compatible with attitude generalization (Bettencourt *et al.*, 1992; Miller *et al.*, 1985). However, I fear that even this may be too easy an answer. To begin with, the experiments which have supported the decategorization model have only employed ad hoc laboratory groups with probably rather little psychological significance for their members. This may have made it relatively easy for the participants to shed these group identities in the conditions favouring "personalized" interaction. In real intergroup settings, such as multi-ethnic schools, it may not be so easy to distract people's attention from their group memberships. Moreover, in those experiments there was probably more than a vestige of group salience even in the decategorized conditions. For example, in the Bettencourt *et al.* (1992) experiment, team members wore large badges around their necks for the duration of the study, proclaiming their original group affiliations. Likewise, the "strangers" viewed on the video recording. This need to maintain some cognitive link between those with whom one has interacted and the wider outgroup is also recognized by Gaertner *et al.* (1993). In discussing the generalization question they suggest that there may need to be a trade-off between the salience of the original group identities and the new superordinate group identity which is intended to subsume them. Without this, they concede, interventions designed to reduce prejudice may have only context-specific effects.

Conclusions

What, then, can we conclude about Tajfel's contribution to the more positive aspects of intergroup relations, the conditions which promote intergroup co-operation and the reduction of ingroup favouring biases? It should be clear from the above that his direct involvement with such issues was minimal. However, *indirectly*, his work has exerted an enormous influence in this direction.

Primarily this has stemmed from his pioneering research on categorization and his insistence on the psychological primacy of this process in all intergroup perception and judgement. As I hope I have shown, categorization processes are in principle exploitable as much for the purposes of prejudice reduction as they are responsible for the aetiology of prejudice in the first place. His work on social identity has also proved to be important for researchers interested in improving negative intergroup relationships, although not perhaps in the way he had originally envisaged. His main insight here was to realize how important it was for group members to be able to see their ingroup in a positive light and to warn of the possible negative consequences of a threat to their social identities (see Brown, 1995 for a more detailed treatment of this question). However, some of these predicted effects of a threatened identity—in particular, those stemming from perceived similarity to an outgroup—have proved to have been less serious than we originally thought. Except at extreme levels of similarity, or under very unstable conditions, any potential threats to identity seem to be outweighed by the more conventionally positive effects of shared values and comparable status. Finally, Tajfel's hypothesis that interpersonal and group processes are qualitatively different has proved to be an important addendum to the contact hypothesis. For it was this suggestion which gave us the first clues as to whether and how positive attitudes generated in an encounter with a few outgroup members could be extended to the many other members of that same outgroup one has not met.

These, in my view, have been real advances. However, this improved understanding of how intergroup conflicts can be lessened has been accompanied by a sober realization of the limitations of a purely social psychological level of analysis. This is particularly evident in the crossed categorization research where, as we saw, the neat solutions suggested by our cognitive interventions in the laboratory rarely hold up in the more complex web of overlapping categories in the real world. And perhaps this is a fitting note on which to finish. For, tireless ideologue for social psychology though he was, Tajfel rarely forgot to remind us to be modest in our aspirations for the discipline. As he wrote in one of his last articles:

> The psychological study of these problems, which will manage to combine some of our traditional preoccupations with an increased sensitivity to the nature of social realities, is one of our most important tasks for the future.
>
> (Tajfel, 1982, p. 32).

References

Allen, V. L., and Wilder, D. A. (1975). Categorization, belief similarity, and group discrimination. *Journal of Personality and Social Psychology*, **32**, 971–977.

Allen, V. L. and Wilder, D. A. (1979) Group categorization and attribution of belief similarity. *Small Group Behaviour*, **10**, 73–80.

Allport, G. W. (1954) *The nature of prejudice*. Reading, MA.: Addison-Wesley.

Amir, Y. (1976). The role of intergroup contact in change of prejudice and ethnic relations. In P. A. Katz (Ed.), *Towards the elimination of racism*. New York: Pergamon.

Berry, J. W., Kalin, R. and Taylor, D. M. (1977). *Multiculturalism and ethnic attitudes in Canada*. Ottawa: Supply and Services Canada.

Bettencourt, B. A., Brewer, M. B., Croak, M. R., and Miller, N. (1992). Cooperation and the reduction of intergroup bias: the role of reward structure and social orientation. *Journal of Experimental Social Psychology*, **28**, 301–309.

Billig, M. (1985). Prejudice, categorization and particularization: from a perceptual to a rhetorical approach. *European Journal of Social Psychology*, **15**, 79–103.

Billig, M. G., and Tajfel, H. (1973). Social categorization and similarity in intergroup behaviour. *European Journal of Social Psychology*, **3**, 27–52.

Brewer, M. B. (1991). The social self: on being the same and different at the same time. *Personality and Social Psychology Bulletin*, **17**, 475–482.

Brewer, M. B., and Campbell, D. T. (1976). *Ethnocentrism and intergroup attitudes: East African evidence*. NY: Sage.

Brewer, M. B., Ho, H.-K., Lee, J.-Y., and Miller, N. (1987). Social identity and social distance among Hong Kong schoolchildren. *Personality and Social Psychology Bulletin*, **13**, 156–165.

Brewer, M. B., and Miller, N. (1984). Beyond the contact hypothesis: theoretical perspectives on desegregation. In N. Miller and M. B. Brewer (Eds) *Groups in Contact: the psychology of desegregation*. NY: Academic Press.

Brown, R. J. (1978). Divided we fall: an analysis of relations between sections of a factory workforce. In Tajfel, H. (Ed.), *Differentiation between social groups*. London: Academic Press.

Brown, R. J. (1984a). The effects of intergroup similarity and cooperative vs. competitive orientation on intergroup discrimination. *British Journal of Social Psychology*, **23**, 21–33.

Brown, R. J. (1984b). The role of similarity in intergroup relations. In: H. Tajfel (Ed.), *The social dimension*, Vol. 2. Cambridge: Cambridge University Press.

Brown, R. J. (1988). *Group Processes: dynamics within and between groups*. Oxford: Blackwell.

Brown, R. J. (1995). *Prejudice: its social psychology*. Oxford: Blackwell.

Brown, R. J., and Abrams, D. (1986). The effects of intergroup similarity and goal interdependence on intergroup attitudes and task performance. *Journal of Experimental Social Psychology*, **22**, 78–92.

Brown, R. J., and Turner, J. C. (1979). The criss-cross categorization effect in intergroup discrimination. *British Journal of Social and Clinical Psychology*, **18**, 371–383.

Brown, R. J., and Turner, J. C. (1981). Interpersonal and intergroup behaviour. In J. C. Turner and H. Giles (Eds), *Intergroup behaviour*, Oxford: Basil Blackwell.

Brown, R. J., and Wade, G. S. (1987). Superordinate goals and intergroup behaviour: the effects of role ambiguity and status on intergroup attitudes and task performance. *European Journal of Social Psychology*, 17, 131–142.

Bruner, J. S. (1957). On perceptual readiness. *Psychological Review*, **64**, 123–151.

Byrne, D. (1971). *The attraction paradigm*. New York: Academic Press.

Byrne, D., and Wong, T. J. (1962). Racial prejudice, interpersonal attraction and assumed dissimilarity of attitudes. *Journal of Abnormal and Social Psychology*, **65**, 246–253.

Campbell, D. T. (1956). Enhancement of contrast as a composite habit. *Journal of Abnormal and Social Psychology*, **53**, 350–355.

Cook, S. W. (1962). The systematic analysis of socially significant events. *Journal of Social Issues*, **18**, 66–84.

Cook, S. W. (1978). Interpersonal and attitudinal outcomes in cooperating interracial groups. *Journal of Research and Development in Education*, **12**, 97–113.

Deschamps, J.-C., and Brown, R. J. (1983). Superordinate goals and intergroup conflict. *British Journal of Social Psychology*, **22**, 189–195.

Deschamps, J.-C., and Doise, W. (1978). Crossed category memberships in intergroup relations. In H. Tajfel (Ed.), *Differentiation between social groups*. London: Academic Press.

DesForges, D. M., Lord, C. G., Ramsey, S. L., Mason, J. A., van Leeuwen, M. D., West, S. C., and Lepper, M. R. (1991). Effects of structured cooperative contact on changing negative attitudes towards stigmatized groups. *Journal of Personality and Social Psychology*, **60**, 531–544.

Diehl, M. (1988). Social identity and minimal groups: the effects of interpersonal and intergroup attitudinal similarity on intergroup discrimination. *British Journal of Social Psychology*, **27**, 289–300.

Diehl, M. (1990). The minimal group paradigm: theoretical explanations and empirical findings. In W. Stroebe and M. Hewstone (Eds), *European review of social psychology*, Vol.1. Chichester: Wiley.

Doise, W. (1976). *L'articulation psychosociologique et les relations entre groupes*. Brussels: de Boeck. Translated as *Groups and individuals: Explanations in social psychology*. Cambridge: Cambridge University Press, 1978.

Dollard, J., Doob, L. W., Miller, N. E., Mowrer, O. K., and Sears, R. R. (1939). *Frustration and aggression*. New Haven: Yale University Press.

Duck, S. W. (Ed.) (1977). *Theory and practice in interpersonal attraction*. London: Academic Press.

Festinger, L. (1954). A theory of social comparison processes. *Human relations*, **7**, 117–140.

Gaertner, S., Dovidio, J. F., Anastasio, P. A., Bachevan, B. A., and Rust, M. C. (1993). The common ingroup identity model: recategorization and the reduction of intergroup bias. In W. Stroebe and M. Hewstone (Eds), *European review of social psychology*, **4**. Chichester: Wiley, pp. 1–26..

Gaertner, S. L., Mann, J., Murrell, A., and Dovidio, J. F. (1989). Reducing intergroup bias: the benefits of recategorization. *Journal of Personality and Social Psychology*, **57**, 239–249.

Gaertner, S. L., Rust, M., Dovidio, J. F., Bachman, B., and Anastasio, P. (in press). The contact hypothesis: The role of a common ingroup identity on reducing intergroup bias. *Small Group Research*.

Gluckman, M. (1956). *Custom and conflict in Africa*. Oxford: Blackwell.

Grant, P. R. (1993). Reactions to intergroup similarity: examination of the similarity–differentiation and the similarity–attraction hypotheses. *Canadian Journal of Behavioural Science*, **25**, 28–44.

Hagendoorn, L. and Henke, R. (1991). The effect of multiple category membership on intergroup evaluations in a North-Indian context: class, caste, and religion. *British Journal of Social Psychology*, **30**, 247–260.

Hendrick, C., Bixenstine, V. E., and Hawkins, G. (1971). Race vs. belief similarity as determinants of attraction: a search for a fair test. *Journal of Personality and Social Psychology*, **17**, 250–258.

Hewstone, M., and Brown, R. J. (1986). Contact is not enough: an intergroup perspective on the contact hypothesis. In M. Hewstone and R. Brown (Eds), *Contact and conflict in intergroup encounters*. Oxford: Blackwell.

Hewstone, M, Islam, M. R., and Judd, C. M. (1993). Models of crossed categorization and intergroup relations. *Journal of Personality and Social Psychology*, **64**, 779–793.

Insko, C. A., Nacoste, R. W., and Moe, J. L. (1983). Belief congruence and racial discrimination: Review of the evidence and critical evaluation. *European Journal of Social Psychology*, **13**, 153–174.

Islam, M. R., and Hewstone, M. (1993). Dimensions of contact as predictors of intergroup anxiety, perceived outgroup variability and outgroup attitude: An integrative model. *Personality and Social Psychology Bulletin*, **19**, 700–710.

Johnston, L., and Hewstone, M. (1992). Cognitive models of stereotype change (3): Subtyping and the perceived typicality of disconforming group members. *Journal of Experimental Social Psychology*, **28**, 360–386.

Joly, S., Tougas, F., and Brown, R. (1993). L'effet de la catégorisation croisée sur la discrimination intergroupe en milieu universitaire. Unpublished manuscript, Université d'Ottawa.

LeVine, R. A., and Campbell, D. T. (1972). *Ethnocentrism: Theories of conflict, ethnic attitudes and group behaviour.* NY: Wiley.

Marcus-Newhall, A., Miller, N., Holtz, R., and Brewer, M. B. (1993). Cross-cutting category membership with role assignment: a means of reducing intergroup bias. *British Journal of Social Psychology*, **32**, 125–146.

Miller, N., Brewer, M. B., and Edwards, K. (1985). Cooperative interaction in desegregated settings: a laboratory analogue. *Journal of Social Issues*, **41**, 63–79.

Minard, R. D. (1952). Race relationships in the Pocahontas coal field. *Journal of Social Issues*, **8**, 29–44.

Mummendey, A., and Schreiber, H. J. (1984). Social comparison, similarity, and ingroup favouritism: a replication. *European Journal of Social Psychology*, **14**, 231–233.

Newcomb, T. (1961). *The acquaintance process.* NY: Holt, Rinehart and Winston.

Pettigrew, T. F. (1971). *Racially separate or together?* New York: McGraw-Hill.

Roccas, R., and Schwartz, S. H. (1993). Effects of intergroup similarity on intergroup relations. *European Journal of Social Psychology*, **23**, 581–595.

Rokeach, M. (1960). *The open and closed mind.* New York: Basic.

Rokeach, M., and Mezei, L. (1966). Race and shared belief as factors in social choice. *Science*, **151**, 167–172.

Rokeach, M., Smith, P. W., and Evans, R. I. (1960). Two kinds of prejudice or one? In M. Rokeach (Ed.). *The open and closed mind.* NY: Basic Books.

Rothbart, M., and John, O. P. (1985). Social categorization and behavioural episodes: a cognitive analysis of the effects of intergroup contact. *Journal of Social Issues*, **41**, 81–104.

Stein, D. D., Hardyck, J. A., and Smith, M. B. (1965). Race and belief: an open and shut case. *Journal of Personality and Social Psychology*, **1**, 281–289.

Stephan, W., and Stephan, C. W. (1985). Intergroup anxiety. *Journal of Social Issues*, **41**, 157–175.

Struch, N., and Schwartz, S. H. (1989). Intergroup aggression: its predictors and distinctiveness from in-group bias. *Journal of Personality and Social Psychology*, **56**, 364–373.

Tajfel, H. (1959). The anchoring effects of value in a scale of judgements. *British Journal of Psychology*, **50**, 294–304.

Tajfel, H. (1966). Cooperation between human groups. *Eugenics Review*, **58**, 72–84.

Tajfel, H. (1969). Cognitive aspects of prejudice. *Journal of Social Issues*, **25**, 79–97.

Tajfel, H. (Ed.) (1978). *Differentiation between social groups: Studies in the social psychology of intergroup relations.* London: Academic Press.

Tajfel, H. (1982). Social psychology of intergroup relations. *Annual Review of Psychology*, **33**, 1–39.

Tajfel, H., Flament, C., Billig, M. G. and Bundy, R. P. (1971). Social categorization and intergroup behaviour., *European Journal of Social Psychology*, **1**, 149–178.

Tajfel, H. and Turner, J. (1986). The social identity theory of intergroup behaviour. In S. Worchel and W. G. Austin (Eds), *Psychology of intergroup relations.* Chicago: Nelson, pp. 7–24.

Tajfel, H., and Wilkes, A. L. (1963). Classification and quantitative judgement. *British Journal of Psychology*, **54**, 101–114.

Triandis, H. C., and Davis, E. F. (1965). Race and belief as shared determinants of behavior intentions. *Journal of Personality and Social Psychology*, **2**, 715–725.

Turner, J. C. (1978). Social comparison, similarity and ingroup favouritism. In H. Tajfel (Ed.), *Differentiation between social groups: studies in the social psychology of intergroup relations.* London: Academic Press.

Turner, J. C. (1981). The experimental social psychology of intergroup behaviour. In J. C. Turner and H. Giles (Eds), *Intergroup behaviour*, Oxford: Blackwell.

Vanbeselaere, N. (1991). The different effects of simple and crossed categorizations: a result of the category differentiation process or differential category salience. In W. Stroebe and M. Hewstone (Eds), *European review of social psychology*, Vol. 2. Chichester, Wiley, pp. 247–278.

Van Oudenhoven, J. P., Groenewoud, J. T., and Hewstone, M. (in press). Cooperation, ethnic salience and generalization of interethnic attitudes. *European Journal of Social Psychology*. University of Nijmegan.

Vivian, J., Brown, R. J., and Hewstone, M. (1994). Changing attitudes through intergroup contact: the effects of membership salience. Unpublished manuscript, University of Kent.

Vivian, J., Hewstone, M., and Brown, R. (in press) Intergroup contact: theoretical and empirical developments. In R. Ben-Ari. and Y. Rich (Eds), *Understanding and enhancing education for diverse students: an international perspective*. University of Dar Ilan Press.

Weber, R. and Crocker, J. (1983). Cognitive processes in the revision of stereotypic beliefs. *Journal of Personality and Social Psychology*, **45**, 961–977.

Wilder, D. A. (1984a). Predictions of belief homogeneity and similarity following social categorization. *British Journal of Social Psychology*, **23**, 323–333.

Wilder, D. A. (1984b). Intergroup contact: the typical member and the exception to the rule. *Journal of Experimental Social Psychology*, **20**, 177–194.

Wilder, D. A., and Shapiro, P. N. (1989). Role of competition-induced anxiety in limiting the beneficial impact of positive behavior by an outgroup member. *Journal of Personality and Social Psychology*, **56**, 60–69.

Worchel, S., Axsom, D,. Ferris, F., Samaha, C. and Schweitzer, S. (1978). Factors determining the effect of intergroup cooperation on intergroup attraction. *Journal of Conflict Resolution*, **22**, 429–439.

7

Power: An Essay in Honour of Henri Tajfel

Sik Hung Ng

Department of Psychology, Victoria University of Wellington

Contents

A personal note is in order. I began my doctoral research with Henri at the beginning of 1974. Prior to that, I had been introduced to his works by my former professor at the University of Hong Kong, who co-edited and prefaced a book with him while they were both at Oxford (Tajfel and Dawson, 1965). In the early months of 1974, I was able to update my knowledge of Henri's works, principally those which he later presented in his Katz-Newcomb lectures (Tajfel, 1974). Like his earlier works on intra- and interserial effects, categorization and prejudice, his more recent work on the emergent social identity theory was inspiring to say the least. It let in a breath of fresh air to what was becoming for me a rather dull social psychology. The theory confirmed my cultural belief in the values of the "group" to the lives of its members. It also indicated the possibility of how "intergroup" behaviour and the "group" might provide some of the missing links between the individual and society, links which had always intrigued me in my study of psychology and sociology. Perhaps most important of all, the theory conveyed to me a deep intellectual commitment to issues confronting subordinate minority groups, with which I was only too familiar from my experience as a Chinese "minority" person in the British colony of Hong Kong.

It would appear then that I had every reason to make social identity theory my doctoral research topic. But this was not to be. As far as I could make out, at the heart of social identity theory was a sequence of statements relating to the shared constructions of social reality (through social categorization), the negotiation of group-based social identity, and the making of social comparisons. It purported to predict what courses of collective action individuals would take to deal with common problems of (evaluative) status. That was fine. Yet it had nothing to say about power beyond the acknowledgement that power is different from status and an important part of the social context in which intergroup behaviour occurs. In this respect, the theory was heading away from the perspective espoused by Sherif (1962):

> In seeking perspectives on special areas of intergroup relations through the consideration of the systems of which they are parts, we immediately encounter the *power* dimension, which has been one of the most neglected aspects of small group research. . . . The differentiated statuses which define any organization from an operational point of view are positions in a power dimension, whatever else they may be. As such, every group is a power group, even though means and instrumentalities of sanctions do differ in formal and informal organizations.
>
> (pp. 16–17, original italics)

The omission of power from social identity theory worried me considerably even though I could also see that the theory was in many ways a theoretical advance over Sherif's rationalist approach to intergroup competition and conflict.

To my mind at that time, not only should social identity theory distinguish power from status—which it had—but having done that, it should also treat power as an equally if not more fundamental dimension than identity, social comparison, and both intra- and intergroup differentiation. What use to minority group members is a "positive" or "psychologically distinct" identity without their group achieving parity of power with relevant (oppressive) outgroups? In what sense can their subordination and their deprivation of an autonomous voice be adequately compensated by a gain in status? Would the compensation liberate them from, or simply trap them in, their subordination? Have their views been solicited by researchers? My reading of Fanon (1965), Malcolm X (1964), and the contemporary history of China under western impact made me very sceptical of identity formulations that were void of power. By the same token, social comparison on "valued" dimensions minus the power dimension made little sense to me; it also ignored the fundamental role of power comparison in intergroup conflict (Sherif, 1966; Simmel, 1950). As for the importance of power in intra- and intergroup differentiation, from what I had learnt of sociological and political theories, especially those relating to social stratification and social change, I was sure of the correctness of my position. At the same time, though, I did not believe that social psychology, not even *social* social psychology as it was then emerging in Europe, should be asked to become sociology or political psychology. Nor should European social psychology be asked to become Asian social psychology or the social psychology of the Third World.

Nonetheless I was brave enough (I was relatively young then) to talk to Henri of my reservations about social identity theory, not knowing how he would respond, or if indeed he would take offence. To my pleasant surprise, he did not take offence at all! More surprising still, he actually encouraged me to work on the topic of power for my doctorate. This I eventually did by incorporating aspects of social identity theory and Mulder's theory of power distance mechanisms into my thesis (Ng, 1977). My subsequent research interest in the power dimension, which has lasted to this date, owes much to Henri's intellectual broadmindedness and, up until his death in 1982, his generous encouragement.

Conversational Interaction

Elsewhere I have written about the power dimension in minimal group experiments with the aim of posing new questions, such as: what makes intergroup discrimination possible (as distinct from what causes intergroup discrimination)? Would political categorization enhance power change beyond the level achievable by social categorization? (Ng, 1978, 1982, 1984). These earlier works took a structural view of power and operationalized it as a given, independent variable.

Later I became interested in the power of talk (Brooke and Ng, 1986), linguistic sexism (Ng, 1990), and the relationship between majority/minority situations and ideological legitimation (Ng and Cram, 1988). These interests marked the beginning of a discursive turn in my study of social power aimed at extending some of the ideas that I had developed at Bristol (Ng, 1980) to map the multiple relations between power and language. In a collaborative study with James Bradac, several power–language relations were examined, and these were discussed in Ng and Bradac (1993) under five headings. In brief, the first relation is that language *reveals* power: the language behaviour (e.g. accent) of speakers may be taken as an indication of their powerful or powerless condition by hearers. Second, language *reflects* power: the prestige of a language rises or falls with the power of its users, and the reaction of message recipients is affected by their belief about the power or powerlessness of the communicator (e.g. a threat is threatening only if the communicator is believed to have punishment power over the message recipient). Third, language *creates* power: talk and rules of discourse practice are potential resources that users can draw upon to advance individual and collective goals, to influence or control the behaviour of group members, and to negotiate or compete with other groups. Fourth, language *depoliticizes* power: language is used simultaneously to attain power and to cover up the power attempt (e.g. dishonest speech, mitigated or masked communication). Fifth, language *routinizes* power: the dominance of one group (e.g. adult males) over others becomes embedded in everyday discourse practices, the routine use of which will make the dominance seem normative, natural, and eventually unmarked and invisible (e.g. linguistic sexism). All of these can be found in different measures in a variety of human communication, one of which—importantly here as this is the focus of the present chapter—is face-to-face conversation.

As Heritage (1984) and others (e.g. Argyle, 1969) have pointed out, "the social world is a pervasively conversational one" (Heritage, 1984, p. 239). Perhaps conversations are so common in everyday life we tend to take them for granted without realizing that our social reality is largely constructed and renewed in conversations, or that our interpersonal relationships, career and self-esteem may rise or fall depending on our involvement in and management of our daily conversations. As far as research goes, despite the pioneering work of Bales (1950), conversational interaction has not been accorded a great deal of attention in small group research. In my study of conversational interaction, I have found it helpful to consult conversation analysis (e.g. Atkinson and Heritage, 1984; Sacks *et al.*, 1974), speech act theory (e.g. Austin, 1962; Searle, 1969), and what may be loosely called interactional sociolinguistics (e.g. Brown and Levinson, 1978; Gumperz, 1982) and discourse analysis (e.g. Coulthard, 1977; Labov and Fanshel, 1977). These (and other) sources are of course not new to social psychology. Clark's (1985) chapter in *The handbook of social psychology*, for example, contains a lucid account of relevant ideas from these sources, as does Potter and Wetherell's (1987) book on discourse analysis. Importantly, the recent works by Giles and his associates under communication accommodation theory is also a rich reference of ideas rooted in similar sources and in social identity theory (Gallois *et al.*, 1988, 1995; Giles and Coupland, 1991).

Below, I will explore some aspects of conversational influence and control that are particularly relevant to the language-creates-power theme. The materials for the present discussion are largely based on Ng and Bradac (1993). In the main, the discussion will centre on relatively non-hierarchical situations where the power distance among individuals either does not exist or, if it does, is vulnerable enough to allow power to be subverted, negotiated or strategically enacted on the spot. As an illustration, consider the following event. One New Zealand Maori group from a tribe in which women had the right to speak in formal ceremonies visited another that denied women such rights. After the hosts had opened the oratory, it was the guests' turn to speak. The speaking turn fell on the guest with the most senior rank, an elderly woman chief.

> After a moment's hesitation she began to speak. Immediately there was a protest from the hosts. Calmly ignoring them, the chieftainess continued her speech to the end and then said: "You Arawa men, you tell me to sit down because I am a woman, yet none of you would be in the world if it wasn't for your mothers. This is where your learning and your grey hairs come from!" Then, turning her back on them she bent over and flipped up her skirts in "the supreme gesture of contempt."
>
> (Salmond, quoted in Coulthard, 1977, p. 48.)

In a conversation, participants engage each other in their respective speaker and hearer roles. These conversational roles circulate in the group during the course of the conversation as participants take turns at talking. As the conversation unfolds, what is being talked about becomes the current focal topic that will in due course develop into or be replaced by another topic. In short, to do conversation, conversationalists have to engage each other in speaker/hearer roles, construct and take turns, and develop as well as change conversational topics (Ng and Bradac, 1993). From this performative point of view, conversations are not just words but are words-in-action and action-in-words that are sequentially enacted in the stream of social actions through which conversationalists both act on and react to each other.

Conversational roles, topics and turns are the major areas of conversational interaction. As such, they are the principal avenues or mechanisms by which conversationalists influence and control each other. There are, of course, other areas of interaction and it is possible that these too can serve as mechanisms for influence and control. For example, communication accommodation theory, to which mention has already been made, proposes four categories of interactional strategy which collectively cover an extremely wide range of such possibilities. Of these categories, the category of approximation strategies (e.g. speech convergence and divergence) is the "oldest" in research that has led to the development of the communication accommodation theory (Giles and Powesland, 1975; Bourhis *et al.*, 1979). Whilst its link with contextual, power-related variables is clearly articulated in the framework of ethnolinguistic vitality (Harwood *et al.*, 1994), its relevance to conversational influence and control remains relatively unexplored. On the other hand, the remaining three categories of interactional strategy are more directly relevant to conversational influence and control.

Firstly, interpretability strategies enable speakers to respond to their conversational partner's ability or inability (actual, perceived or stereotyped) to understand and deal with interaction (interpretive competence). Thus, for example, when talking to infants (or foreign students, elderly people, and persons with disability) speakers may adopt the interpretability strategy of baby-talk (speaking louder and slower in simpler and shorter sentences, etc.). The effect of using this strategy, despite good intentions, is to subject the addressees to patronizing talk that severely limits their opportunity to participate as equal partners. Secondly, discourse management strategies enable speakers to respond to their partners' conversational needs through the management of the field (topic), the tenor (interpersonal positions, roles, and faces) and the mode (turn allocation). Finally, interpersonal control strategies would either increase or decrease the conversational partners' discretion or freedom to play out specific interactional roles. Despite the wide range of possibilities of conversational influence and control envisaged by communication accommodation theory, it would appear that these overlap substantially with the triad of roles, topics and turns proposed in the present chapter.

Except in formal conversations such as school debates and official ceremonies, conversationalists do not have a referee to manage their roles, turns and topics. Instead, they are on their own to negotiate with one another on a moment-by-moment basis, sometimes collaboratively and other times contentiously or even confrontationally. That is, conversational interactions often entail the overcoming of resistance even though they may appear to be smooth and unproblematic on the surface. Hence a closer examination of conversational interactions in relatively non-hierarchical situations, however mundane they may seem, can be informative as to the operation of influence and control.

The operation of conversational influence and control can be observed both during and after a conversation, as will be shown in the second and third sections, respectively. Specifically, the second section will discuss how role engagement and topic control are communicatively negotiated and strategically enacted in the stream of conversational actions. Turns can also be included here, but for present purposes, they will be discussed in the third section, which deals with how conversational influence and control in a non-hierarchical situation will, over time, lead to the formation of an influence hierarchy among conversationalists. The emergence of intragroup power differentiation at the end of interaction will provide an index of the cumulative effect of the operation of conversational influence and control.

Negotiation and Enactment of Power Through Role Engagement and Topic Control

Conversational roles

It is not always an easy task for conversationalists to engage one another in their respective intended speaker and hearer roles. Consider the following excerpt of conversation provided by Pearce (1976, p. 28).

(1) *Tom*: Hey, did you hear what happened downtown today?
(2) *Dick*: Tell me.
(3) *Tom*: No, I was asking you.
(4) *Dick*: Oh, well, there was a demonstration at the post office . . .

At turn 1, Tom requested information of Dick by trying to cast Dick in a newsteller role. He could have done so directly by saying, "Dick, I hereby request you to tell me what has happened downtown today". Instead, he issued an *indirect* (more polite?) request encoded in question form. Dick interpreted the indirect request not as a genuine request for information but as Tom's pre-announcement for telling what he—Tom—had already known about happenings in town. That is, Dick missed what Austin (1962) has called the indirect illocutionary point of Tom's utterance and, in its place, (mis)understood Tom as expecting him to listen. "Tell me", Dick responded, thereby assuming a hearer role. In the next available turn (3), Tom tried to realign the conversation by explicitly casting Dick into the information-giver role. It was only then that Tom succeeded in doing what he had originally set out to do.

Tom's eventual success in role engagement qualifies as an act of power in the sense defined by Russell (1938), namely, power is the *production of intended effects*. This definition of power does not require the power wielder to overcome resistance or to act against another person's interest. Similarly, Heider's (1958) conception of power does not require resistance or conflict of interest. It even drops the requirement of intentionality: power, in Heider's view, is what a person *can* cause. Both definitions have their critics (see Depret and Fiske, 1993; Ng, 1980); but for present purposes, they will serve as bottom-line definitions for some of the power acts that we will be discussing below.

In the interaction between Tom and Dick that we have just read, Dick was only too willing to comply with what he believed were Tom's intentions. As we shall see, in other situations, collaboration may be lacking and role engagement may in fact be resisted, either of which would make the power play more apparent. "I want to talk to you, Michael Lamont Brown!", the teacher shouts in her attempt to summon Brown, a pupil who has behaved badly in class. However, Brown can avoid uptaking the addressee role (see below) by looking or moving away, or his classmates may come to his rescue by engaging him in *their* conversation, thus shutting the teacher out. A more experienced teacher might ask the class to stand, tell all except Brown to sit down, and only then begin to address her target. The latter is caught, as it were, by being cast into an addressee role that will oblige him to respond and will also restrain, momentarily at least, others from speaking. This places the teacher in a strategic position to exercise her official authority by reprimanding the pupil for wrong-doing.

In reaching an interactional position that allows her to overcome the target pupil's reluctance of being engaged in talk, the teacher has achieved power in the Lewinian sense: power is the *possibility* of inducing forces to overcome the target's resistance (Lewin, 1959). In Lewinian field theory, power is separated from its effects and used to refer to the possibility of inducing forces. A comprehensive account of the various power bases for inducing forces from a field theoretical perspective can be found in Raven's (1992) power/interactional model of interpersonal influence. The point to note here is that although one or more power bases (e.g. legitimacy) might have been activated in the sequence of events that eventually placed the teacher in a strong position to exercise her authority, what is more pertinent to the purposes of the present chapter is to describe those events in order to gain an understanding of how power is negotiated and enacted on the spot. By the same token, I will pass over social exchange theory (Jones and Gerard, 1967; Thibaut and Kelley, 1959) and other theories of power (e.g. Emerson, 1962).

It is also worth noting that in the classroom situation referred to above, the teacher intends to engage the pupil in a responsive rather than a non-responsive or evasive hearer role. A fine-grained distinction of hearer roles would be useful for throwing light on how particular hearer roles can be engaged to achieve strategic effects. Clark and Carlson (1982) distinguish three hearer roles. The *addressee* is a hearer to whom the speaker is addressing directly. The *participant* is a hearer whom the speaker intends to take part on a supportive basis in the conversational act that is directed at the addressee. The *overhearer* may be an eavesdropper from whom the speaker wants to conceal the message, or an audience that the speaker wants to address indirectly. Clark and Carlson (1982) give the following kind of example to illustrate how a speaker can cast hearers into the various hearer roles to achieve a strategic effect. Two friends, Ann and Charles, saw some deer-stalker caps in a departmental store and both came to the same conclusion that the caps looked absurd. Later, at the check-out counter, they saw the store manager wearing one of the caps. In front of Charles and with other customers overhearing, Ann addressed the store manager, saying: "What a handsome deer-stalker cap you are wearing!" In doing so, Ann cast the manager in the addressee role, Charles in the role of an ingroup participant, and the customers who were nearby in the overhearer role. This enabled Ann and her friend to constitute the manager as the subject of a sarcastic remark without impunity to themselves. The value of a fine-grained conceptual differentiation of hearer roles is that it provides a useful way of understanding the subtle multilayered goals that are achievable through the strategic casting of conversational roles.

In a similar vein, speakers may better protect themselves from accusation by casting a hearer into an overhearing role. For example, two men may exchange a homosexual joke intended to pour ridicule on a gay man who is nearby, but without referring to or addressing the latter. That is, they can cast their target in an overhearer role, thereby constituting him as the subject of a sexist discourse while at the same time making it difficult for him to accuse them of harassment.

The concept of multiple hearer roles implies that there is more than one party out there whom the speaker has to "deal with". Depending on what stakes the speaker has in the respective parties, he or she may adjust the talk to maximize the yield from the stakes. For example, in televized political debates, politicians have a greater stake in winning over the audience than in winning an argument *per se*. For this reason, when addressing directly their opposite number or the host, speakers also have to address the audience indirectly. Those who can do this will be able to project a positive public face, win the audience over, and achieve greater electoral power (see Heritage and Greatbach, 1986; Wilson, 1990).

Just as there is more than one hearer role, the speaker role can also be cast in multiple forms. Goffman (1981) distinguished three roles (interactional footings) that a speaker, by adopting the corresponding talk-production format, can perform: The animator is the person who is presently saying (animating) the words, which in turn are composed by the author and express the viewpoint or attitude of the principal. When Jesus said, "It is written, but verily I say unto you . . . ", he was fusing all three roles into one. Speakers who do this achieve identity with their words—they and their words are one and the same thing. This has the advantage of being able to project an image of spontaneity and conviction compared to reading from a script.

On the other hand, however, there are situations where it is more advantageous for speakers to dissociate themselves from what they have to say by adopting only the animator role. The advantage here is that the animator cannot be held personally responsible for the content of the speech. For example, by quoting from an incrimination, an innuendo, or a gossip (e.g. "he said she had said . . ."), the animator minimizes the risk of being taken to court. A more subtle display of the use of animation to advance a conversational agenda while minimizing direct personal confrontation is shown in the following segment of a conversation from a political interview provided by Clayman (1988). The immediate context of the conversation is a discussion about violence among South African blacks. IR is the interviewer, IE is the reverend Boesak, one of the interviewees, and the ambassador referred to in the discussion is the South African ambassador to the United States, who is a co-interviewee.

IR: Reverend Boesak let me pick up a point
1→ the ambassador made. What assurances can you give us that talks between moderates in that country will take place when it seems that any black leader who is willing to talk to the government is branded
2→ as the ambassador said a collaborator and is then punished?
IE: The ambassador has it wrong. It's not the people . . .

IR begins by adopting an animator role (at arrow 1) and attributing the upcoming assessment to the co-interviewee, the ambassador. Later, IR renews the animator role and attributes key words (collaborator and punished) to the ambassador again (at arrow 2). In this way, IR animates successfully an evaluative statement while maintaining journalistic neutrality. In his speaking turn, IE accepts IR's animator role while at the same time rebuts the animated assessment and directs his rebuttal at the ambassador and not at IR. By accepting IR's animator role, IE colludes with and thereby enables IR to stage a mediated debate in advancing the agenda of the interview.

The discussion so far has been mostly confined to the initial engagement of conversational roles in situations that are relatively free of conflict of interest. Not surprisingly, the associated power play is relatively undramatic. Beyond this "honeymoon" encounter, however, conversationalists may become reluctant to continue in their initial roles. This may be due to boredom with the initial roles or to a variety of other reasons. For example, a conversationalist who has been playing the role of an overhearer may interrupt an ongoing dialogue in order to add a point to the current topic, raise a new topic, or simply to force others to acknowledge his or her presence. Secondly, in the heat of an argument a speaker may switch from an animator to a principal role in order to state "what I really feel about racist bigots like you!". Whenever conversationalists change their initial roles, a realignment of roles has to be worked out that would require further, and perhaps more dramatic, power play.

The engagement and realignment of roles are closely linked with interactional goals. To analyse roles more deeply, one has to go beyond the kind of speaker roles and hearer roles that have been discussed thus far. Importantly, one has to examine the broader social functions of conversational roles in relation to longer-term interactional goals. For example, the goal of ending a two-party dispute may require a third party to play a meditator role, the function of which is to reconcile, to heal, and to assist the disputants with finding a non-zero-sum solution. Alternatively, in trying to end the dispute the third party may play the role of an arbitrator, whose function will be confined to passing a judgment on the rightfulness of claims and counter-claims. Because the two functions require different communicative skills for speaking and hearing effectively, a person who can act powerfully as an arbitrator may perform poorly as a mediator, and vice versa.

Topic control

Conversationalists have a stake in promoting topics that will advance their respective or collective conversational agenda. Equally, they also have a stake in preventing or discouraging topics that will otherwise embarrass them, put them at risk, or frustrate the group's collective conversational agenda. Both cases call for the negotiation of a particular topic, and not just any topic.

Speakers who have successfully raised a topic can promote it further by lengthening the current turn. One way to lengthen a turn is to minimize turn-yielding non-verbal cues (see Duncan and Fiske, 1977). Another is to claim completion right through pre-announcement, saying, for example, that "There are at least seven points that need to be addressed, but I'll confine myself to only just four. The first is, . . .". However, extended monologistic turns are relatively infrequent; even if they do occur, the time they consume can be more effectively used by co-ordinating a series of shorter interactive turns that involve other members talking actively about the same topic. In any case, it would be very rare for a single conversationalist to monopolize a conversation in one extended speaking turn. The question arises as to how a raised topic can be strategically kept alive and developed socially over a series of turns.

One way of developing the topic in a subsequent turn is by means of an adjacency pair. Examples of adjacency pairs are question–answer and offer–reply. The first part (e.g. question) constrains the content of the second part to the extent that some complementary second actions, but not others are "specially relevant for next turn" (Sacks *et al.*, 1974), or "preferred" (Heritage, 1988). The ability of adjacency pairs in directing subsequent turns to the desired topic is relatively strong in question–answer pairs, which is one of the reasons why questions are commonly used in courtroom trials and other situations where topic control is crucial to success (Philips, 1987). However, even with the success of any one adjacency pair, directionality becomes uncertain as soon as the turn containing the second part ends.

To develop a topic beyond the second turn, the previous speaker ("A") may attempt to regain the turn on his/her own initiative and effort, or the current speaker ("B") may return speakership to the previous speaker. Success in either case will produce an $A_1B_2A_3$ turn sequence. This pattern of alternate turns between a dyad may be extended a fourth time ($A_1B_2A_3B_4$) and even more. When this happens for long enough, the yoked dyadic talk between the same two individuals would provide a strong basis for a topic to be developed between the same pair of members in the first instance, and then later, through the serial engagement of other group members, in a more collective form by the group as a whole. In this way, the resultant group interaction is organized around clusters of yoked dyadic talk. A conversationalist who can create a series of co-operative dyads and be involved in them most of the time will effectively shape the group agenda to gain greater topic control. A co-operative clique is at the heart of this form of topic control, and the underlying mechanisms are collaborative role engagement and successful turn allocation. The yoked dyadic talk may also underpin the dynamics of intragroup power differentiation to be discussed in the next section.

By securing an extended dyadic discursive space in the development of a particular topic, speakers are in a position to more fully express their own views and, where necessary, refute opposing views. The development of a particular topic will also mean that less opportunity will be left for the raising of other, unwanted topics. When this is combined with pre-emptive speech acts that exclude unwanted topics from the floor (e.g. "The purpose of this meeting is to examine means of achieving positive discrimination, not the morality of positive discrimination."), a form of agenda control is in the making. That is, some topics will be organized into talk while unwanted topics will be organized out. This form of topic control is reminiscent of non-decision-making power in politics:

> Of course power is exercised when A participates in the making of decisions that affect B (decision-making power). But power is also exercised when A devotes his (or her) energies to creating or reinforcing social and political values and institutional practices that limit the scope of the political process to public consideration of only those which are comparatively innocuous to A (non-decision-making power). To the extent that A succeeds in doing this, B is prevented, for all practical purposes, from bringing to the fore any issues that might in their resolution be seriously detrimental to A's set of preferences.
>
> (Bachrach and Baratz, 1962, p. 948. Remarks in brackets have been added.)

Where an unwanted topic is already on the floor, attempts will normally be made to change it. Changing the topic can be enacted in a passive or an active way, both of which can be equally effective. The passive way is to show apathy by withdrawing talk-supportive cues (e.g. eye contact, smiling, "yeah yeah") and declining to take the next speaking turn. In this silent mode, the message of "let's us not talk about it any more" is communicated loud and clear. It is often an effective way of causing a topic to wither away. Indeed, in scientific discourse, many a paradigm or theory die precisely in the same way, rather than as a result of being disproved. A more active way of changing the topic is to replace the current (unwanted) topic with another topic either at the next available speaking turn or by interrupting the current speaker (see next section). Asking questions is a common and potentially effective way of raising a new topic to replace the old. In addition to replacing a topic, a question can also restrict the response and thereby control the information that is allowed to reach the floor. Walker (1987) summarized three forms of question that attorneys use in controlling the information that is to come out of the witness. Open-ended "WH" questions (e.g. "What did you do on the night of I January, 1995?") are the least controlling.

More controlling are disjunctive questions (e.g. "Was it red, black, blue, or white?") and yes–no (YN) questions (e.g., "Was it red?"). Still more controlling are yes–no/what questions that allow the attorney to assess the answer immediately and shift freely from one topic focus to another while making the witness appear foolish or unco-operative:

> . . . if the witness gives you a WH answer to a yes–no/what question, you can fall back on the YN form and say, "Just answer the question yes or no. All I asked you was: Do you remember how fast the car was going." On the other hand, if the witness responds to the YN embedding question with an unadorned "Yes", you can sit back, wait in silence, look quizzical, and then say, "Well? How fast was it going?". In either case, it is a no-win situation for the witness, and no matter which way he jumps, he's wrong. Now, that's control.
>
> (Walker, 1987, p. 77.)

Similarly, in doctor–patient interactions, doctors can establish and maintain topic control by structuring their questions and by assessing the patient's response (Mishler, 1984; ten Have, 1991).

One of the problems facing conversationalists who want to replace an ongoing topic is that the action would make them appear to be impolite and also cause the current speaker to lose face (Brown and Levinson, 1978). To enact topic change while minimizing the threat to own face and other's face, group members may make use of pre-acts that function as transition markers, such as, "One more thing," "Incidentally," and "You know what?" (see Crow, 1983). Or they can make use of topic-shading devices to create the impression that what they are about to say has some linkage with the ongoing topic. According to Tracy (1985), linkage may be based on schematic or script knowledge shared by group members, on a particular idea that has already been expressed by the current speaker, or on a meta-issue of which both the ongoing and the new topics are parts. These linkages can also reduce the perceived uncertainty of the direction in which the conversation is heading. As Berger and Bradac (1982) have pointed out, uncertainty reduction is important to conversationalists as this would give them a sense of the predictability of, and collective control over, the ongoing interaction.

So far we have been looking at topic control solely from the point of view of speakers who want to develop or change to a particular topic. The response of other relevant parties has not been considered yet. Unlike the questioning of witnesses by attorneys, in everyday conversations extreme imbalance of power between conversationalists is rare. This allows a high degree of contestability in the control of topics. The contestable nature of topic control can be illustrated by political interviews in which the interviewers attempt to open up controversial topics with the aim of extracting explicit, quotable admissions from the politician interviewees. Instead of co-operating with the interviewer in the Gricean manner (tell only the truth as required, clearly and to the point), the interviewees tend to give vague answers, dodge the question, or stray off to a new topic altogether (Greatbach, 1986). An indication of the prevalence of not replying to questions is shown in Bull and Mayer's (1993) study. Over eight political interviews given by Margaret Thatcher (British prime minister, 1979–1990) and Neil Kinnock

(British Labour Party leader, 1983–1992) during the 1987 British general election campaign, Thatcher and Kinnock did not reply to 56% and 59% of the interviewer questions, respectively. Harris (1991, cited in Bull, 1994) found a similarly high level of evasive behaviour in a different set of political interviews. To pursue and pin down evasive interviewees, interviewers may use a challenge to put the latter on the defensive and, in subsequent turns, reformulate the initial challenge in a more emphatic or aggravated manner to enforce explicitness of reply. An illustration of this can be found in the following question sequence taken from Blum-Kulka (1983, pp. 139–140):

> *Mishal*: Mr Gur . . . you have repeatedly stated that you consider yourself qualified to become prime minister. Tonight you have talked about objective qualifications for the job. What makes a person qualified to become prime minister?
> [Gur's answer]
> *Mishal*: Let's be more practical. If . . . will you present your candidacy?
> [Gur's answer]
> *Mishal*: Do you see yourself as one of the candidates?

Blum-Kulka (1983, p. 146) summarized the reformulations as follows.

> The reformulations seem in effect to be saying "We understand what you mean, i.e. what you have conversationally implied—and the audience is probably aware of the implication too, but our norms require that you should state your propositions instead of implying them (which would be acceptable under normal conditions), so say it. If you do, we'll move on to a different topic, possibly also have you quoted in the news; if you don't, we'll continue to challenge you."

Politician interviewees, of course, do not easily succumb to challenges or reformulations in the contest for topic control. They may attack the question, decline to answer, or, more subtly, equivocate and make a political point (see Bavelas *et al*., 1990; Bull and Mayer, 1993). Consider Gur's reply in the excerpt below (Blum-Kulka, 1983, p. 143):

> *Mishal*: . . . Are you satisfied with the current leadership of the Labour Party?
> *Gur*: There are several things which in my opinion need improvement. But we shouldn't ignore the fact that towards the last elections we grew as a party and drew to us many forces . . . . I think that the coming period will be crucial for the leadership of the party. In my estimate the year and a half (till the next election) will suffice for our leadership to pull the party together and move it forward.

Mishal's question implied criticism of the present state of the Labour Party and called for a strong defence. Gur's immediate response gave the impression that he was going to comply ("There are several things which in my opinion need improvement.")

> The remainder of his move, however, was framed in terms of the party's past ("grew" and "drew") and future ("coming period") not its present. In this way, he shifted the topical focus away from the touchy area of the present to relatively innocuous issues; afterwards, he danced around, as it were, the bait set down in the interviewer's nominated topic. At the same time, he countered the interviewer's implied criticism by portraying the party as one that had a track record of achievement and would continue to make even greater progress in the future. While doing all this, he used referential objects ("party" and "leadership") already contained in the interviewer's question as semantic bridges to create the impression of both semantic and ideational coherence.
>
> (Ng and Bradac, 1993, p. 87)

Power Differentiation Within Groups

The amount of talk tends to be distributed unevenly among group members. Research on leader emergence in initially non-hierarchical situations shows that group members who have talked the most stand the best chance of becoming leaders (Bales, 1956; Hollander, 1985; Mullen *et al.*, 1989). In the first of a series of experiments on the same subject, Brooke and Ng (1986) examined the role of talk in leader emergence and compared it with that of speech styles. Groups of about four unacquainted university students were shown a video about a controversial topic and asked to discuss issues raised in the video. Afterwards they rated each other on social evaluation measures of competence, trustworthiness, social attractiveness, convincingness, and social dynamism. They also ranked their own as well as each other's influence. The internally derived measure of influence ranking was deemed to be more meaningful than one based on judgments made by observers, even though the latter has been commonly adopted in similar research.

In all the six groups that have been tested, the hierarchy of influence ranking passed the concordance test, which indicated a high degree of intragroup consensus on the relative rankings. Compared to low-ranking members, high-ranking members were rated more positively on all five measures of social evaluation, and significantly so on the first two (competence and trustworthiness). To find out what sorts of conversational behaviour might account for the influence rankings, the authors transcribed the conversations for detailed analysis. Consistent with the leader emergence literature, participation level (number of words spoken) was significantly greater among high- than low-ranking members. By contrast, the two categories of members did not differ significantly on stylistic features (polite forms, hedges, tags, intensifiers, terminal-rising intonations) that have been traditionally associated with "powerless" speech (Erickson *et al.*, 1978; Lakoff, 1973). The negative results of speech style made the positive results of the amount of talk stand out even more prominently.

Nevertheless, further analysis of the results by Brooke and Ng (1986) showed that the importance of the quantity of talk was only skin deep. As it turned out, the amount of talk was directly determined by the number of speaking turns. The size of turns did not differ between high- and low-ranking members, but the number of turns was significantly greater among the former than the latter. That is, high-ranking members were better able to gain turns and, as a result, spoke more than did low-ranking members. What appears to be more important is not the amount of talk, but the ability to gain turns. Swann (1988) reported a similar result showing the primacy of turns over words that underlay the dominance of boys over girls in classroom talk.

Theoretically, one may argue that turns are critical to intragroup power differentiation because the successful allocation of every speaking turn would give the speaker one chance to engage self and others in their respective roles, raise or control a topic, advance the group task, and influence the subsequent transfer of the turn to another speaker. That is, every speaking turn, once obtained, immediately becomes a potential resource for the enactment of influence and control, even though the eventual success of the enactment will depend on message-related variables (Bradac, 1989), on the prevailing needs of the group (Bales, 1976), as well as on the responses of other conversationalists. Other things being equal, the greater the number of turns, the greater will be the potential resources and opportunities for influence and control.

The idea that turns are resources for enacting conversational influence goes back to the discourse analytic work of Labov and Fanshel (1977) and, more recently, research that views conversational events as resources (Edelsky and Adams, 1990; Wilson *et al.*, 1984). Furthermore, the activities associated with getting a turn—as distinct from the resource afforded by the turn—may in themselves constitute another source of influence. This is because the act of getting a turn draws attention from group members to self, and the manner in which the turn is gained may also exude leader-like qualities. To explore these possibilities, it would be useful to examine the conversational mechanisms that underlie the allocation of turns.

According to Sacks *et al.* (1974), turn-allocation is one component of turn-taking. The other component, turn-construction, is the content of the current speaking turn until a "transition-relevance place" is reached, at which the next speakership is allocated. Participants in a conversation allocate turns in such an orderly pattern that they appear to be following certain (implicit) conversational rules. These rules are: either the current speaker selects the next speaker, or a listener self-selects as the next speaker; when neither of these occur, the current speaker may, but need not, continue; but if the current speaker does continue, the above procedure "reapplies at the next transition-relevance place, and recursively at each transition-relevance place, until transfer is effected" (Sacks *et al.*, 1974, p. 704).

Sacks *et al.* (1974) posited the above rules in order to account for what they believed was an apparent fact common to all conversations: overwhelmingly, one and only one party speaks at a time. However, they underestimated the prevalence and significance of simultaneous speech, in which two or more speakers talk at the same time (Dunne and Ng, 1994). One type of simultaneous speech is interruption, through which a second speaker gains (steals?) a speaking turn by butting in to render the current speaker's turn-construction incomplete (Roger *et al.*, 1988). Sacks *et al.* (1974) mentioned interruptions but did not regard them as part of the turn-allocation mechanisms, presumably because of the "unrule-ly" nature of interruptions that does not fit their rule-based model.

In an attempt to test if turns obtained by successful interruption were as effective as other, non-interruption-turns in determining influence rankings, Ng *et al.* (1993) replicated the experiment of Brooke and Ng (1986). The results, again based on concordant influence rankings reported by group members themselves, first confirmed the finding that the emergent influence ranking was due to the total number of turns. Then, turns were disaggregated into interruption-turns (turns obtained by successful interruptions) and non-interruption-turns for further analysis, the results of which showed that whilst both were related to influence rankings, the relationship was in fact stronger for interruption-turns.

The strong effect of interruption-turns is counterintuitive to the extent that interrupters are stereotypically viewed as inconsiderate, non-listening and disruptive loud mouths, which would suggest that interrupters cannot be unanimously recognized as leaders. However, available evidence suggests otherwise. As extant research on language attitude has already demonstrated, solidarity and power are orthogonal dimensions—speakers who are disliked may nevertheless be accorded high influence (Brown, 1965; Ng and Bradac, 1993). Further, in Ng *et al.*'s (1993) study, group members who interrupted more frequently were not disliked any more than those who rarely interrupted. They both received the same degree of social attractiveness and trustworthiness ratings. These results and others—see below—suggest that it is the traditional negative stereotype of interruptions, rather than the contribution of interruptions to leader emergence, that should be questioned.

The contribution of interruption-turns (and also non-interruption-turns) to leader emergence has been confirmed in a third study carried out by my associates and myself (Ng *et al.*, 1995). This study also examines, among other things, the positive functions of successful interruptions beyond that of gaining speaking turns for the interrupter. By definition, a successful interruption disrupts the turn of the current speaker while allowing the interrupter to complete his or her turn. There is little doubt that the disruption can be hurtful to the current speaker and detrimental to the flow of the conversation. But this is not the whole picture. Further analysis of the discourse surrounding individual interruptions shows a high degree of altruism, enthusiasm and collaborative talk on the part of the interrupter. For example, there are specific instances where the current speaker appears to be running out of things to say but is unable to gracefully yield the floor. An interruption at this point gets the faltering speaker off the hook, as it were, and saves the conversation from impending moments of awkward silence or dysfluency. The interruption-turn may or may not continue with the current topic; nevertheless it performs an altruistic rescue function at the point when it is needed most (see speaker S1's behaviour in extract 1 below). Interruptions can also have an enthusing function—to promote a current topic by butting in rather than wait until it dries up or dies out for lack of enthusiastic collaboration (see speaker S4's behaviour in extract 2 below). Both types of function are highly constructive, and both require interrupting the current speaker for their implementation. [*Note*: (.) indicates a pause of about 0.5 second; (1.0) shows a 1-second pause; (unclear) identifies an unclear word or words; **I** marks the start of an overlapping speech.]

Extract 1:

S2: . . . so th they i think a lot of people may not even necessarily have their own views but they (.) feel they have their own views because of their christian beliefs? **I** (.) i dunno (.) does
S1: **I** yeah
S2: anyone **I** else (unclear)
S1: **I** yeah actually i think that is true too cos if um as they're saying with the blessed Catholic church

Extract 2:

S3: and like the people on um the left that were anti um euthanasia they (1.0) they um y'know they were saying things like there's not a demand for it (.) people don't really want to die and if they decide they want to die one minute the next minute they rnight decide t they want to live t yknow to say that is just pathetic (.) if you've come to the decision you're going to die i mean i'm sure you don't think oh wake up the one morning i'm going to die today i've just decided it y'know (.) its insulting **I (unclear) yeah**
S4: **I** its like abortion (.) you don't just say i don't want my baby today

The constructive pragmatic functions of interruption-turns may explain partly the positive effect these turns have on leader emergence. (Other constructive functions are also possible, for example, to interrupt talk that has strayed off the agenda in order to keep the group on task, to cut short the unpopular talk of a disliked (outgroup?) member, and such like.) Another explanation is that interruption-turns are the marked form of turn allocation that draws attention to the interrupter. The non-verbal situation immediately surrounding the interruption is usually associated with emphatic prosodic features: a faster speech rate and higher vocal amplitude than the outlying discourse (see also French and Local, 1983; Roger, 1989). Interruptees could either return competition for the disputed turn by talking slower and louder simultaneously, or relinquish the turn by talking softer. In any case, the prosodic marking may make the episode particularly salient to group members, and more easily recalled when they are later asked to rank each other on relative influence.

It is worth noting that in all three of the studies of conversational influence carried out by my associates and myself, there were no significant gender differences in either the number of non-interruption-turns, interruption-turns, or influence ranking. The absence of gender effects in interruption-turns contradicts the claim of male conversational dominance made by Zimmerman and West (1975), but is consistent with the result of James and Clarke's (1992) review of other relevant studies.

To sum up thus far: The formation of an influence hierarchy among members of a newly-formed group is an outcome of the unequal allocation of speaking turns within the group. Turns are allocated by current-speaker-selects-next, or by listener-self-selects either at the first available transition-relevance place or by interruptions. Regardless of how they are obtained, turns create the opportunity or resource necessary for enacting conversational influence through the casting of conversational roles and the control of conversational topics in ways illustrated in the preceding section. Turns also attract group attention to the extent that group members are more attentive to speakers than to hearers; such group attentiveness may also contribute to leader emergence. Contrary to the negative stereotype of interruptions, turns obtained by interruptions are more effective than non-interruption-turns in determining members' influence ranking, possibly due to constructive pragmatic functions and memorable prosodic features associated with the gaining of interruption-turns.

The research reviewed above deals with turn-allocation mechanisms that can be called upon to explain *how* turns are distributed in the group. Further analysis is needed to throw light on *why* turns are distributed unevenly in the group. Part of the answer may be found in individual differences in the ability and motivation to take turns. For example, persons with a "dominant" personality may be better able and more strongly motivated to talk (Roger, 1989). Another part of the answer may lie in certain group processes that enable some prototypical members to talk more often than other, less prototypical members (Hogg, in press). Alternatively, other different group processes may link exceptional or charismatic personal qualities, not prototypicality, to speaking rights. Thirdly, as Fowler (1985) has argued in another context, wider ideologies or discourse rules may favour some particular stance or way of addressing a topic while discouraging other stances and ways of talking. Clearly, personal, group dynamic, and ideological factors need to be addressed in order to develop a fuller understanding of the uneven distribution of turns in non-hierarchical situations.

Another approach to finding the causes of the uneven distribution of turns can be derived from the observation that pairs of speakers tend to alternate their talk over a number of tums. The $A_1B_2A_3$ turn sequence, in which speakers A and B alternate turns, has been found to be the most common pattern of speaker transfer in four-person groups (Parker, 1988). Even in six-person groups where there are as many as four other persons who can potentially displace A in the A_3 turn, the $A_1B_2A_3$ sequence still far exceeds any other sequence (Stasser and Taylor, 1991).

Further, the $A_1B_2A_3$ sequence has more than a 50% chance of extending to the $A_1B_2A_3B_4$ sequence. Eventually the multiturn sequence between the same two speakers will give way to a new sequence involving either a member of the current dyad and a new member, or two new members. To the extent that conversational interaction is organized around clusters of multiturn talk between the same dyad rather than based on a collection of sporadic single- or two-turn talk, it is in the former that one should look for an explanation of the uneven distribution of turns. From this point of view, a conversationalist will obtain a disproportionate number of turns by expanding an interaction into a multi-turn interaction with the same partner, and by getting involved in multiturn interaction with different partners at different times. The sort of conversational behaviour that will achieve these functions is not the same as those kinds of behaviour that will secure single turns or extended interaction with one and only one partner. Or at least it seems that way.

Concluding remarks

As noted in the first section, conversational interaction has never been a hot topic in mainstream, experimental social psychology. Its future in the recent revival of small group research remains dim (Moreland *et al.*, 1994). On the other hand (side?), discursive social psychology, since its rise to popularity in recent years, has been quick to embrace conversation. In particular, the function of conversation in the discursive construction of *social reality* has been stressed (e.g. Harre, 1992; Shotter, 1992; Wetherell and Potter, 1992; see also Mead, 1934).

In the present chapter I have explored the link between conversation and *power*. The discussion has centred on mechanisms of influence and control that operate through role engagement, topic management and turn allocation. To delineate these mechanisms, I have concentrated on relatively non-hierarchical situations where the interpersonal power distance is either non-existing or not big enough to determine who can have access to the mechanisms. In these situations, to use the by now familiar phrase, power is communicatively negotiated and strategically enacted on the spot. The power act that is constituted in the process is always a joint accomplishment between two or more persons, rather than a unilateral act of force or dominance imposed on a person by another.

In conclusion, it would be fitting to point out the limitations of the triad of mechanisms and to indicate some future direction of research. Among the mechanisms, turn allocation is a necessary condition of the others; in this sense it is of special importance to conversational influence and control. But since speakership alone does not guarantee role engagement or topic control, the latter two mechanisms are also important in themselves. That applies to relatively non-hierarchical situations. The same mechanisms, however, may not be fully applicable to situations where a strong asymmetrical power relation already exists among group members. In these highly hierarchical situations, low-power members tend to orientate themselves and direct their communication towards the high-power members (Fiske, 1993; Mulder, 1977; Shaw, 1981). In extreme but by no means uncommon cases, low-power members speak in the voice of those who have power over them, animating the latter's ideas and views. This bottom-up complicity will strengthen further the high-power members' access to speakership, role engagement and topic control. For this reason, access to the mechanisms will be correlated with the existent power relation, that is, access will require less effort from high- than from low-power members. This allows high-power members direct access to topic control with a minimal number of speaking turns. Unlike emergent leaders in non-hierarchical situations, high-power members in hierarchical situations can be conversationally powerful without having to talk much. The interesting questions posed by hierarchical situations are those concerning the relations between interaction and social structure: how conversations reveal, reflect, and routinize existent structural dominance with the help of the complicity of low-power members.

The non-hierarchical and the hierarchical situations referred to above are not meant to be dichotomies, but are rather the two ends of a continuum of power distance. The closer a situation is to the non-hierarchical end (minimal power distance), the more negotiable and contestable the mechanisms of influence and control will become. In the extreme case, the situation becomes a "homogeneous social medium of freely floating individual particles" (Tajfel, 1979, p. 188). Conversely, the closer a situation is to the hierarchical end of the continuum (maximal power distance), the more responsive are the mechanisms to the existent power relation among the parties. The extreme case here would be that the mechanisms are subservient to the existent power relation with the complicity of low-power members. A movement along the hierarchical–non-hierarchical continuum may occur owing to power differentiation or power change within the group over time. As we have seen, power differentiation can occur fairly quickly in newly formed conversational groups. Other studies, though not focusing on conversational groups, have also found that hierarchical differentiation develops rapidly soon after most of the groups are formed (e.g. Barchas and Fisek, 1984; Sherif, 1966). Subsequent power change may increase, decrease, or even reverse the power distance among members. The process of power change that occurs after the initial power differentiation is an important albeit difficult research question, and will certainly require other conceptual tools in addition to those presented in the present chapter.

Despite their limitations, the mechanisms are useful for uncovering conversational control where none appears to exist on the surface. Here lies one direction for future research. As an example, consider the case of intergenerational communication directed from young to elderly people, otherwise known as *elderspeak.* Research has shown that elderspeak resembles adult-to-baby talk (baby-talk) in the frequent use of high pitch, exaggerated intonation, simplified syntax, simpler vocabulary, slower speech fluency punctuated with fillers and fragments, and repetitions or paraphrasing of messages (Caporael, 1981; Kemper, 1994). In elderspeak, as in baby-talk, the speakers adjust their speech behaviour towards the elderly person out of good intentions: to facilitate comprehension, to convey a sense of nurturing and warmth, to express solidarity with the addressee, and so forth.

The linguistic analysis of elderspeak has been confined to sounds and words with little or no regard to the surrounding conversation. As such, the analysis is inadequate for the understanding of why most elderly people consider elderspeak to be patronizing, demeaning and disrespectful; nor can it illuminate the process whereby elderspeak may reduce the communicative competence of elderly people and hasten their social ageing. It is necessary to include the surrounding conversation and the context in the analysis (Coupland *et al.*, 1991). In this wider conversational approach, it becomes apparent that elderspeak, despite the good intentions of the speakers, is in fact conversationally controlling in a detrimental way for the elderly recipients (Ng, 1994; Ryan *et al.*, 1995). For example, a middle-aged man casts an older woman in a passive hearer role by talking past her as if she does not exist, and by talking about her through a third person when in fact she is perfectly capable of playing an active speaker role. An older man is denied speaking turns from time to time. At other times, the turn available to him has been discursively framed by the younger woman in such a way that a nominal response of "yes" or "no" is all that is called for from the older man. In these instances—as in most everyday conversation—the motive of control may be absent and yet the behaviour is controlling in effect. The mechanisms of conversational influence and control discussed in the present chapter provide a way of analyzing how elderspeak is enacted and—more importantly—how it may be resisted or prevented from occurring.

References

Argyle, M. (1969). *Social interaction.* London: Methuen.

Atkinson, J. M., and Heritage, J. C. (Eds) (1984). *Structures of social action: Studies in conversation analysis.* Cambridge: Cambridge University Press.

Austin, J. (1962). *How to do things with words.* Oxford: Oxford University Press.

Bachrach, P., and Baratz, M. S. (1962). Two faces of power. *American Political Science Review,* **56,** 947–952.

Bales, R. F. (1950). *Interaction process analysis: A method for the study of small groups.* Reading, MA: Addison-Wesley.

Bales, R. F. (1956). Task status and likeability as a function of talking and listening in decision making groups. In L. D. White (Ed.), *The state of the social sciences.* Chicago: University of Chicago Press, pp. 148–161.

Bales, R. F. (1976). *Interactive process analysis.* Chicago: Chicago University Press.

Barchas, P. R., and Fisek, M. H. (1984). Hierarchical differentiation in newly formed groups of rhesus and humans. In P. R. Barchas (Ed.), *Essays towards a sociophysiological perspective.* Westport: Greenwood Press, pp. 23–33.

Bavelas, J. B., Black, A., Chovil, N., and Mullett, J. (1990). *Equivocal communication.* Newbury Park: Sage.

Berger, C. R., and Bradac, J. (1982). *Language and social knowledge: Uncertainty in interpersonal relations.* London: Arnold.

Blum-Kulka, S. (1983). The dynamics of political interviews. *Text,* **3,** 131–153.

Bourhis, R. Y., Giles, H., Leyens, J. P., and Tajfel, H. (1979). Psycholoinguistic distinctiveness: Language divergence in Belgium. In H. Giles and R. St. Clair, (Eds) *Language and social psychology.* Oxford: Blackwell, pp. 158–185.

Bradac, J. J. (Ed.) (1989). *Message effects in communication science.* Newbury Park, CA: Sage.

Brooke, M. E., and Ng, S. H. (1986). Language and social influence in small conversational groups. *Journal of Language and Social Psychology,* **5,** 201–210.

Brown, P. and Levinson, S. C. (1978). Universals in language usage: Politeness phenomena. In E. N. Goody, (Ed.), *Questions and politeness..* Cambridge: Cambridge University Press, pp. 56–310

Brown, R. (1965). *Social psychology.* London: Macmillan.

Bull, P. (1994). On identifying questions, replies, and non-replies in political interviews. *Journal of Language and Social Psychology,* **13,** 115–131.

Bull, P., and Mayer, K. (1993). How not to answer questions in political interviews. *Political Psychology,* 14, 651–666.

Caporael, L. R. (1981). The paralanguage of caregiving: Baby talk to the institutionalized aged. *Journal of Personality and Social Psychology,* **40,** 876–884.

Clark, H. H. (1985). Language use and language users. In G. Lindzey and E. Aronson (eds), *The handbook of social psychology,* 3rd ed. New York: Harper and Row, pp. 179–231.

Clark, H. H., and Carlson, T. B. (1982). Hearers and speech acts. *Language,* **58,** 332–373.

Clayman, S. E. (1988). Displaying neutrality in television news interviews. *Social Problems,* **35,** 474–492.

Coulthard, M. (1977). *An introduction to discourse analysis.* London: Longman.

Coupland, N., Coupland, J., and Giles, H. (1991). *Language, society and the elderly: Discourse, identity and ageing*. Oxford: Basil Blackwell.

Crow, B. K. (1983). Topic shifts in couples' conversations. In R. T. Craig and K. Tracy (Eds), *Conversational coherence: Form, structure and strategy*. Beverly Hills: Sage, pp. 136– 156.

Depret, E., and Fiske, S. T. (1993). Social cognition and power: Some cognitive consequences of social structure as a source of control deprivation. In G. Weary, F. Gleicher, and K. L. Marsh (Eds), *Control motivation and social cognition*. NY: Springer Verlag, pp. 176–202.

Duncan S. Jr., and Fiske, D. W. (1977). *Face-to-face interaction: Research, methods, and theory*. Hillsdale, NJ: Lawrence Erlbaum.

Dunne, M., and Ng, S. H. (1994). Simultaneous speech in small group conversation: All-together-now and one-at-a-time? *Journal of Language and Social Psychology*, **13**, 45–71.

Edelsky, C., and Adams, K. (1990). Creating inequality: Breaking the rules in debates. *Journal of Language and Social Psychology*, **9**, 171–190.

Emerson, R. H. (1962). Power–dependence relations. *American Sociological Review*, **27**, 3141.

Erickson, B., Lind, A. E., Johnson, B. C., and O'Barr, W. M. (1978). Speech style and impression formation in a court setting: The effects of "powerful" and "powerless" speech. *Journal of Experimental Social Psychology*, **14**, 266–279.

Fanon, F. (1965). *The wretched of the earth*. London: Macmillan and Kee.

Fiske, S. T. (1993). Controlling other people: The impact of power on stereotyping. *American Psychologist*, **48**, 621–628.

Fowler, R. (1985). Power. In T. A. van Dijk (Ed.), *Handbook of discourse analysis: Discourse analysis in society*. London: Academic Press, pp. 61–82.

French, P., and Local, J. (1983). Turn-competitive incomings. *Journal of Pragmatics*, **7**, 17–38.

Gallois, C., Franklyn-Stokes, A., Giles, H., and Coupland, N. (1988). Communication accommodation theory and intercultural encounters: Intergroup and interpersonal considerations. In Y. Y. Kim and W. B. Gudykunst (Eds), *Theories in intercultural communication* Newbury Park, CA: Sage, pp. 157–185.

Gallois, C., Giles, H., Jones, E., Cargile, A., and Ota, H. (1995). Accommodating intercultural encounters: Elaborations and extensions. In R. Wiseman (Ed.), *Intercultural communication theory*, Thousand Oaks, CA: Sage, pp. 115–147.

Giles, H., and Coupland, N. (1991). *Language: Contexts and consequences*. Milton Keynes: Open University Press.

Giles, H., and Powesland, P. F. (1975). *Speech style and social evaluation*. London: Academic Press.

Goffman, E. (1981). *Forms of talk*. Philadelphia: University of Pennsylvania Press.

Greatbach, D. (1986). Aspects of topical organization in news interviews: The use of agenda-shifting procedures by interviewees. In R. Collins, J. Curran, N. Gamham, P. Scannell, P. Schlesinger, and C. Sparks (Eds), *Media, culture and society*, Beverly Hills, CA: Sage, pp. 441–455.

Gumperz, J. J. (1982). *Language and social identity*. Cambridge: Cambridge University Press.

Halliday, M. A. K. (1976). In G. Kress (Ed.), *System and function in language*. London: Oxford University Press.

Harre, R. (1992). What is real in psychology: A plea for persons. *Theory and Psychology*, **2**, 153–158.

Harwood, J., Giles, H., and Bourhis, R. Y. (1994). The genesis of vitality theory: Historical patterns and discoursal dimensions. *International Journal of the Sociology of Language*, **108**, 167–206.

Heider, F. (1958). *Psychology of interpersonal relations*. New York: Wiley.

Heritage, J. (1984). *Garfinkel and ethnomethodology*. Cambridge: Polity Press.

Heritage, J. (1988). Explanations as accounts: A conversation analytic perspective. In C. Antaki (Ed.), *Analysing everyday explanation*, London: Sage, pp. 127–144.

Heritage, J., and Greatbach, D. (1986). Generating applause: A study of rhetoric and response at party political conferences. *American Journal of Sociology*, **92**, 110–157.

Hogg, M. (in press). Social identity, self-categorization, and the small group. In E. H. Witte and J. Davis (Eds), *Understanding group behaviour* Vol. 2: *Small group processes and interpersonal relations*, Hillsdale, NJ: Erlbaum.

Hollander, E. P. (1985). Leadership and power. In G. Lindzey and E. Aronson (Eds), *Handbook of social psychology*, Vol. 2. New York: Random House, pp. 485–537.

James, D., and Clarke, S. (1992). Interruptions, gender, and power. A review of the literature. In K.

Hall, M. Bucholtz, and B. Moonwoman (Eds), *Locating power: Proceedings of the Second Berkeley Women and Language Conference*, Vol. I. Berkeley, CA: Berkeley Women and Language Group, University of California, Berkeley, pp. 286–299.

Jones, E. E., and Gerard, H. B. (1967). *Foundations of social psychology*. New York: Wiley.

Kemper, S. (1994). Elderspeak: Speech accommodations to older adults. *Aging and Cognition*, **1**, 17–28.

Labov, W., and Fanshel, D. (1977). *Therapeutic discourse: Psychotherapy as conversation*. New York: Academic Press.

Lakoff, R. (1973). Language and woman's place. *Language in Society*, **2**, 45–80.

Lewin, K. (1959). In D. Cartwright (Ed.), *Field theory in social science: Selected theorative papers*. London: Tavistock.

Malcolm X (1964). *The autobiography of Malcolm X*. Harmondsworth: Penguin Books.

Mead, G. H. (1934). *The social psychology of George Herbert Mead*. Chicago: University of Chicago Press.

Mishler, E. (1984). *The discourse of medicine: Dialectics of medical interviews*. Norwood, NJ: Ablex.

Moreland, R. L., Hogg, M. A., and Hains, S. C. (1994). Back to the future: Social psychological research on groups. *Journal of Experimental Social Psychology*, **30**, 527–555.

Mulder, M. (1977). *The daily power game*. Leiden: Martinus Nijhoff.

Mullen, B., Salas, E., and Driskell, J. E. (1989). Salience, motivation, and artifact as contributions to the relation between participation rate and leadership. *Journal of Experimental Social Psychology*, **25**, 545–559.

Ng, S. H. (1977). Power: The dimension of ranking in interpersonal and intergroup behaviour. Unpublished PhD thesis, University of Bristol.

Ng, S. H. (1978). Minimal social categorization, political socialization, and power change. *Human Relations*, **31**, 765–779.

Ng, S. H. (1980). *The social psychology of power*. London: Academic Press.

Ng, S. H. (1982). Power and intergroup discrimination. In H. Tajfel (Ed.), *Social identity and intergroup relations*. Cambridge: Cambridge University Press, pp. 179–206.

Ng, S. H. (1984). Social psychology and political economy. In H. Tajfel (Ed.), *Social dimension: European Contributions to social psychology*, Vol. 2. Cambridge: Cambridge University Press, pp. 624–645

Ng, S. H. (1990). Androcentric coding of *man* and *his* in memory by language users. *Journal of Experimental Social Psychology*, **26**, 455–464.

Ng, S. H. (1994). *"You are too old to drive, dear!" Elderspeak and ageism in an ageing society*. Victoria University of Wellington Inaugural Addresses New Series XII. Wellington: Victoria University Press.

Ng, S. H., Bell, D., and Brooke, M. (1993). Gaining turns and achieving high influence ranking in small conversational groups. *British Journal of Social Psychology*, **32**, 265–275.

Ng, S. H., and Bradac, J. J. (1993). *Power in language: Verbal communication and social influence*. Newbury Park, CA: Sage.

Ng, S. H., Brooke, M., and Dunne, M. (1995). Interruption and influence in discussion groups. *Journal of Language and Social Psychology*, **14**, 369–381.

Ng, S. H., and Cram, F. (1988). Intergroup bias by defensive and offensive groups in majority and minority conditions. *Journal of Personality and Social Psychology*, **55**, 749–757.

Parker, K. C. H. (1988). Speaking turns in small group interaction: A context-sensitive event sequence model. *Journal of Personality and Social Psychology*, **54**, 965–971.

Pearce, W. B. (1976). The coordinated management of meaning: A rule-based theory of interpersonal communication. In G. R. Miller (Ed.), *Explorations in interpersonal communication*. Beverly Hills: Sage, pp. 17–35.

Philips, S. U. (1987). The social organization of questions and answers in courtroom discourse (On the use of wh questions in American courtroom discourse: A study of the relation between form and language function). In L. Kedar (Ed.), *Power through discourse*. Norwood, NJ: Ablex, pp. 83–111.

Potter, J., and Wetherell, M. (1987). *Discourse and social psychology: Beyond attitudes and behaviour*. London: Sage.

Raven, B. H. (1992). A power/interaction model of interpersonal influence: French and Raven thirty years later. *Journal of Social Behaviour and Personality*, **7**, 217–244.

Roger, D. (1989). Experimental studies of turn-taking behaviour. In D. Roger and P. Bull (Eds), *Conversation: An interdisciplinary perspective*. Philadelphia, PA: Multilingual Matters, pp. 75–95.

Roger, D., Bull, P., and Smith, S. (1988). The development of a comprehensive system for classifying interruptions. *Journal of Language and Social Psychology*, **7**, 27–34.

Russell, B. (1938). *Power: A new social analysis*. London: Allen and Unwin.

Ryan, E. B., Meredith, S. D., MacLean, M. J., and Orange, J. B. (1995). Changing the way we talk with elders: Promoting health using the communication enhancement model. *International Journal of Aging and Human Development*, **41**, 87–105.

Sacks, H., Schegloff, E. A., and Jefferson, G. (1974). A simplest systematics for the organization of turn-taking for conversation. *Language*, **50**, 696–735.

Searle, J. R. (1969). *Speech acts*. Cambridge: Cambridge University Press.

Shaw, M. E. (1981). *Group dynamics: The psychology of small group behaviour*, 3rd edn. New York: McGraw Hill.

Sherif, M. (1962). Intergroup relations and leadership: Introductory statement. In M. Sherif (Ed.), *Intergroup relations and leadership*. New York: John Wiley, pp. 3–21.

Sherif, M. (1966). In *Common predicament: Social psychology of intergroup conflict and cooperation*. Boston: Houghton-Miflin.

Shotter, J. (1992). Social constructionism and realism: Adequacy or accuracy? *Theory and Psychology*, **2**, 175– 182.

Simmel, G. (1950). *The sociology of Georg Simmel*. Glencoe, IL: Free Press.

Stasser, G., and Taylor, L. A. (1991). Speaking turns in face-to-face discussions. *Journal of Personality and Social Psychology*, **60**, 675–684.

Swann, J. (1988). Talk control: An illustration from the classroom of problems in analysing male dominance of conversation. In J. Coates and D. Cameron (Eds), *Women in their speech communities: New perspectives on language and sex*. London: Longman, pp. 123–140.

Tajfel, H. (1974). Intergroup behaviour, social comparison and social change. Unpublished Katz-Newcomb lectures, University of Michigan, Ann Arbor.

Tajfel, H. (1979). Individuals and groups in social psychology: Social or psychological? *British Journal of Social and Clinical Psychology*, **18**, 183–190.

Tajfel, H., and Dawson, J. (Eds) (1965). *Disappointed guests*. Oxford: Oxford University Press.

ten Have, P. (1991). Talk and institution: A reconsideration of the "asymmetry" of doctor–patient interaction. In D. Boden and D. H. Zimmerman (Eds), *Talk and social structure* pp. 138–163.

Thibaut, J. W., and Kelley, H. H. (1959). *The social psychology of groups*. New York: Wiley.

Tracy, K. (1985). Conversational coherence: A cognitively grounded rules approach. In R. L. Street, Jr. and J. N. Capella (Eds), *Sequence and pattern in communication behaviour*. London: Edward Arnold, pp. 30–49.

Walker, A. G. (1987). Linguistic manipulation, power, and the legal setting. In L. Kedar (Ed.), *Power through discourse*. Norwood, NJ: Ablex, pp. 57–80.

Wetherell, M., and Potter, J. (1992). *Mapping the language of racism: Discourse and the legitimation of exploitation*. London: Harvester Wheatsheaf.

Wilson, J. (1990). *Politically speaking*. Oxford: Basil Blackwell.

Wilson, T. P., Wiemann, J. M., and Zimmermann, D. H. (1984). Models of turn taking in conversational interaction. *Journal of Language and Social Psychology*, **3**, 159–183.

Zimmerman, D. H., and West, C. (1975). Sex roles, interruptions and silences in conversation. In B. Thorne and N. Henley (Eds), *Language and sex: Difference and dominance*. Rowley, MA.: Newbury House,. pp. 105–129.

8

"Let the Wheelchair Through!": An Intergroup Approach to Interability Communication

SUSAN ANNE FOX

Western Michigan University, Kalamazoo
and

HOWARD GILES

University of California, Santa Barbara

Contents

The fruits of Henri Tajfel's academic labours are, of course, immense, and have been used to explain the intergroup experiences of individuals from different nationalities, religions, ages, genders, ethnicities, occupational groups and so forth. In addition, his work has influenced other, more behavioural, traditions inside as well as outside social psychology, including studies of language and communication patterns—mainly in intercultural and intergenerational settings (see, for example, Fox and Giles, 1993; Giles and Coupland, 1991; Gudykunst, 1986; Harwood *et al.*, in press; Hogg and Abrams, 1988; Semin and Fiedler, 1992). This chapter continues the interdisciplinary focus on communicative issues in a Tajfelian frame with a concern for an understudied intergroup context in this tradition (see, however, Abrams *et al.*, 1990; Szivos and Travers, 1988), namely, interactions between persons with disabilities and those without these disabilities. Hereafter, we shall term such encounters "interability" situations or communications.

In this chapter, we focus upon the following: (1) historical reasons why many people with disabilities have been differentiated into a distinct social group; (2) attitudes associated with this intergroup categorization; (3) communicative features of interability communication; (4) theories which are offered to explain interability situations; and (5) a social identity approach and research agenda which highlights communicative and contact characteristics of interability situations.

Given the breadth of studies conducted on and about people with disabilities, it is important for us at the outset to offer a context in which this discussion of interability situations will be addressed. There are many different types and gradations of cognitive, behavioural and physical disabilities that are the subject of volumes of work in the fields of special education, rehabilitation and medicine. Of these defined disabilities, this chapter will focus mainly upon those people who experience group differentiation due to a physical abnormality which limits their mobility, but who do not have speech, hearing, or cognitive impairments. Furthermore, although not classified by the field of special education as physical disabilities (see, for example, Haring, 1990), we do, nonetheless, include herein facial and body deformities—even obesity. These usually do not directly affect one's everyday motor functioning, yet such appearance stigmas, described by Goffman (1963, p. 5) as "undesired differentness", are many times viewed as "abnormal" (see shortly) and can affect social interactions and relationships. Because of the literature available, we restrict our discussion to North American studies, although some intercultural data do exist (Thomas *et al.*, 1985; Walker, 1983) inviting further exploration.

In sum then, the only differences between people without disabilities and this target group of people with disabilities is that the latter possess a physical disability or appearance stigma which may, or may not, limit their motor functioning, but it in no physical manner impedes their communication. While, for the purposes of the present analysis, we tend to overinclude people with grossly different disabilities and their attending variable origins and consequences into one social category, we readily acknowledge the possibility that very different cultures are implicated and grossly different forms of discriminatory practices may be involved in this variability. Yet society at large, through its historical invocation of the label, "physically disabled", also tends to operate in this homogenizing fashion. Actually, language used in describing people with disabilities (e.g. "handicapped", "otherly abled", "disabled", and "physically challenged") is a contemporary issue given the pressure to conform to "politically correct" terms (Longmore, 1985), even though variable uses have not been found to have an effect upon the attitudes towards people with disabilities (Patterson and Witten, 1987). This is not to suggest that an intergroup communication perspective would not be just as relevant to other groups with communicative deficits, such as persons who are deaf (see Siple, 1994) or visually impaired (Coupland *et al.*, 1986), or others who have particular kinds of diseases, such as individuals known to possess the AIDS virus.

In addressing one last definitional issue from this perspective, it is necessary that at least one member of the interaction finds a possible disability *salient* for the encounter to constitute an interability interaction. Self-stigmatization may also be detrimental to "normal" communication and Dudley Moore, the movie star, accurately exemplifies an aspect of this. He has struggled to overcome his feelings of inadequacy and insecurity because he was born with congenital talipes (a club foot). Although the majority of persons coming into contact with him do not view him as a person with a disability, he nonetheless at times reports he interacts differently because his disability is salient to *him*. Kleck and Strenta (1980) experimentally examined the effects of self-stigmatization when studying the effects of applying, temporarily, an imitation facial scar on women. After applying a simulated facial scar and then removing it without the women's awareness (under the pre-text of re-fixing the make-up), they found that women reported that they were subsequently treated less favourably when, in reality, there was no differential treatment.

People who are physically stigmatized, whether it be a situation such as a person who is quadriplegic or someone with a port-wine birthmark on his or her face, are many times judged and communicated with differently because of their physical anomalies. But first, it seems informative to consider the reasons for differential attitudes about and communicative behaviour towards persons with disabilities.

Reasons for the Rejection of People with Disabilities

A number of theories claim to explain the differential treatment people with disabilities may receive. Wolfensberger's (1972) analysis of the historical roles of "deviant persons" are the most commonly cited reasons in the field of special education. These include perceptions of the physically disadvantaged person as: (a) a subhuman organism, (b) a menace, (c) an unspeakable object of dread, (d) an object of pity, (e) a holy innocent, (f) a diseased organism, (g) an object of ridicule, and (h) as an eternal child.

Viewing people with disabilities as somehow subhuman organisms is typified by stories of "the changeling", "little people", or as "vegetables". These subhuman perceptions can change expectations of intelligence and social skills, which can contribute to the subsequent behaviour and communication that occurs in interability situations. The view that people with disabilities are a menace, either individually or sociologically, can contribute to the feelings that people without disabilities are a burden on their parents or tax-payers. The passage of the Americans with Disabilities Act in the United States, which provides federally enforced antidiscrimination protection for persons with impairments, is thought, by some, to be creating a backlash of negative attitudes as people and businesses spend time and money creating "handicapped accessible" environments (Fowler and Wadsworth, 1991).

As an unspeakable object of dread, studies have documented how people with disabilities may be seen by people without disabilities as a source of shame and guilt. For instance, Richardson (1976) discusses how a mother's shock and inability to react to the deformity of a newborn child can affect her interaction with the child. Mothers have, in general, been found to show less positive, and more muted affection to a child with disabilities as compared to mothers of non-disabled children (Rogers, 1988). Wasserman *et al.* (1985) found that mothers of physically handicapped children were more likely to ignore their child than mothers of healthy children, and that children with facial anomalies were most likely to be ignored by their mothers.

When perceived as objects of pity, people with disabilities are often treated with benevolence, compassion and acceptance, although it may be at the cost of recipients' dignity and self-respect. Though perpetuating the "deserving of charity" stereotype may be an effective way to raise money for disability research (e.g. the Jerry Lewis Muscular Dystrophy Telethon), it may override the "independent" perception which many people with disabilities strive to achieve (Haller, 1993). Social attributions such as holy innocents, children of God, or saints are also a historical view placed upon people with disabilities. In this way, they may not be viewed negatively, but actually attain a demigod status, as though they are specially blessed by God. Even some New Age philosophers portray people with disabilities as "master teachers" who are trapped in deformed bodies or with underdeveloped minds to teach life lessons to people without disabilities (MacLaine, 1985).

The description of people with disabilities as diseased organisms is also a prevalent one. The effects of this are that people without disabilities will see people with disabilities as ill or incompetent and in need of treatment, unable to fully function in the community, or as people best avoided for fear of contracting the disease (see also Braithwaite, in press). As an object of ridicule, people with disabilities are often made targets of amusement for people without disabilities. The award winning movie *The Elephant Man* is a depiction of a deformed person suffering others' taunts in this way. Interestingly, even the doctor who was trying to help John Merrick (the "elephant man") was accused of removing him from carnival ridicule simply to subject him to a more exalted form of ridicule before members of the medical profession. Regardless of the context of ridicule, people with disabilities are many times put in a one-down, or inferior, position wherein they are an unwilling source of amusement or education, unable to contribute positively to society.

Finally, persons with disabilities are frequently believed to be eternal children. In such a paradigm, people with disabilities are held to low intellectual and emotional expectations. It is arguable that programmes such as the Special Olympics, which assigns people with disabilities to non-disabled "buddies", may in some ways promote this eternal child view. The buddies chaperone the special olympians to their events, cheer them on, and in many ways "take care" of persons with disabilities.

Although Wolfensberger's views are cited most often, other paradigms exist. Wright (1983) also reviewed and critically discussed six possible origins of variable attitudes toward persons with atypical physiques (some of which overlap somewhat with the foregoing) as follows: (a) reactions to physical deviancy among lower animals; (b) atypical physiques in primitive and non-occidental societies; (c) so-called "requiredness in cause–effect relations" (i.e. the need to blame victims in a "just world"); (d) "the different and the strange" (as it relates to conformity, stigma and spoiled identities); (e) childhood experiences; and (f) socioeconomic factors. The first position expresses the idea that people react negatively toward people with disabilities because reactions to physical deviancy among some lower animals is negative, many times resulting in the killing of non-normal animals. Therefore, appealing to a belief that human nature follows animal nature, this would explain our ostracization of persons with physical disabilities. Wright (1983) argues, though, that there is not sufficient evidence to support this claim when there is "a heterogeneity of reaction among various species" (p. 252), with examples such as: wolves neither attack nor physically avoid atypical wolves; sharks will eat other wounded sharks; goldfish with amputated fins live "happily" among other goldfish; and baboons are ruthless toward physically inferior others.

A related position is one which supposes that our primitive societies treated physical deviances with ostracization and abandonment. There are some societies which practice infanticide and abandonment, but there are others which view persons with abnormalities as lucky, "innocents of God", or are "held to be under the guardianship of special supernatural agents" (Wright, 1983, p. 254), much like Wolfensberger's view. Wright argues that although, on the whole, negative attitudes would display a preponderance of negative behaviour toward people with disabilities, anthropologists may be predisposed to record the shocking or anomalous treatment of persons with physical abnormalities, whereas normal and benign attitudes would most likely go unrecorded. Consequently, there is no convincing evidence to suggest a consistent pattern of negative treatment toward physically disabled persons by primitive societies. One point Wright makes in regard to primitive cultures, as well as "more civilized" cultures, is that there are no societies in which congenital or "naturally"-acquired physical deformities are seen in a positive and "beautiful" light. (There are cultures which use scarring and other manipulated methods as a form of beautification and/or particularly as a symbol of status (e.g. foot binding of Chinese women, but these are chosen and manipulated deformities.) This "body-beautiful" or "body-whole" idea may be partially culture specific, but the idea that all mothers begin the relationship with their newborns by counting the number of fingers and toes to make sure their baby is "whole" gives rise to the notion of a universal idea that a physically intact body is the most desired. This idea seems to be especially applicable in Western societies where a great emphasis is often placed upon appearance.

The "requiredness in cause–effect relations" illustrates the need for explaining the events in our lives. The aphorism that "bad things happen to bad people" still permeates many religious groups and New Age philosophies that use the notion of "bad karma". Even though the medical professions can offer biological explanations for some disabilities, there does seem to exist a further need to socially attribute causes for physical disabilities beyond the result of bad luck or random chance (see Lerner, 1980 for a discussion of "blaming victims" in a "just world"). Consequently, we may behave toward people with disabilities as if there is something inherent in them that has caused their disability. This seems especially true of the physical quality of obesity, where people are commonly assumed to be in control of their weight (DeJong, 1993).

The "different and strange" approach views rejection toward people with disabilities as a result of people's need and liking for conformity bonding. Wright (1983) explains—somewhat simplistically perhaps, that a law of humankind is that "no one wants to be different" (p. 262) in a socially-undesired way, and those who are dissimilar and unfamiliar are therefore disliked. Heider (cited in Wright, 1983) attributes the negative effects of unfamiliarity to uncertainty (which will be discussed at length below when viewing uncertainty reduction theory) and the aesthetically pleasing need to retain the status quo and be cognitive and behavioural misers. Thus, it is easier, and takes less effort, to eliminate uncertainty by avoiding its source—that is, people who possess a "difference" or "strangeness".

Wright's notion of childhood experiences feeding into negative attitudes toward people with disabilities is based on socialization practices. This approach assumes that during a child's development, some differences are historically deemed socially acceptable (e.g. hair colour, left-handedness, being tan), but others are not (e.g. being obese, using a wheelchair). If a child learns from either parents or the media that people with disabilities should be pitied, that will affect his or her future reactions. In the same way, if people with disabilities are involved in regular classrooms in a non-stigmatized way, this will also affect their future interactions. Finally, Wright suggests that the causes of the rejection of people with disabilities is based on economic and cultural factors. In societies which value production and the utility of people, if people with disabilities are thought of as an economic burden, they are ascribed a lower position. In other cultures, which have adequate or fruitful economies to lessen the competition between individuals or groups, people with disabilities are protected and given adequate care.

In another analysis, McDaniel (1976) offered two bases for attitudes toward people with disabilities: (a) the prejudice or minority approach, and (b) the "body-concept" view. The first approach asserts a devaluation of disabled members of society on the part of the ethnocentric "normal" population, in much the same way as other minorities are assigned inferior status. This position is only partially supported by existing studies (e.g. Grand *et al.*, 1982; Lukoff and Whiteman, 1971; Sillar and Chipman, 1964). The second approach is one which views a person's body self-concept as a determining factor in his or her attitudes toward persons with body abnormalities. There is some supporting evidence (e.g. Eisenman, 1970; Garske and Thomas, 1990; Richardson *et al.*, 1974) that people with a low self-concept in general have a higher tendency to reject minority groups (including people with disabilities). Although this may be useful as a personality variable, it does little to account for specific behaviours toward people with disabilities.

A final theory seeking to explain how views about people with disabilities are created is the "competence–deviance theory" which attempts to explain the anomalous social acceptance of physical deviances (Haring, 1990). This theory posits that in *some* cases social status and competence can overshadow a person's "disability" status. A deviance may be more tolerated if a person is high in competence or social status, as is exemplified by Stephen Hawking's academic status, which overshadows the fact that he is severely physically disabled.

In sum, we have noted that there are different approaches to explaining the reasons for the differential treatment of people with disabilities. Wolfensberger's (1972) eight historically-based views can be present to varying degrees and at different times, depending on the interability circumstances. These views of people with disabilities as worthy of pity (and therefore charity), as eternal children, as diseased organisms, or as a menace, permeate the subsequent attitudes that people without disabilities hold toward people with disabilities. Wright's (1983) view suggests that people with disabilities are given differential treatment because of socialization and evolutionary factors. McDaniel (1976) provides sociological reasons based on ethnocentricity or body concept. One, or a number, of these factors may be affecting how non-disabled people interact with people with disabilities. These "non-normal interactions" begin for people born with a disability from the moment the disability is recognized, or when a disability is acquired. No matter what reason one subscribes to for explaining why people with disabilities are rejected, people without disabilities have attitudes toward people with disabilities which support the notion that they see these people as a separate social group. Before looking at the actual behaviour occurring in interability situations, let us turn briefly to a discussion of the research on attitudes towards disability which can mediate the communication patterns we shall focus upon shortly.

Attitudes Toward People with Disabilities

Although arguably a common bias in all kinds of intergroup work, most interability studies are based upon the attitudes people without disabilities hold towards people with disabilities, and not so much vice versa (Braithwaite, in press). It is not the purpose of this chapter to review this research extensively (for reviews see Altman, 1981; Makas, 1988; Richardson, 1976; Yuker and Block, 1986), but rather to provide a flavour of the area as a whole. This research finds that people with disabilities are often viewed negatively by others without disabilities, the latter seeing them as closed, defensive, and alienated (Wright, 1983), and blaming them sometimes for non-existent failings or mistakes (Farina *et al.*, 1968). Centers and Centers (1963) found that students had more rejecting attitudes toward amputees and rated them as the "saddest" in the class. Burden and Parish (1983) found that children infrequently described persons with physical disabilities as happy, although they frequently described them as dumb, foolish, yet nonetheless (overtly perhaps) jolly. Children without disabilities believed children with disabilities to be more honest, awkward, great, and wise, while children with disabilities rated themselves as more handsome, strong, bad, bitter, and careless (Parish and Morgan, 1984). Hazzard (1983), using eight- to twelve-year-olds, found verification for a "pathetic" stereotype for people with disabilities: different, helpless, and distressed, who deserve or desire pity. Emry and Wiseman (1987) claim that these negative attitudes come in the form of stereotypes that project people with disabilities as dependent, socially introverted, emotionally unstable or depressed, hypersensitive and easily offended. This "shopping list" approach to cataloguing attitudes has achieved little in ameliorating the behavioural effects of these negative attitudes. Moreover, such studies (as they relate, for example, to "happy" versus "jolly") reveal that attitudes towards persons with disabilities are both complex and multidimensional.

However, not all studies find that people with disabilities are viewed negatively. de Appodaca *et al.* (1985), using a high school sample of children without disabilities, found that children with orthopaedic disabilities were rated significantly higher than peers without disabilities on two of twelve peer rating scales, and directionally higher on eight of the twelve scales. Ray (1953, cited from Wright, 1983) found that people without disabilities evaluated boys in wheelchairs as: a better friend, more even tempered, a better class president, more conscientious and more religious; though also more unhappy, and liking parties less. These results show that attitudes towards people with disabilities are not always negative in nature and that there may be (as has been shown with other intergroup attitude contexts; see Hummert, 1994) different subtypes of people with disabilities (e.g. "disabled saint" versus "bitter" stereotypes) that past research has, as yet, not identified.

These findings notwithstanding, Richardson (1976) noted that there is no research needed to argue the disadvantages of being physically disabled in initial social encounters, due, in part, to the negative attitudes people without disabilities hold toward their counterparts with disabilities. Altman (1981), in her review of attitude change studies, also concluded that prior interability contact has been inconclusive in predicting attitude change. However, contact does seem to increase positive attitudes toward people with disabilities in *some* situations (Eposito and Peach, 1983; Gillies and Shackley, 1988; Kleck, 1969; Newberry and Parish, 1987). Furthermore, the type of disability and situational context can also be important factors in attitudes directed toward people with disabilities (Gordon *et al.*, 1990). For instance, Grand *et al.* (1982) found more positive reactions toward people with disabilities in work-related contexts than in dating or marriage contexts. Likewise, Stovall and Sedlacek (1983) concluded that reactions to people with disabilities differed depending upon whether the context was social or academic in nature. Even with the emphasis placed on attitude and contact research, interability research has been inconclusive in proving that the "mere contact" approach to interability contact reduces negative attitudes in all contexts.

The attitudes that people with disabilities hold toward people without disabilities are related to the reasons offered earlier for the rejection of persons with disabilities. For example, the "deserving of pity" view Wolfensberger (1972) points out aligns well with Hazzard's (1983) finding that students viewed people with disabilities as different, helpless, distressed, and deserving or desiring pity. Even some of the results of the more positive attitudes, such as people with disabilities being more conscientious or making a better friend, can find support in Haring's (1990) competence–deviance notion. Regardless of the reasons, these attitudes can translate into expectations about the intelligence, social skills and character which people with disabilities are believed to possess, and subsequently affect the behaviour of people without disabilities toward people with disabilities.

Features of Interability Communication

At a very early age and throughout their schooling, people born with a disability develop a different set of communicative behaviours than do people without disabilities. Wasserman *et al.* (1985) found that mothers of children with disabilities were more initiating, less responsive, more encouraging, but also more ignoring toward their children. Non disabled children allow children with disabilities "more breaks" in games and other interactions (Weitz, 1972). When the only choice for a playmate is a child with disabilities, children without disabilities will engage in more isolated play (Gentry, 1983; Peterson and Haralick, 1977). Thompson (1981, 1982) found that there are low amounts of interactions between interabled peers, even in integrated or mainstreamed classrooms, which contributes to deficiencies in listener-adapted communication. Children with disabilities assume a subordinate position in exchanges with children without disabilities, and it is reasonable to believe that in some instances this learned behaviour continues throughout the life of a person with disabilities (Coleman and DePaulo, 1991; Guralnick and Paul-Brown, 1980).

The different expectations that people without disabilities have toward people with disabilities have been examined in terms of the verbal and non-verbal aspects of interability communication. Given the large number of studies that address attitudinal variables related to people with disabilities, surprisingly few have assessed *communicative* aspects of interability situations. Of these few, many use confederates who do not have a disability role-playing a person who does (Grove and Werkman, 1991; Kleck, 1969; Sigelman *et al.*, 1986). Therefore, this research is highly suspect as to whether it is generalizable to real-life interability settings. Much interability behaviour is typified by anxiety and uncertainty, which can often inhibit the non-verbal behaviour of a person without a disability toward people with disabilities (Barker *et al.*, 1953; Emry and Wiseman, 1987; Kleck, 1968), especially in stranger or first encounters. The following non-verbal behaviours, usually instigated by a person without a disability, are not indicative of "normal" communication, but have been found to be prevalent in adult interability communication (for a more extensive review, see Coleman and DePaulo, 1991):

(1) Shorter interactions which are often terminated abruptly without adopting common leave-taking behaviours (Comer and Piliavin, 1972; Farina *et al.*, 1968; Mills *et al.*, 1984; Thompson, 1982).
(2) Increased physical proximity in interactions between people with and without disabilities (Kleck, 1969; Kleck *et al.*, 1968).
(3) Less eye contact by persons without disabilities toward persons with disabilities (Kleck *et al.*, 1968), but more staring if the person with disabilities is unaware (Houston and Bull, 1994; Sigelman *et al.*, 1986).
(4) Less smiling toward people with disabilities (Comer and Piliavin, 1972).
(5) Greater galvanic skin response arousal by non-disabled persons (Kleck *et al.*, 1966).

Furthermore, *verbal* characteristics of interability interactions have been an area of scant research. First, people without disabilities often express points of view that are less representative of their own in order to seem more similar to those held by people with disabilities (Kleck, 1968; Ray, 1985). People without disabilities, who hold negative attitudes toward people with disabilities, use lower verbal immediacy (a measure of the psychological distance by one's word choice) when speaking to and about people with disabilities (Feinberg, 1971). What is more, people without disabilities also seek less information and show less attention toward people with disabilities than their counterparts without disabilities (Grove and Werkman, 1991). Therefore, interability situations, especially first time interactions, may be strained—both verbally and non-verbally.

In addition to the above, research has focused on the subject of acknowledging a disability (Belgrave and Mills, 1981; *et al.*, 1979; Royse and Edwards, 1989; Sagatun, 1985; Thompson and Seibold, 1978; see Thompson, 1982 for a review of earlier studies). This work is based on the assumption that if people without disabilities are anxious about interacting with a person with disabilities, then mentioning the disability in the interaction should have the effect of lessening this anxiety and increasing the liking for, and acceptance of, people with disabilities. This strategy has been moderately successful in alleviating interability anxiety for the person without a disability. However, it necessarily places the responsibility of disclosing personal information upon persons with disabilities without taking into account the effect of the revelation upon them (Braithwaite, 1991).

Actually, relatively little is known about the communicative behaviour occurring in interability situations. Beyond the above mentioned features, a small number of studies allude to patronizing speech, an area which has been frequently researched in intergenerational settings (e.g. Giles *et al.*, 1993; Ryan *et al.*, 1991; Ryan and Cole, 1990). Being the recipient of patronizing speech has been documented as inappropriate by people with disabilities (Fichten and Bourdon, 1986; Fox, 1994). A few studies have alluded to this speech phenomenon (DePaulo and Coleman, 1986; Fichten and Bourdon, 1986; Strenta and Kleck, 1985), but these have employed their own definitions of patronizing talk. Research on "baby talk", often viewed as patronizing, has found that speech addressed to retarded adults is similar in a variety of ways to speech addressed to six-year-olds (DePaulo and Coleman, 1987). A small component of another study examined the attributions of patronizing behaviour, when defined loosely as "the degree to which the person without a disability's comments appeared to be sincere vs. patronizing" (Strenta and Kleck, 1985, p. 134). The authors found that people (with and without disabilities) who viewed a videotape of a person either in a wheelchair or with a leg cast perceived that the former was more patronized by a person without disability than the latter, even though the actual communications were held constant between the two conditions. Fichten and Bourdon's (1986) research found that inappropriate behaviours included patronizing behaviour as exemplified "by asking the wheelchair user to do an unnecessary task to make him or her feel useful in a group, insisting that socializing is 'good' for the wheelchair user" (p. 330). In Weinberg's (1983) description of social inequity within interability situations, an instance of patronizing speech (although not specifically described as such) may be evident in the quote, "How did you lose your leg, you poor girl?" (p. 368). Although people with disabilities may be consistent in what they determine to be patronizing speech, it should be kept in mind that this label is based on the attribution by the person patronized; that is, it is in the ear of the beholder.

Only recently has there been a formal study to determine what kinds of talk people with disabilities define as patronizing (Fox, 1994). Interviews of people who use wheelchairs yielded three types of patronizing speech described by people with disabilities: (1) baby talk (being called "honey"; "how are *we* doing today?"); (2) depersonalizing talk ("let the wheelchair through" instead of "the person in the wheelchair"); and (3) third-party talk ("At a restaurant the waitress spoke only to the able bodied person (I was with) and not to me") (cf. Adelman *et al.*, 1987; Coe and Predergast, 1985).

Despite the reasons for, attitudes involved, and communicative research on interability situations, the area of interability communication begs for a cohesive explanation for the motivations and behaviours of people with and without disabilities who are involved in interability communication. There have been a few attempts at theoretical explanations of interability communication, but none has yet been able to integrate and adequately predict the communication patterns occurring in interability communication situations.

Existing Theoretical Frameworks

Given that research in the field of disabilities is predominantly descriptive, we need a robust framework for explaining the what, when, and why, of interability communication. Theories invoked in the past, such as uncertainty reduction theory (Dahnke, 1982) and positive outcome value (Grove and Werkman, 1991), are useful building blocks, but to our minds have fallen short in promoting interability research and do not comprehensively explain the transactional nature of interability situations. Emry and Wiseman's (1987) intercultural approach is of this ilk, yet it takes more group and not individual bases for the motivations and behaviours in interability communication. Below we review and critique these theories.

Uncertainty Reduction Theory

Dahnke (1982) proposed a deductive theory of communication to better understand the interaction patterns between people with and without disabilities. He used uncertainty reduction theory (URT) to explain why initial interability interactions can be strained and uncomfortable (see Berger, 1979). The theory assumes "that when unfamiliar persons initially interact, they are primarily concerned with reducing their own uncertainty in order to predict, explain, and ultimately control the effects of their respective communication behaviours" (Dahnke, 1982, p. 107). Therefore, there is a positive association between uncertainty and information seeking. The theory defines affiliation, status, and responsiveness as driving factors in the desire to reduce uncertainty. Dahnke offers sixteen axioms and fifteen testable theorems related to uncertainty reduction and interability communication, which explain that uncertainty and anxiety are high and interpersonal attraction low for people without disabilities involved in interability communication (as opposed to "normal–normal interactions"). Therefore, increases in verbal and non-verbal affiliation by one person (either with or without a disability) can positively affect both the perceived and actual feelings of certainty, anxiety, and attraction to another person. These theorems, for the most part, presuppose that you must manipulate affiliative behaviours in order to lessen the uncertainty and anxiety in initial interability encounters, but does little in offering any pragmatic suggestions as to how this can be achieved.

URT is an interpersonal theory established upon the assumption that the uncertainty an individual feels when involved in an interaction motivates a person to reduce it. Although this effort is useful because of its heuristic nature, it assumes that if factors are manipulated certain results will follow, without addressing why these factors exist. Another problem with this approach, as Dahnke himself admits, is that the propositions are "associational, rather than lawlike causal statements" (p. 109). For Dahnke's approach to fully succeed, it needs to include other motivational factors, besides uncertainty, which drive people to interact. A second problem with this approach is that although theoretically viable, it not supported when tested against another theory, *positive outcome value*, which is addressed next.

Positive Outcome Value Theory

Sunnafrank (1986) reviewed over 100 studies testing URT's axioms and theorems and found that only about half provided any supporting evidence for the theory. Because of this, he re-evaluated and recast the role of uncertainty to a secondary position and used predicted costs and rewards as the driving force for reducing uncertainty. Therefore, predicted outcome values (POVs) are said to "lead to communicative attempts to expand and truncate, respectively, both the conversation and the relationship" (Grove and Werkman, 1991, p. 509).

Grove and Werkman (1991) tested URT and POV by having women without a disability as confederates (trained to use a wheelchair) feign a disability or remain non-disabled when interacting with a non-disabled participant. They found that respondents sought more information and were more aware of the behaviour of the non-disabled confederate. These results supported POV theory in that less positive predicted outcomes led to less information seeking behaviour. POV is an important addition to URT, but there is not yet enough convincing evidence from Grove and Werkman's (1991) study employing confederates to merit generalization from this one experiment to naturally-occurring interability interactions. Their approach is also unidirectional and does not address the transactional nature of the interactions occurring between persons with and without disabilities. It focuses on the person without a disability without regard to the information-seeking or uncertainty a person with disabilities is experiencing, or strategies that either may adopt to change levels of uncertainty.

Intercultural approach

Emry and Wiseman (1987) construed interability communication as an intercultural experience in which "conflicting demands and stereotypes result in a series of regressive spirals for both communicators" (p. 8). Using Rohrlich's (1983) three-tier model of intercultural communication, Emry and Wiseman examined the intrapersonal, interpersonal and systemic levels (i.e. "outcomes beyond the intent of the communicators", p. 17) which contribute to less than normal interability communication.

The intrapersonal level of Rohrlich's model takes into account cultural experiences that lead to a person's attitudes, roles and values in cognitively experiencing a subjective "reality". However, in interability communication there are conflicting social demands and norms; to treat people with disabilities with kindness, and to treat them as equals. People with disabilities have conflicting feelings of dependence and independence which make interactions difficult. Emry and Wiseman believe these conflicting social demands and norms may lead persons to experience approach-avoidance feelings in interactions between people with and without disabilities.

Social stereotypes also create intrapersonal conflict for interability communicators. These stereotypes do not only include personality traits, but also behavioural expectations of how people with disabilities will react in a conversation e.g. that they will be bitter and angry about their disability (Belgrave and Mills, 1981). People with disabilities are also aware of how they are viewed as "different", which increases their feelings of dissimilarity and how interpersonally attractive they appear. Therefore, social stereotypes and social demands can create "double-binds" in which those with and those without disabilities feel they cannot be socially correct with either choice of interaction strategy.

Even though the intrapersonal level is the most important for explaining specific communicative behaviour, there are other levels which need to be addressed. For example, at the interpersonal level interability communication may itself be "disabled" due to lack of social skills by both parties. People without disabilities, operating within stereotypes, may be unclear as to what constitutes appropriate behaviour, and their subsequent behaviour may then be constrained. Because people with disabilities generally have less opportunity for interactions, the behaviour of people without disabilities has more of an effect on the person with disabilities than vice versa.

There are both pros and cons to Emry and Wiseman's approach. On the one hand, its transactional view highlights people with and without disabilities as contributing equally to the communication event, and addresses the role of stereotypes and social norms. On the other, it fails to assess individual motivations and behaviours that occur when interability interactions are successful, and instead views all interability communication as strained, awkward, and as reinforcing pre-existing stereotypes. Furthermore, it also fails to offer possible theorems, hypotheses, or a model of the transactional nature and effects of interability communication that is sorely needed in this field of study.

An Intergroup Communication Approach to Interability Situations

The extant theories have a number of lacunae, as we have tried to argue. We need, therefore, a more robust intergroup theory which can incorporate individual factors yet retain the idea that interability communication can often be an intercultural, "group"-driven experience. Towards this end, we believe an amalgam of social identity (SIT), communication accommodation (CAT), and intergroup contact theories may better explain the communication occurring within, and the consequences of, interability situations. Quite briefly, SIT can assist us with the motivations persons with and without disabilities have when confronting interability situations. CAT can begin to piece together past research on interability communication and explain communicative behaviour in terms of people's goals and intentions. Intergroup contact theory can explain when and if people's contact will result in positive attitude and behavioural change. Addressed separately and then combined into a cohesive compilation, all three approaches can provide us with a valuable new framework and research agenda for studying interability communication.

Social Identity Theory

SIT (Tajfel, 1978) maintains that individuals, through a series of processes, derive their identity (either personal or social) by belonging to, and maintaining membership in, certain groups (see Hogg and Abrams, 1988 for a comprehensive overview, and Hogg and Abrams, 1993 for further developments). It follows, then, that social identity is an important part of one's self-concept, and that people strive to positively differentiate their group from another as a means of further maintaining a positive self-esteem. As people invest their energy into various group memberships, it is evident that they possess many different social identities; context renders different identities to be more important at different times. Social identity is established through a comparison of one group against another, and if an individual senses that their identity is threatened (see Branscombe and Wann, 1994; Dubé-Simard, 1983), they will attempt to differentiate behaviourally and/or communicatively from any group which threatens their identity.

The hierarchical nature of a social structure is also an essential element in the development of one's social identity. "It (social structure) maintains that society comprises social categories which stand in power and status relations to one another" (Hogg and Abrams, 1988, p. 14). The dominant group has the potential to impose its value system and ideology upon subordinate groups for its own ends. Only when a member of the subordinate group feels as though they are socially mobile (i.e. can rise from one group to another) will they attempt to assimilate and become a member of the dominant group. If the subordinate group feels that the social boundaries are impermeable, they may, through social creativity or social competition, attempt to improve their group's social status. One socially creative strategy is for a subordinate group to compare itself to an even lower-status group. For example, people with physical disabilities may wish to compare themselves against people with mental impairments in an effort to increase their status in relationship to a perceived "inferior" other group.

SIT, then, can be of use in explaining interability situations. First, it can help to explain the intrapersonal conflicts that persons with and without disabilities feel when interacting with each other. For persons who do not possess a disability, the possibility of interacting with a person with a disability can possibly create a threat to their social identity. This can occur for any number of reasons; for example, the threat of one day becoming a person with a disability can cause anxiety. Another reason, which Emry and Wiseman (1987) acknowledge, is that associating yourself with a person with disabilities can be damaging to your social standing with others, in this case your non-disabled "in-group", in much the same way that associating with African Americans in earlier times led to pejorative accusations in the United States (e.g. being called a "nigger lover"). Also, there is a sense of uncertainty whenever an interability opportunity presents itself. A few readily-available interability communication scripts come to mind; internal tensions arise within the person without disabilities caused by conflicting agendas he or she may possess to "be kind" yet "treat as equal" (Braithwaite *et al.*, 1984). By a combination of any or for all of these reasons (along with the possibility of assimilating with people who are less than "whole"), the person without a disability may feel that his or her social identity is threatened by the prospect of an interability interaction, and will therefore wish to psychologically and communicatively differentiate from the person with disability. This differentiation may take the form of culturally or psychologically creating a construct that places people with disabilities in a subordinate help–recipient position which could manifest itself communicatively in the form of patronizing speech (see CAT below).

Given their dominant group position, people without disabilities will not readily attempt to assimilate with the subordinate group of people with disabilities. Yet, some types of interability interactions may cause them to feel and derive a more positive social identity by interacting with people with disabilities. An example of this could be illustrated by those people in North America who volunteer to assist in Special Olympics events or Easter Seals Telethons as a way to reinforce part of their social identity without threatening their own group identity. Because the dominant "abled" group possesses power over the subordinate "disabled" group, they are seen as "helping out" the subordinate group. Their identity is not threatened, and their personal and social identities benefit from the intergroup experience. Therefore, if the motive of the person without a disability is to maintain a positive social identity, he or she can differentiate from the subordinate disabled group by interacting with them in a dominant "help-giving" way.

What is more, SIT can explain the motives and behaviours of the subordinate disabled populace. Research shows that people with disabilities see themselves as a separate group (Beail, 1983; Braithwaite, 1990; Fichten *et al.*, 1989). This may occur as a result of people with disabilities comparing themselves to people without disabilities or when the non-disabled majority imposes on the disabled minority the opinion that, in this social hierarchy, they are members of a subordinate group. Braithwaite's (1990) interviews reveal that people who acquire a disability are acutely aware of the change they have experienced in moving from a majority to a minority group status. Beail (1983) discovered that when people with disabilities described their self-concept there was a "rejection of the dominant group attitude" (p. 57). Fichten *et al.* (1989) found that, in general, people with disabilities have positive self-images, although these are unlikely to be maintained when they compare themselves to people without disabilities. They reason that people with disabilities, at least in developing their self-concepts, may view themselves in relation to other people with disabilities who may be even more disabled than they are—thus creating an even "lower-status" disabled group (as was mentioned above).

People with disabilities may also evaluate their identities in comparison to those who do not possess disabilities. They perceive the non-disabled majority to be the dominant group, discover for themselves that there is a degree of social mobility between the two groups and, intending, consciously or not, to strengthen their personal identity, attempt to assimilate into the dominant group. So-called "elective" surgeries, such as plastic surgery, breast implants, or even artificial limbs used by people with disabilities not for mobility but for aesthetic purposes, are often expressions of an attempt to conform to the dominant group's "ideals" and, historically, people with disabilities have exercised these and other measures to lessen their membership in the subordinate group. Therefore, being a member of a group identified by a disability may not be an identity that people wish to maintain. There may well be a pronounced desire by people with disabilities to assimilate socially, more so than to differentiate, from the dominant non-disabled group.

"Jerry's Orphans", a group of Americans with disabilities who consciously reject the Jerry Lewis Telethon, illustrates the use of social creativity within the community of people with disabilities. These people are attempting to differentiate from both the group and stereotypes of "Jerry's Kids", which they believe contribute to a negative stereotype of people with disabilities as needy and helpless. Similarly, persons with disabilities who engage in ingroup-only activities (e.g. wheelchair basketball, "goal ball") may be asserting their identities as active, highly skilled sportspersons, thus not attempting to assimilate into dominant group spheres. Furthermore, the Americans with Disabilities Act was created as a direct result of social competition, perceptions of injustice, and feelings of illegitimate treatment. People with disabilities fought for their civil rights. They now have recourse, as a group of persons who possess either physical or mental impairments which limit their life activities, to federally enforced antidiscrimination policies for their protection (Parry, 1990).

During interability situations, people with disabilities may believe that the best way to assimilate with people without disabilities is to follow the conversational lead of the person without disabilities. This would explain, in part, why many people with disabilities may not assert themselves against patronizing speech and allow it to pass without comment. Asserting and differentiating themselves as members of a subordinate group makes it more difficult for people with disabilities to assimilate into the dominant group. It may be that people who have a positive social identity relating to their disability (e.g. the identity that they have overcome hardships that people without disabilities have not) would be more likely to be assertive and to respond with disapproval to patronizing speech in interability situations.

Given the different possibilities listed above, it is important that research recognizes the different types of identities that people with and without disabilities are attempting to maintain during interability situations. People without disabilities may see their role as "helper" to people with disabilities as a way to most positively maintain their identity (as well as their dominant group-status), even though norms of independence are prevalent. Hence, SIT can aid in explaining the motivations of people with and without disabilities as they seek to maintain and reinforce a positive social identity.

Communication Accommodation Theory

Communication accommodation is, in part, a process by which SIT is manifest communicatively and sociolinguistically (Giles *et al.*, 1991). This approach assumes that "people are motivated to adjust their speech styles (or accommodate) as a means of expressing values, attitudes, and intentions toward each other. It is proposed that the extent to which individuals shift their speech styles toward or away from those of their interlocutors is a mechanism by which social approval or disapproval, and group loyalty is communicated" (Giles *et al.*, 1987, p. 117). Therefore, if one wishes to assert a positive social identity, one can do so behaviourally, via communication accommodation. Based upon the communicative strategies of convergence and divergence, CAT suggests that people employ or adjust their speech and/or behavioural style to achieve their intentions. Convergence has more recently been defined as "a strategy whereby individuals adapt to each other's communicative behaviours in terms of a wide range of linguistic/prosodic/non-vocal features including speech rate, pausal phenomena and utterance length, phonological variants, smiling, gaze, and so on" (Giles and Coupland, 1991, p. 63). Divergence, on the other hand, refers to the accentuation of these communicative differences between individuals.

A number of explicit goals are described as the motivating factors that promote the practice of convergence and divergence. Individuals may seek: (1) social approval; (2) to attain communication efficiency; and (3) to maintain positive social identities. Convergence and divergence may also be driven by the desire to be seen as attractive, supportive, intelligent and involved, and can be mediated by the socially and culturally inherent power structures of the interactants. The idea that a person can accommodate to what they *believe* is the behaviour of another group adds further complexity to the theory. Supporting this idea is the finding that people without disabilities conform their opinions to those which they believe people with disabilities hold (Kleck, 1968). The assumption—and one that is clearly not proven—may be that people with disabilities have less communicative competence (e.g. shorter interactions, less verbal immediacy, less eye gaze). On the other hand, people without disabilities could also be attempting to psychologically diverge by differentiating from "normal–normal" behaviour by using speech with less communicative competence (although this is unlikely given a desire to have a positive, and most likely competent, social identity). Holmes *et al.* (1990), in explaining why people without disabilities stand at a greater distance from people with disabilities, claim that they may be adapting to presumed proxemic rules which exist (although this lower affiliative behaviour may also be attributable to the person without a disability's desire to differentiate).

The same complexities are evident in the behaviour of people with disabilities. Because of the desire to assimilate into the non-disabled dominant group, they may converge to the speech of the person without a disability, even if that speech comes to them in the form of patronization. Persons with disabilities feel that they have to be cheerful to reduce the discomfort of others (Wright, 1983; Elliot and Frank, 1990), which can be viewed as accommodating to a "happy stereotype" that people without disabilities may hold about people with disabilities. It is evident that many different possibilities exist and it is, therefore, important to investigate the motivations and strategies (both psychological and communicative) that interactants are using to promote positive social identities in interability situations.*

Patronizing speech toward people with disabilities, in itself an expression of over-accommodation, may be mediated by several conditions. First, as implied earlier, people without disabilities all too often find the prospect of interacting with a person with a disability as anxiety-provoking and predict few value outcomes emerging from it. Consequentially, they may want to diverge from the speech of people with disabilities. Second, the expectation that people with only one physical disability are seen as possessing other disabilities can cause people

*Patronisation is not a one-way street—as has been documented in the intergenerational arena (Giles and Williams, 1994). In other words, the possibility also exists that certain persons *with* disabilities can, on occasion, patronize persons without disabilities—particularly on dimensions where the latter may be incompetent and vulnerable. This might be "successful" to the extent that it does not incur retaliation from its recipients, who might feel that verbal wrath directed towards "unfortunate others" would be socially unacceptable in public situations. It also allows the patronizer to engage in breaking social taboos and thereby exhibit a unique and valued sense of frankness and directness. That said, it could be resented and attributed negatively by patronizees as an indication of bitterness.

without disabilities to think that a person with a physically disability also has a mental disability (Belgrave and Mills, 1981). This anxiety, lowered communicative expectations associated with negative stereotypes, and minimal predicted outcome value may be compounded by the need for people without disabilities to both differentiate from the subordinate group and conform to the norms of their own group as being "charitable" toward less fortunate groups. Ironically, these circumstances make patronizing speech toward people with disabilities, especially in initial encounters, a logical (as well as rationally justifiable) communicative response.

CAT assists in understanding the motivations and behaviours of people in different communicative circumstances (see Gallois *et al.*, 1995). Although some interability communication experiments have looked at certain communicative behaviours (e.g. information seeking and opinion convergence), again, these have not been developed from an accommodation framework. This approach helps to explain interability communication, and achieves a more coherent framework than has been achieved by URT, POV, and intercultural theories. At the same time, the approach being advanced here acknowledges the potency of constructs inherent in those theories.

Intergroup contact theory

SIT and CAT contribute to our understanding of the motivations and communicative behaviour of interactants in interability situations, but cannot account for the subtle changes in attitude and subsequent behaviour which may occur as a result of such interactions. Contact theories are largely concerned with determining whether contact between different groups will lead to more positive attitudes and, subsequently, more positive interactions and further understanding between groups. Hewstone and Brown (1986), in reviewing other contact work, conclude that the following conditions should lead to positive attitude change: (a) contact involving equal status between groups; (b) pursuit of common goals; (c) social and situational support; (d) intimate rather than casual contact; and (e) pleasant and rewarding contact. Although this type of contact may lead to positive attitude change toward the immediate person or subgroup involved, it may not necessarily generalize to *the group as a whole*. Contact situations are also context-based and behaviours, likewise, may not generalize to other situations. Also, intimate contact may be seen as "interpersonal" contact, and the more atypical a person sees another group member, the less likely he or she will be to perceive this contact as representative behaviour of the whole group. Consequently, people may view these outgroup members as exceptions to the rule and still preserve their stereotypes of the whole group.

Hewstone and Brown's (1986) intergroup contact theory maintains that unless the person(s) involved in intergroup situations are seen as "typical" of the whole group, attitude change will not be generalized to the whole group. Hence, mainstreaming programmes (in which children with disabilities are placed in "regular" classrooms) may not work if the assumption is that mere contact alone will lead to greater understanding and more positive attitudes by people without disabilities. As mentioned above, contact and attitude change studies, on the whole, have failed to support the assumption that mere contact will lead to more perceived similarities between the groups, and subsequently more liking, attraction, and affiliation. More importantly, contact studies have not actually demonstrated that positive change is generalized to a whole group or maintained over time (Fox and Giles, 1993).

When a potential interability situation arises, a person without a disability may choose one of three approaches: non-interaction, interaction with differentiation (often divergent), or interaction with assimilation (often convergent). Assuming that people without disabilities desire to differentiate themselves from the subordinate group with disabilities, the first and second options are the ones most likely to occur. Studies have shown that children with disabilities are chosen less often as friends and playmates (Gentry, 1983; Peterson and Haralick, 1977) which supports the "non-interaction" path. When interaction does occur, the communicative behaviour of persons without a disability can create self-fulfilling prophecies which reinforce stereotypes and override disconfirming evidence, resulting in no significant attitude or behavioural change. If disconfirming evidence *is* attended to, the person without a disability may discount the person with disabilities as an exception and not as a "typical" person with disabilities, thereby failing to generalize their change in attitude to the whole group.

Due to the lack of research employing an intergroup approach to interability contact situations, it is, at present, unwise to assume that any attitude change found by past studies has been generalized to the whole group and not just to the person(s) involved in the immediate contact situation. [Studies involving intergenerational contact have made the distinction that "known" elderly are more positively evaluated than "general" elderly (Kocarnik and Penzetti, 1986; Weinberger and Millham, 1975). We have yet to see this distinction made in interability research.] Therefore, in predicting the future behaviour of interability interactants, uncovering whether the outgroup member is seen as "typical" or "representative" of the whole group must be made the critical determinant of group-based attitude change.

It is important to view interability contact situations using Hewstone and Brown's framework which recommends equal status contact in situations that are seen as intergroup and not interpersonal in nature. Some more recent studies support this notion of equal status, although they do not explicitly involve contact theory in their discussion of interability contact situations (Amsel and Fichten, 1988; Fichten *et al.*, 1991; Westwood *et al.*, 1981). Donaldson (1980) found that in seven of eight studies, positive attitude change resulted from equal status contact. In situations where equal status is not possible (such as helping situations), Fichten and Amsel (1986) suggested that reciprocity or a superordinate goal could be used. Be that as it may, intergroup contact theory is an essential part of studying interability interactions and for determining whether the people involved can achieve a generalized behaviour change toward a group as a whole (see also Fox and Giles, 1993).

Theoretical Synthesis and Application

SIT, CAT, and intergroup contact theory can be interwoven to create an explanatory model of why interability communication may result in non-equal status situations. We will use as an example situations in which people without disabilities patronize people with disabilities, although other interability situations are equally relevant. The internal motivation driving a person without a disability may most often be to promote their social identity as not only a fully functioning person without a disability, but also that of a helpful and charitable person toward persons with disabilities. Therefore, people without disabilities may be attempting to differentiate from their counterparts with disabilities and assert a positive non-disabled identity. This identity can be reinforced linguistically by attempting to converge to a stereotype by means of the language they believe that people with disabilities would both expect and like to hear. The expectation held by the person without a disability is that the person with a disability is worthy of charity. This sentiment can be expressed linguistically through patronizing speech which may be thought to be nurturing and considerate. A positive identity is therefore maintained by the person without a disability through speaking in a patronizing way. If the person without a disability views the person with a disability as typical of all members of the group, the attitude will be reinforced, as may be the behaviour directed towards other people with disabilities in the future.

The person with a disability is placed in a dilemma each time they encounter patronizing speech in an interability episode. If they find it nurturing, and if it helps them maintain their positive self-identity as a person with a disability, then they may accept, converge, and accede to this speech. This convergence could be behaviourally manifest in language which is passive and accommodating, accepting of the one-down position that the patronizing speech imposes on the person with the disability. However, it may be difficult for people with a disability to react to patronizing speech which they find insulting and threatening to their positive self-identity. They may want to diverge from the speech by asserting themselves, and linguistically confront the patronizer. But, as Weinberg (1983) found, the most common reaction to inappropriate behaviour was to "let it pass" without comment, attributing the behaviour of the patronizer to being well-intentioned. Research on helping situations has found that people with disabilities allow people without disabilities to help even when it is not necessary because "able-bodied people often feel good if they can help somebody in need, (and) that playing the Good Samaritan enables them to feel positive about themselves" (Weinberg, 1983, p. 367). In this way, people with disabilities may feel that they are asserting a positive social identity by supporting a member of the group to which they would like to assimilate.

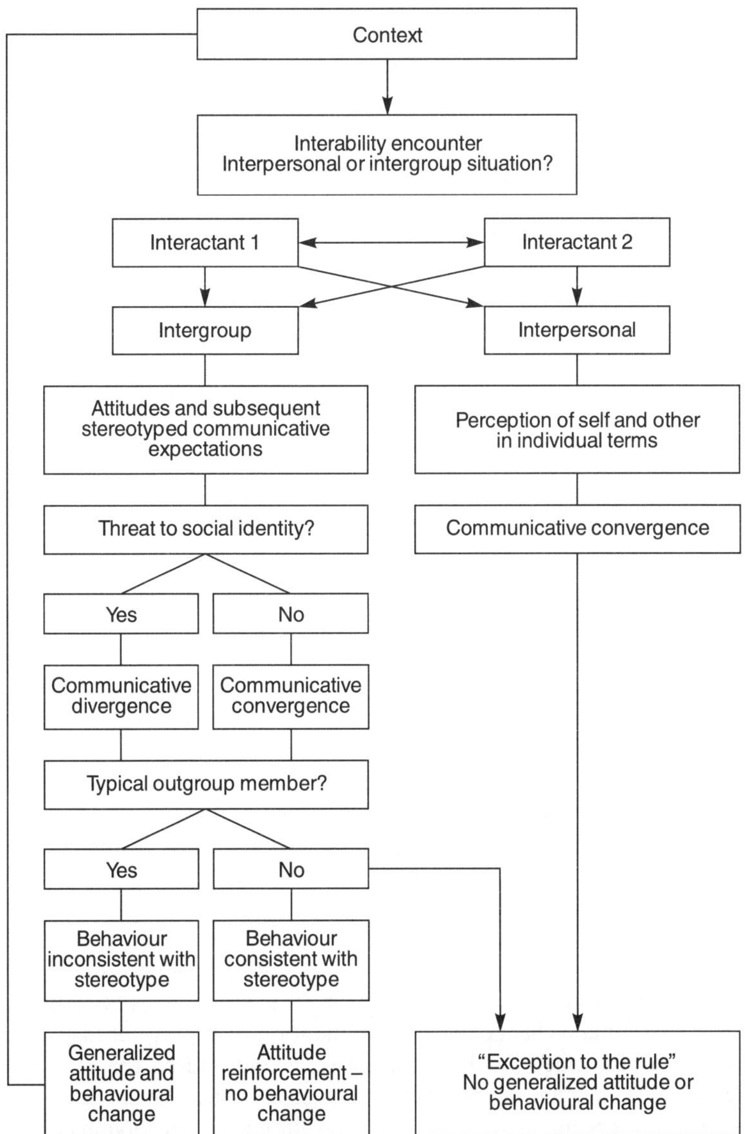

FIG 8.1 Interability communication model.

Intergroup contact theory comes into play when interability interactants assess the other group member and the interaction in which they have participated. If people without a disability see the person with a disability as a typical group member, their attitude, and arguably their future behaviour, will generalize to all members of the group. On the other hand, if the person with a disability is seen as atypical, his or her behaviour will likewise be discounted as being unrepresentative of the whole group, and thus the behaviour and attitude of the person without a disability will remain intact. Therefore, even if a person with a disability asserts that patronizing speech is not appropriate, the assertion will not necessarily have an impact on the behaviour of the person without a disability toward other people with disabilities.

The complexities of SIT, CAT, and intergroup contact can work together in explaining the motivations, attitudes, and behaviour of interactants involved in interability situations. From these theories, a model of interability communication (Figure 8.1) can schematically represent the concepts important to these theories. Hypotheses regarding the attributions, attitudes, and behaviours of interactants can be derived from these theories and this model.

Our schematic model incorporates the constructs discussed above. It first considers whether or not the situation is seen by the interactants as intergroup or interpersonal in nature (Tajfel and Turner, 1986). It is important to note that one person can understand the situation to be interpersonal in nature, while the other can simultaneously believe it to be intergroup. If the situation is perceived as interpersonal, perceptions of the self and other person are assumed in terms of the individual and not by group stereotypes. When perceived as intergroup in nature, attitudes toward the group and associated stereotypes are deemed salient, which may cause a threat to the social identity of the interactant(s). If the interactant's identity is indeed threatened, anxiety is felt, and if value outcomes predicted are either low or negative, communication divergence may possibly be dispensed by the person without disabilities in the form of communicative distance, interactional avoidance by connecting with a third party, or even subtle disparagement. When the identity is not threatened, communication convergence may occur, although that may be via convergence toward what the person without a disability *believes* is appropriate communication toward a person with a disability, that is (over-accommodated) patronizing speech to a communicatively incompetent other. Following the interaction, depending on whether the interactants view the other as typical or atypical of the group, attitude change may or may not result. If the outgroup member is seen as representative of the whole group, attitude change (whether in the form of positive change, negative change, or reinforcement) and subsequent behaviour will be generalized to the whole group. If the outgroup member is not seen as typical, he or she can be seen as a proverbial "exception to the rule," and no attitude or behavioural change will result. Finally, if the behaviour is generalized, it will, depending on the context (thus the arrow), feed into subsequent interability situations.

Future Research

The rest of this chapter will be devoted to setting an agenda arising out of our interability communication model and begins with a discussion of how past research can be re-evaluated using this perspective. First, let us consider mainstreaming, which is an educational attempt to integrate students with disabilities into all classrooms. It is "based on the assumption that through contact between handicapped and non-handicapped students constructive relationships will be built, and the students' competencies to relate effectively with each other will be increased" (Johnson and Johnson, 1981, p. 344). Hiroshige (1990) points out that in mainstreamed schools, "positive peer relations have been described as the most important aspect of the school's curriculum" (p. 3), and should also contribute to socialization of values, attitudes, competencies, and perceptions of the world (Johnson and Johnson, 1981). Frederickson and Woolfson (1987) found that nine- to twelve-year-old students with disabilities spent less time in groups and more time with other students with disabilities, so that even in mainstreamed classrooms there appears to be social segregation of groups based upon ability. Our interability communication model could be used to investigate the effectiveness of mainstreaming programmes. For example, if students without disabilities feel their identity is threatened by the integration of people with disabilities (e.g. perhaps they believe the teacher is spending large quantities of time with the students with disabilities), this will affect the expectations, attitudes, and behaviour of both interactants.

Second, and as also mentioned earlier, there have been a number of studies that have examined the effects of self-disclosure by a person with disabilities on certain interaction variables such as anxiety and liking (see p. 225 for citations). The premise of this research is that non-disabled people are anxious about interacting with people with disabilities because they may have strong emotional reactions to their disabilities (Braithwaite, 1991; Thompson, 1982; Thompson and Seibold, 1978). Subsequently, mentioning the disability in the interaction should have the effect of lessening this anxiety and increasing liking and acceptance of people with disabilities. Strategies which use the acknowledgement of a disability have been moderately successful in alleviating the anxiety which non-disabled people feel about interacting with a person with disabilities, but have not been examined in terms of how they affect the social identities of the people involved. If a person with a disability acknowledges his or her disability, it may dissipate the threat the person without a disability may feel, and the desire to differentiate from the person with a disability. On the other hand, it makes salient a definition of the situation in intergroup terms, leading to the potential for discomfort of how to respond to the agendarizing of the issue. Moreover, sometimes the lack of an acknowledgement of a disability by the person with a disability may lead the latter to feel his or her problems are being underaccommodated. How acknowledgement issues can be negotiated and resolved satisfactorily is a concern that could be investigated profitably from our perspective.

Third, reducing the anxiety that people without disabilities feel toward certain disabilities has been accomplished through disability simulation (Israelson, 1980; Wesson and Mandell, 1989; Wilson, 1971; Wilson and Acorn, 1969). Disability simulation involves becoming temporarily disabled in an attempt to understand the feelings and frustrations that are associated with physical disabilities. The purpose of this method is to increase people's awareness of a disability which should, in turn, increase empathy and thus heighten communicative awareness toward people with disabilities. Disability simulation may be a good method of helping people without disabilities understand the physical limitations of a disability, although it may serve to contribute to increased feelings of pity toward people with disabilities. Research needs to evaluate this procedure as it affects people's social identities and the subsequent behaviour of the interability interactants.

Moving now briefly to furthering the model itself, the following issues seem important to pursue. First, context is a crucial component of the model. Braithwaite (1990) has found that managing helping situations was a frequently admitted problem for people with disabilities. Obviously, each context brings its own special problems that relate to equality, identity management and so forth and it is important to attend to contextual issues in tests or applications of the model.

Second, it is important to understand further when interability interactants define an encounter in more or less "intergroup" terms. This type of research could utilize and expand work by Fichten and her colleagues concerning the thoughts people with and without disabilities have toward interability interactions. Thus far, their research has examined the self- and other-referent thoughts of people in interability situations without adopting an intergroup approach (Amsel and Fichten, 1988; Fichten and Amsel, 1988; Fichten and Bourdon, 1986; Fichten *et al.*, 1989). Her agenda, to identify the types of cognitions which inhibit or facilitate social interactions, dovetails with our interability communication model.

Third, although much is known about the attitudes people have toward people with disabilities, much less is known regarding people's expectations about an interability communication situation. Furthermore, while much is known about the thoughts that people without disabilities have about possibly interacting with people with disabilities (e.g. Fichten *et al.*, 1989), these have not been examined in terms of the types of communicative expectations (e.g. topics one thinks should be discussed and avoided) that both people with and without disabilities possess. It would also be useful to study variability in expectations that people feel govern interability communication, especially in light of the passage of the recent civil rights acts (e.g. the Americans with Disabilities Act). Are attitudes, and thus norms, changing so that people with disabilities are viewed more positively, or is there a backlash in the norms such that the dominant group of people without disabilities view people with disabilities as even *more* in need of charity? It would be useful to understand how a person without a disability chooses the social norms which promote either the independence of persons without a disability (e.g. not offering assistance) or their dependence (e.g. offering help). If the norms are changing, it is also important to discover the medium by which these changes are occurring (e.g. mainstreaming in schools, media portrayals of people with disabilities). The social norms people have are thus an important part of the formation of people's social identity and consequently the expectations and behaviour with which they may engage.

Fourth, past research has failed to address the questions of "how" and "when" people with and without disabilities accommodate to each other. Thus far, little mention has been accorded to gender, and the manipulation of this variable via confederates in interability communication experiments has caused little comment—yet should be considered in future accommodation research. Richardson (1976) claims, on the basis of his review, that in general, females were more tolerant of persons with disabilities than males. This contradicts an earlier study of his (1970) which found the opposite with respect to social impairments (e.g. facial disfigurements and obesity). Clearly, it would be worthwhile to investigate the mediating effect of gender more closely in communicative studies aimed at different kinds of disabilities.

Alluded to in studies above, patronizing speech, a form of overaccommodation, is perceived by people with disabilities to be a frequent occurrence in interability situations (Fox, 1994). Even if this is not the case in the real world, the *perception* that it does occur frequently may be having an impact on people's attitudes, communicative expectations, and subsequent interactions. Though the contexts differ, of course, depending on the life circumstances and degree of activity which a disability permits, the prevalence of patronizing speech is an issue worthy of study. It is important to determine what long-term effects patronizing speech have on people with disabilities. Does it create, through constant interaction with patronizers, a "group-fulfilling prophecy" in which the patronizee becomes the dependent, needing of charity person with a disability which people without disabilities may be expecting? Although the long-term effects of patronization in interability communication are not yet known, their effects on ageing have been speculated. The conjecture in intergenerational communication literature is that patronizing communication is part of a process of constructing old age (Coupland and Coupland, 1990; Harwood *et al.*, 1993; Ryan *et al.*, 1995). The effects of long-term patronizing speech on people with disabilities may include decreases in self-esteem, social identity, and life satisfaction. Regardless of the long-term effects, in the short term patronizing speech can frustrate many people with disabilities and therefore probably plays a part in making both interability interactants uncomfortable.

One of the more direct applications for this research is to formulate strategies which reduce the frequency of non-disabled persons using patronizing speech in interability communication. Research needs to address when and why people with disabilities react toward patronizing speech in an assertive or non-assertive manner—and the implications for a positive social identity based on these linguistic choices. Determining who would be most likely to alter their behaviour would likewise be a component of this research. It may be that people involved in charitable functions directed toward people with disabilities (e.g. The Jerry

Lewis Telethon) would be less open to changing patronizing behaviour because of their communicative stereotypes of interability communication. Care-givers and personal attendants, who many times have extensive contact with people with disabilities, would be a viable group to target for this applied, longitudinal research which should, of course, explore long-term consequences of attitudinal and behavioural change.

Epilogue

The present approach to interability communication is an attempt to explain the motivations for, social identities relevant in, and attitude changes which occur in interability situations. Theoretically, this research incorporated three frameworks new to this research area, all of which are heavily indebted to Henri Tajfel for their forms. They are important building blocks to the thoughts, motivations and speech which occur in, and subsequent changes in behaviour resulting from, interability interactions. There is so much more to be mined here and we have but scratched the surface of what Tajfel's ideas hold out for this domain, which we feel sure he would have received much pleasure in seeing applied.

Given legislation such as the Americans with Disabilities Act in the United States and its emergent counterparts elsewhere in the world (including Britain), which serves to redress the personal liabilities and physical mobility of people with disabilities, the likelihood of interability interactions is increasing (see Braithwaite and Labrecque, 1994). With this increase in interability interactions, there also exists a corresponding need for competency between and among the interactants of all interability communication. Therefore, future research needs to focus on ways to make interability communication encounters more efficient (and possibly satisfying) for both interactants.

We would, however, make one final challenge to people interested in the study of interability relations. Many times, as researchers, we have a tendency to view issues from our own particular vantage point—this being cognitive, communicative, educational, or rehabilitational depending upon the academic disciplines that we inhabit. The most beneficial advancements in knowledge in this area (as well as others) must draw on the strengths, while being aware of the weaknesses, that only an interdisciplinary approach can accomplish. Furthermore, such eclecticism must not only include the organization of thought but also the dissemination of knowledge in these various areas. Through this approach, which Tajfel passionately endorsed and modelled, we can decrease the duplication of information and build knowledge relevant from, and to, a number of different perspectives.

Acknowledgements

We wish to express our gratitude to Dawn Braithwaite, Jim Bradac, the late Tom Haring, and Peter Robinson for their insightful comments on previous drafts of this chapter.

References

Abrams, D., Jackson, D., and St. Claire, L. (1990). Social identity and the handicapping functions of stereotypes: Children's understanding of mental and physical handicaps. *Human Relations,* **43**, 1085–1098.

Adelman, R. D., Greene, M. G., and Charon, R. (1987). The physician–elderly patient–companion triad in the medical encounter: The development of a conceptual framework and a research agenda. *Gerontologist*, **27**, 729–734.

Altman, B. M. (1981). Studies of attitudes toward the handicapped: The need for a new direction. *Social Problems*, **28**, 321–337.

Amsel, R., and Fichten, C. S. (1988). Effects of contact on thoughts about interaction with students who have a physical disability. *Journal of Rehabilitation*, **54,** 61–65.

Barker, R. G., Wright, B. A., Myerson, L., and Gonick, M. R. (1953). Adjustment to physical handicap and illness: A survey of the social psychology of physique and disability (2nd edn.). Social Science Research Council Bulletin, 55.

Beail, N. (1983). Physical disability: The self and the stereotype. *International Journal of Rehabilitation Research*, **6**, 56–57.

Belgrave, F. Z., and Mills, J. (1981). Effect upon desire for social interaction with a physically disabled person of mentioning the disability in different contexts. *Journal of Applied Social Psychology*, **11,** 44–57.

Berger, C. R. (1979) Beyond initial interaction: Uncertainty, understanding, and the development of interpersonal relationships. In H. Giles and R. N. St. Clair, (Eds), *Language and social psychology*. Oxford: Blackwell, pp. 122–144,

Braithwaite, D. O. (1990). From majority to minority: An analysis of cultural change from able-bodied to disabled. *International Journal of Intercultural Relations,* **14,** 465–483.

Braithwaite, D. O. (1991). "Just how much did that wheelchair cost?": Management of privacy boundaries by persons with disabilities. *Western Journal of Speech Communication*, **55,** 254–274.

Braithwaite, D. O. (1995). "Persons first": Explaining communicative choices by persons with disabilities. In E. B. Ray, (Ed.), *Communication and the disenfranchized: Social health issues and implications*. Hillsdale, NJ: Erlbaum, in press.

Braithwaite, D. O., Emry, R. A., and Wiseman, R. L. (1984). Able-bodied and disable-bodied persons' communication: The disabled persons' perspective. ERIC document reproduction service No. ED 264 622.

Braithwaite, D. O., and Labrecque, D. (1994). Responding to the Americans with Disabilities Act: Contributions of interpersonal communication and training. *Journal of Applied Communication Research,* **22**, 287–294.

Branscombe, N. R., and Wann, D. L. (1994). Collective self-esteem consequences of outgroup derogation when a valued social identity is on trial. *European Journal of Social Psychology,* **24**, 641–657.

Burden, P. R., and Parish, T. S. (1983). Exceptional and normal children's descriptors of themselves. *Education*, **104**, 204–205.

Centers, L., and Centers, R. (1963). Peer group attitudes toward the amputee child. *Journal of Social Psychology*, **61**, 127–132.

Coe, R. M., and Predergast, C. (1985). The formation of coalitions: Interaction strategies in triads. *Sociology of Health and Illness*, **7**, 236–247.

Coleman, L. M., and DePaulo, B. M. (1991). Uncovering the human spirit: Moving beyond disability and "missed" communications. In N. Coupland, H. Giles, H., and J. M. Wiemann, (Eds) *"Miscommunication" and problematic talk*. Thousand Oaks, CA: Sage, pp. 61–84.

Comer, R. J. and Piliavin, J. A. (1972). The effects of physical deviance upon face-to-face interaction: The other side. *Journal of Personality and Social Psychology,* **23**, 33–39.

Coupland, N., and Coupland, J. (1990). Language and later life. In H. Giles and W. P. Robinson, (Eds), *Handbook of language and social psychology*. Chichester: Wiley and Sons, pp. 451–470.

Coupland, N., Giles, H., and Benn, W. (1986). Language, communication and the blind: Cuelessness and beyond. *Journal of Language and Social Psychology*, **5**, 52–63.

Dahnke, G. L. (1982). Communication and handicapped and nonhandicapped persons: Toward a deductive theory. In M. Burgoon (Ed.), *Communication yearbook*, Vol. 6. Thousand Oaks, CA: Sage, pp. 92–135.

de Appodaca, R. F., Watson, J. D., Mueller, J., and Isaacson-Kulles, J. (1985). A sociometric comparison of mainstreamed, orthopedically handicapped high school students and non-handicapped classmates. *Psychology in the Schools,* **22**, 95–101.

DeJong, W. (1993). Obesity as a characterological stigma: The issue of responsibility and judgments of task performance. *Psychological Reports*, **73**, 963–970.

DePaulo, B. M., and Coleman, L. M. (1986). Talking to children, foreigners, and retarded adults. *Journal of Personality and Social Psychology*, **51**, 945–959.

DePaulo, B. M., and Coleman, L. M. (1987). Verbal and nonverbal communication of warmth to children, foreigners, and retarded adults. *Journal of Nonverbal Behavior*, **11**, 75–88.

Donaldson, J. (1980). Changing attitudes toward handicapped persons: A review and analysis of research. *Exceptional Children*, **46**, 504–514.

Dubé-Simard, L. (1983). Genesis of social categorisation, threat to identity and perception of social injustice: Their role in intergroup communication. *Journal of Language and Social Psychology,* **2**, 183–205.

Eisenman, R. (1970). Birth order, sex, self-esteem, and prejudice against the physically disabled. *Journal of Psychology*, **75**, 145–155.

Elliott, R. R., and Frank, R. G. (1990). Social and interpersonal reactions to depression and disability. *Rehabilitation Psychology*, **35**, 135–147.

Emry, R., and Wiseman, R. L. (1987). An intercultural understanding of able-bodied and disabled person's communication. *International Journal of Intercultural Relations*, **11**, 7–27.

Eposito, B. G., and Peach, W. J. (1983). Changing attitudes of preschool children toward handicapped persons. *Exceptional Children*, **49**, 361–363.

Farina, M., Sherman, M., and Allen, J. G. (1968). Role of physical abnormalities in interpersonal perception and behaviour. *Journal of Abnormal Psychology,* **73**, 590–593.

Feinberg, L. B. (1971). Nonimmediacy in verbal communication as an indicator of attitudes toward the disabled. *Journal of Social Psychology*, **84**, 135–140.

Fichten, C. S., and Amsel, R. (1986). Trait attributions about college students with a physical disability: Circumplex analyses and methodological issues. *Journal of Applied Social Psychology*, **16**, 410–427.

Fichten, C. S., and Amsel, R. (1988). Thoughts concerning interaction between college students who have a physical disability and their nondisabled peers. *Rehabilitation Counseling Bulletin*, **32**, 22–40.

Fichten, C. S., and Bourdon, C. V. (1986). Social skill deficit or response inhibition: Interaction between disabled and nondisabled college students. *Journal of College Student Personnel,* **27**, 326–333.

Fichten, C. S., Robbillard, K., Judd, D., and Amsel, R. (1989). College students with physical disabilities: Myths and realities. *Rehabilitation Psychology*, **4**, 243–257.

Fichten, C. S., Robbillard, K., Tagalakis, V., and Amsel, R. (1991). Causal interaction between college students with various disabilities and their nondisabled peers: The internal dialogue. *Rehabilitation Psychology*, **36**, 3–20.

Fichten, C. S., Tagalakis, V., and Amsel, R. (1989). Effects of cognitive modeling, affect, and contact on attitudes, thoughts, and feelings toward college students with physical disabilities. *Journal of the Multihandicapped Person*, **2**, 119–137.

Fowler, C., and Wadsworth, J. (1991). Individualism and equality: Critical values in North American culture and the impact on disability. Special issue: Disability policy and the laws: Implications for professional practice in the 1990s: II. Implications for professional practice. *Journal of Applied Rehabilitation Counseling*, **22**, 19–23.

Fox, S. (1994). Patronizing others in intergroup encounters: The experiences and evaluations of people in interability situations. Unpublished PhD dissertation, Dept. of Communication, University of California, Santa Barbara.

Fox, S., and Giles, H. (1993). Accommodating intergenerational contact: A critique and theoretical model. *Journal of Aging Studies*, **7**, 423–451.

Frederickson, N., and Woolfson, H. (1987). Integration: The social dimension. Educational *Psychology in Practice,* **3**, 42–48.

Gallois, C., Giles, H., Jones, C., Cargile, A., and Ota, H. (1995). Accommodating intercultural encounters: Elaborations and extensions. In R. Wiseman (Ed.), *Theories of intercultural communication (International and intercultural communication annuals*, Vol. 19). Thousand Oaks, CA: Sage, pp. 115–147.

Garske, G. G., and Thomas, K. R. (1990). The relationship of self-esteem and contact to attitudes of students in rehabilitation counseling toward persons with disabilities. *Rehabilitation and Counseling Bulletin*, **34**, 67–71.

Gentry, B. (1983). Does mainstreaming insure integration? Lawrence, KS: University of Kansas Early Childhood Institute. ERIC document reproduction service No. ED 231 108.

Giles, H., and Coupland, N. (1991). *Language: Contexts and consequences.* Milton Keynes: Open University Press.

Giles, H., Coupland, N., and Coupland, J. (1991). Accommodation theory: Communication, context, and consequence. In H. Giles, J. Coupland, and N. Coupland, (Eds), *The contexts of accommodation: Developments in applied sociolinguistics*. New York: Cambridge University Press, pp. 1–68.

Giles, H., Fox, S. A. and Smith, E. (1993). Patronizing the elderly: Intergenerational evaluations. *Research in Language and Social Interaction*, **26**, 129–150.

Giles, H., Mulac, A., Bradac, J., and Johnson, P. (1987). Speech accommodation theory: The first decade and beyond. In M. L. McLaughlin (Ed.), *Communication Yearbook*, Vol. 10. Thousand Oaks, CA: Sage, pp. 113–148.

Giles, H., and Williams, A. (1994). Patronising the young: Forms and evaluations. *International Journal of Aging and Human Development*, **39**, 33–53.

Gillies, P., and Shackley, T. (1988). Adolescents' view of their physically handicapped peers—a comparative study. *Educational Research*, **30**, 104–109.

Goffman, E. (1963). *Stigma: Notes on the management of spoiled identity.* Englewood Cliffs, NJ: Prentice-Hall.

Gordon, E. D., Minnes, P. M., and Holden, R. R. (1990). The structure of attitudes toward persons with a disability, when specific disability and context are considered. *Rehabilitation Psychology*, **35**, 79–90.

Grand, S. A., Bernier, J. E., and Strohmer, D. C. (1982). Attitudes toward disabled persons as a function of social context and specific disability. *Rehabilitation Psychology*, **27**, 165–174.

Grove, T. G., and Werkman, D. L. (1991). Conversations with ablebodied and visibly disabled strangers: An adversarial test of predicted outcome value and uncertainty reduction theories. *Human Communication Research*, **17**, 507–534.

Gudykunst, W.B. (ed.) (1986). *Intergroup communication.* London: Edward Arnold.

Guralnick, M. J., and Paul-Brown, D. (1980). Functional and discourse analyses of nonhandicapped preschool children's speech to handicapped children. *American Journal of Mental Deficiency*, **84**, 444–454.

Haller, B. (1993). The misfit and muscular dystrophy: The 1992 Jerry Lewis Telethon as text. Paper presented at the 79th Annual Meeting of the Speech Communication Association, Miami, FL.

Haring, T. G. (1990). Overview of special education. In N. G. Haring and L. McCormick, (Eds), *Exceptional children and youth.* Columbus, OH: Merrill Publishing Company, pp. 3–45.

Harwood, J., Giles, H., and Ryan, E.B. (1995). Aging, communication, and intergroup theory: Social identity and intergenerational communication. In J. F. Nussbaum and J. Coupland, (Eds), *Handbook of communication and aging research.* Hillsdale, NJ: Erlbaum, pp. 133–159.

Harwood, J., Giles, H., Ryan, E. B., Fox, S., and Williams, A. (1993). Patronizing young and elderly adults: Response strategies in a community setting. *Journal of Applied Communication,* **21**, 211–226.

Hastorf, A. H., Wildfogel, J., and Cassman, T. (1979). Acknowledgment of handicap as a tactic in social interaction. *Journal of Personality and Social Psychology*, **73**, 590–593.

Hazzard, A. (1983). Children's experience with, knowledge of, and attitudes toward disabled persons. *Journal of Special Education*, **17**, 131–139.

Hewstone, M., and Brown, R. J. (1986). Contact is not enough: An intergroup perspective on the contact hypothesis. In M. Hewstone and R. Brown (Eds), *Contact and conflict in intergroup encounters*. Oxford: Blackwell, pp. 1–44.

Hiroshige, J. A. (1990). The effects of direct instruction of social skills and peer facilitation on recess intervention of students with physical disabilities. Unpublished PhD dissertation, School of Education, University of California, Santa Barbara.

Hogg, M. A., and Abrams, D. (1988). *Social identifications: A social psychology of intergroup relations and group processes*. London: Routledge.

Hogg, M. A., and Abrams, D. (1993). *Group motivation: Social psychological perspectives*. London: Harvester Wheatsheaf.

Holmes, G. E., Karst, R. H., and Erhart, S. A. (1990). Proxemics and physical disability: Etiology of interactional barriers. *Journal of Applied Rehabilitation Counseling*, **21**, 25–31.

Houston, V., and Bull, R. (1994). Do people avoid sitting next to someone who is facially disfigured? *European Journal of Social Psychology*, **24**, 279–284.

Hummert, M.L. (1994). Stereotypes of the elderly and patronizing speech. In M. L. Hummert, J. M. Wiemann, and J. F. Nussbaum (Eds), *Interpersonal communication in older adulthood*. Thousand Oaks, CA: Sage, pp. 162–164.

Israelson, J. (1980). I'm special too: A classroom program promotes understanding and acceptance of handicaps. *Teaching Exceptional Children*, **13**, 35–37.

Johnson, D. W., and Johnson, R. T. (1981). The integration of the handicapped into the regular classroom: Effects of cooperative and individualistic instruction. *Contemporary Educational Psychology*, **6**, 344–353.

Kleck, R. (1968). Physical stigma and nonverbal cues emitted in face-to-face interaction. *Human Relations*, **21**, 19–28.

Kleck, R. (1969). Physical stigma and task oriented interactions. *Human Relations*, **22**, 53–60.

Kleck, R. E., Buck, P. L., Coller, W. L., London, R. S., Pfeiffer, J. R., and Vukcevic, D. P. (1968). Effect of stigmatizing conditions on the use of personal space. *Psychological Reports*, **23**, 111–118.

Kleck, R. E., Ono, H., and Hastorf, A. H. (1966). The effects of physical deviance upon face to face interaction. *Human Relations*, **19**, 425–436.

Kleck, R. E., and Strenta, A. (1980). Perceptions of the impact of negatively valued physical characteristics on social interaction. *Journal of Personality and Social Psychology*, **39**, 861–873.

Kocarnik, R. A., and Penzetti, J. J. (1986). The influence of intergenerational contact on child care participants' attitude toward the elderly. *Child Care Quarterly*, **15**, 244–250.

Lerner, M. J. (1980). *The belief in a just world: A fundamental delusion*. New York: Plenum.

Longmore, P. K. (1985). A note on language and the social identity of people with disabilities. *American Behavioral Scientist*, **28**, 419–423.

Lukoff, I. F., and Whiteman, M. (1971). *The social sources of adjustment to blindness*. New York: American Foundation for the Blind.

MacLaine, S. (1985). *Dancing in the light*. New York: Bantam Books.

Makas, E. (1988). Positive attitudes toward people with disabilities: Disabled and nondisabled person's perspectives. *Journal of Social Issues*, **44**, 49–61.

McDaniel, J. (1976). *Physical disability and human behavior*. New York: Pergamon.

Mills, J., Belgrave, F. Z., and Boyer, K. (1984). Reducing avoidance of social interaction with physically disabled persons by mentioning the disability following a request for aid. *Journal of Applied Social Psychology*, **14**, 1–9.

Newberry, M. K., and Parish, T. S. (1987). Enhancement of attitudes toward handicapped children through social interactions. *Journal of Social Psychology*, **127**, 59–62.

Parish, T. S., and Morgan, H. G. (1984). Ascriptions by handicapped and nonhandicapped children to themselves, normal children, and handicapped children. *Journal of Genetic Psychology*, **146**, 279–280.

Parry, J. (1990). The Americans with Disabilities Act (ADA). *Mental and Physical Disability Law Reporter*, **14**, 292–298.

Patterson, J. B., and Witten, B. J. (1987). Disabling language and attitudes toward persons with disabilities. *Rehabilitation Psychology*, **32**, 245–248.

Peterson, M. L., and Haralick, J. G. (1977). Integration of handicapped and nonhandicapped preschoolers: An analysis of play behaviour and social interaction. *Education and Training of the Mentally Retarded*, **12**, 235–245.

Ray, B. M. (1985). Measuring the social position of the mainstreamed handicapped child. *Exceptional Children*, **52**, 57–62.

Richardson, S. A. (1970). People with cerebral palsy talk for themselves. *Developmental Medicine and Child Neurology*, **14**, 425–435.

Richardson, S. A. (1976). Attitudes and behavior toward the physically handicapped. In D. Bergsma and A. E. Pulver, (Eds), *Developmental disabilities: Psychological and social implications*. New York: Alan R. Liss, pp. 15–30.

Richardson, S. A., Ronald, L., and Kleck, R. E. (1974). The social status of handicapped and nonhandicapped boys in a camp setting. *Journal of Special Education*, **8**, 143–152.

Rogers, S. J. (1988). Characteristics of social interactions between mothers and their disabled infants: A review. *Child-Care, Health and Development,* **14**, 301–317.

Rohrlich, P. E. (1983). Toward a unified conception of intercultural communication: An integrated systems approach. *International Journal of Intercultural Relations*, **7**, 191–209.

Royse, D., and Edwards, T. (1989). Communicating about disability: Attitudes and preferences of persons with physical handicaps. *Rehabilitation Counseling Bulletin*, **32**, 203–209.

Ryan, E. B., Bourhis, R. Y., and Knops, U. (1991). Evaluative perceptions of patronizing speech addressed to elders. *Psychology and Aging*, **6**, 442–450.

Ryan, E. B., and Cole, R. (1990). Evaluative perceptions of interpersonal communication with elders. In H. Giles, N. Coupland, and J. Wiemann (Eds), *Communication, health, and the elderly.* Manchester: Manchester University Press, pp. 172–190.

Ryan, E. B., Hummert, M. L., and Boich, L. H. (1995). Communication predicaments of aging: Patronizing behaviour toward older adults. *Journal of Language and Social Psychology*, **14**, 144–166.

Sagatun, I. J. (1985). The effects of acknowledging a disability and initiating contact on interaction between disabled and non-disabled persons. Special issue: Social aspects of chronic disease and disability. *Social Science Journal*, **22**, 33–43.

Semin, G., and Fiedler, K. (Eds). (1992). *Language, interaction, and social cognition*. London: Sage.

Sigelman, C. K., Adams, R. M., Meeks, S. R., and Purcell, M. A. (1986). Children's nonverbal responses to a physically disabled person. *Journal of Nonverbal Behavior*, **10**, 173–186.

Sillar, J., and Chipman, A. (1964). Factorial structure and correlates of the attitude toward disabled persons scale. *Educational Psychological Measurement,* **24**, 831–839.

Siple, L. A. (1994). Cultural patterns of deaf people. *International Journal of Intercultural Relations*, **18**, 345–367.

Stovall, C., and Sedlacek, W. E. (1983). Attitudes of male and female university students toward students with different physical disabilities. *Journal of College Student Personnel,* **24**, 325–330.

Strenta, A. C., and Kleck, R. E. (1985). Physical disability and the attribution dilemma: Perceiving the causes of social behaviour. *Journal of Social and Clinical Psychology*, **3**, 129–142.

Sunnafrank, M. (1986). Predicted outcome value during initial interactions: A reformulation of uncertainty reduction theory. *Human Communication Research*, **13**, 3–33.

Szivos, S., and Travers, E. (1988). Consciousness raising among mentally handicapped people: A critique of the implications of normalization. *Human Relations*, **41**, 641–653.

Tajfel, H. (Ed.) (1978). *Differentiation between social groups*. New York: Academic Press.

Tajfel, H., and Turner, J. C. (1986). The social identity theory of intergroup behaviour. In S. Worchel and W. G. Austin (Eds), *Psychology of intergroup relations*. Chicago: Nelson-Hall, pp. 7–24.

Thomas, S. A., Foreman, P. E., and Remenyi, A, G. (1985). The effects of previous contact with physical disability upon Australian children's attitudes toward people with physical disabilities. *International Journal of Rehabilitation Research*, **8**, 69–70.

Thompson, T. L. (1981). The development of communication skills in physically handicapped children. *Human Communication Research*, **7**, 312–324.

Thompson, T. L. (1982). "You can't play marbles—you have a wooden hand": Communication with the Handicapped. *Communication Quarterly*, **30**, 108–115.

Thompson, T. L., and Seibold, D. R. (1978). Stigma management in normal-stigmatized interactions: Test of the disclosure hypothesis and a model of stigma acceptance. *Human Communication Research,* **4**, 231–242.

Walker, S. (1983). A comparison of the attitudes of students and non-students toward the disabled in Ghana. *International Journal of Rehabilitation Research*, **6**, 313–320.

Wasserman, F. A., Allen, R., and Solomon, C. R. (1985). The behavioural development of physically handicapped children in the second year. *Journal of Developmental and Behavioral Pediatrics,* 6, 27–31.

Weinberg, N. (1983). Social equity and the physically disabled. *Social Work,* **28**, 365–369.

Weinberger, L. E., and Millham, J. (1975). A multi-dimensional, multiple method analysis of attitudes towards the elderly. *Journal of Gerontology*, **30**, 343–348.

Weitz, S. (1972). Attitude, voice, and behaviour: A repressed affect model of interracial interaction. *Journal of Personality and Social Psychology*, **24**, 14–21.

Wesson, C., and Mandell, C. (1989). Simulations promote understanding of handicapped conditions. *Teaching Exceptional Children,* **22**, 32–35.

Westwood, M., Vargo, J., and Vargo, F. (1981). Methods for promoting attitude change toward and among physically disabled persons. *Journal of Applied Rehabilitation Counseling*, **12**, 220–225.

Wilson, E. D. (1971). A comparison of the effects of deafness simulation and observation upon attitudes, anxiety, and behaviour manifested toward the deaf. *The Journal of Special Education*, **5**, 343–349.

Wilson, E. D., and Alcorn, D. (1969). Disability simulation and development of attitudes toward the exceptional. *Journal of Special Education,* **3**, 303–307.

Wolfensberger, W. (1972). *The principle of normalization in human services.* Toronto: National Institute on Mental Retardation.

Wright, B. (1983). *Physical disability: A psychosocial approach*, 2nd edn. New York: Harper and Row.

Yuker, H. E., and Block, J. R. (1986). *Research with the attitude toward disabled persons scales (ATDP), 1960–1985*. Hempstead, NY: Hofstra University.

9

Children and Racism: Beyond the Value of the Dolls...

DAVID MILNER

Division of Psychology, University of Westminster

Contents

Social psychology's interest in children's racial attitude development began, indirectly, with Bruno Lasker's study of American adults in the late 1920s (Lasker, 1929). From their recollections of childhood experiences, he concluded that the child is:

> ... certain to have his (*sic*) mind canalized, even before he starts going to school, into habitual acceptance of the prevailing racial attitudes of the group within which he lives. ... the average child is made to notice outer differences and to accept them as signs of inner differences in value.
>
> (p.127)

With an acuity of perception and understanding which was remarkable for his time, Lasker anticipated much of what later flowed from direct studies of children's racial attitudes. Horowitz and Horowitz (1938) and Clark and Clark (1947) pioneered this work, using an assessment method that was to dominate the field for fifty years. These early workers rightly reasoned that young children lacked the cognitive and linguistic apparatus necessary to respond to questionnaires and attitude scales, nor would they be able to handle the complex concepts around the race issue. What was necessary, therefore, was to use some graphic, concrete, recognizable way of representing race to children, for example, dolls or pictures, in order that researchers might elicit their reaction to these figures, and to the racial groups they represented.

In the post-war period, and through the 1950s and 1960s, variants of these methods (dolls, puppets, pictures, line-drawings, photographs) were deployed in studies across the US and elsewhere. A remarkably consistent and coherent picture emerged, summarized by Goodman (1964) in her three-stage schema of racial attitude development. There was indeed an early development of *racial awareness* (the simple ability to distinguish racial differences) from two to three years old, followed by *racial orientation,* or *"incipient attitude"* (the first evidence of positive or negative feelings towards different racial groups) from four to five years, and finally *true attitude* (where these rudimentary dispositions have been fleshed out with more information and with stereotypes) at around eight years old, much as Lasker had broadly anticipated.

Goodman's schema had the virtues of simplicity and of an appropriate emphasis on the affective dimension of the child's attitudes. By the same token, however, it neglected to connect this process with the child's unfolding cognitive capacities. Both an understanding of cognitive development *and* its relation to affective learning are essential. Within Goodman's terms, the notion that it was possible for the child to attain racial awareness within a society (i.e. a perceptual/ cognitive element), without at the same time absorbing some notion of the way society *valued* the groups that awareness focused upon (i.e. an affective element), was an unlikely one, but that is what is implied in the sequential arrangement of racial awareness and racial orientation. Overlap, at least, seems more plausible.

Katz (1976) went some way to rectify this imbalance with an eight-stage schema of an altogether more cognitive kind, though without explicit reference to classical Piagetian milestones. Further elaboration of the cognitive perspective has been provided by, for example, Ramsey (1987) and Aboud (1987, 1992).

Certainly it seems that in the early years, the foundations of racial attitudes are primarily affective. Katz (1987) suggests that attitudes "may developmentally precede cognitions about ethnicity (Zajonc, 1976) or may occur at the same time (Katz, 1983)" (p. 93). The utopian notion of attitude formation as a logical, rational process of weighing up information is nowhere to be seen if feelings do indeed precede facts. There are good reasons to suppose this to be the case. Tajfel and Jahoda (1966) looked at six- to seven-year-olds' preferences for other *nations* in relation to their grasp of the simplest items of factual knowledge about those countries, and found that the children "... agree(d) rather more about which countries they like and dislike than about practically anything else about those countries" (p. 24); and this with abstract entities like nations, with whom the child has no direct contact and is aware of no visible physical differences.

Again, Lewis and Brooks (1975) present evidence which suggests that children as young as ten months old already exhibit same-gender preferences.

There appear to be no a priori reasons why racial dispositions should not also be identified at a similar stage, given that they depend on similarly (or perhaps in an age of greater androgyny, *more*) pronounced cues.

In any event, while the argument about the primacy of affective or cognitive factors is theoretically interesting, it involves an artificial separation. For many children, particularly those who have no direct contact with other ethnic groups, the sources of information about them do not necessarily separate fact from feeling. It is improbable that parents convey meticulously neutral information to their children about other social groups, without any tinge of their own attitudes colouring the picture.

It has been argued elsewhere that the complexity of the early stages of racial attitude acquisition has been exaggerated:

> At one level, the learning process is a simple marriage of two pairs of concepts: good–bad and black–white (as applied to people). The very simplicity of this scheme of things cuts directly through all the conventional objections to the idea that children can have racial attitudes (on the grounds that the issues are too complex for them to handle). The good–bad concept is one of the simplest (and one of the first) pairs of polar opposites that the child meets. Yes–no, positive–negative, smiling–frowning are all expressions of the same contrasting evaluations and are present in parent–child communication—in both directions—from the very beginning. One of the first things which parents try to teach their children is the concept of "no" in relation to fires, cookers, stairs, electric plugs or valued objects of their own. Even earlier they may show disapproval of something the child does. All of this is a long time before the child has produced any speech, so it is done at an almost non-verbal level through facial expression and tone of voice. Thus children become very discriminating concerning their parents' affective tone and from early on can discern from these things alone what is approved of and what evokes disfavour. It is with this well-developed ability to grasp what is positive and what is negative, what is liked and what is disliked, just from parental tone and gesture, that the child attends to parents' and others' information and comments about black people and white people.
>
> (Milner, 1983, pp. 111–112).

Children's Racial Attitudes and Social Identity Theory

The general picture of majority children's racial attitude development is entirely compatible with social identity theory (SIT), though not entirely explained by it. Tajfel would have been the first to point out that to posit a sociopsychological process within groups which causes them, inevitably, to discriminate against out-groups, is to suggest a kind of group "instinct", that illusory trump card in the whist of behavioural explanations. However, to demonstrate a *disposition* which will be enhanced or suppressed by particular economic, cultural and sociohistorical conditions, while a more modest claim, provides a plausible and useful level of explanation.

If we suppose the existence of a society where there is racial disprivilege and an accompanying climate of racial hostility, we would want to suggest that part of the competitive/hostile attitudinal and behavioural relations between the groups may be explained in familiar SIT terms (as regards the origins or the maintenance of the conflict or both), but much more by the classic "realistic" determinants of group conflict: power, money, resources, territory, etc.

Given these characteristics of the *adult* world, children in the society are then, theoretically, subject to two kinds of encouragement to adopt their elders' perspectives: (1) via all those mechanisms responsible for the transmission of adult attitudes in the course of the socialization process, direct tuition, observational learning, identification and role-learning, reinforced by normative pressure from beyond the family; and (2) the development of friendship groups, which contain all the elements in microcosm of the larger inter-group situation. With the developing ability to socially categorize and the stimulus to social comparison, and positive distinctiveness therein, the pieces are in place for junior intergroup conflict.

Clearly, these two sets of pressures operate in parallel, and because they do it seems far more likely that children's selection of outgroups with whom to compete for positive social identity will follow in their parents' footsteps, given how persuasively it is signposted for them. Thus (1) is helping to target the competitive/hostile feelings from (2), while (2) is providing a local arena for the acting out of (1). In other words, intergroup attitude development may be a necessary part of: (a) social development, through (b) the need for a positive social identity, and (c) existing adult social categorizations help to satisfy this "hunger".

Until relatively recently, the process of children's racial attitude development has been depicted as a one-way street; one in which children passively absorb information and attitudes from their immediate environment and take them as their own. It is like the conventional *tabula rasa* view of children in the socialization process and it is at odds with the last twenty-five years of research and theory; our increasing recognition of the active role of children in constructing a view of their social world must be acknowledged. There are, in any case, some problems with the conventional account of the sources of information and attitudes that are the building blocks of the child's own attitudes. It is a matter of whether our account of parental and social influence, reinforced by a battery of wider cultural influences—books, comics, television, films and newspapers—is adequate. The implicit model is one of racial attitudes being formed like a stalagmite by accretion: the drip, drip of salts from many cultural fissures. It is as though we have recognized that there many kinds of media which convey more or less racist messages and we have shown, empirically, that children may develop more or less racist attitudes, and in a simple-minded way equated the two, without proper consideration of (a) how that might happen, and (b) what alternative, supplementary or intervening factors should be taken into account.

There are two other problems with this formulation:

(1) The *variety* of children's experience with others and exposure to different cultural products does not square well with the relative homogeneity of their racial attitudes. Whatever its shortcomings, fifty years of research on children's racial attitudes has established a notably uniform pattern of

development through childhood, which seems to be relatively immune to variations in local conditions. This supports the cultural part of the argument, but at the same time detracts from the role of parental and immediate social influence, where greater variation in individual experience may occur. It suggests, in other words, that wider cultural forces may be more influential than parents, which, in the case of young children, is intuitively open to doubt.

(2) Even were we to accept the notion that cultural media have the leading role in children's racial attitude development, there would remain some major problems. When we "unpack" the cultural products which are held to be the principal racist messengers, we find that some of them cannot be responsible (as far as young children's attitudes are concerned), for they are simply inaccessible to them. As adults we may squirm at the implicit racial biases of newspaper editorials, or at the skewed and victim-blaming "problem perspective" surrounding black people in television documentary/discussion programmes; but these are, for the most part, subtle nuances, the racist significance of which may well escape the majority of viewers, let alone their five-year-olds. This is not to minimize the explicit racism of the all-too-accessible tabloids, but to pose the question of whether the "cultural" account can sustain the role it has been given, particularly since a number of watchdog bodies have begun to expunge the more obvious racism from some media, for example children's literature.

What is argued here is that we have conceived of children passively absorbing parental influences and cultural teaching, and internalizing the racist feelings and beliefs therein, as if by some kind of permeation process. The culture's racist beliefs and sentiments are drawn through the child's "skin" by an inevitable osmosis. Described like this it appears to be a slow affair, a process of seepage, which the metaphor somehow defines in a way which implies uniformity among children. Individual differences can only be explained if we posit a greater concentration of racism in a particular environment, or a more permeable membrane. The osmosis metaphor breaks down here, according to the conventional view, for that process involves the passage of molecules from a less concentrated solution to a more concentrated one. However, it is retrieved by a different perspective, which would see elements of "racism" as emanating from within the child and seeking out elements in the surrounding environment. This does not imply any "instinct" for racism. Nor is it solely reducible to those psychopathological effects of an austerely authoritarian upbringing which might make the child more vulnerable to ethnocentric or even fascist ideologies. Rather, it is an extrapolation of some central ideas of social identity theory back into childhood, beyond even the secondary school years whence it came (Tajfel *et al.*, 1971).

What is proposed here is a model of children's racial (and more general intergroup) attitude development which is altogether more "driven" by the child than in previous conceptions of the process. Perhaps children *actively* seek out targets and initiate social categorization processes so that they can make social comparisons, and make their "groups" and (by implication) themselves "positively distinct" in the process. Much of what we know about adults' social comparisons and social identity needs applies to children with still more force: they are *par excellence*, the people with the least established social identity, other than that often unsatisfactory (and generally powerless) one of "child" in relation to countless powerful elders. Perhaps, then, it is precisely the need to understand the complexity of the social world *and* locate oneself at an acceptable station within it that drives the child to seek knowledge of existing characterizations and ally him/herself with them. The notion that children were *actively* searching out precisely those aspects of adult conversation and behaviour, or of cultural products, which directly address groups and their status relations (i.e. how "we" view social groups) would help to resolve the problem described above.

There may be a partial parallel in the area of gender relations. Here, too, there are powerful social norms and ideologies which influence children's alignments with gender groups, encourage identification with them, and prescribe appropriate behaviours.

Children's passage from infancy, where play is relatively undifferentiated by gender, through to the early years of primary school, where it is increasingly segregated along gender lines, is open to a number of interpretations. Undeniably, the internalization of adult attitudes and values, and conformity with social norms provide a large part of the explanation for this transition. However, this account of the relatively passive absorption of social influences might also be supplemented by a more active view of the child, based on identity needs. In other words, it is not only that a persuasive social climate guides the child towards appropriate gender alignment; it is also that gender alignment brings with it increments of self-definition and positive identity that satisfies children's emerging needs to locate themselves in relation to others in their world and view themselves positively.

Children have a far more restricted range of attributes and category memberships from which to construe their identity than do adults and so it follows that those which are available assume relatively more importance. It may be argued that children will purposefully seek out the few categorizations and alignments which are relevant to them, rather than simply acquiesce in the application of category labels to them and their behaviour. For young children there is security in the group, and security in seeing oneself as a category member. The painful experience of sociometric "isolates", of marginal group members, or of being the last one picked by *either* side for a playground football match, underlines that the need for *belonging* (and being seen to belong) may be as important to the child as the need for companionship *per se*, or participation in the group activity itself.

In the light of the needs satisfied by the process, it seems plausible that it is impelled from within the child, not simply imposed from without by society.

Certainly the demonstration of a "drive" towards categorization, based on identity needs, would enhance the explanation of racial attitude development in children. This would be hard to achieve empirically, though not because it would be difficult to foment categorization amongst children: we now have countless examples of how easy that process is, on the most spurious bases. Indeed, the willingness of subjects to orient their behaviour on categorization into groups on the basis of dot-judging, coin-flipping, or Klee/Kandinsky-preferring could be argued as evidence for an appetite for categorization, quite as much as it reflects the power of the experimenter to call the shots. Rather, the difficulty lies in the interpretation of the categorization behaviour. In other words, if we could demonstrate a "drive towards categorization", how could we show it to originate, unambiguously, in the identity needs of the child, as opposed to (a) an experimenter effect/demand characteristic, (b) a simple modelling of divisions of older children and adults into teams, groups etc., often for competitive purposes, or (c) an expression of the child's need for companionship, or specific group activities, rather than satisfying identity needs?

Of course there is a model for this kind of enquiry in an earlier enterprise. It was Sherif and Sherif's (1953; Sherif *et al.* 1961) meticulously detailed reporting of their classic boys' camps experiments which allowed Billig (1976) to uncover aspects of the intergroup relations which had eluded the Sherifs themselves. While the Sherifs' attention was drawn to the phase in which they had institutionalized competition between the two groups of boys (and which gave rise to negative intergroup attitudes and behaviour, as per their theory), Billig detected an appetite for competition in the reports of the boys' behaviour in *the previous phase*, before they were "supposed" to be feeling competitive (i.e. before the competition had been institutionalized by the researchers). This suggested that simply the business of categorization into groups set in motion a train of comparative and competitive processes, a corollary of which was the development of negative intergroup attitudes and behaviours, which of course became one of the central themes of social identity theory.

It might be possible, following Billig's lead, to extrapolate back even further. In the same way as he identified a clamour for competition before it was officially sanctioned, we may look in the previous phase for an appetite for groupness, division and categorization before the fact. Certainly observers of young children, who found Billig's discovery only too plausible, would have little problem in confirming a still earlier stage in the intergroup process in which there is an active desire to divide into groups.

Regrettably, Sherif's (1966) account of phase 1 is less detailed than any other. The only material which signifies an appetite for division into groups is the survey of the boys' preferred activities, in which it is clear that competitive team games are the most popular. Clearly, this may reflect the intrinsic appeal of these games and sports as much as the need to group and compete, insofar as these are separable. However, when we consider the fuller account of phase 2, it seems clear that the enthusiasm with which each group of boys immediately threw themselves into the generation of an ingroup culture—and in determined contradistinction to the other group—is unlikely to have materialized overnight, and almost certainly not solely from the *fact* of division into groups. In other words the division satisfied a pre-existing appetite by allowing its expression.

As well as developing a recognizable hierarchy of status within each group, both developed strong internal affective bonds: ingroup feelings of loyalty and solidarity between fellow group members. The boys chose names to distinguish the groups: the Red Devils and the Bull Dogs. Sanctions were brought to bear against members who fraternized with boys from the "enemy": they were threatened and branded "traitors". Food parcels and confectionery sent from home were shared within the group and the cabins were now called "home", and boys were given nicknames, like any family group or long-standing gang of friends. Each group came to favour and adopt their own songs, arrived at their own codes of behaviour (and punishment), drew up their own oaths of allegiance and secrecy (*vis-à-vis* the other group), allied themselves with group colours, and used these things in every possible way to affirm (a) their groupness, and (b) their difference from the other group. In short, each developed its own characteristic culture, which was not coincidentally different from the other, but determinedly so.

Even with minimal direct contact with the other group, "they" were a central topic of conversation. These references were usually comparative ("we" versus "they"), and competitive in that they were evaluative comparisons, invariably in terms of better/worse, and in which the ingroup was favoured. Apparently, there soon appeared an upswell of demand for competition with the other group in which, each believed, their own group's superiority would be established.

SIT would argue that, in this situation, categorization/grouping opens a door; what bursts through are some individual/group appetites for intergroup comparison for the purposes of building individual/group self-esteem, and the arena or vehicle for their expression has already been socially defined and constructed: intergroup competition through competitive team games.

There appears to be something going on here beyond a love of softball, or the dubious attractions of completing washing-up more efficiently than a group of peers, or even the pleasure of ingroup companionship. The central goal seems to be *relative* superiority *vis-à-vis* the other group, hence relative status and relative self-esteem. This is achieved at the behavioural level through victory in competition, and attitudinally through disparaging the other group while overvaluing their own.

When Stephen Sondheim wrote, "When you're a Jet, you're a Jet", it was not tautology. It simply expressed (rather more succinctly than we are accustomed to) that group membership gives the individual social identity, social belonging and support, a set of obligations, and much else besides. In *West Side Story*, the Jets and the Sharks compete for territory—or do they? These were not the days of drug "turfs", and so territory simply denoted power and status. What of the Montagues and Capulets, on whom they were based? There appears to have been no economic or territorial reason for enmity, so we may assume the commodity at stake was honour and repute (or as we might say, status, positive distinctiveness, social identity and group/self-esteem—which even Shakespeare would have strained to accommodate within iambic pentameter). The Playboys and the Echo Park Gang, two elements of the burgeoning gang subculture of south–central Los Angeles, show much in common with the Sherifs' Bull Dogs and Red Devils in terms of group dynamics and emblems of identity, however favouring drive-by shooting rather than points and prizes as a way to establish superiority. The same thread, however, runs through countless social fabrics: self-respect can be gained or enhanced through membership of a group with a positive social identity and this may be secured at the expense of other groups. Every increment of outgroup devaluation pays an equal dividend in relative ingroup superiority and self-esteem. More broadly, those appetites can be satisfied by existing ideologies concerning group differences, like race differences which are socially defined and indelibly marked, through the "epidermalization" of status.

Children of Minorities

Since the very beginning of research into children's racial attitude development there has been a paradox, and one which, at first sight, does not square with the central tenets of SIT. While majority-group children have consistently preferred and identified with their own group and tended to disparage outgroups, to a greater or lesser extent, minority-group children have not always followed this pattern. Until the early 1970s, black American children frequently made choices on doll or picture tests which favoured the white figures when choosing friends and companions, and disparaged the black figures in stereotypical ways. The most dramatic expression of this orientation emerged from one of the very earliest studies, when Clark and Clark (1947) asked their subjects which of a pair of brown and white dolls "looks most like you". Around one third of these black children indicated the white doll. The finding was regularly replicated through the 1950s and 1960s, although there was less agreement as to its meaning. While at one extreme it was argued that it was an experimental artifact, at the other it was taken to be early evidence of identity-conflict presaging later psychiatric disturbance. Most writers inclined towards the view expressed by Goodman (1946):

> The relative inaccuracy of Negro identification reflects not simple ignorance of self, but unwillingness or psychological inability to identify with the brown doll because the child wants to look like the white doll.
>
> (p. 626).

Here then was evidence of the intensity and pervasiveness of racism: it was apparently real to five-year-old children, or younger, and not only persuaded white children that their group was superior and preferable, but persuaded black children to explicitly devalue their own group, and by implication, themselves.

So the argument ran, and it was a small step to conclude that these forces would erode the child's self-esteem and undermine educational achievement and life-chances. The equations were too glibly made, on insufficient empirical evidence, but it is easy to see how this occurred within the (then) context of psychologists' images and beliefs about black people generally. Many of these ideas were drawn from clinical practice with individuals, very much reinforced by an ethnocentric picture of black family life as disorganized, inadequate and pathogenic. Nevertheless, the notion that "misidentification" by black children represented some profound intrusion of racism into young children's lives, indeed into their very view of themselves, was a persuasive one. The identification task and the child's response were both simple and dramatic; this stark reversal of logic and denial of objective reality must surely have a deeper significance. It was perhaps not surprising that this rather graphic scenario caught the imagination. It proved to be a very portable image, in microcosm, of the black experience, and its effectiveness was most dramatically demonstrated in the US Supreme Court, when it was an important part of the testimony brought to bear in favour of desegregating the American school system.

Misidentification was by no means an exclusively American phenomenon. It was replicated in New Zealand (Vaughan, 1964), South Africa (Gregor and McPherson, 1966) and Britain (Milner, 1973), widely differing cultural contexts, yet with the common factor of a disprivileged racial "minority", subject to virulent racism.

When the same phenomenon is not only reliably found by different investigators using somewhat different materials in different parts of a country, but remains stable over a period of 30 years, *and* is replicated in three other continents, we might justifiably call it a robust finding, and note that its solidity is shared by rather few other social psychological findings. When, in addition, it radically changes over a short period in ways which directly reflect changes in the social context *and* this too is replicated cross-culturally, we might conclude that here was a rather sensitive and responsive method of research. For a number of reasons, this was not the conclusion drawn.

From 1939 to the late 1960s, American studies had consistently shown a significant minority of black children misidentifying. In the early 1970s, following after the Civil Rights Movement, Black Power and "black is beautiful", black children's misidentification dropped to negligible levels; this profound change was echoed in both Britain (Milner 1983) and New Zealand (Vaughan, 1978), though somewhat later than in the US, and reflecting both domestic and international developments in the profile of black people.

In America, the new generation of findings, while welcome, seemed to provoke not plaudits for the research tool involved, but rather a barrage of criticism. Through the 1970s in particular, there appeared to be a concerted attempt to undermine the earlier generation of findings; as ever, the vehicle of criticism was methodology, though it was not too hard to discern that ideology was sometimes behind the wheel. This debate, and in particular the critique of Banks (1976) is reviewed elsewhere (Milner, 1983).

It is arguable whether the criticisms detract very much from the methodology, whose simplicity is both its virtue and its vice. In any event, the criticism was really directed more at the findings (pre-1970) than the method that had produced them. But if history could be re-written by exposing a flawed method then that would suffice. We will leave to one side the contradiction of savaging a method for its results in one era, while embracing the (acceptable) results from the same method a few years later.

Why was it necessary? The subtext seems to have been that there was felt to be something somehow shameful about misidentification and it needed to be struck from the record. More importantly (and rightly) it was necessary to prevent the finding of misidentification becoming part of a stereotype of black children: a negative and apparently demeaning stereotype, and fettered with the leg-iron of low self-esteem; and to update the picture with an image of black children, proud of their race and themselves.

It is certainly true that too easy an equation had been made between misidentification and low self-esteem. It was an interpretation that had been placed upon misidentification rather than an empirically demonstrated correlation, something which was precluded by the fact that self-esteem and identification were seldom measured concurrently. Nevertheless, when Ward and Braun (1972) measured both racial preferences and self-concepts among seven- to eight-year-old black children, they found that those children with more white-oriented racial preferences tended to have lower self-concept scores; perhaps the earlier speculations about misidentification were not so far from the mark.

The drive to assert a positive black identity in this period (from which the notion of misidentification apparently seemed to detract) was necessary, and entirely predictable within SIT terms, as we shall see. However, the "purging" of misidentification and the counter-assertion that there had never been an identity problem for blacks was illogical, flew in the face of the evidence, and did a huge disservice to our understanding of the effects of inferiorization on oppressed groups. Leaving aside the misidentification findings *per se*, some more general questions need to be asked, and answered:

(1) Four hundred years of racism, operating through social, political and economic institutions, permeating through the culture and all its products, and cleaving the social life of the people, has sustained a variety of highly negative attitudes and beliefs about black people amongst the white population. Given the socialization and lifetime immersion of black people within the same broad sociocultural climate, is it not more likely that some will have internalized these values than that all will have been completely immune to their message?

(2) If black identity was never in question, if there were no negative or ambivalent elements, why was there any need for the black pride and black-

is-beautiful movements of the 1960s, acknowledged by many to have been as important a part of black liberation as the political and economic gains initiated by the Civil Rights Movement?

Question 2 is rhetorical and question 1 is nearly so: to resist the press of racism and emerge unscathed and unmarked by it would be almost unique in human history. Indeed, rather lesser oppressions have been successful in psychologically subjugating their victims.

It does not take an unreconstructed Marxist to identify the central role of economics in the genesis of racism. Nevertheless, the psychological dimension soon becomes important, in constructing an ideology which rationalizes maltreatment by the creation of different (and lesser) beings (whose human or natural resources are required by the oppressor), and generating a gallery of stereotypes of suitable hate-objects—again justifying hostile attitudes. Racism works best when the oppressor does not have to police the oppressed, when individual and institutional racism by the majority do not have to be constantly reinforced, because there is an acceptance of the status quo by the minority. In other words, when the minority members have *internalized* some of the majority values, including the picture of them and their place within society. Through inferiorization and the limitation of minority self-belief and expectation, racism achieves its highest (or lowest) expression: the oppressor has persuaded the oppressed to oppress themselves.

As Jahoda (1961) wrote, of the colonial and neocolonial periods in Africa:

> (the African) now comes to look at Africans and African culture to some extent through they eyes of those European educators who determined the manner and content of the teaching he received; but the price he pays for this partially enlarged vision is psychological inferiority.
>
> (p. 115)

And lest this be thought a Eurocentric perspective, Fanon (1986) confirms the argument, as a voice of the oppressed:

> The feeling of inferiority of the colonized is the correlative of the European's feeling of superiority. Let us have the courage to say it outright: it is the racist who creates his inferior.
>
> (p. 93)

Why should these processes not apply to the subjects of "internal colonization"? African-Americans, Afro-Caribbean and South Asian settlers in Britain, Maoris in New Zealand, have all experienced the pressures, not only of discrimination, disadvantage and disprivilege, but *also* of disparagement, of living their lives in a climate of *inferiorization*, which is the psychological thrust of racism. To invade the minority's self-belief and to supplant it with the majority's demeaning stereotype, is the goal of that thrust. In a real sense it is an important part of what racism is *for*, and to argue that it has had no success in penetrating black psychology or black identity over the generations since slavery and beyond, is frankly improbable. Indeed, some of the most eloquent black voices in literature, both radical and mainstream, have testified as to how it happened, through the undermining of all things black, and inculcation of white standards.

Malcolm X (1968) said:

> As anti-white as my father was, he was sub-consciously so afflicted with the white man's brainwashing of Negroes that he inclined to favour the lighter ones, and I was his lightest child. Most Negro parents in those days would almost instinctively treat any lighter child better than they did the darker ones. It came directly from the slavery tradition that the "mulatto", because he was visibly nearer to the white, was therefore better.
>
> (Haley, 1968, pp. 82–83)

And later:

> I endured all of that pain, literally burning my flesh with lye, in order to cook my natural hair until it was limp, to have it look like a white man's hair.
>
> (p. 138)

James Baldwin (1964) described similar experiences:

> One's hair was always being attacked with hard brushes and combs and Vaseline: it was shameful to have "nappy" hair. One's legs and arms were always greased, so that one would not look "ashy" in the winter time. One was always being scrubbed and polished, as though in the hope that a stain was thus washed away—I hazard that Negro children of my generation, anyway, had an earlier and more painful acquaintance with soap than any children anywhere. The women were forever straightening and curling their hair, and using bleaching creams. And yet it was clear that none of this effort would release one from the stigma and danger of being a Negro; this effort merely increased the shame and rage. . .One had the choice of "acting just like a nigger" or of *not* acting just like a nigger—and only those who have tried it know how impossible it is to tell the difference. . .And the extraordinary complex of tensions thus set up in the breast, between hatred of whites and contempt for blacks, is very hard to describe. Some of the most energetic people of my generation were destroyed by this interior warfare.
>
> (p. 74).

These "literary" accounts, of course, do not constitute scientific data. Somehow we hold them to be suspect, preferring the data we strain to gather from laboriously-collected subjects, performing bizarre or transparent tasks in artificial conditions which control out reality. Yet compare the quality of information we will obtain from our average recalcitrant laboratory subject with the testimony of the author, alive or dead, who is passionately concerned to communicate the texture of experience through reportage, commentary, analysis and synthesis; or through biography, autobiography, fiction or even drama. Of course they will not give us hard data; but they will give us insight, hypotheses, and soft data validated by hard experience.

Fanon (1986) wrote:

> All round me the white man, the sky tears at its navel, the earth rasps under my feet, and there is a white song, a white song. All this whiteness that burns me. . . .

What does this express? That it is "whiteness" that burns the black person, indeed *makes* them black; that this white heat is searing, agonizing, cauterizing and shrivelling; that it is surrounding, all-pervasive and inescapable, assailing all the senses; and that the black person is almost powerless, writhing in its grip. There are further layers of meaning, but even this much provides a more vivid—and economical-account of racism than any number of attitude scales, surveys or, for that matter, doll-tests. In a real sense it enables us to understand rather better how it feels to endure racism. The language creates, momentarily, a vicarious experience which is powerful and affecting: the reader is subtly changed by it, something which rather few journal articles manage to achieve.

It is not that these accounts definitively establish the existence of identity problems amongst oppressed minorities. They simply provide a persuasive backdrop to the era of misidentification among (some) black children, by demonstrating that among (some) adults there were a number of parallels, some ambivalence about racial identity and some wishful orientation towards whiteness. They certainly make it inadvisable to discount that generation of findings, as the critics sought to do.

There are, arguably, reasons for attributing to them more, rather than less, importance. It may or may not be coincidence that it was one of the more revolutionary black leaders in recent history, Malcolm X, who painfully admitted to his pro-white orientation, not only in childhood but into his early adult years. There are grounds for arguing a connection between misidentification and, later, enhanced pro-black allegiance. For example, some of the eight-year-old black subjects who misidentified in Milner's original (1973) study were prominent in the race-related disturbances in St. Paul's, Bristol, ten years later. In another arena, many gays, who were forced to deny their sexual identity (including, in many cases, to themselves) to avoid discrimination, ostracism and prosecution, later chose to assert their homosexuality in the most public and militant ways possible. The Women's Movement, too, provides many examples of those whose militancy has been in direct proportion to their earlier experience of inferiorization.

Whether or not "misidentification" represented a wishful desire to be white (or simply a desire to have the privileges that white people have), it is hard to argue against the opposite side of that coin: that it signified a degree of repudiation of one's own group, a desire *not* to be identified with it. However, this orientation, for a child or an adult, is fraught with difficulties, and ultimately doomed. The emotional difficulty of not wanting to be what you are, simultaneously negating self, family and culture, is compounded by the practical problems of being anything else. For the misidentifier, the temporary escape (if that is what it is) into a fantasy white world is soon ram-raided by the reality of being black, and treated as such. When that is ultimately accepted, when black identity is indelibly inscribed, what does the person do with the knowledge of their former feelings? They will likely experience shame and guilt, and seek to achieve a denial of the denial, through the most overt and determined demonstration of their identification with their own group. Through that identification can the earlier denial of identity be expunged. However, there is a somewhat wider argument here: not only is early misidentification likely to fuel an enhanced ingroup identification subsequently, but *any* intrusion of negative, stereotypical, inferiorizing elements into the child's self-beliefs (whether or not they happen to misidentify on doll tests) will tend to drive the child in the same direction, where there is social support for this orientation and an ideological climate which helps to externalize blame. In other words, while not all minority children misidentify, all have to construct an acceptable identity within a racist climate. All have to cope with the inferiorizing pressures on their beliefs about themselves and their groups. To the extent that the majority group can (properly) be blamed for their predicament, minority-group esteem can be retrieved and maintained, identity enhanced, and competitive action against the majority justified.

In summary, misidentification is not seen here as an artifact, but as: (a) one indication of identity pressures experienced by minorities, pressures which are an essential part of our understanding because they are part of the driving force *behind* minority identity development, part of the engine of psychological liberation; and b) a telling index of social change, which has enabled us to map the transition from one era to another—from the pre-civil rights period, when black inferiorization was at its worst, to the 1970s and 1980s, when the black identity movement has helped to relieve those pressures on black people.

Minority Groups and Social Identity Theory

Social identity theory is at its strongest and its weakest when it deals with the case of minority groups who have an unsatisfactory social identity. Tajfel and Turner (1986) outline three strategies by which individual/group identity (and self-esteem) can be retrieved: individual mobility, social creativity and social competition.

Individual mobility

This usually implies attempts, on an individual basis, to achieve upward social mobility, to pass from a lower to a higher status group . . . the most important feature of individual mobility is that the low status of one's own group is not thereby changed: it is an individualist approach designed, at least in the short run, to achieve a personal, not a group solution. Thus individual mobility implies a disidentification with the erstwhile ingroup (Tajfel and Turner, 1986, p. 21).

This is a familiar strategy, a matter of common observation, where members of (for example) lower social castes or classes "make it" further up the social ladder, by dint of study, commercial success or sheer good fortune. It is more difficult within rigidly stratified societies, and harder still when the minority group carries markers of skin colour, culture or gender, which preclude them from "passing", even where they are willing to slough off their backgrounds, the inevitable admission price to higher status. Indeed not only must disidentification be complete, it may be necessary to evince the characteristics of the higher group more thoroughly and overtly than they do themselves.

An extreme and graphic example of individual mobility was provided by the then British prime minister, Margaret Thatcher. Her strategy in "passing" into (and up through) the male-dominated political system was unprecedentedly successful. Her management style in running her government was muscularly masculine. And it was certainly an individual strategy in that other women benefited little from her elevation, either in terms of policies to improve women's conditions or the promotion of women to government office. It is said that, when necessary, she did use feminine wiles to get her way, and even that a senior Conservative fell under her spell, but the overwhelming impression was of an overly macho man in all but anatomy.

Without becoming embroiled in an argument about the relative force of racism and sexism, it is difficult to say how good this analogy is for the individual mobility of black people. Certainly Thatcher was an exceptional personality; equally certainly, it would require a black person of similar driving force to become prime minister. What they have in common is the individual's triumph over the conspicuous marker he or she carries, one which formerly restricted him or her to a disadvantaged social group. However, exceptionality is the point for all who would be individually mobile (writ large in the case of the ascent to high office); a handful of individuals scale the ladder in this way, but many more are rebuffed.

Social creativity

These several strategies involve the minority group in "re-defining or altering elements of the comparative situation. . . . It is a group rather than an individualistic strategy" (op. cit., pp. 19–20).

Comparing the ingroup to the outgroup on some new dimension

While there is evidence of this strategy in many majority/minority situations, it is perhaps the weakest of the three. It is usually possible to find dimensions on which the minority will compare more favourably with the majority, but by definition, these are *not* the dimensions that the society values most highly. In Britain, the Afro-Caribbean community could derive a more satisfactory social identity by comparing themselves with whites on dimensions of religious observance (for older members), or on the racial composition of the Olympic team or the current music charts. The fact remains that black people have always been "allowed" to succeed in sport and music; the graph of relative income distribution between the communities tells a different story, and a more persuasive one for social valuation purposes.

Changing the values assigned to the attributes of the group, so that comparisons which were previously negative are now perceived as positive

It has become a truism if not a cliché to cite the "black is beautiful" movement as the prime example of this strategy. Of course, truisms are true, and they become clichés through repetition in appropriate circumstances, so the fact of repetition should not detract from their value, but enhance it. It *was* the case that "black" was a term of abuse, long before "nigger", and of course it is no coincidence that it was reclaimed and made positive (as indeed has "nigger", though strictly amongst black people themselves). It is the ultimate repudiation of the negative past and assertion of the positive present and future.

Similarly, long before political correctness, it was unthinkable for adult liberals to label male homosexuals as "queers". Now militant gays positively embrace the word, sometimes appearing to enjoy the discomfort of those who struggle to take it on board after generations of proscription. Likewise, in the late 1960s, when "black" became "beautiful", whites struggled to abandon the previous euphemism "coloured" with great difficulty. What's in a name; but in a real sense it is the most public statement of identity, and therefore to consciously change the group name to one which was previously despised, and proclaim it positive, is as direct a kind of evidence for this aspect of SIT as one could wish.

Changing (or selecting) the outgroup with which the ingroup is compared

There can undoubtedly be some compensatory increments of positive social identity derived from comparing the ingroup with another *more* lowly group. There is also scope for creativity in *making* another group inferior by re-appraising its attributes, indeed this is an important aspect of white–black racism in the first place. These processes have been held to account for "poor white" racism, and may also underlie hostility between Afro-Caribbean and South Asian communities in Britain. Neither are they restricted to race-related conflicts; the social identity of the British Labour Party (not to mention their numerical status in Parliament) was badly dented by successive Conservative electoral victories, and as a result their antipathy towards the weaker Liberal Democrats has never been greater, despite the increasing overlap of their policies. Obviously there are other factors at work, but we can seldom find absolutely pure examples of SIT (or any other theory) in the real world.

Social competition

> The group members may seek positive distinctiveness through direct competition with the outgroup. . . . To the degree that this may involve comparisons related to the social structure, it implies changes in the groups' objective social locations.
>
> (op. cit., p. 20).

Relocation in the social hierarchy obviously provides the most direct and effective antidote to a negative social identity. It is also the most difficult strategy to realize because it requires (a) concerted group action in (b) social, political and economic spheres in which the minority is *relatively* powerless, resisted by (c) a powerful majority who wish to preserve their resources, privileged status and social identity; thus on every front they will try to co-opt, resist or reverse the minority's progress. It is a formidable list of constraints; indeed it seems almost insuperable, until we remember that this is precisely what black South Africans have achieved in the last few years. As a result it is rather unlikely that Gregor and McPherson's (1966) finding of misidentification amongst black South African children would be replicated now.

How well does the SIT minority group schema sit with the literature of children's racial identity development discussed earlier? To resume, briefly, the discussion of misidentification: it is clear that SIT presents a framework in which to accommodate those findings, and the interpretation which has been placed on them here. Misidentification is, *par excellence*, an instance of *psychological* individual mobility. It is an unrealistic fantasy escape from the ingroup identity and all it connotes. Like most instances of individual social mobility, it is doomed to failure. Reality obtrudes and the majority group rejects.

SIT is at its weakest where it fails to account adequately for the processes of transition *between* stages. The high face-validity of the various stages is compromised by a less-than-full account of the dynamic propelling minority group members from one to the next. The most glaring example of this is the transition from *individual mobility* to *social creativity*, when the conditions described in the former actually appear to be the antithesis of those necessary for the latter to appear, and this is acknowledged:

> Insofar as individual mobility implies disidentification, it will tend to loosen the cohesiveness of the subordinate group . . . the low morale that follows from negative social identity can set in motion disintegrative processes, that, in the long run, may hinder a change in the group status.
>
> (op. cit., p. 21.)

It is easier to accept the partial vacuum between stages two and three because this must largely be filled by factors beyond our remit: economic, political and social structural; but the transition from stages one to two is from the *individual* to the *social* levels of behaviour, and this is the single most insistent theme—rationale even—of social psychology. Tajfel himself argued as much (Tajfel and Fraser, 1978), in addressing the work of Dollard and Miller (1939) and Adorno *et al.* (1950).

Social action (as in stages two and three) does not happen without *motivation*, sufficient to thrust the individual outwards, to connect with those who have had similar experience (and, I should add, those who have not attempted individual mobility but have been thoroughly identified with their group in the first place, a curious omission from SIT). It seems more than plausible to suggest that the necessary propulsion comes precisely *from* the experience of identity denial (and shame engendered by its failure), or lesser degrees of self-devaluative introjection, and from resentment and hostility from direct experience of rejection and disprivilege.

Secondly, this motivation amongst minority group members must be harnessed and articulated, socially *organized* and collectively expressed, and to the extent that social creativity, let alone direct competition, represent new departures for the group, they must be evangelized and wider support gathered. The organization of discontent is a complex process and does not always conform to a single, simple model. It usually involves the joining together of those with common interests, the fostering of group consciousness, initial political steps through single-issue politics and protest rather than wholesale electoral campaigns, pressure group activity, raising the group profile through media penetration, defining leaders and spokespersons who can represent their case, embarking on "test-case" legal actions to redress grievances, seeking direct political representation and building an independent economic base through developing business organizations. While this appears to be first and foremost a political and economic process, it is clear that there is an integral process which is equally social psychological. Increments of positive identity achieved by its progression in turn reinforce and encourage further progress with enhanced self-belief. Political and economic liberation go hand-in-hand with psychological liberation, and so it is perhaps surprising that as social psychologists we have tended to "bale out" at the point where "social competition" begins to engage with other disciplinary territories.

Again it seems likely that those who have been most scarred by racism, have been turned against their own group or even themselves, will ultimately be the most active repudiators of racism and their group's negative image: in other words, become leaders, or the kind of committed consistent minority (within the minority) which successfully argues for innovation and change, *qua* Moscovici. Those for whom race has been most salient, most affecting, those whose minds and lives have been most shaped by its excesses, it is argued, are most likely to be drawn to a commitment to that very issue, in political behaviour as well as attitudes. Activism and commitment require a driving force which is greater than mere belief or sympathy with a cause; by "action" and "reaction", racism may, for some minority members, produce just this kind of psychological dynamic.

It is an empirical matter to determine scientifically whether misidentification amongst the children of oppressed minorities anticipates later militancy, as argued here, and supported in literature (as opposed to *the* literature). At the very least it is a powerful metaphor for the basis of the motivational thrust behind "the social dimension" to SIT's account of minorities. For those who have not experienced, at close hand, the crushing effects of a negative identity, and the shame and rage it engenders, it is worth recalling Henri Tajfel's own early wartime experience: for the sake of survival he was compelled to deny his Jewish identity, and he was quite clear that this experience was one of those which shaped not only his later identity, but also his thinking and research, which this volume serves to celebrate.

References

Aboud, F. (1987) The development of ethnic self-identification and attitudes. In J. S. Phinney and M. J. Rotheram (Eds), *Children's ethnic socialisation*. Newbury Park: Sage Publications.

Aboud, F. (1992). *Children and prejudice*. Oxford: Blackwell.

Adorno, T. W., Frenkel-Brunswik, E., Levinson, D. J., and Sanford, R. N. (1950). *The authoritarian personality*. New York: Harper and Row.

Baldwin, J. (1964). *Nobody knows my name*. London: Michael Joseph.

Banks, W. C. (1976). White preference in blacks: a paradigm in search of a phenomenon. *Psychological Bulletin,* **83**, 1179–1186.

Billig, M. (1976). *Social psychology and intergroup relations*. London: Academic Press.

Clark, K., and Clark, M. (1947) Racial identification and preference in Negro children. In T. M. Newcomb and E. L. Hartley (Eds), *Readings in social psychology.* New York: Holt.

Dollard, J., Miller, N. E., Doob, L. W., Mowrer, O. H., and Sears, R. R. (1939). *Frustration and aggression*. New Haven: Yale University Press.

Fanon, F. (1986). *Black skin, white masks.* London: Pluto Press.

Goodman, M. E. (1964). *Race awareness in young children*. New York: Collier Books.

Goodman, M. E. (1946) Evidence concerning the genesis of interracial. *American Anthropologist,* **48**, 624–630.

Gregor, A. J., and McPherson, D. A. (1966). Racial preference and ego-identity among white and Bantu children in the Republic of South Africa. *Genetic Psychology Monographs*, **73**, 217–253.

Haley, A. (1968). *The autobiography of Malcolm X.* Harmondsworth: Penguin Books.

Horowitz, E. L., and Horowitz, R. E. (1938). Development of social attitudes in children. *Sociometry* **1**, 307–338.

Jahoda, G. (1961). *White man.* London: Oxford University Press.

Katz, P. A. (1976). *Towards the elimination of racism.* New York: Pergamon Press.

Katz, P. A. (1983). Development of racial and sex-role attitudes. In R. Leahy (Ed.) *The child's construction of social inequality.* New York: Academic Press.

Katz, P. A. (1987). Developmental and social processes in ethnic attitudes and self-identification. In M. J. Rotheram and M. S. Phinney (Eds), *Children's ethnic socialization.*, Newbury Park: Sage Publications.

Lasker, B. (1929). *Race attitudes in children.* New York: Holt.

Lewis, M. and Brooks, J. (1975). Infants' social perceptions: a constructivist view. In L. Coven and B. Salatapek (Eds), *Infant perception: from sensation to cognition*. New York: Academic Press.

Milner, D. (1973). Racial identification and preference in black British children. *European Journal of Social Psychology,* **3**, 281–295.

Milner, D. (1983). *Children and race: Ten years on*. London: Ward Lock Educational.

Ramsey, P. (1987). Young children's thinking about ethnic differences. In M. J. Rotheram and M. S. Phinney (Eds), *Children's ethnic socialization*. Newbury Park: Sage.

Sherif, M. (1966). *Group conflict and co-operation: Their social psychology.* London: Routledge and Kegan Paul.

Sherif, M., Harvey, O., White, B. J., Hood, W. R., and Sherif, M. (1961). *Intergroup conflict and co-operation*: The robber's cave experiment. Norman, OK: University of Oklahoma Press.

Sherif, M. and Sherif, C. (1953). *Groups in harmony and tension*. New York: Harper and Row.

Tajfel, H., Flament, C., Billig, M., and Bundy, R. (1971). Social categorisation and intergroup behaviour. *European Journal of Social Psychology,* **1**, 149–178.

Tajfel, H., and Fraser, C. (1978). *Introducing social psychology.* Harmondsworth: Penguin.

Tajfel, H., and Jahoda, G. (1966). Development in children of concepts and attitudes about their own and other nations: a cross-national study. Proceedings of the XVIIIth International Congress in Psychology, Moscow, symposium 36, 17–33.

Tajfel, H., and Turner, J. C. (1986). The social identity theory of intergroup behaviour. In S. Worchel and W. G. Austin (Eds), *The psychology of intergroup relations*. Chicago: Nelson-Hall.

Vaughan, G. M. (1964). Ethnic awareness in relation to minority-group membership. *Journal of Genetic Psychology,* **105**, 109–130.

Vaughan, G. M. (1978). Social change and intergroup preferences in New Zealand. *European Journal of Social Psychology,* **8**, 297–314.

Ward, S. H., and Braun, J. (1972). Self-esteem and racial preference in black children. *American Journal of Orthopsychiatry,* **42**(4), 644–647.

Zajonc, R. B. (1976). Family configuration and intelligence. *Science*, **192**, 227–236.

10

Constructing Social Identities: The Individual/Social Binary in Henri Tajfel's Social Psychology

MARGARET WETHERELL

Faculty of Social Sciences, Open University

Contents

For me as for other contributors, this memorial volume for Henri Tajfel is an opportunity to acknowledge important intellectual debts. It is also an invitation to engage in debate, a chance to look back and re-evaluate Tajfel's ideas, theories and arguments and understand their place in social psychology. My interest is in the way Henri Tajfel narrated his discipline; the conceptual dilemmas, logics, gaps and absences in his account of what social psychology should and could be. Because Tajfel was a master craftsman, the pattern of his account is revealing and not just about the ways in which social psychology was understood in the 1960s and 1970s. Tajfel could tell a good story and there is still an enormous amount to be learned from the way in which he worked the various epistemological currencies of his time—the "individual and the social", "levels of analysis" and the demand for a "systematic science" based on experimental method. He was an artful arguer and thinker, a passionate rhetorician, and someone who set, and continues to set, the intellectual horizon for his students and colleagues.

As the use of terms such as "narration", "stories" and "accounts" suggests, my re-evaluation of Tajfel's contribution to social psychology will work from the vantage point of social constructionism, discourse analysis and post-structuralism and the ways in which these emphases are developing in social psychology. What does Tajfel's work look like in light of recent moves towards a more contextual and relational social psychology based on the study of discursive forms, joint action and social practices (e.g. Billig, 1987; Gergen, 1985; Harre and Gillett, 1994; Parker, 1992, Potter and Wetherell, 1987; Shotter, 1993)? And, what would Tajfel have made of these recent developments?

Some hints of his likely reaction can be found in *Human groups and social categories* (1981), where he sketched out a reply to some of the early moves in this field. Tajfel took issue in the Introduction to that volume with Rom Harre's efforts during the late 70s to build an "ethogenic" approach to social psychology (Harre, 1977). Tajfel's point was that in stressing autonomy over mechanism and the process of "self-making" as the proper subject for social psychology, Harre was in danger of individualism. He objected, too, to one of the principal claims of ethogenics that people's common sense understandings of social life should be respected and made an object of study rather than dismissed or treated with contempt. Like Michael Billig (1977), Tajfel argued that this empathetic stance ruled out serious critical work on phenomena such as fascism. In Tajfel's view, the possibility that some people's understandings of social life were indeed contemptible should be left open in social psychology.

Tajfel's attack on what he saw as the individualism of the "new social psychology" was trenchant.

> Individual autonomy as the core of the "political process", and of many aspects of social behaviour, is a myth. In many social situations, we are buffeted here and there by powerful social forces beyond our control. . . . Individual autonomy (deciding *not* to steal) has strict limits for a child living in a vast slum of an immense city. Or when you have internalized, as a soldier, the powerful social prescription that the enemies are not quite human. Or—as a guard in a concentration camp—that the inmates are a virus in the social "organism". These are, of course, extreme cases. My point is that they are no more than one end of a long continuum. Any society which contains power, status, prestige and social group differentials (and they all do), places each of us in a number of *social* categories which become an important part of our *self*-definition. In situations which relate to those aspects of our self-definition that we think we share with others, we shall behave very much as they do.
>
> (Tajfel, 1977, p. 654, cited in 1981, p. 14)

Although this is a selective reading of "new social psychology", aspects of Tajfel's diagnosis of individualism and his critique seems to me justified. Much of the new work in the 1970s emerged in tandem with humanistic psychology and its critique of behaviourism. It carried with it many of the liberal political assumptions of that tradition with the same absences when it came to theorizing ideology and collective constructions. This humanistic tradition is still influential among many "new social psychologists" of the 1990s, but there also has been a wholesale deconstruction of the individual and the social since 1981 building on the earlier work of, for example, Mead, Bakhtin, Vygotsky, Harvey Sacks and Wittgenstein, along with the recasting of "self-making" and "commonsense understandings". Ironically, this recasting seems to me to illustrate more clearly the tensions in Tajfel's own conceptions of the individual and the social and allows us to see some of the characteristic logic of this particular binary.

In this chapter I want to argue that Tajfel's commitment to social analysis (which was extremely important for the development of social psychology) was at odds with other key principles in his epistemology. These principles and this tension sometimes drew him to modes of explanation and to theoretical choices which in retrospect appear paradoxical—highly psychologized and individual focused (c.f. also Henriques, 1984; Michael, 1990; Taylor and Brown, 1979, for a discussion of this element of Tajfel's work). In revisiting this territory, I want to look, first, at some of the key principles in Tajfel's social psychology, then at the minimal group studies and the transition made in that research from "normative" explanations to the "process" account as an instance of these tensions. Finally, I want to briefly examine some of the ways in which discourse analysis reworks these concerns.

Terms of the Debate

The foundations on which Tajfel built his theory and method are clear in much of his writing but were articulated most explicitly in his chapter "Experiments in a social vacuum" written in 1972 (also reprinted in Tajfel, 1981). In this chapter we find, first, a strong recognition of the social construction of reality combined with an equally forceful affirmation of the experimental method as the basis of social research, along with a commitment to a "levels of analysis" specification of the social psychologist's domain of study. Each of these "non-negotiable principles" needs examination in detail.

Importance of the social context

> . . . in an infinite variety of situations throughout his (*sic*) life an individual feels, thinks and behaves in terms of his social identity created by the various groups of which he is a member and in terms of his relation to the social identity of others, as individuals or *en masse*. It is equally obvious that this social conduct is determined to a large extent by the relations between the groups to which he belongs as well as other groups, and that the nature of these relations is in turn largely due to the socially shared regularities of intergroup conduct. . . . The social setting of intergroup relations contributes to making the individuals what they are and they in turn produce this social setting; they and it change and develop symbiotically.
>
> (Tajfel, 1981, p. 31)

As the reference to symbiotic individual and social change suggests, Tajfel saw the social context as decisive in the formation of individual psychology. He recognized a number of possible influences. First, most simply, material factors— an individual's class and economic position—would determine not just what range of actions was possible but the valence or meaning ascribed to those actions. As the example raised above of the slum child's decision to steal suggests, people's position in economic and social structures will condition the nature of their choices in a direct sense.

Tajfel was also interested in what he called "norms" or, sometimes, "rules" of appropriate conduct. These collective constructions were seen as crucial to the connection of the individual to the social, mediating between the two. He argued that social action will be determined by what the individual considers to be appropriate behaviour for a situation. This sense of appropriateness, however, will not depend on individual constructions alone but is always a reworking and instantiation of collective conceptions of appropriate behaviour, "prevailing systems of norms and values" (1981, p. 36).

On some occasions, these collective constructions (informed by values) would become ideologies or systems of belief which would mobilize people for collective action. Tajfel was particularly interested in social movements and the process by which a group's conception of itself and of its opposition would lead to the critical point required for mass action. This mass action might take place either on the symbolic front, in the formulation of new representations of the group situation such as the positive ideologies of a minority group, or in direct agitation for social change. Linked together, therefore, in Tajfel's writings were notions of material position, social norms, collective action and the possibility for social change understood as the "social context".

This sense of the social was the basis on which he attacked many other developments in social psychology including frustration–aggression theory, authoritarian personality research and work on political values. He argued, for example, that Eysenck and Wilson's (1978) studies of the psychological basis of political beliefs were fundamentally flawed because their research embodied a "vision of society as consisting of randomly interacting individual particles or 'personalities'" with "no room in this vision for the socially or culturally shared cognitive organizations of a social system based on a commonly perceived social location in that system". (1981, p. 16).

What is unclear, however, in Tajfel's analysis is the degree of influence he wanted to attribute to the social context and to these "socially shared cognitive organizations". To what extent are human minds socially constructed? What are the boundaries to this constructive process? Some of his writing suggests that he saw social influence as entirely pervasive, crucial to very definition and understanding of emotions, motivation, thought process or cognition and other psychological states. In his attack on exchange theories in social psychology, for example, Tajfel argued that a theory of reinforcement based on people's dealings with their physical environment could not be carried over in any simple way to social relationships. Social interaction, he pointed out, brought about a *qualitative* transformation of individual understanding. Even very basic states of motivation and perception of reward were social and cultural in origin. He argued, too, that social factors are present from the beginning of the child's life, so that to say what was social and what was in some sense "pre-social" was a difficult task. He also referred approvingly to Schacter's (1970) work which suggested that cultural and social understandings organize the experience of emotion and even the perception of bodily states.

These themes in Tajfel's work align him with contemporary social constructionism and with lines of work in psychological anthropology, post-structuralism and developmental psychology which have explored the social formation of mind and self-understanding and which have examined how collective representations become personalized as individual motivations, emotions, fantasies and subjectivities (c.f. Bruner, 1990; Kvale, 1992; Schwartz *et al.*, 1992; Wertsch, 1991). Other trends in Tajfel's writing, however, suggest a very different direction and emphasize a very different understanding of individual psychology and the social context.

Drawing on a common formulation of his times, Tajfel was critical of what he called "sociological determinism" or "sociological reductionism". He argued that sociologists were in danger of assuming a *tabula rasa* or empty organism model of the individual. In his view, the assumption that social processes could be simply inscribed on the blank slate of individual minds involved a naive understanding of psychology. This formulation of the dangers of sociological determinism (and the notion of autonomous levels of analysis in academic inquiry which it implies) led Tajfel to a model of the individual and the social where there were clear limits to social constructionism. Specifically, it encouraged him to develop a "form and content" understanding of the individual and the social. Basic individual psychological processes with their own independent shape and structure were seen as providing the form, the tools to think with, while society and collective constructions provided the content. In Tajfel's work, then, we begin to find an ambiguity around the social construction of the individual—whole-hearted support combined with moderation of that support when it is seen to lead to "sociological determinism". And, this ambiguity is linked to claims about "levels of analysis".

Levels of analysis

> Questions about human social behaviour can be considered as being on a continuum which ranges from biological through psychological and sociopsychological to sociological.
>
> (Tajfel, 1981, p. 24)

As a rhetorical device, the notion of levels of analysis in academic inquiry, with each discipline having its own distinctive problems and phenomena to study, does some useful work for the social psychologist. It protects territory while allowing co-existence with other psychologists and social scientists and it also opens up a debate about just who is a proper social psychologist.

Tajfel thought that the appropriate topic for the biologist was the genetic and physiological basis of social behaviour, while psychologists should focus on general laws of functioning which are unique to humans. Tajfel stated that these would be laws relating to language and socialization, socially derived secondary motivation, social cognition, imitation, the relationship between frustration and aggression, and so on. Sociologists, on the other hand, working at their own level, should look at how the broad economic and social organization of society affects social behaviour.

What is left, then, for the social psychologist? Tajfel argued that large and crucial areas of social conduct remain

> . . . which are uniquely characteristic of the sociopsychological *homo* in the sense that they present empirical discontinuities with his biological background, with his non social psychological functioning and with the conception of him as being fully accounted for by the social system of which he is part.
>
> (Tajfel, 1981, p. 25)

From his point of view, problems arose when these areas of social conduct were explained by the biologist, psychologist and sociologist in ways which did not respect their particular nature as sociopsychological phenomena. Tajfel argued that these other levels of analysis set the range of what was possible in social behaviour but did not determine the manifestations or the specific forms that social behaviour takes. Developing an analogy with the history of art, Tajfel suggested that just as paintings and sculpture take the shape they do because people have two hands and ten fingers, social behaviour takes the shape it does because of basic laws of human biological and psychological functioning. Yet in the same way that anatomy is not an adequate explanation of the diversity of artistic styles found across the world, basic psychological and biological laws do not explain social behaviour.

As he put it in another formulation, the biologist and the psychologist are concerned with aspects of social behaviour which are preliminary to social man (*sic*), "that are no more "social" in their origin than is colour vision or the generalization of conditioned responses", but "social behaviour would not have been what it is if these processes were not what they are." (Tajfel, 1981, p. 28).

How does this relate, then, to the debate about the individual and the social? On the one hand, Tajfel identified a set of processes studied by psychologists and biologists which are in some sense non-social but which have to do with social behaviour. These processes were said to have their own autonomy and level of analysis (although all levels also interact). There seems, in other words, to be a separate logic to the individual part of the individual—social dichotomy and thus some kind of limit on the social construction of individual psychology. Furthermore, "genuine" social psychological phenomena were identified which are not the province of sociology or mainstream psychology and it is a mistake for the social psychologist to try and reduce these to the basic processes of biology and psychology.

This rhetoric of levels of analysis (along with the dichotomy of the individual versus the social) as a way of narrating social psychology creates a number of dilemmas, questions and cul-de-sacs, not least about the status of these psychological processes, which are in some sense non-social but which supposedly intertwine with social influences from birth. It is unclear, too, what non-reductionistic biological and psychological analyses of social behaviour would look like, yet that possibility is central to the logic of levels of analysis Tajfel outlined. A major rhetorical advantage here, however, is that talk of levels of analysis allows the opposition to be both right and wrong. Tajfel's critique of frustration–aggression theory, for example, illustrates just how these themes could be worked.

Frustration–aggression research (e.g. Berkowitz, 1962) is wrong, Tajfel argued, because it does become reductionistic and tries to break down the complexity of intergroup behaviour into an underlying psychological relationship between frustration and response to frustration. The theory thus ignores the specific ways in which frustration and aggression are interpreted in an intergroup situation and how these interpretations act on and change the basic relationship. Yet Berkowitz and his colleagues are also right, Tajfel claimed, because they have discovered a law of psychological functioning at the psychological level of analysis, a level with its own autonomy and rightful questions. Frustration–aggression theory, in Tajfel's view, is thus right but irrelevant to the social psychologist. The basic process cannot be disputed but its generalizability to social psychological phenomena can be placed in doubt.

One of the reasons, I suspect, why this move was so useful for Tajfel concerns the third basic principle underpinning his approach—the importance of experimental method. Since frustration–aggression theory was based on experimental findings, it had to be in some sense true. But, since, from Tajfel's perspective, the theory was also patently false and an obstacle to developing the kind of social psychological analysis he preferred, levels of analysis was a way of explaining why frustration–aggression research needed to be surpassed.

Experimental Method

> . . . the aim of the present chapter was to express my preoccupations as a social psychologist whose work has been almost entirely within the experimental tradition of the discipline and who continues to believe that, amongst the approaches to social behaviour open to us, theories which can be tested experimentally contain the least doubtful promise for the future.
>
> (Tajfel, 1981, p. 18)

Tajfel's concerns with ideology, with cultural and group based frameworks for making sense and with people's interpretations of appropriate conduct suggest an affinity with anthropology and with ethnography. Tajfel was adamant, however, that a "descriptive" science of this kind was not sufficient for social psychology. His stated aim was to develop theories of empirical regularities in social behaviour which would identify the law-like processes he assumed were generating the observable patterns. Social psychology should be a "systematic" rather than a "clinical" science (1981, p. 27).

This emphasis, however, presented him with some problems given that his focus was, at least in part, on human interpretative work and given, too, his arguments concerning levels of analysis and the distinctive nature of social psychological phenomena. One way of resolving these difficulties was to argue that any dissatisfaction with the attainments of social psychologists was not due to their reliance on experimental method, but arose because these experiments were conducted "in a social vacuum". Tajfel tried to develop a new understanding of the social psychological experiment which would allow for more social relevance while retaining key methodological features such as the operationalization of variables and hypothesis testing.

What kind of laws, for example, would social psychological experiments discover? Tajfel argued that social psychological laws would fall somewhere between universal applicability and specificity to particular social situations. Unlike the biologist, or possibly the mainstream psychologist, social psychologists would not be able to claim general human applicability for their findings. But nor would their findings be entirely specific to the particular social situation set up and investigated in the experiment.

In formulating their findings, social psychologists would have to consider the ways in which the participants in the study understood, interpreted and defined their social situation. How they understood, for example, their ingroup and outgroup, the norms of social behaviour offered by their culture, and so on. These understandings would be collective and regular and would interact with "general processes" (so laws were possible) but also would be specific to some extent.

> . . . the general case is an impossible myth as long as human beings behave as they do because of the social expectations with which they enter an experiment—or any other social situation. If these expectations are shared—as they always are by definition to some degree in any social context—I shall obtain data from my experiment which are neither "general" nor "individual". The observed regularities of behaviour will result from the interaction between general processes and the social context in which they operate.
>
> (Tajfel, 1981, p. 21)

Once again social and cultural constructions seem to be understood as a "content" which fills out the "general processes" of individual psychology. These constructions are seen as in some sense separate from these psychological processes. What is not clear from Tajfel's description is whether the general processes he mentioned are the laws of cognition and so on he associated with the psychological level of analysis, in which case interaction with the "social context" produces the distinctive social psychological phenomena he wanted to study, or whether the "general processes" are in some way laws already at the "social psychological level" which then interact further with "social context".

Both of these readings of social identity theory as an example of a genuinely social psychological theory have been offered at various points. Categorization, comparison and the desire for positive self-esteem (the building blocks of social identity theory) have been presented as basic individual psychological processes (c.f. Tajfel, 1979) which are then interpreted in certain ways in specific social situations to produce *social* identity, *social* comparison, and so on. And the social categorization, social comparison and social identification sequence has been presented as a distinctive social psychological law or general process in its own right.

From the standpoint of discourse analysis (Potter and Wetherell, 1987) and with the advantage of hindsight, what is interesting about Tajfel's move to include participants' meanings as part of the field which the experimentalist must investigate is that this shift does represent the beginning of the end for experimental method. Once it is acknowledged that people's actions and interpretations transform and come to constitute social situations along with "the social environment" then the operationalization of variables and hypothesis testing become fraught, as does the assumption of generalizability.

To summarize my argument so far, when we look at the way in which Tajfel narrated his social psychology, the discursive moves, constructions, dichotomies and logics he outlined, we can see how these led him to take up an ambiguous position to the relationship between the individual and the social context. On the one hand, Tajfel stressed the constitutive role of social influences in the construction of individual minds so that what was individual and what was social could not be disentangled. On the other hand, he stressed the separation of the individual and the social into "form" and "content", into basic universal psychological processes and social constructions added to these general processes.

I am not arguing that these inconsistencies and contradictions in Tajfel's social psychology should be seen as mistakes or indicative of incomplete conceptual work. In my view, they are a logical outcome of the non-negotiable theoretical principles of the day, such as levels of analysis and the experimental method. Indeed, Tajfel's working through of these, to my mind, represents a highly creative and original attempt to build a progressive social psychology from these starting points. In the next section I want to examine how the nexus of conceptual dilemmas which made up Tajfel's metatheory of social psychology became instantiated in the interpretation of the minimal group studies and then structured the shape assumed thereafter by social identity theory.

Minimal Groups: Collective Constructions and General Processes

In 1970, in his article for the *Scientific American*, Tajfel set out his first version of a theory of intergroup psychology based on the minimal group findings. He was trying to explain why the mere introduction of a group distinction, in the absence of any history of intergroup conflict and personal interest, seemed to be sufficient to cause his experimental subjects to discriminate against an outgroup. The explanation he developed at that point to account for these findings was essentially a normative one. He argued that the regularity across cultures of discrimination against outgroups implied that there was some underlying psychological factor in this behaviour—the individual's internalization of specific social norms or expectations.

Tajfel suggested that during socialization children come to locate themselves in the established "social construction of reality". The child's categorization of the social environment into groups is overlaid by society's definition of these groups as "we" and "they". Value judgements inevitably come to be associated with the group categorizations. In other words, the child internalizes a "generic norm" of behaviour towards outgroups. And, whenever the child is faced with a situation which contains an explicit group categorization such as the minimal groups experiment, she or he is likely to behave in a way which is consistent with this generic norm, discriminating, for example, against the outgroup, while regulating this behaviour in relation to other prevalent norms such as fairness.

Tajfel was to reject this explanation in favour of the account which later became social identity theory, but it is interesting to see how the early normative explanation meshes with a number of his broader epistemological concerns discussed in the previous section. In the normative account there is an emphasis, for example, on what the subject brings to the experiment. The subject's prior understandings of appropriate conduct are seen as interacting with the variables in the experimental situation to produce the behaviour the experimenter observes. These understandings were described in 1970 as a "generic norm" but there is a clear affinity with Tajfel's later references to "socially or culturally shared cognitive organizations of a social system" which are "based on a commonly perceived social location in that system." (1981, p. 16). Moreover, norms were linked to values in Tajfel's early explanation; there is some relation to the ideological climate in which a child is raised. His explanation in 1970 prefigured a great many of his later concerns with the way in which groups, particularly minority groups, come to position themselves in an established social reality and his concern, also, with the ideological functions served by outgroup stereotypes.

Tajfel's conclusions in his 1970 article reflected, too, the influence of Sherif and Sherif's arguments of the 1960s. Sherif and Sherif (1969) analysed intergroup behaviour as a complex response to the objective material situation, a response which would be mediated by the group's definition and understanding of its interests and, crucially, by prevailing cultural and social norms, in particular by the ways in which these have been taken up by the group to become an ingroup code of conduct. Ingroup norms combined with the objective goal relationship between groups would dictate an appropriate response whether this was intensely discriminatory and pejorative in the case of, say, many conflicts around "race", or based on appeals to reason, fairness, the importance of negotiation, and so on.

This "normative" and indeed "constructive" approach to understanding intergroup action which demands an in-depth investigation of the cultural, ideological and material situation in order to understand a group's response seems to me eminently sensible from a discourse analytic position. It made sense too when, as a graduate student, I tried to understand the results obtained from our minimal group experiments in New Zealand (c.f. Vaughan, 1978; Wetherell, 1982). The research we conducted with Maori and Pacific Island children failed to replicate the minimal group pattern emerging in studies across Europe and the USA. These children from a very different cultural background chose to maximize the *joint profit* of both groups rather than maximize ingroup profit or the difference between groups. They did not consistently discriminate. This result is commensurate with the cultural and social frameworks of Maori and Pacific Island people and the ways in which co-operative and competitive patterns are embedded in these cultures. I now understand it as a demonstration of the Sherifs' point that social and cultural norms refracted through the ingroup are a crucial aspect of intergroup action. In terms of Tajfel's normative explanation, we had found not a "generic norm of discrimination", but certainly variation which was clearly related to the prior understandings the subjects brought to the experiment.

I find it much more difficult to understand these results in terms of the claims embedded in social identity theory which Tajfel went on to develop with John Turner once he had rejected the normative account. That is, to see the Maori and Pacific Island children's responses as caused by an automatic and supposedly universal social psychological process of categorization, identification, comparison and attempts to maximize self-esteem through differentiation manifested usually, but not necessarily, as ingroup favouritism and outgroup discrimination. It is possible that at some "deep" level the children we studied were "really" competing, engaging in social comparison and in maximizing self-esteem, differentiating if not discriminating by being generous to both groups and awarding money irrespective of group designation. But this is, of course, to privilege the psychological process over social and cultural constructions as the true generator of the behaviour and to privilege it, too, as the source of meaning. In a fundamental sense it seems to me social identity theory has become a search for an explanation in individual and psychological (social cognitive) terms.

In 1978, Tajfel described his reasons for his shift from normative accounts to social identity theory. He explained why he had rejected the picture he had painted in 1970.

> Two simple and overlapping explanations were available at that time to account for these results: a "normative" one and a "learning" one. The first was that our schoolboy subjects, aged 15 to 16 years, saw the situation as one of "team competition" in which one should make one's own team win at whatever cost. The second was, that—in a new situation—they engaged in ingroup behaviour which had been reinforced on countless occasions in the past. Both these explanations are sensible; they are also quite "uninteresting"—uninteresting because they are not genuinely heuristic. If our subjects had chosen strategies of choices leading to maximum joint profit, the same explanations could still serve in one form or another. If they had chosen only the strategy of fairness without that of ingroup favouritism, one could still "explain" their responses starting from norms and previous reinforcements. The argument put forward here is not that these explanations are invalid. It is rather that, in addition to their capacity to explain all kinds of results, they are at a level of generality which prevents them from serving as a point of departure for new and more searching insights about intergroup processes.
>
> (cited in Tajfel, 1981, p. 271)

The rest, as they say, is history—from these reinterpretations of the minimal group findings, and as a result of this rejection of the normative account, emerged the apparatus of social identity theory as we know it today, with its strong individual–social dichotomy and with its emphasis on universal psychological processes underlying intergroup behaviour. I would argue that with the shift to social identity theory Tajfel had sided with the elements in his social psychology which led him away from social constructionism.

It is certainly the case that within the epistemological and methodological frameworks in which Tajfel was working, exploring social, ideological and cultural constructions and their psychologic (the "normative and learning environment") would indeed have seemed difficult and "uninteresting". To begin with, there were few recognized methods available in social psychology for exploring these constructions or few likely to be acceptable to journal editors. Perhaps more importantly, this aspect of the "social context" was undertheorized, understood simply in social psychology as "norms". It also seems to me, as I tried to argue above, that the particular weave of Tajfel's metatheory, its contradictions, the focus on experimental investigation and on levels of analysis with their own autonomy, as well as social forces, inevitably drew his attention away from the social and ideological context towards the "general psychological processes" thought to interact with this social context.

Social Constructionism and Intergroup Psychology

One of the main achievements of social constructionism and discourse analysis (along with recent work on social representations) in the years since Tajfel's death has been to take up and develop the issue of collective meaning. Tajfel's research placed questions of ideology, "belief structures" and the relationship between identity and collective significations on social psychology's list of legitimate topics. His analyses of complicated "real-life" group situations and the ways in which people came to be placed within these were, in my view, some of his best work. I like to imagine that discourse analysis and the study of rhetoric can be seen as continuing these themes, albeit with a more congenial methodological and theoretical apparatus.

The key here has been the reformulation of language, its nature, function and place in social life. For Tajfel, it is probably fair to say, language was not an issue. It was interesting to see, for example, that in his 1972 chapter he placed language along with motivation and basic cognitive activities in the category of quintessentially *psychological* processes. Language was presented as a good example of those "general processes" which made social life possible just as the anatomy of the human hand produces art of a certain kind. But these processes were seen as ultimately belonging to the psychological level of analysis rather than the sociopsychological.

This treatment of language reflects the orthodox view in psychology at the time embodied in Chomsky's (1965) psycholinguistics and in his structuralist framework. Language was understood as an abstract system of rules, an autonomous and independent mechanism, a form of knowledge which could be codified in dictionaries and grammar textbooks. As David Graddol (1994) notes, if we take a structuralist view, then we come to see language as a kind of self-contained machine made up of components (phonemes, sentences, clauses, adjectives, verbs) which go together in certain patterns to make the system work.

Standing alongside this structuralist model of language was the concept of "communication" developed in the 1950s. This combined approach saw the use of language as a relatively straightforward and "non-social" matter. Language was seen as acting as a neutral medium or "transport system" conveying messages from ear to ear (or from mind to mind in the case of writing rather than speech). I have a thought which I want to communicate to you. I encode that thought in words, you then decode the words to find the original message. In this model of communication, people were assumed to be independent of language. They were seen as pre-existent characters who *use* language. Language was the vehicle which carries the objects along as they are communicated, faithfully reflecting them from one mind to another. Expression was seen as an individual matter, with people struggling by themselves to find the right words. There was a strong distinction in these approaches between talk and doing, between words and action. Words are used to describe and convey, action happens elsewhere and might be the subject of the communication.

In contrast, discourse analysis and the study of rhetoric (c.f. Billig, 1987; Edwards and Potter, 1992; Potter and Wetherell, 1987) is based on the assumption that language is pre-eminently a *practical activity*, a form of social action in its own right. Indeed the use of the term "discourse" signals this shift from a focus on language as an abstract system to a focus on practice, what people actually do. Communication becomes seen as a form of social engagement which acts back on those communicating and constructs their nature. Discourse is thus *constitutive* of both objects and people. Talk and writing are not merely about actions, events and situations, they are creative of those actions, events and situations. Descriptions, accounts, evaluations, as Edwards and Potter put it, build worlds.

In talking, people are constituting their social realities and collective cultures, manufacturing and constructing their lives, and are themselves manufactured as personalities and subjects in the process. Through this negotiation, the social world becomes populated with characters which are given certain attributes. Relationships become formulated as being of certain kinds, some forms of relating become defined as problematic and some as constructive and positive, and so on. Social life in this way is in no sense separate from the words. Talk is not neutrally recording. Discourse comes to constitute social life as we know it.

Exploration of the constitutive and indexical properties of discourse and its pragmatics makes it clear how meaning is a collective, interactional and historical accomplishment. Discourse is personal and social, private and public, inside and outside simultaneously, so that to build a world is to build a self and a mind (Edwards and Potter, 1992). As Edwards and Potter note, this approach to language breaks down the idea that there are certain classes of utterances which refer to some set of events in the world, for instance, and other classes of utterance (perhaps confessional or revelatory) which are interesting for what they tell us about self, motivation and cognition. Versions of the self and the world are mutually dependent.

These points about the nature of discourse and "social constructions" raise, of course, all kinds of complex ontological and epistemological issues concerning the foundations of reality and the nature of truth. Issues arise, too, about the human subject and questions of passivity, activity, agency and determination which cannot be explored here in depth. But, from my point of view, as we tried to demonstrate in our work on racism (Wetherell and Potter, 1992; see also Marshall and Wetherell, 1989), what is exciting in relation to the concerns of social identity theory is that here is a productive route for studying in detail, at first-hand, the operation of power, the process of categorization, the creation of identity and movements for social change.

The promise of this work for understanding the social and collective constructions which interested Tajfel is clearly illustrated in the work of Billig *et al.* (1988) on ideological dilemmas, and in Michael Billig's work on patterns of collective arguing and thinking (Billig, 1987). It is illustrated, too, in recent post-structuralist feminist work which has examined in detail the construction of identity, the stories which sustain "feminine and masculine fictions" and the ways in which these become embedded in people as "subject positions" (e.g. Hollway, 1984, 1989; Walkerdine, 1990). This work has not assumed that the generative process comes from deep within a universal human nature, below the "surface" of social life; but it has nonetheless been interested in "depth", in the psyche, and the ways in which subjectivity becomes layered, developing contradictory formations through the process of social construction.

This work has begun with the social and the movement of the social "inwards" but it has not assumed, as Tajfel feared, a simple social dope model of the cultural subject. Rather, as Michael Billig has found, and our own work on racism shows, the process of incorporation into the various "normative fields" which make up social life is effective because those fields are fractured, multiple and pluralistic, structured by dilemmas, inconsistent, rather than homogeneous or easy to absorb. The process is one which works through the active dialogue, debate and negotiation of many "arguers and thinkers" and combines moments of resistance with transformation in complex patterns of sedimentation. There is no one "generic norm" but a shifting patchwork of interpretative resources and ideological practices and out of these social categories intergroup strategies and group identities coalesce.

These new developments can be read as a decisive break with some of Tajfel's most central preoccupations. They certainly depended on breaking the stranglehold of the experimental method in social psychology. But they can also be read as continuing his concerns. Neither a discontinuous nor continuous history of social psychology seems adequate at this point and, in conclusion, as we celebrate Tajfel's life and work in this volume I want to note the potential for a double reading of Tajfel's contribution to social psychology. His work in many respects was antithetical to the development of social constructionism, but social identity theory also acted as an important precursor and Tajfel's concerns in particular helped legitimate and stimulate these new lines of research.

References

Berkowitz, L. (1962). *Aggression: A social psychological analysis.* New York: McGraw-Hill.

Billig, M. (1977). The new social psychology and "fascism". *European Journal of Social Psychology,* **7**, 393–432.

Billig, M. (1987). *Arguing and thinking.* Cambridge: Cambridge University Press.

Billig, M., Condor, S., Edwards, D., Gane, M., Middleton, D., and Radley, A. (1988). *Ideological dilemmas: A social psychology of everyday thinking.* London: Sage.

Bruner, J. (1990). *Acts of meaning.* Cambridge, MA: Harvard University Press.

Chomsky, N. (1965). *Aspects of a theory of syntax.* The Hague: Mouton.

Edwards, D., and Potter, J. (1992). *Discursive psychology.* London: Sage.

Eysenck, H. J., and Wilson, G. D. (Eds) (1978). *The psychological basis of ideology.* Lancaster: MTP Press.

Gergen, K. (1985). The social constructionist movement in modern psychology. *American Psychologist,* **40**, 266–275.

Graddol, D. (1994). Three models of language description. In D. Graddol and O. Boyd-Barrett (Eds), *Media texts: Authors and Readers.* Clevedon: Multi-lingual Matters and Open University.

Harre, R. (1977). On the ethogenic approach: Theory and practice. In L. Berkowitz (Ed.), *Advances in experimental social psychology,* Vol. 10. New York: Academic Press.

Harre, R., and Gillett, G. (1994). *The discursive mind.* Thousand Oaks, California: Sage.

Henriques, J. (1984). Social psychology and the politics of racism. In J. Henriques, W. Hollway, C. Urwin, C. Venn, and V. Walkerdine (Eds), *Changing the subject: Psychology, social regulation and subjectivity.* London: Methuen.

Hollway, W. (1984). Gender difference and the production of subjectivity. In J. Henriques, W. Hollway, C. Urwin, C. Venn, and V. Walkerdine (Eds), *Changing the subject: Psychology, social regulation and subjectivity.* London: Methuen.

Hollway, W. (1989). *Subjectivity and method in psychology.* London: Sage.

Kvale, S. (Ed.) (1992). *Psychology and postmodernism.* London: Sage.

Marshall, H., and Wetherell, M. (1989). Talking about career and gender identities: A discourse analysis perspective. In S. Skevington and D. Baker (Eds), *The social identity of women.* London: Sage.

Michael, M. (1990). Intergroup theory and deconstruction. In I. Parker and J. Shotter (Eds), *Deconstructing social psychology.* London: Routledge.

Parker, I. (1992). *Discourse dynamics.* London: Routledge.

Potter, J., and Wetherell, M. (1987). *Discourse and social psychology.* London: Sage.

Schacter, S. (1970). The assumption of identity and peripheralist–centralist controversies in motivation and emotion. In M. Arnold (Ed.), *Feelings and emotions.* New York: Academic Press.

Schwartz, T., White, G. M., and Lutz, C. (Eds) (1992). *New directions in psychological anthropology.* Cambridge: Cambridge University Press.

Sherif, M., and Sherif, C. (1969). *Social psychology.* New York: Harper and Row.

Shotter, J. (1993). *The cultural politics of everyday life.* Milton Keynes: Open University Press.

Tajfel, H. (1970). Experiments in intergroup discrimination. *Scientific American,* **223**, 96–102.

Tajfel, H. (1972). Experiments in a social vacuum. In J. Israel and H. Tajfel (Eds), *The context of social psychology: A critical assessment.* London: Academic Press.

Tajfel, H. (1977). Social psychology and social reality. *New Society,* **39**, 653–654.

Tajfel, H. (Ed.) (1978). *Differentiation between social groups.* London: Academic Press.

Tajfel, H. (1979). Individuals and groups in social psychology. *British Journal of Social and Clinical Psychology,* **18**, 183–190.

Tajfel, H. (1981). *Human groups and social categories.* Cambridge: Cambridge University Press.

Taylor, D. M., and Brown, R. J. (1979). Toward a more social social psychology? *British Journal of Social and Clinical Psychology,* **18**, 173–179.

Vaughan, G. (1978). Social change and intergroup preferences in New Zealand. *European Journal of Social Psychology*, **8**, 297–314.

Walkerdine, V. (1990). *School-girl fictions*. London: Verso.

Wertsch, J. (1991). *Voices of the mind*. London: Harvester Wheatsheaf.

Wetherell, M. (1982). Cross-cultural studies of minimal groups: Implications for the social identity theory of intergroup relations. In H. Tajfel (Ed.), *Social identity and intergroup relations*. Cambridge and Paris: Cambridge University Press and Editions de la Maisons des Sciences de l'Homme.

Wetherell, M. and Potter, J. (1992). *Mapping the language of racism: Discourse and the legitimation of exploitation*. London and New York: Harvester Wheatsheaf and Columbia University Press.

11

Social Identity and Time

SUSAN CONDOR

Department of Psychology, Lancaster University

Contents

Introduction

When, in 1979, I first arrived at Bristol as a postgraduate student the little that I knew of Henri Tajfel's work had been gleaned from a lecture on "prejudice" in my undergraduate degree course at Cardiff. At my first supervision session Henri handed me a copy of the then recently-published *Differentiation between social groups* (which, it appears, I never got round to returning) and (somewhat more prudently) a photocopy of his chapter "Experiments in a vacuum" from *The context of social psychology.* I was instructed to "go away and tell me what you think". I duly went away, and stayed away for the next six months. The problem was that, although I scanned the pages of these texts painstakingly and even obsessively (I recall at one stage calculating that I had read Tajfel's chapters in *Differentiation* at least twelve times), I was quite unable to see what Tajfel was saying, much less think anything about it.

Eventually my vision of Tajfel's theory* of social identity and intergroup relations became clarified through information picked up from other postgraduates and researchers at Bristol. I came to realize that, in order to see what Tajfel was saying, I needed radically to readjust my intellectual focus and expectations. I had to stop searching for the bogus pipelines, reinforcement schedules and overheard snatches of cocktail party conversation which had stood out so solidly in my undergraduate texts. After a lengthy process of acculturation I came to learn about the various things I might expect to find in Tajfel's work: a concern for widespread patterns in human behaviour; a critique of attempts to explain phenomena such as racism or anti-Semitism in terms of reductionist psychologies; a "dynamic" theory which recognized the flexibility and context-dependence of human action; a perspective which recognized human agency and the responsibility of social actors for constructing the world in which they live; a perspective which recognized macrosocial context and the process of social change; a perspective which, while it focused on ideology and (inter)subjectivity, nevertheless did not deny the material aspects of relations between "real life" social groups; a theory which, in so far as it naturalized (and thereby implicitly justified) collective identities and action (especially "minority group" action) provided theoretical and empirical ballast against the existing ("American") social psychological hegemony and its (implicit) ideological support of the status quo.

Many of these themes are not foregrounded explicitly "in" Tajfel's written texts although they are explicated most clearly in Tajfel's personal reflections on his work in *Human groups and social categories*. This perhaps explains why there are now so many different versions of what Tajfel "really meant" which are used to authorize a particular reading of his work. In undertaking to write this chapter, I find myself at something of a rhetorical disadvantage. Throughout most of my time at Bristol I attempted (usually successfully) to avoid any contact with Henri which might risk exposing the depths of my ignorance, the extent of my misunderstanding, the fact that I did not possess the true, subtle insider-knowledge necessary in order to pass as a bona fide social identity theorist. As a consequence, I now do not have any basis for warranting any claims I might wish to make concerning what Tajfel's work might "really" have been about. Instead, I am forced to rely largely on the texts of Tajfel's written work, which I read, if no longer as a complete "outsider", at least without the benefit of daily communication with other social identity theorists who can tell me what to think.

This causes particular problems with respect to the theme that I have (probably unwisely) chosen for this chapter. Given the nature of this Festchrift—a reflection back over Tajfel's career, a consideration of work taking place "today"

*It is conventional for Tajfel's work on social identity and intergroup relations to be described as a "theory" or "model" although it is not clear that his work does, in fact, have the characteristics implied by either of these terms. For the sake of convenience I shall retain the use of these terms when referring to Tajfel's work, although the pedantic readers may, if they prefer, place these terms in imaginary scare quotes.

in the context of this intellectual heritage, a speculation on future "developments" yet to come—it would seem pertinent to address the issues of time and history as they figure in Tajfel's own work. The question of time surfaces repeatedly throughout Tajfel's writing on intergroup relations, although it is not at all clear that Tajfel himself adopted any clear "position" on the issue. Tajfel was, for example, clearly concerned with the issue of historical transformation and "social change" (see Reicher, this volume). Tajfel also recognized and stated a concern for the specificity of the historical and cultural present (see Billig, this volume). In this chapter I shall be focusing on the ways in which Tajfel addressed the issue of time as it pertained to the "dynamic" nature of psychological functioning and to the understanding of social groups as temporal processes. Although Tajfel's work was prescient in so far as he acknowledged these considerations, he did not develop these ideas to any great extent in his written work. In discussing the issue of time as it relates to social identity I shall take Tajfel's work as a point of departure. However, in the process of attempting to follow these ideas through I shall come to explore a number of issues which have not, traditionally, been considered by social identity theorists. These include issues such as the serial character of social life, the significance of technology to the conceptualization and organization of large-scale social collectivities, and the temporal aspects of the subjective self-concept. None of these issues is, I think, incompatible with Tajfel's original interests.

Psychological Flexibility

> The Marivaudian being is . . . a pastless futureless man, born anew every instant. The instants are points which organize themselves not a line, but what is important is the instant, not the line.
>
> (Barthelme, quoted by Lasch, 1979)

During the stock-taking "crisis" of the 1970s, a number of commentators criticized existing social psychological perspectives for presenting an essentially static picture of psychological functioning and of social life (e.g. Gergen, 1973; Moscovici, 1972). Tajfel, similarly, argued against reified models of psychological functioning: "the greatest adaptive advantage of man is his capacity to modify his behaviour as a function of the way in which he perceives and understands a situation" (Tajfel, 1969, p. 81). Tajfel (e.g. 1972, 1978a) in particular took issue with attempts to explain prejudice—and intergroup relations more generally—with recourse to enduring psychological characteristics of particular individuals, or with recourse to supposedly generic (acontextual) psychological processes. In discussing the context-contingent character of human subjectivity Tajfel distinguished two "idea types" of situation: those in which people act in terms of their unique individuality, and those in which they think, feel and act in terms of a sense of collective self. Tajfel typically used the minimal group studies to illustrate this potential for people to respond flexibly to social context: he suggested that the findings from these studies showed how in some (particular) situations people will perceive the world (and act) in terms of intergroup distinctions (the implication being that, in other contexts, they would not do so). In his theoretical work Tajfel (e.g. 1980a) argued that social categories should not be treated as "static variables", but as dynamic, continuously changing, relational ways of orienting to the social world. Similarly, he argued that social identifications should be seen to be fluid and variable over time: "the psychological existence of a group for its members is a complex sequence of appearances and disappearances, of looming large and vanishing into thin air" (Tajfel, 1982a, p. 485). In this respect, Tajfel's work may be seen to have prefigured those more recent ("postmodern") developments in social psychology which have promoted the notion of decentred subjectivity and have stressed the radically context-contingent nature of human subjectivity and social behaviour (e.g. Henriques *et al.*, 1984; Potter and Wetherell, 1987).

This emphasis on the situated, occasional nature of social and self-perception has not always been followed through in empirical research. In particular, it is interesting to note how research on "real life" intergroup relations has tended to bracket the issue of the flexibility of subjectivity. Instead, researchers seek to examine social identity in "the field" through the application of survey technology; most usually by the application of scales designed to gain an insight into social imagery (e.g. Bourhis and Hill, 1982) or instruments designed to measure (and compare) individuals in terms of the strength of their identification with a given social category (Condor, *et al.*, 1987). The assumption behind these methods is that social perception and identification may be regarded as relatively enduring ("reliable") facets of individual psychology.

The question of the flexibility and context-contingency of subjectivity has, however, been emphasized by researchers adopting Turner's self-categorization approach to group processes (e.g. Turner *et al.*, 1987, 1994) who foreground the question of category salience (see e.g. Hogg and Turner, 1987; Oakes, 1987; Oakes *et al.*, 1991; and see Tajfel, 1982a for an account of the importance of salience to his own theoretical concerns). Self-categorization theory treats self and social perception as radically context-contingent, dependent not only upon the expectations and motives that an individual subject brings to a situation ("perceiver readiness") but also upon the perceived relevance of a particular category to any (perceived) context. The perceived relevance or "fit" of a particular category is, according to self-categorization theory, a function both of the extent to which a particular level of categorization best captures the relative differences between stimuli ("the principle of metacontrast") and of the extent to which the specific characteristics of the stimuli match the perceivers' background knowledge about the categories ("normative fit") [see Oakes *et al.*, 1994; Turner *et al.*, 1994; and see also Tajfel's (1980b) original attempt to utilize Bruner's work on perceiver readiness and fit to explain variations in self and social perception]. This theoretical emphasis on category salience has been accompanied by an empirical project aimed at the elucidation of the context-dependence of social and self-perception in a series of imaginative laboratory experiments. These studies have reliably demonstrated that self-description and stereotypic perception may be influenced by variations in local context (as illustrated, for example, by the effects of manipulating the specific instructions given to subjects or to variations in the comparative frame of reference provided by the experimenters) as well as events taking place in the "wider social context" (e.g. Haslam *et al.* 1992).

The self-categorization perspective certainly avoids problems of reification and, to some extent, essentialism which often bedevil social psychological accounts of social behaviour. However, in common with many other approaches which emphasize the flexibility of subjectivity and action in microtime, this approach leaves us with the problem of accounting for (or even conceiving of) continuity *over* time. Is it meaningful to speak of social identities, stereotypes, categories and groups as anything other than fleeting, ephemeral phenomena? Certainly, some recent statements by self-categorization theorists suggest that it is not: "[the] content of a stereotype is not a fixed set of attributes applied in an all-or-none manner, but is shaped selectively by the context of its application" (Oakes *et al.*, 1994, p. 123); "there is no psychologically based stability, continuity, or unity in the self from situation to situation" (Turner *et al.*, 1994, p. 459).*

Oakes and her colleagues (1994) have recently broached the question of the temporal continuity of social perception and action, albeit in a rather parenthetical manner. They suggest that stability in stereotypic judgement may arise from, amongst other things, "the stability of intergroup relationships", and from "the higher-order knowledge frameworks used to give coherence to varying instances of group behaviour. . ." (p. 199). This sort of perspective, which essentially locates "continuity" at the level of macrosocial relations or at the level of intrapsychic processes effectively brackets the question of the temporal linking of local microsocial "contexts" or episodes. Self-categorization research focuses on documenting the synchronic moment. There is no account of how specific moments can be seen to fit together diachronically. This is due in large part to the fact that, in self-categorization theory, the "social field" or "context" is treated (or at least spoken of) as if it were essentially external to the perceiving subject: a stimulus display which individual subjects view, a set of instructions to which they respond, rather than a process of which they are a part. More generally, we can note how laboratory studies of category salience—in common with most empirical social psychological research—achieve an image of social life as composed of discrete "contexts" and "moments" both through the application of particular technical devices (forms of analysis which bracket any movement or change within the experimental episode; see Antaki *et al.*, in press),

* As something of an aside, it is worth considering the historical and ideological context in which current theories of the "flexibility" of the human subject are proposed. In addition to Tajfel (1972) several other of the "crisis" authors have pointed to the ways in which academic models of psychological functioning reflect, and possibly ideologically support, the politicocultural status quo (e.g. Moscovici, 1972; Sampson, 1977). Bearing this in mind, it is tempting to point to the correspondence between emerging social psychological emphases on the "flexibility" of the individual subject, and the requirements of post-Fordist labour markets for "flexible" workforces.

and textually, by reporting the experimental episode as if it were entirely divorced from the prior or subsequent activities of the participants. Through the imposition of an artificial beginning and ending, social psychologists construct a "plot" for their research stories which show how all the elements hang together and "make sense" within the context of the research episode itself (cf. Billig's 1976 account of experimental studies of intergroup relations).

At this stage I should like to point to the first of several tensions which I perceive in social identity theory's attempts to deal with the problem of time. It is clear from Tajfel's work that the issues he sought to address (large-scale social categories, prejudice, intergroup differentiation and conflict, social movements and so forth) need to be seen as relatively enduring (although possibly developing and transforming) *over time*. If we focus on flexibility in microtime at the expense of continuity over macrotime there is a distinct danger that the social problems which "loom large" at the outset of our work, and to which we commonly refer to when justifying an interest in social identity and intergroup processes (racism, anti-Semitism, class relations, international conflict, etc.) may, in effect, "disappear into thin air" the moment we start to interrogate them. Certainly, we should not return to theories which treat human actors as if they were constrained by rigid psychological hardware which prevents them from responding to changes in the social environment. However, if we are at all concerned with large-scale social processes neither can we afford to regard our research subjects as Marivaudian beings.

Social groups as processes

> Structure. . .is encountered in becoming, and one cannot illustrate it except by pursuing this process of becoming.
>
> (Durkheim, 1933, p. 323)

It is clear from Tajfel's writing that, whilst he acknowledged psychological flexibility in microtime, his major concern was to theorize social relations in macrotime. In order to avoid reifying social structures (and hence denying the moment-to-moment variability of human cognition and conduct), Tajfel emphasized how social relations are *realized over time* ("social groups are not 'things'; they are processes" (1982a, p. 485)). Tajfel suggested that even apparently stable systems of social relations rely upon continuous social reproduction over time:

> Even in the most rigid caste system. . .the social distinctions which may appear very stable are related to a continuously dynamic psychological situation in which a superior group can never stop working at the preservation of its distinctiveness.
>
> (1974a, p. 77)

Apart from its apparent voluntarism (a point I have discussed elsewhere, see Condor, 1989, 1990, and see below) this perspective would appear to have much in common with some current sociological and anthropological perspectives which regard the formation of social collectivities as ongoing processes. These include Philip Abrams' (1982) account of "structuring" and

Giddens' (e.g. 1979, 1984) rather better-known analysis of the process of "social structuration". In addition, currently popular "network" approaches in anthropology (Hannerz, 1992) and the social studies of science (Knorr-Cetina, 1981; Latour, 1986, 1987) also emphasize the need to regard social life as a temporal trajectory rather than as a static set of positions. These perspectives (and others like them) regard social action as essentially *serial* in character (e.g. Heller, 1982, 1984). The serial character of social action may involve some measure of routine repetition of action over time, as exemplified, for example, in Bourdieu's (1977) analysis of "habitus" and Giddens' discussion of the way in which social institutions are chronically reproduced through the mundane repetition of activity in daily life. Such perspectives do not suggest that individual social actors are locked within rigid, unchangeable "roles", and they do not deny the potential for innovation or creativity. What they do emphasize is the fact that large-scale systems of social relations do not exist (and persist) independently of their reproduction by human subjects in the course of their daily lives. In this, these approaches have some apparent parallels with Tajfel's approach to intergroup relations and Turner's approach to the process of self-categorization (both of which stress the importance of established "shared norms" in regulating social activity).

Where these approaches to social process differ from social identity theory is in stressing the ways in which the social world is constructed through the serial linking of events, and the serial transmission of action and information *between* social actors and local domains. Social identity theory currently lacks what Carr (1991) terms a "relay model" of social life: it does not address the question of how wide-scale (macrosocial) phenomena may be effected through the "chaining" of microsocial episodes (Knorr-Cetina, 1988). This sort of "relay" perspective may be illustrated with reference to the notion of "translation" which is commonly employed in actor network theory (e.g. Callon and Latour, 1981; Latour, 1986, 1987). The construct of "translation" refers to the way in which orders, claims, artifacts and so forth come to be spread over time and space through a continuing process of being handed on, and taken up, by different social actors. Each of the social actors* through whose metaphorical hands these ideas, statements, texts and artifacts pass is regarded as a "multi-conductor" (Latour, 1987, p. 140) who shapes them according to his or her own local projects. Claims, identities, ideas and practices cannot endure over time or spread over space without being taken up by successive social actors. But each of these social actors will effectively "translate" (drop, transfer, corrupt, modify, add to or appropriate) these practices in the course of taking them up and passing them on.

* In the interests of simplicity of exposition I am, for the time being, bracketing the issue of what or who constitutes a social "actor". It should be noted, however, that actor network theorists do not necessarily assume that an "actor" will be an individual human subject. In actor network theory, the construct of an "actor" is applied to any person or object that functions within a network as a unitary or homogeneous entity. An "actor" may, then, refer to a corporate entity, a machine or a natural phenomenon as well as an individual human being.

This sort of analysis of social process is rather different from the model of social life proposed in either Tajfel's or Turner's approach to the process of social identification. Certainly, remarkably few social identity theorists have considered the ways in which intra- or intergroup processes may unfold and transform over time (for exceptions, see Brown and Ross, 1982; Taylor and McKirnan, 1984; Reicher, 1987). There seem to be two reasons why social identity theorists have generally neglected to analyse social groups as ongoing processes.* The first is theoretical, and derives from Tajfel's reluctance to adopt reductionist models which analyse "large-scale" intergroup phenomena in terms of the dynamics of "small group" behaviour. The unfortunate consequence is that social identity theorists have largely excluded the microsocial domain of human activity from their theoretical model *tout court*.† In general, social identity theory posits a direct line of communication between the individual and the macrosocial by effectively cutting out the microsocial middle-man (see, for example, Turner and Oakes, 1986). Ironically, at the same time that social identity theorists have been arguing for a need to exclude considerations of microsocial processes from theories of macrosocial relations, elsewhere in the social sciences theorists have been suggesting that macrosocial relations cannot be properly understood without a consideration of microsocial (small group) activity. In particular it is argued that, in order to appreciate the *processual* character of widescale (macrosocial) relations, it is necessary to consider the process of communication within, and the dynamic and multiple links between, the microsocial fora in which these processes routinely operate (e.g. Callon and Latour, 1981; Giddens, 1984; Knorr-Cetina, 1988).

The second reason why social identity theorists have, by and large, neglected to consider the ways in which intergroup processes come to be constituted over time pertains to issues of methodology. Although Tajfel himself remained a champion of laboratory experimentation (e.g. 1972, 1980a) he did acknowledge that this technology was limited in its ability to illuminate diachronic process, especially processes taking place over a long period of time. The problem here (as Tajfel, 1972 suggested) is not so much with the technique of experimentation *per se* as with the ways in which experimentation is routinely conceived and practised within social psychology. Laboratory experimentation, and, in particular, the way in which "findings" are constituted by particular technologies of data gathering, statistical analysis and report writing, tends to result in reified representations which, as I have already argued, are accomplished by the bracketing of the "movement" of phenomena under investigation within the

* There is, of course, much talk in the literature about "social identity processes", "intergroup processes", the "process of differentiation", and so forth. It seems that, in general, such discussions are confined to an explication of intrapsychic processes (the way in which an individual "reacts" to a dynamic social field) rather than to the dynamics of the social field itself.

† The question of "small group" behaviour re-emerges when attempts are made to explain microsocial activity in terms of the sorts of social identity processes which are used to explain the individual's relationship to large-scale, abstract, social categories (see, for example, Hogg, 1992; Turner *et al.*, 1987).

experimental setting (Antaki *et al.*, in press, and see Bourdieu, 1977, for an account of how the treatment of time in research contexts leads to the reification of social scientific constructs). In addition, the practices associated with experimental research exclude any analysis of the *distal* precursors to, and consequences of, activity taking place within particular microsocial episodes.* Unlike Bruno, Latour (1987), social psychologists rarely follow either the researchers or their subjects into and out of the specific research episode in order to construct an open-ended account which charts the trajectory of actions over time and through the social body.

Unintended consequences of serial social action

> [Decisions] in a board room impinge on the life situation of an aboriginal population without that board's or its corporation's having any place in the cognized world of the population so affected or, indeed, probably vice versa.
>
> (Barth, 1992, p. 20).

In this section I shall turn to consider one particular consequence which stems from this neglect to consider the ways in which social action may be successively "translated" by various social actors. When they test their theories in the laboratory, social identity theorists typically attempt to explain social activity in terms of *local* cause-and-effect sequences, which often entail a consideration of the motives of social actors. When they turn to consider distal (large-scale, macrosocial) social constructs, social identity theorists often attempt to explain these, too, with recourse to the intentions of social actors. In particular, intergroup theorists often imply that the stability or disruption of systems of social relations represent a direct consequence of activities designed expressly to "maintain stability" or to "institute change". This is particularly the case in those analyses which have attempted to use Tajfel's (e.g. 1975a, 1978b) account of minority group "strategies" in order to explain the occurrence of actual historical change in the relations between social groups (e.g. Williams and Giles; cf. Condor, 1989). A similar problem may also be identified in Tajfel's (1981b) own treatment of the "social functions" of stereotypes, in which he tends to conflate the actual social outcomes of particular social representations with the (conscious or unconscious) intentions of the people who formulate and use these representations (see Condor, 1990). In this, social identity theorists often come close to espousing voluntaristic and teleological models of history and social change which neglect the ironic character of human social activity: the fact that, in the ongoing process of translation over time and dispersal over space, our actions may come to have (or at least, contribute to) consequences that we never anticipated.

If we appreciate the ways in which texts, arguments and artifacts become dispersed over space and translated over time through the linking of

* In fact, the logic of "ethical" experimentation assumes that there need be no distal consequences of the research episode (see Condor, 1991).

microcontexts, we can begin to appreciate the ways in which purposeful social action may come to have unintended social consequences. Certainly, it is difficult to argue that such long-term, wide-scale, social processes such as warfare (Knorr-Cetina, 1981), industrialization, democratization and globalization (Elias, 1991) were envisioned by, or even conceivable to, the individual and corporate social actors whose behaviour contributed to their realization. Conversely, strategies directed at implementing political change (such as that evidenced in the sorts of new social movements discussed by Tajfel) can come to have outcomes which are different, and often quite contrary, to original expectation (Giddens, 1984).

In order to illustrate the problems which may arise if we try to account for the eventual (distal) outcomes of a serial social process in terms of the intentions or motives of individual (or collective) social actors, let us reconsider Tajfel's original minimal group experiments. There are, as is well known, many plausible stories concerning the motives of the boys who, when assigned to arbitrary social categories, tended to display ingroup favouritism. Tajfel himself provided two different accounts: first, that the boys were complying with general cultural norms of group behaviour which dictated "competition" between social groups (e.g. Tajfel, 1970; Tajfel *et al.*, 1971), and alternatively, that the boys behaved as they did in order to achieve a satisfactory social identity (e.g. Tajfel, 1974a, 1974b). In both of these accounts, however, the causal* processual story is curtailed: we know that social categorization "caused" intergroup differentiation and ingroup favouritism, but then the trail goes cold. The experiment is terminated, the subjects debriefed, and we hear no more about what happened next. Brown and Ross (1982) attempted to address the question, "what happens next?" by extending the time-scale of the laboratory episode. But this still restricts the sort of story that can be told by effectively limiting the analysis to the interactions which take place *within* (rather than between) particular local contexts.

What if we were to follow the course of the particular acts which took place within the microcontext of the experiment (awarding money to anonymous others on the matrices) as they are translated by social actors and transferred between social episodes beyond the confines of the experimental laboratory? For the sake of simplicity, I shall draw a fairly gross distinction between the two classes of social actor involved in the minimal group studies: the schoolboys and the experimenters (Billig, 1976). For the sake of convenience, let us assume that, for the boys, the experimental episode constituted a form of social "sequestration". By this, I mean that the events which occurred were effectively packaged-off from their everyday lives by virtue of occurring in a "special" place (the

*More properly, I should call this an "effective" story, since I am considering how particular social acts can come to constitute enabling or constraining conditions on subsequent action. Although I am arguing for a need to see social action as "chained", I am not suggesting that one social act automatically or necessarily "causes" or leads to any other particular act. For a discussion of the distinction between causal and "effective" histories, see Dean (1994).

laboratory) and time (the duration of the experiment)*. For the social psychologists, however, the experimental episode was part of the process of their everyday (working) lives. The social psychologists did not ignore or forget what had happened in the laboratory as soon as they had debriefed their subjects. On the contrary, at this stage the social psychologists set about implementing a set of translations—interpreting and broadcasting knowledge of the experimental episode. In the first place, they translated the social actors into "subjects" and then into corporate "conditions". They also translated the boys' choices on the matrices into "strategies" (or "pulls"). The various independent acts which took place during the study were collapsed and reconstituted under labels such as "MD", "MJP" and so forth. These were then translated again into a single summary "finding": the "phenomenon of gratuitous discrimination in favour of the ingroup" (p. 173). At this point we may stop to consider whether the individual, physically isolated, boys who took part in the study actually anticipated that their acts would contribute to the aggregate outcome identified ("discovered") by the researchers. There is some reason to suppose that they did not. After all (as Tajfel and his colleagues tell us) the boys seemed to be of the opinion that "everyone else" would "naturally" opt for the MJP strategy. In the absence of communication with their fellows, they would have no way of knowing that their isolated acts would, in effect, contribute to an overall *tendency* to favour the ingroup.

So what happened next? Henri Tajfel, Mick Billig, Robert Bundy and Claude Flament then enlisted (to borrow Latour's term) this "fact" to support their own local projects. One of these local projects was to make a particular claim about the social psychology of intergroup processes (other "local projects" may have been things like, "to get an article in *Scientific American*", or "to keep my job"). Let me at this stage risk stating the obvious: these various local projects for which the *researchers* enlisted the boys' behaviour (now transformed into "data") were quite different from the local projects that had influenced the boys' initial actions (which may have included things like, "to please the experimenters", "to avoid looking stupid", "to achieve a satisfactory sense of self", or whatever).

Of course, the effective trajectory does not end with the publication of Tajfel's *Scientific American* article in 1970. The claims made in this article were subsequently to be reiterated, taken up, challenged, absorbed, tested, reinterpreted, misinterpreted and ignored by successive generations of social psychologists all over the world. The boys who took part in the minimal group studies may have had many different reasons for acting as they did, and in order to understand why the boys acted as they did in the minimal group situation we would need to know what these local motives were. However, the fact remains that we *cannot* explain the multiple, distal *effects* of their acts simply in terms of their original

* Tajfel and his associates (1971) certainly assumed this to be the case. They noted that the subjects "knew that on return home in their minibus, and later, they would revert to the pattern of their previous interactions which were entirely unrelated to the categorizations used in the experiments. . ." (p. 175).

motives in the particular situation in which this action took place. After all, had Tajfel's subjects not displayed Kandinski-chauvinism, I would not be sitting here writing this chapter today.* But it would be ludicrous to suggest that the boys acted as they did *in order to* enable the development of a "school of thought" within academic social psychology.

The Temporal synchronization of social life

> An American will never meet. . .more than a handful of. . .fellow-Americans. He has no idea what they are up to at any one time. But he has complete confidence in their steady, anonymous, simultaneous activity.
>
> (Anderson, 1983, p. 31)

Whatever the reasons for the neglect, it seems that, in the absence of a clear understanding of social groups as serial process, and social life in terms of a series of diffusions and translations within and between social groups, social identity theorists often tend to fall back on reified, static constructions of "group behaviour". At this stage I should like to explore a second tension which I see in Tajfel's account of social identification and (inter)group behaviour as it pertains to issues of time. On the one hand, as we have seen, Tajfel appears to suggest that widescale (geographically dispersed) social groups are reproduced and transformed in a dynamic manner over time. On the other hand, Tajfel's primary understanding of the nature of social "group" activity emphasized the manifestation of similarity among group members at *the same moment in time.* Throughout his work Tajfel repeatedly claimed that widescale collective activity takes the form of "people acting and feeling more or less in unison" (e.g. 1984 p. 712), and repeatedly raised the question of "why so many people behave in unison" (e.g. 1977, p. 654). This perspective appears to be shared by many of the most influential contemporary intergroup theorists: "intergroup behaviour is typically homogenous or uniform. . . . The songs and chants of striking miners against the police in the British coal dispute of 1984–1985 provide a graphic illustration of behavioural uniformity" (Brown, 1988, p. 5). The assumption that "group" or "collective" activity is manifested in synchronic uniformity has also been adopted by Turner in his self-categorization approach to group processes: "participants will often seem to act and feel in a spontaneously unitary fashion. Their behaviours may seem co-ordinated and concerted almost as if there were some single, directing consciousness (or unconsciousness)" (Turner, 1987, p. 3). Elsewhere I have questioned the assumption that "group" behaviour should be understood in terms of similarity (the appearance of "uniform", "consensual" or "equivalent" activities on the part of individual group members, Condor, 1990, and see also Billig, 1976). I shall broach this issue again here, but for the time being I should like to focus on the issue of the *synchronization* of self-perception and social action.

* For the sake of simplicity I have, of course, bracketed the fact that social outcomes tend to have multiple causations, or as historians say, many "microdescents" (Braudel, 1980).

At this stage let us recall the rationale behind the social identity approaches to intergroup behaviour (as presented by Tajfel) and to group membership (as presented by Turner and his colleagues). Both of these approaches are advertised as especially pertinent for the analysis of those "virtual" groups [or, to borrow Anderson's (1983) term, "imagined communities"] in which individual group members are chronically geographically dispersed (e.g. nations, ethnic groups, social classes, occupational categories such as "university lecturer", or disciplinary subcategories such as "social identity theorist"). The question then arises as to *how* the members of geographically dispersed social categories *can* come to act in an apparently "spontaneously unitary fashion". This question has not, as far as I know, been raised by social identity theorists.

If synchronized activity is seen to result from some form of planned event (such as an anniversary, or, more specifically, 11 am on Remembrance Day), this would presuppose the existence of a synchronized social time to which individual social actors could refer in calculating when to act. The synchronization of social time is not, however, a "natural" or self-evident phenomenon which requires no explanation. People today (or, at least those who are likely to be reading this book) tend to take it for granted that there is a single "world time" (which, for example, enables us to conceive of onset of the "year 2000" as a global rather than a local event): however, the notion of a single "world time" was only established as late as 1884 (Zerubavel, 1982) in response to the organizational requirements of European expansionist bureaucracies and the global expansion of markets.

It is clear that social identity theorists would not regard all (or even most) synchronized social activity as planned. How, then, is such synchronization effected? One way in which we might attempt to answer this question is by suggesting that there exist types of salience-provoking "context" which can transverse large spatial distances in short periods of time. In the absence of some theory of morphic resonance, this would appear to suggest that the "context" is likely to be transmitted across space through some medium of mass communication. As it stands, this sort of explanation would not conflict with the assumptions behind either Tajfel or Turner's approach to social identity, although, as I have noted already, social identity theorists have generally been reluctant explicitly to enter "communication" as a variable in their accounts (presumably due to some concern that this would somehow draw them back into psychological reductionism). Moreover, in so far as social identity theorists do acknowledge the existence of systems of mass communication, these are not accorded any special theoretical concern. They are treated simply as a taken-for-granted (and uninteresting) component of the "wider social context". However, once again it seems that this might need some explication. In particular, we might note that, in order for unplanned collective behaviour to be synchronized in the sense that people "act and feel more or less in unison", the medium of communication would have to be virtually instantaneous. This would seem to imply that unplanned collective behaviour is dependent upon relatively historically novel forms of technology (the telephone, radio, satellite TV, etc.). I shall return to consider this issue in the next section of this chapter. For the time being we can concede the existence of media-enabled synchronic uniformity in human behaviour. Doubtless, on the exact moment that Germany was knocked out of the 1994 World Cup, several thousand German men, living all over the world, groaned simultaneously. Moments such as this are, however, rare and are in any case hardly central to the concerns of most social identity theorists.

A third possibility is that when social identity theorists speak of behaviour as being "concerted" or of people acting "in unison" they may be thinking of a rather broader time-zone. Maybe they do not mean that human activity will be *precisely* synchronized in time, but rather that members of a particular social category will come to exhibit similar behaviour *averaged over* a period of time. A close reading of Tajfel's work suggests that, in some places, his understanding of "the social context" in which people act "in terms of group" actually refers to a relatively long historical period or "generation" (cf. Abrams, 1982). In these cases, Tajfel did not attempt to explain either how "changes" in ideological or historical "context" were effected, nor how these changes come to influence the common sense of social actors (see Condor, 1989). I shall not consider this issue in any detail here, save to note these sorts of "social uniformity" in ideology and action exhibited over the *longue duree* (Braudel, 1980) cannot easily be explained entirely in terms of the mechanics of social identification. The sorts of "group differences" to which Hogg and Abrams (1988), for example, refer (speaking a particular language, wearing particular sorts of clothes, living in a particular place) do not always, or necessarily, reflect processes of "group identification". They may often represent—as Bourdieu (1979) would suggest—the mundane "habitas" of the social actors. The actors themselves may not even recognize how their everyday practices (which may be experienced phenomenologically as personal "taste" or "normal" human behaviour) differentiate them as a category from others.

Irrespective of how, exactly, social action comes to be synchronized, if we accept recent claims made by self-categorization theory concerning the sensitivity of self-categorization and stereotyping to (relatively small) variations in local context, it seems that we are still left with the problem of explaining how geographically separated social actors can come to act and feel "in unison". For example, even if a number of spatially-dispersed social actors were to be confronted by the same (media-transmitted or previously established) "context" (say, for example, the outbreak of a war, or a Royal wedding) there is no reason to suppose that all of—or even most of—the social actors would react "in the same way" to this information. In fact, from the premises of self-categorization theory, it would seem that this would be very unlikely to be the case. For one thing, each of these individual social actors would be presented with this information in a slightly different *local* context which, as we know, would influence their reactions. Moreover, each social actor would be interpreting the message in the light of the ideologies, goals and interests that they brought to the situation (what self-categorization theorists describe as "perceiver readiness"). As research on audience activity has demonstrated, people are quite capable of interpreting images and messages in various and often (for the analyst) quite surprising ways (e.g. Fiske and Hartley, 1990; Jhally and Lewis, 1992). Furthermore, it would seem that any social identification is open to multiple interpretations. There is no good reason to believe, for example, that all women perceive womanhood in the same way (Condor, 1984), nor that all Britons perceive their own Britishness in the same way (Condor, in press) even in the "same context". It may be that, in some situations, the existence of communication between social actors might diminish this variability in the interpretation of a situation (by establishing and transmitting a "party line") but there is no guarantee that this will be the case (Reicher and Hopkins, in press). As Handler (1994, p. 30) says:

> For any imaginable social group—defined in terms of nationality, class, locality or gender—there is no definite way to specify "who we are", for "who we are" is a communicative process that includes many voices and varying degrees of understanding. . .the uttering of every statement about "who we are" changes, if only slightly, our relationship to who we are.

There is, then, absolutely no reason to believe that, even averaged over an extended period of time, individual social actors acting on the basis of the "same" salient identity would necessarily display "similar" behaviour.

So the question remains: how do dispersed social actors come spontaneously to demonstrate consensual or equivalent self-perception and action? The simple answer is that they do not. It is in practice very difficult to think of situations in which a number of spatially separated, and non-communicating individuals do, in fact, act "in a unitary fashion". It is significant, I think, that the work within social identity theory which has done the most to explain the processes of collective activity is Stephen Reicher's (e.g. 1982, 1987) work on *crowd* behaviour. Crowds are, by their very nature, not "imaginary communities" (although they may come to symbolize them)—they are composed of spatially co-present social actors. Moreover, as Reicher has demonstrated so potently, behaviour within crowds is not characterized by simultaneous uniformity. Rather, within the crowd there is an ongoing negotiation of the meaning and appropriate nature of collective activity.

More generally, it is possible to argue that synchronic uniformity in action is not, on the whole, a normal feature of large-scale social categories. Certainly, the media, politicians, social movement activists and social scientists may, on occasions, construct images of "the public sphere" in which members of a dispersed social category are presented *as if* they exhibited a synchronic unity [see, for example, Anderson's (1983) account of the construction of "the nation" as a synchronic "community"]. Such representations involve the construction of images which essentially air-brush out individual and temporal variation in order to achieve a picture of an homogenous "us, now". At this stage we might consider the claims made by social identity and self categorization theorists when they assert that they have illustrated the existence of "uniform" behaviour amongst their experimental subjects in the laboratory. It is possible to argue that the minimal group studies and salience experiments do not so much reveal as *construct an image of* "uniform" responses to an experimental manipulation. As Danziger (1990) has argued, the use of aggregatory statistics (which present individual differences as "error variance") effectively allows the researcher to construct a fictive collective subject ("the experimental group"), which is then treated *as if* it constituted a veridical representation of each of the individual subjects at the point of testing.

I am not denying that spatially dispersed social actors do sometimes "act in a unitary fashion". However, the occasions on which this occurs are rare and usually take the form of a ritual display of collective identity. Such displays may be relatively spontaneous (as was the case, for example, with Brown's chanting miners), but in such cases it is notable that the actors are usually co-present, or at least able to coordinate their activity through networks of communication. Identity displays may also take the form of routine enactments as is the case, for example, when "the British nation" (or, rather, a sizeable number of British people) observes two minutes' silence for the war dead on Remembrance Day. Such ritual displays of collective unity do not, I would argue, simply involve the co-incidence of the psychological functioning of a number of independent, dispersed and non-communicating social actors (cf. Abrams and Hogg, 1990, p. 4). Rather, they indicate the operation of various forms of *social organization.* Unlike Turner (see p. 296) I do not think that such activity simply *appears* co-ordinated, I would argue that it actually *is* co-ordinated. This co-ordination occurs not through the operation of a "unitary consciousness" (or unconsciousness) in, but by communication between, social actors. This organization may, on occasions, be directed (often literally) from "above", in which case the appearance of synchronized uniformity may be carefully stage-managed and enforced through some form of external scrutiny (see, for example, Peukert's 1987 analysis of parades in Nazi Germany). On other occasions, the co-ordination of the social field may be effected more democratically. This would be the case, for example, when miners jointly arrange to collect on a picket line, or when a long-standing arrangement is made for people to buy poppies and for elective crowds to gather at, and live television to be transmitted from, the Cenotaph.

Time and social organization: Largescale social groups as sociotechnical systems

> . . . I should, therefore, be grateful if you could come for an interview at 3.00 PM on Thursday 16th. On second thoughts, it might be better if you came on Tuesday 14th as I shall not be here on Thursday.
>
> (Letter from Henri Tajfel inviting me to interview)

Instances of synchronic activity—occasions when members of social categories "do the same thing"—should not be regarded as the only (or even the prototypical) form of group or collective activity. Rather, these might better be understood as one (perhaps rather peculiar) example of a more general mode of social co-ordination which Giddens (e.g. 1987, 1990) terms the "time–space zoning" of social life. This refers to the ways in which large-scale social activity is routinely effected through co-ordinating the activities of social actors in terms of time and place. This involves the synchronization of social activity (which may or may not involve different social actors "doing the same thing" at the same time), and also the management of the sequencing, rate and timing of the acts of individuals and groups.

In order to illustrate some of the ways in which social life is routinely organized through the management of time and space,* let us consider Hogg's (1992) account of the way in which his own everyday activities are influenced by "group memberships". Hogg cites several examples of mundane "group" activities: committee meetings, rendezvous with friends, watching a live rugby match, driving and observing traffic flow. What is significant is that *all* of these activities require not only a subjective sense of social identification on the part of individual actors, but also require some mechanism for the *temporal-co-ordination* of the actions of the different individuals involved. In the first place, all of these examples presuppose the existence of devices which allow us to measure and "know" time, and they also presuppose the existence of a single synchronized social time to be "known". Without this, it would be impossible to arrange to meet other people in a particular place at a particular time. In addition, all of these social events require the use of time-management devices such as diaries, appointment books, table bookings, sporting event programming and TV scheduling. A good deal of this activity is delegated to individual social actors [we all possess watches, and undertake to be punctual (Shaw, 1994)], although it should be noted that responsibility for the more integrative and complex systems of social time–space co-ordination (transport timetabling, TV programme scheduling, the organization of urban traffic flow through the precise timing of traffic lights, imposition of speed limits and so forth) is often delegated to expert systems (Giddens, 1990).

This leads to the second point that I wish to make: in order to understand the behaviour of people as members of large-scale social categories we need to consider the role of technology in human social life. Social identity theorists, like social theorists more generally (Johnson, 1988; Latour, 1991; Law, 1991), tend to overlook the ways in which technology is intimately and necessarily implicated in modern social life. However, as Adam (1992, p. 176) argues:

> Science and technology are implicated in almost every aspect of contemporary western life. They constitute its rationality. Machines, nuclear power and telecommunication are defining features of our age. Clocks and the social interactions structured to their rhythm, global time-zones, the almost instantaneous communications via satellites, and the simultaneity of the past, present and future created by television are all inconceivable outside the framework of scientific technology . . . technology manifests and shapes not just objects and nature but social relations . . . it infuses our everyday reality and our understanding of it.

* It is very difficult to discuss time independently from space. However, for want of both space and time, I shall not be foregrounding the issue of space in this chapter.

At the very basic level, mundane social coordination requires devices for the measurement of time (calendars, clocks) and for the keeping and transmission of records (literacy, and various techniques for reproducing and distributing the written and spoken word). These should not be simply taken for granted: human life would be (and has been) very different without these technologies (Clark, 1974; Landes, 1983; Luhmann, 1989; Zerubavel, 1981). The forms of social co-ordination which, in effect, serve to erase spatial distances between social actors as members of dispersed social categories are in fact very recent sociotechnical accomplishments initiated with the development of the telegraph, radio and telephone between 1880 and 1918 (Kern, 1983). Had I been paying attention to Brunel's architecture when I arrived in Bristol for my interview with Tajfel, I might have noticed that there are two clocks at Bristol's Temple Meads station: one to indicate the time in Bristol, and the other to indicate the time in London. It was not until rapid transport and communication became commonplace that there was a need to establish a single "national time".

More specifically, many of the forms of social co-ordination that we now witness (and largely take for granted) in late modern societies depend *entirely* upon the availability of forms of rapid communication (fax, satellite TV, the Internet) which can transverse large distances in virtually no time (Adam, 1992; Nowotny, 1992, 1994). We could, in fact, go so far as to argue that the existence of "large-scale" social categories, both as cognitive constructs and as "real" forms of social organization, depends upon (and only exists because of) systems of rapid transport and communication which enable human beings effectively to bracket the existence of space in their conception of, and dealings with, one another (see Calhoun, 1991). In an important sense, then, the very phenomena which social identity theory attempts to explain (the behaviour of people as members of spatially dispersed "imaginary communities") are, themselves, the result not of universal sociopsychological processes, but of socio*technical* systems which are peculiar to modernity.

Social identity and being in time

> In order to have a sense of who we are, we have to have a notion of how we have become, and of where we are going.
>
> (Taylor, 1989, p. 3)

Up to this point I have considered the flexibility of human behaviour in response to changing environmental contingencies, and have argued that social identity theorists should not focus on the question of psychological plasticity in microtime at the expense of appreciating trajectories of human (psychological and physical) activity over macrotime. I have identified a tension between Tajfel's suggestion that social groups should be regarded as ongoing processes and the tendency on the part of social identity theorists to revert to reified constructions which bracket the historical dimension of social life. Finally, I argued that collective behaviour cannot be explained solely with recourse to the intrapsychic process of social identification, and argued that we need to take account of the ways in which both local and widescale social behaviour comes to be co-ordinated through the organization of time.

Whilst I have questioned the utility of relying on "social identification" *per se* as an explanation of regularities in widescale social activity, it was not my intention to suggest that the co-ordination of social behaviour does not involve some form of reflexive self-monitoring and self-regulation on the part of human beings (aided and abetted by technological devices). In this section I shall turn to focus on the question of human subjectivity. In particular, I shall consider the phenomenological questions corresponding to the ("objective") social scientific issues outlined above: how do people reflexively experience them*selves*? As radically decentred subjects whose being is confined to the transitory, ephemeral moment?; or, as coherent beings-over-time? And how do people conceive of social categories (and, by extension, their own category membership)? As synchronic collections of individuals co-existing and acting in parallel at any moment in time?; or, as serial "generations" of social actors? And what can this tell us about the sorts of behaviour that people engage in when they act on the basis of these subjective understandings?

In asking these questions, I am aware that I am opening one of social identity theory's many "black boxes" (c.f. Latour, 1986). Tajfel often stated explicitly that he did not wish to "enter into endless and often sterile discussions of what 'is' identity" (e.g. 1978a, p. 63). In what follows I shall, then, be resisting this attempt at conversational closure. My aim in opening this "black box" is not to destabilize Tajfel's carefully constructed "social identity" argumentative edifice (c.f. Latour, 1986). Rather, I hope to show that an explication of these issues may lead to the construction of an even more radically "anti-individualist" understanding of human identity than that currently employed by social identity theorists.

Let us start with the question of the phenomenology of "flexibility". Notwithstanding recent discussions of "postmodern" decentred subjectivity (Henriques *et al.*, 1984; Shotter and Gergen, 1989), most theorists still suggest that a (possibly the) central feature of human identity involves a subjective sense of endurance over time and space. As Gergen and Gergen (1983, p. 255) suggest, "[the] fact that people believe they possess identities fundamentally depends on their capacity to relate fragmentary occurrences across temporal boundaries". Even momentary self-images involve a simultaneous awareness of the present (self-in-context), the past and the anticipated future (Brockelman, 1985; Heidegger, 1962). A sense of identity—of being oneself—hence necessitates both retroactive and proactive memory (Collins *et al.*, 1993; Conway, 1990; Freeman, 1993; Gillis, 1994). I am not arguing that a sense of identity-over-time precludes a phenomenological awareness of flexibility nor of change. As Brockelman (1985, p. 64) notes, the "temporal extendedness or thickness of personal identity means that 'I' am neither simply a sheer continuity (a same and single 'me' over time) nor simply fragmented into a series of different 'me's, but both" (see also Giddens, 1991). Indeed, it would not be possible to regard ourselves as "flexible" nor as "changing" if we did not have some sense of our own continuous existence over time.

This phenomenological sense of ontological continuity is not confined to individual ("personal") identity, but also constitutes an important aspect of social identification. This may become apparent when an individual exhibits a sense of commitment to a particular social identity (Moreland *et al.*, 1993): a sense that they have "always" belonged to a particular social group and/or that they will continue to do so in future. This sort of sense of enduring group membership was, to some extent, captured in Tajfel's account of "situations of social change" (in which individuals experience their category membership as binding). Of course, not all group memberships are necessarily experienced as enduring and endurable components of the self—however, it is possible to overstate the extent to which people in contemporary societies regard identities as voluntary or transient (c.f. Lasch, 1979). Even objectively voluntary and mutable group memberships may, at least on occasions, be phenomenologically experienced as enduring identities to which one has a long-term commitment. This was apparent in some recent work in which Mark Levine and I (Condor and Levine, submitted; Levine and Condor, 1995) studied the social identities of supporters of various British football teams. One interesting finding concerned the ways in which football supporters typically presented their allegiance to a particular club not as a voluntary (and modifiable) "choice", but as an inevitable, enduring (life-long) commitment:

> Once you have identified with a team and seen them a couple of times you naturally feel no need to look elsewhere, so you are lumbered with the first one you saw.
>
> (Aston Villa supporter)

> I'm a firm believer in the idea that the team you support is governed by your upbringing and that you as an individual have very little choice. Otherwise we'd all support Rangers or Man United.
>
> (Raith Rovers supporter)

> I just had this feeling for Leicester City, I think they represented my roots, my sense of being who I am. Leicester City are a part of my identity. Leicester City are my first love in football and I will support them to my dying day.
>
> (Leicester City supporter)

This sense of permanent commitment was often accomplished by tracing the roots of one's identification with a club to formative childhood influences (as illustrated by the above quotations), or through constructing this identity in terms of metaphors of kinship:

> I saw them with my dad when I was five and it was love at first sight. I had a brief dalliance with Chelsea once, but I soon came home to my true love, and I havn't strayed since. It's unthinkable to me now that I could ever desert my club. I'll stick by her through sickness and in health to death us do part.
>
> (Ipswich Town supporter)

> It's like being part of a family. Like you don't chose [sic] your parents and they don't chose [sic] you, but you love each other anyway and stick together through thick and thin. That's how I see my relationship with Derby.
>
> (Derby County supporter)

In addition, we are capable of conceiving of social categories as ontologically continuous irrespective of the continuity of our own category membership. As social actors we are, on occasions, capable of understanding imaginary communities as historical phenomena: stretching back in time, and forward into the future. Many theorists have explored the role of historiography, collective memory and the invention of tradition to the construction of collective identities (e.g. Connerton, 1989; Hobsbawm and Ranger, 1983; Schwartz, 1982; Wright, 1985). The notion that social categories may be subjectively understood as historical processes has figured in some subsequent developments of Tajfel's work on intergroup relations. The question of the perceived durability of social categories is raised both in Breakwell's (1983) analysis of "threatened identities", and in Bourhis' development of Giles' work on "ethnolinguistic vitality" (Bourhis *et al.*, 1981; Sachdev and Bourhis, 1993). Both of these bodies of work have, unfortunately, been somewhat marginalized from mainstream approaches to intergroup theory.

A sense of ontological continuity involves not just a sense of a past self but also of a future self. A faith that "I" (or "we") will *continue to be* in the near and the distant future may be manifested in a sense of self as an ongoing career or as an unfinished project (Goffman, 1968; Harre, 1979), a concern for reputation (Emler and Hopkins, 1990) and a sense of personal responsibility (Tappan, 1991), including the responsibility for inventing, maintaining and changing our selves (Lury, in press). In so far as we have faith in the future continuity of our selves—as individuals or as collectivities—our behaviour may be anticipatory as well as reactive. As Cohen (1968, p. 262) points out, "subjective future is proposed in all our activities. Without a tacit belief in tomorrow nearly everything we do today would be pointless". Similarly, collective activity may be based on a projection of social identities into the future. The motive (which may not necessarily be conscious) behind this activity may be simply to reproduce a social group or category across time. More generally, though, in post-traditional societies in which the future appears unpredetermined, actions initiated in the name of a collectivity may involve *planning for the future*, including behaviours such as resource management, insurance against possible future contingencies, and actions explicitly directed towards the management (or implementation) of social change (Giddens, 1990). Tajfel was, of course, concerned with the future-oriented nature of social activity when he attempted to account for the strategies employed by social movements aiming at the achievement of a positive social identity. Similarly, several of the authors who have subsequently adopted Tajfel's approach to "minority group" activity or the "social functions" of social stereotypes have stressed how the activity of a particular social group may not simply reflect an attempt to satisfy immediate "needs" for positive ingroup distinctiveness, but may reflect a (rhetorical) strategy aimed at achieving social transformation in the near, or distant, future (Bourhis and Hill, 1982; Breakwell, 1983; Condor, 1984; van Knippenberg, 1984; van Knippenberg and Ellemers, 1993).

At this point we may distinguish two ways in which social categories (and category membership) may be subjectively perceived by social actors. The first involves a sense of synchronic co-existence (or co-evalness to borrow the anthropological term) of category members. I have already noted that, in his discussion of nationalism, Benedict Anderson (1983) points to the way in which a sense of national "we-ness" may be based, at least in part, on an illusion of simultaneity. Similarly, a sense of global identity (what self-categorization theorists might term a "superordinate level of self-categorization") may rely on a sense of global co-evalness (Fabian, 1983; Friedman, 1985). A second way in which lay social actors (as well as academic social scientists) may subjectively perceive social groups is as comprised of successive generations of social actors. Although generational models of social life may be particularly salient amongst people living in traditional societies (Lasch, 1979; Shils, 1981; Strathern, 1992), we should not underestimate the extent to which social participation is still understood as a generational phenomenon in late modern societies. By way of illustration we may note the persistence of terms (often metaphors) of kinship for describing and understanding an individual's relationship with a group. I noted above how soccer supporters may construct their relationships to their teams in terms of kinship, and more familiar examples abound ("the fatherland", "Uncle Sam", "daughters of the American revolution", "brothers in arms", "sisterhood is powerful", "family of man").

Once a social category is subjectively understood as being comprised of successive generations of social actors, it then becomes possible for social identity to be experienced not only as a sense of co-evalness (of synchronic co-existence with other ingroup members) but also in terms of serial connectedness with other ingroup members. As Carr (1991) put it, "my social existence not only puts me in contact with a co-existing multiplicity of contemporaries: it connects me with a peculiar form of temporal continuity . . . which runs from predecessors to successors. This sequence extends beyond the boundaries of my life, both into the past before my birth and into the future after my death . . . the *we* with whose experience the individual identifies can both pre-date and survive the individuals that make it up" (pp. 113–114). It is, perhaps, not unreasonable to argue that one of the particular features of social (as opposed to personal) identity lies in this potential for a sense of self to be projected (potentially infinitely) across time. This issue has often been discussed with reference to the particular case of national identity. Game (1990), for example, has suggested that national identities may involve a sense of continuity and connectedness which transcends individual mortality, "the desire to which nation speaks is one of transcendence over particularity, continuity as opposed to the discontinuous existence of individuals" (p. 105).

The significance of this to an understanding of social behaviour becomes apparent when we consider how the (future-oriented) actions of collectivities are often directed towards an imaginary distal future beyond the lifetimes of existing category members. Notwithstanding recent suggestions that contemporary social life lacks concern for posterity (Lowenthal, 1992) and is composed of individuals living for the moment (Lasch, 1979), we can still identify ways in which individuals and organizations may (in the name of social identities) defer (and even sacrifice) immediate or short-term gratification in order to ensure the future for unknown others who are yet to come. We experience a sense of stewardship over the "heritage" of the social groups to which we belong, and see it as our duty to protect this heritage for future generations, even if it is not clear why, or if, our successors might want it (Condor, in press). On a bureaucratic level, members of collectivities often forecast and plan for future worlds in which they, *as individuals*, will never live. In recent years, these imagined futures for which we plan, but in which we (as individuals) will not live, have become increasingly distal. The development of nuclear power, for example, has been associated with a vast expansion of the timespan of our concern: from the few generations of imaginable human actors, to the millennia, by which it is currently estimated that radioactivity will outlive the human race.

This leads me to my final point. Since the time that Tajfel was writing in the 1970s, we have witnessed the development of new social movements whose focus of concern extends far beyond the contemporary "identity" of their members. Many of these social movements evidence a sense of responsibility for humankind—what Turner would call a "superordinate" or "interspecies" level of self-categorization. Giddens (1991, p. 27) points to the way in which this "death of the other" may be seen as a consequence of the general cultural and technological changes associated with late modernity: "late modernity produces a situation in which humankind in some respects becomes a 'we', facing problems and opportunities where there are no 'others' ". However, the collective identity of new social movement activists is not even limited to a sense of "brotherhood of man". Rather, in cases such as the ecology movement, we can see how people assert a trans-species identity: they build associations with animals, and with "nature" itself. On some occasions these superidentities are used as symbols of existing human social identities. Game (1990), for example, points to the way in which constructions of Australian national identity may accomplish a sense of "timelessness" by identifying "the nation" with the physical terrain. In other cases, though, the future on whose behalf social actors speak stretches over and beyond the sphere of human social relations. As Connolly (1991, p. 166) suggests, such movements can evidence a "sense of identity with *life* itself that stretches below and above any particular identity". The potential scope of the identities which guide our action are effectively limitless. We are not confined to speaking as members of groups with particular interests, nor as members of the human race. On occasions, our identities may extend over space and time to embrace nature, the planet, life, the universe and everything.

Twenty-five years on: Some thought on the diffusion and translation of Tajfel's social identity theory

> We live in a world in which the processes of unification and diversification proceed apace, both of them faster than ever before. In some ways, large-scale human groups communicate with each other more than ever. . .and have become increasingly interdependent. At the same time, there is a powerful trend, to be seen virtually all over the world, aiming at the preservation or the achievement of diversity, of one's own special characteristics and "identity". . .
>
> (Tajfel, 1978a pp. 1–2)

> . . .the gap that has been created between our discipline and other social sciences (such as anthropology, sociology, linguistics or economics) has led to a situation of ignorant expertise. The questions we ask are most often very restricted; and if it happens that important problems are taken up, we manage to transform them again to minor questions. . .But all this does not seem to disturb anyone, since it appears that we have achieved our principle aims of applying correctly the rules of the art of experimentation and of receiving for this the approval of our own little group
>
> (Moscovici, 1972, pp. 62–63)

Tajfel's theory of social identity and intergroup processes was clearly a product of its intellectual generation (see Billig, this volume, and P. Abrams, 1982 for an account of "generations" in social life). Having said this, we should be wary of assuming an intellectual synchronicity: the existence of a single "academic time" (c.f. e.g. Adam, 1992). Radical social psychologists often suggest that social psychological theorizing is, in some important respects, "behind the times"—failing to appreciate important changes which have taken place in the social world, and trailing sadly in the wake of "developments" taking place elsewhere in the social sciences (e.g. Sampson, 1989). In this respect, Tajfel's work can be seen to have been remarkably "ahead of its time" in terms of social psychological theorizing. I have already noted similarities between Tajfel's concern with psychosocial flexibility and "postmodern" theorizing on the subject of human identity and social life (see also, Billig, this volume). More specifically, it is possible to identify a host of interesting parallels between Tajfel's social identity theory of intergroup processes and work that was taking place about the same time elsewhere in the social sciences. For example, Tajfel's concern for the comparative nature of social categorization has clear parallels with developing approaches in poststructuralism (e.g. Derrida, 1972). Tajfel's work also has much in common with those perspectives which stressed the way in which "the self" is understood in contradistinction to "the other", amongst the most notable examples of which are Said's (1978) work on "Orientalism" and de Beauvoir's (1953) earlier account of "the second sex". In his later work Tajfel himself noted the clear parallels between his work on intergroup differentiation and the work of Bourdieu (1979) on the dynamic process of social distinction.

I have already noted that Tajfel's concern for "wide-scale" social categories has certain points of similarity with other attempts to understand the identities of spatially-dispersed groups of people, most notably with Anderson's (1983) construct of the "imagined community". In addition, Tajfel's attempt to delineate different types of group boundaries has much in common with Douglas' (1978, 1982) anthropological perspective on group/grid distinctions in social life.

Tajfel's emphasis on the importance of human agency and social change (see Reicher, this volume) had much in common with the work of the British Marxist historians such as E. P. Thompson who, writing in the 1960s, attempted to explain how human beings "made their own history" (see Kaye, 1992). Tajfel's account of what have since become known as "new social movements" was, in contrast, somewhat ahead of its time in the social sciences. It is only more recently that social theorists have begun to reflect on the character and existence of (rather than to adopt somewhat unreflexively a position within) various forms of "identity politics".

Although it is not altogether clear whether Tajfel himself was aware of all of these particular developments outwith social psychology, the existence of these parallels can certainly be attributed to the fact that Tajfel kept up to date with general theoretical developments taking place throughout the social sciences. Tajfel's work was always notably "cosmopolitan" (c.f. Merton, 1957). In his writing he integrated insights from anthropology, sociology and history and, in so doing, took on the role of an intellectual "cultural broker" (c.f. Wolf, 1956), passing these insights on to his local network of social psychologists. The distinctiveness and intellectual quality of Tajfel's social identity theory stands as a testament to what may be gained from academic hybridization.

Over the past twenty-five years, Tajfel's work has exerted an enormous influence on social psychology. It has become diffused throughout the imaginary community of social psychological scholars, and has been enlisted for a multiplicity of projects by hundreds of different academics over the globe. In the process of diffusion, Tajfel's theories have, of course, been translated in a multitude of ways, as each social psychologist (or team of psychologists) attempts to utilize social identity theory for their own ends. As in all social networks, this process of translation has not been undisputed. As the various chapters in this volume attest, the social identity "school" is characterized by schism and struggle, as each author asserts a right to enlist Tajfel as a founding-father for his or her own intellectual product. However, notwithstanding the extent to which Tajfel's theory has become diffused within social psychology, his work has not attained much in the way of recognition outside our own little group. Many of the (apparently similar) contemporaneous theoretical developments which took place outside social psychology have, in contrast, permeated disciplinary boundaries to a far greater extent. The writings of Bourdieu, Anderson and Douglas, for example, have been enlisted by scholars originating from a variety of different disciplinary homelands, as academics have come to communicate with each other more than ever before, and as ideas, texts and terminologies come to be freely exchanged in the global academic marketplace.

There are many possible reasons why Tajfel's work has not received the sort of interdisciplinary recognition that it so clearly deserves. At the risk of oversimplification, I should like to suggest that this has partly been due to the maintenance of academic trade barriers on the part of subsequent social identity theorists. It is clear that, since the time that Tajfel was writing, social identity theorists typically emphasize the distinctive aspects of "their" theory in order to establish a distinctive identity within the imaginary community of "social psychology". One need not look beyond the preface of many recent books to see that the audience that the author addresses tends to be confined to his or her own little group. We need only look at the reference lists from the more recently-published work to see how the textual friends (c.f. Shotter, 1993) and enemies that authors enlist tend to be drawn almost exclusively from the psychological community. Moreover, when describing their "approach", social identity theorists regularly claim to be carving out a distinctively "social psychological" turf: they stress the importance of maintaining a distinction between (their) "social psychological" approach to intergroup processes and perspectives which exist elsewhere in the social sciences. Authors may refer in passing to the "need" to consider historical, sociological or anthropological perspectives at some juncture, but the assumption seems to be that there is no real need to establish, nor to utilize routinely, rapid media of interdisciplinary communication and exchange. The implication is that, at some point, the separate pieces of the intellectual jigsaw will fall into place. But the responsibility for this integrative work is radically deferred: it is assumed to be the responsibility of some other academic agent working at some unspecified point of time in the future.

Working under conditions of self-imposed academic apartheid, social identity theorists now rarely seem to feel the need to keep up to date with developments taking place in other corners of the academic globe. Hence, for example, when Hogg and Abrams (1988) attempted to consider the social identity approach in relation "to other perspectives in social science" (p. 18), it is notable that the "other perspectives in social science" which they discussed were limited almost entirely to the work of early theorists of modernity, including Marx (1844), Durkheim (1893), Weber (1930) and Parsons (1951).

There are two things worth noting about this. The first is that Hogg and Abrams fail to consider how the "social world" for which Tajfel attempted to account was already, in many ways, very different from "the social world" as it existed in (and was described by theorists of) the nineteenth and early twentieth centuries. The second thing worth noting is that Hogg and Abrams appear to assume that whereas social psychological theorizing continues to "progress" (they are clearly concerned to cite recent references and to map out how particular bodies of work have "developed" over time) the same is not also true of "other perspectives in social science". The assumption seems to be that, since 1930, sociologists have done no more than simply muse on the significance of the Protestant work ethic.

But the world and theorizing in the social sciences has, of course, changed enormously over the past fifty years. And there is a danger that, if we do not continuously reconsider, modify or reject our own constructs in the light of these practical and theoretical developments it may well be that, at that point "in the future" when we do sit down to engage in dialogue with these "other" social scientists, we will find ourselves with nothing relevant to say. Unless social identity theorists are prepared continuously to translate Tajfel's original work on the relations between people as members of widescale social categories with a view to considerations such as the temporal organization of social life, the dynamics of sociotechnical systems, and the development of global (and trans-species) identities, it may be that, in another twenty five years time, social identity theory will be significant only as a transcended moment in the history of our own (extinct?) little group.

Acknowledgements

I should like to thank Mick Billig, Mark Levine, Mike Michael, Peter Robinson, Mary Smyth and all the members of the Klee and Kandinski groups, without whose help this chapter could not have been written.

References and Further Reading

Abrams, D., and Hogg, M. (1990). An introduction to the social identity approach. In D. Abrams and M. Hogg (Eds), *Social identity theory: Constructive and critical advances*. New York: Harvester Wheatsheaf.

Abrams, P. (1982). *Historical sociology*. Open Books.

Adam, B. (1992). Modern times: The technology connection and its implications for social theory. *Time and Society*, **1** 175–191.

Anderson, B. (1983). *Imagined communities: Reflection on the origins and spread of nationalism*. London: Verso.

Antaki, C., Condor, S., and Levine, M. (in press). Social identities in talk. *British Journal of Social Psychology*.

Barth, F. (1992). Towards greater naturalism in conceptualizing societies. In A. Kuper (Ed.), *Conceptualizing society*. London: Routledge.

Bat-Chava, Y. (1994). Group identification and self-esteem of deaf adults. *Personality and Social Psychology Bulletin*, **20**, 494–502.

Billig, M. (1976). *Social psychology and intergroup relations*. London: Academic Press.

Bourdieu, P. (1977). *Outline of a theory of practice*. Cambridge: Cambridge University Press.

Bourdieu, P. (1979). *La distinction: Critique sociale de jugement*. Paris: Editions de Minuit.

Bourhis, R., Giles, H., and Rosenthal, D. (1981). Notes on the construction of a subjective vitality questionnaire for ethnolinguistic groups. *Journal of Multilingual and Multicultural Development*, **2**, 144–155.

Bourhis, R., and Hill, P. (1982). Intergroup perceptions in British higher education: A field study. In H. Tajfel (Ed.), *Social identity and intergroup relations*. Cambridge: Cambridge University Press.

Braudel, F. (1980). *On History*. Chicago: University of Chicago Press.

Breakwell, G. (1983). *Threatened identities*. Chichester: Wiley.

Brockelman, P. (1985). *Time and the self*. USA: Crossroad Publishing Co.

Brown, R. (1988). *Group processes: Dynamics within and between groups*. Oxford: Blackwell.

Brown, R., and Ross, G. (1982). The battle for acceptance: An investigation into the dynamics of intergroup behaviour. In H. Tajfel (Ed.), *Social identity and intergroup relations*. Cambridge: Cambridge University Press.

Calhoun, C. (1991). Indirect relationships and imagined communities: large-scale social integration and the transformation of everyday life. In P. Bourdieu and J. S. Coleman (Eds), *Social theory for a changing society*. Boulder: Westview Press.

Callon, M., and Latour, B. (1981). Unscrewing the big Leviathan: how actors macrostructure reality and how sociologists help them to do so. In K. Knorr-Cetina and A. Cicourel (Eds), *Advances in social theory and methodology*. Boston: Routledge and Kegan Paul.

Carr, D. (1991). *Time, narrative and history.* Bloomingbton: Indiana University Press.

Clark, D. (1974). Technology, diffusion and time-space convergence: the example of the STD telephone. *Arena*, **6**, 181–184.

Cohen, J. (1968). Subjective time. In J. Fraser (Ed.), *The voices of time*. London: Allan Lane.

Collins, A., Gathercole, S., Conway, M., and Morris, P. (Eds), (1993). *Theories of memory.* Hove: Lawrence Erlbaum.

Condor, S. (1984). Womanhood as an aspect of social identity. Unpublished PhD thesis, University of Bristol.

Condor, S. (1989). "Biting into the future": Social change and the social identity of women. In S. Skevington and D. Baker (Eds), *The social identity of women*. London: Sage.

Condor, S. (1990). Social stereotypes and social identity. In D. Abrams and M. Hogg (Eds), *Social identity theory: Constructive and critical advances*. Brighton: Harvester Wheatsheaf.

Condor, S. (1991). Sexism in psychological research. *Feminism and Psychology*, **1**, 430–434.

Condor, S. (in press). "Having history": A social psychological exploration of Anglo–British autostereotypes. In C. Barfot (Ed.), *National and ethnic stereotypes*. Leiden.

Condor, S., Brown, R., and Williams, J. (1987). Social identification and intergroup behaviour. *Quarterly Journal of Social Affairs*, **3**, 299–317.

Condor, S., and Levine, M. "Nobody likes us we don't care": Soccer supporters' constrictions of social identities. In submission.

Connerton, P. (1989). *How societies remember.* Cambridge: Cambridge University Press.

Connolly, W. (1991). *Democratic negotiations of political paradox.* Cornell University: Cornell University Press.

Conway, M. (1990). *Autobiographical memory.* Buckingham: Open University Press.

Danziger, K. (1960). *Construction the subject* . Cambridge: Cambridge University Press.

Davis, J. (1992). History and the people without Europe. In K. Hastrup (Ed.), *Other Histories.* London: Routledge.

de Beauvoir, S. (1953). *The second sex.* London: Cape.

Dean, M. (1994). *Critical and effective histories.* London: Routledge.

Derrida, J. (1972). *Positions.* Paris: Editions de Minuit.

Douglas, M. (1978). Cultural bias. Occasional Paper 35, Royal Institute of Anthropology, London. (Reprinted in M. Douglas (Ed.) (1982). *In the active voice.* London: Routledge and Kegan Paul.)

Douglas, M. (Ed.) (1982). *Essays in the sociology of perception.* London: Routledge and Kegan Paul.

Durkheim, E. (1893). *The division of labour in society.* (English edition: 1933. New York: Macmillan.)

Eiser, J. R. (1986). *Social psychology: Attitudes, cognition and social behaviour.* Cambridge: Cambridge University Press.

Elias, N. (1991). *The society of individuals.* Oxford: Blackwell.

Emler, N., and Hopkins, N. (1990). Reputation, social identity and the self. In D. Abrams and M. Hogg (Eds), *Social identity theory: Constructive and critical advances.* London: Harvester Wheatsheaf.

Fabian, J. (1983). *Time and the other.* New York: Columbia University Press.

Fiske, J., and Hartley, J. (1990). *Reading television.* London: Methuen.

Freeman, M. (1993). *Rewriting the self: History, memory, narrative.* London: Routledge.

Friedman, J. (1985). Our time, their time, world time: The transformation of temporal modes. *Ethnos*, **50**, 168–183.

Game, A. (1990). Nations and identity: Bondi. *New Formations*, **12**, 105–121.

Gergen, K. (1973). Social psychology as history. *Journal of Personality and Social Psychology*, **26**, 309–320.

Gergen, K., and Gergen, M. (1983). Narratives of the self. In T. Sarbin and K. Scheibe (Eds), *Studies in social identity.* New York: Praeger.

Giddens, A. (1979). *Central problems in social theory.* London: Macmillan.

Giddens, A. (1984). *The constitution of society.* Cambridge: Polity Press.

Giddens, A. (1987). *Social theory and modern sociology.* Cambridge: Polity Press.

Giddens, A. (1990). *The consequences of modernity*, Cambridge: Polity Press.

Giddens, A. (1991). *Modernity and self identity.* Cambridge: Polity Press.

Gillis, J. (1994). *Commemorations: The politics of national identity.* Princeton, NJ: Princeton University Press.

Goffman, E. (1968). *Asylums*. Harmondsworth: Penguin.

Handler, R. (1994). Is "identity" a useful cross-cultural concept? In J. Gillis (Ed.), *Commemorations: The politics of national identity*. Princeton, NJ: Princeton University Press.

Hannerz. U. (1992). The global ecumeme as a network of networks. In A. Kuper (Ed.), *Conceptualizing society*. London: Routledge.

Harré, R. (1979). *Social being: A theory for social psychology*. Oxford: Blackwell.

Harré, R. (1993). Identity projects. In G. Breakwell IEd.), *Threatened identities*. Chichester: Wiley.

Haslam, S., Turner, J., Oakes, P., McGarty, C., and Hayes, B. (1992). Context-dependent variation in social stereotyping 1: The effects of intergroup relations as mediated by social change and frame of reference. *European Journal of Social Psychology*, **22**, 3–20.

Heidegger, M. (1962). *Being and time*. Oxford: Blackwell.

Heller, A. (1982). *A theory of history*. London: Routledge and Kegan Paul.

Heller, A. (1984). *Everyday life*. London: Routledge and Kegan Paul.

Henriques, J., Hollway, W., Urwin, C., Venn, C., and Walkerdine, V. (1984). *Changing the subject: Psychology, social regulation and subjectivity*. London: Methuen.

Hobsbawm, E., and Ranger, T. (Eds), (1983). *The invention of tradition*. Cambridge: Cambridge University Press.

Hogg, M. (1992). *The social psychology of group cohesiveness*. London: Harvester Wheatsheaf.

Hogg, M., and Abrams, D. (1988). *Social identifications: A social psychology of intergroup relations and group processes*. London: Routledge.

Hogg, M., and Turner, J. (1987). Intergroup behaviour, self-steorotyping and the salience of social categories. *British Journal of Social Psychology*, **26**, 325–340.

Jhally, S., and Lewis, J. (1992). *Enlightened racism*. Boulder: Westview.

Johnson, J. (AKA B. Latour) (1988). Mixing humans and nonhumans together: The sociology of the door-closer. *Social Problems*, **35**, 298–310.

Kaye, H. (1992). *The education of desire: Marxists and the writing of history*. New York: Routledge.

Kem, S. (1983). *The culture of time and space 1880–1918*. London: Weidenfeld.

Knorr-Cetina, K. (1981). Introduction: The micro-sociological challenge of micro-sociology: towards a reconstruction of social theory and methodology. In K. Knorr-Cetina and A. Cicourel (Eds), *Advances in social theory and methodology*. Boston: Routledge and Kegan Paul.

Knorr-Cetina, K. (1988). The micro-social order: towards a reconception. In N. Fielding (Ed.), *Action and structure*. London: London: Sage.

Landes, D. (1983). *Revolution in time: Clocks and the making of the modern world*. Cambridge, MA: Harvard University Press.

Lasch, C. (1979). *The culture of narcissism*. New York: Norton.

Latour, B. (1986). The powers of association. In J. Law (Ed.), *Power, action and belief*. London: Routledge and Kegan Paul.

Latour, B. (1987). *Science in action: How to follow scientists and engineers through society*. Cambridge MA: Harvard University Press.

Latour, B. (1991). Technology is society made durable. In J. Law (Ed.), *A sociology of monsters*. London: Routledge and Kegan Paul.

Law J. (Ed.), *A sociology of monsters*. London: Routledge and Kegan Paul.

Levine, J. M. (1995). "Till death us do part": constructions of social identity and commitment by British soccer supporters. Paper presented at the Social Psychology Section of the BPS annual conference, York, September.

Lowenthal, D. (1992). The death of the future. In S. Wallman (Ed.), *Contemporary futures: perspectives from social anthropology*. London: Routledge.

Luhmann, N. (1989). *Gleichzeitigkeit und Synchronisation*. Vienna: Institut for Soziologie.

Lury, C. (in press). *Possessing the self*. London: Routledge.

Marx, K. (1906). *Capital*. Chicago: Kem.

Merton, R. (1957). *Social theory and social structure*.

Moreland, R., Levine, J., and Cini, M. (1993). Group socialization: the role of commitment. In M. Hogg and D. Abrams (Eds), *Group motivation: Social psychological perspectives*. London: Harvester Wheatsheaf.

Moscovici, S. (1972). Society and theory in social psychology. In J. Israel and H. Tajfel (Eds), *The context of social psychology: A critical assessment*. London: Academic Press.

Nowotny, H. (1992). Time and social theory. *Time and Society*, **1**, 421–454.
Nowotny, H. (1994). *Time: The modern and postmodern experience*. Cambridge: Polity Press.
Oakes, P. (1987). The salience of social categories. In J. C. Turner *et al.* (Eds), *Rediscovering the social group: A self-categorization theory*. Oxford: Blackwell.
Oakes, P., Haslam, A., and Turner, J. (1994). *Stereotyping and social reality*. Oxford: Blackwell.
Oakes, P., Turner, J., and Haslam, A. (1991). Perceiving people as group members: The role of fit in the salience of social categories. *British Journal of Social Psychology*, **30**, 125–144.
Parsons, T. (1951). *The social system*. Glencoe, IL: Free Press.
Peukert, D. J. K. (1991). *The Weimar Republic*. London: Allen Lane.
Potter, J., and Wetherell, M. (1987). *Discourse and social psychology*. London: Sage.
Reicher, S. D. (1982). The determination of collective behavbiour. In H. Tajfel (Ed.), *Social identity and intergroup relations*. Cambridge: Cambridge University Press.
Reicher, S. D. (1987). Crowd behaviour as social action. In J. C. Turner *et al.* (Eds), *Rediscovering the social group: A self-categorization theory*. Oxford: Blackwell.
Reicher, S. D., and Hopkins, N. (in press). Seeking influence through characterising self-categories: an analysis of anti-abortionist rhetoric. *British Journal of Social Psychology*.
Sachdev, I., and Bourhis, R. (1993). Ethnolinguistic vitality: Some motivational and cognitive considerations. In M. Hogg and D. Abrams (Eds), *Group motivation: Social psychological perspectives*. Brighton: Harvester Wheatsheaf.
Said, E. (1978). *Orientalism*. London: Routledge and Kegan Paul.
Sampson, E. E. (1977). Psychology and the American ideal. *Journal of Personality and Social Psychology*, **35**, 767–782.
Sampson, E. E. (1989). The challenge of social change for psychology: Globalization and psychology's theory of person. *American Psychologist*, 914–921.
Schwartz, B. (1982). "The people" in history. In R. Johnson *et al.* (Eds), *Making histories*. London: Hutchinson.
Shaw, J. (1994). Punctuality and the everyday ethics of time. *Time and Society*, **3**, 79–97.
Sherif, M., and Sherif, C. (1953). *Groups in harmony and tension*. New York: Harper.
Shils, E. (1981). *Tradition*. London: Faber.
Shotter, J. (1980). Action, joint action and intentionality. In M. Brenner (Ed.), *The structure of action*. Oxford: Blackwell.
Shotter, J. (1993). *Cultural politics of everyday life*. London: Open University Press.
Shotter, J., and Gergen, K. (1989). *Texts of identity*. London: Sage.
Strathern, M. (1992). *After nature*. Cambridge: Cambridge University Press.
Tajfel, H. (1969). Social and cultural factors in perception. In G. Lindzey and E. Aronson (Eds), *The handbook of social psychology*, 2nd ed, Vol. 3. Reading, MA: Addison-Wesley.
Tajfel, H. (1970). Experiments in intergroup discrimination. *Scientific American*, **223**, 96–102.
Tajfel, H. (1972). Experiments in a vacuum. In J. Israel and H. Tajfel (Eds), *The context of social psychology: A critical assessment*. London: Academic Press.
Tajfel, H. (1974a). Social identity and intergroup behaviour. *Social Science Information*, **13**, 65–93.
Tajfel, H. (1974b). Intergroup behaviour, social comparison and social change. Katz-Newcomb Lectures, Ann Arbor (unpublished).
Tajfel, H. (1975a). The exit of social mobility and the voice of social change: Notes on the social psychology of intergroup relations. *Social Science Information*, **14**, 101–118.
Tajfel, H. (1975b). Social psychology and social processes. Paper presented at a conference on Methods in Social Psychology, Bologna, December.
Tajfel, H. (1977). Social psychology and social reality. *New Society*, **39**, 653–654.
Tajfel, H. (Ed.) (1978a). *Differentiation between social groups: Studies in the social psychology of intergroup relations*. London: Academic Press.
Tajfel, H. (1978b). *The social psychology of minorities*. London: Minority Rights Group.
Tajfel, H. (1980a) Experimental studies of intergroup behaviour. In M. Jeeves (Ed.), *Survey of social psychology, No. 43*. London: George Allen and Unwin.
Tajfel, H. (1980b). The "New Look" and social differentiation: A semi-Brunerian perspective. In D. Olson (Ed.), *The social foundations of language and thought: Essays in honor of J. S. Bruner*. New York: Norton.
Tajfel, H. (1981a). *Human groups and social categories: Studies in social psychology*. Cambridge: Cambridge University Press.

Tajfel, H. (1981b). Social stereotypes and social groups. In J. C. Turner and H. Giles (Eds), *Intergroup behaviour.* Oxford: Blackwell.

Tajfel, H. (1982a). Instrumentality, identity and social comparison. In H. Tajfel (Ed.), *Social identity and intergroup relations.* Cambridge: Cambridge University Press.

Tajfel, H. (1982b). Social psychology of intergroup relations. *Annual Review of Psycholgy,* **33**, 1–39.

Tajfel, H. (1984). Intergroup relations, social myths and social justice in social psychology. In H. Tajfel (Ed.), *The social dimension: European developments in social psychology,* (Vol. 2). Cambridge: Cambridge University Press.

Tajfel, H., Billig, M., Bundy, R., and Flament, C. (1971). Social categorization and intergroup behaviour. *European Journal of Social Psychology,* **1**, 149–177.

Tappan, M. (1991). Narrative, authorship and the development of moral authority. In *New Directions for Child Development,* **54**, 5–25.

Taylor, C. (1989). *Sources of the self.* Cambridge: Cambridge University Press.

Taylor, D., and McKirnan, D. (1984). A five-stage model of intergroup relations. *British Journal of Social Psychology,* **23**, 291–300.

Thompson, E. P. (1963). *The Making of the English working class.* New York: Vintage Books.

Turner, J. C. (1982). Towards a cognitive redefinition of the social group. In H. Tajfel (Ed.), *Social identity and intergroup relations.* Cambridge: Cambridge University Press.

Turner, J. C. (1987). Introducing the problem: individual and group. In J. C. Turner *et al.* (Eds), *Rediscovering the social group: A self-categorization theory.* Oxford: Blackwell.

Turner, J. C., Hogg, M., Oakes, P., Reicher, S., and Wetherell. M. (1987). *Rediscovering the social group: A self-categorization theory.* Oxford: Blackwell.

Turner, J. C., and Oakes, P. (1986). The significance of the social identity concept for social psychology with reference to individualism, interactionism and social influence. *British Journal of Social Psychology,* **25**, 237–252.

Turner, J. C., Oakes, P., Haslam, S. A., and McGarty, C. (1994). Self and collective: Cognition and social context., *Personality and Social Psychology Bulletin,* **20**, 454–463.

van Knippenberg, A. (1984). Intergroup differences in group perceptions. In H. Tajfel (Ed.), *The social dimension: European developments in social psychology,* Vol. 2. Cambridge: Cambridge University Press.

van Knippenberg, A., and Ellemers, N. (1993). Strategies in intergroup relations. In M. Hogg and D. Abrams (Eds), *Group motivation: Social psychological perspectives.* Brighton: Harvester Wheatsheaf.

Weber, M. (1930). *The Protestant ethnic and the spirit of capitalism.* London: Allen and Unwin.

Wetherell, M. (1982). Cross-cultural studies of minimal groups: Implications for the social identity theory of intergroup relations. In H. Tajfel (Ed.), *Social identity and intergroup relations.* Cambridge: Cambridge University press.

Wolf, E. (1956). Aspects of group relations in a complex society. *Americal Anthropologist,* **58**, 1065–1078.

Wright, P. (1985). *On living in an old country.* London: Verso.

Zerubavel, E. (1981). *Hidden rhythms: Schedules and calendars in social life.* Chicago: University of Chicago Press.

Zerubavel, E. (1982). The standardization of time: A sociohistorical perspective. *American Journal of Sociology.* **1**, 1–12.

12

Social Identity and Social Change: Rethinking the Context of Social Psychology

STEPHEN REICHER

Department of Psychology, University of St Andrews

Contents

A Return to the Repressed

If a concept is a tool, and if its significance depends upon the explanatory work it is designed to perform, then the very idea of social identity is all too frequently misunderstood. On the one hand, it is easy to overextend the concept by ignoring the context of its usage. Social identity was not intended as a general model of identity *per se*. In introducing the concept, Tajfel (1978) explicitly seeks to avoid "endless and often sterile discussions as to what 'is' identity" (p. 63). He acknowledges that there are many other fascinating questions as to the origins and development of identity. However his explicit and limited interest is in how aspects of the self are relevant to his particular concern with the psychology of intergroup behaviour. More recently, it could be argued that self-categorization theory has extended the use of the social identity to an explanation of group psychology in general (Turner *et al.*, 1987, 1993). Nonetheless, it remains true that social identity remains a useful concept precisely because its field of applicability is limited but clearly delineated.

On the other hand, a constricted view of context can lead to social identity being conceptualized too narrowly. In part, at least, this relates to a question of method. As with most social psychology, research in the social identity tradition has been dominated by laboratory experimentation. Whatever the strengths and weaknesses of such methods (see, for instance, the interchange between Billig, 1994 and Spears, 1994), there are certain things they are not very good at. One is the exploration of a historical dimension to human action. For reasons of practicality and in order to avoid a profusion of conditions, laboratory experiments are predominantly one-shot interventions. If history is excluded, then an awareness of social change necessarily goes with it.

This may go some way towards explaining a puzzle that goes to the heart of social identity research. In one of the earliest discussions of the issue, Tajfel (1972) stresses that social identities are not simply means of simplifying a complex social reality. Rather, they are a means of both creating and defining one's place in a dynamic social world. Above all, and the original phrase is stressed in italics, social identity *"is a guide to action"* (p. 298). Such a perspective impels one forward, for not everybody can be satisfied with their social place, and even if they are it needs work to be maintained. Therefore, to talk of social place inevitably raises the issue of whether social change will be sought or impeded. And, if social identity is bound up with the analysis of social place, it must also be bound up with the analysis of social change. In a later chapter that builds upon his earlier sketch, Tajfel makes this quite explicit: "social identity is understood here as an intervening causal mechanism in situations of 'objective' social change [c.f. Tajfel, 1972]—observed, anticipated, feared, desired or prepared by the individuals involved" (1978, p. 86).

For Tajfel, then, the notion that people will strive to achieve positive social identity by positively differentiating the ingroup from the outgroup was merely the prelude to asking further questions relating to social change. What happens when group members find themselves negatively defined in relation to other groups? What are the conditions under which they will remain passive as opposed to active? When will they adopt collective as opposed to individual strategies of change? What are the options for collective action? It was with how and when the oppressed and the marginalized (more neutrally described as "minorities") can change their lot that Tajfel was concerned both intellectually and personally. Yet, for all this, the emphasis on social change has been lost—if not repressed—in the ever-burgeoning field of "social identity" research.

In 1987 a "Social Identity Conference"—the only one of its kind—was held in Exeter. Of the thirty-five papers and presentations only four even touched on the issue of social change and only one had it as the central concern. By contrast, the number of references to the "minimal group experiments" (where allocation of people to groups on trivial or even random grounds leads participants to give greater rewards to ingroup members than outgroup members, even at the cost of reducing absolute level of reward to ingroup) was striking. Even more striking was a tendency to refer to "social identity theory" as if it were limited to an explanation of the differentiation found in these experiments in terms of social identification, social comparison and the desire for positive social identity. In other words, what for Tajfel was a point of departure was widely treated as an end in itself and social change therefore dropped off the agenda.

On those occasions where the issue of social change is addressed, the work shares two characteristics. First of all, it is largely confined to investigating whether Tajfel's various assertions about relationships between variables can be empirically grounded. Such questions include whether collective action is related to collective identification (Kelly, 1993; Kelly and Breinlinger, 1995), whether the adoption of collective as opposed to individualistic change strategies is related to such factors as the permeability of group boundaries and the stability of intergroup status relations (Ellemers *et al.*, 1990, 1992; van Knippenberg, 1987), and whether Tajfel is correct in his identification of strategies of social change (Williams and Giles, 1978). This is in marked contrast to other areas of social identity research where the forward development of concepts and theory predominates over retrospective validation.

Secondly, as Kelly and Breinlinger (1995) note, psychologists remain reluctant to venture out of their laboratories even when they are looking at social change. Field studies of when and how people participate in collective action are remarkably rare. Characteristically, the researcher will manipulate such variables as group salience, ability to pass between groups and ability to challenge intergroup inequalities, and then observe the results in terms of group action. Hence, the key parameters of context are fixed in advance and social action is seen as a dependent variable. This makes it hard to see how social structural variables—and the ways in which they are perceived—may themselves arise out of social action. It is even harder to observe the reciprocal process by which action and context constantly impinge upon each other.

Thus, the same methodological constraints which have marginalized the study of change within social identity research are employed even where the importance of change is recognized and they serve to limit the way in which it is conceptualized. It may seem particularly ironic to study social dynamics in a way that excludes the processes by which people create and re-create the conditions of their social being. Perhaps it is a warning for a discipline which often seems to prioritize the tools of enquiry over the jobs they are meant to do. As Moscovici (1972) noted, psychology is afflicted by a fetishistic attachment to the one method of laboratory experimentation, seeing it as the sole mark of true science. Yet, he argues; "social psychology will be unable to formulate dangerous truths while it adheres to this fetishism. This is its principal handicap, and this is what forces it to focus on minor problems and to remain a minor pursuit. All really successful sciences managed to produce dangerous truths for which they fought and of which they envisioned the consequences" (p. 66).

The aim of this chapter is to reassert the importance of social change to social identity research. Indeed it should be a criterion for the adequacy of any social psychological theory, and especially a theory relating to groups, that it provides an account of change. After all, for all the attempts to hold back the tide, society and human understanding never stand still. Moreover, whether we look microsocially or at the major events that change our world, collective action is always to the fore: 1789, 1830, 1848, 1917, 1989—these dates alone are sufficient to make the point.

In arguing for putting change back at the core of the agenda where it rightfully belongs, I am not simply arguing for a return to Tajfel's promised land from which we have somehow erred. Part of my argument is that, while Tajfel may have stressed the importance of change and described some of its elements, he never did provide an *explanation* of the phenomena. The supposition that he did has hamstrung the continuing trickle of research on change from a social identity perspective. Moreover, I shall argue that an adequate account requires us to reassess central concepts within this perspective such as "context" and even "social identity" itself.

However, before moving on to these arguments, a personal note on "dangerous truths" is in order. My first acquaintance with Henri Tajfel, with traditional group theory, and with the social identity tradition came in my first year as an undergraduate at Bristol University. It was a period where student radicalism, albeit in decline, was still alive. In the midst of the course there was an occupation of Senate House (the University administration building) over the specific issue of nursery provision and a general concern with equal access for women to university. Two things struck me from this coincidence of events. The first was a sense of the contradiction between what mainstream psychology was saying about groups and my own experience of group action. Although group theories described collective action as intellectually impoverished if not downright irrational, I had never come across the level of intellectual debate in mass meetings which would stretch on—sometimes throughout the night. And if psychologists implied that groups were at best conservative and at worst socially destructive, my overwhelming experience was one of transformation—on a personal level, in that my own understanding and sense of self altered dramatically through participation, but also on a social level in that the occupation went some way towards altering the institutional position of women. At least some women could come to university who previously were excluded.

If this mismatch provided a basis for challenging group psychology, the motivation to do so was enhanced by the active way in which traditional psychological ideas were employed during the events. This is the second thing that struck me. As we were inside Senate House, so the authorities sought to discredit the occupation as mindless. Variously the activists were described as getting carried away, as innocents misled by agitators and as professional activists with ulterior motives. While the language was less technical, these arguments faithfully reproduced the various conceptual strands which I met in the lecture room. Thus, traditional psychological ideas did not only omit the possibility of social change in theory, they were actively used in practice to undermine collective attempts at social change.

If this is a relatively trivial example, it nevertheless illustrates a larger point. A concern with social change is not just an abstract intellectual exercise. To imagine change is, as Tajfel (1978) indicates, one of the conditions for its occurrence and psychology cannot avoid its place within the cultural imagination. Therefore we can serve either to reify the status quo and pathologize anything that stands outside it, or else envision alternative worlds and explicate the processes by which they are achieved. Whether or not a psychology of social change will produce dangerous truths is an open question. However, it is certain that its absence will condemn us to conservatism. For political as well as for intellectual reasons, a return to the repressed priorities of social identity theory is long overdue.

Social Change in the Social Identity Tradition

The nearest thing to a manifesto for the emergence of a distinctively European tradition in social psychology was Israel and Tajfel's (1972) text *The context of social psychology.* The book can be read as a critique of reification in social psychology: the way in which human behaviour is considered without reference to its social context and the resulting consequences. First of all, the social determination of behaviour is ignored. Secondly, because an examination of social significance is possible only if the links between actor and social world are considered, the meaningful and symbolic character of human action is eliminated. Thirdly, since the removal of action from a specific location renders it timeless and universal, social change is also ruled out of court.

The critique also has a reflexive element. Traditionally, there is a tendency to ignore the socially situated nature of psychological theory: how our ideas are shaped by current models of the human subject, how our research questions, methods, and analyses are influenced by our values and, perhaps most crucially, what the social significance of our work might be. That is why Tajfel's introduction suggests that, although the book has no dedication, had there been one it would have read "to our students and colleagues who care, whether they agree or disagree" (1972, p. 13).

These arguments informed both the concerns of early European social psychology and the ways in which they were addressed. If the problem is a desocialization of psychology through ignoring context, then it is necessary to explore the social dimensions of human being through considering actors in context. Consequently, the issues of social determination and, especially, social change rose to the top of the agenda. Indeed, it is worth quoting from Tajfel's introduction again: "Ideally the central issue of social psychology should be the study of psychological processes accompanying, determining, and determined by social change" (1972, p. 4). Such ideals were translated into practice in the work of the two best known European social psychologists: Moscovici and Tajfel himself.

Moscovici's work on social representations (e.g. Moscovici, 1961, 1984, 1993) deals with the inherently consensual and ideological nature of individual understanding but it is also concerned with the way in which understanding is transformed, how the unfamiliar becomes familiar and how familiarity itself mutates. Moreover, his work on minority influence (Moscovici, 1976) starts from the observation that conventional models always imply that influence serves to reproduce existing social relations. As a counter-balance, Moscovici seeks to examine how active minorities may succeed in redrawing the social landscape.

Social identity theory posits the social determination of individual psychology on at least two levels. In the first place, the very concept of social identity as "that part of an individual's self-concept which derives from his knowledge of his membership of a social group (or groups) together with the value and emotional significance attached to that membership" (Tajfel, 1978, p. 63) relates selfhood to a broad ideological context. If, on the one hand, social identities are intensely personal in the sense of defining who we are and where we stand (to the extent that people are even prepared to die for the good of social collectivities such as religions and nations (Reicher, 1993a,b), then, on the other hand, the meaning of any social identity cannot be reduced to any particular individual. What it means to be British, Catholic or whatever is something that is a historical function of politics, economy and culture. In the second place, social identity theory (Tajfel, 1978, 1982; Tajfel and Turner, 1986) as well as its development into self-categorization theory (Turner *et al.*, 1987, 1993) acknowledges that the meanings of any given category will be a function of the immediate social situation: groups define themselves through comparisons with such other groups as are present in a given context.

However, as I have stressed, Tajfel was equally interested in social change (Tajfel, 1974, 1978, 1981). Moreover in his hitherto unpublished Katz-Newcomb lectures of 1974—probably the most comprehensive of his accounts—Tajfel stresses once again that this is not a secondary interest within social identity theory. If anything, it is the theory's *raison d'être*. The very concept of social identity is understood as a mediating variable in the explanation of change.

What Tajfel means by this is that, if group members desire positive social identity, then a tension arises when they discover themselves to be negatively defined in relation to other groups. It is this tension which provides the dynamic for change. However, it does not automatically follow that change will occur, nor is it inevitable that the change will be collective. Before this happens a number of conditions must be met. Tajfel's account is essentially a description of what the crucial conditions are.

First of all, where individuals find themselves to be subordinated as members of a group, they might be expected to adopt an individualistic strategy of seeking personal advancement by denying group identity (what Tajfel (1975) following Hirschman (1970) calls "exit"). However, such an approach is only feasible where group boundaries are perceived to be permeable and where the individual is not automatically limited because of his or her group membership. In Tajfel's terms, the strategy of "exit" depends upon a belief structure of social mobility. Conversely, the precondition for a collective strategy of seeking personal advancement by changing the position of the group as a whole (which Tajfel, 1975, again following Hirschman, terms "voice") will depend upon seeing group boundaries as impermeable. For Tajfel, the strategy of voice depends upon a belief structure of social change. Thus, he uses the example of South Africa under apartheid as a situation in which the oppressed black majority can only advance by challenging its structural exclusion and he quotes the work of Danziger (1963) and Geber (1972) who use a technique of "future autobiographies" to show that, in consequence, black people speculate about their fate in collective as opposed to individual terms (Tajfel, 1978).

A belief that individual mobility is impossible may be necessary but it is not sufficient for collective action to occur. It is also necessary that a change in the group's position is seen as both morally desirable and practically possible. To take the two in turn, Tajfel argues that it is only when domination is seen as illegitimate that comparisons with the dominant group become possible and hence the issue of change arises. Where hierarchical or unequal social relations are seen as legitimate (as an example, the Indian caste system is invoked) change is not even a matter at issue. On the question of practicality, Tajfel employs the term "cognitive alternatives" to denote a situation in which group members can envisage a future in which they are no longer subordinated, which renders their present situation contingent or "insecure" and which makes action for change a realistic option.

Where all these conditions are satisfied, collective action is predicted to ensue, but the form this action will take remains open. Three options are outlined—subordinate group members may try to: redefine themselves in terms of the characteristics of the dominant group; redefine characteristics previously seen as negative in positive terms; or else adopt a strategy of "social creativity" whereby, through the diffusion of new ideologies, new group characteristics are made which have a positively valued distinctiveness from the superior group. Tajfel also deals with dominant group members—albeit less fully. Very rarely will they accept the injustice of their dominance and either leave the group or else accept challenges from the subordinate group. Much more frequently, they will respond to any challenges by increased discrimination and by the creation of new ideologies which differentiate them from the subordinate group as well as justifying repression.

In sum, Tajfel presents us with the factors involved in a psychology of social change: belief structures, perceptions of legitimacy, cognitive alternatives and strategies of action. More properly, he presents some of the factors that are involved, since recent research in the social movement literature points to the importance of additional variables such as, perceptions of collective action as legitimate, perceptions of the forms of collective action that are proposed as potentially successful, and self-identification as an activist (Kelly and Breilinger,

1995; Klandermans, 1989; Klandermans *et al.*, 1988; Morris and McClurg-Mueller, 1992).

However, the important thing is not so much the number of factors in Tajfel's account, but rather the status of the account as a whole. In effect, it is a list of (some of) the psychological ingredients that go towards producing social change. However it cannot in itself be characterized as a psychological model, let alone a theory, of social change. Indeed, if it were to be taken as such, there are dangers that crucial issues may remain unexplored and the consequent vision of change—both in terms of means and possibilities—would be severely limited. There are at least three major areas in which Tajfel's account would need to be elaborated before the term "model" could properly be applied.

First of all, the very concept of change requires clarification. It is not simply that the account is limited to the psychological precursors of psychological change as opposed to the factors which lead to involvements in movements for structural change (after all, the various civil rights movements are as much if not more about changing laws, altering institutional practices, challenging exclusion and redistributing resources as they are about members evaluating themselves positively), but also that the vision of psychological change is itself limited.

In a book that is often taken as a call for black separatism, Carmichael and Hamilton (1967) argue that black people must come together in order to challenge those psychological and structural impediments that stop them participating on equal terms with whites. In other words, autonomous organization may be a means, but the end is to render irrelevant racial categorization. Similarly, Michael Farrell—a founder member of one of the radical republican organizations in Northern Ireland—argues that it is futile to try and get Catholic and Protestant workers to unite in a sectarian state. Rather, the priority must be to organize amongst those who are willing to challenge the nature of the state and hence create the conditions for future unity (Farrell, 1980). It would be easy to find similar examples elsewhere. The general point is that even where people organize around a particular form of difference (be it racial, ethnic, national, religious or whatever) that does not mean that action is limited to redefining the terms of that difference. Rather, their aim may be to destroy the system of difference entirely and reassert another. Perhaps the most famous expression of this view is Nelson Mandela's statement at the Rivonia trials of 1964. After arguing that "political division, based on colour, is entirely artificial and, when it disappears, so will the domination of one colour group by another", he concludes with the oft-quoted words: "During my lifetime, I have dedicated myself to this struggle of the African people. I have fought against white domination and I have fought against black domination. I have cherished the ideal of a democratic and free society in which all persons live together in harmony and with equal opportunities. It is an ideal which I hope to live for and to achieve. But if needs be, it is an ideal for which I am prepared to die" (1978, p. 175). As Mandela's recent donning of a Springbok shirt at the rugby World Cup final makes clear, now as then the category "African" involves both "black" and "white". Moreover, it supersedes them.

In limiting change to the redefinition of group characteristics, the definition of social identity is reduced to a set of characteristics whose major importance is whether they are evaluated positively or negatively. To define social identity in such terms sits uneasily with Tajfel's arguments elsewhere that identity is something involved in the dynamics of practice: "a guide to action". How can a set of traits, attributes, or whatever allow one to organize and manipulate the complexities of our shifting social relations? Moreover, such a static conception makes it difficult to see how identity is bound up with the processes of social change. I argued above that the very conception of social identity helps overcome the dualism of self and society. I shall argue below that this conception needs to be refined if we are to overcome the dualism of social determination and social change (c.f. Reicher, 1987a).

The second set of issues which needs to be elaborated has to do with the interactions between terms. Most obviously, Tajfel outlines the possible strategies of change that may be adopted by subordinate and dominant groups. However, no mention is made of the way in which the strategy of each group may be affected by the actions of the other. Similarly, there is little consideration of the ways in which other variables—such as belief structures, perceptions of legitimacy and cognitive alternatives—may be affected by the responses to initial forms of collective action. For instance, there is much evidence that early modern rioting was often done in the name of the king or queen in order to reclaim what were seen as traditional rights (Stephenson, 1979). Whether their sense of loyalty was undermined or not depended upon the way in which officers of the monarch responded. Similarly, as Therborn (1980) points out, revolutionary movements rarely if ever start off with a blueprint of a new society—or even any sense of a new society. It is only through their actions, the retaliations of those in power or else their impotence in the face of mass actions, that the existing regimes are delegitimized and possible futures are glimpsed. What is more, many struggles involve more than two parties and it is essential to examine the more complex interplay between them. For instance, the rise of the Muslim League culminating in the partition of India and the creation of an independent Pakistan can easily be mystified as expressing an essentialist Muslim identity [see, for instance, the Lahore resolution (Khan, 1988) as a key expression of Muslim nationalism] unless one examines the role of the British Imperialism. The League gained power and credibility only when the British gave them political office as a means of undermining the Congress Alliance's "Quit India" movement (Singh, 1987). All in all, no model of social change can hope to explain what any single party does apart from the interaction between them all.

This raises the third and possibly the most crucial issue. As things stand, the variables of interest are simply stated as if they confront the subject from without and constitute "entry conditions" for the process of social change. Before the mass acts they must see individual progress as futile, inequality as illegitimate and alternatives as possible. But where do these understandings come from? How do they develop? Unless these questions are answered, any model of social change must ultimately defeat itself. The explanation founders upon pre-given understandings which are either a feature of the structural and ideological context, or else derive from stable intrapsychic beliefs. Either one has a social determinism which ultimately denies the agency of actors and makes them puppets of transcendental understandings, or else a pure voluntarism whereby action pays no heed to social reality.

On the whole, where Tajfel does give illustrations, it is to point to the importance of contextual factors. Thus beliefs of social change derive from the structural barriers of apartheid, or else perceptions of legitimacy reflect the hegemony of the caste system in India. For social change as for social determination, Tajfel is concerned to put behaviour back in its social context. His stress is on the way in which various aspects of this context influence the occurrence or non-occurrence of social change. Billig (1987) points out that the meaning of any term is dependent upon the argumentative context in which it is expressed. Against the background of a psychology which systematically decontextualized human understanding and action, it is entirely understandable why Tajfel should have wished to stress the importance of context to the extent of overstressing its fixity and solidity. However such a concept is clearly inimitable to his project of explaining change.

This tendency is not limited to early versions but is equally apparent in the most recent developments of the tradition. Thus, one of the key propositions of self-categorization theory (Haslam and Turner, 1992; Haslam *et al.*, 1992; Oakes *et al.*, 1994; Turner *et al.*, 1987, Turner *et al.*, 1993) is that the definition of social identity will be a function of the comparative context in which groups find themselves. This means that, far from being rigid and unchangeable, group level perceptions (stereotypes) will systematically vary as a function of who else is present in the context. This variability does not display the distorted nature of stereotyping—quite the opposite. Stereotypes reflect social reality and it is because reality is relational that stereotypes alter as relations change.

There is much to recommend this view—most notably its attack on the mainstream social cognition view of group perception as inherently faulty (just the most recent in the long history of psychologies which propose that the individual is always superior and hence preferable to the collective). However, as I have argued elsewhere (Reicher, 1993a; Reicher and Hopkins, in press a,b), the problem is that social reality is taken as self-evident and hence the relationship between reality and categorization is entirely one way: reality determines self-categorization. This is to ignore that the definition, both of context and of who is included within it, is often a matter of fierce controversy. It is also to ignore that context is made up of the ways in which subjects categorize themselves and these categories also form the basis from which people seek to restructure the context.

Rather than seeing context as something external to and determining of human understanding in general and social identity in particular, it is necessary to develop a perspective which acknowledges how context may itself be made of identities and the actions which flow from them. What we need is a new way of looking at context and its relation to identity. However, in order to do so, we need to take on board the other two issues that I have raised. First of all, any new perspective must involve an interactive element and must also consider the development of interactions over time. Secondly, such a perspective must change our view, not only of context but also of social identity. In order to elaborate these points I shall use some work on change in crowd contexts as illustration.

Crowds, contestation and the context of change

It may seem ironic to root an analysis of social change in the study of crowds. After all, the traditional view has it that crowd members lose all sense of self, all control over behaviour and hence are "only powerful for destruction" (Le Bon, 1895, translated 1947). Even those who repudiate the Le Bonian approach still maintain a distinction between crowds and social movements, with only the latter seen as motors of change (Milgram and Toch, 1969; Tajfel, 1978). Such a distinction is, however, difficult to maintain if one considers that crowd incidents may often instigate social movements—the rise of the gay liberation movement after Stonewall being perhaps the most significant recent example. Moreover, crowd action may often form an ideologically coherent and politically effective component of such movements: E. P. Thompson's resonant phrase "collective bargaining by riot" summarizes the point with admirable brevity (Thompson, 1971, 1991). More recently, it could be argued that, for all the ways in which they were condemned as irrational and counter-productive at the time, the American riots of the 1960s and 1970s did more to generate responses to the exclusion of at least a section of the black population than a decade of boycotts, sit-ins and peaceful demonstrations (Allen, 1970; Frazier, 1962). Even Martin Luther King, who eschewed all but non-violent tactics, acknowledged that the riots were "the voice of the oppressed".

If this is so, then it can be argued that those traditional theories which characterize crowds as generically irrational serve not only to obscure the social character of mass action but also act politically to silence the oppressed. It was with these twin concerns in mind that my initial studies of the crowd were undertaken (Reicher, 1982, 1984, 1987a). Much of this work concentrated on the so-called St. Pauls riot of 1980. This was the first of the British inner city disturbances of the 1980s and took place in an area of the city of Bristol in which there was a relatively large black population. The "riot" arose out of a police raid on a black-owned cafe and the arrest of its owner. Events lasted over eight hours, during which the police were driven out of the area, police officers and police property was stoned, and widespread looting took place.

In brief, I argued that people do not lose their identity in the crowd but rather shift from acting in terms of personal identity to acting in terms of the relevant social identity. Correspondingly, people do not lose control over their behaviour in the crowd, but rather control shifts to those values and understandings by which this identity is defined. It may be that the situational meaning of this identity within the crowd context needs to be elaborated and that a variety of interpretations are possible. Nonetheless, the range is limited for there are many interpretations that would clearly be dissonant with the broader identity.

In short, crowd action is socially meaningful because people act in terms of shared social self-definitions. Correspondingly, we should not dismiss crowd action as senseless but rather listen carefully to what it tells us about the understandings of groups whose views are characteristically ignored. As the historian Reddy has written of working class crowds in Rouen: "the targets of these crowds thus glitter in the eye of history as signs of the labourers' conception of the nature of society" (1977, p. 84).

Whatever their merits in terms of reasserting the social coherence of mass action, these studies are vulnerable to criticism on grounds of social change. To start with, the issue of change is largely ignored. Analysis of St. Pauls concentrates on one phase of the events, when conflict with the police had started and before the police withdrew. The question of transitions from phase to phase, therefore, does not arise and possible differences between phases are excluded from study. This empirical limitation is matched by an analytic focus upon the way in which a pre-given identity determines the shape of crowd behaviour. Even if some room for manoeuvre is allowed in terms of situational interpretations, the contours of the superordinate identity are taken as fixed. Once again, the question of how self-understanding may itself change through the process of crowd action is not addressed.

Nonetheless, even where it is not sought, the issue of social change is hard to repress entirely. Like grass through tarmac, it always manages to poke through. The day after the "St. Pauls riot" there was something akin to a victory party on the green where conflict had started. The music that was played was specifically anti-authority and it was matched by the behaviour of the crowd members who smoked cannabis openly in front of the watching police. The significance of such acts was encapsulated by the ways in which participants talked about the "riot" itself: "we took on the police and beat them. They will never again treat us with contempt . . . they will respect us now", or else: "The colour of your skin determines everything. We can't beat them in the court, but we defeated them on the streets" (Reicher, 1984, p. 16). In other words, if the conflict arose over what were seen by participants as unwarranted police interventions into the life of the St. Pauls community, and if crowd action was specifically directed at agencies of external control, so the event was seen as redefining relationships with these outsiders. The party was both a celebration and an assertion of this changed relationship.

What renders this all the more significant is the fact that participants did not only refer to social change in terms of social relations, they also referred to themselves in similar terms. When asked to describe crowd members or else to define their identity, no-one responded in terms of attributes or traits. Rather, they talked of "being from St. Pauls" in terms of their social location (Reicher, 1987a,b). The predominant way of doing so was in relation to the position of being black in Britain. Sometimes this was explicit. Thus, one youth argued that being from St Pauls was like being black in terms of being denied jobs, being harassed by the police and generally being discriminated against. Another participant claimed of the crowd as a whole that "politically they were all black". Sometimes, the link was stated more generally. As one crowd member put it: "I think it was quite honestly a case of us against them. Us, the oppressed section of society, if you like, against the police, against authority basically" (Reicher, 1984, p. 13). At yet other times, the link was with the core experience of black people. When Desmond Pierre of the St. Pauls Defence Campaign was asked about the rationale for the organization, he responded that "we are defending ourselves on a lot of issues, but the main one is the right to lead a free life" (Reicher, 1984, p. 14). If a racialized form of oppression defines being from St. Pauls, then defending St. Pauls means the reassertion of autonomy and control.

This way of conceptualizing identity has much in common with Billig's (1995) view of national stereotypes and self-stereotypes. He argues that they are not so much descriptions as theories about the social world. Similarly, I would argue that for the people of St. Pauls, and for people more generally, identity is a model of where one stands within a system of social relations. It is therefore simultaneously a theory of the way in which the world works and an analysis of the options and actions open to the subject given his or her position in it. Moreover, the model involves evaluative stances: in the case under consideration, oppression is wrong, autonomy is a right, resistance is permissible if not required. In this sense, identity is more than a passive reflection of what is. It is a statement of what ought to be. Social identity is always, in part, an active project.

The advantage of such a formulation is threefold. First of all, it is adequate in terms of Tajfel's original formulation of social identity as "a guide to action" (Tajfel, 1972). Unlike a trait adjective checklist, identity as a model of self in social relations prescribes both what one can do and what one should do. Secondly, it overcomes a contradiction between identity process and identity content which continues to characterize work in the broad social identity tradition. Thus, even if recent studies of stereotyping in the self-categorization tradition insist that the group definition depends upon and varies with the social relations obtaining in context, they continue to operationalize (if not conceptualize) identity as a set of traits (e.g. Haslam and Turner, 1992; Haslam *et al.*, 1992; Oakes *et al.*, 1994). But if social identity is a function of social relations, it is surely more consistent to see it as represented in terms of social relations. Thirdly, and of most direct concern here, such a conception carries us forward in searching for an understanding of social change.

I have argued that the major problem for social identity theorists in explaining social change lies in the separation of context from the self and a one-way flow of determination from the former to the latter. By defining identity in relation to the structure of social reality and by acknowledging the two-sided nature of this relation (identity is both a theory of how things are and a project for how they should be) then at least we start with concepts addressed to the problems they are meant to solve. The question of how action based on a socially determined identity achieves social change can then be reformulated as, "how can action on the basis of a particular model of self in social relations change the nature of those social relations"? An answer is to be found in the fact that different groups differ in their understandings. The dynamics of identity and change need to be explored in the relationship between these various understandings and the consequent development of interactions between the parties involved. Our recent studies of crowds (Drury, 1994; Reicher, in press; Reicher and Stott, 1991) may help to make this more concrete.

In a number of different situations—such as student demonstrations, football fans at the World Cup and anti-Poll Tax rallies—we have found a similar pattern of interaction. The student demonstration can serve as illustration of this more general pattern (Reicher, 1996). This demonstration was in response to government plans for a scheme to progressively replace grants to students with repayable loans. The event had initially been billed as a lobby but was much larger than expected. As a result, the plans were changed such that the students were to march to a park in South London where a rally would be held. However, as the demonstration crossed over the river Thames, there was a breakaway from the official route and some 5000 students ended up on Westminster Bridge—just over the river from the Houses of Parliament. On the bridge they were met by a cordon of police. The ensuing conflict between students and police was front page news and the subject of extended political debate.

Initially, the mass was heterogeneous and consisted of many groups of people who considered themselves in terms of specific affiliations (Exeter students, Labour students, groups of friends) rather than in terms of a single superordinate category membership. However one categorization which was repeatedly stressed divided "ordinary students" who were simply seeking to have their concerns heard by parliament from those "political students" who called for and who initiated confrontational acts.

As a consequence of such acts, the authorities—the police in particular—applied containing or else repressive tactics towards crowd members. Their progress was blocked and rows of police were used to force back any students who sought to approach parliament. Critically, however, the police acted against the crowd as a whole. Therefore many people who opposed confrontation were treated along with those who might have initiated it. Everybody was treated with hostility and stopped in their activity irrespective of what that activity might have been. The consequence of this was that an initially passive majority perceived outgroup action as illegitimate, considered their rights to have been violated and hence sought to reassert their rights even if this meant joining in confrontations that they originally eschewed. Concerted attempts were made to breach police lines. More importantly, these attempts were broadly supported. Previously parochial categorizations had given way to a general sense of grievance as students.

In addition, the sense of power engendered by forming part of a common category with the mass in general—rather than being, as previously, fragmented into small groups—gave people the confidence as well as the reason to challenge authority. Students surged against police lines, they joined in to wrestle free other students (whether they knew them or not) who had been arrested. This escalating challenge confirmed initial police fears of and repression towards the crowd as a whole. Police reinforcements were called up, mounted reserves were brought into action. The conflict escalated on both sides and culminated with a mounted police charge into the student crowd, causing a number of injuries. For many of the students, especially those who initially saw themselves as non-confrontational, the result was to effect a profound change in their view of the police and of society in general, but also in their views of themselves. Moreover, the two were interlinked. The police were no longer seen as neutral upholders of an order in which the concerns of ordinary people are as important as the defence of parliament. Instead, they came to be seen as part of a repressive state apparatus which is used to deny the rights and interests of powerless groups such as students. Just as the general model of social relations changed from the consensual to the conflictual, so the self-location of the students themselves had to shift. Their identity had changed from the loyal to the oppositional with all the political and moral implications which flow from such a stance.

The aim of this extended description is not to suggest that all crowds or even all crowd confrontations will follow this pattern. Clearly, there is no more a generic pattern to crowd interaction than there is to crowd behaviour. Rather, the aim is to show how our conceptual approach to change needs to be developed in order to account for what happened in this and like instances.

The dynamic originates in the fact that merely by acting as part of the crowd, members change their social relationship to others. Thus, in other contexts, students may be perceived and treated by others in general and the police in particular as articulate, responsible members of society. In the crowd they constitute a threat, a potential if not actual challenge to social order. In part, this is due to the power of numbers. In part it is due to the dissemination of ideologies which portray the crowd as either made up of troublemakers or else liable to come under their sway (Cronin, 1995; Stott, 1995). This sets up a number of asymmetries between the perceptions of those parties involved in the crowd event. If insiders (at least initially) see themselves and respectable and non-confrontational, the police see and treat them as dangerous. If insiders see the crowd as heterogeneous and the majority divorce themselves from those who are seen as confrontational, the police tend to see and treat the crowd as homogeneous—especially in situations where conflict has been initiated. Lastly, what students see as their legitimate rights (to demonstrate, to be heard in parliament) are seen as illegitimate (a threat to order, the possibility of disrupting parliament) by the police.

It is important that we don't stop with the observation of asymmetry for, while it may set a dynamic in motion, it is necessary to explore how this dynamic is played out. Perceptions of self and other, as I have argued, are not simply descriptions but guides to action. Moreover, the groups involved in any event do not only differ in their understandings, but also in their ability to act upon them. In particular, the police have the technology, the means of communication and co-ordination, and also the institutional support, to impose their understandings on the crowd—at least initially. Thus the perception that a crowd is homogeneously dangerous and illegitimate in its actions means that it is treated as such. A police cordon stops everyone passing, irrespective of their actions or intentions. A police sweep clears everyone away, and everyone is equally liable to be hurt, crushed or roughly handled as a consequence. To use a familiar term, police action imposes a common fate on crowd members.

However, it is equally important that we don't reify groups and power differences between groups as determining the interaction. Another point that clearly emerges from examining the development of crowd encounters is that relations are reconstituted in the course of an event. Thus, in imposing a common fate on the student crowd, the police create a context in which crowd members redefine themselves in terms of a common category membership. This redefinition serves to alter the power relations between groups; it allows the student mass to resist police actions and to at least attempt to impose its own understanding of rights. Insofar as identity is conceptualized as a representation of one's place in a system of social relations, this reconstitution of social relations is also a reconstitution of selfhood. Hence both the context and the psychological basis for future action is in constant movement. The self-understanding of groups, the relation between those groups, and even the nature of the categories involved may shift from one round of interaction to the next.

At one level, this analysis may seem very different to Tajfel's. However it is worth noting that there are similarities between both in terms of the key variables that are postulated as relevant to the occurrence of collective action. Where Tajfel talks of "belief structures of social change" it is argued here that people will act together collectively where they are treated (and consequently see themselves) as equivalent, irrespective of any interpersonal differences. Where Tajfel refers to legitimacy, I propose that groups will enter into conflict with others in order to assert rights which are illegitimately denied them. And where Tajfel invokes "cognitive alternatives", I suggest that the sense of possibility engendered by collective empowerment is crucial to crowd grievance becoming crowd action.

Thus, in terms of critical variables, the difference between the two approaches is not so much what they are but how they are conceptualized. For Tajfel, they are listed as conditions for the onset of collective action. Here they are seen as emerging in the process of collective action itself. Consequently, where Tajfel's terms are characterized as states of the mass in itself, here they are characterized much more in terms of features of intergroup relations: how insiders can act in the light of outgroup action; what people feel they should be able to do in relation to what they are allowed to do; and what people can do in the face of the opposition of others.

More generally, in order to examine the dynamics of social change, the broader conceptual basis through which social identity theory approaches social change has been reconceptualized in relational terms. First of all, it is suggested that both change and social identity itself be thought of in terms of social relations. Change is a matter of shifting social relations and is directly linked to identity insofar as social identity is a representation of one's place in a system of social relations.

Secondly, it is argued that an analysis of change needs to be rooted in situated studies of interactions between groups. Moreover, such studies need to be historical and examine the development of these interactions. Only in this way is it possible to see how action on the basis of social identity may alter the relations between groups and set up a process in which the successive responses of each group to the other progressively redefine the groups themselves and the ground on which they act.

Thirdly, and lastly, such a historical and developmental approach breaks down the traditional opposition between subject and context. In situations of social conflict, the context in which human beings act is made up of the actions of other human beings. This is especially obvious in crowds where those others are physically present and the constraints they impose take a direct and visible form, such as cordons of officers, squads in riot gear, and so on. However, it is no less true in other situations where human activity has been formalized into institutional practices and regulations. Thus, subject and context are not different orders of reality. Indeed, what derives from the subjectivity of one set of actors forms the context in which others act and in which their subjectivity is formed. Thus, the self-conceptions of the police as upholders of order in the face of student threat leads them to mount a cordon of officers in the students' path and push back any who seek to progress. This, then, is the physical context in which students act, in which they develop their own self-understandings from which flow the actions that constitute the context for further police action.

Viewed in this way, the distinction between subject and context refers to the social distribution of conscious human practice over space and time. What is the action of some subjects is the context of others. What is context at one point in time resolves into action at another. It is perhaps only because psychology has been so bad at studying interactions and has viewed behaviour ahistorically that these connections are obscured, subject and context are torn apart and the dynamics of social change become so elusive. Conversely, it follows that only by defining our concepts in relational terms, adopting methods that can incorporate interactive and historical dimensions, will we avoid the dualism of subject and context and be able to understand social change.

Conclusions

The foregoing has been long, so I will be brief. This chapter has sought to do three things. The first was simply to remind us of the central place that understanding social change had in the origins of social identity theory and to argue that this priority needs to be restored. No social psychological theory which ignores change is intellectually adequate. No theory which implicitly or explicitly denies change is politically acceptable. The second aim was to argue that Tajfel may have insisted on the importance of change but his was more the prolegomenon to any future model rather than a psychological model of social change in itself. I have argued that such a model requires us to elaborate if not change some of the fundamental concepts of social identity theory. In particular, the notion of context, which in its early stages may have been the basis for overcoming the reifications of traditional psychological theory, is now in danger of becoming a major impediment to progress. It is essential to overcome the notion of context as external to and determining of self-categorization and to substitute an understanding of the two as mutually implicative of the other. I have also argued that the study of social change needs to look at the interactions between groups in a historical perspective. Thirdly, and finally, I have provided one illustration of such a study and how it can help elucidate the process of social change. As I stressed, this example is in no way intended as a template for all social change. There may be many different forms of social interaction which lead to change and there may be many similar forms of interaction in which change does not occur. What is now necessary is to undertake detailed historical studies of different interactive relations in order to elucidate the conditions under which change occurs and the forms it takes. If this chapter encourages anyone to undertake such studies, it will have succeeded in its purpose.

References

Allen, R. A. (1970). *Black awakening in capitalist America.* New York: Doubleday.

Billig, M. (1987). *Arguing and thinking*. Cambridge: Cambridge University Press.

Billig, M. (1994). Repopulating the depopulated pages of social psychology. *Theory and Psychology,* **4**, 307–335.

Billig, M. (1995). *Banal nationalism.* London: Sage.

Carmichael, S., and Hamilton, C. V. (1967). *Black power: The politics of liberation in America.* New York: Random House.

Cronin, P. (1995). Police perceptions of crowd events. Unpublished manuscript, University of Exeter.

Drury, J. (1994). The new roads war: the experience of the "no M11" campaign. Paper presented to the Conference of Social Economists, Leeds, July.

Danziger, K. (1963). The psychological future of an oppressed group. *Social Forces*, **62**, 31–40.

Ellemers, N., Doosje, A., van Knippenberg, A., and Wilke, H. (1992). Status protection in high status minority groups. *European Journal of Social Psychology*, **22,** 123–140.

Ellemers, N., van Knippenberg, A., and Wilke, H. (1990). The influence of permeability of group boundaries and stability of group status on strategies of individual mobility and social change. *British Journal of Social Psychology*, **29**, 233–246.

Farrell, M. (1980). *Northern Ireland: Orange state.* London: Pluto.

Frazier, E. F. (1962). *Black bourgeoisie.* New York: Collier.

Geber, B. (1972). Occupational aspirations and expectations of South African high school children. Unpublished PhD thesis, University of London.

Haslam, S. A., and Turner, J. C. (1992). Context-dependent variation in social stereotyping 2: The relationship between frame of reference, self-categorisation and accentuation. *European Journal of Social Psychology*, **22**, 251–277.

Haslam, S. A., Turner, J. C., Oakes, P. J., McGarty, C., and Hayes, B. K. (1992). Context-dependent variation in social stereotyping 1: The effects of intergroup relations as mediated by social change and frame of reference. *European Journal of Social Psychology*, **22**, 3–20.

Hirschman, A. O. (1970). *Exit, voice and loyalty.* Cambridge, MA: Harvard University Press.

Israel, J. and Tajfel, H. (1972). *The context of social psychology.* London: Academic Press.

Kelly, C. (1993). Group identification, intergroup perceptions and collective action. *European Review of Social Psychology*, **4**, 59–83.

Kelly, C., and Breilinger, S. (1995). Identity and injustice: exploring women's participation in collective action. *Journal of Community and Applied Social Psychology*, **5**, 41–57.

Khan, S. A. (1988). *The Lahore resolution: Arguments for and against.* Karachi: Royal Book Company.

Klandermans, B. (1989). Grievance interpretation and success expectations: the social construction of protest. *Social Behaviour*, **4**, 113–125.

Klandermans, B., Kriesi, H., and Tarrow, S. (1988). *From structure to action: Comparing social movement research across cultures. International social movement research*, Vol. 1. Greenwich, CT: JAI Press.

Le Bon, G. (1895; translated 1947) *The crowd: A study of the popular mind.* London: Ernest Benn.

Mandela, N. (1978). *The struggle is my life.* London: IDAF.

Milgram, S., and Toch, H. (1969). Collective behaviour: crowds and social movements. In G. Lindzey and E. Aronson (Eds), *Handbook of social psychology*, Vol. 4. Reading, MA: Addison-Wesley.

Morris, A. D., and McClurg-Mueller, C. (1992). *Frontiers in social movement theory.* New Haven: Yale University Press.

Moscovici, S. (1972). Society and theory in social psychology. In J. Israel and H. Tajfel (Eds), *The context of social psychology.* London: Academic Press.

Moscovici, S. (1961). *La psychanalyse: Son image et son public.* Paris: Presses Universitaires de France.

Moscovici, S. (1976) *Social influence and social change.* London: Academic Press.

Moscovici, S. (1984). The phenomenon of social representations. In R. Farr and S. Moscovici (Eds), *Social representations.* Cambridge: Cambridge University Press.

Moscovici, S. (1993). Razon y Culturas. Speech given in acceptance of an honorary doctorate, University of Seville.

Oakes, P. J., Haslam, S. A., and Turner, J. C. (1994). *Stereotyping and social reality.* Oxford: Blackwell.

Reddy, W. M. (1977). The textile trade and the language of the crowd at Rouen 1752–1871. *Past and Present*, **74**, 62–89.

Reicher, S. D. (1982). The determination of collective behaviour. In H. Tajfel (Ed.), *Social identity and intergroup relations.* Cambridge: CUP, and Paris: Maison des Sciences de l'Homme.

Reicher, S. D. (1984) Social influence in the crowd: an explanation of the limits of crowd action in terms of a social identity model. *European Journal of Social Psychology*, **14**, 1–21.

Reicher, S. D. (1987a). Crowd behaviour as social action. In J. Turner, M. Hogg, P. Oakes, S. Reicher, and M. Wetherell (Eds), *Rediscovering the social group.* Oxford: Blackwell.

Reicher, S. D. (1987b). From minimal group experiments to mass social action. Paper presented at the International Conference on Social Identity. Exeter.

Reicher, S. D. (1993a). On the construction of social categories: From collective action to rhetoric and back again. In B. Gonzalez (Ed.), *Psicologia cultural.* Seville: Eudema

Reicher, S. D. (1993b). The national constitution: An argumentative approach to the definition and salience of national identities. Workshop on "National Identities in Europe", Lisbon.

Reicher, S. D. (1996). The Battle of Westminster: Developing the social identity model of crowd behaviour in order to deal with the initiation and development of collective conflict. *European Journal of Social Psychology.*

Reicher, S., and Hopkins, N. (in press, a). Constructing categories and mobilising masses: An analysis of Thatcher's and Kinnock's speeches on the British miner's strike 1984–5. *European Journal of Social Psychology.*

Reicher, S. and Hopkins, N. (in press, b). Seeking influence through characterising self-categories: An analysis of anti-abortionist rhetoric. *British Journal of Social Psychology.*

Reicher, S., and Potter, J. (1985). Psychological theory as intergroup perspective: a comparative analysis of 'scientific' and 'lay' accounts of crowd events. *Human Relations*, **38**, 167–189.

Reicher, S. D. and Stott , C. (1991). *How crowd conflict starts.* Paper presented to 4th International Conference on Conflict Management, Den Dolde, Netherlands.

Singh, A. I. (1987). *The origin of the partition of India.* New Delhi, Oxford University Press.

Spears, R. (1994). Why "depopulation" should not (necessarily) be taken personally: A commentary on "repopulating the depopulated pages of social psychology". *Theory and Psychology*, **4**, 337–344.

Stephenson, J. (1979). *Popular disturbances in England 1700–1870.* London: Longman.

Stott, C. (1995). *Intergroup dynamics of crowd behaviour.* Unpublished PhD thesis, University of Exeter.

Tajfel, H. (1972). La categorisation sociale. In S. Moscovici (Ed.), *Introduction a la Psychologie Sociale*. Paris: Larousse.

Tajfel, H. (1974). *Intergroup behaviour, social comparison and social change.* Unpublished Katz-Newcomb lectures. University of Michigan, Ann Arbor.

Tajfel, H. (1975). The exit of social mobility and the voice of social change: notes on the social psychology of intergroup relations. *Social Science Information,* **14**, 101–118.

Tajfel, H. (1978). *Differentiation between social groups.* London, Academic Press.

Tajfel, H. (1981). *Human groups and social categories.* Cambridge: Cambridge University Press.

Tajfel, H. (1982). *Social identity and intergroup relations.* Cambridge, Cambridge University Press and Paris, Maison des Sciences de l'Homme.

Tajfel, H., and Turner, J. (1986). An integrative theory of intergroup relations. In S. Worchel and W. G. Austin (Eds), *Psychology of intergroup relations.* Chicago: Nelson-Hall.

Therborn, G. (1980). *The ideology of power and the power of ideology.* London: Verso.

Thompson, E. P. (1971). The moral economy of the English crowd in the eighteenth century. *Past and Present*, **50**, 76–136.

Thompson, E. P. (1991). *Customs in common.* London: Merlin.

Turner, J. C., Hogg, M., Oakes, P. J., Reicher, S. D. and Wetherell, M. (1987). *Rediscovering the social group.* Oxford: Blackwell.

Turner, J. C., Oakes, P. J., Haslam, S. A., and McGarty, C. (1993). Self and collective: cognition and social context. *Personality and Social Psychology Bulletin*, **20**, 454–463.

van Knippenberg, A. (1987). Social identities and social mobility. Paper presented at the International Conference on Social Identity. Exeter.

Williams, J., and Giles, H. (1978). The changing status of women in society: an intergroup perspective. In H. Tajfel (Ed.), *Differentiation between social groups.* London, Academic Press.

13

Remembering the Particular Background of Social Identity Theory

MICHAEL BILLIG

Department of Social Sciences, University of Loughborough

Contents

The place of Henri Tajfel in social psychology is secure. His experiments and theories continue to inspire research. A younger generation of experimentalists dedicates itself to developing the details of social identity theory and to exploring its intricacies with further research programmes. The report of the earliest minimal group experiment has become a "citation classic" (Billig, 1992). Whilst this side of Tajfel's work is receiving due recognition, there is a further dimension which is sometimes overlooked today. Tajfel, in addition to his experimental programmes, articulated a broad vision of social psychology. This broader vision is vital for understanding the depth of Tajfel's thought as a social theorist. However, it includes themes which might be thought to sit uneasily with aspirations to complete the experimental programmes. Indeed, it contains a number of intellectual similarities with the sort of social constructionism often seen to represent a very different type of social psychology than social identity theory.

In his broader views on the nature of social psychology, Tajfel insisted upon the historical nature of social psychological phenomena. In general terms, rather than in specific detail, his arguments about the importance of historical understanding resemble those of Gergen (1973, 1994). Also, as will be seen, Tajfel insisted on the limitation of social psychology. In his view, social psychology on its own was insufficient for understanding important social phenomena; nor could social psychology ever hope to produce complete explanations. Tajfel did not elaborate these themes as some sort of peripheral activity, undertaken as a break from the important business of experimentation. Quite the contrary, they are of a piece with some of the most deep-seated aspects of this thinking, so much so that the depth and originality of his work is diminished if this broader vision is ignored.

The Limitations of "Explanation"

In considering Tajfel's social thought, there are two key texts: the introductory chapter to *Human groups and social categories* (Tajfel, 1981), which was entitled "The development of a perspective"; and the article "Experiments in a vacuum", which was originally published in Israel and Tajfel (1972) but which Tajfel used as the second chapter in *Human groups and social categories*. When referring to "Experiments in a vacuum" here, references will be taken from the republished version. This was the version which Tajfel intended to be read alongside the introductory remarks, which he specially wrote for *Human groups*.

"Experiments in vacuum" criticized the practice of conducting experiments for their own sake and the tendency to ignore the social context of experimentation. Experiments, argued Tajfel, would not provide universal truths, for each experiment was itself socially and historically situated. Experimental subjects came to the laboratory with the outlook of their times. Unless social psychologists took note of the social and historical contexts of psychological phenomena, including the phenomena demonstrated in their laboratories, they would produce a discipline, that trivialized its subject matter. Tajfel's argument went beyond making methodological points. He was presenting a vision of social psychology which insisted on the historical and social nature of its subject matter.

Later researchers who have been developing social identity theory have tended to treat the message of "Experiments in a vacuum" as peripheral to their concerns. For example, Hogg and Abrams (1988) mention the article only in passing, and then in relation to Moscovici and Faucheux's (1972) reinterpretation of Asch, rather than in respect to Tajfel's own work (p. 169). Likewise Turner *et al.*, in their book *Rediscovering the social group*, give the article brief mention (1987, p. 148). Again, the reference is unconnected with Tajfel's own theorizing, which, of course, dominates that book. Critics of orthodox social psychology have taken the reverse approach to the article. They have cited it with approval as a methodological critique of experimentalism without discussing it in the context of Tajfel's other work. For example, Gergen (1994a) in *Toward transformation in social knowledge* cites "Experiments in a vacuum" several times, but does not mention any other of Tajfel's writings.

Tajfel, in presenting his own work in *Human groups and social categories*, strikes a different tone from that which can sometimes be found in the writings of his later followers. Tajfel explicitly stressed the limitations of social psychological explanation. In the introductory chapter, Tajfel deliberately circumscribed the scope of his own work, and that of social psychology in general. He stressed that "a *modest* contribution can be made to . . . the unravelling of a tangled web of issues" (italics in original, p. 7). He asserted: "I do not believe that 'explanations' of social conflicts and social injustice can be mainly or primarily psychological" (1981, p. 7). The italicizing of *modest* was as rhetorically significant as the apostrophising of "explanations".

Later theorists have often described the aims of their work, and of social psychology in general, somewhat differently. They have written of their hopes for integrated, unified theories. John Turner and colleagues introduced their own detailed development of social identity theory by emphasizing that "it is important to produce . . . a unifying, general theory of the group" (Turner *et al.*, 1987, p. 43). Hogg and Abrams (1988) outlined the achievements of social identity theory, informing readers that "the social identity approach is vibrant and flourishing, and continues to provide an exciting impetus for the theorizing and research of a growing number of social psychologists" (p. 217). Because the approach "circumvents" individualism, "the unit of analysis becomes transformed", and, in consequence, "the approach opens the way for a more integrated and complete analysis of the social psychological functioning of individuals in society" (pp. 217–218).

These promissory notes for unified, integrated and complete theories seem to differ from the self-ascribed theoretical modesty of Tajfel's rhetoric, which, by its use of apostrophes, doubts whether "explanations" of social conflict can ever properly be explanations. Why this should be the case is interesting. The differences between Tajfel's modest vision of limitation and the more confident visions of unification are not matters of personality. Nor does the modest vision reflect the caution of a pioneer who does not have the benefit, afforded to followers, of seeing where the new discoveries would lead. Tajfel's insistence on theoretical caution goes well beyond methodology, for it reflects some of the most profound issues facing those who wish to study social conflict in the twentieth century.

Background of a Theory

In the introductory chapter of *Human groups and social categories*, Tajfel described how his psychological work reflected his own background. He was not merely giving his personal history, but, in so doing, he was making the general point that social history conditions thought. Psychology was no exception, for, as Tajfel argued, psychological thinking will reflect the social backgrounds of psychologists. In consequence, "a 'neutral' social psychology is hardly possible"; indeed, neutrality in the social sciences often amounted "to the implicit taking of a position" (Tajfel, 1981, p. 7). If psychological theories are products of their social background, then, so long as there are psychologists from different social backgrounds, there will be different psychologies. Tajfel recognized the implication: unity within psychology could only be established by abolishing the social diversity of backgrounds. In describing the development of European social psychology, Tajfel stressed that the aim was not to create a unified social psychology, but to encourage a diversity of perspectives which would reflect the political, social and linguistic diversities of Europe. Thus, Tajfel wrote of the "need for a diversity of social and cultural perspectives" (p. 6). Unequivocally, he asserted that "there cannot be, and should not be, any kind of a unified European, or any other, social psychology" (p. 5).

Such comments possess a tenor which is now commonly called "post-modernist". Tajfel's remarks celebrate differences of insight and of perspective. The intellectual heterogeneity reflects a heterogeneity of locality and identity. Tajfel was warning against the dangers of uniform truths (or what Lyotard, 1984, would call "meta-narratives"), which threaten to overwhelm difference. Instead, he hoped for moments of insight, which, significantly, he did not describe in terms of "scientific" facts. Also, Tajfel was acknowledging the provisional, situated nature of social psychological insights, including his own. In this respect, he was displaying a reflexive awareness, which again has become characteristic of postmodern theorizing, especially within social psychology (Ashmore, 1989; Gergen, 1991, 1994b; Michael, 1991, 1994).

In the domain of European social psychology, there appears to be a paradox. The *post* is *ante*, as the tones of postmodernism are to be heard in the words of the founder, rather than in the followers who pursue the modernist ambition of a unifying theory. As will be suggested, this inversion of the familiar sequence is not fortuitous. It, too, reflects a social and historical background. In particular, it reflects proximity, and subsequent distance, from the history which, as Tajfel wrote in his introductory chapter, was his own background.

The beginning of the introductory chapter to *Human groups and social categories* contains some of the most moving passages which Tajfel ever wrote. The words, picked with utmost care, suggest a hesitancy, as if the message could not be communicated, especially to those of us readers born safely after the events described. Tajfel was writing of the destruction of his own "social background": even that familiar sociological phrase suggests a distanced formality. Tajfel was referring to the murder of European Jews in the Holocaust, which he narrowly and fortuitously escaped. He specifically mentioned his reactions when released from a prisoner-of-war camp at the end of the war: "I soon discovered that hardly anyone I knew in 1939—including my family—was left alive" (p. 1).

If Tajfel was writing of the destruction of his "social background", then the destruction of background was itself to become the background of his thinking. Tajfel described how be became an academic "almost in a fit of absent-mindedness" (p. 1). He learnt a new jargon, a new way of looking at the world. He thought that he had become enfolded in the security of British academia: "And, yet, when I look back today, I know without any doubt that this has never been true" (p. 2). If there had been any forgetting, it had only been temporary and incomplete. What might have seemed absent-mindedness was not properly so, for some things could never be absent from the mind and would continue to be expressed in his formal thinking.

Tajfel's choice of research topics—prejudice, conflict between groups—was not haphazard. That much appears clear. In addition, as the introductory chapter states, Tajfel showed an impatience with explanatory impostors—with intellectual systems that claim to have discovered the full significance of events, so that those events can be comfortably labelled as "explained". The introductory chapter has a sub-text which arguably separates it from the rhetoric of some later works on social identity theory. Tajfel, as he introduced his own theory, was careful to make statements of limitation, rather than advertising its limitless possibilities. The direction of explanation moves from background to theory, not vice versa. The theory is to be understood in terms of its background. He made no claim that the theory, then, can be used to understand—to explain—the background.

As Zygmunt Bauman (1988, 1992) and others have written, the optimistic assumptions of modernism, whether expressed culturally, politically or philosophically, were shaken in the mid-twentieth century. A confident belief in scientific advancement and progress towards the unity of knowledge seems untenable in the shadow of the Holocaust. Science was mobilized in the cause of the premeditated, repeated slaughter of innocents. This most systematic barbarism known to history did not occur on the periphery of what Europeans have long been accustomed to call the "civilized world". It happened in one of modernity's central homelands. If the Holocaust, above all other aspects of modern history, seems to demand psychological "explanation", nevertheless, its essence, as Tajfel knew, must always lie beyond the scope of psychological theory.

Critique of Explanations

No intellectual theory can be properly understood merely in terms of what the theorist is proposing, but it also needs to be seen in terms of rival ideas which the theorist is opposing. Tajfel's theoretical work is no exception. Its strength cannot be assessed merely in terms of experimental evidence; it should also be seen, and assessed, as an argument against other theories. Tajfel was especially critical of approaches which ignored the particularities of history and which absorbed all social phenomena into general, or universal, categories of psychological explanation, especially those which reduced the social to the individual. Above all, he was critical of approaches which appeared to explain away the one historical event, which, above all others, should not to be dismissed as "understood".

It is easy now to overlook the extent to which Tajfel, as he formulated his cognitive approach to social psychology, was arguing against biological explanations. His classic article, "The cognitive aspects of prejudice", is explicit in its attack upon biologism (see also Tajfel, 1976). Tajfel criticized approaches that explain wars and social conflicts in terms of biological urges for aggression and which, thereby, reduce the sweep of human history to the expression of inbuilt, unchanging instincts. According to Tajfel, "the general climate of opinion favours the blood-and-guts model which at present is having quite a run" (1981, p. 129). Significantly, Tajfel's example of a blood-and-guts theorist was the ethologist Konrad Lorenz, whose writings on "man-as-an-instinctual-animal" gained an immense popularity in the 1960s. Tajfel made brief, but telling, points against Lorenz, arguing that general statements about aggressive instincts do not take analysts far in understanding particular social conflicts.

There was, of course, a further "background". Instinctual theories, for all their pretensions to offer explanations for large-scale social aggression, can only approach an event like the Holocaust in bad faith. Either the victims must be presumed to carry identical instinctual urges as their oppressors, for such urges are claimed as being endemic to the human condition; or, if the victims are said to lack such forces, then, biologically, they are being branded as being less-than-human or lacking in necessary, forceful human qualities. There is a further point. The tradition of blood-and-guts theorizing was itself deeply implicated. Nazism as a political ideology made use of a quasi-biologism, which postulated that instinctual and racial factors were the prime movers of human history (Kuhl, 1994; Poliakov, 1974). The choice of Lorenz in Tajfel's critique was significant. Lorenz's popular *Sturm und Drang* prose contained echoes. Early articles, which Lorenz published in Germany during the Nazi period, consciously used Nazi terminology to outline those themes of biological strength and weakness which would be developed in the post-war bestsellers; indeed, Lorenz even praised the Nazi regime for what he took to be its understanding of racial factors (Billig, 1981; Müller-Hill, 1988).

There were political undercurrents in Tajfel's repudiation of Eysenck's theories of ideology. When Tajfel was writing the introduction to *Human groups and social categories*, Eysenck and Wilson (1978) had recently published an edited volume *The psychological basis of ideology* (Eysenck and Wilson, 1978). As Tajfel recognized, the main concern of Eysenck's work was to discover why some individuals hold extreme political views. By reducing questions of ideology to those of individual difference, Eysenck was ignoring the social and historical context of human action. In introducing the re-publication of "Experiments in a vacuum", Tajfel made it plain why such a reduction can only contribute a minor understanding (and a major misunderstanding) to the events of which he was writing but a few pages earlier. He wrote:

> Authoritarian or tough-minded personalities may have contributed to the development of national socialism in Germany; but the question as to why *psychologically* the movement had such an enormous popular success in its time is left just as wide as before.
>
> (1981, p. 16, emphasis in original)

Tajfel went beyond making a methodological point about individual theories of personality. He pointed out that Eysenck and Wilson were attempting to explain individual differences of belief in terms of genetics. Tajfel was scathing about this. Eysenck and Wilson could only cite one tentative study to support their confident conclusions: "So much for scientific objectivity", commented Tajfel pointedly. He went on: Eysenck and Wilson's work "far from dealing with *the* 'psychological basis of ideology' reflects much more closely the ideological basis of *some* psychology" (1981, p. 16, emphases in original). Again, there were echoes. Implicitly, Eysenck's work was dividing people biologically, and, given the implied evaluative nature of his categories, the groupings carried more than a hint of biological desirability and undesirability. Tajfel was appalled to find that Eysenck and Coulter (1972), in a key paper which claimed to discover the psychological properties of extremism and which was reprinted in *The psychological basis of ideology*, was openly quoting with approval the ideas of E. R. Jaensch, the Nazi and deeply anti-Semitic psychologist (Billig, 1981, 1982). In criticizing Eysenck's work, Tajfel was doing more than claiming to assess the empirical evidence. He was giving expression to his belief in the historical and ideological nature of social psychology.

If biologism is culpable as an explanation of ideology, then there are other theories which Tajfel criticized for their wide-eyed innocence. Such theories denied the importance of ideology, unreflexively claiming to put themselves beyond the reach of ideology. In particular, Tajfel wrote strongly against theories of social psychology which reduced large-scale social conflicts to interpersonal relations. In looking only within the minds of individuals when attempting to understand social processes, psychologists narrow their own perspectives. They ignore that the beliefs and mental states of individuals are historically created and situated. As a result, the social psychological study of individuals should lead outwards to a historical and ideological study of socially shared beliefs.

For example, Tajfel criticized frustration–aggression theories, which linked mass violence to individually experienced feelings of frustration. What such theories ignored was that mass violence depends upon shared beliefs and collective identities (Tajfel, 1981, pp. 39–40). When victims are selected, discriminated against or murdered *en masse*, one sees not so much the power of individual frustrations, but the power of cultural myths: "These myths, be they called *représentations collectives*, social representations or *social* (as opposed to individual) stereotypes, constitute . . . a crucial part of the background affecting the collective aspects of social behaviour of masses of individuals" (Tajfel, 1984, p. 696, emphases in original).

Tajfel, in criticizing social psychological theories for overlooking the importance of social myths or representations, was pointing to the necessity to study groups rather than individuals. There is a further point that relates to the universalism of many social psychological theories. Myths are culturally and historically specific: not all cultures and all historical periods share the same beliefs. Thus, the analysis of social phenomena in terms of myths should lead the analyst to consider the specificities of ideological and historical location. However, universal theories of psychology, which are phrased in general terms and whose variables are presumed to be applicable for all social contexts, bypass the analysis of historical specificity: they presume a universal psychology. (For a discussion of the differences between universal and particular theories in social psychology, see Billig, 1991, Chapter 3.)

Tajfel, in critically analysing other social psychological theories, discussed the drawbacks of both reductionism and universalism. For example, he took equity theory to task, especially in the form of its variant, the theory of the "just-world". Equity theories tend to be phrased in universal terms, as they stipulate universal principles of human behaviour. As Tajfel (1984) pointed out, equity theories propose as a general principle that harm-doers want to believe that their victims accept their treatment as justified. This assumption, according to Tajfel, makes all sorts of cultural assumptions about the relation between harm-doer and victim. Above all, it makes a nonsense out of the events, lying behind Tajfel's own psychology. Whether the victims accepted their fate was "hardly an important worry for the perpetrators of the systematic massacres of the last war" (Tajfel, 1984, p. 698). An ideology had decreed the victims to be worthless, just as Nazi doctors had defined the mentally ill and handicapped as unworthy of the right to live (p. 709).

Etienne Balibar (1991) has argued that there is no racism without "theories", for the racist makes assumptions about the reality and nature of "races". Thus, the Nazi doctors were putting their "theories" into practice, when medically murdering those they considered as "worthless". In so doing they were not "concerned with interpersonal exchange" as indicated by equity theory, for they "were not concerned with goods and services between themselves and their patients" (Tajfel, 1984, p. 709). Again, as Tajfel criticized a theory that was unaware of its own ideological basis, his sarcasm was evident. Equity theories might well describe certain modes of relating in liberal, capitalist, North American society (see also Sampson, 1977, 1993). In the manner of ideologies, such theories universalize the relationships of their own historical context into general statements of human nature. When the theory is applied to a social and political context which is very different from its own background, the inadequacies become clear.

One last example of Tajfel's critique can be given. Cultural myths, as social theories, typically embody "theories" of social explanation. Tajfel (1981, p. 156) gave the example of Nazi anti-Semitism and the belief in a worldwide Jewish conspiracy. Anti-Semitic conspiracy theorists depict Jews as a powerful, united group of conspirators, planning to dominate the world: the Jewish conspirators, then, in the mind of the conspiracy theorist, are to be blamed for all manner of evils. This mythology has a long, unhappy history (Billig, 1978; Cohn, 1967; 1989; Katz, 1980; Poliakov, 1974). Superficially, the analysis of such myths would appear to cover the same ground as "attribution theory". The conspiracy theorist offers explanations, as social events are attributed to the hidden machinations of the conspirators. Attribution theorists are also interested in the ways that individuals explain their social world. However, the study of the ways in which cultural myths such as the conspiracy theory suffuse the thinking of their believers, and provide them with the means for interpreting the world, is a far cry from what is conventionally termed as attribution theory (for recent critiques of attribution theory, see Antaki, 1994; Edwards and Potter, 1993 and Potter and Wetherell, 1987).

Again, the example of Nazism provides a test case. Tajfel (1982), in his concluding summary for *Social identity and intergroup relations*, discussed critically the contribution of Horwitz and Rabbie (1982). Horwitz and Rabbie had illustrated the propositions of attribution theory. They had suggested that Germans, during the Nazi period, would have treated Jewish friends differently from non-Jewish ones. The Jewish friends would be considered to be "unresponsive to German needs" and would be treated as members of a social group, rather than as individuals. Tajfel commented that it was hardly such attributions "which played a central role, or could even be seen as 'incipient' in what happened to millions of people, Jews and others, during the Second World War" (1982, p. 486). Such millions were marked off from the definition of being human, not because attributions about motives were made. As Tajfel commented, "no attributions need to be made at all, no more than attributions are made about insects subjected to a DDT treatment" (p. 487).

Something crucial is lost if analysts explain the social mythology of anti-semitism in terms of "attributions" or "motives for equity". The specificity of history escapes theoretical attention. The ferocity of the anti-Semitic tradition—together with what Tajfel called more generally "the power of deeply entrenched cultural myths" (1982, p. 709)—is transmuted into something more homely, altogether cosier: mythology becomes a thin-grained personal calculation. Events which two generations later should continue to disturb the consciousness of the so-called "civilized world", are reduced. "What did the Nazis think of the Jews?" becomes a question with a comfortingly clichéd answer: they made attributions, just like everyone else; they blamed the Jews, because, just like everyone else, they wanted to believe the world is a just place. But the Nazis' ideology, and the murderous pursuit of that ideology, were not just like everything else. Any psychological theory which suggests otherwise offers the enticement of a soothing collective amnesia for a history which, across generations, should not be collectively forgotten.

Social Identity Theory and Universalism

At first sight, social identity theory would seem to share features with some of the approaches, which were rejected by Henri Tajfel as being inadequate for understanding large-scale social conflict. Social identity theory is a universal theory, both in terms of its key concepts and its core assumption about individual motivations. Also, as will be suggested, the theory cannot appropriately be applied to offer explanations for its own background.

The key terms in universal, social psychological theories refer to phenomena which are not historically or culturally restricted. Thus, a theory of "prejudice" is a universal theory, for "prejudices" typically are assumed to be discoverable in all eras and all historical contexts. On the other hand, a theory of "fascism" is a particular theory, in that fascism, as a political movement, belongs to the twentieth century. Clearly, by this criterion social identity theory is a universal theory. It discusses identification with "ingroups" and differentiation from "outgroups". The very terms "ingroup" and "outgroup" imply universality, as does the general term "intergroup relations": social scientists use these terms to indicate that their theories are not bound to a particular social or historical context (Breuilly, 1985).

Tajfel's theory assumed that the processes of intergroup comparison and intergroup differentiation, which lie at the heart of social identity theory, depend upon a universal motive for a positive social identity: "It can be assumed that an individual will tend to remain a member of a group and seek membership of new groups if these groups have some contribution to make to the positive aspects of his (*sic*) social identity" (Tajfel, 1981, p. 256). This assumption is phrased universally: all individuals, whatever their historical location, are presumed to share this basic motivation.

Some social identity theorists have interpreted the theory in terms of a strategy to discover universal, psychological processes, which are presumed to lie behind different forms of group identity. They have considered the differences between instances of group identity to be less interesting than the search for similarities. For example, Hogg and Abrams (1988) begin their book *Social identifications* by discussing how ingroups distinguish themselves from outgroups. To illustrate the point, they mention a variety of different sorts of groupings where such intergroup distinctions operate: "national groups (Italians, Germans), religious groups (Buddhist, Muslim, Protestant, Catholic), political groups (socialist, conservative), ethnic groups (Karen, Lahu, Akha in Thailand), sex groups (male, female), youth groups (punk, skinhead), university faculty groups (Science, Arts, Law) and so on" (p. 2). They declare that the essential social psychological question is "*how* do people identify with a group, and precisely what are the consequences of such identification?" (p. 2, emphasis in original). Thus, the task is to find the underlying psychological similarities behind the outward differences.

In "Experiments in a vacuum", Tajfel discussed the problems associated with a universal strategy for social psychological investigation. Every social phenomenon, he argued, is both unique and not unique—or, to use Lewinian terminology, it possesses both a distinctive phenotype and is an instance of a more general genotype. Universal theories, with their search for nomothetic laws, stress the genotypic features: particular phenomena are only interesting to the extent to which they illustrate general processes. When theorists put too much stress on the general features of a particular instance, then a problem arises. Psychological processes are abstracted from their historical contexts in order to be treated as instances of generalities. The result is that the historical particularities are flattened. Of course, theoretical gains can be made by seeking general laws, but, as Tajfel argued in "Experiments in a vacuum", the resulting theories deal with mythical phenomena: "the general case is an impossible myth", for the general can never occur except in a particular instance (1981, p. 21; see also, Billig, 1994 for a similar argument regarding the rhetoric of experimental social psychological reports). Thus, theories that treat social reality in generalities only are making mythic descriptions.

The question is not whether it is empirically correct or incorrect to adopt a strategy which places prime emphasis upon searching for universals, even if such universals can only be found in a mythic form. What is at stake is a matter of intellectual strategy. Every historical event—indeed, every human being—is both singular and comparable. As Aristotle (1976) argued in *Topica*, statements of quality and statements of quantity are always possible. Similarly, it is possible for social scientists to approach any topic nomothetically or ideographically: the theorists can subsume the particular under some general heading, or can concentrate upon the particularity. This perennial possibility for making judgements of singularity or comparison (for particularizing or categorizing) lies at the root of the two-sidedness of human thinking (Billig, 1987a). To insist on the uniqueness of a given event is not to suggest that the event is totally unique in every respect, and that comparisons cannot be made. It is to suggest that the essence of the matter lies in the uniqueness and the comparisons miss that essence (Billig, 1987a). Thus, the question is not whether it is possible to categorize or particularize, but what are the consequences of so doing. This is question faced by everyday thinkers, as much as by social psychological theorists.

In the case of "intergroup relations", the strategy of universalizing can lead to the neglect of historical factors, which Tajfel himself warned against and which act as defence against the tendency to theoretical immodesty. The example of nationalism can be used as an illustration (see Billig, 1995, for more details). National loyalties can be considered as examples of more general "ingroup loyalties". As Benedict Anderson (1983) has argued, nations are "imagined communities". Social identity theory stresses that all groups depend upon members' feelings of commonality, and that there is no "reality" to groups apart from their psychological reality (Turner, 1982; Turner *et al.*, 1987). As Tajfel

(1981) wrote, a nation will only exist if a body of people feel themselves to be a nation (p. 229). From this, one might say that all groups are similar to nations, in that they are "imagined communities", and the issue is then to search for the psychological commonalities of such social imaginings.

An opposing strategy, however, is possible. This would insist on exploring the particularities of the nationalist imagination. As Benedict Anderson suggests, communities are to be distinguished "by the style in which they are imagined" (1983, p. 16). The great religious communities of the Middle Ages were imagined in different terms than the modern nation. The imagining of "Christendom" involved different "theories", representations of morality and assumptions about the nature of the world, than are involved in the imagining of the modern nation. The imagining of the Islamic *umma*, before the age of nationhood, differed crucially from the imagining, and creation, of Islamic nation-states today (Zubaida, 1993).

The concept "nation" involves imagining a mixture of uniqueness and similarity. Each nation imagines itself to be unique (an "us" differentiated from others), but also to possess the properties of nationhood, which are shared with other nations. These "theories" of nationhood are historically particular, having become the accepted political common-sense of the modern era; they would have been foreign to the common-sense of mediaeval Europe (Billig, 1995; Harris, 1990). When leaders of social movements that seek to attain political independence declare their particular "group" to be a "national people", they are making political declarations which involve assumptions about nationhood, political entitlements and the "naturalness" of these entitlements. Such declarations are understood internationally, for the "theories" of nationhood are today internationally shared as a worldwide contemporary ideological common-sense (Gellner, 1983, 1987). Without these "theories" and without the establishment of the world of nation-states, national identities, which appear so familiar and "natural", would not be possible. National identity, in this context, is not an individual feeling, but a form of life (Billig, 1995). The question is not whether "national identity" is an instance of "group" identity; it is clearly is. The question to ask about national identity is why, in our age, it has seemed so "natural" to value this "identity" above life itself, so that this "identity" has lain behind slaughter on a scale and intensity unknown to other ages and their "identities".

Smaller range identities also imply theories, representations and, thereby, forms of social life. Academics cannot classify themselves as "biochemists" or "professors" without making assumptions about academic disciplines, institutions, professions and, indeed, about the nature of knowledge itself. All these imaginings depend upon wider ideological beliefs. In consequence, grammatically similar statements of identity can have very different meanings. "I am a sociologist", uttered at a professional gathering of anthropologists carries a different meaning from the famous declaration of the US president, John Kennedy, "*Ich bin ein Berliner*". To say that both are similar statements of group identity would close down analysis at precisely the point at which it should begin.

The point is not necessarily how individuals categorize themselves, but how the categorizations are categorized—what cultural myths they perpetuate. Such an analysis requires a move from the universal to the particular, so that the particularities of history, through which community is imagined, can be studied. Moreover, such an analysis involves examining the particularities of discourses in ways which social identity theorists have often been reluctant to acknowledge. Social categorization is not an abstract process, but, as Edwards (1991) has argued, categories are for talking. Social distinctions, comparisons and categorizations are constituted within, and accomplished by, acts of language. Thus, the phenomena described in universal terms by social identity theory can be observed in their concreteness, as people make utterances about themselves, other groups, their groups and so on (Widdicombe and Wooffitt, 1995). The meanings of such discourses cannot be stipulated in advance, but have to be discovered in the situated detail of their utterance.

As discourse theorists have stressed, utterances are rarely, if ever, simple expressions of individual belief, but, in making an utterance, speakers (or writers) are engaged in complex social and rhetorical activity (Billig, 1987a; Edwards and Potter, 1992, 1993; Parker 1992; Potter and Wetherell, 1987; Shotter, 1993). This can be seen, for example, in the complexities of racist discourse. Speakers, in making claims about "them" and "us", and about "fairness" and "unfairness", not only use "theories" of race and culture, but are also making claims about themselves, often attempting to display discursively their own claims for "reasonableness" (Billig, 1991; van Dijk, 1992, 1993; Wetherell and Potter, 1992). This discursive activity must be understood in relation to its context of utterance. This context includes not merely the immediate interpersonal, or conversational, context but also the wider ideological context, as speakers take up and use discursive resources which they themselves have not created, but which bear an ideological history (Billig, 1991; Fairclough, 1992). And, as Tajfel stressed in the opening chapters of *Human groups and social categories*, the ideological context is always a historical context. Again, social psychology, in considering such matters, should open itself up to the study of ideology.

Psychology and Separation

When Tajfel was arguing to restrict the explanatory ambitions of social psychological theories, he was emphasizing that no social psychological theory which was proposed as universal could produce a full explanation of whatever it tried to analyse: it can offer partial insight only. Indeed, the psychological insights might not even be the most important form of insight, for the psychological aspects always need to be set in their historical and social contexts.

Different intellectual strategies might follow from this warning of limitation. One intellectual strategy that is becoming common amongst social psychologists is to recognize this limitation in theory, but to act as if the limitation could be set aside in academic practice. Thus, researchers claim to pursue the goal of the integrated, pure social psychological theory while conceding that, to obtain a full explanation of any social phenomenon, the social psychological theory will have to be combined, in ways unspecified, with theories from other disciplines. The concession, however, is made as a justification for putting aside the particularities of history. Hogg and Abrams (1988) state their recognition of the importance of "other perspectives in the social sciences", including history: "It is not possible to predict or explain content or culture by recourse to psychological processes alone" (p. 18). This statement appears towards the beginning of their book; for the rest, the psychological processes are then presented as if they stand alone and, as if for methodological reasons, they can be bracketed off from the other perspectives. Hogg and McGarty (1990), outlining their approach to social identity theory, state that "we as social psychologists" are only concerned with social institutions and social groups "to the extent to which they are psychologically represented"; they comment that "the study of specific groups in their own right is perfectly proper, but it is largely the task of other disciplines (e.g. sociology)" (p. 24).

This sort of claim functions as a justification for academic specialization: social psychologists are to act as social psychologists, pursuing their universalist theories while leaving other matters to other disciplines, which in their turn conduct their business in intellectual isolation. It is a vision of independent crafts, each labouring in their own workshops, and each nurturing their own professional identities ("we social psychologists", "we sociologists", etc). Broader ideological concerns become minimized in the work of narrow specialisms. This practice of specialization has left its rhetorical imprint in the way that social psychology is currently being written. A glance at the bibliographies in the most prestigious journals of social psychology would confirm that the specialist texts of social psychologists tend only to cite other social psychological studies. In this way, the discipline is becoming a self-enclosed intellectual culture with its own rhetorical rituals (Billig, 1994). The other perspectives intrude only minimally.

To be sure, traces of this strategy can be found in Tajfel's writings, especially as he sought to establish social psychology as a recognized intellectual discipline in Europe. On the other hand, as can be seen in the early chapters of *Human groups and social categories*, he also explicitly opposed the strategy, recognizing that the particularities of history could only be bracketed out of social psychological investigation at the cost of dealing with "impossible myths". Most importantly, Tajfel's own writings exemplify the desire to open up, rather than enclose, social psychology, whose historical and ideological origins he explicitly recognized. Tajfel's references range across the social sciences and, most notably, he cited history in ways which are rare today in social psychological texts. This breadth of scholarly reference was never a rhetorical adornment but was crucial to Tajfel's vision of social psychology. In this respect, his writings resemble those of Serge Moscovici, who, likewise, seeks to create social psychology as "an anthropological and historical science" (1984, p. 948). The constant references to history while apparently illustrating theoretical points, draw attention to the limitations of theory, warning against the dangers of immodest "explanation". They help to break the illusion that the pure, universal theory can be constructed as anything but myth.

Singularity of Background

Tajfel's concern to limit the theory which he was constructing needs to be set against its own background. As he wrote, the murder of European Jews and others was always present in his intellectual thinking. Yet, he did not turn around the theory, which was so imaginatively produced, in order to "explain" the background. There is no social identity "explanation" of the Holocaust in Tajfel's writings. Nor could there be one, unless it were to reproduce the same characteristics which he so emphatically criticized in other theorists.

The very words of social identity theory seem inappropriate for the purposes of explaining the theory's own background. As Tajfel so often wrote, the theory aims to illuminate "intergroup relations", and, indeed, to establish the importance of intergroup relations in the minds of social psychologists, who have so frequently been preoccupied by interpersonal relations. The concept of "intergroup relations" bears its own rhetoric. It suggests groups in some sort of relationship with each other, such as the boys' groups in the famous Sherif experiments (Sherif *et al.*, 1961). The word "relations" seems inappropriate for episodes of gross inequality and violence. The rape victim and the rapist hardly share a "relation" in the act of rape: to call it a "relation" diminishes the crime. And so it is with the most extreme of mass slaughter. As Jews were systematically collected and led with force to their deaths, this was no mere episode in "intergroup relations", as if Jews and Germans were in some sort of "relationship". The enormity of the crime demands that the conventions of language be stretched: in this context, even the word "crime" seems inappropriate.

The search for positive social identity, too, seems inadequate if offered as an explanation. To "explain" Nazism in terms of the Germans searching for a "positive social identity" after the defeat of the First World War would be as trivial as offering an explanation in terms of "attributions". Of course, glimpses of psychological insight can be gained. As Tajfel (1981) recognized, the need for outgroups to be constructed in distinction to the ingroup can be recognized in Hitler's "invention" of the Jews "as a social category", as it can in other myths about outgroups (pp. 249–250). However, as Tajfel was quick to point out, the similarities between Nazism and other examples of national identification were accompanied by profound differences. Recognition of the similarities in no way ended the matter, even from a social psychological perspective. The particular ways in which Nazism "invented" Jews, and the ways in which this invention, which itself was also a historical repetition, was able to take root in the minds of millions of Germans, still needed to be explored.

The problem is that universal psychological theories can trivialize social events, as the general theoretical categories absorb the particulars. Nazism would become another "group prejudice", the Holocaust another example of "discriminatory behaviour". Tajfel's own theory of categorization (itself one of the most important universal theories in social psychology) illustrates the process. As Tajfel argued, categorization involves absorbing a particular instance into a wider category (Tajfel, 1959; Tajfel and Wilkes, 1963). The act of categorization encourages the categorizer to exaggerate the similarity between all instances which are categorized together, whilst exaggerating their differences from instances of other categories. The theoretical concepts of social psychology tend to operate in this manner. As theorists categorize actions theoretically, so these actions are interpreted as instances of something more general (Billig, 1994). The theorists, then, tend to ignore the particularities of those actions, as the particularities disappear into the universal.

But how can the Holocaust be categorized? How can it be absorbed by theory? Any attempt to do so involves a loss of the sense of historical uniqueness. As Geoffrey Hartman, himself a survivor, has written, the Holocaust should not be considered as "just another calamity". It is distinguished from other massacres "because of its magnitude, its blatant criminality, its co-ordinated exploitation of all modern resources, cultural and technological" (1994, p. 3). Glimpses of familiar psychological processes can be recognized in the pattern of events: there are Milgram-style acts of obedience, acts of frustrated aggression, distorting projections of enemies, even instances of "attribution". These glimpses cannot be combined into an overall theory which has been tested on other events. In the words of Alain Finkielkraut, the Holocaust is "un assassinat sans équivalent dans l'histoire" (Finkielkraut, 1989, p. 30).

If there is no precise historical equivalence, then there is no general category for description. Nor can there be general explanations, unless the reasons for resisting judgements of historical equivalence are ignored. Any general category would reduce the Holocaust to a similarity with other calamities; its uniqueness would be diminished, even forgotten. In this respect, to quote Saul Friedlander, the Holocaust "carries an *excess*" (1994, p. 262, emphasis in original). Every explanation—every judgement of comparison—threatens to abolish that excess.

Even comparisons with other genocides can be problematic. Some social scientists have attempted to produce general sociologies or social psychologies of genocide, investigating the similarities between the Nazi persecutions and, for example, the genocide of Armenians in Turkey or of Tasmanians at the hands of British colonialists (Chalk and Jonassohn, 1990; Du Preez, 1994; Kuper, 1981; Staub, 1984). If a general term, such as "genocide" is employed, then the

Holocaust can be absorbed into the generality. Du Preez (1994) writes that genocide is "psychologically intelligible and, to that extent 'normal' response to a particular kind of social and political crisis" (p. iii). The Nazi genocide, he writes, was an example of "ideological genocide"; and "in the twentieth century the models for genocide are those of Nazis and the Soviets" (p. 80). The uniqueness—the particular excess—is being worn away by the categorization and comparison. And the crimes of the Soviets are being condemned by the comparison.

Linguistically, the term "*the* Holocaust" retains the sense of uniqueness (the uniqueness is doubly stressed by using the Hebrew term "the Shoah"). Writers can draw attention to the severity of other holocausts to the extent that these are "holocausts", to be compared with *the* symbol of excess. For example, Tajfel (1981) in his introductory chapter wrote that since 1945 there had been "many new massacres and also some new holocausts" (p. 7). Chalk and Jonassohn (1990), who argue that "the Holocaust is part of a larger category of genocide", stress, nevertheless, its uniqueness both theoretically and semantically: it was "the ultimate ideological genocide", perpetrated "in post-enlightenment Europe by a people steeped in Western culture and rich in scientific knowledge" (pp. 323–325).

Again, it is a matter of judgement. It is not technically impossible to offer explanations, as Du Preez illustrates. However, the explanations themselves carry an excess—in this case, an ideological and ethical excess. There has been fierce debate amongst German historians about the uniqueness of the Holocaust. Some historians, such as Nolte, Fest and Hillgruber, have been stressing the similarities between the Holocaust and other political murders, especially the crimes of Stalinism (see Maier, 1988 for a review). Nolte has compared Nazism with the State of Israel—a comparison which has been more usually made by extreme left-wing writers, for whom Zionism is the target (Billig, 1987b). Nolte has even attempted to depict Nazism in terms of "intergroup relations", as if Hitler's programme against the Jews were a reaction against Jewish actions (Maier, 1988, p. 46).

It is not the possibility of comparison which is debatable but, as Maier points out, "the purpose of comparison is what is at stake" (p. 54). As critics such as Jurgen Habermas have argued, the comparisons with other massacres carry a political direction; they "normalize" and "historicize" the Holocaust, thereby lessening German responsibility. If Nazism is considered as a response to Jewish actions, then the victims can start being seen to be implicated in their own destruction. It is no coincidence that "revisionists", such as Nolte, put their arguments in the context of the need for Germans to rediscover their national identity and their national past. If, as Nolte has suggested, every major nation has its Hitler-equivalent, then Germans need not transmit a unique sense of shame in their history. Once the Holocaust ceases to symbolize the worst excess imaginable (indeed, if the numbers of victims can be reduced, or even if the very existence of the crime is questioned), then German national history and national identity become correspondingly more comfortable. As Maier (1988) states, the argument for comparability "opens the way to apologetics" and "facilitates a literature of evasion" (p. 1).

All this bears directly on the fear of "explanation". In the social sciences, any explanation promises to dispose of the events to be explained. Their particularities may be absorbed into familiar, universal categories. The "explanation" seems to reduce the need for further thinking; it even obviates the need for memory. The "explanation" can now be remembered, as the particular serves the purpose of the general theory. As far as psychological explanations are concerned, there is an additional danger. They offer an invitation to empathy: *tout comprendre, c'est tout pardonner.*

The claim of a complete explanation is a claim to discard the excess; it presents the social world as captured, or tamed. There is a strong case for saying that the Holocaust should represent a past which is "unmasterable"; it is to be remembered beyond understanding (Friedlander, 1994). Over twenty-five years ago, Emile Fackenheim made a similar point, suggesting that Auschwitz is the rock on which all rational explanations will crash and break apart (1968, p. 31). An analogous sentiment was being expressed indirectly, when Tajfel, in introducing some of the most brilliant theories of social conflict in the history of social psychology, implicitly warned lest the theories absorb their background—his theories, his background.

Concluding Remarks

If Henri Tajfel, in common with others from his background, sought to draw insights from the inexplicable, then these differ from the search for explanations. Perhaps, then, it is not inappropriate to seek general lessons regarding the limitations of theory from the background of social identity theory. As Tajfel stressed, the psychological dimension is crucial for understanding social conflict: this dimension, most notably, includes the ways in which myths, explanations, accusations and justifications are uttered. The search for insight can also impel a search for general theories of explanation, for there can be no insight without the sifting of similarities and differences. However, general theories bring appropriation as much as they promise explanation. They threaten to rob the explananda of their particularity. Each imagined community which collectively remembers its history and identity is transformed into a "group" or "society" or "nation"; each individual becomes a "subject", an "attributer", a "group member"; the singularities are to be considered methodologically irrelevant and to be eliminated in theory. In this way, the categories of theory can only achieve their gains at the cost of appropriation.

Sometimes the ideological cost of this appropriation is too great to be paid, for it is an appropriation of memory, whether the memory of individual experience or that transmitted through collective culture. For us, the pupils of Henri Tajfel, there is also another question of payment: how to repay the debts, both personal and intellectual, to a teacher who demonstrated how to think creatively. One way of course is to continue refining his theories, following his methodological examples, as if the work could be completed. Another way is to guard against completion, to respect the gaps and limitations, remembering that they did not arise in the first place through forgetfulness.

References

Anderson, B. (1983). *Imagined communities*. London: Verso.

Antaki, C. (1994). *Explaining and arguing*. London: Sage.

Aristotle (1976). *Topica*. London: Loeb Classical Library.

Ashmore, M. (1989). *The reflexive thesis*. Chicago: University of Chicago Press.

Balibar, E. (1991). Is there a "neo-racism"? In E. Balibar and I. Wallerstein (Eds), *Race, nation, class*. London: Verso, pp. 17–28.

Bauman, Z. (1988). *Modernity and the holocaust*. Cambridge: Polity Press.

Bauman, Z. (1992). *Intimations of postmodernity*. London: Routledge.

Billig, M. (1978). *Fascists: a social psychological view of the National Front*. London: Harcourt, Brace, Jovanovich.

Billig, M. (1981). *L'Internationale raciste: De la psychologie a la "science" des races*. Paris: Maspero.

Billig, M. (1982). *Ideology and social psychology*. Oxford: Basil Blackwell.

Billig, M. (1987a). *Arguing and thinking*. Cambridge: Cambridge University Press.

Billig, M. (1987b). Anti-Semitic themes and the British far left: some social–psychological observations on indirect aspects of the conspiracy tradition. In C.F. Graumann and S. Moscovici (Eds), *Changing conceptions of conspiracy*. New York: Springer Verlag, pp. 115–136.

Billig, M. (1989). The extreme right: Continuities in the anti-Semitic conspiracy tradition. In R. Eatwell and N. O'Sullivan, (Eds), *The nature of the right*. London: Pinter, pp. 146–166.

Billig, M. (1991). *Ideology and opinions*. London: Sage Press.

Billig, M. (1992). The baseline of intergroup prejudice ("citation classic"). *Current Contents: Social and Behavioral Sciences*, **24** (4), 8.

Billig, M. (1994). Repopulating the depopulated pages of social psychology. *Theory and Psychology*, **4**, 307–335.

Billig, M. (in press). *Banal nationalism*. London: Sage Press.

Breuilly, J. (1985). Reflections on nationalism. *Philosophy of the Social Sciences*, **15**, 65–75.

Chalk, F., and Jonassohn, K. (1990). *The history and sociology of genocide*. New Haven: Yale University Press.

Cohn, N. (1967). *Warrant for genocide*. London: Chatto Heinemann.

Du Preez, P. (1994). *Genocide: the psychology of mass murder*. London: Boyars/Bowerdean.

Edwards, D. (1991). Categories are for talking. *Theory and Psychology*, **1**, 515–542.

Edwards, D., and Potter, J. (1992). *Discursive psychology*. London: Sage.

Edwards, D., and Potter, J. (1993). Language and causation: a discursive action model of description and attribution. *Psychological Review*, **100**, 23–41.

Eysenck, H. J., and Coulter, T. (1972). The personality and attitudes of working-class British communists and fascists. *Journal of Social Psychology*, **87**, 59–83.

Eysenck, H. J., and Wilson, G. D. (1978). *The psychological basis of ideology*. Lancaster: MTP Press.

Fackenheim, E. L. (1968). Jewish faith and the Holocaust. *Commentary*, August, pp. 30–36.

Fairclough, N. (1992). *Discourse and social change*. Cambridge: Polity.

Finkielkraut, A. (1989). *La Mémoire Vaine du Crime contre l'Humanité*. Paris: Gallimard.

Friedlander, S. (1994). Trauma, memory and transference. In G. H. Hartman (Ed.), *Holocaust Remembrance*. Oxford: Blackwell, pp. 252–263.

Gellner, E. (1983). *Nations and nationalism*. Oxford: Blackwell.

Gellner, E. (1987). *Culture, identity and politics*. Cambridge: Cambridge University Press.

Gergen, K. J. (1973). Social psychology as history. *Journal of Personality and Social Psychology*, **26**, 373–383.

Gergen, K. J. (1991). *The saturated self.* New York: Basic Books.

Gergen, K. J. (1994a). *Toward transformation in social knowledge*, 2nd edn. London: Sage.

Gergen, K. J. (1994b). The limits of pure critique. In H. W. Simons and M. Billig (Eds), *After postmodernism.* London: Sage, pp. 58–78.

Harris, N. (1990). *National liberation.* London: I. B. Tauris.

Hartman, G. H. (1994). Introduction: darkness visible. In G. H. Hartman, (Ed), *Holocaust remembrance.* Oxford: Blackwell, pp. 1–22).

Hogg, M. A., and Abrams, D. (1988). *Social identifications.* London: Routledge.

Hogg, M. A., and McGarty, C. (1990). Self-categorization and social identity. In D. Abrams and M. A. Hogg, (Eds), *Social identity theory.* New York: Springer Verlag pp. 10–27.

Horwitz, M., and Rabbie, J. M. (1982). Individuality and membership in the intergroup system. In H. Tajfel (Ed.), *Social identity and intergroup relations.* Cambridge: Cambridge University Press, pp. 241–274.

Israel, J., and Tajfel, H. (Eds) (1972). *The context of social psychology.* London: Academic Press.

Katz, J. (1980). *From prejudice to destruction: Anti-Semitism*, 1700–1933. Cambridge, MA: Harvard University Press.

Kuhl, S. (1994). *The Nazi connection: Eugenics, American racism and German national socialism.* Oxford: Oxford University Press.

Kuper, L. (1981). *Genocide.* New Haven: Yale University Press.

Lyotard, J.-F. (1984). *The postmodern condition.* Manchester: Manchester University Press.

Maier, C. S. (1988). *The unmasterable past: History, Holocaust and German national identity.* Cambridge, MA: Harvard University Press.

Michael, M. (1991). Some postmodern reflections on social psychology. *Theory and Psychology*, **1**, 203–221.

Michael, M. (1994). Discourse and uncertainty: postmodern variations. *Theory and Psychology*, **4**, 483–404.

Moscovici, S., and Faucheux, C. (1972). Social influence, conformity bias and the study of active minorities. *Advances in Experimental Social Psychology*, **6**, 149–202.

Moscovici, S. (1984). The myth of the lonely paradigm: A rejoinder. *Social Research*, **51**, 939–967.

Muller-Hill, B. (1988). *Murderous science.* Oxford: Oxford University Press.

Parker, I. (1992). *Discourse dynamics.* London: Routledge.

Poliakov, L. (1974). *The aryan myth.* London: Chatto Heinemann.

Potter, J., and Wetherell, M. (1987). *Discourse and social psychology.* London: Sage.

Sampson, E. E. (1977). Psychology and the American ideal. *Journal of Personality and Social Psychology*, **35**, 767–782.

Sampson, E. E. (1993). *Celebrating the other.* Hemel Hempstead: Harvester Wheatsheaf.

Sherif, M., Harvey, O. J., White, B. J., Hood, W. R., and Sherif, C. W. (1961). *Intergroup conflict and co-operation.* Norman, OK: University of Oklahoma.

Shotter, J. (1993). *Conversational realities: Studies in social constructionism.* London: Sage.

Staub, E. (1984). *The roots of evil: The origins of genocide and other group violence.* Cambridge: Cambridge University Press.

Tajfel, H. (1959). The anchoring effects of value in a scale of judgements. *British Journal of Social Psychology*, **50**, 294–304.

Tajfel, H. (1976). Against biologism. *New Society*, **37**, 240–242.

Tajfel, H. (1981). *Human groups and social categories.* Cambridge: Cambridge University Press.

Tajfel, H. (1982). Instrumentality, identity and social comparison. In H. Tajfel (Ed.), *Social identity and intergroup relations.* Cambridge University Press: Cambridge, pp. 483–507.

Tajfel, H. (1984). Intergroup relations, social myths and social justice in social psychology. In H. Tajfel (Ed.), *The social dimension.* Cambridge: Cambridge University Press, pp. 695–715.

Tajfel, H., and Wilkes, A. L. (1963). Classification and quantitative judgement. *British Journal of Psychology*, **54**, 101–114.

Turner, J. C. (1982). Towards a cognitive redefinition of the social group. In H. Tajfel (Ed.), *Social identity and intergroup relations.* Cambridge: Cambridge University Press, pp. 15–40.

Turner, J. C., Hogg, M. A., Oakes, P. J., Reicher, S. D., and Wetherell, M. (1987). *Rediscovering the social group.* Oxford: Blackwell.

van Dijk, T. A. (1992). Discourse and the denial of racism. *Discourse and Society*, **3**, 87–118.

van Dijk, T. A. (1993). *Elite discourse and racism.* Newbury Park: Sage.

Wetherell, M., and Potter, J. (1992). *Mapping the language of racism*. Hemel Hempstead: Harvester Wheatsheaf.

Widdicombe, S., and Wooffitt, R. (1995). *The language of youth subcultures*. Hemel Hempstead: Harvester Wheatsheaf.

Zubaida, S. (1993). *Islam, the people and the state*. London: I. B. Tauris.

Postscript

W. PETER ROBINSON

Department of Psychology, University of Bristol

I first met Henri in the late 1950s when he was demonstrating that sticks could have their perceived lengths changed by the category labels assigned to them. He was full of excitement about the accentuation effects which he had found. Subsequently, we met occasionally for drinks. Unfortunately, as a diffident postgraduate, I registered his intellect as being categorically superior to mine, in cleverness and sense, and as a consequence did not seek opportunities to talk and think with him about his puzzles or mine. To my disadvantage and regret, this deference influenced our not infrequent encounters over the next thirty or so years. It was not Henri's fault. He was as eager to discuss my concerns as his own, and there were never any acts to signify distinctiveness and superiority. On the contrary, it was problems that dominated discussions. These never ran off into displays of personal cleverness or scholarly triviality, and there was always a feeling that if one could really understand minimal group effects and combine these insights with the contributions of the other social sciences and history, one might be able to understand voting patterns at the United Nations, and help to make life better for the victims of the conflicts within and between states. That the pattern of alliances and antagonisms of states explained their voting better than the rhetorics of justice and decency, used by their political protagonists to justify their positions, was illustrated on more than one occasion by Henri.

My final conversation with him in St. Mary's hospital was a typical occasion. He had accepted the imminence of his death. The conversation drifted in and out of shared experiences, recollections of Oxford and Bristol, and of the European Association and its growth. We laughed about his earlier impish proposal that the headquarters of the European Association of Experimental Social Psychology should be on a yacht moored in the Mediterranean. That might have helped to lessen conflicts about deciding where committee meetings should be held. But somehow it emerged that I had a puzzling question on hand: why did groupings of anti-school teenagers have abusive names for the outgroup of their academically committed peers, but escape any reciprocating label? The ambience switched, and there was a total focus upon this asymmetry, its explanation, and its relevance to social identity theory. The pace of talk accelerated, the customary zest was renewed, and there was some laughter at implausible suggestions. Something then reminded Henri of his days as a rehabilitation officer, and the boys he had helped in that role. He mentioned that occupationally this had been the most satisfying part of his life. It was a fine but sad farewell.

As several authors have mentioned, Henri was a European intellectual, in the best sense of that phrase, and the breadth and depth associated with that statis informed his social psychology in a manner and to an extent that no undergraduate education in present-day Britain can begin to approach.

He was also a very positive thinker about the development and significance of social psychology. His optimism encouraged him to ignore the fact that social psychologists in Britain were a low-status, small minority outgroup within psychology, within universities, and within the society. This has been illustrated quite recently in Sutherland's *Irrationality* (1992). What Henri Tajfel had to do with Stuart Sutherland during their overlapping period in Oxford, I do not know. Not a lot, I imagine. For much of his career Sutherland epitomized the disdain in which social psychology has been held by many, but not all, of the elite at the so-called "hard end" of the discipline. Just as Cambridge physiology and Oxford philosophy were disposed towards the dismissal of the academic pretension of what used to be called experimental psychology, so some of the practitioners of the latter liked to kick the social dog. There are still signs, in slips of the pen in Sutherland's text, which appear to betray a continuing denigratory attitude, even though many of his well-chosen examples of irrationality derive directly from the social psychological literature on social discriminations, comparisons and evaluations.

Henri had a single citation in the Sutherland references, but in fact social identity theory and its elaborations would, in combination with other social psychological theories, explain many of the results in Sutherland's book. The text is an excellent and socially relevant synthesis; the paradox is that it should be founded so heavily on social psychology, as well as on people's problems with statistical reasoning, but with the former gaining much less acknowledgement. This intellectual discrimination never seemed to worry Henri, and certainly he was not discouraged from realizing his dreams for the subject.

Like immigrants, protagonists of new subjects can expect to have to struggle to become assimilated by the host institutions, and it would seem that the older and more status-conscious the institutions in which change is sought, the more arduous the struggle. Witness the contrastive growth of social psychology in the USA and, more recently, in those countries which have thrown out totalitarian regimes. Henri would have been delighted by this aspect of "perestroika", and he helped enormously by laying the foundations of the European developments, first through his founding father role in the European Association of Experimental

Social Psychology, and later through the integration of Central and Eastern Europeans into the Association. Social psychologists generally can be pleased that they were so early into first western and then pan-European networking.

While the extra-British developments meant hard work, this seemed to proceed much more constructively than the earlier and continuing battles at home. Henri was one of what was literally a handful of emigre academics, who found themselves promoting the cause of establishing social psychology in Britain. They had to do so in the face of opposition from both the British Psychological Society and the universities generally. Fortunately, Bristol gave Henri a chair from which he was able to fulfil his ambitions to develop the subject, to attract and inspire a younger generation with his own enthusiasm, and to promote social psychology in Europe. In all three his success was enormous.

What he did not try to accomplish, and would have failed had he attempted to achieve, was a shift of the academic or wider British culture into an appreciation of the importance of social psychology, both as a field of study and a source of intelligence for developing a society rationally and realistically. One of the absurdities of the politics of post-war Britain has been its focus on the attempted understanding and manipulation of the economy without an appreciation that a society is made up of people with social and personal identities. Government failures to see, or act upon, the fact that the elimination or reduction of intergroup conflicts about the distribution of rationed resources and opportunities in a society is crucial to the quality of life for its members, stem from an ignorance and arrogance about the human sciences, and a simultaneous lack of imagination about the future. Earlier, Labour governments were as insensitive to these issues as their recent Conservative successors. In pre-war Britain railwaymen were proud of their distinctive regional lines, each of which had its positive stereotype. Road hauliers were proud of their trucks and their service. Nationalization into anonymity in the cause of efficiency and ideology were sure recipes for disaster in the new systems, in the absence of corresponding steps to secure positive social identities linked to quality of performance; likewise, the consequences of the ideological dogmatism of the New Right, in counting the cost of everything. Nursing and teaching were both professions where the satisfactions of doing a worthwhile job well were what made their occupants tolerant of their low salaries. The morale of both is now at a very low ebb, and the quality of the service offered by both must decline unless the intrinsic commitment is restored.

Such examples could be multiplied many times, more so in some countries than others. The excessive and too rapid cultivation of individualism and interpersonal competitiveness is typically associated with rises in the indicators of social breakdown. Whether political and other elites know this perfectly well and see it as ways of entrenching their privileges, or whether they are simply ignorant about social experience and behaviour is, of course, an issue of considerable longevity. Somewhere I picked up the idea that the duty of Old

Testament prophets was to preach and teach. They could not be held responsible for those who did not listen to or heed what they had to say. In so far as social psychology has messages for societies and their members, it might be argued that social psychologists could assume similar duties. The writings of Henri Tajfel have very profound messages for those who choose to read them. He has left a living memorial in the European organizations and institutions he worked so hard and successfully to create, and through the continuing work of the colleagues and students he helped to inspire.

Bibliography of Publications of Henri Tajfel

RUPERT BROWN, ANGELIKA SCHIPPER and NILS WANDERSLEBEN

Centre for the Study of Group Processes, Department of Psychology, University of Kent

Contents

In the twenty-eight years of his professional career, from his graduation in 1954 to his death in 1982 (and then posthumously), Henri Tajfel published seven books (six edited volumes, one of his own collected work) and over ninety articles and book chapters. In his own curriculum vitae he organized these into three sections: social perception; intergroup relations; and other publications. We have followed his lead in this and simply added a fourth section: unpublished work. The latter consists of several papers we unearthed in his personal effects, together with some influential but never formally published writing (e.g. his 1974 Katz–Newcomb lectures). The material is organized into date order within each of the four sections.

The chapters of this Festschrift are sufficient testimony to the enormous influence of Tajfel's work on international social psychology. To those let us just add three small statistics which may serve as a final affirmation of his continuing impact on our discipline. We consulted the Social Science Citation Index for the years 1976–1990 (all that was immediately available to us). In each of the first five years of this period there were an average of seventy-one Tajfel citations; in the next five there were an average of 113; and from 1986–1990, by which time

Tajfel had been dead for over four years, there were no less than 188 per annum. Doubtless the more quantitative of our readers will be able to calculate the precise exponential rate with which this citation count is increasing. But the rest of us will simply note with some pleasure that the ideas of this great social psychologist are reaching and affecting an ever growing and appreciative world audience. And long may they continue to do so.

Published work 1957–1987

Intergroup relations

Tajfel, H. (1959). A note on Lambert's "Evaluation reactions to spoken languages". *Canadian Journal of Psychology*, **13**, 86–92.

Tajfel, H. (1960). Nationalism in the modern world: The nation and the individual. *The Listener*, **63**, No. 1624.

Tajfel, H. (1963). Stereotypes. *Race*, **V**, 3–14. Reprinted in J. O. Whittaker (Ed.), (1972). *Recent discoveries in psychology.* Philadelphia: W. B. Saunders.

Tajfel, H. (1964). Cognitive aspects of the development of nationalism. Proceedings of the XVth International Congress of Applied Psychology, Ljubljana.

Tajfel, H., Sheikh, A. A., and Gardner, R. C. (1964). Content of stereotypes and the inference of similarity between members of stereotyped groups. *Acta Psychologica*, **22**, 191–201.

Jaspars, J. M. F., Van de Geer, J. P., Tajfel, H., and Johnson, N. B. (1965). On the development of national attitudes. University of Leiden, Institute of Psychology, Report 01–65. Reprinted in *European Journal of Social Psychology* (1973), **3**, 347–369.

Tajfel, H. (1965). Some psychological aspects of the colour problem. Chapter 10 in *Colour in Britain.* London: BBC Publications.

Tajfel, H. (1966). Children and foreigners. *New Society*, June. Reprinted in A. Etzioni and M. Wenglinsky (Eds), (1970). *War and its prevention.* New York: Harper and Row.

Tajfel, H. (1966). I pregiudizi di colore in Gran Bretagna: l'esperienza degli studenti d'Africa, d'Asia et delle Indie occidentali. *Rivista di Sociologia*, **3**, 53–82.

Tajfel, H. (1966). Co-operation between human groups. *The Eugenics Review*, **58**, 77–84. Reprinted in *Magyar Filozofiai Szemle* (1967), **3**.

Tajfel, H., and Jahoda, G. (1966). Development in children of concepts and attitudes about their own and other nations: a cross-national study. Proceedings of the XVIIIth International Congress of Psychology, Moscow, Symposium 36, pp. 17–33. In translation in *Ceskoslovenska Psychologie* (1966), **11**, 437–444.

Simon, M. D., Tajfel, H., and Johnson, N. B. (1967). Wie erkennt man einen Österreicher? *Kölner Zeitschrift für Soziologie und Sozialpsychologie,* **19**, 511–537.

Tajfel, H. (1969). The formation of national attitudes: a social psychological perspective. In M. Sherif (Ed.), *Interdisciplinary relationships in the social sciences*. Chicago: Aldine, pp. 137–176.

Tajfel, H. (1969). Cognitive aspects of prejudice. *Journal of Biosocial Sciences*, **1**. Suppl. Mon. No. 1, *Biosocial aspects of race*, pp. 173–191. Reprinted in *Journal of Social Issues* (1969), **XXV** (No. 4), 79–97; and in P. Watson (Ed.), (1973). *Psychology and race*. Harmondsworth: Penguin Books.

Johnson, N. B., Middleton, M., and Tajfel, H. (1970). The relationship between children's preferences for and knowledge about other nations. *British Journal of Social and Clinical Psychology*, **9**, 232–240.

Middleton, M., Tajfel, H., and Johnson, N. B. (1970). Cognitive and affective aspects of children's national attitudes. *British Journal of Social and Clinical Psychology*, **9**, 122–134.

Tajfel, H. (1970). Aspects of national and ethnic loyalty. *Social Science Information*, **IX** (3), 119–144.

Tajfel, H. (1970). Experiments in intergroup discrimination. *Scientific American*, **233** (5), 96–102. Reprinted in R. C. Atkinson (Ed.), (1971). *Contemporary psychology*. San Francisco: W. H. Freeman.

Tajfel, H., Nemeth, C., Jahoda, G., Campbell, J. D., and Johnson, N. B. (1970). The development of children's preferences for their own country: a cross-national study. *International Journal of Psychology*, **5**, 245–253.

Tajfel, H., Flament. C., Billig, M. G., and Bundy, R. P. (1971). Social categorization and intergroup behaviour. *European Journal of Social Psychology*, **1**, 149–178.

Tajfel, H. (1972). Vorurteil. In *Lexikon der psychologie*, Vol. 111. Freiburg: Verlag Herde.

Tajfel, H., Jahoda, G., Nemeth, C., Rim, Y., and Johnson, N. B. (1972). Devaluation by children of their own national or ethnic group: Two case studies. *British Journal of Social and Clinical Psychology*, **11**, 235–243.

Jaspars, J. M. F., Van de Geer, J. P., and Tajfel, H. (1972). On the development of national attitudes in children. *European Journal of Social Psychology*, **2** (4), 347–369.

Billig, M., and Tajfel, H. (1973). Social categorization and similarity in intergroup behaviour. *European Journal of Social Psychology*, **3**, 27–52.

Bourhis, R. Y., Giles, H., and Tajfel, H. (1973). Language as a determinant of Welsh identity. *European Journal of Social Psychology*, **3** (4), 447–460.

Tajfel, H. (1974). Social Identity and intergroup behaviour. *Social Sciences Information/Information sur les Sciences Sociales*, **13** (2), Apr, 65–93.

Tajfel, H., and Billig, M. (1974). Familiarity and categorization in intergroup behaviour. *Journal of Experimental Social Psychology*, **10**, 159–170.

Tajfel, H. (1975). The exit of social mobility and the voice of social change: Notes on the social psychology of intergroup relations. *Social Science Information/Information sur les Sciences Sociales*, **14** (2), 101–118. Reprinted in *Przeglad Psychologiczny* (1979), **22** (1), 17–38.

Tajfel, H. (1976). Exit, voice and intergroup relations. In L. Strickland, F. Aboud and K. Gergen (Eds), *Social psychology in transition.* New York: Plenum Press.

Tajfel, H. (1976). Against biologism. *New Society,* **37**(No. 721), 240–242.

Tajfel, H. (1977). Human intergroup conflict: Useful and less useful forms of analysis. In M. von Cranach, K. Foppa, W. Lepenies and D. Ploog (Eds), (1979). *Human ethology: The claims and limits of a new discipline.* Proceedings of a symposium held at the Werner-Reimers-Stiftung, Bad Homburg, October 1977. Cambridge: Cambridge University Press.

Bourhis, R. Y., Gadfield, N. J., Giles, H., and Tajfel, H. (1977). Context and ethnic humour in intergroup relations. In A. J. Chapman and H. C. Foot (Eds), *It's a funny thing, humour.* Oxford: Pergamon.

Tajfel, H. (1978) The social psychology of minorities. London: Minority Rights Group, report no. 38.

Tajfel, H. (Ed.) (1978). *Differentiation between social groups: Studies in the social psychology of intergroup relations.* London: Academic Press.

Chapter 1 (H. Tajfel): Introduction.

Chapter 2 (H. Tajfel): Interindividual behaviour and intergroup behaviour.

Chapter 3 (H. Tajfel): Social categorization, social identity and social comparison.

Chapter 4 (H. Tajfel): The achievement of group differentiation.

Bourhis, R. Y., Giles, H., Leyens, J.-P., and Tajfel, H. (1979). Psycholinguistic distinctiveness: Language divergence in Belgium. In H. Giles and R. St. Clair (Eds), *Language and social psychology.* Oxford: Blackwell.

Gadfield, N. J., Giles, H., Bourhis, R. Y., and Tajfel, H. (1979). Dynamics of humor in ethnic group relations. *Ethnicity,* **6**, 373–382.

Tajfel, H., and Turner, J. C. (1979). An integrative theory of intergroup conflict. In W. G. Austin and S. Worchel (Eds), *The social psychology of intergroup relations.* Monterey, CA: Brooks Cole. Also revised in S. Worchel and W. G. Austin (Eds), (1986). *Psychology of intergroup relations.* Chicago: Nelson Hall, Chapter 1 H. Tajfel and J. Turner: The social identity theory of intergroup behaviour.

Turner, J. C., Brown, R. J., and Tajfel, H. (1979). Social comparison and group interest in ingroup favouritism. *European Journal of Social Psychology,* **9**, 187–204.

Brown, R. J., Tajfel, H., and Turner, J. C. (1980). Minimal group situations and intergroup discrimination: Comments on the paper by Aschenbrenner and Schaefer. *European Journal of Social Psychology,* **10**, 399–414.

Tajfel, H. (1980). Experimental studies of intergroup behaviour. In M. Jeeves (Ed.), *Survey of psychology,* No. III. London: George Allen and Unwin.

Tajfel, H. (1981). *Human groups and social categories: studies in social psychology.* Cambridge: Cambridge University Press. German, Portuguese, Spanish and Italian translations: Stuttgart: Klett-Cotta; Lisbon: Livros Horizontos; Barcelona: Herder; and Bologna: Il Mulino.

Tajfel, H. (1981). Social stereotypes and social groups. In J. Turner and H. Giles (Eds), (1981). *Intergroup behaviour.* Blackwell: Oxford. Translated and reprinted in Tajfell, H. (1982). Stereotype spoleczne I grupy spoleczne./ Social stereotypes and social groups. *Studia Psychologisczne,* **20** (2), 5–25.

Vaughan, G. M., Tajfel, H., and Williams, J. (1981). Bias in reward allocation in an intergroup and an interpersonal context. *Social Psychology Quarterly,* **44**, 37–42.

Tajfel, H. (1982). Social psychology of intergroup relations. *Annual Review of Psychology,* **33**, 1–39.

Tajfel, H. (Ed.) (1982). *Social identity and intergroup relations.* London/New York: Cambridge University Press. Preface and Introduction: H. Tajfel. Chapter 16 H. Tajfel: Instrumentality, identity and social comparisons.

Tajfel, H. (1983). Prejudice. In R. Harré and R. Lamb (Eds), *The encyclopaedic dictionary of psychology.* Oxford: Blackwell.

Social perception and related topics

Tajfel, H. (1957). Value and the perceptual judgement of magnitude. *Psychological Review,* **64**, 192–204. Reprinted in M. D. Vernon (Ed.), (1966). *Experiments in visual perception.* Harmondsworth: Penguin Books; C. W. Backman and P. F. Secord (Eds), (1966). *Problems in social psychology.* New York: McGraw-Hill; G. Hunyady (Ed.), (1972). *Szocialpszichologia.* Budapest: Gondolat; J. R. Torregrosa (Ed.), (1973) *Teoria e investigacion en la psicologia social actual.* Madrid: Instituto de la Opinion Publica.

Tajfel, H. (1959). Quantitative judgement in social perception. *British Journal of Psychology,* **50**, 16–29. Abbreviated and translated in D. Jodelet, J. Viet and P. Besnard (1970). *La psychologie sociale.* Paris: Mouton.

Tajfel, H. (1959). The anchoring effects of value in a scale of judgements. *British Journal of Psychology.* **50**, 294–304.

Tajfel, H., and Cawasjee, S. D. (1959). Value and the accentuation of judged differences. *Journal of Abnormal and Social Psychology,* **59**, 436–439.

Tajfel, H. (1962). *Social perception.* Chapter 1 in G. Humphrey and M. Argyle (eds), *Social psychology through experiment.* London: Methuen.

Tajfel, H., and Wilkes, A. L. (1963). Classification and quantitative judgment. *British Journal of Psychology,* **54**, 101–114.

Tajfel, H., and Winter, D. G. (1963). The interdependence of size, number and value in young children's estimates of magnitude. *Journal of Genetic Psychology,* **102**, 115–124. Reprinted in F. Dambrot, A. Friedman and J. A. Popplestone (1965). *Readings for general psychology.* Wm. C. Brown Book Co.

Tajfel, H. (1964). Human "judgment" in the laboratory. Categories and stereotypes. *Common factor.* **1**, 1.

Tajfel, H. (1964). Bias in judgment. *New Society,* **4**, 11–12.

Tajfel, H., Everstine, L., and Richardson, A. (1964). Individual judgment consistencies in conditions of risk taking. *Journal of Personality*, **32**, 550–565.

Tajfel, H., Richardson, A., and Everstine, L. (1964). Individual consistencies in categorizing: a study of judgmental behaviour. *Journal of Personality*. **32**, 90–108. Reprinted in P. B. Warr (Ed.), (1970). *Thought and personality*. Harmondsworth: Penguin Books.

Tajfel, H., and Wilkes, A. L. (1964). Salience of attributes and commitment to extreme judgments in the perception of people. *British Journal of Social and Clinical Psychology*, **2**, 40–49.

Bruner, J. S., and Tajfel, H. (1965). Width of category and concept diffferentiation. *Journal of Personality and Social Psychology*, **2**, 261–264, 266–267.

Tajfel, H. (1966). Study of cognitive and affective attitudes, final report. Grant AF-EOAR 64–59.

Tajfel, H. (1966). The nature of information in social influence: an unexplored methodological problem. Proceedings of the XVIIIth International Congress of Psychology, Moscow, Symposium 34, 50–57.

Tajfel, H., and Bruner, J. S. (1966). The relation between breadth of category and decision time. *British Journal of Psychology*, **57**, 71–75.

Wilkes, A. L., and Tajfel, H. (1966). Types de classification et importance du contraste relatif. *Bulletin de C.E.R.P.*, **15**, 71–81.

Tajfel, H. (1967). Similarity and dissimilarity. BBC (August).

Tajfel, H. (1968). Social perception. In *International encyclopaedia of the social sciences*. Vol. XI, 567–575.

Tajfel, H. (1969). Social and cultural factors in perception. Chapter in G. Lindzey and E. Aronson (Eds), *Handbook of social psychology*, Vol. III, 2nd edn. Cambridge, MA: Addison-Wesley, 315–394.

Tajfel, H. (1972). La catégorisation sociale. In S. Moscovici (Ed.), *Introduction à la psychologie sociale*. Paris: Larousse (Translation).

Tajfel, H. (1976). Social psychology and social processes/La Psicologia sociale e i processi sociali. *Giornale Italiano di Psicologia*, **3** (2), 189–221. Reprinted in A. Palmonari (Ed.), (1976). *Problemi attuali della psicologia sociale*. Bologna: Il Mulino.

Tajfel, H., and Forgas, J. P. (1981). Social categorization: Cognition, values and groups. In J. P. Forgas (Ed.), *Social cognition: Perspectives on everyday understanding*. European Monographs in Social Psychology, No. 26. London: Academic Press.

Other Publications

Peters, R. S. and Tajfel, H. (1957). Hobbes and Hull—metaphysicians of behaviour. *British Journal for the Philosophy of Science*, 30–44. Reprinted in L. I. Krimerman (Ed.), (1969). *The nature and scope of social science*.

New York: Appleton-Century-Crofts; and M. Cranston and R. S. Peters (Eds), (1972). *Hobbes and Rousseau: A collection of critical essays*. New York: Doubleday.

Tajfel, H. (1958). The teaching of psychology in social science courses. *Bulletin of the British Psychological Society*, **24**, 23–28.

Bruner, J. S., and Tajfel, H. (1961). Cognitive risk and environmental change. *Journal of Abnormal and Social Psychology*, **61**, 231–241. Reprinted in R. J. C. Harper, C. C. Anderson and S. M. Hunka (Eds), (1964). *The cognitive processes*, NJ: Prentice-Hall and J. C. Mancuso (Ed.), 1970. *Readings for a cognitive theory of personality*. New York: Holt, Rinehart and Winston.

Tajfel, H. (1964). Problems of international co-operation in social psychological research concerned with new and developing countries. *Mimeo Report*, 1–91.

Tajfel, H. (1964). Die Entstehung der kognitiven und affektiven Einstellungen. In *Vorurteile: Ihre Erforschung und ihre Bekaempfung*. Politische Psychologie, Band 3. Europaeische Veranstaltung, Frankfurt a.M., 1964, Reprinted in Tajfel. H. (1987). The formation of cognitive and affective attitudes. In Werner Bergmann (Ed.), *Error without trial: Psychological research on antisemitism*, Vol. 2. Berlin, Federal Republic of Germany: Walter de Gruyter, pp. 542–546.

Tajfel, H., and Dawson, J. K. (Eds.) (1965). *Disappointed guests: essays by African, Asian and West Indian students*. Oxford University Press. Preface and Epilogue by H. Tajfel and J. L. Dawson.

Tajfel, H. (1966). International co-operaion in social psychology: Some problems and possibilities. *Bulletin of the British Psychological Society*, **19**, 29–36.

Tajfel, H. (1968). Second thoughts about cross-cultural research and international relations. *International Journal of Psychology*, 213–219.

Eiser, J. R., and Tajfel, H. (1972). Acquisition of information in dyadic interaction. *Journal of Personality and Social Psychology*, **23** (2), 340–345.

Israel, J., and Tajfel, H. (1972). *The context of social psychology: A critical assessment*. London/New York: Academic Press (published in co-operation with the European Association of Experimental Psychology).

Tajfel, H. (1972). Some developments in European social psychology. *European Journal of Social Psychology*. **2** (3), 307–321.

Hoffman, S., Leontief, W., and Tajfel, H. (1975). Book II in *Social sciences policy, France*. Paris: O.E.C.D. (Published simultaneously in French)

Tajfel, H., and Moscovici, S. (1976). The renaissance of old myths in social psychology. *Zeitschrift für Sozialpsychologie* (in German translation), **7**, 292–297.

Tajfel, H. (1977). Social psychology and social reality. *New Society*, **39**, 757, 31 Mar, 653–654.

Tajfel, H. (1977). Social psychology. In A. Bullock and O. Stalleybrass (Eds), *The Fontana dictionary of modern thought.* London: Fontana and New York: Harper.

Tajfel, H., and Fraser, C. (Eds) (1978). *Introducing social psychology: An analysis of individual reaction and response.* Harmondsworth: Penguin. Reprinted in 1987.

Chapter 1 (H. Tajfel and C. Fraser): Social psychology as social science.

Chapter 12 (H. Tajfel): The structure of our views about society.

Chapter 16 (H. Tajfel): Intergroup behaviour: I. Individualistic perspectives.

Chapter 17 (H. Tajfel): Intergroup behaviour: II. Group perspectives.

Tajfel, H. (1979). Individuals and groups in social psychology. *British Journal of Social and Clinical Psychology*, **18**, 183–190.

Tajfel, H. (1980). Nachwort zur Neuauflage. (Foreword; German translation.) In Fritz Bernstein (Ed.), *Der Antisemitismus als Gruppenerscheinung: Versuch einer Sociologie des Judenhasses*, Königstein/Taunus: Jüdischer Verlag im Athenäum Verlag. (First edition 1926).

Tajfel, H. (1980). The "New Look" and social differentiations: A semi-Brunerian perspective. In D. Olson (Ed.), *The social foundations of language and thought: Essays in honor of J. S. Bruner.* New York: Norton.

Tajfel, H. (1982). Social justice in social psychology. In Paul Fraisse (Ed.), *La psychologie du futur.* Paris: Presses Universitaires de France.

Tajfel, H. (Ed.) (1984). *The social dimension: European developments in social psychology*, 2 Vols. Cambridge: Cambridge University Press.

Chapter 1 (H. Tajfel, J. Jaspars and C. Fraser): The social dimension in European social psychology.

Chapter 33 (H. Tajfel): Intergroup relations, social myths and social justice in social psychology.

Unpublished

Tajfel, H. (no date). Social categorization.

Tajfel, H. (no date). Distinctiveness of social categories and intergroup discrimination: a rejoinder to Gerard and Hoyt in a context of some wider issues.

Tajfel, H. (no date). Memorandum containing suggestions for a motivational study on motor oil purchasing for Dorland Advertising Ltd.

Tajfel, H. (no date). Memorandum on a motivational study concerned with the promotion of a new type of motor-car tyre for Dorland Advertising Ltd.

Tajfel, H. (no date). A crisis of identity. First draft.

Tajfel, H. (1974). Intergroup behaviour, social comparison and social change. Unpublished Katz-Newcomb Lectures, University of Michigan, Ann Arbor.

Author index

References to the works of Henri Tajfel are ubiquitous and are therefore not given page references.

Subject index